The Enigmatic Chancellor

Drawing of Theobald von Bethmann Hollweg by Olaf Gulbransson.

THE ENIGMATIC CHANCELLOR

Bethmann Hollweg and the Hubris of Imperial Germany

by Konrad H. Jarausch

New Haven and London, Yale University Press, 1973

Designed by John O. C. McCrillis
and set in Baskerville type.
Printed in the United States of America by
The Vail-Ballou Press, Inc., Binghamton, N.Y

Published in Great Britain, Europe, and Africa by
Yale University Press, Ltd., London.
Distributed in Canada by McGill-Queen's University
Press, Montreal; in Latin America by Kaiman & Polon,
Inc., New York City; in India by UBS Publishers'
Distributors Pvt., Ltd., Delhi; in Japan by John
Weatherhill, Inc., Tokyo.

To H. L. F.

Contents

Preface

At the center of the debate about the continuity of German history lies the riddle of Bethmann Hollweg's personality and politics, since it holds the key to the tragedy of the Wilhelmian Empire. Even more than the demonic greatness of Bismarck or Hitler, the failure of the fifth chancellor's reforming conservatism reveals the structural causes of Germany's inability to find a place among the European nations and to develop a liberal constitutional system. The moral ambivalence in the mainstream of German politics of which he was both representative and victim, makes Bethmann's struggle a paradigm of the essential inadequacy of the German solution to the problems of the present century. Pondering the meaning of his people's tortured past after the second holocaust, Thomas Mann cautioned against both vindictive condemnation and tearful compassion. "There are not two Germanies, a bad one and a good one." Perhaps he was thinking of Bethmann's fate when he elaborated: "They are but one and the same whose best becomes its worst through diabolic guile. The bad Germany is the errant good one, the good one in misfortune, guilt, and disaster."

The recent contributions of political, social, and psychological analysis necessitate a fresh concept of biography that transcends the traditional life and times approach. A legacy of the nineteenth century, the genre can no longer suffice as a chronicle of the inner development of a hero or as a hagiographical apology of a statesman. Going beyond the exploration of personal motives and ideas, the reconstruction of decisions and actions in their ideological and social structural setting will contribute to a fuller understanding of the dynamics of an era. Social position fashions the backdrop, economic interests provide the material foundation, constitutional and legal structures furnish the framework, cultural and intellectual leitmotivs sound the timbre, subconscious psychological forces reveal the inner compulsions; but the individual remains the looking-glass. As a systematic heuristic collage, biography, describing and analyzing the nature of an individual's interaction and convergence with society, can draw upon other historical and social scientific methods. Impersonal forces such as social configurations, political systems, statistical trends, or chains of ideas do not have lives of their own; they are incarnate in specific persons and peculiar events at particular times and under special circumstances. But the very singularity of an individual fate, if strategically chosen, can synthesize the conflicting views of an age.

The destruction of Bethmann's personal _Nachlass_ in Hohenfinow during the Soviet occupation and the survival of an abundance of official documents have dictated the form of presentation of this study. Insufficient for psychobiography, the nature of the material permits a double focus on decisions and structural constraints proceeding outward from the antihero toward Imperial Germany as a whole. Since strict adherence to chronology throughout would have obscured the larger relationships, I have divided Bethmann's chancellorship into thematic slices despite my conscious effort to expose the complex interplay between domestic and foreign policy. To retain the flavor of Bethmann's personality, his own words are used wherever possible; since the events themselves litter the pages of textbooks, only the clarification of their nuances can capture his elusive personal role. Because the massiveness of archival evidence if cited individually at each appropriate point would interrupt the flow of ideas and cause much needless duplication, the unorthodox form of collective citation seemed perferable, even if it is occasionally irritating to the specialist. To facilitate the tracing of sources, letters and papers quoted are listed in order of their appearance in the text, and additional documentation as well as references to other literature follow at the conclusion of each footnote. The existence of numerous detailed guides to the field, as well as the exigencies of space, have prohibited the inclusion of a traditional bibliography, but comparative titles are frequently mentioned in the critical notes. As compensation for this shortcoming and as introduction to the generalist, a short essay on sources appeared to me to be more useful than long tables of cryptic archival signatures. Touching on several chapters, the case study of Bethmann's middle-european order, his occupation policy toward Belgium, and the reestablishment of Poland forms the appendix.

The intellectual and practical debts of a study of such scope are legion. For adding a personal dimension to it, I must gratefully acknowledge the assistance of Felix von Bethmann Hollweg and Frau Baronin von Sell, while I would like to thank Mrs. Howard E.

White for her kind permission to cite the Riezler diary. Moreover, I am deeply indebted to the archivists who unselfishly gave of their time and vast holdings, such as Drs. Gehling, Mommsen, Enders, Weiser, Branig, Neck, Schottenloher, Gönner, Schlechte, Stahl, Haselier, Miss Agnes Peterson, and Mark G. Eckhoff. Similarly, I would like to express my gratitude to the custodian of the E. M. House Collection, to the director of the manuscript collection of the Deutsche Staatsbibliothek, and to all other librarians who assisted my bibliographical efforts. To Dr. A. von Harnack, Robert and Dr. Wolfgang Haussmann, Marlene Freifrau von Weizsäcker, and Frau Professor Hildegard Rassow, I owe permission to consult the papers of their fathers. The generous help of other scholars like W. Gutsche, E. von Vietsch, W. J. Mommsen, and K. Hildebrand, as well as the benevolent advice of the principals of the Fischer controversy, greatly aided my inquiry. Only the financial support of the graduate school of the University of Wisconsin, the Deutscher Akademischer Austauschdienst, the Faculty Improvement Program of the University of Missouri, and the American Philosophical Society, and the creative leisure supplied by the Shelby Cullom Davis Center for Historical Studies at Princeton University made the completion of this work possible. Among the numerous people who have helped with the mechanical preparation of this manuscript, I would like to single out Barbara Folsom for her spirited copyediting and David Cotter and Lore Amlinger for their construction of the index. Finally, I must give credit to two mentors on opposite sides of the Atlantic, each of whom possesses a special living insight into the German problem, Professors Franz Petri and Theodore S. Hamerow.

At the height of the first controversy over the *Kriegsschuldfrage* Max Weber deplored the fact that "every new document which comes to light after decades revives the undignified lamentations, the hatred and scorn, instead of finally allowing the war to be buried, at lest morally." Writing to a young scholar, Bethmann agreed that only "objectivity, fairness, and above all dignity" would help future historians to escape the vicious circle of sterile recriminations. "In my opinion the 'responsibility for war' must now be treated dispassionately by all. Any other method is suspect."

List of Abbreviations

AA	Auswärtiges Amt, Bonn, Politisches Archiv
AB	*Alldeutsche Blätter*
AHR	*American Historical Review*
BA	Bundesarchiv Coblenz
BDs	Gooch-Temperley, *British Documents*
BHStA	Bayrisches Hauptstaatsarchiv Munich
BM	*Berliner Monatshefte,* formerly *Kriegsschuldfrage*
BT	*Berliner Tageblatt*
CEH	*Central European History*
DAZ	*Deutsche Allgemeine Zeitung*
DSB	Deutsche Staatsbibliothek Berlin
DZA Me	Deutsches Zentralarchiv, Abteilung Merseburg
DZA Po	Deutsches Zentralarchiv, Abteilung Potsdam
FDs	*Documents diplomatiques françaises*
FRUS	*Foreign Relations of the United States* (supplement)
FZ	*Frankfurter Zeitung*
GDs	Kautsky et al., *Deutsche Dokumente zum Kriegsausbruch*
GK	*Geschichtskalender*
GLAK	Generallandesarchiv Karlsruhe
GP	*Grosse Politik*
"Gutsbuch"	Felix von Bethmann Hollweg's estate chronicle
GWU	*Geschichte in Wissenschaft und Unterricht*
HHStA	Haus- Hof- und Staatsarchiv, Vienna
HJ	*Historical Journal*
HZ	*Historische Zeitschrift*
IBZ	Hoetsch, *Internationale Beziehungen*
IFA	Matthias-Morsey, *Interfraktioneller Ausschuss*
Isv	Stieve, *Der Diplomatische Schriftwechsel Iswolskis*
JCEA	*Journal of Central European Affairs*
JCH	*Journal of Contemporary History*
JGOE	*Jahrbücher für Gesshichte Osteuropas*
JMH	*Journal of Modern History*
KPs	Kiderlen Waechter Papers, House Collection, Yale University
MGM	*Militärgeschichtliche Mitteilungen*
NA	National Archives, Washington D.C.
NAZ	*Norddeutsche Allgemeine Zeitung*
Oe-U	Bittner et al., *Oesterreich-Ungarns Aussenpolitik*

xiii

PrGStA   Preussisches Geheimes Staatsarchiv, Dahlem
RDs   Siebert, *Benkendorffs Diplomatischer Schriftwechsel*
SDs   Boghitschewitsch, *Die Auswärtige Politik Serbiens*
S-G   Scherer-Grunwald, *L'Allemagne et les problèmes de la paix*
SHStA   Sächsisches Hauptstaatsarchiv Dresden
StAPo   Staatsarchiv Potsdam
UA   Untersuchungsausschuss der dt. Nationalversammlung
UF   Schraepler-Michaelis, *Ursachen und Folgen*
VJHfZG *Vierteljahrshefte für Zeitgeschichte*
WaG   *Welt als Geschichte*
WHStA   Württembergisches Hauptstaatsarchiv Stuttgart
WP   Wahnschaffe protocol of party leader briefing
WUA   *Werk des Untersuchungsausschusses*
ZfG   *Zeitschrift für Geschichtswissenschaft*
ZfMG   *Zeitschrift für Militärgeschichte*

CHAPTER 1

The Shadow of Responsibility

"I take the liberty of asking the Allied and Associated governments to direct against me the proceedings which they intend to initiate against His Majesty, the Emperor. For that purpose I place myself completely at the disposal of the Allied and Associated Powers." Former Chancellor Theobald von Bethmann Hollweg thus addressed Premier Georges Clemenceau three days before the signing of the Treaty of Versailles. With this gallant gesture Bethmann offered himself in place of William II to be tried for Germany's role in the unleashing of World War I: "According to the constitutional laws of the empire, I bear entire responsibility for the emperor's political actions during my tenure of office as chancellor. Since the Allied and Associated Powers propose to sit in judgment on these actions, I feel entitled to ask that they hold me alone responsible." [1] Attempting to live up to his motto, "As long as I can serve my country, I bear even injustice willingly," the ex-chancellor considered it his right and duty to stand by the consequences of those decisions made by him, not the kaiser or the generals. "Since I am solely accountable for imperial policy, I wish to refute the Allied accusation that we committed grave violations of international law, and appeal to universal morality by defending Germany's honor before a hostile tribunal." [2]

After a long inner struggle, Bethmann Hollweg had resolved to override Chancellor Scheidemann's and Foreign Minister Brockdorff Rantzau's veto, based on their fear that his selfless offer would be construed as an admission of German guilt and as a recognition of Allied jurisdiction. [3] Since the Entente's pressure on Holland for extradition of the refugee kaiser had grown nearly intolerable, the former chancellor felt he could no longer wait. "Legal niceties cannot stand in my way. More significant is the ethical imperative that I must take on myself the responsibility for the emperor without regard for the consequences." Although his demarche was not likely to meet with anything but derision, "It *might* stiffen Holland's stand; encourage the opponents of the kaiser's extradition in England,

1

America, and the neutral countries; counteract moral depression at home; and in the far future pave the way for a juster evaluation of our own guilt." Not devotion to William II, whose limitations he knew only too well, but anguish over the spiritual crisis of his people inspired Bethmann's unsolicited self-sacrifice. "Our present situation is so desperate that even impractical steps have to be taken as long as they do not wreak *further* damage and might contribute to raising our moral standing in the world." [4]

The former chancellor's unprecedented step embarrassed the Allied statesmen gathered in Paris. On June 28, 1919, the very day of the signing of the Versailles treaty, the Big Five searched for an appropriate answer. "This is the best thing that he has ever done," President Wilson charitably remarked, while Prime Minister Lloyd George conceded, "He has never been one of the worst." Only Clemenceau was not disposed toward leniency: "No doubt, Bethmann Hollweg is on the list of those that should be tried." But Wilson overruled *le Tigre:* "I do not believe that; he does not fit any category of defendant we intend to indict. There are, in fact, on one hand the kaiser, accused of violating Belgian neutrality and on the other hand those guilty of breaking the laws of warfare. Neither of these two major accusations applies to Bethmann Hollweg." Invoking British custom, Lloyd George admitted that Bethmann's argument was correct according to the letter of the constitution; but the American president scoffed, "Unfortunately for that thesis we know how the German constitution worked in practice." Ignoring both the language of the document and its implementation after William's collapse in the *Daily Telegraph* Affair, Clemenceau insisted that "the German emperor has said often enough that he was the master, that his will ruled all." To head off further discussion Wilson quickly offered a compromise. "We could write that we render homage to Bethmann Hollweg's intention, but that we cannot accept his interpretation of the German constitution. I myself have studied that document very closely and know it well." Brushing aside the objection of the Japanese representative, Baron Makino, the American president then suggested charging Secretary of State Lansing and the Commission on Responsibility with a polite refusal.[5]

This expedient instruction, which sidestepped the issue of the moral validity of the war guilt and trial clauses of the Versailles treaty, governed the formulation of the commission's answer. The

American delegate, Dr. Scott, insisted that only the emperor was to be judged. "His former chancellor can neither appear before this tribunal as defendant nor determine the guilt or innocence of his erstwhile master." Acknowledging that Bethmann's offer was "highly creditable to him as a man," he nevertheless concluded, "This proposal is inconsistent with the terms of the treaty." [6] Fearing an erosion of the ethical basis of the peace settlement and knowing that an enraged public would demand a scapegoat for the bloodshed, the delegates of the Big Five decided in a meeting on July 15 that "there can be no question of modifying Articles 227-230 of the Treaty of Peace." The special tribunal was solely empowered to condemn the emperor. "The principal Allied and Associated Powers would exceed their authority if in the solution of these difficulties, they should substitute themselves for the special tribunal provided by Article 227." [7] Two weeks after this preliminary draft, the Naval Communication Service laconically wired to Washington, "The Council decided that no answer be made to von Bethmann Hollweg regarding his personal responsibility for the outbreak of the war." The evasiveness of the Big Five obscured the ex-chancellor's courageous initiative since, by claiming to condemn Imperial Germany's transgression before all mankind, the victorious allies were not above using justice for their own political ends.[8]

"The curse of responsibility for German policy before and during the war" placed Bethmann's enigmatic personality and politics into the center of contemporary and posthumous controversy.[9] While wartime Entente propagandists pictured him as "a political sleepwalker" whose incompetence hastened the carnage,[10] his domestic Pan-German opponents predicted that he would become the gravedigger of Germany:

> Weh Deutschland, dass zur Schicksalsstunde
> Dich ein 'Geheimrath' dirigiert!
> Und wieder klafft die alte Wunde,
> Und wieder wird das Volk verführt.*

As remedy, the anonymous poet [11] prayed for a true *Führer:*

> *Woe, Germans, that in fateful hour
> A bureaucrat stands at your head!
> Again the old wound saps your power
> Again the people are misled.

> Wann naht der Held, der sicher ahnend
> Die alte Wunde mit dem Speere schliesst?
> Der Held, der neue Zukunft bahnend,
> Für Deutschland unser Blut vergiesst.*

In contrast a few moderate voices [12] struck a sympathetic note:

> Die Zeit wird kommen, Dich zu richten,
> Wir wissen dies: *Ein Mann der Pflichten*
> Hietst Deinem Volk die Wacht
> Durch tiefer Kriegsgefahren Nacht:
> Du treuer Mann von Hohenfinow.†

The chancellor's first biographies were written as weapons in the struggle for peace and reform, to popularize his austere personality and spur him into further action. In a slim volume distributed at the front, the South German Catholic historian Gottlob Egelhaaf called for "a victorious, powerful, and peaceful Germany." [13] The Protestant clergyman and Christian Socialist Hermann Kötschke, as a former schoolmate offering glimpses of the chancellor's youth, urged him to become a true *Volkskanzler* by ending the bloodshed and liberalizing the Prussian vote.[14] But after 1918 the authoritative voice of the Borussian tradition, conservative historian Fritz Hartung, charged in the official biographical dictionary that Bethmann's weakness and lack of statemanship had squandered the splendors of the Second Empire. "All in all he was a Hamlet nature in which the native hue of resolution was all too often sicklied over by the pale cast of thought. It was his and Germany's tragedy that he was called upon to right a disjointed time." [15] On the other hand, speaking for a minority of prorepublican intellectuals, Friedrich Thimme, editor of *Die Grosse Politik,* attributed the responsibility for the collapse to the fist-thumping and sabre-rattling of the Right, and deplored as the chancellor's central flaw his "failure to combat military interference in the political sphere more resolutely." [16] But in Weimar

---

*When comes the hero, who confiding
Closes the old wound with his spear?
The leader who into the future striding
Sheds our blood for Germany so dear.

†The time shall show in all its beauty
What we now know: *A man of duty*
You watched over your people's plight
Throughout the darkness of war's night,
You loyal man of Hohenfinow.

and Nazi Germany the majority saw Bethmann through Alfred Rosenberg's eyes, as "the headless chancellor: a sad chapter of German history." [17]

Overshadowing the holocaust of World War I, the *Götterdämmerung* of Hitler's short-lived thousand-year Reich nevertheless intensified the intellectual debate over Bethmann's role in the perversion of the Bismarckian tradition. Although seeing him as "a scrupulous, contemplative, judicious, scholarly man, standing with mild skepticism above the worldly confusion . . . a stoic, carrying the burden of an overpowering fate and almost in harmony with darkness and despair," Werner Frauendienst still took him to task for being "basically unpolitical, lacking the passionate urge to act and to create, not a leader at the helm of a great empire during its hour of crisis." [18] Going beyond the traumas of the older generation, younger scholars broke with the traditional obsession with the leadership of individual statesmen. "Chancellor Bethmann Hollweg's limits sprang less from his pensive nature than from the immaturity of the people and the unwillingness of his political enemies to follow his ideas of national unity and inner rejuvenation." [19] Behind the chancellor began to emerge the "structural calcification of Wilhelmian Germany cut off from the influx of regenerative forces and hence incapable of creative change." [20]

In a dramatic attempt to grasp the continuity leading from 1914 to 1939, the Hamburg historian Fritz Fischer interpreted World War I as a concerted German bid for world power, manifesting itself with horrifying clarity in annexationist dreams. "Essentially, German war aims were not merely an answer to the enemies' war aims, made known in the course of the war, nor the product of the war situation, created by the *Burgfrieden* (domestic truce) and the blockade; they are explicable only in light of factors operating since 1890 or even earlier—naval policy, the 'policy of bases,' colonial, eastern, Balkan and European economic policies, and the general political situation which—primarily as an effect of Germany's own policy—produced after 1904 and 1907 the attempt to overthrow Germany by 'encircling' her." As a by-product of this outraged and massive indictment Fischer exploded the traditional picture of the "philosopher in the chancellor's chair" and, though allowing that he appeared as a moderate "liberal imperialist," made Bethmann the mastermind of, not just the reluctant accessory to, annexationist crimes. "A man whom his contemporaries saw as a well-meaning bureaucrat, given to self-doubt and vacillation, now emerges as a cool and calculating Machiavellian statesman whose bumbling moderation was a mere front for sinister aims." [21]

Fischer's provocative theses touched a raw nerve of German historical consciousness, implicitly challenged the legitimacy of a German national state, and sparked the most intense scholarly controversy of the Bonn Republic.[22] Hailing him as a prophet of sick capitalist society, East German historians only mildly quibbled with Fischer's inconsistent economic infrastructure,[23] while Western scholars gratefully found their suspicions of German apologetics justified; [24] but the majority of West German professors assailed their Hamburg colleague's ethical rigorism as "the clouding of national historical consciousness." [25] Once again Bethmann's responsibility became the involuntary focus of a public struggle, spilling over into the pages of *Die Zeit, Die Welt,* and *Der Spiegel,* conducted with the weapons of history while feeding on the taboos and neuroses of the painful *Bewältigung der Vergangenheit* (clarification of the past).[26] In his magisterial analysis of militarism, the dean of the older generation, Gerhard Ritter, devoted his third volume to that "tragedy of statecraft," Bethmann's wartime chancellorship. "What was revealed to our eyes was not a weak personality desirous of pleasing everyone and finally alienating all, but the gripping tragedy of a highly admirable statesman who, with desperate effort but never in despair, led his nation out of an endless labyrinth"; he thus sought to do justice to his political intent. "What determined his failure was not his alleged weakness of will, but the problem which is at the center of this inquiry: the curse of German militarism." [27]

A second major opponent, Egmont Zechlin, more cautiously saw Bethmann's policy as a tightrope act "between reason and public pressure," picturing him as a cabinet diplomatist, a flexible and cautious *Realpolitiker,* misled by the illusion of limited war. "Bethmann maintained a strong reserve toward the war aims programs submitted to him from all sides and did not commit himself to a firm series of goals." [28] Although Fischer countered adeptly that "the almost exclusive concern with the conflicts of conscience and fatalistic sighs of a Bethmann Hollweg or a Kühlmann appears highly one-sided," the structural debate about Wilhelmian imperialism nevertheless focused on the political goals, motives, and decisions of the fifth chancellor, since larger conceptual theories regarding the demise of Imperial Germany had to be tested against specific decisions and individual actions.[29] Using the unpublished diary of Bethmann's imaginative adlatus Kurt Riezler, Karl Dietrich Erdmann built a countercase in which he described the fifth chancellor as *Weltpolitiker wider Willen,* a statesman "who administered power without becoming its slave." [30] As these positions escalated, Fischer charged passionately in a second imposing tome: "Without a doubt, the war unleashed by the German politicians in July 1914 is not a preventive war 'out of fear and desperation,' but rather an attempt to subjugate the enemy powers before they grew too strong and to realize by force political goals which may be subsumed under the term of German hegemony over Europe." In an ironic reversal, Bethmann, who was initially condemned as a lackey of the Left, had now turned into the diabolic villain of the Right.[31]

While reflecting the convulsions of German consciousness, the debate over Bethmann's responsibility also gradually produced a differentiated picture of the fifth chancellor. In a ponderous *Habilitationsschrift* the Marxist scholar Willibald Gutsche attempted to do justice to the struggles within the Wilhelmian leadership. "The chancellor, for domestic and international reasons, followed a diagonal policy which resembled a flexible, liberal approach based upon an economic form of hegemony desired by German imperialism, but which represented the general interest of the ruling classes concerning the power political goals of expansion." [32] Analyzing the limitations of Bethmann's power, W. J. Mommsen, in a systematic inquiry into the problem of political leadership before the war, stressed the lack of organized communication between government and public as the fatal weakness of the chancellor's methods. "In its incessant attempts to find a middle road between the political aims of different camps and to prevent them from airing their sharp differences publicly, the Bethmann government contributed to the creation of an almost unreal political atmosphere, whose victim it finally became." [33] Going beyond social constraints and political limitations, the American historian Fritz Stern described the chancellor as "a puritan gambler," deplored "that to a large extent he accepted the values of the very system he criticized," stressed the pessimistic fatalism that made him "unwittingly, probably unconsciously—a front for the very forces which he detested," and concluded that "his historic role abetted the disastrous course of Germany's history in this century." [34] Although a methodological step backward, the chancellor's first full biography, written by the archivist Eberhard von Vietsch, focused on the conflict between power and morality in the ethical politics of the statesman. "In the final analysis the whole Weltanschauung of classical German idealism failed with Bethmann on the highest political level." [35] At last the fifth chancellor had found a portrait consonant with his own self-image; but Bethmann was too honest not to reject metaphysical flattery. "Do you know into which groups Goethe divides public officials?" he queried whimsically. "There are fools, philistines, and knaves. Perhaps you will find out which I am." [36]

Despite two generations of research and debate, Bethmann's responsibility for the tragedy of Imperial Germany remains elusive. One historian has counseled dejectedly, "Perhaps it is now time to recognize that his inconsistency is not without precedent in human affairs and that the search for Bethmann's 'real' position may be doomed to failure." [37] Others have countered, "The sphinx of the chancellor is fascinating as representative of German political culture, and an explanation of his undoubtedly contradictory policy and person would help deepen our understanding of German history from Bismarck to Hitler." [38] As a private man Bethmann may well remain an unresolvable enigma. But as a political type, the fifth chancellor manifested the basic paradoxes of the Second Empire with unusual clarity. Confronted with the central dilemma of Wilhelmian imperialism, Bethmann was forced to wrestle with the problems of Germany's place in Europe and the world, the constitutional form of its politics, the social polarization between masses and elites, and the legitimacy of its independent intellectual tradition. Because of his position at the center of the political machinery of Imperial Germany, he, more than others, had the opportunity to resolve the conflicts constructively. His successes and failures, his hopes and despairs, his goals and actions, his motives and inspirations were not only an outflow of his private being but the result of larger forces working on and through him—hence the enigma of his person merges into the riddle of the entire age.[39]

"What is the good of looking backward? I hate moralizers and an old Cato is a repulsive sight." Bethmann set high standards for himself. "Great men are ahead of their times and those who are not must attempt to move with it. But they who bring up the rear—*habeat sibi*. Chronicles and collections of anecdotes will recall them, but they will accomplish nothing and be a useless subject, even if their convictions are sincere." [40]

CHAPTER 2

In Search of Himself

"As you begin, so you will remain./Though powerful are duty and need,/stronger yet is the force of birth," Gerhard von Mutius stamped the imprint of ancestral heritage on his cousin Theobald von Bethmann Hollweg. Like that of other successful German burghers, his family had risen from common origins to patent nobility two generations earlier and adopted the revealing motto, *Ego et domus mea serviemus domino*. The male line of Hollweg, first documented in the Hessian university town of Giessen in the mid-1500s, had been prosperous artisans, tradesmen, and Protestant divines before moving to the larger city of Frankfurt late in the seventeenth century.[1] Dating back to 1426 in the former imperial fortress Goslar, where they had been city counselors, the female lineage of Bethmann settled in the imperial city in the mid-eighteenth century and soon played a prominent role in the financial circles of the Main metropolis. Their most illustrious member, the personally knighted Simon Moritz, reknowned as "Frankfurt's first citizen," was Napoleon's and Metternich's banker, Russian consul general, and the leading gentile competitor of the Rothschilds.[2]

His daughter Susanna Elisabeth, a "woman of high and noble spirit," attracted to her elegant salon such luminaries as Johann Wolfgang von Goethe, Wilhelm von Humboldt, and Mme de Staël. In 1780 she married Johann Jacob Hollweg, a diligent banker and pietist, who after adopting the double name, assumed the directorship of the Bethmann bank, a stately neoclassical building behind a massive wrought iron gate. A man of deep religiosity, Theobald's great-grandfather was interested in more than commercial success and attempted to refute the frivolous secularism of the *Aufklärung* in a tract entitled "Hope for a Future Life Proven by the Resurrection of Jesus." At the threshold of the nineteenth century, the Bethmann Hollwegs, transformed from small town bourgeoisie to cosmopolitan patriciate, represented the growing power and self-assurance of the wealthy urban bourgeoisie.[3]

In order to acquire the prerogatives of *Bildung* (education) as well,

9

his youngest son, Moritz August von Bethmann Hollweg, following his father's spiritual interests, abandoned the banking business and ventured into the world of legal scholarship. Inspired by Karl Friedrich von Savigny's historical jurisprudence, he pursued a brilliant university career at Berlin, and later at Bonn, by investigating the origins and theories of civil litigation.[4] A religious awakening during his studies inspired him with a strong pietistic faith that provided an ethical foundation for his legal mind and involvement in ecclesiastical affairs. After receiving a sizable inheritance from his mother, he was knighted in 1840 and bought the picturesque castle of Rheineck. Personal friendship with Frederick William IV and revulsion at the revolutionary "tempest and turmoil" of 1848 drew him into politics. At first an outright reactionary, Moritz August soon became a reforming conservative opposing the intransigent *Kreuzzeitung* with the moderate *Preussische Wochenblatt*.[5]

Searching for a middle way between the doctrinaire liberalism of the Left and the stubborn conservatism of the Junkers, Bethmann Hollweg argued for a pro-British policy during the Crimean War and was therefore appointed minister of culture during the New Era in 1858. But because his irenic nature and his advocacy of greater self-government in the Protestant church were no match for the raging passions of the constitutional conflict, he resigned to return to jurisprudence on the appointment of the Iron Chancellor.[6] Fearing Bismarck's "va banque" policy in 1866, Moritz August warned Frederick William IV against the danger of a fratricidal war with Austria. Despite Prussian victory, he refused to exult in the ultimate success of such unprincipled *Realpolitik*, "because it does not rest on moral and legal grounds." For intellectual as well as temperamental reasons, Theobald's grandfather sought to reconcile natural law with the essence of German idealism. "Formal freedom or self-determination is the precondition of true ethical freedom, in which man harmonizes with the will of God." Liberals saw only restraint and caprice, while conservatives fell into the opposite error of religious and political legalism. "The future of state and church, of law and [society] depends upon free morality." [7]

Since they preferred the simplicity of rural life to "the shallow pleasures of high society," Moritz August's sons, Theodor and Felix, sought to become gentlemen farmers in the East, a necessary step for acceptance into the Prussian nobility. While vacationing in the

Swiss Oberhofen on the Thuner See, the younger Felix was so charmed by the "prettiness and sensitivity" of Isabella de Rougemont in a tableau vivant that he answered his mother's suggestion "that she might be a good wife" with, "Yes, I have already thought so." [8] Soon afterward, in November 1853, Felix won her hand, and after returning from an extensive honeymoon trip to Rome, the couple acquired the *Rittergut* Hohenfinow, a scarce two hours from Berlin. The estate of around 7500 acres included the lands of Tornow and Sommerfelde and cost the considerable sum of 400,000 Thaler, a measure of the family's wealth.[9]

Headstrong and sometimes given to domestic tyranny, Felix possessed "a highly developed drive for independence and a strong desire for hard work"; while the French-speaking Isabella, having a more impressionable and social nature, suffered from the harsh climate and the bigotry of the neighboring Junkers and often longed for her sisters' more glamorous life in Paris. Her warmth complemented her husband's impulsive gruffness and added a touch of cosmopolitanism to the simple rusticity of Hohenfinow.[10] With all his grumpiness, her husband was content to pour his robust energies into the improvement of the estate. By building new stables, establishing a trout-hatchery and a steam sawmill, and experimenting with new crops, he restored Hohenfinow to its former prosperity. Hence Felix von Bethmann Hollweg was respected by his neighbors as an improving landlord, and in 1874 he was appointed *Landrat* (district magistrate) for the district of Oberbarnim.[11]

Nevertheless, this outward conformity to Junker life hid an independent spirit. Broadly politically conscious, he deplored the fall of Richmond and the defeat of the South in the American Civil War, "not because of the disappearance of slavery, but because of the subjugation of the energetic and able Southerners to Northern democracy." Opposed to egalitarianism, he confessed, "I do not know whether I am more repelled by the depravity of slavery or that of Northern democracy!" Similarly, during the Austro-Prussian War, he wrote, "We are endangered less by the undoubtable stupidity of the reactionaries than by the unpatriotic doctrinairism of the progressives." He was not a true Prussian conservative, deploring the king's *Gottesgnadentum* (the divine right of kingship) because of his own national vision, "We fight for our existence and for Germany's future." In contrast to his father's ethical objections to Bismarck's unscrupulous Realpolitik, Felix admitted, "My younger blood delights in power and energy; so far Prussia has never grown in a strictly lawful and ethical manner and in the future it will need enterprising, perhaps even revolutionary, leaders to gain control of Germany." He gloated over the disappointment of his Frankfurt relatives' Austrian sympathies and rejoiced at the sudden victory of Sadowa, exclaiming enthusiastically: "If only we are not too moderate now! All of Germany stands open to us."

A German rather than a Prussian patriot, Felix applauded the progress of unification. "All of this [has come about] through one energetic man, Bismarck, and the successes of our victorious army." Although he had cautioned against a war with France, since he could not see any direct advantage to it, he enlisted as a volunteer in the medical corps and directed a military hospital in 1870–71. And despite his opinion "that the French are a disgustingly superfluous and not very respectable people," he pleaded for restraint in victory. If he echoed the prejudices of his class, and if his role in the Reichstag as a member of the Free Conservatives was ephemeral, Theobald's father nevertheless clashed with the obscurantist views of his reactionary neighbors. "The social hubris rampant in those circles antagonizes me so much that I do not want to belong to them. This is the same barrier which constantly separates me politically from the conservative landowners of our district." Despite his support for Bismarck's *machtpolitische* unification, Felix von Bethmann Hollweg "could not share the Junkers' special caste ambitions and sympathies for the *Kreuzzeitung*, even if I am a conservative like most of them." [12]

For half a century, the center of Felix's labors, the estate of Hohenfinow, was a microcosm of Prussia's retarded social development and pretentions to *Kultur*. Only thirty miles from Berlin, it appeared to the visitor like a rural Tusculum amidst the bustling industrial landscape of the late nineteenth century. "The estate encompasses part of the village with its sprawling buildings, among which the well-designed riding stable with manège stands out." Prosperous straw-roofed cottages huddled around a thirteenth-century village church, whose foundations were older than the neighboring abbey, Chorin. A majestic avenue of linden trees led to the manor, a spacious, three-story brick building from the seventeenth century, recently renovated with a Renaissance façade. Modest but warm, the interior was accented by a glass-ceilinged gallery and harmoniously blended an ample new staircase with baroque stucco ceilings, rococo paintings, and occasional hand-carved furniture, left by a procession of previous owners. Stately and massive though a mixture of styles, the manor "rested on the ruins of a castle of the Ostmark that protected the Oder crossing against Slavic heathens." The showpiece of the estate was the spacious park, dotted with meadows and ponds and extending toward a steep bluff overlooking the Oder. "The marshes lie like a barrel cut by three water arms: the stagnant, the old, and the new Oder, dammed up by mountains here and there which surround the green pastures like so many wooden staves," the peregrine Fontane recalled the scene. "For miles only meadows, no fields, no villages, nothing but haystacks growing smaller and grayer until they merge into a grazing herd on the horizon. Only grass; from time to time a few willows, perhaps a boat gliding across some branch of the river and here and there an ox-cart, loaded with hay, or a tiled roof, whose redness punctuates the landscape." [13]

But this idyllic picture was deceptive. With Felix von Bethmann Hollweg's purchase in 1855, a new spirit had entered the quiet rural world. The fifteen hundred souls living on the estate were relieved about the return of "a respectable family to Hohenfinow." The speculation and neglect of Huguenot Venezobren and the decadent sprees of their successor, Jacobi-Cloest, had driven the docile peasants to rebellion in 1848! "Stern and just, a frugal landlord, an enemy of laziness and indulgence, of hypocrisy and flabbiness," the new master, Felix, "educated through the example of his personality." Moreover, his business acumen, his ambition, and his openness to modern technology disrupted the semifeudal tranquillity and made the estate profitable once more by introducing agrarian capitalism. Encouraging the construction of a railroad station at Niederfinow, he revived the subsidiary agrarian industries of brick-burning, sawmilling and liquor distilling. Felix also bought the steel mill of Karlswerk, which had gone bankrupt during the hectic speculation of the 1870s, but his attempts to revive its production failed and it was turned into housing for seasonal laborers. The extensive forest, covering slightly more than half of the domain, produced considerable profits while draining the Oder marshes, and the establishment of a pumping station increased the hay output. But most striking to the eye were the endless wheat fields, which belied the poverty of the "sandbox of the Holy Roman Empire." In the first four decades of Felix's administration Hohenfinow yielded the following annual gross income:

Agronomy	28,729.00 Marks
Brickyard	21,702.00 Marks
Forestry	12,339.00 Marks
Sawmill	5,412.00 Marks
Gristmill	863.00 Marks
	69,045.00 Marks

No longer a purely agricultural enterprise, the estate provided the family with a modest but comfortable living until World War I when, because of Bethmann's political activities, it was placed under a trusteeship. Unable to compete with the vast estates in Pomerania, Hohenfinow nevertheless produced solid wealth and confronted its owners with the problems of landed gentry in an industrial age.[14]

"In November 1856 mother went from Berlin to Hohenfinow for Isabella's labor, the birth of our dear Theobald, the heir of his grandfather's love of learning," Moritz August proudly noted in his autobiography. Disappointed in his landowning sons, he enjoyed the boy's inquisitive spirit and provided him with intellectual and religious nourishment. "My grandfather . . . and I had much in common and he was a shining example for my inner life because of his loving interest, which only few men can experience," Theobald wrote after his death in 1877. "Now he has passed away and his spirit which ennobled the whole family has left a precious memory as well as a painful void." His deep affection had inspired Theo's kindred soul with a desire for knowledge and a high regard for ethical values. But after 1870 Moritz August seldom talked of politics and at best influenced Theo only indirectly through his example.[15]

On the other hand, Theo's temperamental father, proud of his success in improving the estate and respected as Landrat by his constituency, heaped most of his attention upon the oldest son. Although not devoid of intellectual interest like other Junkers—he read Auerbach and Gustav Freytag—Felix inspired awe rather than love in his children. For his birthday in 1865, Max, Theobald, Margarethe, Hildegard, and Felicia offered their congratulations in a

little rhymed play. As the most verbal, Theo praised their father's
business acumen, and wished:

> Nun verschenken was wir haben
> Kopf und Hand hat es gemacht;
> Und auch unsere kleinen Gaben
> Nimmt der Vater gern in Acht.*

Since Theobald shared only Felix's passion for music and not his
other intellectual tastes, the second son often seemed a stranger in
his father's house. "Since my grandfather is no longer, I feel increasingly alienated from my family, although I love them strongly."
Despite this inner distance, many of Theobald's political opinions
reflected his father's preoccupations, and his eulogy upon the latter's
death in the "Gutsbuch" is so spontaneous and warm as to preclude
the existence of any severe conflict.[16]

His elegant and sensitive mother, a ray of French sunlight in the
foggy clouds of the Mark, attempted to lighten the discipline of her
harsh husband and came closer to fulfilling her son's longing for a
warm human relationship. On her death in 1908, Theobald confessed, "I have lost a friend and comforter in physical and psychological suffering." [17] If, however, the bourgeois origins of the family in
the more liberal atmosphere of Frankfurt and his French heritage
prevented the boy from falling under the spell of a Junker existence,
they were only muted motifs. This varied background, neither
wholly Prussian nor entirely free-city, neither gentleman farmer
nor professional scholar, formed contradictory strains in Theobald's
character.

Although he was overshadowed by his more affable brother Max,
Theo had an untroubled childhood and caused his parents "little
concern over health or ease of instruction." Nannies with starched
aprons, gnarled domestic servants, wild games with the village children, entertaining visits of the cousins Sommerfeld, Mutius, and
Pourtalès, endless Sunday sermons in the Gothic church, and the joys
and adventures of rural life made up his universe. A memorable
event recorded in the "Gutsbuch" was a violent thunderstorm: lightning set ablaze one of the towering linden trees of the park and sent
the children running to safety behind their mother's skirts at the

---

* What our heads and hands make,
  Gifts that are but small,
  Father joyfully does take.

fireside. Their regimen was strict. "Rising at five or six in the morning, the brothers had a cold bath, a simple breakfast and studied hard; their father exercised them in sports, hunting, and riding. Games and pranks with the village boys relieved this discipline only too seldom." But soon Theo was big enough to vacation away from home "at the sea spa Trouville with his aunt Cecile Bérard in order to cure his insistent headaches." Such trips to Berlin, Rheineck, and Paris widened his horizons. While away, "Theobald often writes nice and childlike letters, whereas his older, more superficial brother leaves much to be desired." The formative political experience of his youth was seeing the magnificent spectacle of victorious Prussian troups parading in Berlin in 1866. "The Royal Castle and the Lustgarten were truly great and beautiful," illuminated by hundreds of chandeliers and decorated with massive statues of the Great Elector, the Hohenzollern kings, and a giant Borussia. "This imposing sight" etched into his impressionable mind the splendor of the monarchy and the popular enthusiasm of German unification.[18]

Education was taken seriously at Hohenfinow. Max and Theo prepared for the gymnasium with private tutors and were examined on their accomplishments by the famous classical scholar Perthes. The first *Hauslehrer* (tutor), a candidate of theology named Mühlensiepen, was highly respected as "a fine and polite gentleman"; but their father was critical of his successor, Boyde. "He is an intelligent and gracious man, and with more inner modesty and less democratic views he would be an even more pleasant house fellow." The tutors found "Theo a lovable and gifted youth and it was a pleasure to instruct him. In spite of all sensitivity, he was boyishly active and always ready for a gay prank. No doubt he owed his tact and deep feeling to his mother, and the highly developed sense of authority and duty to his father." Characterized by a strong desire to please, Theo possessed "a quick grasp of essentials and a good memory as natural endowments. He learned foreign languages with ease and already at the age of twelve congratulated his grandfather in Latin on a special occasion." The heavy crates of folios that accompanied Moritz August on each visit fascinated the young Theobald. Conscientious, obedient, and lovable, the boy would have seemed too perfect, if his sharp-eyed grandmother had not exposed one weakness: "What will become of Theobald? He is so ugly!" But lest his son become too bookish, Felix attempted to stimulate his technical interest by installing a room telegraph and by taking him on the hunt. "Today I took Theo along and shot twelve partridges and he hit one of them." [19]

This sheltered, if not completely uneventful childhood, ended abruptly when the twelve-year-old was sent to the old *Fürstenschule* Pforta, in the fall of 1869. One of the elite schools of Protestant Germany, Schulpforta counted such luminaries as Klopstock, Fichte, Ranke, and Nietzsche among its alumni. Mainly serving the sons of the nobility and *haute bourgeoisie,* Pforta was steeped in the traditions of neohumanism and German idealism. As the prototype of classical education, centering upon mastery of Latin and Greek, the curriculum was demanding and in the upper grades reached a level unrivaled in Germany. The entrance examination was rigorous, but once Theobald had been admitted to the *Quarta* (fourth form), the real trial began. Although living as externs with Pastor Beseler, during their initial years Max and Theobald experienced all the hazing and restrictions that characterized nineteenth-century boarding schools. Summer vacations in Hohenfinow or travels such as a *Wanderung* through the Harz Mountains with their former tutor only seldom interrupted this monastic existence.[20]

Under such pressure, the more outgoing Max faltered and was forced to repeat a grade, whereas Theobald conscientiously—if sometimes grudgingly—mastered the material and, through his success in school, began to capture the affections of his father.[21] Although he made few close friends at Pforta except for the historian Karl Lamprecht [22] and the younger Wolfgang von Oettingen, he was respected by his classmates, not only for his studiousness but also for his independence of judgment. High-strung, idealistic, full of unexpressed emotions, Theobald owed less to formal instruction than to his independent reading of Kant and Schopenhauer. Despite his scholastic achievements, he was popular, since he possessed a lively sense of humor and was always ready to engage in harlequinades. During the annual Martini dramatic production, Theo played the lead, a dashing Frenchman in Gutzkow's *Königsleutnant.* His forte was rhetoric. In a debate about the merit of objective versus subjective history, he "so overwhelmed his opponent with his quick, adroit, and sweeping oratory that the latter no longer dared utter a word"—not that he had been right, but he possessed an intuitive insight into his audience's mind which made his sophisms effective. In 1875 he was graduated *primus omnium* after completing a long valedictorian thesis on "Aeschylus's 'Persians' in the light of Aristotle's Poetics," an enterprise which tested his mental powers to their limit.[23]

Throughout his later life, Bethmann retained a warm interest in his alma mater, "since I loved the old Pforta very much . . . I could not tear my thoughts from her." His partly enforced and partly voluntary study of the classics made him a representative of the "tyranny of Greece over Germany," and the neohumanism of Humboldt, with its elitist, esthetic, and ideal preoccupations, permanently marked the habits of his mind. The political spirit of the school was strictly monarchist. "Becoming civil servants of the crown, possibly also of the church, seemed almost self-evident to the alumni of Pforta." Although it provided the basis for many of his philosophical and political beliefs, this experience was not entirely happy: he later complained about suffering from "his exclusive position" at Pforta. More concretely, he "had always abhorred its gossip," and deplored the "impertinence and impudence, the boyish boorishness and that clubby spirit so typical of Pforta." Theobald's idealistic bent was offended by the "commonness and uncouthness" of many fellow pupils and their lack of higher aspirations. Moreover, outward regimentation all too often snuffed out the flames of intellectual enthusiasm. "At one time I wrote harshly about Pforta and did not even leave the small unpleasantnesses untouched," Theo confessed to a friend. But he continued to recommend its education to his relatives, and his harsh criticism of the elite school was, as a former teacher pointed out, "unconsciously the best plaidoyer for Pforta." [24]

Following in Goethe's footsteps, Theobald celebrated his liberation from philological drudgery by a grand tour through Italy. In the company of a family friend, he deeply inhaled the spirit of antiquity and the incense of Catholicism's majestic churches. To a younger schoolmate at Pforta, who had remained behind in gray and rainy Germany, Theobald enrapturedly described his impressions. "I wish you were here and could swim with me down the Rhone to the azure Mediterranean." He wrote from Geneva, "in order to help you see this Paradise, since I cannot describe it to you, I shall be content to tell you in dry words that I found everything in Italy which I had unknowingly searched for earlier in the cold North." His two months in Rome, where he was received by Prussian Minister Keudell, were "simply splendid. It is indescribable what magic hovers over the walls of this eternal city! The great historical past that one encounters at every step through the magnificent ruins imbues everything with a seriousness and dignity which contrasts poignantly with the life of the present Italian people, and especially with the intrigues of the Catholic Church." Full of postromantic admiration, Theobald was not offended by "this contradiction; it rather lets one feel all the suffering and joy of this world without a touch of sentimentality." The irony of Catholic women saying their rosaries in the Pantheon, built by Agrippa for Augustus, struck a mystical, pantheistic chord in his impressionable mind. "The most precious gain one can bring home from Italy is that one learns to suppress sentimentality before the majesty of history and nature," he confessed to Oettingen, exhorting his precocious friend to cross the Alps. "There you will recapture health." Theobald lyrically wrote of the Pyramid of Caius Cestius, ringed by cypresses in which the evening breeze "sounds like a death chant for those buried below. On the graves bloom thousands of camellias, red and white." Recalling Hoelderlin and Nietzsche, these lines testified to the genuine force of his encounter with enchanting Italy.[25]

This personal and intellectual liberation was short-lived. In late 1875 Theobald enlisted in the 15th Ulanen to fulfill his military obligation as *Einjähriger* (reserve officer candidate). "At present I am playing miles gloriosus in old Strasbourg and am drilling ad nauseam," he reported to Oettingen. "Sergeants and superficial comrades make up my social life, and I am deteriorating spiritually. If I were not a Philistine I would not refuse the demands of this sensual world . . . I have not yet tasted that poison." Rereading the opening verses of Heine's *Buch des Leidens* hardly compensated for "the boring and vexing military service," and in retrospect the unending stable and barracks duty appeared to be "a true desert and void." At the same time Bethmann enrolled in the university but "hardly attended lectures and actually was a student only on his calling cards." The unending "service, which does not satisfy me, and the lack of any true friendship," were repugnant to him. However, although he found neither personal nor intellectual fulfillment during his military duty and desultory studies in Strasbourg, Theobald rejected self-pity. "Perhaps it is the prerogative of youth to be happy only because one exists and because one sees other people live and enjoy themselves." Compared to the sheltered cloister walls of Pforta and the majesty of the Alps, Bethmann now saw his life as problematical. "I have lost much of my frivolous optimism. . . . So far life has tossed me about wildly and often the vortex has pulled me along. But I have never made progress in these odysseys." As he thus overdramatized his experiences, Bethmann was approaching the threshold of a personal crisis.[26]

Although he never abandoned his social position or lost sight of his practical goals, Theobald now entered a phase of severe self-doubt and inner struggle. "While reading Strauss, Darwin, and Haeckel, I have suddenly stumbled into a realm of ideas and principles completely different from my earlier ones, so that I am presently in the hopeless situation of believing everything and nothing," he explained to Wolfgang von Oettingen. "And yet I must confess that I feel more serene and happy than before and hold to the blasphemous belief that this earth is not only far from the vale of tears of theologians but that it can be quite pleasant and beautiful here." Shattering his previous philosophical and religious certainties, the encounter with the iconoclast David Friedrich Strauss "has thrown me into my present orbit," and produced "inchoate and revolutionary" ideas in Theobald's mind. Moreover, Darwin's stress on struggle rather than Aristotelian harmony, and Haeckel's espousal of vulgar materialism challenged Bethmann's idealism, his conventional neoclassicism, and the moderate, pietistic Protestantism of his grandfather. Because Theobald romantically overvalued the ideal of Platonic friendship with one kindred soul, his intellectual anguish assumed personal dimensions as well. "In Strasbourg a radical reaction against this ideal took place, so much so that I lost myself for some time in the crowd, drifting along in frivolous and sometimes dissolute *Jugendrausch*." Later he reflected on his overreaction. "In order to strip off my own onesidedness, I embarked with sails too full; I lost many a precious thing, but I rejoiced when the storm battered me and night and flood were about to devour me." Unfulfilled by the high-flown idealism of Pforta, Bethmann flung himself into student life, celebrating the disintegration of his spiritual moorings by "living like a heathen." For most *Studiosi* only harmless diversions, for Bethmann these escapades assumed metaphysical significance.[27]

Because he had found little response among his fellow students, Theobald thirsted for someone to whom he could bare his innermost thoughts. The younger Wolfgang von Oettingen fulfilled this need because of his literary and artistic sensitivity. "For the first time in a long while have the strings of my *Gemüth* been touched, which once whispered most treasured melodies and filled my life with sparkling joy." Theobald thanked Wolfgang: "I know so few people who follow me in my moods, and recently the silence of death has darkened my soul and stifled my emotions. Now you offer your friendship and I can hardly say how wondrous and at the same time painful this feels." Not a face-to-face friendship with a fellow student, but rather a letter-relationship, their exchange was conducted in *Sie,* the polite form of address. Not until a year later did Bethmann suggest using the familiar *Du,* "since *Sie* is so formal and we do not exchange formalities." The correspondence revolved, not around gossip or political speculation, but around poetry of surprising talent:

Spätsommer

Es weht die Luft so schwül im Hain
Bang zittert der Wind in den Bäumen.
Und ich mit meinem Schmerz allein
Geh hin in trüben Träumen.

Die Blümlein alle blau und roth
Sie nicken still im Winde
Sie ahnen ihren frühen Tod—
Und nicken still im Winde.

Ihr Blümlein, Blümlein weinet nur
Bald müsst auch ihr verderben.
Der Herbstwind rasselt in der Flur.
Und dann—dann müsst ihr *sterben.*

Ihr Blümlein, Blümlein weint um mich
Und weint um meine Schmerzen
Auch meines Glückes Lust verstrich
Ich fühl den Tod im Herzen.*

*Indian Summer

The air hangs sultry in the grove,
An anxious wind rustles the trees.
And once again in pain I rove
Alone with my dreary dreams.

The flowers clothed in blue and red
Silently nod in the breeze,
Knowing they will soon be dead—
Silently nod in the breeze.

Full of Weltschmerz, presentiments of death and sorrow, these late romantic lines reveal less personal suffering than the self-consciousness of a sensitive youth searching for "a great and holy enthusiasm into which I could submerge my soul as into purifying fire." The poems' recurring themes of stormy or wintry nature, the darkness of night, the passions of *Liebeswonne* and *Jugendlust,* and the longing for heroic sacrifice are largely conventional, and Bethmann in cooler moments found it impossible to sustain literary inspiration. Free from the restrictions of the gymnasium, and not yet sobered by professional responsibility, he could allow himself for a few precious years to savor his chaotic emotions and to suffer the anguish of "feeling that one could be something and is nothing!" In youthful fashion, his love of humanity remained abstract, "like someone walking through a village in the evening after a day's hike and looking through the windows into the lighted rooms of the inhabitants." In general, Bethmann felt a basic distance, a lack of warmth, a difficulty in sustaining human relationships, which accounted for much of his tendency to withdraw and meditate.[28]

This introspective pessimism also rendered Theobald's relationships with the opposite sex difficult. "You should know how trying it is for a passionate soul like myself who either gives and takes completely or not at all, to seek and find a friend who is willing to do likewise, and gladly accepts some of my rough edges and nastiness." To Oettingen he preferred to dramatize:

> Oh könnt ich lieben!
> Könnt ich eine Nacht
> Voll heisser Jugendglut
> Im Arme meiner Liebsten schlafen,
> Und mit der Morgenröte
> Weckt mich ein früher Tod
> Aus süssem Liebestraume.
> Und träge auf des Nachtwinds Flügeln

> Blossoms, oh blossoms, shed your tears!
> You, too, soon here will lie.
> When autumn's frigid hand appears,
> Then you will have to die.

> Flowers, oh flowers, weep for me
> Shed tears for all my pains.
> My joy and happiness did flee,
> I feel death in my veins.

Die wonnetrunkne Seele sanft
Zum ewig freud- und leidenlosen Nichts——
Wie wohl geschähe mir . . . ! *

And he continued his rapturous fantasies in prose: "Always only to surmise happiness but never to taste it is a harsh fate. And the god does not grant me in this suffering the gift of describing my agony." More imagined than real, this inferno nevertheless agitated the twenty-year-old deeply and led him to premature skepticism: "La vie est une chaine d'illusions et de déceptions et quelle sottise que de se plaire dans les illusions?!" But he was repeatedly tempted. "Child, yesterday I beheld a girl—but oh! threefold iron shielded my heroic breast," he related one encounter to the younger Wolfgang. It was the daughter of Paul Heyse the poet, who inspired another vision of a romantic pilgrimage to Rome to atone for real and imagined sins. "Then I would weep and sink / before you my own queen, / you Venus born of foam, / you mistress of my heart." Although Bethmann pleaded poetically—"Oh! open your lips/ and say the saving word!"—absolution never came. Despite his own awareness that "a beautiful spring and a little love" would overcome his self-doubt and periodic fits of depression, Theobald did not succeed. "I have done everything possible. I skated with all the young girls of Berlin: either they were timid or coquettish, but few were really beautiful." His exaggerated notion of female beauty and purity created a chasm which made it impossible for him to find satisfaction in mere reality. "I find it disquieting that, despite some criminal desires of my brain, I have reached my twenty-fifth year without ever having loved passionately, especially since I regretfully know sensuality." Bored with the shallow prattle "of the young girls who still fear the switch of the nursery or bring the aesthetic ignorance of the finishing school into the ballroom," Theobald began to take an interest in young matrons, although—unlike Werther—he was far from endangering any mar-

*Oh, could I love!
Could I one night
Full of youth's fire
Lie in my beloved's arms,
While at dawn
Early death would wake me
From sweet passion's dream.
And carry on the wings of wind
My blissful soul gently
Into eternal joy and painless void——
How wondrous that would be!

riages, "since Lady Venus did apparently not grace my cradle." Not until his own wedding in 1889 did Bethmann find a satisfactory compromise between the ideal and the real in love.[29]

Escape into the fancied world of "romantic raptures, dreams of Italy and beautiful women," failed to still Theobald's metaphysical hunger. Realizing reluctantly that "there are many things between heaven and earth, not dreamed of by school wisdom," he buried his excessive exultation and returned to his preoccupation with "the crumbling of my moral convictions about me." Although the realist critique of idealist fantasy distressed him, "I am not too sad about it [since] *reality is so beautiful* and only those who can see it with healthy eyes do not need forced idealization through clouded and diseased imagination." In an attempt to save some of his intellectual heritage from the confrontation with atheism, materialism, and Darwinism, Bethmann maintained that "realistic imagination" was part and parcel of reality, not a romantic invention: "I perceive it in Goethe, Shakespeer [*sic*] and in the really good and old works of Greek sculpture, no longer in Apollo Belvedere, where the god has become an actor *qui pose*." Only rampant, "unjustified fantasy" had to be rejected because it created a "painful, haunting consciousness of human depravity, imperfection, and weakness," whereas the former produced "the joyful sensation of how beautiful reality is." This groping attempt to recover the balance of German classicism was predicated on Haeckel's theory "that there is no dualism, only a monism in this world, that we are all beings of one kind who strive to reach perfection, or at least ought to do so." The popular notion of nature as beautiful as long as "man does not intrude with his suffering" was a pious fiction of those "who offer us nothing but empty phrases about 'a better afterlife.'" Leading him in passionate hours to the maxim, "Eat, drink, and be merry for tomorrow we die," this partial break with idealism made Bethmann confess: "I love life, the world, and men, although I have had to suffer much from them. Yes, you see that I have become a very modern child of this world!" At last, Zeller's history of German philosophy, "a splendidly written work which gives a synopsis of the systems with great clarity," and some lectures helped him to come to the reassuring conclusion, "Only now do I find out how little I know in [philosophy], since many a doubt with which I wrestled desperately is here lightened and resolved through historical reflection." Nevertheless his contradictory synthesis between idealism and realism left much unanswered. "How I envy people with a good, firm faith! As I must admit," he wrote to Oettingen, "I am still horribly far from it. Despite much activity, my life leads me deeper and deeper into these underground mines." [30]

Nevertheless Bethmann's legal studies progressed smoothly. In October 1876 he moved to Leipzig to pursue jurisprudence in the shadow of the new *Reichskammergericht* (imperial supreme court) "content as far as one can be and fairly conscientious in my work, which far surpassed my expectations." The ancient Saxon university, at the time the largest institution in the empire, possessed the most distinguished law faculty and enjoyed the reputation of requiring hard work. Because legal study meant learning by rote rather than independent penetration, the lectures he had to attend were "fairly dry," and since the true ethos of Wissenschaft seldom inspired professorial dictations, the high-strung Bethmann soon grew dissatisfied. "Officially I am studious, but I live in scholarship like a wanderer and am not at home with it." While he often found the art historian Anton Springer or the economist Karl Roscher more scintillating, Theobald did assimilate many of the fundamental legal concepts of his teachers. Adolf Wach, in whose house he was a frequent guest, confronted him with a muted natural law critique of the Hegelian and Treitschkean primacy of the state. Even if there was no earthly power above it, he argued for the existence "of a law, which born with us, a guide inherent in the state, flowing from its rational order," constituted "an eternal measuring rod for the government's intent and action." Much of his later rhetoric was also heavily indebted to the leading apologist of the liberalized monarchical bureaucratic state, Rudolf von Gneist. Despite his prominent liberal role in the Reichstag suspicious of parliamentary power, the anglophile Berlin professor advocated honorary self-government, relying on the fusion of the propertied and educated bourgeoisie with the natural aristocracy. Rationalizing the Prussian constitutional compromise, he propagated a reform of the local administration to strengthen representation on the *Kreis* level and, because of his deep belief in the *Rechtsstaat* (rule of law) insisted on legal review of administrative decisions. But in spite of all criticism of royal absolutism, aristocratic egotism, and bureaucratic irresponsibility, Gneist saw the Prussian three-class suffrage as "the total product of the social, moral, and legal ideas of a nation on a specific level of development, which manifests itself in the formulation of a legal norm in a certain political crisis and which is accepted since a different one *cannot* be found." The tension between the ethically normative and politically expedient roles of law remained unresolved.[31]

Since he often felt "true, genuine enthusiasm lacking and much mediocrity," Theobald flung himself into the pleasures of student life. Although he thought the difficulty of making real friends, "next to the dirty trade-Jews and coal pollution Leipzig's greatest drawbacks," he considered "the splendid Gewandhaus concerts a steady delight and the theater, which is not altogether to my taste, nevertheless stimulates me each time to small critical reflections." Since the one-time rebellious *Burschenschaften,* the champions of national and liberal reform, had become pale copies of the boisterous traditionalism of the *Landsmannschaften* (regional fraternities), whose duelling and drinking ritualistically controlled student custom, he found little to choose among the erstwhile enemies. Although more progressively oriented, the independent *Finkenschaften* (loosely or nonorganized students) lacked social cohesion and colorful costumes. Abandoning his search for ideal companions, Theobald therefore joined his older "brother's friends, a circle of former fraternity students, necessitating a fairly closed social life." Aware of the limitations of his social position, he felt obliged not to stray too far even if he was unwilling to undergo the ritual of membership in one of the corps. "You know that I am not *standesvornehm* [of noble blood], but when all external life functions move in a privileged circle it is imprudent and false to step out of line even with one foot." Somewhat more mature in his attitude toward student frolics, he wrote in 1877: "I found myself again without sentimental egotism or Philistine weakness. Now I can join occasionally in shallow student fun; since I no longer take it to heart, I even enjoy drinking bouts [*Kneipabende*] and mischievous pranks." Nevertheless intellectual entertainments such as the reading of Kleist's "Prince of Homburg" were his chief delight, while he found psychological release in his passion for hunting, which made him forget "many pensive stupidities. You know how much I love nature; its solitude reawakens slumbering words in me and the contrast of the sensual pleasure of the chase with my inner emotions heartens me and bans weak sentimentality." Nevertheless such diversions were all too short-lived, and "the goddess with the scales has again replaced her sister with the bow and I sit behind my books with customary dedication." [32]

The laborious process of "freely forming my own world" was not complete until Theobald developed a conception of society and politics. While fancying himself a "man of passion" during the period between adolescence and adulthood, he remained unpolitical and generally shared the prejudices of his class. Thus he benevolently admitted that Fritz Reuter's description of "the daily life of the 'common' people" warmed his heart and that the patriarchical "distribution of Christmas presents to the poor children with their radiant little faces made me feel happy." As a self-conscious Protestant, he wondered about "poor" Pius IX's death, "if he is not relieved to have left the masquerade of infallibility behind. Now a new one will repeat the mass of lies which the stupid world will continue to adore. Shame!"

However, the second assassination attempt on William I by the self-styled socialist Dr. Karl Nobiling crystallized Theobald's political consciousness in an intensely emotional confession at Rheineck. "Dearest friend, what a great event of world history has unfolded before our eyes during the past few days!" At least he hoped it would "be a milestone for our inner development on which the despicable socialists and unclear doctrinaire liberals will smash their heads. I cannot believe that our beloved German people is incapable of being one *Volk* and one state." Theobald hoped for a reversal of the "simpering, petty spirit among us," but he knew "that we need a complete regeneration and this warning is especially directed to us young men." Deploring the general lack of idealism, "the apathetic indifference," and "the frivolity and lack of concentration," he alluded to his own former conflicts, "We play with socialist ideas, with materialistic atheism, unaware of their danger, and the other side is too stupid to decide what is to be thrown out as reactionary vagaries and what must be reformed as treasured ideals." But the student response to the crime made him immensely proud: "During the past week such a unanimous wave or patriotic enthusiasm and dedication to a great cause swept through us that we felt ennobled in common duty to our common fatherland, despite our sadness and revulsion. These were magnificent days, I tell you, which defeated all cowardice!" Caught up in the emotional surge, Bethmann poured out his heart to his friend: "You, my dearest, will feel with me how strongly these events so contrary to my expectations have inspired me." [33]

This sudden awakening of enthusiastic patriotism provided the leitmotiv of Bethmann's political beliefs throughout his life. "Late at night, at the open window, looking from the castle to the river flowing majestically in the moonlight," Theobald thanked Oettingen for expressing a kindred feeling. Only the lonely voice of a nightingale broke the enraptured silence, and from a distant village ribald songs echoed in the dark valley. "My whole being and life are more and more determined and uplifted by my Germanness and by my desire to be a true and brave son of my Germany according to my profession. I cannot and will not think of a life without a fatherland." Carried away by his patriotism, Theobald denounced the "Israelitic cosmopolitan tendency . . . which espouses as ideal the utopia of dissolving the individual fatherlands in a general world murk," calling it a "lie and an impossibility which at one time almost ensnared me. But now, I think, I am cured forever."

Despite this outburst of unreflective, emotional nationalism, Bethmann's critical mind refused to be swept into right-wing hysteria. "These incredibly stupid reactionaries," he compained the next evening to Oettingen, and apologized for having sounded like one of them. "I am far from adopting the views of the *Kreuzzeitungsritter* and Co., who render any progressive evolution impossible by their prejudice." Even at a moment of high patriotic exultation, Bethmann was already searching for a middle way: "Can one really believe that these people consider that everything created in the last twenty or thirty years is false and must be burned to make things better?" On the basis of German unification, Theobald rejected Prussian particularism, since it attributed all evils to the Liberals and demanded a return to "the good old days." "These idiots! They really act as if they had not lived and experienced anything, for them the great book of history does not exist, and they seem to have forgotten that there once was a French Revolution!" Already striking chords that would later be so central to his political work, he continued, "They will fail to put their insane reactionary ideas into practice because the people are not clay dolls that one can shape as one pleases; their rantings create immense harm since they stoke the flames of partisan hatred."

Rejecting as alien the prescriptions of socialism and liberalism, and dissastisfied with the unreconstructed stand-pattism of the Conservatives, Bethmann idealistically prayed for a unified patriotic response which would lead the fatherland to domestic unity and foreign peace. Nevertheless, these passionate pages hint at what was to become his key political weakness. "The lovely silhouette of the

Siebengebirge, the green mountain paths toward the Eifel with its desolate, melancholy ruins and burnt-out craters" made wild desires surge up in him. "Do not berate me; unfortunately I never turn these wild thoughts into wild deeds." He confessed his inability to act, "O God, were I to do it, could I do it, I believe I would be healed!" [34]

Soon harsh reality in the guise of his approaching state examination put an end to all his poetic and patriotic raptures. In early fall of 1878 young Bethmann moved to the Prussian capital and "issued a severe law for myself which will put a strict rein on my fantasy, but it is an exceptional law with a firm terminal date." To relieve the strain of preparation, he "acquired a roomate, a true friend and an old love—the antique head of the young Augustus." This magnificent bust, in whose features "youthful innocence and Caesarism are wondrously mixed," was his "entire joy, daily delight, and a true refreshment." Similarly, he adored the casts of the treasures of Olympia, especially the Hermes and Nike attributed to Praxiteles; they "united classical restraint with cheerful, godlike manhood in a delightful degree." To ease the boredom and routine of legal memorizing, he worked with Detlev von Bülow, later a high official, "a good man, true as gold and the archetype of a Nordic explorer." But mounting pressures of mindless cramming made him "prosaic and dull," sometimes even glum. "I sit almost the whole day at home and learn boring things in an exasperating manner without thoroughness and joy." He attended few lectures, "since I lack time and since one breathes more human stench than wisdom there," and when he did hear Hobbes and Pufendorf he encountered such a "lack of spirit that would have made the old gentlemen turn in their graves had they still been able to hear." Not even the kaiser's parade, with all its "magnificence and turmoil," could shatter his dismal mood because "last summer in Leipzig I undertook a major scholarly work which interested me very much, but I have been forced to abandon it, too, since I thought it too risky to tie myself down before the exam." To his younger cousin, the writer Gerhard von Mutius, who lived in the same house during these trying months, he appeared as "an older, benevolently superior, tolerant bachelor with a black beard." He recalled him "walking the streets of Berlin in a black greatcoat, slightly stooped, somewhat nearsighted, looking at the showcases through his pince-nez. Sometimes I also saw him at dinner or at my aunt's. He did not always quite belong in the elegant circle that assembled there. He remained aloof and was not without pride in his isolation." The "unedifying work" reinforced Theobald's distance from others, made him "a dull fellow" who only hoped to end his misery by "enrolling for the examination in March." [35]

"Rendering the necessity of a new Adam quite clear," the approaching hour of reckoning "gave practical significance to the eighteen-hundred-year-old question 'what shall I do?' " Still unsure "if and what in my studies will satisfy me," Bethmann decided to "hasten the end as much as I can in order to try some kind of work and find out if I can accomplish something and then either continue with success or retire." The enforced solitude made him "think neither of traveling nor spring, neither of love nor blooming apple trees; I slave from morning till night like a carriage horse." Even a short vacation at Hohenfinow, where "I recited tragedies and poems to my ladies," a trip to the "Leipzig fair, distasteful with its fleas and Jews," and visits to the opera, which made "me curse graphically about Wagner's *Rheingold* and *Walkurie*," did little to relieve his "unpleasant state of overwork and examination fury." But on June 18, 1879, he could finally write to Oettingen that his "farflung and difficult examination paper" was completed and that the *Staatsexamen* itself had "a happy outcome. Now . . . you must rejoice with me that I have moved this unpleasant weight from me." His patient labors had such success that he was rewarded with the grade *excellent* and encouraged to continue immediately with his doctoral orals at Leipzig. Hoping that "my whole life will then assume another and more quiet character," he presented himself in late July. "I passed the oral examination," he wrote Oettingen in November, "and I am still waiting for the result of the dissertation," which had been begun in spring but needed more polish. After the customary bureaucratic delays, Theobald, now barely twenty-four, was promoted to doctor of law in February of 1880, with a thesis reminiscent of his grandfather's scholarly interests, "Gegenstand und Inhalt des Pfandrechts an dinglichen Rechten. Nach römischem Recht." To enjoy four fleeting weeks of freedom before entering the austere state service, he "traveled as hunter to the Carpathians, that is, as knowing roué to Vienna and [Buda-]Pest." Even though the Hungarians seemed all too superficial, he admired "the landscape's godlike nature and the holy stream, the Danube. The solitude of the mountains has been an immense balm, and a foreign country with strange customs was a precious experience for me, a Nordic beaver." Indulging for a last time the inner turmoil and outward folly of his student days, Bethmann was "enraptured with Hungarian wine and gypsy songs." [36]

With the successful completion of his studies in 1879, Theobald's *Wanderjahre* were over. "The realization that all the thoughts, the high-flung ideas which in earlier years rushed through my mind were only the straw-fire of youth," though still painful, revealed that he was beginning to find himself. His idyllic and sheltered childhood at Hohenfinow was now but a fond memory. The intellectual flights of humanistic Pforta inspired an occasional postcard in Latin and an idealized familiarity with the classics. The storms and stresses of his effort at poetic creativity, his struggle for sexual, philosophical, political, social, and professional emancipation had soldered a new metal in the fire of youthful enthusiasm: Bethmann's often baffling personality. Despite his self-dramatization, much of his childhood, adolescence, and youth had been conventional. Birth on a quiet estate, education first by tutor then in an elite classical school, a grand tour of Italy, military service in a distinguished cavalry regiment, the study of law in Leipzig, as well as the return to the political and social capital of Prussia for examination, even the obligatory doctorate, comprised the typical upbringing of the fortunate sons of the aristocracy or the *Grossbürgertum*.

Yet Theobald's reaction to these experiences had not always been predictable. Although the rivalry with his older brother intensified his learning efforts, he apparently enjoyed the cloistered world of Schulpforta more genuinely than most of his peers. As a self-styled intellectual, he rejected the personal demands of militarism, and in contrast to those of Bismarck, his student escapades were tame. Refusing to join a fraternity, he lived in his own imagination, preferring the world of ideas and ideals to prosaic reality. A young man of uncommon aspirations, Theobald, because of his failure at sexual adjustment, literary self-expression, and formalized scholarship, assumed a character both cold and fervent, cynical and idealistic, conservative and reformist. At twenty-three he was both astonishingly old and personally naive, and was ready to concretize his "hazy ideas about the future." Lacking other attractive alternatives, Bethmann pragmatically resolved "to dedicate [his] efforts to the service of the state." [37]

CHAPTER 3

The Making of a Chancellor

Because the newly united German Empire possessed only an embryonic bureaucracy, Prussian administration remained a favorite career of the jeunesse dorée. Public officials, having developed from timid royal servants into wielders of power at the fulcrum of the state, dominated the ill-defined but vast realm of politics which lay between Hohenzollern prerogatives and infrequent parliamentary review. Although *Geheimrat* (privy councilor) liberalism had largely been purged and a self-perpetuating "noble-bourgeois aristocracy of office" taken its place, the duty ethos of this self-proclaimed "universal estate"—a curious amalgam of Kant and Hegel—still provided aspiring youths with the purpose of service to higher ideal.

But Bethmann found his legal apprenticeship "dry and boring," saw himself not as "a well-appointed *Referendar* [junior law clerk] but rather as an underpaid typewriter of the judges," and lamented that his court appointment at the Berlin *Kammergericht* turned him into "a simpleton for all eternity." Grateful to be "neither husband or debtor," the chief targets of civil litigation, Theobald enjoyed his leisure by reading widely in French and English, and made a few friends with whom he could discuss "the alpha and omega of physics and ethics." Already in 1880 Bavarian ambassador Hugo von Lerchenfeld had recorded Bethmann's name as that of "an official capable of assuming some first-rate position in the future." Longing for an end to "this butterfly existence" and disillusioned with the judicial busywork from which he "learned nothing," Bethmann made an unconventional decision. "The manifold and often disparate social contacts with colleagues, relatives, students, and officers never leave me a quiet hour, and render me so distracted that in order to preserve a few illusions for my later life, I want to move to a smaller town." In stark contrast to the majority of his ambitious peers, who frequented the salons of the Prussian and German capital in order to secure favorable appointments in the military or the foreign service, Theobald preferred the tranquility of Goerlitz in Upper Silesia, where he could better "decide if I want to remain with the courts or change over into administration." Annoyed by the pettiness of the judiciary, he tended toward the latter career, sighing: "Had I only a material basis and a profession which I like and in which I could accomplish something. Until now I have been looking at life like a cow at a new gate."[1]

Though less exciting, life in provincial Prussia was more satisfying for Bethmann. Since Goerlitz had no openings, he was sent to the *Bezirksgericht* (district court) in Frankfurt on the Oder, where the old councilor, Falcke, welcomed him and his eventual successor Georg von Michaelis with the profound question, "Do you know the *noedus forensis,* the court knot," used to tie packets of files together? Since work was not demanding, Theobald had ample time to mingle with the future administrative elite of Prussia, among whom Wilhelm von Waldow and Georg von Rheinbaben later occupied high offices. "The general spirit of our Referendar society is, to be true, hardly more than average, but some of its members are interesting in terms of intellect and character. Moreover, we share a true camaraderie, and for the first time in my life I feel free, independent, and self-reliant with my fellows without possessing an exclusive position." Before the turn of the century Frankfurt's social life was "harmless, small town, divided into cliques gossiping about everybody, and offering little beauty and less spirit." Hence Theobald "danced, stayed awake, and groaned throughout carnival," and only escaped the arrow of Cupid "because I had girded my chest with triple steel." With such lively if provincial diversions, work "at least in its noncraftsmanlike aspects" had to take a backseat. "To be sure, I have sighed through many a file, but have never found the philosophers' stone. In half a year," he confided to Oettingen in March 1881, "I confront the decision whether I want to become judge or official." And, in a first stirring of responsibility, he added significantly, "The latter career might lead to statesmanlike action and I shall probably embark upon it, since my inclination and, as I believe—perhaps blasphemously— also my calling, draw me toward it."[2]

After the obligatory two years' apprenticeship following the first state examination, Bethmann was admitted to the second Staatsexamen in June 1884. His superiors in Frankfurt testified to his "good legal knowledge, diligence and industry, practical astuteness and private probity," and considered him "an excellent addition to state officialdom." Upon completing his introduction into the district bureaucracy, he was sent to Freienwalde to complete his practical initiation into local administration. In Frankfurt, at his father's request, he followed the traditional preparation for state service in the district president's office, the church and school department, the direct taxes, domain, and forest division, and the main governmental payroll office. *Regierungspräsident* (district president) Heyden regarded Bethmann as "not only the most gifted but also one of the most industrious of all the *Referendare* trained here." When the day of reckoning arrived, Bethmann shone as usual. "During the examination the committee flattered me and my official superiors considered me God knows what," he wrote to Oettingen. Indeed, the examining committee was impressed with his answers to their questions about the legal status of the organs of the Protestant and Catholic churches, and "which reasons speak for or against granting state officials an active or passive right of election to parliament?" His thesis of over four hundred pages, written in six weeks and revealing "an industrious, thorough and, on the whole, successful effort," persuaded the examiners to grade it "good" despite some minor criticism of his argument for restricting the passive right of election for officials. The oral part, ranging widely over Prussian civil and administrative law, was so successful that Minister of the Interior Puttkammer telegraphed Theobald's joyful father: "Your son has just passed with distinction. Congratulations." First transferred to the district administration in Potsdam, the new *Regierungsassessor* (probationary administrator) was temporarily appointed Landrat of Oberbarnim to fill his father's vacancy. After a second setback in a Reichstag election, the older Bethmann had resigned, "disavowed by the district, which I administered with energy and success." Since his only competitor had been sent to Schwerin, "Theobald came here as commissary administrator and in August, I think, after a unanimous request of the Kreistag, he was [permanently] appointed as Landrat." Parting reluctantly from his intellectual aspirations, the twenty-nine-year-old bachelor had only the "hope that the work which fully satisfies my will also heal my soul." [3]

Besides being a new step toward personal independence and maturity, Theobald's decision to begin at the bottom of domestic administration rather than to join the glamorous foreign service unwittingly launched him on a spectacular career. Self-consciously withdrawing from his former friends "and seeking to go my way alone," he felt "older, unfortunately very old, and much worse. I always think of a butterfly whose colorful dust has been brushed from his wings." But these sensitive ruminations to Oettingen grew fewer and fewer in number, "since with all the inner pain, my outward life moved forward with a certain luster." On a gray September day in 1877, he had first met Crown Prince William, who had accepted a hunting invitation to Hohenfinow. Seeking to escape female tutelage and eager to prove his manhood because of his crippled right arm, the eighteen-year-old prince replied to Felix's offer to kill a deer, "Are the bucks close enough for me to shoot one?" Despite his host's careful provision of half-tame deer in the preserve, young William was so excited about his first hunt that he missed three or four times. The older Bethmann dreaded the royal wrath at this disappointment, but when dusk began to fall the forester announced another buck. Approaching as near as eighty paces, William rested the rifle on Felix's shoulder, sighted, "and the buck collapsed under his fire." Having thus proved his markmanship, William always remained grateful to the Bethmanns for his first trophy. "This little episode provided the impetus for a lasting relationship, founding a gracious friendship toward me and my family until the present day," Theobald's father wrote in 1890. Indeed, the emperor returned often to the chase at Hohenfinow, "repeating his cordiality upon every visit and acting like a friend toward Theobald at every opportunity." The Bethmanns' "position of trust" with William II did not harm Theobald's professional advancement, although there is no evidence of the kaiser's direct intervention in his favor.[4]

Theobald's appointment as Landrat "especially pleased" his father, since he "wanted him to be my successor in the district after Max's failure." The professional disgrace of his more affable and seemingly favored older brother profoundly affected Theobald's self-image and his attitude toward Hohenfinow. After his *Abitur,* the easy-going, good-looking Max had so enjoyed the delights of riding, soldiering, and carousing with the notorious fraternity, Saxo-Borussia at Bonn, that he had barely passed his first legal examination. In 1883, rather than face the shame of failing his second Staatsexamen, he suddenly decided to flee—to America! When the family learned of this rash decision, father, mother, and Theobald intercepted him at Calais. Their long discussions with him were fruitless, however, and "I convinced myself that a change to completely new surroundings was necessary for Max, and we agreed that he should launch a commercial career in New York." Although he was unable to persuade him to return home, his father at least wanted to give Max an easier start in the New World by providing him with introductions to American banking circles and paying him 150,000 Marks, his share of the inheritance. After sustaining some initial disappointments on Wall Street, Max moved to the expanses of Texas, where he bought large tracts of land to sell to German immigrants—again with little success. In 1897 he died prematurely of stomach cancer. The two brothers' relationship recalled their father's lines about his own older brother, Theodor. "We two got along fairly well in life but were never very close, since we were too differently endowed, and each went his special way; but I often felt hurt by the pride of the smarter brother and oldest son of the family." Now Theobald was the sole heir to the family tradition and occupied the Landrat residence, renovated at considerable expense by his father, "in the hope that one of my sons would relieve me." [5]

The tasks awaiting the "highly gifted" Landrat in Freienwalde, the spa of the Mark Brandenburg, were challenging. During the previous decade his father's all too generous spending (necessitated by the negligence of his predecessor Haeseler), had brought the district deeply into debt; but through strict economies, Theobald was able to show a profit of 4,000,000 Marks by the end of his term. The work of internal colonization of the Oder marshes, begun by Frederick the Great, called for incessant efforts at drainage, the building of pumping stations, the winning of new land; and in 1892 Theobald applied for a professional assistant to help him in his task. The ambitious road-and-bridge-building program undertaken by his father had to be continued, a branch of the railroad from Berlin to Frankfurt/Oder constructed, new schools and hospitals established. The conservative and parsimonious peasants, the undertaxed nobles, and the liberal townspeople more often resisted than helped Bethmann's efforts, but he succeeded in acquiring a reputation for fairness by taxing his fellow landowners according to the true value of their estates. When *Kreistag* (local council) or *Ritterschaft* (council of nobles) were deadlocked, Theobald could use his persuasiveness to good advantage, and when confronted with intractable opposition, he learned the fine art of political compromise. Later a bitter opponent, the young assistant Cuno Westarp regarded his only slightly "older superior very highly as Landrat and as a man, and . . . remained grateful for his introduction into the practical work of district administration." Patriarchical conservatism, though open to the growing problems of industrialization, informed Bethmann's warnings "that it is imperative to stem the social-democratic propaganda" which was beginning to threaten even the relative stability of Oberbarnim. In this report Theobald followed the political ideas of his Free Conservative father, appointed to the Herrenhaus in 1889. His practical success and moderation so endeared him to the district administration that he was already noted in 1888 as one of the promising young Landräte of whom much could be expected in the future.[6]

Despite the limited intellectual and artistic pleasures of Freienwalde, these were the happiest years of Bethmann's life. In contrast to his father, who had "played the pike in the carp pond," he was well liked in the district. But more importantly, among the neighboring nobility and childhood family friends he met his wife Martha. In 1886 he had congratulated Oettingen on his engagement with the bittersweet lines, "The more I miss it in my own life, the more I delight in the happiness of a friend"; but three years later his father could report: "On June 17, 1889, Theo married Martha, the youngest daughter of the first marriage of Pfuel-Wilkendorf, a pretty and cheerful girl, whom we receive with open arms into our family. In happy marriage she completely shares the cares of her husband concerning his district, work, and election." The lighter and more sociable nature of his Junoesque wife complemented Theo's tendency to brood and awoke in him a sense of humor that few of his closest friends had suspected to exist. The couple's happiness grew when, "after a long delay, their first child, a healthy boy, was born on June 4 [1890], and was baptized August Friedrich." But death and disease did not respect the rural idyll, and on May 6, 1892 their second child was taken from the young parents. Theobald himself had just undergone a severe attack of appendicitis and felt the need to unburden his heart. "You know," he said to his younger cousin Gerhard von Mutius, "it is strange when that moment comes in life when one feels: I can go on no longer! In nothing, not even in ideas!" The student laughed off such dark forebodings, but he later admitted, "He was and remained in all phases of his life a lonely man." Only the "radiant appearance, the warmhearted figure" of

Martha von Pfuel dispelled his recurring pessimism, since she was, in the eyes of Hohenfinow's pastor, "the archetype of noble femininity, inner piety and true motherly love." [7]

Having lost his seat in the Reichstag to the liberal Friedrich von Schroetter after two terms, the older Bethmann urged his son to run for parliament in 1890. After some maneuvering, a competitor, Baron von Eckardtstein, withdrew from the race and "Theobald was unanimously nominated as candidate of the Conservatives and National Liberals . . . after a good electoral speech." His chances appeared favorable, "since Theobald is very well liked in the district and probably all progressive Liberals will vote for him for fear of the Social Democrats." The district had been disputed between the moderates and the Right, but against the threat of a Left victory the former archenemies closed their ranks behind Bethmann, since "the mass of common people and workers is too overwhelming." An eloquent speaker, Theobald voiced his family's moderate conservatism on the defensive against the agitation of the *Reichsfeinde* (enemies of the empire). "What will the world come to if the poison of the all too human sins of avarice and envy spread even among our farm workers," his father lamented, skeptical about the outcome of the campaign. "As war between nations cannot be avoided, so also internal strife will have to be resolved by powder and lead, since the permanent rule of the Social Democrats is impossible as long as we remain sinful men." Because the secret ballot weakened the control of the Junkers in their own districts, when the vote was counted, Felix had to admit, "I was too sanguine." To be sure Theobald had received 7,201 votes, the absolute majority, but the election was contested and thrown out in the Reichstag committee, since he had drawn only one vote over 50 percent. Disgusted with the fickleness of the electorate, Theobald refused to run again, and the bickering of the Right led to a resounding Progressive victory in the runoff election. [8]

Theobald's short venture into the Reichstag was ephemeral, but his disappointment was overshadowed by the news of the Iron Chancellor's fall. Father and son in Hohenfinow "were deeply moved and saddened that the great man had to come to this end after *such accomplishments* and such self-sacrifice." "Finally I *had* to dismiss him" was William II's emotional plea for understanding from the older Bethmann in May 1890. Bismarck's deceitful dealings with foreign diplomats "bordered on high treason," and "regarding the grave social questions, all he could advise was to shoot the Social Democrats without mercy, chase the insolent Reichstag away, and set the debated military demands so high that a break had to take place." Referring to the disputed cabinet order of 1852, the kaiser complained, "The situation was so chaotic and the ministers so afraid of him that no one dared speak a word." Presenting his version of the events leading to the final rupture, William feigned surprise that the chancellor who had just asked to retire on the grounds of ill health should have recovered so miraculously that he was now negotiating with his parliamentary archenemy, the Center Party leader Ludwig Windhorst. When the kaiser asked to be informed about such dealings in the future, "since it is embarrassing for me to find out such important matters through third persons," the aging Bismarck snapped back, "such a demand was unheard of . . . and he forgot himself to such a degree that I feared the inkwell would hit my head any moment." Agitatedly the chancellor continued, "he had to refuse my order emphatically and demand his dismissal, if I insisted on it." This quarrel between emperor and chancellor "rendered the situation impossible, business was at a standstill since no minister dared act and inform me." When William insisted on abrogating the cabinet order that had forced ministers to report only through the chancellor, Bismarck positively "refused to turn [the document] over to me; otherwise he would have to insist on leaving." Recounting the final tragicomedy of the chancellor's stubborn refusal to give this disputed paper to a minor royal official, William concluded his tirade with the words, "thus I was forced to grant his request for retirement," and decried the fallen chancellor's version of the story in the press as "very unfitting and saddening." Theobald's father, who had listened to the kaiser's effusive self-justification with sympathy and regret, understood the inevitability of the clash. "After the eternal successes which he had gained through his mighty personality, Bismarck could not and perhaps would not renounce the fullness of power, and the emperor would not and could not subordinate himself because of his energetic and excitable nature, understandable because of his youth." Nevertheless William's obsessive justification of the "dropping of the pilot" only spurred both Bethmanns to urge a public reconciliation between the founder of the empire and the young sovereign.[9]

The new kaiser's lack of "inner seriousness, personal effort, and devotion," to the task of government made Bethmann foresee dire consequences "since Europe resembles a powder keg and as far as I can tell is approaching general war, while social democracy continues to make inroads." William's all too frequent refrains, *sic volo, sic jubeo* and *suprema lex regis voluntas,* "made intelligent people shake their heads and considerably weakened the monarchical sentiment of our people which had been strengthened so wonderfully by the old kaiser." In 1893 the Bethmanns found the monarch more settled and less impulsive but continuing to vent his irritation at Chancellor Georg Leo von Caprivi's handling of the controversial school reform bill, "I can tell you, it is quite difficult to get along with this fathead." Because Bismarck's successor proved to be more than a front for the *persönliche Regiment,* the emperor threatened that Caprivi's days were numbered; but he praised Johannes Miquel's intelligence and lauded Karl Heinrich von Bötticher, since he proved more pliable. "This is characteristic of the perspective from which the kaiser judges *everything,*" Theobald's father complained to the "Gutsbuch." "He insists that everything be done according to his own, if mortal, views by spineless and supplicant ministers; *any* criticism is forbidden." He added prophetically: "It is this from which we suffer and which must lead gradually to our collapse. Even if the emperor appears to know much, his comprehension is often superficial and, because of his conviction of personal infallibility, all the more blind." The blame for this self-deception must partially be attributed to Bismarck who crushed all individuality; but the emperor enjoyed and encouraged the fawning of his advisers, making the older Bethmann wish, "If he were only spared the sycophants in his partly horrible entourage." Although he possessed considerable insight into the demands for social and political change, William preferred to remain passive, "expecting the impulse for the reform of [Prussian] suffrage to come from below." From repeated royal visits and long political conversations with his father, the young Landrat knew the emperor's strengths and weaknesses; but for him they remained personal foibles to be borne with patience, and Theobald echoed his father, "More and more the kaiser captures my heart and undoubtedly matures in many ways." [10]

In recognition for his dedication as Landrat, William II personally bestowed the Order of the Red Eagle, fourth class, on Theobald in 1893—"more than I really expected," as his father noted proudly. Although the royal promise "One day I'll make a minister out of your son!" was most likely apocryphal, this unusual honor indicated that Bethmann's career would soon extend beyond the narrow horizon of his district of Freienwalde. Indeed, on April 16, 1896, the aspiring official was called into the provincial administration at Potsdam as *Oberpräsidialrat* (provincial councilor). An impromptu poem by Judicial Counsel Toll expressed the esteem of his former colleagues. Beginning with the prophecy of a friend, "Some day this man will become something extraordinary," it continued to exemplify how the prediction had come true because of his "rare intelligence," coupled with "untiring zeal," uncommon "perceptiveness," and "persuasive power."

> Gross und weit war stets sein Blick,
> Ausserordentlich sein Geschick,
> Zu verhandeln mit den Leuten
> Auch mit gerade nicht gescheuten.
> Über's Lob erhaben steht
> Seine Objektivität,
> Und herunter bis zum Knecht
> Jeder sagt's: er war gerecht.*

This conventional and somewhat heavy-handed flattery omitted as much as it revealed. There was no word about the defense of agrarian interests, no reference to that schnapps-drinking conviviality cherished by the Junkers, no hint of any sense of humor. The same serious probity that brought the forty-year-old Bethmann the honorable offer of the higher salaried *Landesdirektorium* (provincial directory) of the Mark—which he refused—often antagonized his peers.[11]

The years spent in the provincial administration in Potsdam, under the shadow of crown and court, were a second apprenticeship for Bethmann. Under the liberal *Oberpräsident* (provincial president), von Achenbach, and the conservative minister of the interior, von der Recke, he was introduced to the intricate secrets of Prus-

---

*His vision was always acute and grand
And extraordinarily skillful his hand
In dealing with his opposite part,
Even with men not especially smart.
Above all praise we think to be
His penchant for objectivity,
And down to the servant everyone must
Say unmistakably: He was just.

sian high bureaucracy. With his roving assignments, including the Provincial Council, *Ritterschaftskasse* (loan association for the nobility), and the Council of Agriculture, he internalized the spirit and shared the substantive concerns of the Prussian administration. Benevolently autocratic, the bureaucracy still carried the fading heritage of the Freiherr von Stein, and insisted upon its own incorruptible objectivity; but tradition as well as social composition inclined it to favor the existing order in city and countryside. Not the years as Landrat, but his experience in the civil service strengthened Bethmann's preference for closely reasoned memoranda, expert opinions, and endless meetings over the heat of parliamentary debate. In training, inclination, and appearance almost the stereotype of a privy councilor, he soon attracted the attention of the minister of the interior. "As Landrat he has proven himself in every respect and fulfilled our expectations. He is known as a civil servant of exceptional gifts, rich knowledge, great industry, practical ability, and polished manners. These attributes prepare him for advancement into a higher position, ahead of all others." But when the senile chancellor "Uncle Chlodwig" von Hohenlohe offered him a ministerial position, he wisely refused. As the right hand of Achenbach, Theobald quickly distinguished himself, so much so that his superior recommended him "highly for the office of *Regierungspräsident* (district president) even in the most difficult district" because of his reputation "of acting without haste and on the basis of thorough deliberation." Appointed head of the district administration of Bromberg in West Prussia in May 1899, he was confronted with the nationalities problem of the Wilhelmian Empire, the strained symbiosis of Germans and Poles. When thanking the magnate, Count Hutten-Czapski, he feigned modesty: "To my distress I see that well-meaning people have created a reputation for me which I will be unable to live up to. Nevertheless, I gladly assume the new office, the difficulties of which I do not underestimate." The new district president unfortunately did not have enough time to become thoroughly familiar with the vexing Polish question, since in October of the same year, Bethmann was recalled to Potsdam, this time as Oberpräsident of the Mark Brandenburg, the highest administrative office in Prussia.[12]

At the age of forty-three, Bethmann Hollweg was the youngest governor in Prussia. To one of his close collaborators, Joachim von

Winterfeld-Menkin, he appeared to be "the born Oberpräsident. He possessed . . . universal education. Showing off was anathema to him; the simpler a man acted, the more he prized him. His dark voice underlined the effect of his diction." Nevertheless he often felt ill at ease with his rapid advancement—he rejected the ministry of the interior in 1901—and complained to the trusted Oettingen, "You are someone who is truly devoted to his work and nevertheless does not reach the position in which he can give his best to the world; and I, on the contrary, have never been up to the multitude of tasks confronting me and, therefore, became a dissatisfied dilettante who nevertheless received position after position, effortlessly and indiscriminately." Musing over his astounding success, he queried, "When will the gods' envy become apparent, or do I have to do penance for my guilt by not being able to enjoy my undeserved luck fully and purely?" In a flash of self-insight he added, "Or is it by painfully experiencing the disparity between my ability and my duty every day?" As before, Bethmann attempted to silence his lingering self-doubts by undertaking his new tasks with the same concentrated devotion that had characterized him at Schulpforta. With his father's death in 1900, the responsibility for the estate was added to the burden of his official work. "Compared to my public duties, Hohenfinow has remained a stepchild," since "I live elsewhere and lack the natural ability as well as the preparation for the practical questions of agriculture." In the last pages of the "Gutsbuch" he mused in 1904, "Had it not been for my mother's loving care for the people, the house, and the garden, which upheld the old traditions, many of those bonds would have been dissolved which are essential for the survival of the whole." His appointment as governor and his establishment as head of estate and family ended the long apprenticeship. Now Theobald would have to fulfill his promise.[13]

Administering the Mark Brandenburg in 1900 was a difficult task. Just emerging from the *Gründerzeit,* Berlin was growing at an unprecedented rate, devouring the surrounding villages and towns and posing large problems of urban reorganization and welfare. Responsible for defending provincial interests against the urban sprawl, Bethmann was a central figure in the negotiations for the creation of a greater Berlin; and with his immediate superior, Ernst Baron von Hammerstein, he visited London and Paris to gather comparative material. On his return he observed, "After both countries, the horizons of one's fatherland seem somewhat narrow." Growing public demands on the civil service, as well as the Berlin press, which was ever ready to expose some inefficiency, made him request an increase in staff. "Abhorring radical measures," the new governor rejected the idea of transferring the provincial government to Berlin where it would be lost in the mass of agencies, "whereas here in Potsdam we have a dominant position." To find a compromise between the antiquated prerogatives of the nobility, the dynamic demands of the haute bourgeoisie, and the growing needs of the working and urban poor, required tact and imagination. While confronted with the problems of modern social change, Bethmann continued to cultivate his relations with the landed proprietors by attending the Council of Agriculture and taking an interest in the sturdy yeomen farms, the pride of the rural regions of his province. He was faced once more with the nationalities question in the form of Catholic services being conducted in Polish in Charlottenburg, and had to investigate whether they sprang from nationalism or were a result of real ignorance of German; when they appeared to be the latter, he allowed them to continue. Accepting social democracy as a negative fact of urban life, Bethmann watched the spreading agitation in the countryside with growing apprehension, as he feared that the Red plague might undermine the social basis of the manors, but he also showed humane concern for the dismal lot of migrant farm laborers. In his relations with his subordinates, he was just and impartial, not asking them to campaign for any specific state-supporting party, because he did not regard them as political agents except when quelling subversion. His refusal to punish the recalcitrant Landräte who had opposed the construction of the Mittelland canal connecting the Ruhr basin with Berlin because of conservative class interests (fearing the collapse of grain prices) stemmed from his high concept of their office rather than from his love for the Junkers.[14]

The daily routine of the governorship consisted "not of earth-shaking work but of busy loafing, as Goethe calls all bureaucracy, while not affording that concentrated leisure," necessary to rekindle Bethmann's former intellectual interests in literature and antiquity. Reflecting upon his office, he often felt out of place: "For years I have been suffering from this feeling, especially because in my profession I should not lag behind my time but hurry ahead of it. Sometimes I believe I am doing it in some respects." But Prussian field and central administration did not breed a spirit of optimistic confidence in the people and in the natural evolution of democratic institutions. Sensitive and perceptive men like Bethmann deplored "the subjection of our political, religious, and artistic life to democracy *and* Byzantinism," but knew of no alternative to the rule of the *profanum vulgus* or irresponsible tyranny. "When I observe how the great and the humble carry on, I doubt time and again whether my hope" that this horrible dilemma "will give way to a free and, in the best sense, aristocratic development, is based upon the course of history, or upon reactionary ideas." Not agrarian but esthetic and intellectual nobility, in Plato's sense, was Bethmann's ideal political goal. Hence he often complained to Oettingen: "Because of the pressure of business I have been forced to let my innermost [feelings] wither, and when I attempt to listen in a favorable moment for the vanished melodies, I realize to my dismay that I have never *known* enough to penetrate beyond superficial emotions. And what little I have known, I have forgotten by now." Bethmann continued in words typical of an age that considered itself imitative, "in such a mood I long to refresh my spirit with a strong time and with strong men." Perhaps realizing a personal handicap, he asked his long-time friend: "Suggest a work about the Italian Renaissance regarding politics and culture. It should not be too popular, but if possible grant an insight into the sources." Because of the intellectual limitations of his official position, he remained grateful for Oettingen's scintillating, witty, and sarcastic writings, "My laity perhaps prevents me from understanding everything, but I discover personal insights which remain hidden to others." [15]

It was because he was known as "a good Oberpräsident . . . a man of high culture and personal charm," that chancellor Bernhard von Bülow called upon Bethmann to leave the quiet Priesterstrasse in Potsdam and replace Freiherr von Hammerstein as Prussian Minister of the Interior in 1905. Following his own advice to Friedrich Wilhelm von Loebell, "under no condition can you avoid this higher mission," Bethmann swallowed his fear of "the turmoil of high politics," which had been aggravated by the struggles over social policy and protective tariffs, and refused no longer. "So Theobald Bethmann is his successor," commented the Baroness of Spitzemberg, one of the leading women of court society. "At any rate, he has accepted only reluctantly the difficult and responsible po-

sition which he had already once declined after Miquel's death."
Thanking Oettingen for his congratulations, Bethmann stressed,
"you will understand that this change in my life is in many respects unpleasant. The cultivation of the inner man has suffered
enough already and it will be completely impossible in the near
future. I find this outwardly honorable position thoroughly repugnant." But the challenge of creative statesmanship beckoned
nevertheless: "The hope of bringing one's own convictions to bear
more widely and effectively is enticing even if I only succeed in adding a new wrinkle to the machine of [Prussian] bureaucracy." As
he had earlier warned Loebell, he repeated, "I am not oblivious to
the frictions I will encounter because of my opinions, which do not
fit into the Prussian scheme of things." Despite all self-criticism and
occasional bouts of pessimism, Bethmann entered the new office
"with a certain joyous confidence, which would be greater if I
could rely somewhat more on my health." Reflecting the good will
of the court circles, Baroness Spitzemberg welcomed that the minister of the interior "is in the emperor's good graces; he is an eminently important, highly cultured man, neither a stubborn bureaucrat nor a Junker, but unfortunately of poor health. They say he
is a future chancellor, and it would be too bad if he consumed himself beforehand as minister." [16]

Both by background and inclination conservative, Bethmann shared
the basic political convictions of Bülow's cabinet. Traditionally
held by a conservative, the Ministry of the Interior, which controlled the Prussian bureaucracy, demanded a man who reflected
the prevailing sociopolitical views of the Junkers and the haute
bourgeoisie. In his first bills and administrative orders, Bethmann
did not disappoint these expectations, although his more moderate
tone made the "uncrowned king of Prussia," Conservative leader
Ernst von Heydebrand, denounce him as "the wrong man. He is
a confused philosopher, but for the Ministry of the Interior we
need a strongman [*Polizeiknüppel*]." In his maiden speech in the
Landtag Bethmann struck a new chord when he called "the development of national welfare one of the most serious tasks," achievable
only "through liberation from the fetters of bureaucracy and free
participation of all levels of the population." Stressing voluntary
cooperation, he added, "We already punish too much anyway." While
formally conciliatory, Bethmann nevertheless sought to safeguard
Prussia against subversion by defending the deportation of Russian

revolutionaries in 1906: "The royal state government is unanimously of the opinion that the mass migration of elements lacking a secure livelihood, who are partly illegitimate and partly connected with the revolutionary machinations in the neighboring monarchy, cannot be tolerated, economically or politically." In a telling comment he ridiculed public opinion as the "confusion arising from the differently colored blinders that men wear." Proud of the "great increase in our prosperity despite higher taxes," and admitting "that I am not an overly great friend of police measures in general," he sponsored an extensive reform of the legal preparation required for civil service and of the tax structure of circles, communes, and provinces of Prussia. The new minister of the interior fully subscribed to the Bismarckian synthesis, and sought to strengthen it through a modicum of practical progress; but he declared in the Landtag, "I for my part am bold enough to consider many of the demands of extreme liberalism very reactionary." [17]

Since the Socialist gain of twenty-five Reichstag seats provoked industrial and Conservative cries for governmental action, Bethmann's first major legislative concern was the establishment of effective measures against further subversion. Based on existing legislation, commissary negotiations between the concerned ministries had to investigate "if and how one can counteract the partly open, partly underground Social Democratic agitation in favor of imitating the Russian Revolution, and undermining the empire and military discipline by general strikes and resistance within the army during a state of emergency." His catalogue of accusations against the party was lengthy: the corruption of youth; agitation among civil servants; indoctrination of the lower orders; vilification of the government; glorification of crime; preparation for revolution; invitation to draft resistance; and propagation of the general strike. But the minister of the interior was opposed to any resumption of Bismarck's measures, "since they would shackle the bill with the odium of an *Ausnahmegesetz* (exceptional law)," a measure outside the bonds of common law. Not an extreme reactionary clamoring for a counterrevolutionary coup d'état, Bethmann sought to rescue the Wilhelmian Reich with the weapons of the Rechtsstaat, and concluded "that social democracy must be combatted on the basis of common law." During the interministerial negotiations, a deadlock arose over precisely this question, since only extralegal measures promised to be effective. Not revolutionary intent, but revolutionary action could be the basis of legal persecution, and Bethmann's legal training convinced him that subjective criteria had to be replaced by objective ones. Defending his stand adamantly in several *vota*, he argued that placing certain groups outside the law would only increase the very lawlessness that the government was combatting. When it proved impossible to develop new restrictions within existing laws, and the Bülow bloc won a crushing electoral victory over the Social Democrats in 1907, Bethmann's initiative was shelved. But although he favored new police measures against subversion, the minister of the interior also strongly championed the introduction of a law alleviating the plight of migrant farm workers.[18]

In the debate over the continuation of a forceful settlement policy to counteract the rapid increase of the Polish population in the eastern provinces, Bethmann also defended Bismarck's divisive legacy ("Not until the Germans have permanently secured their dominance politically and economically can real pacification take place"). Because of his experience in Bromberg, the minister did not favor extreme repression, but maintained that a relentless policy of Germanization be carried out. Confessing in the Landtag that "a policy of petty pin-pricks is very much against my grain," he nevertheless warned the Polish deputies, "Do not arouse the quiet, loyal, industrious, and progressive Slavic population against state and authority—then we will have the peace which I desire as much as you!" Bethmann's treatment of the school strike in Poznan followed a similarly moderate line, both in form and in substance. In a lengthy printed memorandum on settlement policy in December 1906, he attacked the general pessimism about the German position in West Prussia. Citing the number of eighty thousand German settlers and the foundation of fifty villages each year as evidence, he emphasized that dropping the settlement policy would be a grave mistake, since at last it was beginning to show signs of success. Correctly analyzing the conflict as a struggle between Polish farm laborers and German peasants, he was nevertheless class-bound enough to call "the maintenance of a healthy German landed gentry in the Ostmark indispensable. . . . Hence only a mixture of latifundia and peasant holdings can be considered a sound policy." Unable to resolve the contradiction between the nationalist demand of settling as many small farmers as possible and the Junker desire to preserve large estates worked by cheap Polish labor, Bethmann could offer no creative solution. Because he insisted on the systematic continuation of the strategic buying of *Güter,* albeit at lower prices, the minister could not avoid the logical consequence of such a stand, "If one believed that the upholding and strengthening of the German influence in the eastern provinces was a question of survival for the Prussian State and the German Empire," one had to demand "that the settlement commission be allowed to exercise its right of expropriation." In both the struggle against socialism and that against the Poles, the Wilhelmian Empire stretched the limits of legality and only postponed ultimate failure.[19]

If so far he dared to differ from the ultraconservatives only in tone, Bethmann took an independent stand on the crucial question of Prussian electoral reform. Having inherited the promise of action from Hammerstein, he ordered work to be continued on the minor modifications initiated by his predecessor. Bethmann was unwilling to challenge the fundamental political structure of Prussia, a task that had defied veteran prime ministers. So he contented himself with reforming the most glaring abuses without coming to grips with the underlying irrationality of the three-class system, which was considered a bulwark against the egalitarianism of Reichstag suffrage. To insure smoother practices and remedy the grossest inequalities of districting due to urbanization, the new minister proposed dividing the most populous districts in half, a measure which would add ten seats to the Landtag. Already disappointed by the tokenism of his reforms, the progressive public was enraged when Bethmann maladroitly assured the deputies "that the adoption of [equal] Reichstag suffrage is unacceptable to us," for reasons of historical development. Although he admitted "that a bitter feeling of disgust poisons our public life," he sought its source in excessive leveling rather than in inequality. "It is something thoroughly unhealthy, it is a misfortune, that we make every political decision dependent upon its effect on the Social Democrats." According to "that great aristocrat of the spirit, Kant," the future will belong to those "forces which shape our nation, not by tearing down but by striving upward." Reflecting less class prejudice than the teaching of constitutional lawyers like Gneist, Bethmann's political philosophy concluded: "One can deeply feel the serious necessity of electoral reform, even if one does not believe we can solve it in the impatience of the moment according to one blueprint. All progressive and creative segments of our nation must gather together, and there can and will not be a suffrage law unless it is based upon their open and honest cooperation." Progressive, National-Liberal and Center Party parliamentarians were dismayed by such unabashed elitism, and only the *Deutsche Industrie Zeitung* rejoiced: "All those considers the one-sided democratic trend . . . an anathema must be extraordinarily grateful to the Prussian Minister of the Interior for having, in his name, confessed the serious desire of the government to counteract this danger." [20]

"I was fully conscious that with this speech I would stir up a hornet's nest and put myself in political jeopardy," Bethmann explained to Oettingen. "Our Prussian suffrage is impossible in the long run, and although it produces a parliament capable of acting, its conservative majority is animated by such a banal spirit and is so complacent in its power, humiliating any progressively minded man, that we *must* search for a new basis." In startling contrast to his public utterances, the minister was obviously well aware of the need for change. But his reforming conservatism was isolated in the Prussian hierarchy, since "even for this principle I find no understanding in the Staatsministerium (Prussian ministry of state, i.e. cabinet), nor probably with H.M., and of course under no circumstances with the majority of the Landtag." Intellectually he found himself at an impasse because of his rejection of universal suffrage, "It is enormously difficult to come up with a suitable form for the reform, which is impossible in the near future anyway." And in an insight typical of his later chancellorship, he added, "All *that* I could not say openly, and yet I did not want to deny myself a small glimpse into the future even while introducing the modest bill intended to serve practicality and not to accomplish any reforms." As he could not mention positive goals and only indicated certain abstract guidelines, he was "completely shipwrecked" by the criticism of the press. Although the impact of such frankness on the House was greater than it appeared in the newspapers and increased his personal influence upon the parties of the Right, Bethmann was pessimistic whether he could reach what he desired. "We must drive the Conservatives forward and guide the Liberals away from party phrases and shibboleths—but I despair of this possibility when I see how my words are maliciously misinterpreted and turned around." As philosophical basis for later reforms, his speech had misfired. "The relationship between world-view and politics has become completely unfathomable for the people, and one courts vindictive criticism when making a modest reference to it." [21]

Responding to the challenge of finding a third way between the plutocratic three-class system and egalitarian universal suffrage, Bethmann drafted a lengthy memorandum on electoral reform in March 1907. "It is imperative that the Prussian Ministry of State recognize openly and clearly the need for the reform of the Prussian suffrage and declare itself ready for appropriate legislative action." The old system could survive no longer, since "a large part of the people regards three-class suffrage as the ultimate expression of East Elbian Junkerdom." Exposing the dangers of continued identification of the Prussian government with the party interests of the Conservatives, Bethmann deplored "that . . . in its manners and aspirations this caucus still acts as the specific representative of old Prussian Junkerdom," whose hubris, prejudice, castelike seclusion, and opposition to any liberal movement antagonized all other parties. Realizing the immense "danger of committing the gravest of all political mistakes by missing the right moment," the minister pleaded for gradual evolution. Prussia had to choose between dangerous immobility or reformist survival. Skeptical of a Conservative mellowing under Heydebrand, Bethmann urged the ministry, "Imperial policy demands a liberal regime in Prussia." Still not prepared to make the jump to Reichstag suffrage, he proposed a system which could evolve in this direction if need be. Since proportional suffrage would not allow such a transformation, "there remains the idea of plural suffrage, graduated according to age, possessions, and education. . . . Not essentially different from universal suffrage, it avoids the latter's greatest weakness by preventing the rule of sheer numbers." Pioneered in Belgium and Sweden and "meeting the demands of the middle classes," a plural voting system would break the Conservative stranglehold without delivering the government into the hands of democratic or socialist radicalism. It would offer the long-needed opening to the Left and shift the social basis of the monarchy from nobility to bourgeoisie, thus excluding equally plutocracy and the "subversive tendencies emanating from the Poles and Socialists." Counteracting the leveling trend toward *Vermassung,* it would found the state on the rule of a middle class of age, substance, and education and would rejuvenate the monarchy while preserving the positive strains of the Prussian tradition. Although inadequate in the eyes of the Progressives, the solution proposed in the March memorandum marked the beginning of Bethmann's emancipation from traditionalism. "A showdown between the government and the Conservatives can hardly be avoided in the long run, even if the suffrage remains unchanged." [22]

However, the next confrontation in spring and summer of 1907 was not a conflict with the Right but once again a struggle against the Reichsfeinde (in this case, the Social Democrats and the Center Party), which had dared to challenge the bloody suppression of the Herero revolt. To Oettingen, Bethmann commented on this domestic turmoil: "The last few weeks have thrown me into desperate pessimism, otherwise so alien to me. I do not want to elaborate on it since I have not yet reached a clear picture of the possible outcome." Sensing the opportunity for a political triumph, Chancellor Bülow quickly dissolved the Reichstag and called for the patriotic cooperation of Progressives, National Liberals, Free Conservatives, and Conservatives to defeat Catholics and Socialists. The election was a smashing victory for the new Bülow bloc, since Socialist strength was cut in half and the new coalition controlled the Reichstag.[23]

"Under these circumstances, [Vice-Chancellor] Count Posadowsky no longer quite fitted into the cabinet," since his vigorous social legislation had rested on the parliamentary support of the Center Party, now ostracized. Although often rumored, the actual resignation of the man who had guided the domestic policy of the empire for almost a decade was still a surprise. As a bridge for the Bülow bloc, conservative enough for the Prussian Right and yet progressive enough for the *Freisinn,* the emperor favored the young minister of the interior, "who will show a greater practical sense in the conduct of affairs." Bavarian ambassador Lerchenfeld reported that "although Herr von Bethmann is usually counted among the Conservatives, he subscribes to more liberal sentiments than his party friends in Prussia." Contrary to his later memory, Chancellor Bülow praised his "great intellectual scope, his statesmanlike talents, and also his firmness toward the kaiser. His Majesty knows Bethmann from this side exactly and respects him nevertheless." [24]

The offer of the Imperial State Secretariat of the Interior after only two years at the helm of the Prussian bureaucracy embarrassed Bethmann; but once again his sense of duty prevailed and he accepted the post. From a vacation in Bad Kissingen "in which I have for the first time in years tried again to base my life on human sentiments," he thanked Wolfgang von Oettingen for his congratulations. "I have let Goethe's letters, and occasionally the sun and lovely Franconia inspire me, but I am astonished and shocked about the lack of concern with which I am approaching tasks which demanded Posadowsky's extreme intelligence and ascetic work but which are alien to me." Ever since his appointment as Landrat, Bethmann's massive frame had been beset with recurring illnesses, necessitating vacations in the Alps and taking medicine. "When at times the premonitions about what ought to be and will be begin to circle around me like crabs around the bait, my optimism seems like light-hearted blindness and perhaps I do not consider that my political existence is at stake," he confided to his friend. "I have not sought this new burden, but have fought against it until the last [moment]," he admitted tellingly, "but now that it has been placed upon me, I must seek to bear it as I am." Because of his previous experience, he continued, "I do not fear the political work nor the legislation demanded by public opinion as much as the unpolitical sense of our nation, which does not want to abandon preconceived opinions and which must yet be forced to make sacrifices, if we are to succeed in enlisting the cooperation of all vital political elements." All too aware of the empire's inner schisms, which had turned the political parties into economic interest groups jockeying for the spoils of power at the expense of the common weal, Bethmann was not eager to assume the new office. "Please do not speak of him as a future chancellor," his wife protested, "It disconcerts me whenever I hear it, since at the bottom of his heart Theobald does not aim for it at all." But the new secretary of the interior perceptively insisted upon one condition. "That not the oldest minister, but Herr von Bethmann Hollweg has been named Vice-President of the Prussian Ministry of State, is dictated by concern for the present political situation," Chancellor Bülow explained to his ministerial colleagues, and the appointment was understood "as an attempt to guarantee the unity of policy between the empire and Prussia." [25]

When the *Reichsanzeiger* announced Bethmann's appointment as imperial secretary of the interior and vice-chancellor on June 25, 1907, few were surprised. Even the habitually critical *Zukunft* hailed him as "a man of strong gifts and a fortunate hand," adding that "Herr von Bethmann, who offers proposals with a fine skeptical smile to the Reichstag, is the man of the epoch." Considering him "indispensable here for the time being," Bülow had chosen Bethmann to continue the Bismarckian tradition of benevolent *Sozialpolitik* (social policy); but the social composition of the Bülow bloc made such a task impossible, since the Conservatives regarded all welfare measures with suspicion, while the Liberals opposed state intervention in the economy. Since the crusade against Catholicism and socialism could not provide a working program for the disparate coalition, he almost despaired that "my striving for independence and objectivity can escape from this tangle of lies, sensationalism, and playing for popularity." Forced to cooperate closely with the Bundesrat, the Secretariat of the Interior was burdened with wider responsibility and endowed with less power than the Prussian Ministry of the Interior. At a dinner with the representatives of the states, the new state secretary stressed that he would proceed only with the agreement of the member governments, but warned of excessive federalism reminiscent of the Frankfurt Bundestag. When thanking the widow of his earlier predecessor, Boetticher, for sending him a commemorative volume, he wrote, "All of us who are called upon to build upon the work of your late husband see his portrait in the touching and vibrant colors of reality, reflecting his work for kaiser, empire, and his loved ones." Less ideologically oriented than Boetticher or Posadowsky, Bethmann quickly recognized the central issue of domestic politics. To the second Congress of the Christian-Social workers organizations in Berlin he formulated his foremost aim, "I know no greater task for the present than to make the labor movement of our days an integral part of our social order." And to a largely skeptical audience of the *Zentralverband deutscher Industrieller,* he "emphasized the necessity of a resolute continuation of Sozialpolitik." [26]

Too wedded to a preindustrial image of social harmony to cure more than the symptoms of the profound dislocation of Wilhelmine society, Bethmann nevertheless understood that only "positive measures," not propaganda or repression, could check the spread of revolutionary sentiment. Hoping that extraparliamentary community action and rising prosperity would eventually solve the "social question," he publicly criticized the Left for "everywhere playing off class interests against real human beings." Among the specific measures inherited from his predecessor—such as a new trade law, a bill creating chambers of work, an extension of social insurance, and new wine and check regulations—the draft of an associations law posed the first major domestic test to the Bülow bloc.[27]

Demanded intitially by Conservative leader Heydebrand, the proposed bill assumed, under the influence of the Liberals, "the purpose of creating a unified and nonreactionary law for the whole empire." This first draft memorandum still stressed, "Through such measures—curbs on foreign language dailies, the preventive prohibition of assemblies, and the restriction of the use of foreign language in public—the most dangerous excesses of the Polish movement can be restrained." But as compensation for its repressive clauses, albeit "on the basis of common law," the secretary of the interior promised "a liberal law of association and assembly" in all other respects. To simplify the jungle of state laws, Bethmann strove for a common denominator closer to the liberal South German than to the conservative Prussian usage. By removing the restrictions governing political associations and by closely limiting police powers, he sought to increase the unregimented area in civic affairs. Only public assemblies would have to be registered and possess an assembly directorate, but for the first time women and minors were to be admitted, and membership files, no longer required, would not automatically be open to police inspection. Yet Bethmann repeatedly warned against the inclusion of the crucial issue of the right of coalition and opposed the creation of associations of civil servants as well as of rural laborers.[28]

Reflecting the vicissitudes of constitutional evolution, this contradictory blend of progressive and repressive elements in the associations law provoked a mixed reaction in public and parliament. While the Conservatives regretted the curbing of police powers, the National Liberals supported the language clause for chauvinist reasons, the Progressives welcomed the liberal features, the Center Party rejected its anti-Catholic implications and deplored its heavy-handed Germanization attempt, and the Social Democrats denounced it as a new "extraordinary law of the worst kind." But more important than parliamentay criticism was the reluctance of the South German states to tighten their existing system, forcing Bethmann finally to exclude election rallies from the *Sprachparagraph* (prohibition of non-German languages). The heated debates in the Reichstag, straining the very fiber of the Bülow bloc, resulted in further concessions regarding the right of coalition for farm workers and the application of the language paragraph; but the government retained the power to prohibit dangerous assemblies, to require the eventual use of German, and to limit the participation of eighteen-year-olds, when the bill was finally approved by 203 to 168 votes. A modest step toward legal liberalization, the associations law was almost a Pyrrhic victory for the chancellor. "The Conservatives complain that the government dares impose liberal laws on them, while the Liberals consider the acomplishments too modest," Ambassador Lerchenfeld reported perceptively. Reflecting the inner tensions of the coalition of erstwhile enemies and Bethmann's often timid reform conservatism, the *Vereinsgesetz* threw the Progressive Party into a severe crisis.[29]

A similar duality of aims characterized Bethmann's proposal for the reform of workers' insurance. Considerably less than the Left expected but more than the Conservatives were willing to permit, the bill intended to simplify the tangled legal structure and extend the previous coverage. Since a wealth of different institutions ranging from cooperative mutual aid societies to yellow unions and state agencies had developed to serve insurance functions, Bethmann refused to amalgamate the different groups when addressing a conference of insurance agencies and union representatives. "The whole insurance structure must be unified and made more comprehensible," and for this purpose "the local agencies, which are presently splintered into many different places, must be combined into one local office . . . to provide a common substructure." The legal web had rendered the effectiveness of the existing institutions marginal because they had become unintelligible to the insured. Expanding the circle of the workers covered to include farm laborers, domestic servants, druggists' apprentices, musicians, theater personnel, and other service or white-collar workers, the law was equally designed to "remove the appointment to insurance agencies from Social Democratic power," thus depriving the party apparatus of an important sinecure. Despite the inclusion of widows and orphans, the bill aroused the criticism of the Left, the Zentralverband deutscher Industrieller, and the free professions, because Bethmann had insisted on employer-employee parity on all review boards. The secretary of the interior considered it "a comprehensive reform that [struck] a just balance between gain and loss of rights," and intended neither to alienate workers nor employers. But despite the time limit set by the *lex Trimborn,* the *Reichsversicherungsordnung* was not adopted until 1911, when the new secretary of the interior,

Clemens von Delbrück, piloted it safely past all the reefs of Reichstag, Bundesrat, and interest groups.[30]

In his last major proposal as secretary of the interior, Bethmann most clearly revealed his sociopolitical aims. In a circular in the summer of 1908 he suggested the creation of *Arbeitskammern,* reminiscent of chambers of commerce, in order to restore social peace by depoliticizing the wage struggle. "The establishment of chambers of work is predicated on the belief that it will be possible to lessen the hostility between employers and employees that has arisen partly out of misunderstanding and lack of communication, by bringing representatives of both sides together for common problem solving." To move into the direction of orderly collective bargaining he did not envisage "small parliaments which usually create mischief," but professional bodies capable of compromise because of the mutual respect of capital and labor if given true parity. Bethmann based his optimism about the *bourse de travail* on "the experience that even a Social Democrat can accomplish useful tasks when he works within the area of his competence together with bourgeois elements."

Defending his ideas in a major Reichstag speech in January 1909, Bethmann rejected a national *Arbeitsamt* (employment office) and a schematic structure for the whole empire, preferring to restrict the chambers to a single branch of business and to a district in which real need existed. "I believe you have seen that I do not live in social-political fantasies, but I am somewhat optimistic in this regard. I do believe that practical cooperation will have reasonable results." Denying the charge that he was naive enough to believe that peace and harmony would ensue from mere dialogue, the secretary of the interior nevertheless assured: "I am certain that Arbeitskammern are no social-political mirage, that they correspond to a *real political need* . . . and are a tool which will not make *differences* disappear but will *bridge* them to the welfare of the whole." By depoliticizing the wage struggle Bethmann hoped to provide a positive role for the unions, which were interested in tangible gains, thereby drawing the Socialists into the empire. But the composition of the Bülow bloc and the secretary of the interior's timidity were incapable of forcing a major opening to the Left, and the workers' chambers were buried in desultory discussions in the Reichstag until 1917.[31]

The years of his tenure as state secretary of the interior were

Bethmann's politically most creative period. In charge of the internal policy of the empire but still in the shadow of Bülow, Bethmann could strive for gradual constitutional and social evolution without bearing the full burden of responsibility. But because of the "dirt in which the nation has wallowed for a year," Bethmann feared that "disaster will come. Today especially I tremble because of a certain intervention from above." Deploring the kaiser's continued immaturity, he added: "I hope I am seeing too bleakly. But as soon as we begin to accomplish something, then—certainly with the best intention—a hasty hand intervenes and strips the best away." Hence he forecast internal convulsions: "The coming winter will be more difficult than the last, since not even bittersweet coalition harmony will exist—only the difficult financial reform and other matters which bring nobody joy." And, tellingly, he continued, "I personally will have a difficult time because of the social-political impatience," since "in a position like my own one hears either slick flattery or massive abuse, but never reasoned truth." [32]

The darkest cloud on the horizon was the problem of the three-class suffrage, since despite Bethmann's massive memorandum Loebell's advice for postponement had prevailed. Failing to grasp the crucial importance of this issue for the survival of the monarchy, Chancellor Bülow temporized, waiting for a more favorable parliamentary constellation, while Prussian minister of the interior, Friedrich von Moltke, was adamantly opposed. Only after a long struggle did Bethmann succeed in swaying William II to allow the ministry to make a vague commitment to change in January 1908 and to elaborate it in October in the speech from the throne: "It is my will that . . . the suffrage of the lower house be developed in a manner corresponding to the economic development, the spread of education, as well as political maturity and the strengthening of state consciousness." Only Bülow's personal intervention saved the final sentence from the objections of the Prussian ministers, "I consider this one of the most important tasks of the present." By implication shutting the door on true equality of the vote, this declaration of good will to the Liberals did not constitute a decision for action and left the Conservative stranglehold over Germany's largest state untouched.[33]

All the pent-up resentment against William's personal rule broke loose in October 1908 with the *Daily Telegraph* Affair. In order to improve Anglo-German relations, the kaiser had made some indiscreet statements to one of his hunting hosts, Colonel Stuart-Wortley. "The interview was anything but hostile to Great Britain, but contained grave breaches of political tact and claims about German advice for English warfare against the Boers which had to, and in fact did, hurt British pride," the chief of the naval cabinet, Admiral von Müller, said of the document. Despite earlier imperial faux pas, Chancellor Bülow thought that his own vacation at the North Sea spa of Norderney should not be interrupted, and the minor official in the Foreign Office who did read the release did not dare to correct the emperor. Provoking much resentment in England because of its clumsy attempt to butter up the British cousins, the *Daily Telegraph* interview caused even more commotion in Germany. "In unprecedented unity the German press . . . raged with elemental fury against Prince Bülow; his resignation was demanded immediately." In short, Austrian Ambassador Szögyény reported to Vienna a severe chancellor crisis which soon turned into a constitutional conflict. "Never before in Prussian history have *all* circles been captured by such deep resentment against their sovereign, not to mention Germany as a whole, which is only loosely associated."

William II's refusal to cut short his hunting expedition to Donaueschingen only added fuel to the flames. "We have lost a battle," sighed Chief of Staff Helmuth von Moltke. "And what is worse, we do not know how to prevent such incidents in the future." Shocked and outraged at the kaiser's tactlessness, the Reichstag majority, even including the Conservatives, demanded public censure. Dispatched by Chancellor Bülow to head off parliamentary condemnation, Bethmann Hollweg reported back "that it will be impossible to limit the present uproar to the *Daily Telegraph* or to the formal mistakes committed in the treatment of the document" by the Foreign Office. "What is erupting now with primeval force is resentment against the personal regime, dissatisfaction over the emperor's attitude of the last twenty years, of which the conversations in the *Daily Telegraph* are only one among many symptoms." As the leader of German domestic policy, Bethmann entreated the chancellor to take this into account when speaking in the Reichstag. "We can only hope for a good outcome if Bundesrat, parliament, and country receive the distinct impression that I have not merely been concerned with helping the kaiser out of a jam," Bülow wrote later, recalling this dramatic discussion. "The country must be convinced that this incident will produce a turn for the better and that I will ruthlessly fight for such a healing of our domestic malaise." Viewing the affair not as a minor lapse but as a characteristic event, Bethmann pleaded passionately to end the *persönliche Regiment* and make the chancellor alone responsible for policy: "Your Excellency is not only the kaiser's chancellor, but also the chancellor of the empire." [34]

In the showdown in the Reichstag on November 10/11, Chancellor Bülow followed the secretary of interior's advice. With "extraordinary skill" he criticized the monarch for his indiscretions without yielding to parliamentary demands for constitutional reform. Because he blamed William's personality while defending his noble intentions, the angry parliamentarians "understood that a change of chancellors at the present moment would only further complicate the general political situation of the empire." Having thus escaped, Bülow sought to teach the kaiser a lesson. In the session of the state ministry of November 11, "all ministers agreed it is my duty to tell H.M. that crown, empire, and monarchical sentiment will run grave risks unless a fundamental change takes place in this area. The kaiser has to be more reticent." In the critical audience with William II a week later, Bülow found the kaiser "in such a depressed and pessimistic mood that I had to comfort him more than criticize his past conduct." Speaking firmly but compassionately, Bülow stressed that it was not so much the "technical error" of the Foreign Office as the content of the controversial interview that had caused protest. "You are not about to resign?" the dejected monarch questioned. "Remain, help us." Because the kaiser was so crestfallen over the unsuspected result of his well-meaning gesture, Bülow had few difficulties in securing his permission for a notice in the *Reichsanzeiger,* "Accordingly H.M. approved the chancellor's statements in the Reichstag and assured Prince Bülow of his continuing confidence." Not an actual peccavi, but an indirect admission of guilt and an endorsement of Bülow's partially self-serving explanations, this statement was ratified by the Prussian cabinet, where Bethmann Hollweg "expressed the warmest thanks of the State Ministry for the execution of this difficult task." [35]

Bülow's initial victory reestablished the chancellor's ultimate political accountability, which had been endangered through the dismissal of Bismarck, but it failed to meet the Left's demand for ministerial responsibility and parliamentarization of the empire.

Dilatorily, Bethmann Hollweg announced in early December, "The federal governments cannot take a concrete position regarding questions which are so vital to the constitutional basis of our political life, before they have had the opportunity to arrive at a decision of their own, based on firm recommendations from the Reichstag." Since the Conservatives were adamantly opposed to parliamentarization, the Progressive reform initiative "came to nought." The imperial promise "not to interfere in the affairs of state directly without consulting with advisors" cured the symptom but not the cause of the debacle. For Bethmann Hollweg, who had so strongly implored Bülow to remain firm against royal absolutism but who equally rejected the logical consequence of founding the chancellor's authority upon a representative parliament, the *Daily Telegraph* Affair was a disgusting spectacle. Dining with him after his Reichstag speech in early December, Baroness von Spitzemberg found her host, "who is hardly a pessimist, looking into the future with grave misgivings, since he misses a sense of responsibility not only in the emperor but also in the crown prince. However, he also thinks the niveau of the Reichstag depressingly low, as soon as it has to prove its claim to power by its ability to use it. It should, rather, stop criticizing and negating and help the government, and afterwards make its demands." Between the often irresponsible demagoguery of the Reichstag and the rhetorical bluster of the emperor and his son, who publicly referred to their ministers as "real asses," Bethmann found little to choose. "The princes run themselves and the monarchy blindly into the abyss." [36]

Despite all its thunder and lightning, the storm of the *Daily Telegraph* Affair failed to clear the air. After the kaiser slowly recovered from his psychological and physical breakdown, he lent a willing ear to charges that Bülow had not defended him enough "against the unjust and exaggerated attacks" of the Reichstag. The formerly intimate friendship between chancellor and emperor had suffered, and already in November 1908 Austrian Ambassador Count Laszlo von Szögyény-Marich reported, "I believe I'm not wrong when I predict that sooner or later we will have to count upon a change of guard." Privately and semipublicly William began to form his own version of the events under the influence of the camarilla, time and again complaining to intimates about Bülow's lack of backbone, "I became the scapegoat and my chancellor washed his hands in innocence!" But the rumors were premature. With his blustering support of Austria in the annexation crisis of Bosnia and Herzegovina, Bülow won his last foreign political triumph, at the brink of a general war. "From the first moment I was convinced that Germany was isolated and even at the risk of war had to stand at Austria's side," he recalled one year later. "I considered it highly probable that we would preserve peace if we remained firm, and that we would break the net of encirclement which existed more in imagination than in fact." In a long conversation with the emperor on March 11, 1909, Bülow attempted to recapture his thrust by frankly discussing the unfortunate chain of events that had led to the rift between them. Although insisting that he had been wronged for the last time, William II reconciled himself with his most congenial advisor ("Whoever says anything against my chancellor will have to take me on!"). But even the bouquet of roses presented to Bülow's charming Italian wife at an intimate dinner, the dementi in the press, and the chancellor's triumph in the Reichstag could not heal the breach. The intrigues behind his back continued and, moreover, in the spring of 1909 the agile Bülow confronted a domestic task that could not be solved by finesse, "The great problem of the moment is the reform of the imperial finances." [37]

Because of the staggering expense of Weltpolitik, "the *Reichsfinanzreform* became a vital imperative for the German Empire." Bismarck had restricted the central government to indirect taxes and the states had to make up the deficits with matricular contributions from their direct taxes, so the empire had suffered from a financial shortage since its infancy. The secretary of the treasury estimated the needed additional revenue at 500 million Marks annually, a sum which made Bülow remark that the "reform has no favorable prospects." The opposing economic theories as well as material interests of agrarian Conservatives, heavy industrial Free-Conservatives, light industrial National Liberals, and commercially oriented Progressives tested the cohesion of the Bülow bloc as much, if not more, than the eternal irritant of electoral reform. In deference to Conservative wishes four-fifths of the new taxes were to be levied on consumption, which most heavily fell upon the lower and middle incomes. But as a concession to the Liberals, Secretary of the Treasury Sydow insisted upon taxing property, and here the only possible avenue seemed an inheritance tax. The four hundred million levied upon necessities and commerce were approved quickly, but because of the rumors that Bülow's position was no longer firm, the Conservatives balked at the inheritance tax, which primarily weighed on landed property. While the Liberals were intransigent on taxes on consumption and mobile capital, the Center Party viewed Bülow's parliamentary difficulties as an opportunity to escape the oppositional role and to regain influence on policy. When in the Budget Committee on May 13 a new coalition of Conservatives and Center Party voted down a Liberal progovernmental version of the tobacco tax for personal and social reasons, the end was in sight. In his swan song in the Reichstag Bülow "spoke too professorially for the Conservatives, and for the Center his words assumed an almost provocative ring," while he frantically sought to "reassure the Liberals that he would not make the reform without them."

In the final tabulation on June 24, "the inheritance tax was rejected with the slim majority of eight votes against the entire Left." The kaiser was furious at the Conservatives' lack of patriotism, crass interest politics, and speculation that Bülow was "a dying man." ("I am willing to impose the tax laws upon the country if the third reading results in an equally small or even smaller majority against the bill!") But the emperor's threats were in vain, since Bülow had with rare inflexibility committed himself to "forcing the entire financial reform through with the majority of the bloc parties and at any price [wanted] to prevent even a part of the bill being accepted due to Center Party support." His "gravest mistake in domestic policy," the persecution of the Center, and the reliance on the Progressives as governmental party now exacted its price, when Old Prussia refused to be saved by reform. Moreover, the chancellor was unable to use his last trump, since the dissolution of the Reichstag would, in every political observer's opinion, "result only in the increase of social democracy." Although Conservatives and Center Party were willing to substitute taxes on mobile capital, Bülow, unwilling to bend ignominiously under the blue-black yoke, had reached the end of his twisting political journey.[38]

Ambassador Szögény reported the inescapable denouement: "I hear from a completely reliable source that Prince Bülow intends to travel to Kiel tomorrow to ask Kaiser Wilhelm for his dismissal." Compared to his dazzling tenure, the chancellor's last interview with the emperor aboard the royal yacht *Hohenzollern* "was a weak last scene of a grandly conceived final act." In a hurry because he did not want to miss breakfast with the prince of Monaco on the chocolate baron Meunier's yacht, a distraught William listened to Bülow's plea "that the attitude of the Conservative Party has created such a situation that my remaining in office has become impossible." Histrionically proclaiming *"ma vie au roi, mon honneur à moi,"* the chancellor painted a glowing picture of his achievements in foreign and domestic policy, "in foreign affairs we must remain on the course which I have set." Regarding domestic politics, he added soberly, "it will be pivotal to attempt to restore the damage done by the ambition and selfishness of the parties, if possible." The kaiser called the " 'triumph' of the Center Party, brought on by 'the stupidity of the Conservatives,' a 'scandal' " and accepted Prince Bülow's resignation in principle, while insisting that he remain long enough to bear the onus of the misshapen financial reform. During the farewell dinner in honor of the departing chancellor, William II revealed his true motives to Bülow's wife: "You must not believe that the inheritance tax or the [collapse of the] bloc felled Bernhard. You must seek the true reason in the events of November." Although the repudiation of his economic policy by a clerical-conservative Reichstag coalition seriously undermined his position, the fourth chancellor really fell because of William's conviction that "he has insufficiently defended his imperial master." [39]

The final tax compromise was negotiated under the leadership of Vice-Chancellor Bethmann, who had observed the crisis with growing apprehension. "The government's position is false when it knows beforehand that [the inheritance tax] will be rejected. This refusal robs the cabinet of its initiative, strengthens the conservative-clerical position and, in the end, necessitates the acceptance of impossibilities. That is my fear," he wrote to one of his key advisors, the later secretary of finance, Adolf Wermuth. "I do not want to make predictions about the coming developments," since the issue still remained in doubt. "I fear that the new majority will cling to the *Kotierungssteuer,* which will be declared unacceptable; then either the entire reform will be rejected, or only 350 million passed, and the Center Party will postpone the rest until fall. At present the Conservatives are so dependent upon the Center that they can hardly do anything against them." Bethmann's fears proved only too well founded. He anxiously reported the parliamentary defeat of the inheritance tax to the vacationing Wermuth: "The decision has been made. . . . At any rate, now we must negotiate with the new majority," reject the all too impossible Kotierungssteuer, and force the Conservatives to muster a majority which will make suggestions acceptable to the Bundesrat. "They claim to be strong enough for it. I shall believe it for the time being. The reform will be possible with 500 million." The financial need of the empire was such that the government was forced "to take the taxes where it can get them." The revenue compromise worked out with the Conservatives, Center, and federal states was clearly regressive, since it levied taxes on brandy, beer, tobacco, light and matches, tea and coffee, as well as stamp duties on securities, checks, bills, drafts, property exchanges, and even dividends, i.e. consumers and commercial capital. Nevertheless Bethmann counseled acceptance since "postponement would not only extend the fiscal crisis for months, but would jeopardize the entire project." The alternative of no taxes at all was worse than unjust taxation. "If an agreement is reached now . . . the united governments will do a *service to the fatherland,*" despite all justified criticism.[40]

Since "only a few believe that the chancellor's resignation is definite," seasoned observers noted "that the general political situation continues to be very tense." Berlin teemed with rumors about possible successors to Bülow. Bethmann asked his collaborator Wermuth to return "since the future developments *can* become uncertain, even in our ministry." The popular desire for a forceful leader made the former diplomat, Count Wedel, and the Prussian finance minister, Rheinbaben, leading candidates, but the emperor preferred the dynamic ambassador to the quirinal, Count Monts, and was only dissuaded with great difficulty by the chief of his civil cabinet.[41] When Rudolf von Valentini instead suggested Bethmann's name, the kaiser responded, "I know him well; he is always lecturing and pretends to know everything better." The secretary of the interior's loyal support of Bülow in the *Daily Telegraph* Affair made him add, "I cannot work with him." When Hofmarschall August Eulenburg and the senile Botho Eulenburg, a former Prussian prime minister, also refused, the emperor turned to a potential military strongman, the reorganizer of the Turkish army, General Colmar von der Goltz. But he was thought indispensable to German influence on the Ottoman Empire and ordered to continue the reorganization of the Turkish army.[42]

Only after failing with his own candidates did William decide to follow Bülow's advice that "the chief difficulties lie in domestic politics," and that he should therefore appoint the best man for internal affairs, Theobald von Bethmann Hollweg. In court circles this choice caused little surprise "because Bethmann had been known as a future chancellor since his entrance into the cabinet," and during each previous crisis "one expected him to move into the chancellor's palace." Acutely aware of his own shortcomings, Bethmann rushed to Chief of the Chancellery Loebell, who had initially suggested his candidacy, and proposed Minister of Agriculture Schorlemer-Lieser instead. But when Valentini finally came with the royal order on July 8, Bethmann yielded "with grave doubts," after a long and passionate debate. Protesting his "inadequacy," he wrote to William II, "that I can base my acceptance only on my loyalty and love for my emperor and fatherland and my prayer for God's assistance. Moved by such sentiments, I thank Y.M. and place my services at your disposal." In a curious mixture of humility, self-doubt, assertiveness, and desire for power, Bethmann adroitly moved into the center of the imperial stage while Bülow was bowing out. "You will find it natural that I accept this office with a heavy heart," he confided to his friend Karl von Eisendecher a few weeks later. "Only a genius or a man driven by ambition and lust for power can covet this post. And I am neither. An ordinary man can only assume it when compelled by his sense of duty." [43]

Since, compared to some of the high Prussian favorites, Bethmann promised moderation and some progress, "all of Germany received the choice with relief." The perceptive Lerchenfeld did not miss the irony that "in domestic policy he has spun the same thread as Bülow and he is now supposed to accept his inheritance." Knowing him as "a very intelligent, quiet, benevolent, and exceptionally reliable man," Austrian Ambassador Szögény was reassured that "as politician he confessed to conservative, but not reactionary, views with a strong liberal tinge." Although Bethmann was less cosmopolitan in experience and possibly in sympathies than his urbane predecessor, the American envoy Hill expected "that so good a jurist, so experienced an administrator and so just a man as the chancellor appears to be will be considerate of the positions which foreign powers will be obliged to take," and that the excellent relations between the U.S. and the empire "will not be affected in any manner." [44]

Because he had made few enemies as vice-chancellor, the German press was reserved but benevolent, since it was preoccupied with praising Bülow's world political successes. In *Die Alldeutsche Blätter,* Ernst von Reventlow stressed the necessity of "strengthening the government . . . in as far as the new chancellor shows the will to follow a pronouncedly national policy and opposes the trend towards parliamentarization." The moderately national *Grenzboten* commented, "Everywhere he has been received with trust and will himself recognize clearly that he has to earn this faith daily to keep it." Similarly, the *Konservative Monatsschrift* emphasized that "Bethmann appears, as no one else, predestined to unite the divided parties with impartial government and sober legislation." The Center Party reserved judgment on the former champion of the Bülow bloc, while a disappointed National Liberal leader warned that "liberalism has reason to beware." But the progressive Friedrich Naumann argued that "he can say with more justification than his predecessor that he is convinced of the necessity of a certain liberalism in politics, because in his case this conviction does not rest on mere tactics but on moral grounds." Further to the Left, other voices warned against his indecisiveness, and the Socialists denounced him as an exponent of bourgeois *Sammlungspolitik* (consolidation): "In fact the Conservatives have been victorious." To them, Bülow's fall was symptomatic of a wider crisis of Wilhelmine foreign and domestic policy which could not be overcome by the appointment of an educated and sincere bureaucrat: "The hangman still stands before our door!" [45]

Although Bethmann was known for his "moral courage, scrupulousness, thorough education, idealistic enthusiasm, and critical mind," such qualities alone had never sufficed to bring anyone into the Wilhelmstrasse. His impressive rise through the ranks of the Prussian bureaucracy owed just as much to his capacity to internalize its adminstrative ethos, his lack of major mistakes during his official career, and his pragmatic opportunism, adaptable to changing constellations within the wider limits of a liberal conservative tradition. William II's benevolence toward the Bethmann family and Theobald's image as a man never concerned for his own advancement but only committed to doing his duty also speeded his career. His policies as Prussian minister of the interior uncritically continued the Bismarckian practices of persecuting socialism, Germanizing the Poles, and tying political participation to the criteria of birth, wealth, or education, even though he became privately convinced that only a major overhauling of the entire system could in the long run forestall a violent outburst. As domestic leader of the Conservative-Liberal Bülow bloc, Bethmann, during his tenure as vice-chancellor and secretary of the interior, fully shared Bülow's tactical conviction that Old Prussia could only survive rejuvenated by reform, and his legislative proposals concerning a revision of the associations law, the extension of social insurance, and the creation of chambers of work made some attempt to reach this goal. Not compromised in the struggles over the *Daily Telegraph* Affair and the reform of imperial finances, he seemed a logical choice for chancellor because he shared the central assumptions of Wilhelmian Weltpolitik but lacked the domestic blinders and diplomatic frivolity that had brought Bülow down. "The new chancellor is a straw man." The Princess Radziwill echoed the feelings of court society when she commented, "Bethmann's nomination means that the emperor wants to rule himself." "Of course Bethmann is the successor, but not with [Alfred von] Kiderlen, and it is horrible and quite incomprehensible how this conscientious man accepts those new tasks with the mannequin [Wilhelm] von Schoen, who will put both at the kaiser's mercy," Baroness von Spitzemberg similarly lamented. "What that portends, together with the internal bitterness about taxes and the blue-black bloc, makes a partiot's blood run cold." By all standards the new chancellor faced a formidable task. Would the future bear out Bülow, who recommended him "neither as a thoroughbred nor a jumper, but as a good plow-horse, plodding along slowly and steadily, because there are no hurdles in sight," or would it justify Ballin's later quip, "Bethmann is Bülow's revenge"? [46]

CHAPTER 4

In Bismarck's Footsteps

The legacy Prince Bülow bequeathed to his successor was nothing short of dismal. Although in midsummer 1909 the Wilhelmian Empire looked more prosperous and powerful than ever, tensions were mounting behind the imposing façade, which threatened to destroy the Iron Chancellor's supreme accomplishment within the decade. Domestic politics were in disarray and Germany's position in the world was hardly better. Militant Weltpolitik and Friedrich von Holstein's misconception of the "free hand" had gambled away Berlin's dominance on the continent, provoked the construction of a wall of hostile ententes, and hastened Italy's desertion from the Triple Alliance. At home the *Daily Telegraph* Affair had dramatically revealed public discontent with William II's irresponsible personal rule, while Conservative opposition to the inheritance tax showed that Old Prussia was unwilling to make even the slightest concession to social or constitutional evolution. When Bethmann assumed the heavy burden of chancellorship, Imperial Germany was at a crossroads: would it evolve peacefully or stagnate and unleash war?

"He was completely conscious that he would face grave struggles," Szögyény reported Bethmann's grim resolve, "but he knew the terrain on which he had to move and counted on being able to surmount the great difficulties with calmness, patience, and compromise." Known as "thorough, serious and forbidding in appearance, humorous only in his closest circle, old Prussian in his respect for any office *secundum ordinem,* German in his love for the fatherland, and capable of high enthusiasm," the new chancellor was the exact antithesis of his facile predecessor. In contrast to the opportunistic Bülow, he prized "the rustic virtues of tenacity, perseverance and patience," and believed that "in politics, too, there is a long wait between sowing and reaping. Whoever loses confidence in bad weather is as little fit to be a farmer as a statesman." A young official, Kurt Riezler, voiced high expectations. "After the soulless Bülow, [Bethmann is] a relief. If he fails, every idealist must despair in our system." [1]

In his attempt to counteract the hubris of Wilhelmian Germany, Bethmann was forced to work within a network of severe constraints. Though in the hands of Bismarck it had been unassailable, the chancellorship had weakened drastically, as his epigones had let many of its powers slip away. A halfway house in terms of the constitution, the office lay at the center of all the unresolved tensions inherited from the Prussian conquest of Germany. Formally responsible only to the emperor but in fact also dependent on the Reichstag—as demonstrated by Bülow's fall—the chancellor had to reconcile the divergent demands of Prussia and the empire. This pseudoconstitutionalism made him solely responsible for the conduct of imperial foreign and domestic policy; but any chief executive was severely restricted by the *Kommandogewalt* (power of command) and the personality of William II. The institutions of the cabinet system, dealing with civilian, army, and navy affairs, prevented the chancellor's direct access to the kaiser and provided a natural focus for a permanent camarilla. Lacking a federal cabinet and aided only by his representatives, the secretaries of state, the chancellor—as prime minister of Prussia—was primus inter pares in the Prussian Ministry of State. Theoretically, only the executor of the directives of the Federal Council [Bundesrat], which was endowed with ultimate legislative power, he was nevertheless forced to respond to increasingly vocal national opinion, divided into competing parties and imperialistic propaganda organizations. A crippled legacy of the *Stellvertretergesetz,* the imperial chancellery was notoriously understaffed and incapable of fulfilling its multiple tasks of reconciling the imperial secretariats, the Prussian ministries, and the Reichstag. In one crucial area, the coordination of press policy, the chancellery was nearly powerless, and the information office of the Foreign Office proved incapable of controlling opinion on domestic as well as foreign policy. Restricted to the use of indirect taxation, the imperial government was at the financial mercy of the Bundesrat and the Prussian parliament. Even in his proper domain, foreign affairs, the chancellor was subject to the whims of the emperor, the irresponsible planning of the military, the clamor of a chauvinist press, and the pressure of economic interest groups. Instinctively sensing these difficulties, Martha von Bethmann Hollweg exclaimed when she heard of her husband's appointment, "Dear Theo, you cannot do that!" [2]

The gravest liability of the chancellorship was William II's volatile personality and his tendency to reverse policy decisions at a moment's notice when emotionally upset. Although after the *Daily Telegraph* Affair the kaiser's personal regime, i.e., his penchant for unexpected interference, was more fiction than fact, it still required constant ministerial vigilance. "I regret that H.M. has been so temperamental, especially in his statements about Prince Bülow and Russia, since in the end too much becomes public knowledge without doing any good," Bethmann complained to his friend Ambassador Eisendecher three months after his inauguration. "Except in our first discussion regarding Prince Bülow, the high lord has always been sensitive and tactful toward me." In contrast to the sentimental friendship with his predecessor, based on flattery and sycophancy, relations between the kaiser and Bethmann lacked warmth and hardly transcended official correctness. Resentful of Bethmann's pedantic, pensive, and pedagogical strain, William often ridiculed his chancellor, but he could always count on his loyal devotion and fundamental honesty. Although he approached the kaiser in a ritualistically deferential manner, Bethmann could, when necessary, stand up to him and almost always succeeded in convincing him. "The idea that he will ally himself with the princes in order to chastise the Reichstag and eventually abolish it, or that he will send one of his adjutant generals into the Reichstag, if I am not tough enough, constantly crops up in conversations with me," Bethmann lamented in 1913. "I do not take these things too seriously, although they increasingly prevent mutual trust and agreement on the policies to be followed. They personally demand much strength of nerve and give me a certain feeling that this will not go on much longer." The emperor was an unruly horse to be bridled by the chancellor acting as his political and moral conscience, because tradition and character predisposed William II to think of himself as the nearly omnipotent heir of Frederick the Great.[3]

Constitutionally dependent upon the Bundesrat, Bethmann skilfully turned this limitation into a political asset. In temper and general outlook closer to the liberal conservatism of the prime ministers Karl von Weizsäcker, Georg von Hertling, Alexander von Dusch, and Christoph Vitzthum von Eckstädt than to his more obscurantist Prussian colleagues, the chancellor intensively cultivated relations with the non-Prussian courts. Stressing that profederalism needed to be nurtured not only between the states "where it is self-evident" but also in parliament, he added, "To reconcile the opposition resulting from the different political character and habits of North and South is a task which has become more and more important to me during the last two years." Bethmann's mental horizon reached beyond the Mark Brandenburg, since he "greatly regretted the setback in relations between North and South Germany," brought on by the crisis over imperial finances. "The hostile feeling against Prussia, now spreading into Baden, causes me deep concern." Opposed to unitary government, especially in controversial matters such as the revision of domestic shipping tolls, he attempted "to find a way which would be as acceptable as possible to the dissenting states." Moreover, federalism led Bethmann to the conclusion "that the parliamentary system in the empire is irreconcilable with the federal principle of our constitution and would imply the mediatization of the member states." Only respect for states rights could prevent the eventual "erosion of the foundations of Prussia, the key to any healthy imperial policy." The Bundesrat, therefore, remained a mainstay of Bethmann's power throughout his tenure as chancellor. Similarly, Germany's allies and even her enemies trusted Bethmann more than they had ever confided in Bülow. Often a reference to Vienna's support could forestall an incipient chancellor crisis.[4]

Within the imperial government, Bethmann from the outset insisted on his own ascendancy. Dependent on the favor of the chancellor, the state secretaries almost always supported him, except for the secretary of the navy, Admiral Tirpitz, who could count upon the emperor. When colorful personalities like Kiderlen-Waechter sought to follow an independent policy and privately ridiculed Bethmann as *Regenwurm,* they were brought to heel because they needed the chancellor's support vis-à-vis kaiser and Reichstag. By not appointing his erstwhile rival, Prussian Minister of Finance Rheinbaben, vice-president of the State Ministry, Bethmann solidified his grasp on the Prussian cabinet, although Rheinbaben, as minister with longest tenure, was clearly entitled to this honor. To lessen the Conservatives' resistance to his policies in the empire, Bethmann provoked Rheinbaben's resignation one year later and forced the retirement of Minister of the Interior Moltke and Minister of Agriculture Bernhard von Arnim, who were replaced by August Lentze, Johann von Dallwitz, and Clemens von Schorlemer, respectively. "The change of guard has strengthened Bethmann's position considerably," his *adlatus,* Kurt Riezler, noted. "He has understood that 'a statesman must have scalps on his belt.' " Only shortly before the outbreak of the war did he appoint Foreign Secretary Jagow and Secretary of the Treasury Kühn Prussian ministers of state. The opposition of strong personalities such as Colonial Secretaries Dernburg and Lindequist, as well as Secretary of the Treasury Wermuth, resulted inevitably in their dismissal. Considering such threats of resignation insubordinate, the chancellor snapped: "Believe me, dear Wermuth, I also often find unpleasant obstacles in my path. But I have always told myself that offering to resign is a means of pressure which can only be used with the most careful limitation because of [fundamental dictates of] raison d'état." Although the inherent conservatism of the Prussian bureaucracy and ministry severely restricted Bethmann's evolutionary conservatism, since they were counterbalanced only moderately by the somewhat more progressive state secretaries of the empire, within these restraints the fifth chancellor was more powerful than his detractors were willing to admit.[5]

Though theoretically least important, in fact, the Reichstag proved to be Bethmann's most difficult check. Because of universal suffrage tempered only by the practice of runoff elections, Bismarck's stepchild reflected the major social, economic, and ideological forces of the empire; and the transformation of the honorables clubs into mass parties and their capture by interest groups made the Reichstag the focus of major political struggles despite its semi-impotence. The parliamentary budget powers rendered the collaboration between the cabinet and the parties imperative, but the fleeting experience of the *Kartell* and the Bülow bloc had not allowed the emergence of government by majority coalition. "In Germany we will suffer for a long time from a short-sightedness of the parties which is unknown in other countries," Bethmann lamented frequently about "the Reichstag's lack of dignity." He deplored Bülow's fall, which was hastened by parliamentary defeat, as "a dangerous trend" and, unwilling to do business for the Clerical-Conservative "blue-black" coalition, he strove to reassert "the independence and freedom of the government which is absolutely necessary to counteract the dangerous drift toward parliamentarization." Clinging tenuously to the fiction of "government above parties," Bethmann sought to further the reconciliation of National Liberals, Conservatives, and Center Party "through practical work" in order to "make possible the concrete cooperation of all bourgeois parties." By checking the rampant imperialism of the Liberals, breaking down Conservative abhor-rence of liberalization, and nationalizing ultramontane Catholics, he sought to create a solid parliamentary basis for his moderate pol-icies, because he realized that "our difficulties result from lack of a firm Reichstag majority and from the necessity that the chancellor, especially the present one, has to drum up sullen *Landsknechte* from all four corners of the earth for every [legislative] battle." Two con-siderations made "a shift [to the Left] almost impossible: the in-credible stupidity of the Liberals and the kaiser's instability." A structural necessity, a political tradition, and a personal preference, Bethmann's pretense of impartiality ultimately made him the par-liamentary prisoner of the Right.[6]

"Striving to reduce the numerous areas of international friction," Bethmann similarly pursued the domestic aim of healing the divi-sions left by Bülow's fall and of building a consensus for gradual liberalization. Although "it is still too early to judge," the new chancellor hoped that "the gradual sobering which must occur af-ter the political paroxysms of the last months will exert a reconciling influence" on the parties. In his initial meeting with the Prussian Ministry of State, Bethmann programmatically explained that "a fundamental change of policy did not seem necessary." Only "the Conservatives must be helped to correct their errors while retaining their independence, as many Liberals as possible must be drawn into positive cooperation, and participation must be made easier for the Center." Cautious and deliberative, Bethmann proposed no star-tling departures, and while seeking to maintain tolerable relations with his erstwhile mentor, soon emancipated himself from Bülow's preoccupation with tactical success to seek, rather, a more basic and lasting agreement on the goals of domestic politics. In his maiden speech before the Reichstag, the new chancellor refused to propose a grandiose program and to play up to "petty party interests." Claim-ing "that we cannot have a partisan government in Prussia," Beth-mann appealed to those circles "of our people who in the long run do not thrive on political sensation and irritation." Stressing the salutory effect of the financial reform, he continued, "What the people demand most is that this economic and cultural work not be disturbed at home or on the world market through experiments and unrest." Rejecting the slogans of radicalism or reaction as im-pediments to reasonable progress, he rather relied on "the need for creative action which the national community imposes upon all of its members, and this duty will survive the present trials and disturbances." Strongly applauded by the Right, Bethmann's apolitical program assumed that not drastic change, but slow and steady advance would break the fever symptomatic of the deep-seated malaise of Wilhelmian politics.[7]

"A tough nut to crack," the inherited promise of Prussian electoral reform soon tested this self-conscious attempt "at returning to Bismarck's old system of creating ad hoc majorities." Perceptively, the Austrian chargé predicted, "The solution of this problem will be the great touchstone for the initial phase of Bethmann Hollweg's chancellorship." Since the Conservative stranglehold on the Prussian Landtag, resulting from the three-class system, made any progressive policy in the empire almost impossible, the chancellor resolved to make the broadening of the suffrage his first domestic priority. In early November 1909 Prussian Minister of the Interior Moltke presented his draft proposal, arguing that the imperial promise of "organic evolution" excluded any basically different procedure such as universal, proportional, or plural voting from the very beginning. Modest in scope, this reform attempted to eliminate the worst abuses of the existing system, such as indirect balloting and the plutocratic distortions due to the use of tax returns as basis for the division into the three classes of electors. To broaden participation, nevertheless, age, education, and economic independence were suggested as sources of additional votes up to a possible maximum of twelve. Announced in January in the *Thronrede* (the kaiser's opening speech to the Landtag), this minor liberalization was, as Szögyény had foreseen, "too radical for the Right and too timid for the Left," and found few supporters anywhere. Bethmann himself apologized: "The proposal for the reform of the Prussian suffrage will not increase the sympathies of [South Germany]. Hence it is all the more urgent that in this crisis, which the country and I will have to surmount, everything is avoided which could further harm the idea of national unity." Unwilling and for political reasons unable to grant both secret and direct ballot, Bethmann insisted on at least one of these features, coupled with limited anticapitalistic provisions and some easing of access to the vote, in order to strengthen the state-supporting middle and lower middle classes against subversion from below. "The end of agitation for electoral reform is in the common interest of all bourgeois parties." He pleaded for sacrifices from all respectable elements, "Even if the reform will never satisfy the radicals' desire for agitation, it might at least quiet those who support the parties voting for this measure." A minuscule step toward "liberal government" in Prussia, the chancellor's reform bill attempted to break the domestic deadlock with the approval of the Right.[8]

Because of the tactical blunder of not consulting the parties when preparing the suffrage proposal, Bethmann's reception in the Landtag boded ill for the fate of the bill. The chancellor's argument "that it would be more appropriate to give the draft a factually correct form and then introduce it to Parliament" backfired, and when he took the rostrum the far Left shouted angrily, "Traitor to the people," while the Right retorted, "Kick them out!" Dismissing Socialist idealism as "pure will to power" and insisting to the Progressives that "raw numbers are the simplest but not the only criterion for the political rights of a nation," he polemicized against the stereotype of reactionary Prussia by pointing to the progressive income tax, the extension of municipal self-government, the famed incorruptibility of the bureaucracy, and the existence of a Rechtsstaat. "As long as the power of its royalty is unbroken, Prussia will not let herself be dragged into the wake of parliamentarization." Bethmann sought to reassure the restive Conservatives, to whom even such mild medicine was distasteful: "Behind the whole malaise is the feeling that after the rapid advances which we have made, we now find ourselves in *a period of cultural stagnation*." Speaking with the self-assurance of a still unbroken Borussian tradition, he continued, "Has not the democratization of parliament in all countries contributed to the brutalizing and diluting of political morals and to the hamstringing of progress which we need so dearly and to whose advancement the suffrage reform is being introduced?" Slightly misquoting Bismarck, Bethmann stressed that "the God-given dependencies" required a graduated vote and that "not secret but public ballot contributes to a spirit of civic responsibility." Intended to persuade the agrarian, industrial, and educational elites that *"Prussia must preserve herself in consonance with the entire development of Germany,"* these starkly elitist words "could not but evoke a profound impression in the thickly crowded house, in contrast to the negative reporting of the majority of the press." But Bethmann's proud defense of the Prussian heritage by courting the forces of resistance alienated the powers pressing for change and contributed little to "the chief purpose of the reform, which is to pacify the country and to reach a tolerable conclusion." [9]

In the ensuing parliamentary maneuvering, Bethmann soon found himself between all chairs. The chancellor's unwillingness and the structural impossibility of making the reform against the opposition of the strongest party in the Landtag, the Conservatives, assured Heyde-brand the uncrowned king of Prussia, a virtual veto. When, as concession to their new Center allies, they dropped their opposition to secret vote while the Catholics revived indirect ballot, "the grand idea and, so to speak, the backbone of the bill" was crushed. Although distasteful but by no means fatal, the surprising Clerical-Conservative compromise handed the Liberals the tactical key to the situation, "If the National Liberal party showed once more that it could not be relied upon, he considered agreement with the Conservatives and the Center preferable to complete failure." In repeated conversations with leaders of the Right as well as in a declaration in the Lower House, Bethmann stressed that he would accept the secret and indirect ballot, if the educational (i.e. *Kulturträger*) votes were restored and the maximum amount of taxation credited toward classification were limited. By mid-March 1910 the chancellor confessed that he had "completely abandoned hope for an agreement among the major parties," but continued to press for negotiations between Heydebrand and the Liberal leader Eugen Schiffer. "If indirect suffrage is to be kept it is doubly necessary to realize the goal of these reforms by adding cultural votes and restructuring voting districts." Despondent because of the intractability of the Conservatives and the insatiability of the Liberals, Bethmann *"urgently* hope[d] that the Upper House will reach conclusions which I can accept." Although he denounced an attempt to link electoral reform to a stipulation requiring a two-thirds majority for constitutional change in the future as "nothing but a conservative dictatorship," the chancellor only wanted a moderate broadening of the electorate, insisting on safeguards "to bar an excessive influx of Socialists and Poles and to give heavy industry, especially in the Rhineland, a chance to be represented in the Lower House." On April 28 Bethmann pleaded in the Upper Chamber that "the royal government would consider it detrimental to the interests of the state if a negative result" were reached. Because of this personal appeal, the Lords passed an amendment suggested by Schorlemer, setting limits to the controversial *Drittelung* (triple classification of the tax base) which had some chance of being accepted by the Liberals.[10]

The chancellor's "pleasure that these changes move along the lines which the moderate parties prefer" turned into gloom when the bill returned to the Landtag. "The reaction of the National Liberal party to this fait accompli will—according to my conviction—determine not only the vote on the reform but also the future alignment of parties"—Bethmann sought to win the bourgeois Liberals for the Clerical-Conservative compromise. "Now a new platform has been created which offers the possibility of a free decision, be it positive or negative." He added the warning, "I am firmly convinced that only political action guarantees the acquisition of influence." Although the chancellor intensified his efforts to exert pressure on the Conservatives through the Rhine-Ruhr industrialists and to rally the Center "for a compromise supported by the great majority of the bourgeois parties," the government ultimately succeeded in affronting each major faction. The refusal of the Liberals to accept a sham reform, the opposition of the Conservatives to any substantive change at all, and the tactical vacillations of the Catholics between both parties, forced Bethmann to admit, "I could never recommend to Y.M. the approval of a law which in all important stipulations dictated by Conservatives and Center would not even be accepted by the *Neue Fraktion* of the Upper House, would not be supported by the Free Conservatives in the Lower House, to say nothing of the National Liberals, and finally does not meet the justified demands of the government." William II agreed that "by bending under the yoke of a parliamentary majority the authority and reputation of the government would be so damaged that even the failure of the bill must be considered the smaller evil." Unwilling "to accept sizable revisions of the Upper House decisions," to tolerate the Liberal "coupling of direct and secret ballot," or to be content with the blue-black travesty of the bill, Bethmann foundered on the resistance of Old Prussia to the hopes of the majority of bourgeois Germany. "I regret the probable failure of the reform, but more its effect upon our further party development. The chasm between Conservatives and National Liberals will widen and the latter be pushed further to the left. A hardly beneficial reign of Conservatives and Catholics will ensue." There was no room to compromise, since he felt that "the direction of our entire policy is at stake." [11]

The final Landtag debate of May 27, 1910, was only an anti-climactic postlude. Progressive Deputy Fischbeck marveled at "the strange burial which we celebrate today. At the open grave you gentlemen quarrel about whose child it was and who committed the murder. But my political friends will not shed one tear for it." Outwardly possessed but deeply saddened, Bethmann rejected a restrictive Conservative amendment, more radical Liberal suggestions, and the Center Party demand to restore the original decisions of the Landtag. "If the majority of this esteemed assembly is unable to base its deliberations upon the resolutions of the Upper House, I see no prospect for reaching a positive result," the chancellor concluded to the applause of only a few Conservatives. Because these votes created a "gap in the question of *Drittelung*," Bethmann had no alternative left, "I regret to inform Y.M. of the failure of the reform, but since I did not want to squander the prestige of the government, I was required to act as I did." The failure of the first major initiative of his chancellorship was bitter, since he knew what its dangerous long-term consequences would be. "It is not easy in Germany to yield sufficiently but carefully enough to the pressure for democratic reform," he pondered afterward, still hoping to reintroduce a similar measure when he had found the right password. "More important than the content of the proposed changes will be the party constellation that can be won for a proposal. For that reason I let the bill fail last year." The experiment of recreating Bismarck's cartel had not survived the initial test. "I could not and will not be able to make the law without the support of the Free Conservatives of National Liberals." Wanting to reform not discard tradition, the chancellor rejected the option of a Liberal-Center-Free Conservative majority because "it would in fact lead us too far to the left. Hence the problem remains unclear and dangerous, because with their personal, social, religious, and political hubris and intolerance, the Conservatives have succeeded in focusing everyone's disgust and dissatisfaction against the three-class suffrage, which is generally seen as an expression of Junker predominance." Embittered by the Right's blindness to necessary change, Bethmann reasoned, "Perhaps they will first have to pass through the hard school of Reichstag elections." [12]

Although "the relationship between government and the parties and the future course of the National Liberals" remained unresolved, Bethmann immediately tackled another major constitutional problem which had troubled the empire since Bismarck: the reform of the status of the Reichsland, Alsace-Lorraine. Already as state secretary of the interior the new chancellor had written a lengthy and persuasive memorandum arguing "for determined action to develop the constitutional position of Alsace-Lorraine in order not to hinder the inner assimilation of even the Germanophile parts of the population by a feeling of inequality." As long as Alsace-Lorraine remained an object of imperial policy, "it will never psychologically grow into the empire." To counteract the revival of pro-French agitation, Bethmann suggested the creation of a Landtag with full parliamentary powers, the exclusion of the Reichstag from provincial administration, and the province's admission into the Bundesrat, even if the increase in pro-Prussian votes would raise strong opposition elsewhere. Since "previous experience proves that Alsace-Lorraine has not grown into the Reich," Bethmann endorsed Alsatian State Secretary Mandel's suggestions for the establishment of an independent diet, the elimination of the Reichstag's powers, the admission of Alsatian votes into the Bundesrat, and autonomy regarding its suffrage. In his second major speech on domestic policy in the Reichstag, the chancellor stressed that "the empire desires and supports—not only materially but also politically—the development of the Reichsland toward independence." To be sure, the granting of full autonomy required guarantees and a reversal of Francophile agitation, but this process could be hastened only by patient understanding, "The more one stops looking at things on both sides with exaggerated chauvinism, the earlier Alsace will cease to be the battleground of nationalist quarrels and the earlier it will become, as it wishes, a valuable member of the family of German states." [13]

"A legislative proposal concerning the Alsatian constitution is ready," Bethmann announced in March 1910. "Since recent political experiences show what an unpleasant position one can be forced into through small and half measures," he suggested sizable concessions to Stadtholder Count Wedel in order to integrate the disputed province fully into the Reich. The key question of making Alsace-Lorraine a voting member of the Bundesrat, thus upsetting the balance of votes so carefully constructed by the Iron Chancellor, could perhaps be side-stepped by creating an upper house in the Reichsland. "Qualified personalities, under the present circumstances, can be educated in no other way than by responsible participation in the affairs of state." Overriding bureaucratic misgivings, he asserted, "The goal of the reform will always remain the full independence of Reichsland legislation; the earlier it is achieved, the more it can be made to fit into conservative and *staatserhaltende* institutions." In October 1910 the draft proposal reached the Prussian Ministry of State for a full debate. Vice-Chancellor Delbrück stressed the need for moderate reform and refuted Minister of the Interior Dallwitz's arguments that the proposals were too far-reaching by countering that Prussian class suffrage would only strengthen the political weight of the Francophile bourgeoisie. By emphasizing that "the time has finally come to take a decisive step forward," and that the government "must offer something which deserves to be called an improvement," Bethmann convinced his reluctant colleagues to submit a substantial reform to the Reichstag on January 28, 1911. Contrary to his conservative and nationalist critics, the chancellor saw "the slow increase in the independence of Alsace-Lorraine as a means of tying the Reichsland more closely to the empire," and cautioned emphatically: "Do not engage in a policy of all or nothing. It will lead to nothing." The contradiction between offering a liberal plural suffrage in the Reichsland while rejecting it in Prussia was necessitated by Alsace-Lorraine's freer traditions, whereas in Prussia the suffrage had to guarantee "a constant and staatserhaltende policy." [14]

Despite Bethmann's outspoken warnings, the Reichstag commission "shifted the basis of the government proposal" by granting even greater independence than the chancellor could permit. Unwilling to abandon the project and thus suffer a second major defeat, he hit upon the idea of allowing Alsace-Lorraine three Bundesrat votes, with the stipulation that they should not be counted if the presiding power (Prussia) would gain a majority only through them. Since Berlin's influence lay not in its formal votes "but in its historical achievements and its mission," Bethmann was willing to concede this theoretical loss of voting power in return for the expected allegiance of the Alsatians. Although from the very beginning the Conservatives refused to participate in the shaping of the bill, the Reichstag commission, with the approval of all parties including the Social Democrats, accepted the strongly modified government

proposal after Bethmann had once more declared, "I consider the
evolution of the constitution a necessity." To convince William II,
he argued that he had initially preferred the granting of Bundesrat
votes, that the reduced residence requirement would benefit German
officials, and that the potential harm resulting from a failure of the
bill far outweighed the inconvenience of the elimination of plural
suffrage. "The law must not be allowed to fail because of the personal position of the chancellor. The Social Democrats' vote for it
is no objection against it. If I cannot weather the shock which my
position with the emperor and in Prussia receives by this," he consoled himself, "I will go without having anything to forgive myself. Then I bequeath my successor a better bed to lie in than my
predecessor did." The chancellor disarmingly added, "One must
have the courage of one's own mistakes. . . . It would not matter
if one lost everything as long as one remained true to oneself." In
the showdown, only the Conservatives, led by the notorious Junker
Oldenburg-Januschau, decried the reform as "a blow against Prussia's honor and prestige." Angered by charges of a caudinian yoke
and a new *Olmütz*, the chancellor rose to say: "Gentlemen! You
want to cling to a law which has not changed since 1879. I consider
it necessary to take a step forward," and prophetically added, "The
future will show whether those who want to stand still or those who
want to go forward are right!" [15]

Although he could "feel a certain satisfaction that finally the
maxim according to which I have directed policy has proven correct
and the government's prestige and independence have been restored," Bethmann was soon confronted with another ill-fated Bismarckian legacy, the Prussian Poles. "Taking it as self-evident that the
ministry would prefer not to make use of its power to expropriate"
Polish estates, the chancellor, under Conservative pressure, felt
nevertheless bound by Bülow's *Enteignungsgesetz* "to apply the law
if there is no other possibility for settlement." Seeking to strengthen
the German hold on the eastern provinces, he considered "a formal
repudiation of the Prussian Polish policy impossible" since "the continued advance of Polish influence constitutes a grave threat to the
German element." In January 1910 Bethmann justified the trans-
ferral of two officials in Upper Silesia who had voted for Polish candidates in a local election as "the right and the duty of the government to enforce the principles of its policy on its officials even if

they disagree." Crediting the Polish revival with deep spiritual roots, the chancellor disassociated himself from *Ostmarkenverein* (chauvinist eastern league) demands for an aggressive nationalities struggle. "Supported by German national consciousness, steady work will strengthen the German element culturally and economically so that the Polish movement, despite its advances, will not be able to subvert it." Nevertheless, Bethmann's enforcement was drastically milder than that of his predecessor, and he was instrumental in the attempt to reconcile William II with the Polish nobility through creating a royal residence in West Prussia. "Looking back, the Poznan festivities were a success," he said, thanking Hutten-Czapski for his help, "and it was pleasant for me to note that even the press —except for the National Liberal correspondents of course—showed much understanding." Though aware that "we would satisfy only the Pan-German and hatakist sheets through immediate action," during the Morocco crisis Bethmann telegraphed the HKT society a flaming *"numquam retrorsum"* against any changes in official policy. Since "any reasonable politician can raise the justified accusation of weakness if the government does not expropriate," the chancellor finally yielded to nationalist pressure within and without the cabinet and conceded that "the seizure of single estates can no longer be avoided," despite the bad effect this would have on the Austro-German alliance. Caught between the Conservative majority in Prussia and the Liberal preponderance in the empire, Bethmann received an unprecedented Reichstag vote of censure in early 1913, when the first Polish estate was sequestered. In Imperial Germany concessions to the Right fostered not gratitude but contempt.[16]

In other legislative areas, the chancellor's initiative was stymied by the chronic crisis in imperial finances. Although the misshapen *Finanzreform* had netted about 500 million Marks in new revenue, it barely sufficed for running expenses and for interest on the national debt, since the state secretaries felt only very loosely bound by budget plans and estimates. Economy-minded Secretary of the Treasury Wermuth never tired of reminding Bethmann that the "income for the fiscal years raises the fear that actual taxes for 1910 will not even reach the conservatively estimated revenue." No extravagant social reforms could be introduced because of Wermuth's personal pledge "not to accept any new expenditures without an increase in revenue." But Bethmann feared that militarily "this policy of retrenchment, disregarding army and navy needs, cannot be tolerated long

without endangering the vital interests of the empire: we must create
new taxes, unless the existing finances yield more revenue than anticipated." Since further indirect levies were impossible, he thought
"Conservatives and Center Party could do nothing better than to
accept the inheritance tax as soon as possible, not only for the sake
of the state but also for their own partisan benefit," since only such
a sacrifice would "dissipate the deep resentment provoked by their
earlier refusal." Such opposition might be overcome "with an arms
increase, which can only be justified by rattling sabres and creating
a war scare." Pondering the conflicting dictates of defense, peace,
and parsimony, the chancellor asked himself, "Who can today assume the responsibility for brandishing the sword and conjuring up
war as long as he is not compelled to do so by dire necessity?" Since
Minister of War Heeringen did not insist on excessive demands,
Bethmann followed Wermuth's counsel that, at most, "a small increase can be implemented without new taxes" and advised William
II that "the international situation allows us to be content with
proposing only what is *militarily essential.*" According to his pledge
that "the government must now economize within its means and
lay the foundation for the permanent improvement of imperial
finances," Bethmann recommended a modest enlargement of the
peacetime army consisting of some ten thousand men financed out
of running expenses. Because of his commitment to peace and his
respect for the dynamic Wermuth, whose miserliness he sometimes
suspected, the chancellor resisted the temptation to wave the red
flag and supported the secretary of the treasury's austerity budget,
since he did not yet believe *"Hannibal ante portas."* [17]

Committing himself to "the resolute maintenance of the bases of
our economic policy," Bethmann did not dare challenge the social
foundation of German Weltpolitik. "A chancellor at the head of a
Bassermann-Payer phalanx—I do not even speak of Bebel—is as
impossible as a blue-black one. Even Bismarck has repeatedly called
it his task to navigate between the parties," he reflected on the structural limitation of his political options. The slogans "Defense of
national work" and "Support of autarchic agriculture," which justified the 1879 and 1897 compromise between agrarians and industrialists, were the foundations of Bethmann's economic credo. But
it was tempered by some patriarchical concern for the entire body
politic: "Any unprejudiced observer of the outlines of Germany's
economic development must recognize that beyond its splendid

progress no segment of the economy, neither agriculture, nor industry, nor trade, and neither employers nor employees have been stepchildren." Not even the drought of the summer of 1911, which sent the prices of grain, meat, and potatoes skyward in western Germany, could force Bethmann to abandon his optimism. At the same time he was supporting specific remedial measures, he stressed in the Prussian Ministry of State: "The principles of our economic policy must be maintained. We can permit neither a lifting of the agricultural protective tariffs nor a weakening of the restrictions against animal epidemics." While he suggested a cut in railroad fares and a ban on converting potatoes into alcohol, and admitted the need for minor revision in that Junker bonanza, the *Einfuhr-schein* (rebate) system, Bethmann nevertheless maintained in the Reichstag: "Gentlemen, we will energetically resist these [Progressive] attacks *against our economic policy*. The *resolute continuation of our present economic policy* is a duty to the country." This unequivocal support of the socioeconomic bases of the Wilhelmian state appeared mandatory, since "it is highly important to strengthen the position of the staatserhaltende parties in the [coming] election by a government declaration." [18]

Although Bethmann habitually complained about the artificially created "unrest which should serve to open the eyes of all moderate elements about the consequences of the unprincipled nihilism espoused by our press," the chancellor's most vexing irritant was his relationship with the Conservative Party. Despite frequent conversations with Heydebrand, and the efforts at mediation of Count Leo von Buch, Count Winterfeld-Menkin, and Undersecretary of State Wahnschaffe, the differences, at first tactical, soon became fundamental. "Perhaps without realizing it [Heydebrand] advances the parliamentary system in Germany as no one else," Bethmann lamented, "and what is saddest—he no longer has any understanding for those monarchical sentiments which are a tradition of the Conservative Party. In his parliamentary game, he no longer counts the crown in. He is leading his party on a disastrous course." The transformation from a club of dignitaries to an interest group representing the Bund der Landwirte made the party abandon its state conservatism in favor of an unremitting and unconditional struggle to maintain the economic and political status of the Junker and the other survivors of preindustrial society. "Under Heydebrand's lead-

ership the Conservatives have embarked upon a dangerous road,"
Bethmann unburdened himself to Eisendecher. "Every day they lose
conscious and subconscious sympathies in all moderate, not purely
Junker circles. Instead of cultivating the wellsprings of Prussian
conservative power—complete loyalty toward the crown and faithful
cooperation with the government—[Heydebrand] seeks the salvation of his party in dictatorial partisan politics in parliamentary
style." Gravely concerned with the blindness of his peers, Bethmann
predicted: "This must increase bitterness immeasurably, since the
East Elbian Landräte, dependent upon the goodwill of the conservative landowners in their administration, are pawns of Conservative politics and will remain so for a long time despite all Liberal
clamor." Abandoning their special status, the Conservatives were
beginning to use all those demagogical devices the chancellor abhorred most, and because of Heydebrand's often cutting stubbornness and Bethmann's hypersensitivity, reconciliation repeatedly
failed. Since as Prussian prime minister he had to fear their wrath,
the chancellor continued to strive for the preservation of the traditional order, but gradually and painfully he began to emancipate his
policy from the party's militarism and stand-pattism. In the conservative tradition of Stein and Bismarck, he thus incurred the Conservative Party's venomous enmity.[19]

Logically, Bethmann should now have turned to the National
Liberals, since the Free Conservatives, though cooperative, were too
small a party to provide him with sufficient support. Indeed, there
were signs of hope: "Recently the National Liberals are learning
from the mistakes of the Conservatives. As soon as they stopped the
policy of pure obstruction and began supporting the government
instead of cursing it, their shares rose considerably. I hope they will
stick to it." At moments the chancellor was optimistic: "If the
Liberals were moderately clever, they could capture me. They
should support me despite reservations in principle and prepare
themselves in every respect to govern." His collaborator Riezler
was skeptical: "This will be impossible. These epigones do not
care about power and influence but for speeches in county meetings,
and they basically fear abandoning their accustomed opposition
role." Bethmann similarly resented their "political ignorance . . .
parliamentary ambition, and the lack of scruples with which they
are ready at any time to exploit serious national questions for their
partisan interest." Therefore he believed that "there can be no

change until the present ugly mood has been cleared up by elections. Only if the Conservative defeat that I forsee results in the victory of *moderate* liberalism can elections create greater stability." But Ernst Bassermann's personal preference for the swaggering Bülow rendered Bethmann's repeated efforts to woo the National Liberals, through Hutten-Czapski or Schiffer, ineffectual. Too moderate in foreign policy, too conciliatory in his treatment of minorities, too socially concerned, the chancellor could not find his natural allies because of their expansionist imperialism, their repressive nationalism, and their unmitigated exploitation of the proletariat.[20]

"Only the Center Party had political sense," Bethmann praised Hertling's tact in discriminating between patriotism and chauvinism in the Morocco debate of November 1911. Nevertheless, the establishment of a working relationship between the chancellor and the Center had not been easy because of the Prussian suffrage struggle, the divergent political tempers of the Protestant North and the Catholic South, and ill-fated papal intervention in German politics with the Borromäus encyclical. "The incredible New Year's letter of the Pope to Cardinal Fischer" troubled the chancellor for parliamentary reasons. "Rome wants to centralize Catholicism once more and at the same time to ossify it further, thereby ruining it as an independent spiritual force." Nevertheless, he strove to quiet the public uproar. Answering a Free Conservative interpellation calling for withdrawal of the German ambassador to the Vatican, Bethmann admitted that the references to the Reformation were less than politic, but reiterated that "the royal government is intent on doing everything necessary to protect and to maintain confessional peace in the country." Ambassador Szögyény counted as a "great success" the prohibition against the encyclical being read from German pulpits resulting from Bethmann's remonstrations to the Vatican. Latent tensions erupted again over the antimodernity oath, required by the Curia, which had "created a deep uneasiness in Germany." Because of his aim to maintain the Center Party as an organization but to liberate it from Roman tutelage if possible, the chancellor had to "dance on eggs" in the Reichstag when expressing his concern: "If I interpret the feeling in Prussia and Germany correctly, nobody wants a new *Kulturkampf*, although the papal action clearly endangered confessional peace." Despite considerable ill will in the lower ranks of the party, Cardinal Kopp and the Center leadership were satisfied with Bethmann's genuine desire for domestic peace, and the potentially explosive issue was successfully defused. The party was mildly progressive in matters of social legislation, but in budget questions, because of its alliance with the Conservatives in the *Finanzreform*, it had committed itself to an irresponsible opposition to property taxes. Torn between the reformist Left under Matthias Erzberger, the bureaucratic middle under Peter Spahn, and the conservative landed gentry under Bavarian premier Hertling, it often lacked cohesion, but paved the way for many a compromise in the Reichstag. For this reason the uneasy toleration of the first years of Bethmann's tenure gradually developed into a close working relationship—often through Lerchenfeld's services and Hertling's help in Munich. Until Erzberger's sensational reversal, the Center Party offered firm parliamentary support for the chancellor.[21]

Because they had expected more from the chancellor's electoral reform, Progressive leaders Friedrich Naumann, Conrad Haussmann, and Friedrich Payer initially regarded Bethmann with much skepticism. As a sincere monarchist, the chancellor often ridiculed democratic radicalism. "It is typical of our political bitterness, immaturity, and lack of discipline that those papers which more or less openly demanded the kaiser's participation in daily politics in Poznan cannot denounce sharply enough his general pronouncements in Königsberg, inspired by high moral seriousness concerning his and everyone's duty to the fatherland." Although privately outraged at William's latest lapse, Bethmann defended him in the Reichstag against attacks from the Left: "The Königsberg speech . . . contains, not, as has been alleged, the exposition of absolutist ideas irreconcilable with our constitution, but a strong appeal to the monarchical principle on which Prussian law rests, and a confession of deepest religious conviction which broad circles of the population share and understand." Even if such apologies for the divine-right antics of William II did not endear Bethmann to the Progressives, as Naumann's portrait of "the lonely chancellor" reveals, his moral earnestness and his desire to work for slow reform ultimately struck a responsive chord. Although the democratic Left saw Bethmann primarily as a check on Tirpitz or Ludendorff and accepted him faute de mieux, the chancellor's political evolution toward their limited imperialism and domestic gradualism eventually made the Progressives his most reliable base in the Reichstag.[22]

Because "sooner or later we will have to work with the Social

Democrats," Bethmann gradually reversed his stand from proscription to cooperation. Nevertheless he sought a meeting of minds on his terms, since he called for measures such as the establishment of *Fortbildungsschulen* (vocational schools) in order "to compete with the Socialists in this area through organizing youth welfare." Although he authorized abortive ministerial discussions on measures to combat "the contamination of the army reserve with Socialist ideas," and blamed the Moabit riots on "their moral coresponsibility," when the kaiser once again "spoke to him about the Socialist danger and advocated legal repression, he answered that, if the people only remain physically and psychologically sound and healthy, then they will get over socialism by themselves." Riezler thought this reasoning "typical of Bethmann, who not only says it to the kaiser, but believes it. As far as the people are concerned, it is true, but not for the kaiser." First of all, in questions of Sozialpolitik in which they had a special stake, but gradually also in issues like the reform of the Alsatian constitution, the Social Democratic Party emerged from its legislative ghetto, since the government was ever so slowly beginning to treat it as one among other legitimate Reichstag parties. Bethmann wrote to Bülow in 1911: "It is becoming more and more difficult, not only for the other parties but also for the government, to regulate their relationship with the Social Democrats. . . . Within the Socialist Reichstag faction there is great fermentation. Last winter the opposition between the revisionist and radical members grew so violent that they no longer respected customary social forms." Although the chancellor's hope in revisionism was disappointed in all prewar congresses, his conviction grew that "one must cooperate with the Social Democrats from issue to issue. As State Secretary [Delbrück] had done before, he would not take exception to negotiating personally with their leaders." As a result of Bethmann's political realism, a half-century of Socialist isolation was drawing to a close.[23]

Because of the approaching Reichstag elections, the chancellor found it "damnably difficult to force myself into a festive mood" during Christmas 1911. "My oldest son, still a young student, recently said to me with some truth, 'The government must finally become more popular.' I see the necessity. But I am not yet philosopher enough to ask a public, which continually vilifies me, for approval in any other way than by doing what I consider right." Tellingly he added, "Unfortunately I cannot always do that." Because of Conservative obstructionism, the elections "will not bring us anything good. I count upon approximately one hundred Socialists, perhaps more." Although this did not necessarily have to incapacitate the Reichstag, "a popular government must then be established." But what could he do? "It is unfortunate that the ministry can hardly take an active lead during the campaign. The economic slogan has little appeal because it is not contested enough. And the Social Democratic threat is momentarily also unconvincing." The fear of a leftist victory made the kaiser "very angry at me," as the chancellor confided to Kiderlen-Waechter. "He expects a chauvinist campaign for the [projected] arms increase and is more than displeased since I am not about to do that." Since waving the bloody shirt would further strain the explosive international situation, "I would commit a grave mistake if I were to do so." Unwilling to disavow the negotiated Morocco compromise and to save the Conservatives from the consequences of their own folly, Bethmann argued: "If I shoot now, I have no ammunition left if the Reichstag has to be dissolved. Then patriotic agitation might be necessary." Externally "I cannot do it because army increases only advance peace if they are introduced by a government showing quiet confidence." In order to spare the cabinet "the dangerous charge of passivity," and in order to rob the Left of the explosive issue of the rise in food prices, Bethmann approved an uninspiring electoral article by Delbrück in the *Norddeutsche Allgemeine Zeitung* calling for "the continuation of our present economic policy of trade treaties and of protection of national labor," as well as the "furthering of our social policy, the guarantor of a peaceful domestic development." Seeking a theme which could unite the bourgeois parties but allow for a moderate shift toward liberalism, the chancellor could find nothing better than the Red bogey, ineffective because of runoff election agreements between Socialists and Progressives and the latter and National Liberals. Only in Prussia the ultraconservative Minister of the Interior Dallwitz instructed his officials of the necessity of using their voting rights against "any party undermining the foundations of state and law, i.e. Social Democrats, National-Poles, or Danes." Pessimistically Bethmann wrote to Oettingen: "Like craters on Etna, crises arise in our politics in never-ending succession. One is hardly cold before the next erupts. One has to become a Rosario in order to survive between them." [24]

Since in the Hottentot campaign of 1907 the pendulum had swung far to the Right, Bethmann's refusal to whip up chauvinist emotions resulted in a landslide toward the Left in 1912. In the first round Conservative losses destroyed the blue-black bloc, but since moderate liberalism might still be victorious, Undersecretary Wahnschaffe frantically attempted to persuade the middle parties to cooperate in the runoff, and Bethmann ordered a telegram which he sent to Conservative magnate Friedrich von Schwerin-Löwitz to be published in the *NAZ:* "I view your reelection as a good omen for the future. May the bourgeois parties regain their consciousness during the final round." But these halfhearted efforts were in vain. "The outcome of the main voting was no surprise for the chancellor, as he told me," Ambassador Szögyény reported, although the Socialist rise to 110 mandates exceeded his expectations. The chief victims were the parties of the Right, who paid for their resistance to juster taxation, but National Liberals and Progressives failed to profit much in the Conservative debacle. Theoretically a Bassermann-Bebel front possessed a slim majority of three votes, but the right wing of the Liberals was unreliable. On the other hand, the Bülow bloc also lacked enough seats to be reconstituted: "Under these circumstances it will be the task of the government to create majorities from issue to issue." If the lack of any distinct majority in the Reichstag made a working relationship impossible, the disappointed chancellor assured Szögyény that "he intended to dissolve the House and to announce new elections with the agreement of the kaiser, of which he was quite certain." Blaming the degree of the Socialist increase on the doctrinairism of the Liberals, Bethmann refused to follow the trend, stressing that "the government must stand on its own two feet," and rejecting all demands of parliamentarization. "The Empire cannot be governed radically or reactionarily; otherwise we have to exclude one half of our nation from politics." Emphasizing "how confidently H.M. in agreement with his allies, looks into the future despite the recent setback," Bethmann informed the Prussian ambassadors: "The speech from the throne . . . rejects any theory of catastrophe and professes a joyful dedication to the continued support of Germany's world-political interests." [25]

Although the 1912 elections produced a progressive Reichstag, the spiraling arms race on land and sea dominated Bethmann's domestic politics during the Indian summer of peace. Bent on achieving parity with the British navy in order to be free to pursue a militant Weltpolitik, Admiral Tirpitz seized upon "growing popular disgust with Morocco, loss of prestige abroad, and an insufficient fleet" to motivate a new naval law with William II. Concealing the collapse of his risk theory, torpedoed by the British switch to the dreadnought, Tirpitz pleaded that the gap in the annual building rate (to be reduced from four to two) be filled by returning to the hallowed *Dreiertempo*. "If chancellor, Kiderlen, and Wermuth do not want to cooperate, they'll be sacked," the mercurial emperor threatened, calling Bethmann a "hopeless weakling," and urging *"handeln* rather than *verhandeln"* because the proud battleships were his favorite toy and the backbone of his imperialism. Lerchenfeld perceptively deplored the public pressures for armament: "Unfortunately, not only the naval league, but also a considerable number of parliamentarians toot this horn." Bethmann was caught between the millstones of "the demands of the kaiser, the secretary of the navy and a great part of the people dreaming of world domination and naval enthusiasm, and the knowledge that irresponsible acquiescence would lead to political catastrophe." [26]

Although he himself was pessimistically aware "that one cannot eliminate the ultima ratio [of war] from the life of nations," the chancellor nevertheless strove "to postpone it as long as possible." Admiral Müller reported his views to William II: "The chancellor understands that we must upgrade the navy, but he also has to consider finances and the political impression on England. Moreover, he cannot embark upon naval expansion over the heads of the federal states." In his battle against the chauvinist exhortations of naval attaché Widenmann, Bethmann was supported by the colorful Swabian foreign secretary, Kiderlen-Waechter, who loathed Tirpitz "because I fear that his policy will lead to war with England," and by Secretary of the Treasury Wermuth, who enjoyed slashing military expenditures with grim determination. In long and passionate reports, Germany's British ambassador Metternich warned against navalist illusions that "England will retain its proportional advantage," but William II scribbled in the margins: "I do not agree with the judgment of the ambassador! The naval attaché is right!" Indirectly, the threat that "any government commitment to the inheritance tax will make it impossible for the Conservative Party to continue supporting the cabinet," helped the chancellor to drag his feet, since he was supported by the Bundesrat in his resolve to cut naval requests and impose new taxes on property rather than consumption. Because Bethmann succeeded in postponing any decision until after the resolution of the Morocco crisis and the conclusion of the elections, William II grew more and more impatient. "If the chancellor is not willing he must go," he blustered. "I must be my own Bismarck." [27]

The chancellor attempted to drive out the devil with Beelzebub and curb the unavoidable naval increase by the desperate stratagem of making a large addition to the army. Arguing that "the decision will clearly lie with [land war]," Heeringen demanded full training of available manpower while Wermuth tore his hair over Tirpitz's fiscal estimate: "One can only negotiate on this basis if one intends to provoke a deep foreign and domestic crisis." Claiming that he could "not procure Bundesrat approval until the military and financial preparations have been completed," Bethmann won a respite by agreeing to introduce both bills in a special budget at a later time. He urged both departments "to cut down their additional demands to our ability to pay for them," and, in a brilliant move, outflanked Tirpitz by announcing the army increase in the *NAZ*. When William II ranted "The chancellor has betrayed me!" he countered that he was doing his best to speed preparations as long as the bills remained within the framework of those taxes which could be raised. Unwilling to risk war over the means that should prevent it, Bethmann pondered, "We shall do for our arms on water and land whatever our finances possibly permit, not with threatening noises, but as far as we can in industrious silence." [28]

Relieved by his partial success, Bethmann reported to Kiderlen: "Tirpitz and Heeringen have now been ordered to share the 105 million in new taxes that Wermuth has promised to create, of which the army is to receive the lion's share." Since news of both bills had leaked out and Wermuth had hidden 80–100 million Marks of reserves in the budget, he believed that "a naval increase, now limited to 50 million, can be borne, if need be, as long as it is accompanied by a larger army increase!" Nevertheless he sighed: "Actually this entire policy is such that I cannot go along with it. That you know. But I always ask myself whether the situation would not be more dangerous if I were to resign, probably not alone." Adroitly martialing all moderate forces and aided by Wermuth's letter of resignation, Bethmann finally succeeded in whittling down Tirpitz's demand from six to three ships for the next six years thus breaking the primacy of the Dreiertempo. Nevertheless, "the coverage of the arms bills still causes me grave concern. Center Party and Conservatives do not want to learn anything. Despite insistent advice to the contrary, they have again committed themselves against the inheritance tax." Bethmann knew that he had to force the most vocal advocates of naval imperialism to pay part of its cost. Unless some alternative were found, he wrote, "we will drift into a new domestic crisis which will be all the more serious because one cannot rely upon the Liberals. As long as Bassermann and Heydebrand remain leaders, I foresee a bleak future." [29]

The primary stake in the armament struggle was Bethmann's bid for British neutrality. The dramatic Haldane mission held out a brief hope for breaking the vicious circle of imperialist crises; the chancellor remained "full of reservations and maintained the naval bill could not be introduced since the army proposal was still unfinished." But the fact that he had to wait for news from Metternich regarding the outcome of the talks so enraged William II that he fired off a telegram full of "incredible crudities" to the German ambassador demanding immediate publication of the armament plans: "My and the German people's patience has run out." This imperial thunderbolt struck home. In angry despair Bethmann protested against the accusation of "abusing Y.M.'s and the people's trust by protracting the announcement of the arms bills." Since William had interpreted "the withdrawal of British ships from the Mediterranean to the North Sea as a threat of war which [would] be answered by a sharper naval law—three-speed tempo—and eventually mobilization," Bethmann felt he could no longer bear the responsibility for such a policy and offered to resign. "You will not blame the commander-in-chief and the officer, the first role for us Hohenzollerns . . . for his insistence on quickly implementing the arms increases." But the kaiser angrily recoiled and appealed to him as his "highest official, personal friend and nobleman of the Mark Brandenburg to continue to pledge [his] loyalty to Emperor, King, and Margrave." [30]

Although Bethmann declared himself "ready to continue in office in exchange for guarantees" that would strengthen his hand against the chauvinists, "the policy of working for English friendship while demanding new ships from the Reichstag is a fiasco." When it became clear that the price of British friendship was "the reduction of the bill so that it fits into the existing naval law, i.e. practically its abandonment," Bethmann could no longer hold out against full publication of the bills. "The effect of this political clarification was strange. The kaiser was actually glad." Only after the intervention of the empress did the chancellor relent and announce the increases before completing the financial preparations. The crisis had ended in a stalemate between Bethmann's policy of reconciliation, based on fiscal responsibility, and Tirpitz's attempt to obtain parity with the leading naval power at the expense of militarizing domestic politics. The result was neither offensive preparedness nor financial stability, while the kaiser continually complained about "the trying struggles between himself and the chancellor during the winter." [31]

While the Reichstag found no fault with the army and navy increases, the question of taxation proved as troublesome as Bethmann had expected. "In the present constellation everything depends upon finding a form of the *Erbschaftssteuer* acceptable to parliament together with the arms bills." When the Conservatives and the Center Party showed no greater insight than they had three years earlier by continuing to oppose an inheritance tax, and the Prussian cabinet was deadlocked between Wermuth and the conservative wing, Bethmann compromised by suggesting the elimination of the infamous *Liebesgabe,* or tax exemption on schnapps, a perpetual irritant to the Left. The kaiser aptly commented, "The Conservative agrarians will foam at the mouth," but Bundesrat rejection of a subsidiary inheritance tax, to be paid through the contributions of the states, left the chancellor no other choice. Since Wermuth's reserves would cover the balance, Bethmann accepted his resignation and appointed the less forceful and more pliable undersecretary, Kühn, as his successor. In April 1912 he finally proclaimed in the Reichstag, "For Germany, in the heart of Europe, with open boundaries on all sides, a strong army is the most secure *guarantee of peace.*" Although he did not insist on the inheritance tax in order to "find a version to which all bourgeois parties can agree," Erzberger and Bassermann attached a rider to the brandy tax bill demanding a "general taxation on property" within the year. But since the Reichstag also voted the increase of twenty-five thousand men, Bethmann accepted this compromise. The unity of the bourgeois parties revealed, as he reported to William II, "that the nation is resolved to sacrifice everything for its strength and future." But the tax question had not been solved, only postponed.[32]

The outbreak of the first Balkan war and the fear that England might join Germany's enemies threw William II into a nervous frenzy and opened another round in the arms race. "The kaiser has held a war council with his paladins from the army and navy, of course behind Kiderlen's back and mine, and has ordered the preparation of a new army *and navy* increase." Bethmann was aghast. Although he agreed with the need for another army expansion to counteract the French shift to three-year service and the enormous Russian plans, he knew "if H.M. together with Tirpitz wants to make the bond [between London and Paris] unbreakable, he will succeed without difficulty through a new naval law." This genuine war scare, which even led to some premobilization measures rescinded at the demand of the political leadership, hastened preparations for the army increase and provoked a spate of writings on economic and psychological preparedness. But without great difficulty Bethmann succeeded in vetoing Tirpitz's suggestion to resume building three battle cruisers a year. "Aside from the demands of the air force, which are almost imposed upon us bcause of French superiority, the idea of replenishing older cadres in the army through an increased call-up of young, now undrafted men of recruiting age has become so popular that it must be done sooner or later because of the new French army law and the momentous Russian build-up," Bethmann informed Hertling in late December 1912. "I do not yet have definite plans and even if they existed, *I cannot reveal them as long as the tension provoked by the Balkan conflict has not subsided completely.*" Disturbed by this threat to peace, the chancellor was "gravely distressed by our military's assessment of our relative strength in case of war. One must have a good deal of trust in God and count on the Russian revolution as ally in order to be able to sleep at all." In a telling indictment of Wilhelmian hubris, he continued: "Because of the navy we have neglected the army and our 'naval policy' has created enemies around us. We did not need that and could have built ships anyway." Because the Balkan crisis cut psychologically deeper than the Morocco confrontation, Bethmann considered "the army increase indispensable. We cannot afford to leave out any recruit who can wear a helmet. I shall pass the bill as the military demands it, without reductions. Otherwise they will come back next year and General Keim and company will continue to agitate." Subscribing to the traditional maxim, *si vis pacem para bellum,* the chancellor nevertheless opposed irresponsible provocation of war.[33]

In the ensuing struggle between the general staff, spearheaded by the flamboyant Erich Ludendorff, and the Prussian minister of war Heeringen, who was fearful that too rapid an expansion would dilute the class character and spirit of the officer corps, Bethmann played only a mediating role. Since the compromise proposal eliminating three additional army corps would already cost approximately 1000 million Marks for the first year, the chancellor warned "that he could not provide any money beyond it." The funding possibilities once again hinged on the inheritance tax. Since it would only "affront the Conservatives and Center Party," the chancellor on the advice of his collaborators leaned toward taxation of the increase in property value rather than a straight levy on inheritance which could be included in the wider, less provocative formula. But despite his entreaties to Hertling and Vitzthum ("I consider it all the more pressing that we propose a property tax which has a chance of passing the Reichstag") the state governments refused to sanction a *Vermögenszuwachs* (increased property) tax, since it infringed upon their fiscal authority over direct taxation. Seizing upon Kühn's suggestion of a "special property levy, not really a tax but a one-time assessment," the chancellor sought to persuade the states' ministers that the need for "collecting the bourgeois parties in a common front" overrode considerations of federalism. "In the Bundesrat the question of taxation has created considerable difficulties which are basically the fault of the Conservatives and the Center's hatred for the inheritance tax. Especially the Conservatives are incredible people," Bethmann complained, although he still clung to the idea of passing the taxes with the same majority as the military bills. "I cannot conduct a policy based on the grand [Bassermann to Bebel] bloc in tax questions." Hence, after much difficulty, a tentative compromise was reached between the demands of the states and those of the parties, including an "extraordinary" assessment of one billion and a subsidiary property-value-increase tax, levied by the state governments. "I think the Reichstag will accept the military bill and the countrywide levy, but I am still doubtful whether we can get approval this spring regarding the running costs," Bethmann pondered. The government proposal seemed to him the sole path for an agreement between the bourgeois parties which would "put the costs on capable shoulders and not deprive the states of light and air . . . for a healthy future." [34]

Since the increase of 125,000 men was the largest peacetime addition to the German army, Bethmann sounded serious but not threatening notes in his introductory speech to the Reichstag. Referring maladroitly, but with conviction, to a possible conflagration *"which will pit Germans against Slavs,"* the chancellor claimed to present the bill "not because we are at war but because we are at peace and because we intend to be victorious should war come." As the psychosis of encirclement obsessed all bourgeois parties, the military demands met with only minor objections (such as the question of the number of princely adjutants to be granted to the states), and the increase was passed by a majority of the Right. But despite Bethmann's plea for sacrificing party interest "to a strong and peaceful fatherland," the Left strengthened the antiproperty provisions of the Vermögenszuwachs tax and returned it directly to the empire. "The next weeks will be exciting, and although I hope for a good outcome, the army and financial bills contain as many possible crises as the Balkan question," Bethmann predicted. "I shall still hear much criticism, but I think they will pass anyway. We only have to be patient. Unless forced, I would rather steer them through without dissolving parliament." The Reichstag's temporary cut of three of six cavalry regiments "provoked the kaiser to the utmost, and he would like to chase parliament away—or at least threaten to do so. But I consider this wrong."

When a Socialist proposal to tax the princes of the empire in the one-time levy seemed to endanger the entire revenue bill, the chancellor countered by prompting a voluntary sacrifice from them and by obtaining a dissolution order which, partially misunderstood, brought the National Liberals to heel. Similarly, in the Bundesrat only stern warnings against provoking "a severe domestic crisis" and against undermining national defense convinced the states to accept the parliamentary compromise of an imperial property-value-increase tax. "In the Reichstag things are finally coming to a conclusion. I have been working on this matter for many months and in the end one loses one's energy and accepts stupidities just in order to finish things off," he confessed in late June 1913. "Our Imperial deputies have voted disgusting taxes. . . . Nevertheless stubbornness on my part would have been wrong. It is still a positive fact that this democratic Reichstag accepted such a gigantic military bill." Bethmann felt unjustified in provoking a dissolution because the property tax, which he considered inevitable, would have been a poor election slogan for the government. Hoping finally to have satisfied the Liberals' hunger for taxation of landed wealth, he justified accepting soldiers from the Right and taxes from the Left by the stubborn self-isolation of the Conservatives: "They demand that the government march through thick and thin for them but do not want to support it in return." Still pursuing a basically conservative policy, Bethmann was forced to ally himself with the more progressive forces because the narrow class-interest politics of the Conservative Party jeopardized Germany's imperial position. As a result the new tax "reached the upper limit of what property and the states can bear" and "increased the power of parliament . . . immeasurably." [35]

Although he reported optimistically that "the tax compromise reached by the majority of the bourgeois parties may portend a gradual leveling of our political antagonisms," Bethmann soon realized that his concessions to the Left had strained his relations with William II. While the last years had "taken more of a toll than I thought and wanted to admit in the bustle of Berlin life," he could "not deny that the kaiser found my manner of conducting policy more and more irritating everyday, and in the last week it has contributed much to his nervous anxiety. He is much too hasty in his thinking to understand that one can succeed with quiet firmness and deliberation." The chancellor further explained his vexation to Eisendecher: "In the excitement of the moment he does not understand that the practice of banging one's fist on the table presupposes power which does not disappear afterwards." In terms of policy, Bethmann did not consider these outbursts too tragic, although they made cooperation trying and often nearly impossible. But personally, the continual frictions that stemmed from the negative aspects of William's unbalanced personality made him tired and dejected. "Whoever [was] forced to look behind the scenes [was] grateful" that the kaiser was "popular as never before," because the gap between appearance and reality was staggering. While William reluctantly recognized Bethmann's achievement in financing the bill, the chancellor ominously wrote to Oettingen: "In about one week we will move to Hohenfinow. The more distant future is still quite dark." Indeed, Bethmann was again on the verge of resigning, but this time he intended not to return. His personal pessimism was heightened by the international situation: "I shall breathe easier when all is over. I am sick of war, the clamor for war, and the eternal armaments. It is high time that the great nations quieted down again and pursued peaceful tasks. Otherwise an explosion will occur, which no one desires and which will harm all." [36]

A petty incident which shocked the sleepy Alsatian town of Zabern soon interrupted the chancellor's dark thoughts. Despite constitutional reform in Alsace-Lorraine, Imperial Stadtholder Count Wedel predicted, "Only time can dull anti-German sentiment; quiet patience and firm benevolence are the only means to hasten this process of recuperation." However, the trigger-happy military, which viewed the Reichsland merely as glacis for a future war and resented the Francophile leanings of the bourgeoisie, found a kindred spirit in William II: "It has been almost fifty years and things have only gotten worse." A series of military-civilian clashes, typical of the dualistic structure of the Bismarckian Empire, finally culminated in the "military provocation" of a Lieutenant Forstner, who insulted Alsatian recruits by referring to them as *Wackes*. "Military circles do not possess the right sense of responsibility," Count Wedel reported; "the German cause has suffered a severe setback." Word of the incident soon leaked to the press, and the officer's tactlessness came to symbolize the repressive militarism of Prussia. "According to my opinion, the prestige of the army will not suffer, but rather increase, if whatever happened is not covered up but punished," the Stadtholder implored the emperor.

These well-meant warnings came too late. The Zabern garrison had so antagonized the population that local youths jeered Lieutenant Forstner, and Commanding Officer Colonel Reuter ordered indiscriminate arrests of unruly citizens. Bethmann described one incident: "When carpenter Levy, who was eating dinner with his family, heard the roll of drums, he ran downstairs since he believed it was a fire. In front of the house one man was just being arrested. Hence the concierge called Levy to come inside quickly. When Commanding Lieutenant Schadt heard this, he ordered the arrest of Levy. He was seized in his apartment by four men with fixed bayonets." Since "a state of siege had not been declared," it was clear to the chancellor "that without being forced by circumstances, the military [had] transgressed its legal authority." To cool William's militaristic ardor, Bethmann argued, "According to my humble opinion, the principal task of protecting the authority of the army from charges of having violated the law can only be accomplished if the existing violations are corrected immediately." Otherwise "the army and thereby the whole country will suffer severe harm from these events." Thus the chancellor called for a thorough investigation. The army countered "that military action had only become necessary because of the failure of civil authorities." Hence William II, naively unaware of the political repercussions, rejected civilian interference "since it was purely a matter of his Kommandogewalt." By calling for "immediate redress," Bethmann had dared to question the whole military tradition of Prussia.[37]

When the chancellor entered the Reichstag on December 3 to answer Progressive, Socialist, and Alsatian interpellations about the incidents, he walked into a seething volcano. Although he was personally convinced of the "illegality of the military action" and had pleaded with the emperor to "order the army to respect legal boundaries" as the only way to assuage the storm, publicly Bethmann thought it his duty to assert that "the royal uniform must be respected under any circumstances." It was "the conflict of local authorities" which caused the transgressions, although "it is impossible to decide who is in the right." Though hinting at the military investigation, Bethmann's dispassionate speech, which groped for a middle ground between a defense of royal prerogative and civil law, fundamentally misjudged the severity of the outrage. "The impossible is happening. The incomprehensible is being done." Center Party deputy Fehrenbach called the day a disaster for the empire and demanded guarantees. Not the threatened censure but "the danger of creating a cleavage between army and people" made Bethmann plead with William II, "I shall be defenseless if further incidents occur." Only "the cooperation of military and civilian authorities with full respect for their mutual spheres and for law and justice" could prevent future clashes. Replying to Conservative praise of the glories of the Prussian arms, Alsatian deputy Ricklin summed up the mood of the House: "Today it is the German military which has morally lost Alsace-Lorraine for the German Empire." The surprisingly large vote of no-confidence emphasized, as Bethmann admitted, "that the military in fact arrogated to itself power which belongs to the civil authority alone, and thereby acted illegally." Although "on the entire Left nobody expect[ed] or desire[d] a chancellor crisis," something had to be done, since according to Theodor Wolff "things would only get worse." Wahnschaffe persuaded Bethmann to make William II, who had refused to leave his military entourage in Donaueschingen, return to the capital and to launch an explanatory article in the *NAZ* "which will soon restore calm." Unless the military was publicly reprimanded, "the chancellor's position would become untenable and all resentment . . . focus on the bearer of the Kommandogewalt." [38]

Because of the *Daily Telegraph* Affair unwilling to place responsibility where it belonged, Bethmann was caught in the cross fire of imperial wrath and public discontent. "It was a madhouse," the chancellor recalled the scene in the Reichstag. "By their temper tantrums these people believe they can hide their political innocence. The vainglorious Bassermann arm-in-arm with Scheidemann and Erzberger lacks any dignity. Bülow would have set off brilliant fireworks which would have pleased the crowds and singed the wings of kaiser and army." Revealingly, he continued: "I am glad that I did not even try that. The harm to our future would have been immense. Hence I stood in the fiery rain. That is not even so bad. The inner revulsion was much too great for me to feel the cinders." The parliamentary defeat made him confess: "Therefore I am probably not meant to be a politician. But—I am right anyway. And that feeling will stay with me in the future." Unable and unwilling to satisfy the public outcry by open censure of the military, hamstrung as he was by the emperor's sensitivity toward criticism of the army, Bethmann's cautious reassertion of the rule of law and civilian primacy failed to placate the aroused public, who saw Zabern not as a tactical error but as a symptom of the larger political malaise of Wilhelmian Germany. Because of William's opinion that "the journalist pigs are mostly at fault," the chancellor had to use all his powers of persuasion "to paper over the rupture with half-measures" by removing the guilty regiment to a training area outside of Zabern, transferring Forstner, and court-martialing Reuter. Because of this compromise, published in the *NAZ* on December 7, the Reichstag vote of censure remained without practical consequences. "A political judgment" rather than a parliamentary bid for power, the Socialist resolution in favor of the chancellor's responsibility to the Reichstag was no serious threat. As long as William II was unwilling to sacrifice the halfhearted defender of Prussian militarism to parliament, the chancellor had little to fear. Privately "the kaiser does not at all approve of Bethmann's handling of the Zabern affair, since he accuses him of too much partiality for the civilians against the military," Ambassador Szögyény reported. Unintelligible to the public, the chancellor's sinuous middle policy provoked the open hostility of the Conservatives without regaining the lost sympathies of the liberal bourgeoisie. Saxon Ambassador Salza pessimistically predicted, "Considering everything, I believe that we are heading toward another domestic crisis and I fear that Bethmann will no longer be able to master it." [39]

"Politically Alsace-Loraine is a shambles," perceptive observers agreed on the disastrous consequences of the court-martial's dismissal of charges in January 1914. This apparent military triumph over civil law led to bitter attacks on Bethmann's "passivity" on the questions of the inheritance tax, the Braunschweig succession quarrel, Prussian electoral reform, and the protection of strikebreakers.[40] Undaunted, Bethmann urged the minister of war: "In principle, the maintenance of law and order is the responsibility of the civil authorities, and there is no question that according to the rules the army can only intervene, when previously requested by the civil authorities." Hoping "that there will be no further difficulties in the use of weapons," Bethmann attempted to justify the Prussian practice: "According to common law the military in every state must be able to intervene in case of imminent danger when the civil authorities are unable to ask for assistance due to external circumstances. If the state abandons this right, it abandons itself." Nevertheless, he was deeply disturbed by the "arrogance of North German officers. . . . It will not improve here for many years. On the contrary," he insisted, "in military circles there reigns a boundless hubris, deprecating the masses, which is fueled by the irresponsible policy of the Conservatives." Because of his inability to curb the Right, Bethmann had to admit the failure of his liberal assimilation policy in Alsace-Lorraine. To be sure, the cabinet order of 1820 that justified the military transgressions was dissolved and new instructions for the use of weapons ratified. But the appointment of "the strongly conservative and energetic" Dallwitz as Wedel's successor heralded the return to a patriarchical bureaucratic administration. "I do not consider Zabern as tragic as you do," Bethmann belittled the negative consequences of the affair: "Certainly it complicates things in the Reichsländer. But in North Germany it drastically discredits radicalism and the Reichstag." The chancellor's penchant for compromise was no match for "overdeveloped military absolutism and Prussian conservatism." [41]

Fearful that Bethmann's halting gradualism might gamble away their privileges, Conservatives and Pan-Germans spun "secret intrigues [against the chancellor] as assiduously as they [could], supported by Tirpitz who [was] moving in for the kill." The resentment of Old Prussia crystallized in late 1913 in General Gebsattel's long memorandum to the crown prince, a known Bethmann enemy and, as such, receptive to suggestions of a coup d'état. To "reform" the Reichstag suffrage in "Christian, monarchical, and constitutional, nonparliamentary" directions, the Pan-German general suggested provoking a constitutional conflict and reintroducing plural voting in the empire. The racial mixing of Jews and Germans should be prohibited and the Jewish press destroyed in order to prepare the German people for war. With Wahnschaffe's help, Bethmann immediately drafted a coherent and convincing rebuttal stating his political philosophy. Though he admitted the existence of a political malaise, the chancellor affirmed that a coup d'état "is imperative only when the state perishes without it." Condemning a counter-revolution from above as "either a stupidity or a crime," Bethmann continued, "As great as the disgust of earnest people concerned about the welfare of the fatherland is with the *Vermassung,* it does not suffice as basis of a coup d'état." Unequivocally he reiterated, "There is no possibility of changing the electoral law in the near future by a putsch or by some other radical method." Not yet convinced of the need for Reichstag suffrage in Prussia and sympathizing with some of Gebsattel's complaints, he insisted, "Plural suffrage is as theoretically attractive as it is impractical." Workable in small, unified states like Belgium and Saxony, it was illusory in the large, heterogeneous empire. "The memorandum is also too superficial concerning the Jews. It simply declares them aliens and chases them out of the country, after having confiscated their property. It is not really possible to discuss such an idea seriously." Because he was unwilling to overstep the bounds of common law, Bethmann rejected the abolition of the freedom of the press as "fantastic." "Despite some useful suggestions in detail, on the whole the memorandum is quite incredible. It is removed from all reality, misunderstands the force of historical unity, in short: it treats the coup d'état as a trifle and promises castles in Spain for the future." A clear refutation of the domestic program of the far Right, the chancellor's scathing critique of Pan-German dreams as well as Socialist utopias testified to his hope that cautious reform conservatism would eventually prevail.[42]

Although foreign diplomats considered his position firm in the spring of 1914 despite "all dissatisfaction with his domestic policy,"

Bethmann himself was beginning to have second thoughts. "These four years have dealt harshly with me and the last winter and spring with their great tasks have made me weary," he reflected. "Especially the men who should lighten my burden professionally, H.M. and the Conservatives, make things as difficult as they can. I should have resigned in the beginning of July [1913], since it is inevitable sooner or later." Moreover, the style of Wilhelmian politics, the "extensive official and semiofficial business in Berlin, Swinemünde, Hamburg, Kehlheim, Posen, and Breslau make it impossible to find peace and meditation." His daily pace was forbidding: "At seven in the morning he mounts his horse and after a brisk hour-long ride through the Tiergarten, work begins. From nine o'clock on, the chancellor listens to reports, receives ministers, diplomats, parliamentarians, journalists, and works, usually with a short rest at noon until eight o'clock at night," Wahnschaffe recorded. "Then he is not even tired, but sits down to dinner with a few trusted friends or a great number of invited guests, and after several hours of spirited conversation, works deep into the night." Moreover, in the spring of 1914 he was deeply shaken by the failing health of his dear Martha and confessed, "My soul is often not strong enough to be courageous in spite of all this." The doctors could not stop her internal hemorrhage, and on May 11 her suffering ceased. "Certainly work always remains the first duty for a man," the grief-stricken chancellor confided to Bülow, but the loss left a void which could not be filled: "What was past and should have been future, all that was tied to our common life is now destroyed by death. Only the certainty that the good accomplished by her here on earth is eternal sustains me." [43]

Looking back on the first half-decade of Bethmann's chancellorship, his close collaborator Wahnschaffe nevertheless concluded: "The German people, who did not bestow their trust upon Bethmann very quickly, have finally recognized his high gifts and know that in all decisions the emperor could not have a more loyal and reliable counselor than this firm, wise, and tested man." Though a stern taskmaster rather than a dazzling demagogue, the fifth chancellor surpassed all of Bismarck's epigones. Appointed during a severe domestic crisis, his calming influence had succeeded in "bringing about the greatest financial reform and increase in military preparedness [since 1870], despite such bitterly opposed parties." Undoubtedly the failure of Prussian electoral reform was a signal defeat for his policy of gradual liberalization, but the constitution of Alsace-Lorraine, though not as progressive as desired by the Left, included universal suffrage. "The imperative of positive action about which the chancellor spoke has become effective and has firmly unified the parties from Right to Left." Because the very structure, constitution, and spirit of the Bismarckian Reich precluded a policy based upon the Bassermann-Bebel bloc, and reliance on the blue-black Clerical-Conservative coalition would have pent up pressures for change to the point of explosion, Bethmann chose a diagonal policy between the extremes of reaction and revolution. In the tradition of reform conservatism he sought to preserve the monarchy and the Prussian heritage by haltingly adapting it to the demands for increased participation and social justice. It was this fundamental insight which set him apart from the Heydebrands and Westarps and from his ministerial colleagues Dallwitz and Loebell, who adamantly resisted the liberalization of Prussian suffrage. The immense hatred with which the Right pursued Bethmann testifies that something more than a mere tactical difference was at stake. Beyond the social basis and structure of the Prussian state, the monarch himself capriciously limited the chancellor's freedom to move forward, by his impulsive interventions in favor of autocratic and socially conservative measures. Nevertheless, one could claim without too much exaggeration, "In matters of domestic politics, Bethmann's authority has never been questioned." [44]

The limited successes of progressive legislation were vitiated by eruptions such as the *Daily Telegraph* and Zabern Affairs, when the organized chaos of Wilhelmian government was exposed in its full irrationality. Although rare enough to be written off by most contemporaries as accidents, such breakdowns revealed the social, economic, cultural, and political contradictions upon which the imposing edifice of the Wilhelmian state rested. Gerhard Hauptmann's unduly revolutionary commemoration of 1813 affronted the chancellor, who thanked Oettingen for his rebuttal, "written as if from my soul and hopefully bringing many people to their senses." But Bethmann was troubled by the creeping malaise hidden beneath the pomp and festivity of the centennial celebration of the Wars of Liberation. "I breathe easier now that the ceremonies are over. The kaiser can be content with them. He was never so popular as now." But forced as he was to look behind the imposing façade into the inner workings of government, business, and the intelligentsia, the chancellor recoiled in horror: "Why is it so hard for us poor Germans to develop a somewhat satsifying cultural and political life?" This paradoxical premonition of decay and doom during a period of triumphal economic expansion called for sterner medicine than the fifth chancellor could or would administer. In those halcyon years of peace Wilhelmian Germany was reaching not a turning point but a deadlock. While the forces of change were increasing and optimistically clamoring for democratization and greater social justice, the legions of conservatism and reaction, unwilling to yield their political and social privileges without a battle, rallied to counterattack.

This perplexing swelling of the social democratic stream and the conservative countercurrent rendered a middle course more and more hazardous. While progress in specific areas was still possible, the fundamental obstacle to the gradual evolution of the Wilhelmian Empire, the odious class suffrage in Prussia coupled with the economic compromise between Junkers and robber barons, could not be overcome. Although there were no domestic storm clouds threatening in the placid summer sky of 1914, the empire's underlying contradictions had not been resolved and Bethmann could well ask himself if he had succeeded in moving the state forward far enough to forestall an eventual violent outburst. Nevertheless he was determined to continue the struggle: "Now I must see if and how I can go on." [45]

CHAPTER 5

The Mirage of Weltpolitik

"Germany must conduct a Weltpolitik, because its entire national economy depends upon world trade and more than fifteen million Germans earn their livelihood from exchange with overseas countries." Accepted by the vast majority of Wilhelmian elites, this economic rationale inspired a belated imperialism marred by political immaturity and an aggressiveness that stemmed from a sense of inferiority. "We must buy colonial wares, [compensate for] the deficit in our agricultural production, and barter with goods produced by ourselves, namely industrial products," Karl Peters, the controversial colonial pioneer, preached to his landlocked countrymen. Compelling the reluctant Bismarck to carry the imperial black, white, and red to Africa and Asia, the double imperative of raw materials and markets logically required "a strong navy to prevent the more powerful states from forcefully excluding [Germany] from the great markets." Often saturated with Pan-German ideology and popularized by naval, colonial, army, and *Ostmarcken* leagues, this blustering imperialism reached its culmination in Admiral Tirpitz's risk theory. Since any setback in economic imperialism might unleash "internal upheavals, suffering, and social cataclysms," the domestic counterpart of rampant navalism was an uncompromising bourgeois *Sammlungspolitik* against Socialist and Catholic subversion. But increasing obstacles to territorial expansion and rising pressures for constitutional reform led a younger generation of Liberal Imperialists to advocate a "world policy without war," based on economic penetration and redistribution of colonial spoils with England. Because of growing domestic polarization, German foreign policy in the last years of peace witnessed a struggle between the reactionary navalist and moderate imperialist quest for the fata morgana of world power.[1]

Predicated upon the twin illusions of Holstein's "free hand" and of Tirpitz's battle fleet, Prince Bülow's diplomacy, the climax of rampant imperialism, led to the destruction of Germany's international position erected by Bismarck. If the Wilhelmian Empire loomed more massive, prosperous, and imposing than ever, the formation of the Anglo-French and Anglo-Russian ententes had fundamentally altered the European balance of power and had critically narrowed the continental base for German world policy. Despite widespread praise for the departing master diplomat, the permanent officials of the Wilhelmstrasse were pessimistic in their first briefings of the new chancellor. As "the darkest cloud on our political horizon," Anglo-German tension raised the dangerous possibility "that with the help of Russia and France, England might use a minor pretext to maneuver Germany into a position where it would either have to suffer a diplomatic defeat or fight against a coalition of powers, perhaps even including Italy." Not trade rivalry but "the steady and rapid growth of our navy" prompted London's consistent opposition to German colonial designs.[2]

The diplomatic cornerstone of Berlin's system, the Triple Alliance, which "had splendidly survived the test of Algeciras and the last Balkan crisis" was now being eroded by the "shiftiness and unreliability" of the Italian partner. Competing German and Austrian economic interests in the Balkans caused considerable friction, and the slow internal paralysis of the Danubian monarchy rendered the *Dreibund* more and more ineffective. Since the "whole odium of Russia's diplomatic defeat" in the Bosnian annexation crisis fell upon Berlin, the "traditionally cordial relations" between the two Northern Courts had deteriorated to merely "normal, i.e. outwardly correct." Only in Constantinople had Bülow's policy been successful in "gradually regaining our former position" through the military mission of General von der Goltz; and the opening of the first section of the Bagdad railroad raised bright prospects for a new market. Because of the hereditary enmity of France, Russian resentment over the "Nibelungen loyalty" to Austria, and British hostility due to the naval race, the freedom of action for Weltpolitik had shrunk rapidly. Germany had arrived at a diplomatic juncture. A growing segment of public opinion concluded that "the course of English and Prussian history indicates that arms will ultimately have to decide who will rule this planet." But the Foreign Office advised the new chancellor, "For political reasons it is highly desirable to work hand in hand [with the British] in economic enterprises" in Turkey and in Africa in order to break the iron ring of encirclement.[3]

Though "only little acquainted with the complicated machinery of foreign policy," Bethmann set out with much enthusiasm to master the intricacies of *die Grosse Politik*. Despite his training in domestic administration, the chancellor looked beyond the narrow confines of the Mark Brandenburg, since he was fluent in French and English, had traveled widely, and had confronted internal issues spilling over into international problems. To erase the image of Teutonic duplicity created by Bülow, he assured British ambassador Sir Edward Goschen, "On one thing you can thoroughly depend, namely that my policy in foreign affairs will be entirely frank and open." And although his diplomatic procedure was sometimes clumsy, the chancellor did gain a capital of trust for German policy through his honesty. "As long as Bethmann Hollweg is chancellor we will cooperate with Germany for the peace of Europe," Sir Edward Grey assured the British cabinet. Hence the diplomatic response to Bethmann's appointment was generally reserved but benevolent.[4]

This change of style in the Wilhelmstrasse signified a departure in substance as well. "His main effort will be directed toward earning the sympathies of foreign countries and toward reducing the numerous areas of friction in the international arena," Ambassador Szögyény reported. The new chancellor was fundamentally convinced "that in our age policy can only be based upon [rational] interest" rather than upon the vague notions of prestige and power. Austrian Foreign Minister Aerenthal perceptively remarked: "I believe that Bethmann's policy is primarily determined by very sober, purely business considerations. He abhors boundless plans and prefers to concentrate on immediate and practical objects." Since the chancellor's primary concern focused on continental policy, his assurance to Szögyény "that the cultivation of intimate and loyal relations between the allied monarchies was dear to his heart and would always be his lodestar," was more than a polite phrase. Nevertheless, he accepted Bülow's reasoning, that "today Germany needs her place in the sun," and "that the German people must expand" economically and culturally in Asia Minor and Central Africa. Less martial navalism than measured Machtpolitik, his "moderate imperialism" differed fundamentally from the imperial visions of the Right: "On all fronts we must drive forward quietly and patiently in order to regain that trust and confidence without which we cannot consolidate politically or economically. Of course this does not suit our irresponsible politicians," he pondered, "but according to my firm conviction, this is the only possible course for us. Then we shall be able to realize greater aims in colonies and world trade without having to risk our existence." [5]

Because of the fragmentation of power in the Wilhelmian Empire, the execution of Bethmann's clear and independent foreign policy was by no means assured. "The discrepancy between the ideas of the kaiser and the chancellor is blatant," Count Aerenthal predicted. "There will be no lack of friction and the course of German Weltpolitik will fluctuate considerably in the future." By temperament and ideological inclination, William II favored Tirpitz's aggressive naval expansionism, although he possessed a deep-seated respect for peace. Too impulsive to supervise the daily routine of diplomacy, his ill-timed interventions with foreign royalty and statesmen, as well as his public faux pas, created the stereotype of the autocratic kaiser abroad. Lacking the Iron Chancellor's stature, experienced Foreign Secretary Wilhelm von Schoen was weak-willed and compliant; but Alfred von Kiderlen-Waechter, whom Bethmann imposed upon the reluctant emperor, proved just as difficult because of his aspirations of becoming a "Swabian Bismarck." Denouncing the chancellor in private letters to his mistress as a *Regenwurm* and *Buss*-and *Beth*mann, "vacillating between weakness and autocracy," the strong-willed Kiderlen ran the Wilhelmstrasse rather independently, only relying on the chancellor to tame William II and the Reichstag. Although he bore his foreign secretary's insubordination because of his political gifts, Bethmann nevertheless reasserted his authority: "I have always attempted to maintain for you that independence and freedom of action which is indispensable for a leader in diplomatic and military battle. I will neither change this principle for any ministry, nor can I renounce the supreme direction of affairs and the authority to indicate those matters in which I wish to participate personally with the agreement of the chiefs of the ministries." In a more general manner he warned: "I consider the authority of the chancellor as responsible director of the entire policy of the empire highly important. To maintain this power undiminished belongs to the vital duties of my office." Similarly he attempted, albeit with varying success, to keep the other strong personality in the cabinet, Admiral Tirpitz, from interfering: "If you think you cannot avoid conversations with foreign diplomats, I would appreciate your making sure that your statements do not go beyond the outlines of the foreign policy of the empire, directed by me." [6]

Despite his preference for the quiet working of cabinet diplomacy, Chancellor Bethmann Hollweg was increasingly subjected to parliamentary, public, and economic pressures. Although the Reichstag's constitutional role in shaping policy was limited by Bismarckian precedent, the German parliament was demanding a larger voice in foreign affairs and could seriously embarrass the government through budget control and public criticism. But since the rabid imperialist majority created by the Hottentot election of 1907 rejected the chancellor's moderate Weltpolitik, he attempted "to exclude the Reichstag, if at all possible." Lack of actual participation in government often made the parliamentarians' criticism irresponsible and, despite the chancellor's special briefings and his confidential speeches in the Budget Committee, the prestige imperialists in the Reichstag severely limited the government's freedom of action. "You know the excessive susceptibility of German opinion regarding Morocco," Bethmann complained to French ambassador Jules Cambon. "I don't see any reason for it, but I am forced to take it into account." Even if nationalist pressure could be useful as a bargaining device, Socialist and Progressive counterpressures were not strong enough to keep Bethmann's diagonal from often veering to the Right: "We can count on the Pan-Germans, Navy League, etc. to raise a loud hue and cry. That cannot keep us from doing what we consider right, but obviously all our concessions [to England] must be defensible on the basis of our present naval law." [7] In contrast to the Imperial Naval Office, whose press section supplied information for imperialist agitation, the chancellery lacked an effective propaganda arm, because the clash of personalities between Kiderlen-Waechter and Otto Hammann prevented any rational reorganization of the Foreign Office's *Pressereferat*. Since he was often defenseless, the chancellor resented interest group pressures on his policy. In the notorious Mannesmann affair he publicly broke with the Pan-German League: "It is irresponsible that members of an organization such as the Alldeutsche Verband, which claims to be working for the national good, hurl such undignified and unfounded accusations against [the Foreign] Office." Striving for a stance above the parties, the chancellor opposed the use of government power to gain private advantages and only supported economic expansion when he believed it furthered the more general national interest.[8]

The overriding task confronting the new chancellor was to escape the noose of the ententes through an Anglo-German rapprochement. "I completely agree with your judgment regarding [the improvement of] our relations with England," he wrote, thanking Admiral Eisendecher for his concern. "From the first day on, I have been determined to conduct our policy accordingly." Hardly a month after his appointment he sketched the outlines of his foreign political program to the kaiser: "We endanger such vital interests in a war with England that we must attempt to eliminate all causes [of conflict] if possible." Directly attacking the root of the tension, the naval race, Bethmann suggested turning the informal talks between the German shipping magnate Albert Ballin and British banker Sir Ernest Cassel into formal negotiations. By offering the large concession of "legally recognizing British naval supremacy" through limiting the building of dreadnoughts, the chancellor ideally hoped to gain the political compensation of "a treaty of neutrality in which England promises to remain neutral if we are attacked by France and Russia, singly or together, or if we are forced by our alliance to help Austria." Deceiving himself about the magnitude of the reversal of policy demanded from Britain, Foreign Secretary Schoen commented, "By this we are not at all asking England to abandon its friends." In the preparatory discussions Admiral Tirpitz proved surprisingly cooperative, since Bethmann, confessing to a "lack of the necessary naval technical expertise," agreed "that a departure from German naval law as a whole was impossible —because that would run into insurmountable opposition in the Reichstag" and would be vetoed by William II. The wily admiral drew up a formula "for a slowdown in the construction of new ships" to establish a ratio of 1 : 1.45 between German and British dreadnoughts, legally guaranteeing the German fleet a size that it might only reach by straining every available resource in competitive building. From the beginning, naval concessions depended upon a political agreement in Bethmann's mind: "The more we gain in the question [of a peaceful-friendly orientation of British policy], the more easily will we be able to defend a naval agreement against the attacks of our ultras." Dissolving the "Copenhagen Complex," a double agreement "would decisively strengthen our position in the European concert in material and moral terms." Such a "diplomatic revolution" could not but improve the prospects of German Weltpolitik in Africa and Asia.[9]

If the design was grand, the execution fell far short of it. His "honest and straightforward" manner and eagerness for a foreign political success made Bethmann disregard Kiderlen's shrewd warning, "We must not startle the British through too extensive propositions." Already during his first exploratory conversation with Sir Edward Goschen, Bethmann hinted "that the discussion of a naval agreement could lead to no practical result unless it formed part of a scheme for a general understanding and was based upon a conviction on the part, not only of the two governments, but of public opinion in both countries that neither country had any hostile or aggressive designs against the other." Whitehall immediately interpreted the chancellor's "ominous" suggestion as the "desire to limit our right of intervention" and as going "beyond anything we have with France or Russia." The navy scare had planted a strong suspicion against the "Junkers, the militant professors, and the army and navy," in British public and diplomatic minds. When negotiations got down to particulars, the British ambassador could only make the personal suggestion: "H.M.'s Government might state, for instance, that England would not make an unprovoked attack against any Power," a formula clearly disappointing to Bethmann. As price for a British pledge of nonaggression, Goschen demanded a naval agreement which "would not be based on their present naval program." Since Tirpitz was beginning to withdraw his promises, the chancellor was caught in a vicious circle of mutual suspicion which made the navel agreement a precondition for friendship and viceversa. In biting minutes, Whitehall denounced the German initiative as "a paper concession or no concession at all" that implied a "solemn recognition of the territorial status quo," which cost French friendship because of Alsace-Lorraine, and as "a relapse into the bad habits of her former diplomacy" of demanding "fresh concessions in return for being conciliatory." [10]

Bethmann's assurance that he was not "demanding anything from England in contradiction to its ententes" fell upon deaf ears, since the British were more committed to the Franco-Russian alliance than they were willing to admit. The mere slow-down in the building speed seemed "a little one-sided," since an assurance of neutrality would tie "the hands of England . . . so long as the engagement was in force, and Germany, the only aggressive power in Europe, would be free to act when and where and how she pleased, while England remained a discontented and probably angry spectator." Sedan had not been forgotten. English neutrality would guarantee German hegemony on the continent, not only in the chancellor's form of indirect dominance, but also in the Pan-German version of outright rule and annexation. Moreover, when Bethmann broached the delicate matter too rashly, the paranoia of the unbalanced Wilhelm Stumm and the Germanophobia of Sir E. A. Crowe and Sir Arthur Nicolson erected an insurmountable wall of mutual suspicion. Although the trappings were still those of cabinet diplomacy, both governments acted under drastic domestic pressure: "It is most displeasing that England continues to agitate against us officially and unofficially," Bethmann grumbled. While the emperor, the Reichstag majority, and the imperialist public would not allow the chancellor a reduction in the naval program, the crucial concession for England, British public opinion did not allow Whitehall to withdraw into splendid isolation. The only promising alternative, that of colonial arrangements so successful in the ententes, was not attempted until further failures of general agreement had rendered it too late.[11]

The fata morgana of a treaty guaranteeing English neutrality obsessed Bethmann to such an extent that he failed to see the significance of more limited cooperation. Calling the Bagdad Railway "an imperial idea in Germany" and "a great national undertaking," Bethmann replied to Goschen's feeler: "The only way in which an agreement concerning the Bagdad Railway . . . could be made palatable to the German people would be that it should form part of a general political understanding between Great Britain and Germany." Disappointed once again, Bethmann concluded bitterly "that the maintenance of the alleged balance of power policy, which actually results in a limitation of German power, is such a firmly founded principle of British foreign policy that even the most far-reaching concessions regarding our naval armaments are unlikely to be sufficient to make them abandon it." Frustration colored his complaint to the ambassador that, even in cases where both countries' interests were more or less identical, he found London opposed: "I maintain that if the British people had not been *taught* by their government to regard Germany as an enemy, the expansion of the German fleet would have caused them as little anxiety as the expansion of the navy of the United States." Perplexed, Goschen thought it better not to reply in kind: "I could only have told him that if it was irritating to Germans to find Englishmen always in possession, it was equally irritating for Englishmen, wherever they had vested and important interests, to have Germans poking their noses in and demanding shares in concerns and interests which had been built up by years of British hard work and enterprise." Although Bethmann primarily intended to secure the German position on the continent and remove obstacles to peaceful economic expansion overseas, British statesmen viewed his advances in the most sinister light: "They want the hegemony of Europe and to neutralize the only thing which has prevented them for getting it; viz., England's naval strength." Though rejecting the militant imperialism of Tirpitz and the Pan-Germans, the chancellor could not and would not abandon peaceful Weltpolitik. Hence the only fruit of intermittent Anglo-German negotiations was an agreement to exchange naval information, a measure designed to minimize anxities by exploding exaggerated fears. Although the general goal of an Anglo-German rapprochement remained as distant as ever, Bethmann Hollweg tenaciously clung to it as lodestar of his foreign policy: "For one and one-half years I have been working toward this and therefore I believe in it." [12]

Since his initiative toward London had met with only slight success, Bethmann sought to relieve the pressure on Germany by approaching the other members of the entente as well. The removal to Paris of the "more clever than wise, and hyperambitious" Alexander Petrovich Izvolsky, whose personal vendetta against Count Aerenthal had estranged the kaiser from the tsar, and his succession as foreign minister by the "sober and thoughtful" Sergei Sazonov, offered a chance to renew the tie with Petersburg. Suspicious of an Austro-Russian rapprochement, Bethmann saw Nicholas II's visit in November 1910 as an opportunity "to settle our differences with Russia among four eyes." Sazonov's prime objective "of consolidating Russia internally" allowed a meeting of minds on the basis of the status quo. Offering his services as mediator in Balkan disputes between Vienna and Petersburg, Bethmann went so far as to assure "that according to its protestations, Austria does not harbor expansionist designs in the Balkans" and to add, "Should it in the future admit to such ideas, we are neither obligated nor willing to stand up for them." As counterconcession, Sazonov stressed that "Russia will never enter into an anti-German combination with England" and that, despite the historic mission of liberating the Slavs, "Russia strives for nothing but peace and the maintenance of the status quo in the Balkans and would work with all its power toward localizing any eventual conflagration." [13]

The details of the Potsdam agreement included a Russian promise not to undermine the authority of the Young Turk government and a German pledge for support of internal reforms of the Ottoman Empire. Bethmann promised to respect the Russian sphere of interest in Persia as long as German commerce enjoyed full equality, while Sazonov dropped all opposition to the completion of the Bagdad Railway, only reserving the exclusive right to construct a spur-line to Chanikin in Persia. Although the chancellor claimed, "we certainly do not expect a fundamental revision of Russian policy," he hoped for "the reestablishment of close and trusting relations between us, as long as Russia avoids opposing Germany without being forced to do so by its own vital interests." But the Russian refusal to put these general assurances into writing and the somewhat contradictory public explanations of Sazonov and Bethmann revealed that the gulf between the Franco-Russian and the Dual Alliance had become unbridgeable. The success of the specific Persian agreements signed in April 1911 improved the atmosphere temporarily without fundamentally reversing the diplomatic current. Although there was no immediate Russo-German clash of interests, mutual commitments to France and Austria as well as conflicting interests in Turkey prevented a true rapprochement. "The Russian visit went better than expected. Both sovereigns treated each other openly and relaxedly, in best, almost gay spirits; Sazonov, who is a sober, cool, and loyal man, has left a most favorable impression in contrast to Izvolsky." Nevertheless Bethmann concluded, with more hope than realism, "I certainly believe that our position in the world has been substantially relieved." [14]

The *entrevue* of Baltischport in midsummer of 1912 revealed the limitations of personal diplomacy and of well-meant declarations that "nothing can happen in the world if Russia and Germany stand together." The pious communiqué that the meeting "could not change the grouping of European powers whose value for the maintenance of peace has been proven" was an ill-concealed admission that the presence of "the traditionally cordial relations" lacked reality. Nevertheless, "the meeting of the two emperors was harmonious, and I believe I have established and affirmed friendly and loyal relations with Sazonov and Kokovtsev." The pivotal Russian statesmen "above all desire peace for Russia and *therefore,* not because they are in love with us—on the contrary they find us really unsympathetic—they want to be on a friendly footing with us, if possible." Although claiming he had no illusions about Baltischport, Bethmann believed: "Three years ago the wire between Petersburg and Berlin was cut and Petersburg did not consider it important to retie it. In comparison to that, the present situation is much better, especially since the Russians simultaneously calm France." In a similar vein he wrote to his cousin, Ambassador Count Pourtalès: "Russia likes us as little as any other Great Power. For that we are too strong, too parvenu, and generally too repulsive. Even Kokovtsev and Sazonov do not love us. If it were in the Russian interest to make war on us tomorrow, they would do so in cold blood." But he was personally convinced that Russia wanted peace to build "its great and firmly founded future," and that "its *foreign* position is so favorable that it would be more than short-sighted not to use it for domestic consolidation." The settlement of its Asian disputes with Japan, the competition of France, England, and Germany for its favor, and Austria's unwillingness to destroy European Turkey made it "obvious that Germany cannot reap impressive dividends from this constellation. But it is equally clear that we must use the situation to make our relations with Petersburg as friendly as possible, and that alone is the meaning of Potsdam and Baltischport." In one of his rare private ruminations about foreign policy, Bethmann speculated, not in a mood of fearful fatalism but of optimistic candor, "Thereby we calm France, facilitate our rapprochement with England, and will be able to envisage a future resolution of the Balkan question more confidently than if we were enemies." [15]

The chancellor's attempt to normalize relations with Russia was, like his entire policy of peaceful economic expansion, severely limited by German public response. Irritated by press polemics, which made rational assessment of the national interest more and more difficult, Bethmann often pleaded in the Reichstag for "calm reserve" and for "cooperation of the public mood with foreign policy." Although he was optimistic that "in general this necessity is correctly understood in Germany," he resented that after Baltischport "a hyperclever Pan-German felt he had to warn, in alarmist articles reprinted by *Die Post,* against my naiveté and Russian perfidy." In unusually irate marginalia the chancellor castigated the blindness of chauvinism: "Every child knows that the general feeling in Russia is not friendly toward Germany; but our brave Pan-Germans try successfully to worsen it as much as possible. It is equally well known that men like Izvolsky work against us, Finally, at court, in the army, and [in the] bureaucracy there are undoubtedly currents which would, the earlier the better, like to expiate the disgrace of the Japanese defeat, preferably through a war against us rather than against Japan." Nevertheless he had gathered in his conversations with the Russian statesmen that "all of these tendencies are not represented in the present Russian government nor supported by it. . . . Despite the Germanophobe sentiments in Russia, we must attempt to reach as good relations with the Russia *government* as possible." Resenting nationalist pressures not just in Petersburg, Bethmann fundamentally disagreed with both strategy and tactics of the Pan-Germans: "With these idiots one cannot conduct a foreign policy—on the contrary. Together with other factors they will eventually make any reasonable course impossible for us." [16]

To form a judgment independent of yellow journalism, Bethmann traveled not only to the Triple Alliance capitals of Vienna and Rome but also to the personally unknown East. "Nothing in these years has refreshed me so much as the short Russian trip during which I forgot our domestic misery, abandoned myself to new impressions, and was surrounded by friendliness on all sides," he wrote, thanking Pourtalès for his cordial reception. "Moscow fascinated me. This southern city on a northern latitude, with its East Asian culture, its rough-hewn people, and its historical traditions, so large, far-flung, and semibarbaric, is particularly gripping. As simple tourists we have fully enjoyed the three days." But even then his restless mind sought for political meaning behind the picturesque appearances. "My unfortunately too short trip was full of beautiful and great impressions and has cured me of many false prejudices which I too had absorbed from our irresponsible press," he summarized to Eisendecher. "This wealth of natural resources and of inexhaustible human power are factors that especially we, influenced by our effeminate culture, should not fear but also should not underestimate." Impressed by Russian potential, Bethmann did not wish to precipitate a possibly inevitable conflict but rather sought to defuse the tensions and avoid a clash by a rational compromise of political and economic interests. "It is tedious and detailed work without dazzling successes, but necessary." [17]

Sober realism also informed Bethmann's policy toward Germany's western neighbor, the Third Republic. "Certainly [we must have] good and loyal relations with France," the chancellor criticized the crown prince's fantastic proposal of an entente. "But we should under no circumstances *reveal* an undue need for friendship, because that could spoil everything which we have reached recently." Bismarck's unstatesmanlike annexation of Alsace-Lorraine, and more recently the first Morocco crisis, prevented any intimacy beyond formal correctness in Franco-German affairs. In one of his first conversations with French Ambassador Jules Cambon, Bethmann expressed "his desire for cooperation with France in Morocco which had inspired the accord of February 9," 1909, thus recognizing the predominance of French political interest in the North African country but claiming commercial equality for Germany. "He especially repeated his hope for a quick settlement of the indemnities due German tradesmen, which would prove the utility of the agreement for German public opinion." Although in the Mannesmann affair the chancellor sacrificed the economic interest of one firm for the improvement of relations with Paris, French unwillingness to share their new sphere of influence with German business forced him to warn, in December 1910, in the Reichstag, "Do not doubt that we will energetically defend the rights and interests of German merchants." [18]

In contrast to Bethmann's leadership in the attempted rapprochement with England and Russia, German policy in the Morocco crisis of 1911 was almost solely directed by the dynamic secretary of state, Kiderlen-Waechter. Endowed with a "clever and well-balanced solid mind," as well as possessing the reputation of "a strong man," Kiderlen was tempted to reverse the diplomatic defeat of Algeciras and improve the government's domestic situation in the coming Reichstag elections by a dramatic diplomatic triumph.[19] The French punitive expedition to Fez in April 1911 offered Kiderlen the chance to declare the Algeciras Act abrogated and "to resume his entire freedom of action" because "the establishment of a military force for the Sultan, the building of block-houses, and the securing of roads through a native army with French instructors" had to lead to a protectorate. Although the French might have acted in good faith in attempting "to defend endangered Europeans," Kiderlen claimed "that Germany could not agree to a lasting occupation of Morocco and to the Sultan's dependence upon France." Unwilling and, because of domestic pressure, unable to let France formalize her North African empire without some equivalent gain for Germany, Kiderlen and "the Foreign Office correctly assumed that we can only get something respectable from the French, despite their willingness to compensate us, if we seize a *Faustpfand* [trump]." The young diplomat, Riezler, rationalized in his diary: "If we [only] make a proposal, we will receive nothing other than press attacks and cries for war." If the French do not withdraw after a reasonable time, "Germany will send two cruisers to the western coast of Morocco, and peacefully enter the harbors of Mogador and Azemmour." This coup would be justified by the protection of "important" German business interests, which Kiderlen instructed to petition for help. Such a "bargaining chip" necessary because Germany's claims were commercial rather than territorial, left Kiderlen with all options open. "Little by little we will make ourselves at home in the ports and the hinterland and then at the right moment attempt to come to an understanding with France on the basis of the division of Morocco or of compensation by a part of the French Congo." [20]

How did Bethmann react to this dangerous plan, which "could create many difficulties because of the attitude of the other powers, notably England"? According to Riezler "the chancellor will present it orally to the kaiser on the basis of the Foreign Office memorandum—but [he] probably still has misgivings." The emperor was persuaded "that we should make a proposal" to Paris, since the banker Leo Delbrück reported glowingly "that we could have any colonial compensation we wanted . . . as long as we do not interfere in Morocco." But Bethmann instinctively recoiled "from sending ships. And yet it will not work without them." His tactical warning to the French ambassador revealed also serious concern: "Part of German public opinion is very agitated about the [Morocco] question; they say that German interests are not properly defended; and I anticipate the possibility of *extremely grave* difficulties between us, which makes me uneasy about the future." Cambon's answer, "nobody can keep fruit from ripening or Morocco from falling under our influence one day," increased his apprehensions, because it demonstrated that without tangible pressure Germany could not satisfy the appetite of an imperialist public "demanding its part in the division of the world." Despite his scruples against blustering brinkmanship, Bethmann succeeded in convincing himself, "Such political surprises as the mission of the *Panther* are unpleasant for those who make them, but the [naval] demonstration could not be conducted otherwise, since the French would probably have sent a ship to Agadir." Although he left "full liberty of action and entire responsibility" to Kiderlen, Bethmann helped persuade the kaiser that a coup would hasten French concessions, and in late June 1911 the foreign secretary wired laconically, "Ships granted." [21]

The shock and outrage of European opinion over the *Panther's* leap to Agadir revealed that Kiderlen was playing a dangerous game of prestige. Indeed, Jules Cambon now admitted the necessity for negotiations, since the status quo had become untenable, and conceded "that serious colonial compensation" could alone legalize the French protectorate over Morocco. But increasing Pan-German agitation for the annexation of southern or western Morocco, which he himself helped to provoke, limited the foreign secretary's flexibility. "At any rate we will have to take a firm stand in order to reach a favorable result," Bethmann advised the impatient William II. "Without sizeable concessions we cannot leave Morocco to the French. . . . [Otherwise] our credit in the world will suffer unbearably, not only for the present, but for all future diplomatic actions." While Russia, on the basis of the Potsdam talks, only halfheartedly supported France, the possibility of a German port on the Atlantic so disturbed the British that they viewed the confrontation as a test of the Entente and concluded that a German diplomatic victory would mean "definitely the subjection of France." The realization that then Berlin's "hegemony would be solidly established with all its consequences immediate and prospective," prompted London's countercoup, Lloyd George's unequivocal warning against unilateral German action at Mansion House, which disregarded normal diplomatic procedure. Because of this assurance of support, "the French do not want to give up [the Congo]," while "Kiderlen wants to get what he demanded. British intervention seems to have angered him so colossally that he said to Cambon after Lloyd George's speech that now Germany could no longer reduce her demands because of English blackmail." A German call "for the withdrawal of French troops from Morocco," the only alternative to compensation, could "not be accepted by the French, and therein lies the danger of war." Because of these unexpected repercussions "the kaiser, exceedingly unhappy, telegraphed Bethmann and ordered him and Kiderlen to report to him at Swinemünde." [22]

Though gambling for the highest stakes, "Kiderlen informs nobody completely, not even the chancellor," Riezler complained about the foreign secretary's secretiveness. "He speaks when he likes, but not when he should. Bethmann said yesterday, he wanted to give Kiderlen a lot to drink in the evening in order to find out what he ultimately wants." The stratagem worked, but "what he said was very serious, so that the chancellor believes Kiderlen not only considers the possibility of war but wants it." Aroused by the smallness of Cambon's concessions and by the vehemence of annexationist pressure, "Kiderlen's stubbornness is the most important political factor at present. It is elemental and unruly. Considering the confidence that he enjoys, neither the chancellor nor the kaiser can let him go"; Riezler thus analyzed the predicament of German policy. "The second factor is the correct idealist German conviction that the nation needs a war. This is even shared by Bethmann. Hence he has conceded to Kiderlen that we must hold out and accept the risk of war." But in one point the chancellor differed fundamentally from the chauvinist public. "He does not want to precipitate war. That he wanted to have affirmed by Kiderlen." The chancellor's assistant noted: Press chief "Hammann convinced him that Kiderlen was not out to make war. Correctly so. Kiderlen believes in success." While the foreign secretary persuaded the chancellor to remain firm, the kaiser, who had initially objected to gunboat diplomacy, wavered. "Kiderlen is fed up and is ready to throw the whole thing at H.M.'s feet." But by now Bethmann had been won over and "resolved to stick it out and to resign if necessary." Under this pressure from his advisors William caved in. "The kaiser was quite humble in Swinemünde. Kiderlen returned very pleased." [23]

The agreement on forceful brinkmanship remained hollow since Berlin was only willing to bluff, not resort to war. While public passions were rising to a fever pitch and Britain ordered naval preparations, "Paris retreated in the Congo" step by step. The negotiations over compensation were complicated not only by French cabinet crises, but also by the "doubtful importance" of the Congo to Germany. Colonial Secretary "Lindequist does not think much of it and wants Dahomey," adjacent to German Togoland. The colonial administrator was "enraged over his personal humiliation by Kiderlen and intends to resign. Today he is with the chancellor in Hohenfinow, who wants to dissuade him." The ever-louder cry of *West-Morokko Deutsch*, spurred by exaggerated reports of the country's mineral and agricultural wealth, forced Kiderlen to insist on economic safeguards short of a complete French protectorate. After months of exasperating bargaining, the Morocco accords were finally initialed on October 11 and the Congo agreement on November 2, 1911. "Territorial *compensation* in return for our [legal] *concessions* in Morocco," more specifically, the protection of certain economic rights in Morocco and the gain of 263,000 square kilometers of the Congo that formed a bridge to the Congo River, was technically a good bargain for Germany. With the possible future collapse of Belgium, Spanish, and Portuguese colonies, this nucleus for a greater Central Africa justified Bethmann's claim "that when the dust of battle settles, both countries will appreciate the results and Europe will find an assurance of peace in them." But inflamed public opinion denounced the accords as diplomatic defeat. "It is false that in Germany the nation is peaceful and the government bellicose—the exact opposite is true," Jules Cambon reflected with perceptive irony.[24]

Interrupted by laughter and shouts of derision, Chancellor Bethmann Hollweg defended the Morocco agreement in the Reichstag in early November 1911: "We drew up a program and carried it out. Nothing, no influence from outside or inside has made us depart one step from it." Political prudence spoke against the annexation of Moroccan territory, since it would have meant preventive war, which was ridiculed by Bismarck. He concluded proudly: "We expect no praise, but we fear no reproach." But despite his briefings of the party leaders a deluge followed. Colonial Secretary Lindequist's controversial resignation, Lloyd George's unexpected threat, and frustrated dreams of world power aroused the parties in rare unanimity to subject the government to savage criticism. "We now know where the enemy stands," Conservative leader Heydebrand thundered against England, claiming that Bethmann "could have achieved much more" had he only shown more courage. The venerable Socialist, August Bebel, rejected the entire course of the Morocco policy since Bülow: "The great reckoning [*Kladderadatsch*] will come without our help. You are all working toward it." More outspoken than Center Party chief Hertling, National Liberal deputy Bassermann charged: "I consider a thorough *critique of the government's action* not only our right but also our patriotic duty." In the royal box the crown prince and one of his younger brothers demonstratively applauded nationalist charges that the chancellor's policy was "a *defeat,* whether we say so or not." [25]

Although the next day the Progressives rejected "such chauvinistic agitation," their critique of the safeguards for German business in Morocco and of the value of the Congo territory, infested with malaria and swamps, was equally severe. Only the Free-Conservatives accepted the government's claim "that it has indeed achieved everything which it set out to do. But then it should not have encouraged such exaggerated hopes." Because the fundamental direction of his foreign policy was at stake, Bethmann heatedly denied *"accusations of weakness"* and singled out Heydebrand's irresponsible conservatism. "Inflammatory words *lacking any restraint* such as those of Herr Heydebrand (very good) may serve party interests (stormy applause of the Left) but they harm the German Empire (renewed loud approval of the Left)." Raising his frame in genuine fury, the chancellor, with a derisory motion of his hand, continued: "The strong man does not always have to strike with the sword—in his mouth! (stormy acclamation of the Left)." Although he endorsed patriotic idealism, Bethmann made a fundamental distinction: "To heat national passions to the boiling point for utopian annexations or party purposes—gentlemen, that means compromising patriotism (stormy applause of Progressives and Socialists) and throwing away national treasures (renewed stormy approval of the Left and immense commotion)." [26] Not only the Bavarian ambassador considered Bethmann's philippic "a personal triumph" and was deeply impressed by it. Nevertheless, "such public censure of the leader of a party on whose support he has, in ordinary times, chiefly to depend," was in Szögyény's eyes "hardly correct tactically," since it rendered a "patriotic" election campaign impossible.[27]

"The Reichstag was undignified and Heydebrand leads the Conservatives down demagogic paths," Bethmann poured out his heart afterward. "If in our nonparliamentary system the government is not even supported by the Conservatives and moderates, then soon there will be nobody left to carry on." Although "the [treaties] are hardly ideal," the Conservatives "could have kept the national wind in their sails without making such irresponsible noises and distancing themselves so openly from the government. How—that Hertling has shown." In general, he "deplored the immaturity of the Reichstag, which gives us the reputation abroad of unreliability due to disunity and chauvinism, and at home, further postpones the gradual healing of our wounds." Nevertheless he asserted: "My conscience lets me sleep. War for the Sultan of Morocco, for a piece of Sus or Congo or for the Brothers Mannesmann would have been a crime." But there was the one unsettling thought that "the German people have so frivolously played with war this summer. This is serious, this I must oppose. Even at the risk of drawing the wrath of the people upon me." In a similar vein, he revealed to Karl Freiherr von Weizsäcker why he had drawn back from the brink: "If I had driven toward war, we would now stand somewhere in France, our fleet would largely lie on the bottom of the North Sea, Hamburg and Bremen would be blockaded or bombarded, and the entire nation would ask me, why this? . . . And it would rightly string me up on the nearest tree." Nevertheless, Bethmann knew that he was himself partially to blame: "We were driven by the necessity of maintaining our economic interests and of showing the world that we were firmly resolved not to be pushed aside." Intending to liquidate the ill-fated legacy of Algeciras, this *Interessenpolitik* had only succeeded under the grave risk of war by fanning the flames of annexationist imperialism which might be uncontrollable in the future. Hence the chancellor replied morosely to Goschen's question of whether he had time to play his usual Beethoven sonata before going to bed, "My dear friend, you and I like classical music with its plain and straightforward harmonies; how can I play my beloved old melodies with the air full of modern discords?" [28]

In pursuit of his "main goal, the loosening of the Entente," Bethmann now returned his attention to Great Britain, the center of opposition. "Like you, I consider a modus vivendi with England imperative," he confided to Eisendecher, apologizing, "In the last analysis even Morocco was intended to facilitate this and would have hastened it, had not opposition to our government turned our Moroccan policy into a defeat by England, caused indiscriminate naval agitation, and thereby forced our policy into a course of blustering unsteadiness, although it truly demonstrated a good deal of calmness and firmness this summer and fall." Estimating his chances of success, he continued, "The British *parties* favor an understanding with us and I hope to be able to overcome the resistance of Sir Edward Grey and especially his aides in the Foreign Office *in time*— if here everything were not dictated by the mood of the moment and by the political sophistication of a kindergarten." Since Admiral Tirpitz deftly exploited popular embitterment against England to press for an augmentation of the fleet, Bethmann warned his ambassador,

Count Paul von Metternich, "The government will only be able to escape this pressure . . . if England decides on a positive agreement with us and documents this decision by facts." When asked by Sir Edward Goschen what he meant by this reference to "deeds and not words," Bethmann replied "that he had 'everything' in his mind." Because his policy of peaceful expansion was threatened by navalist clamor, the chancellor seized upon Sir Edward Grey's earlier suggestion of "greater colonial gains" to block a "naval increase which, as the British statesmen will have to admit, they themselves irresponsibly provoked." Although his optimism wavered, Bethmann steered determinedly toward an "agreement coming close to a neutrality treaty," because only that could prompt the kaiser and the public to accept a rapprochement.[29]

Despite Count Metternich's warning that "political understanding on a broad basis cannot succeed . . . especially now when we propose a naval increase," negotiations began in earnest in January 1912. Transmitted privately through Sir Ernest Cassel and Albert Ballin, Whitehall's feelers centered on three distinct yet related points: "(1) Fundamental. Naval superiority recognized as essential to Great Britain. Present German naval program and expenditure not to be increased but if possible retarded and reduced. (2) England sincerely desires not to interfere with German colonial expansion. . . . (3) Proposals for reciprocal assurances debarring either power from joining in aggressive designs or combinations against the other would be welcome." But Bethmann's single reservation, "that this year's (1912) estimates must be included in the 'present German Naval Program' in as much as all the arrangements will already have been completed," limited the promise of his cordial invitation to Sir Edward Grey from the outset. To give a more informal character to this "very frank exchange of views," Minister of War Viscount Haldane, who was steeped in German culture, was sent privately to Berlin in early February with the "approval of king and the Cabinet, but merely to talk over the ground." [30]

Impressed by Bethmann's "absolute sincerity and good will," Haldane listened attentively to his plea for "the *establishment of closer relations*," but restricted his host's all too sanguine neutrality formula to "mutual undertakings against aggressive or unprovoked attacks." Replying that "the spirit . . . was everything; and if there was the real spirit, words like these might express all that was necessary," Bethmann stressed "that it was absolutely essential to Germany to have a third squadron in full readiness for war," adding, "my admirals are very difficult." But the chancellor's "evident desire to meet us wherever he could" was not enough for the British visitor, who returned to the two-keel-to-one standard and intimated that some fundamental modification of the naval program was necessary, a measure which Bethmann promised to consider. Success in finding a political formula "would open up a vista of others topics," such as cooperation in Africa on disputed "territorial questions" like Angola, Timor, Pemba, Zanzibar, the Bagdad Railway, and Persia. "For two and a half years he had been striving to bring about an agreement between Germany and England," Haldane described Bethmann's entreaties. "This had been the aim of his policy." This illusory near unanimity was exploded by a second conversation between Haldane and the obstreperous Tirpitz, restrained somewhat by William II, about specific naval concessions, the prime British interest. "Well, can we not spread the *tempo?*" Haldane finally suggested, circumventing Germany's obstinate refusal to sacrifice the naval law. Momentarily persuaded by William's charm that the political "agreement was the key to everything," Haldane once again met with a more subdued Bethmann, who sensed that the concession of a building slowdown as a result of an entente was "too small" to sway the British cabinet. Nevertheless, for a brief moment in the spring of 1912, it seemed that the decades of hate and suspicion between the Anglo-Saxon cousins would be resolved by a triple agreement, essentially on German terms.[31]

The chancellor's optimism evaporated when the personal diplomacy of the well-meaning negotiators was confronted with the realities of conflicting Anglo-German interests. "A promising beginning has been made. I do not yet know what the future will bring. At any rate it was good to have a chance to speak openly with a member of of the British cabinet," Bethmann summarized to a friend. But both domestic pressure for a naval increase and British reluctance to conclude the bargain put him on the defensive. Despite Haldane's insistence "that he understood the necessity of a naval law because of public opinion and the need for a third squadron," the size of the new personnel demands was construed as "great augmentation by the British Admiralty." Refusing to accept the vague postponement of three ships as a naval agreement, Sir Edward Grey distanced himself from the all too generous promises of Haldane. While "the basis [for any agreement] was shifted" by London, Bethmann's free-dom of action was limited by William II's increasing insistence on the immediate publication of the naval law and by his rejection of British desires for its modification as "impudent interference." [32]

When the kaiser instructed Metternich over the chancellor's head, "I shall consider any transfer of the Mediterranean squadron into the North Sea as cause for war and answer with the *increased* building program in its old form and with mobilization," Bethmann had no choice but to declare, "The accusation that I abuse Y.M.'s patience and the trust of the German people by postponing the publication of the content of the arms increases . . . forces me to ask for my dismissal." Beyond the constitutional issue of ultimate responsibility for instructing ambassadors, the entire thrust of his foreign policy was at stake. Unwilling to destroy the slight chance of future success, Bethmann pleaded "that we are duty-bound to con-tinue the negotiations," since a provocative breakdown would "tragically worsen our relations with England and force Germany to launch a preventive attack. In such a war France will enjoy the military aid of Russia and doubtless also of England, while it will not be a casus foederis . . . for our allies." He warned emphatically: "I cannot bear the responsibility for working toward such a goal from our side. Forced into war we will wage it and with God's help not perish. But to conjure up war ourselves without having our honor or vital interests threatened would be a sin against Germany's destiny, even if according to human foresight we could hope for complete victory." Unequivocally rejecting a preemptive strike, the wounded and angry chancellor demanded the cessation of royal interference in foreign policy. He spoke from the deepest convic-tions of his political being when he concluded: "On the basis of the office bestowed upon me by Your Majesty, I bear the responsibility for the policy ordered by Y.M. before the country, history, and my conscience. Even Y.M. cannot relieve me of this responsibility. Since Your Majesty does not allow me to do it justice, I humbly beg to be discharged from my offices." [33]

Bethmann's offer to resign, a supreme effort to force his British policy to prevail over Tirpitz's opposition, temporarily blocked the publication of the naval increase and allowed him to resume nego-tiations. The chancellor's "undeniable successes in foreign policy" neutralized the admiral's counterthreat to resign, and the emperor's angry outburst, "Bethmann is ripe for the sanatorium," only prepared for another Wilhelmian compromise, since both continued in office. Despite Lerchenfeld's advice that "reconciliation with England seems impossible on the basis of the naval law," [34] Bethmann sidestepped Grey's suggestion to move on to the more promising colonial question, since he "still put the main emphasis on a political agreement." Now he was even willing to "accept the Haldane formula, if it is added that in case of impending conflict with other states a timely exchange of views takes place." Puzzled by the clear signs of a German power struggle, Goschen erroneously concluded that Bethmann "may be supposed to be willing to make considerable sacrifices," since he had declared "he wouldn't care twopence what was said about the rest of his work as chancellor." Hence Whitehall refused to go beyond the assurance that "England [would] make no unprovoked attack upon Germany and pursue no aggressive policy against her," which in the chancellor's words "didn't go half far enough; he would simply be laughed at if he produced such a meager little formula as a reason for reducing the demands of the Naval Party, or as the basis of an understanding." The British suspiciously misinterpreted the chancellor's feverish anxiety for an agreement. "Putting two and two together, it looks very much as if they were trying to square us in good time." Unwilling to tie their hands through neutrality, the English statesmen preferred an anti-German balance of power to preserve their own colonial hegemony.[35]

When his second attempt to turn the chimera of British neutrality into tangible diplomatic fact had failed, Bethmann reluctantly agreed "to continue the exchange of opinion on colonial and territorial questions." Although the emperor's wrath demanded the recall of Metternich, a belated victim, colonial negotiations centering on Portuguese Africa and the completion of the Bagdad Railway were indeed begun. "True to his instruction [the new ambassador Baron] Marschall only sounds the terrain and has not yet reported anything decisive aside from his very cordial reception by all the important people," Bethmann noted with growing disappointment in the summer of 1912. Dimly recognizing that the pursuit of a political settlement without adequate naval sacrifices was doomed to failure, he continued to hope, "From a friendly exchange of views on colonial and other questions affecting both of us, we do not only promise ourselves a détente but also the possibilility of finally reaching a [wider] agreement acceptable to both sides." [36]

Despite his ardent courtship of London and Petersburg, the chancellor knew that "the Archimedian point of all of European politics" was "our alliance" with Austria-Hungary. In Bismarck's system offset by the Reinsurance Treaty, the Dual Alliance had become the continental cornerstone of Wilhelmian Weltpolitik, when the formation of the ententes made the dual monarchy Germany's sole great power friend. Any resurrection of the Three Emperors' League was impossible as long as Petersburg demanded "a renunciation of any economic activity, and political influence in the Balkans" from Vienna, and German policy was dominated by "our well-known treaty relationship with Austria." Within the Triple Alliance, the growing Italian interest in the Balkans, as well as rising irredentism, created severe strains despite the Consulta's vociferous assurances that "regardless of the composition of the new ministry, Italian foreign policy will not change." Conscious of "the unreliability of the complicated policy of the slippery Signor Tittoni," Bethmann counseled generosity to the Ballplatz and supported direct negotiations between his two allies "to prevent Italy from intervening independently and willfully in the case of warlike complications in the Balkans." Although the chancellor initially thought "Austria as Balkan power was chiefly responsible for Balkan questions" such as the admission of Turkey into the alliance, he gradually reasserted German leadership within the Dreibund. "Fear of Russia and *the thought* that we could come to an agreement with Russia at its expense had driven Austria into our arms and will keep it there." Bethmann intended to prevent "the resurgence of the old Kalnoky tendency of arrogating to itself the direction of the Triple Alliance which belongs to us." Revealing the inner weakness of the Dual Alliance, he concluded, "Should extreme things come to pass, it would be better if the first attack were directed against Austria, which will then need *our* help, and not against us, so that [the outcome] does not depend upon Austria's [decision] if it wants to be loyal." Though Bethmann assumed the "role of a fireman" toward Viennese adventures, Austria's weakness and growing German economic interests in Turkey forced Berlin to abandon its traditional Bismarckian disinterest in the Balkans.[37]

Bethmann's dual policy of restraining Viennese escapades while assuring the survival of the Hapsburg monarchy was tested severely by the Tripoli war. Unleashed in the wake of the Morocco crisis, Rome's imperialistic attack on Constantinople, the focus of German economic and military interest, placed the chancellor in a quandary. "Although engaged in Asia Minor not only with hundreds of millions [of Marks], but also with its prestige," Germany could not oppose the ill-timed Italian expedition, since Tripoli had been promised to Rome. Despite Germany's influence, Bethmann could not advise territorial concessions "because the age of intervention politics had definitely passed and the new Turkey is especially sensitive toward anything that looks like interference in its domestic affairs." When Italian military incompetence raised the danger of a general Balkan war, Bethmann hoped for "a fait accompli through a quick landing," and telegraphed William II: "Certainly German policy . . . follows the principle that the integrity of the Turkish Empire must be maintained, but only in as far as Turkey *itself* upholds it." Torn between the Turkophile advice of the embassy at the Golden Porte and Gottlieb von Jagow's warnings from Rome that lack of German support would break up the Triple Alliance, Bethmann scrupulously fought for a compromise. "As unpredictable as the momentary situation in Turkey is, I still believe that the desire for peace is increasing on *both* sides. Should Turkey decide to make Tripoli and Cyrenaika independent, then the only possible basis for peace will have been found." Although not officially mediating in the conflict between ally and victim, the chancellor hoped, "If these provinces then come to an arrangement with Italy, it will not cause a revolution in Turkey, as long as the men in power in Constantinople succeed in dampening other unrest in European Turkey. But Italy must be intelligent enough not to insist upon appearances but to be content with any agreement allowing it, on the basis of its actual victory, to expand its influence into those provinces which it had annexed but not yet occupied." The peace of Lausanne, hastened by the thunderclouds of a general uprising in the Balkans, allowed Germany to escape with undiminished influence in Constantinople and led to a premature renewal of the Triple Alliance despite the Austro-Italian dispute over Article 7 regarding compensations in the Balkans.[38]

The "pronounced optimism" with which Bethmann faced the conclusion of the Balkan alliance due to Sazonov's pacific assurances was rudely disappointed by the outbreak of the first Balkan war in the fall of 1912. In long discussions in Buchlau with Aerenthal's successor, the dapper Count Leopold Berchtold, the chancellor attempted to assuage the fear that Austria faced "the painful alternative of either standing firm and risking a conflict which could turn into a cataclysm or giving in, certain of having abdicated as independent power factor and being eliminated from the concern of Great Powers." Despite the increasingly threatening news from the Balkan capitals, Bethmann remained sanguine. "Nobody wants war in Europe, nobody. I hope that if a conflict erupts, we can localize it; the Great Powers should agree in order to bring that about," he stressed to the French ambassador. Even after the outbreak of hostilities in October, Bethmann maintained that "we can await developments calmly," and stressed that the war "must be allowed to take its course and, brutal as it sounded, he hoped it would be very severe and very bloody" to hasten the eventual peace. "The important thing for the Great Powers . . . was to keep in continual contact and above all to keep quiet—he was convinced that there was no danger at all of either Austria or Russia moving unless we—England, France and Germany—set them going by some false move." More concretely, the chancellor supported Anglo-German cooperation, which "would exert a great moral force;" even if the dismemberment of European Turkey could no longer be postponed, it need not lead to European war. Frightened, William II nevertheless thundered, "I shall *under no circumstances march against Paris and Moscow* for the sake of Albania and Durazzo," since "such a goal cannot serve as a slogan for a life-and-death struggle for Germany." This danger seemed remote, since Austria's minimal program—calling for the independence of Albania, no Serbian access to the Aegean, and the safeguarding of Austrian economic interests—was supported by Italy and considered quite reasonable in all capitals. Dispelling exaggerated rumors of war by a strongly worded communiqué in the *NAZ*, the German chancellor viewed the coming Balkan complications with quiet confidence, trusting in Russian moderation and hoping for British cooperation: "There was no longer any possibility of intervention [of the powers], only mediation, but Germany should conduct a policy of restraint." [39]

Nevertheless, Bethmann's foot soon slipped on the tightrope of supporting Austria without antagonizing England, thus provoking a genuine war scare, when he felt compelled to support Vienna in the Reichstag: "If against all expectations [our allies] are attacked by a third party while pursuing their interests and are thereby threatened in their existence, we will have to stand firmly at their side. . . . Then we will fight to maintain our own position in

Europe, our own future, and our security." Without reassuring the suspicious Berchtold, the chancellor's firmness caused consternation in Whitehall since it made Austria more reluctant to compromise. *"A serious situation continues to exist,"* wrote one of the chancellor's advisors, weighing the probability of war. "Russia's real designs are still in the dark and they are pivotal; our whole effort is presently directed at keeping Austria from taking decisive steps which could perhaps . . . turn British opinion against us." When, on December 8, Grey's discreet counterwarning that "England would under no circumstances allow a defeat of the French" reached the mercurial William II, he exploded: "Haldane's conversation with [Prince Karl Max von] Lichnowsky . . . tears away the veil of uncertainty. Because of enmity and hatred of Germany, England will at all costs help France and Russia against us." Conjuring up the image of a *Götterdämmerung* struggle between Latins, Slavs, and Germans in which the Anglo-Saxon cousin would aid the enemy, the enraged and fearful kaiser called a war council of his military advisers and painted a martial picture of a Balkan alliance of Bulgaria, Rumania, Albania, and Turkey joining Austria: "Then we shall be free to fight the war with full fury against France." Chief of Staff Moltke heartily agreed on "war, the sooner the better"; but, more realistically Admiral Tirpitz cautioned "that the navy would prefer to see the postponement of the great fight for one and a half years." Because of the incompleteness of the Kiel canal and the general unpreparedness of the fleet, "the kaiser reluctantly agreed to a postponement," but insisted on the introduction of new army and navy increases, on a search for new allies, and on the preparation of the public for war. Despite the sinister language, which testified to the depth of the war scare, Admiral Müller summarized the ominous conference in the words, "The result was practically zero." [40]

Although William II claimed that the chancellor "had now gotten used to the idea of war," Bethmann denounced the impromptu meeting as an impetuous creation of fear: "Haldane's communication to Lichnowsky was not nearly that serious. It only affirmed what we have long known: *now as before England follows a policy of balance of power and therefore will stand up for France if the latter is in danger of being annihilated by us.*" Encouraging Eisendecher's attempts to assuage the imperial wrath, he continued: "Demanding that England throw herself around his neck, despite his policy, H.M. has gotten terribly excited about this and immediately held a war council with his stalwarts of army and navy, behind my and Kiderlen's back, ordered the preparation of an army *and navy* increase, and broadcast the Haldane conversation, fantastically enlarged, over the whole world." As a dire consequence of this escalation of the arms race, he sarcastically predicted: "If, with Tirpitz, H.M. intends to make the [Anglo-French] bond completely unbreakable, they will succeed without difficulty by their new fleet increase. But given a reasonable policy I do not consider the Haldane statements threatening. In the present crisis England has worked closely and loyally with us and has succeeded in calming Russia." Without belittling the dangers inherent in the explosive situation, Bethmann concluded: "[Britain] wants no continental war because it would be drawn into it and does not want to fight. In that light its obligations toward France perhaps have their positive side. But we must not conduct a nervous jumping-jack policy; otherwise the others' patience will run out one day." [41]

Although the Saxon and Bavarian military attachés warned that the "picture behind the scenes" was darker than official optimism would have it, Bethmann categorically rejected chauvinist propaganda for army and navy increases, demanding that Tirpitz and Moltke, "do not commit themselves behind my back vis-à-vis H.M." Even the vaguest preparations *"cannot be allowed to seep into the public as long as the tension caused by the Balkan crisis has not abated."* But William still suffered from shock at Haldane's warning: "Perhaps it will soon be a matter of life and death for Germany. . . . Therefore we must be ready for any eventuality and miss no opportunity to strengthen army and navy." The kaiser continued ominously, "if the chancellor raises difficulties for which he did not hope, they could become dangerous for him." Despite William's "immense excitement," Lerchenfeld calmly concluded that "there is now no greater danger of war than before." "Categorically denying" rumors that "H.M. pressed for war" lest they become self-fulfilling prophecy, Bethmann attempted to reassert his influence on William II and to prevent a naval increase which would destroy any remaining chance of British neutrality. Although the kaiser was convinced "that *immediate* intervention of England is a certainty," he deferred to the chancellor's judgment that "Germany and England, who have no interests of their own in the Balkans, primarily are called upon to advance the peaceful outcome of the London negotiations through their influence on the belligerents." Although the largest peacetime addition to the Prussian army resulted from the war scare, any naval increase was rejected. Bethmann neither mounted a systematic propaganda campaign, nor did he, as an obedient bureaucrat, prepare for the inevitable diplomatically. "The Powers must see to it that this war is brought to a conclusion, and that all the questions which are now agitating Europe are settled once and for all. We have been on tenterhooks for too long, with war always looming in the background. This state of things is getting on the nerves of Europe and interfering with every sort of social, financial, and political development," Bethmann expressed his grave concern to Goschen in January 1913. "I do not wish to give away any political secrets, but I can assure you that if it had not been for England and Germany, Europe would be in a state of war at this moment." [42]

In contrast to the emperor's exaggerated fears, the resolution of the Balkan crisis vindicated Bethmann's cautious and peaceful policy. With some satisfaction, the chancellor reflected on "the critical foreign situation in which, as I still believe, we have not maneuvered without skill and in which we have succeeded in making the Ambassadors' Conference in London work quite smoothly. Unless Turkey and the Balkan alliance resume their fight and thereby create incalculable new sources of conflict—which I do not believe likely— this [cooperation] has eliminated the danger. Should this be the end of my political career, I have not toiled in vain at least in this regard." Lest the Austro-Russian rivalry push Europe to the brink of war, the chancellor warned Berchtold unequivocally, "I would consider a forceful resolution of the crisis a mistake of immense consequences as long as there is a slight chance to see the conflict through under considerably better circumstances, even if many interests of the Austro-Hungarian monarchy" were pressing for war now. Bethmann tirelessly sought a compromise between the Russian desire to enlarge Serbia and the Austrian wishes to prevent the Balkan Piedmont from obtaining access to the Adriatic Sea. "Your Excellency expresses the fear that we could drift into a world war because of Albania and Serbia," he sought to reassure Lichnowsky. "We will support the Austrian side as far as this seems necessary for the maintenance of the power position of our ally. The possibility of conflict with Russia arises from the fact that tsarist policy is directed toward the diminution of this position." When the surprising extent of the victories of the Balkan Alliance threatened to open the Pandora's box of Asian Turkey, Bethmann hoped that "it will be possible to postpone posing the Near Eastern question. But it will come, and probably sooner than we desire. Only hand in hand with England can we solve it in a manner acceptable to us, since in all our colonial questions as well we are dependent upon collaboration with Britain." Germany's exasperating task was "to solve the Skutari issue through compromise in accord with England without undermining the firmness of our alliance with Austria." As "the lone positive result of the shipwreck of Austrian Balkan dreams," the chancellor consistently endorsed the relatively moderate demand in London for the creation of an Albanian buffer state, and after some territorial concessions, it was accepted by the European Concert.[43]

In spite of Bethmann's diplomatic support of Austrian desires, relations between Berlin and Vienna were becoming strained. "Hoping that a direct Austrian intervention into the Balkan conflict could be avoided," the German chancellor considered Albanian independence a sufficient victory. Hence he intimated strongly that Germany would fulfill her duty as ally only if, despite "a calm, waiting attitude," the Hofburg were the victim of a Serbian attack. In a clear warning to the Viennese war party, Bethmann continued: "I must counsel against the idea of wanting to swallow Serbia, since it will only weaken the monarchy." Moreover, Gottlieb von Jagow's appointment as Kiderlen's successor shifted German policy away from cooperation with Bulgaria toward creating a Rumanian-Greek-Turkish barrier "against the advance of the Slavic flood and of Russian influence" in the Balkans. The notorious unreliability of Bulgarian King Ferdinand, the kinship of the Rumanian and Greek monarchs with William II, and racially based fears of Pan-Slavism, as well as economic interests, persuaded Bethmann to attempt to forge a new Balkan alliance out of the non-Slavic powers to block Russia. But impressed with their complete congruence of interests with Bulgaria and hypnotized by the inevitability of a conflict with South-Slav irredentism, Austrian diplomats rejected the German program as impractical because of Rumanian designs on Transylvania. Despite these Balkan difficulties and quarrels within the Dual Alliance, Bethmann clung to his moderate course: "Our position will long, if not forever, remain difficult. We must hold France in check through a cautious policy toward England and Russia. Of course, this does not please our chauvinists and is unpopular. But I see no other way for Germany in the near future." [44]

Although tensions between the imperialist blocs continued,

Nicholas II's and George V's visit to attend the Hohenzollern-Guelph wedding in mid-1913 was "a considerable success, even if one can expect no practical consequences." Bethmann informed his cousin Pourtalès, "We have suffered so many setbacks from personal mis-understandings and irritations that it is always a step forward if private relations are good." Treating each other "politely as com-rades and relatives," the three monarchs "talked a great deal about politics, especially the tsar, who is far above his British cousin. He felt completely free and was visibly impressed by the friendly re-ception everywhere. "Of course nothing was agreed upon, although H.M. trumpets to the world that he has now solved and regulated the Balkan problem with his cousins and this went so surprisingly well and fast because the stupid ministers were not involved"— Bethmann thus satirized royal diplomacy. "The three high lords shared a strong personal animosity toward Ferdinand and a desire to court Greece while maintaining Asian Turkey intact. With such Hellenophile expectations our allies probably fared badly." Sincere love of peace inspired the tsar's personal assurance to Bethmann, "If we both stick together all will turn out well." In contrast, the conver-sation "with the king remained superficial, but had a decisively friendly undertone, and he unreservedly stated his satisfaction over the improvement of our relations." Symbolically, Bethmann saw "the torchdance of a princess between the tsar and the British king [as] a picture with undeniable historical importance. At any rate the kaiser has reason enough to be content, and I regret that he is nevertheless again very nervous." [45]

William II's apprehensions were not unfounded, since the out-break of the second Balkan war among the former victors once more threatened European peace. Although further strains developed be-tween the Ballplatz and the Wilhelmstrasse, Bethmann's refusal to support Berchtold's demand for revision of the Treaty of Bucharest hastened the eventual settlement. Nevertheless, the chancellor en-dorsed Austria's ultimatum to Serbia, insisting on the execution of the decisions of the London ambassadorial conference. "The German government was not consulted, but afterwards approved the démarche completely," since, in contrast to the earlier boundary quarrels, Albanian independence was vital to the survival of Austria. When this crisis, too, passed because Berlin's defense of Vienna's claims was based on European decisions, "the Greco-Turk relations gave cause for concern." Once again war seemed near. "The Turks have 300,000 fine, well-rested soldiers. The Greeks are tired. The Serbian reservists will hardly let themselves be involved in a new battle. Bulgaria is probably too exhausted to aid the Ottomans actively, but it would grant Turkey all possible liberty for attacking Greece. Hence the chances are favorable for the Turks, and if the Greeks do not make concessions, I fear shooting will begin again." Although the Greco-Turkish quarrel made the program of an anti-Slavic Balkan alliance illusory, Bethmann had no easy solution, sighing, "Providence should let these fellows fight until they cannot go on." Realistic in restraining and supporting Vienna to preserve the Hapsburg monarchy *and* European peace, Bethmann's Balkan policy nevertheless remained barren in its courtship of Rumania and Greece and its suspicious neglect of Bulgaria.[46]

Despite Bethmann's guarded optimism late in 1913 domestic pressures in both empires forced a new crisis in Russo-German relations. Smarting from the Central Powers' diplomatic victory in the Albanian question, the Russian public, and later the tsarist statesmen, took affront at the mission of General Liman von Sanders to the Bosporus to reconstruct the badly battered Turkish army. Since he "never imagined that Russia could be offended by our military mission," Bethmann admitted that "I must blame myself for leaving the generals too much of a free hand in the summer and fall when I was absent." Nevertheless, the chancellor pleaded to Kokovtsev "that he should not think that I intended to contradict my own policy behind my back with the military mission," and thus vitiate his efforts at a détente. Initially reluctant to make any concessions "which, interpreted as retreat in the face of French and Russian threats, would provoke a storm of resentment" at a moment when the Zabern affair made his position precarious, Bethmann was eventually persuaded by Pourtalès's alarmist dispatches that "the General should soon be promoted to a higher rank," thus eliminating his direct control over Constantinople. "It was in our own interest that he laid down the *command,* and one should not have given it to him in the first place," since his task was the reorganization of the Turkish army and not political or military influence on the Sublime Porte. This modification of Liman's position sufficed to calm the waves, because Russian premier Kokovtzev sincerely believed Bethmann's protestation, "Since my appointment as chancellor four years ago, I have made every effort to eliminate the slightest misunderstandings between the two empires united through traditional bonds of loyalty and trust." [47]

The psychological, economic, and political hostility between Berlin and Petersburg had grown too deep to be bridged by personal diplomacy between responsible statesmen. "Russia gives me pause for concern. Its policy is completely unpredictable, since it is impossible to tell whose influence is decisive at present because it fluctuates," Bethmann pondered in February 1914. "Therefore I hope that this strong Pan-Slavist aggressive mood will still cede to reason. But I am not without doubts. Luckily France is, at the moment, peaceful." Mutual distrust, economic rivalry, and military fears crystallized in an alarmist article of the *Kölnische Zeitung* in which the Pan-German correspondent, Ullrich, warned of Russian armaments against Germany that would be completed in 1917. Although the German embassy, as well as Undersecretary Zimmermann, denounced it as "absolutely unofficial, full of misplaced pessimism, and too insignificant to cause concern," the nationalist press echoed the Cassandra call and demanded a more resolute policy against the Slavic danger. "In the case of Russian naval officers, the local officials in Berlin have committed hair-raising blunders. But they are no greater than those of the Russians toward us." The chancellor was inclined to dismiss such incidents: "The editorial of the *Kölnische* was a stupidity. Yet it hardly did any real damage." But an equally bellicose Russian article inspired by Sukhomilov in early June fanned the flames anew and made even Bethmann realize the gravity of the danger: "If so far only the most extreme circles of Pan-Germans and militarists charged Russia with premeditating an attack in the near future, now even more sensible politicians begin to follow this line." The outbreak of new armament fever might even force the cautious chancellor's hand. [48]

As Russo-German antagonism threatened to erupt over any trivial incident, Bethmann sought to strengthen relations within the Triple Alliance: "I consider a clear word to Vienna absolutely mandatory. In its entire policy Austria is beginning to emancipate itself from us somewhat too strongly and must *meo voto* be reined in time." Although William II theatrically assured Archduke Francis Ferdinand of his "Nibelungen loyalty," the chancellor was profoundly disturbed by the Austrian inability to find a modus vivendi with Serbia, "but hoped for a change for the better in this regard." Minimizing the gravity of the Austro-Serbian antagonism, the

German chancellor attempted to dissuade the Ballplatz from making "the future unification of Montenegro with Serbia . . . a question of prestige." Lukewarm toward the Prince of Wied, the newly appointed ruler of strife-torn Albania, the Wilhelmstrasse only reluctantly agreed to a Bulgarian loan. To salvage its Balkan scheme, Bethmann attempted to mediate between Athens and Constantinople in the question of the Greek islands. At the same time he strove to "avoid everything through which the actions of the Triple Alliance would be brought in opposition to the powers of the Triple Entente." Although "he considered the danger of war slight in the near future," the chancellor agonized over the developments in the Southeast. "Rumania is completely antagonized by Austria and Russia is assuming a strong stance in case of a recurrence of the Balkan crisis. If Austria once again embarks upon a prestige policy without backing it up, things can become quite serious," he warned Eisendecher in April of 1914. "Vienna keeps flirting with Sofia—of course without success in the pinch—and cannot get along with Serbia, does not understand that Serbia will finally have to reach the Adriatic anyhow, and thereby provokes, in case of emergency, the opposition of all the Balkans along with the Russians and perhaps finally even Turkey." Concerned not only about the floundering Balkan policy of the Dreibund but also about the danger of a general war, Bethmann concluded: "We must not let this fate overtake us, but fighting against it is hard." [49]

Nevertheless the chancellor refused to panic as long as he was assured of British cooperation. "The ambassadorial conference is pitiful, but it has brought us quite close to England. Of course H.M. wanted to destroy all this once again with a new naval law; Lichnowsky paddles on the surface of the waves, but I do not want to rob him of the illusion that he has created the ocean. So far he is doing well," the chancellor confided to his friend Eisendecher. "Grey is full of the best intentions, but so entangled in Entente policy that we ought to be glad if at least he restrains Russia and France. And that he does." Although cooperation in Balkan matters "was worth more than any naval agreement or political understanding," the unresolved naval question and the trade rivalry limited the rapprochement. "Germany had gradually grown up to be a really Great Power in every sense, especially commercially," Bethmann explained privately to Lord Granville. "A really Great Power with a seaboard could not be a *Landratte;* she *must* have a fleet, and a strong fleet," not just for defense of her colonies "but for the general purposes of her greatness." Since the chancellor fundamentally accepted this credo of navalism, only attempting to modify its form, Winston Churchill's proposal for a naval holiday, as well as renewed informal feelers for limiting naval armaments, fell on deaf ears. But because Germany could only expand commercially with British sufferance, Bethmann suggested "that we should get into the habit of talking more openly and frankly to each other and that we should work together when questions of common interest arise." [50]

The subsequent practical negotiations centered on the eventual division of the Portuguese colonies, an important step toward a German Central Africa, and on the controversial extension of the Bagdad Railway to the Persian Gulf. Because of the hard bargaining of reluctant financial, shipping, and colonial interests, the negotiations, conducted chiefly by the first secretary of the London embassy, Richard von Kühlmann, and only loosely supervised by the chancellor, proceeded slowly. "Without concrete reasons, I have the vague feeling that the improvement of our relations with England has not been reversed but halted temporarily," Bethmann noted dejectedly in the summer of 1913. "It was clear to me from the beginning that this path would be long and arduous." Nevertheless, agreement between Berlin and Paris on spur lines, "reasonable but not spectacular for either side," gradually brought London to terms. "I hope that we will finally be able to agree with England on Bagdad," the chancellor sighed in February 1914. "But the British are tenacious and Lichnowsky often too impatient. Life could be bearable if people were not quite so unreasonable." Two months later he noted more optimistically: "We are making quiet progress with England. But she is very unyielding in her desire not to cold-shoulder France, which is always piqued at the smallest things." [51]

When the compromise on the future partition of Angola was initialed in the spring of 1914, Bethmann could not cash in on his success: he was afraid to appear the dupe, since the British government wanted to publish the Treaty of Windsor guaranteeing Portugal's possessions at the same time. "Well! I do honestly think that public opinion would be upset and that the chancellor's enemies in the Reichstag, always on the lookout for grievances against him, would make hostile speeches and use the opportunity to add a few more nails to his official coffin," Ambassador Goschen predicted.

But a growing group of Liberal Imperialists, following Hans Plehn's slogan "Weltpolitik and no war!" and seeing Germany as "junior partner of the British Empire," agreed with Lichnowsky's justification "that the new treaty can be called an important success of [the chancellor] not only as a further step forward toward our colonial desires but as a significant practical result of the much discussed rapprochement." However, renewed Balkan tensions and rumors of an Anglo-Russian naval agreement tested cooperation between London and Berlin more severely than did anticipated domestic criticism of the colonial accords. "If we both act together as guarantors of European peace, which *as long as we follow this goal according to a common plan* neither Entente nor Triple Alliance obligations shall prevent, war will be avoided," Bethmann instructed Lichnowsky twelve days before Sarajevo. "Otherwise any number of secondary conflicts of interest between Russia and Austria might light the torch of war. A farsighted policy must consider this alternative beforehand." Despite the improvement of the Anglo-German political atmosphere, in June 1914 Bethmann had nothing more tangible than the hope, "Sometimes you [Count Lichnowsky] see things somewhat too pessimistically if you believe that in case of war England will *undoubtedly* be found on France's side against us." [52]

Because the chancellor himself found time to systematize his actions only after the war, the power-political logic of his apparently self-contradictory foreign policy is best seen in the contemporary writings of his foreign policy assistant in the chancellery, Kurt Riezler. Steeped in an idealism tempered by Darwin and Nietzsche, the speculative *Legationsrat* characterized the socioeconomic dynamics behind German imperialism: "A young nation of enormous energy and capacity with a rapidly growing population has awakened to activity. It is making immense progress in the economic realm; its interests enlarge and reach overseas. . . . External necessity and inner vitality force it to engage in Weltpolitik." Echoing the convictions of his generaton, he continued: "Germany cannot allow the areas still open for world political activity to be closed. Accompanied by short-lived success, any attempted exclusion will fail in the long run because of our real power and immense drive." [53] Although he deplored the dangerous political immaturity of his countrymen, Riezler optimistically believed "in the possibility of parallel expansion," allowing European powers to share in the spoils of Africa and Asia: "We live in an age when new countries can still be divided." Because of such opportunities, "Germany centered its Weltpolitik on economic penetration and gained undeniable successes, as is shown by its rapidly increasing trade." Since "risks have grown more than spoils," he asserted that "the present course of the great powers must generally be called a policy of postponing warlike confrontations." Developing an embryonic theory of deterrence, Riezler argued that "wars are no longer fought, only calculated—and the result of the calculations today decides, as once did battles, the advantages or disadvantages for either side." The only major danger of open conflict was either "dire necessity" or "a government's exaggerated bluffing, i.e. *festgebluff*, that it can no longer withdraw, even if that were correct policy. Personal interests, ambition of the governments, or the expected furor of the nationalists can cause a war which objective interest alone would never have justified." Because of this fear of faulty brinkmanship, Germany could only follow Bethmann's moderate imperialism: "In our age victory belongs to the steady, tenacious, and gradual achievement of small successes and a policy which does not insist on prematurely reaping its outward advantage and which executes its movements with power but without provocation." Denouncing this rational economic imperialism as weakness, the Pan-German journalist Franz Sontag countered bitterly: *"Now as before we believe in the liberating deed of a single man, in the victorious genius of that statesman who will once again lead his German people to such heights as when Otto the Unique's mighty genius raised it to a Great Power."* [54]

In his own infrequent statements on Weltpolitik, Bethmann Hollweg claimed "that he had to conduct a policy without a definite, great and tangible goal," because of the irrationality of public opinion and the insufficiency of Germany's economic base. Though personally preoccupied with cautious *Kontinentalpolitik,* he "generally agreed" with Walther Rathenau's fanciful vision of a Middle European customs union and a future Anglo-German alliance, with the goals of Central Africa and Asia Minor complemented by domestic liberalization. To prove that he, too, embraced German expansion, albeit in the indirect manner advocated by the Liberal Imperialists, Bethmann released in December 1913 a letter to his friend, the historian Karl Lamprecht, calling for an "external cultural policy." Like France and England, "Germany must embark upon this path if it wants to conduct a world policy." Because "we are not yet securely conscious of our culture as our essence and national ideal," he believed "that the importance of this task is still too little known to us. We are a young people and perhaps still have too much naive faith in violence, underestimate the finer means, and do not yet understand that what force conquers, force alone will never hold." Himself content with economic and cultural gains, Bethmann was nevertheless propelled toward a more militant stand by the hubris of Wilhelmian elites. "Don't you think that there is a public opinion in Germany which is easy to inflame in questions in which patriotism and self-interest combine?" Bethmann unburdened himself to Jules Cambon. "At any rate be fair enough to admit that I seek to arouse it as little as I try to follow it." Nevertheless, this imperialist mood demanded tangible success: "France has pursued an imperial policy for forty years. . . . During this time passive Germany did not follow this example, but today it needs a place in the sun." Though employed as a tactical argument to prompt French concessions, the chancellor's reference to "the legitimate reward of a growing organism" betrayed his agreement with the Wilhelmian conviction that demographic and economic growth "condemn Germany to expand abroad in some way." Bethmann, too, was spellbound by the glittering mirage of Weltpolitik, even if he pursued it with more moderate means. But did the chancellor's espousal of liberal imperialism imply that he irrevocably steered Germany and Europe toward war? [55]

Agreeing with the title of the French revanchist tract, *Le Germanisme encerclé*, Bethmann openly called Germany's external situation grave when speaking to Lerchenfeld in late June 1914. The failure of an agreement with London over the Benguella railroad in Angola, shrinking capital for political export, the slowdown of the economic boom, anticipated difficulties in German trade policy, Russia's immense armaments, and the excitement of public opinion, all contributed to a crisis psychology and a willingness to look for extreme solutions in Berlin. In April the presidium of the Pan-German League prophesied doom: *"France and Russia prepare the decisive battle against the German Empire and Austria-Hungary and both intend to fight* as soon as they consider the moment opportune." But despite his propensity for martial phrases, William II warned against incidents that might spark an explosion; "therefore *greatest reserve and caution must be the general principle of our policy.* . . .

Whatever the situation, He, *the Emperor, would never unleash a preventive war.*" Nevertheless, the general staff "and many military men consider the present moment still favorable for fighting the irrevocable conflict," and more plainly "want preventive war." In spite of Moltke's desire for a preemptive strike, despite growing business clamor for a showdown, and despite a widespread public impatience with the unspectacular methods of Bethmann, the tsarist ambassador, Sverbejev, was convinced "that the Berlin cabinet does not share the views of the belligerent circles of Germany, who, as I am told, desire to bring about an immediate warlike confrontation with Russia, and that it would prefer to try all peaceful means to reconcile our interest before taking a decisive step." Although the obstacles to peace were growing everywhere in Europe, war was by no means inevitable. In the halcyon summer of 1914 the Russian ambassador concluded optimistically, "I do not doubt that the German government is strong enough to be able to curb the warlike tendencies of the German chauvinists." [56]

Not because of "theoretical leanings towards peace, but [from] considerations of a thoroughly practical nature," Bethmann rejected the idea of preventive war. Refuting Pan-German General Gebsattel's accusations "that our foreign policy . . . strives to maintain peace *at any price* and thereby undermines the dignity and honor of the German Empire," the chancellor irately rebutted: "In no case has the honor and dignity of Germany been violated by another nation. Who desires war without such cause must do so for vital interests that cannot be reached without war," such as the Iron Chancellor's goals in 1864, 1866, and 1870. "Bismarck drastically condemned any prestige policy as un-German. He and we have seen where it leads with Napoleon III." In early summer of 1914 Bethmann did not consider these conditions fulfilled. Already during the height of the war scare of December 1912 his friend Oettingen remarked in his diary: "Bethmann *hopes* that war can be avoided and would consider it a great misfortune. It would mean the outbreak of revolution in Russia." To be sure, war was a legitimate means in his political arsenal. As a nineteenth-century cabinet diplomatist he dismissed "arms limitation between two countries who may have to defend their honor and independence against each other as chimerical." Unable to halt it, he feared the grave consequences of the arms race: "We are reaching the point where the resources of the states will be exhausted and neither their population nor their finances will be sufficient for the necessary sacrifices." Not political idealism, but realism conceived as raison d'état, in the form of pursuit of traditional Kontinentalpolitik broadened into a primarily economic Weltpolitik, made Bethmann strive for peace. "In any war which is unleashed without compelling reason, not only the Hohenzollern crown but the future of Germany is at stake," he eloquently warned the rash crown prince. "Certainly our policy must be led boldly. But to rattle the sabre at any diplomatic entanglement without having honor, security, or the future of Germany endangered is not only bold beyond reason, but criminal." [57]

Because of Bethmann's policy, the deadly scenario of "Michael Wagebald's" *Europe in Flames: The Future German War* remained fiction for the half-decade preceding 1914. "Father! Father! It is war and the British have landed," the book's hero, Niels Hansen, shouts in alarm. "The French have blown up the German cruiser *Frega* off Azemmour with torpedoes . . . [We march] against the hereditary enemy, nobody knows if against them alone, probably also against the Russians." All too soon these words would no longer be the fever dreams of patriotic youth. The outbreak of fighting in early August, the kaiser's promise—"petty discord and egotistical strife pale before the great tasks of the present, and in our soul glows the holy image of the German fatherland"—as well as the Socialist vote for war credits, bore a fatal resemblance to what was to come. But *"Not a single ship of the proud fleet with which Old England ruled the Atlantic saw its home again,"* the magnificent paper victories over France and Russia, and the cutting off of the Suez Canal were to remain elusive visions. Alliance with England, colonial cooperation, inclusion of Holland in the German Empire, ten billion francs as indemnity from France, German rule over Morocco, internationalization of Egypt, gains for German allies, and creation of a "United States of Europe"—what a grim *pax Germanica* to be! William's decision *"to be happy as ruler of a great, free and rich people which had won the right to cooperate, to counsel, and to complete the* [inner] *structure of the empire,"* was a feverish fantasy of naval and liberal imperialism shared by millions of Germans in all walks of life. A reform conservative, Bethmann refused to imbibe much of this chauvinist poison and strove for a moderate alternative in keeping with the basic ideological and economic demands of his time. But, with his reluctant assistance, the nightmare was to turn into a frightful reality.[58]

CHAPTER 6

The Illusion of Limited War

As one of the principal actors in the drama that unleashed World War I, Chancellor Bethmann Hollweg preferred to emphasize the cosmic causes of this conflict, which devoured not only Imperial Germany but the entire nineteenth-century European world.[1] In order to preserve domestic unity, based on the myth of enemy attack he implored Prince Bülow to counteract public criticism of Germany's role in the July crisis. "Charges that this war could have been avoided, that it could have been fought under more favorable auspices, or that it borders on a preventive war leave a sting whenever they are made, and implant themselves firmly the less people consider the larger relationships of history." Reminding his predecessor of his own share in the responsibility, the chancellor explained the catastrophe by the general hypertrophy of imperialism:

> All that belongs to the distant past and led to the coalition against us with and without our guilt; all that increasingly isolated Germany's might while Austria declined and the Entente grew; all that forced us to adopt a policy of utmost risk, a risk that grew with each repetition, first in the Moroccan crisis of 1905, then in the Bosnian quarrel, and once again in the Moroccan confrontation—all these developments seem insignificant compared to the momentous impact of the present [struggle], until a later, peaceful time will slowly recognize the reasons for this fate that is too colossal to have its origin in singular events.

Since he rejected attributing blame for "the failure of reconciliation with England and France on the shortcoming of my personality," Bethmann liked to believe that "this world cataclysm was conjured up, not only through the collective guilt of nations but also through the collective guilt of men and parties within them." But this indictment of the imperialist fever in general and the hubris of Wilhelmian Germany in particular could not silence the nagging question: What personal part did the fifth chancellor play?[2]

Obsessed by his complicity in the great conflagration, Bethmann remained ambivalent about the failure of German policy in July 1914 until the day he died. While firmly denying "the misleading contention that we *encouraged* Austria to attack Serbia, which sounds as if we had taken the initiative, and that is absolutely false," he nevertheless admitted to intimate friends: "This war torments me. Again and again I ask if it could have been avoided and what I should have done differently. All nations are guilty; Germany, too, bears a large part of the responsibility." The suffering of millions of soldiers and civilians may have prompted such soul-searching, but the deeper source of this anguish was his awareness that his own aims and mistakes had heavily contributed to the disastrous outcome. To Conrad Haussmann's question about General Max Montgelas's accusations against the Central Powers, Bethmann replied candidly: "Lord, yes, in a certain sense it was a preventive war. But only if war was hanging over our heads, if it had to come two years later much more dangerously and inevitably, and if the military said today war is still possible without defeat, but no longer in two years," then Germany had no choice but to fight. "Yes, the generals," he sighed, revealing that his hand had partially been forced. "It could only have been avoided by a rapprochement with England, that is still my conviction. But after we had decided for a [common] policy with Austria, we could not desert her in that crisis." And yet in opposition to Kurt Eisner's and Roderich Gooss's revelations from German and Austrian archives, the exchancellor maintained stubbornly: "We honestly and with the greatest effort worked for mediation and peace. May each of Germany's enemies be able to say the same!" [3]

The paradox of Bethmann's aggressively defensive self-consciousness, which reflected the contradictory nature of Wilhelmian society, is largely resolved in the eloquent diary of Kurt Riezler, which provides an impressionistic but accurate record of his moods and motives.[4] "The chancellor [is] a child of the first half of the nineteenth century and an heir of a more idealistic culture," Riezler explained Bethmann's anachronistic probity and sense of measure on the basis of his intimate acquaintance with him. "Strange that with his old-fashioned humanitarianism, his seriousness and incapacity for ostentation, he could have come to power in this neo-Teutonic milieu and could assert himself successfully against politicians and wire-pullers. But he is not at all unequivocal. His cunning is as great as his bungling. Both alternate." Although the popular stereotype of the "philosopher of Hohenfinow" aptly fit Bethmann's aloofness and pensiveness, the chancellor's assistant never underestimated the craftiness and tenacity hidden behind the furrowed brow. "Curious man. He is not at all winning, except with excellent wine, music, and deep conversation. But he possesses much that is morally appealing. However, that is no attraction for our politicians. Unbearable in many ways, [he is] admirable in great things. Privately, I ask his forgiveness for many a judgment," Riezler confessed to himself. Like many contemporaries, "I have basically always thought him a clever and cultured bureaucrat. That is totally wrong. In breadth and independence of mind, he is a great man. He is completely free of prejudice and narrowness and quite independent of public opinion and outside influences." Gradually the surprised assistant grew to understand his mentor. "His judgment forms quite independently. He says only things unsaid and unheard. If only he would not suffer from the vexing habit of faking doubt when he has a firm conviction of his own, and of saying things that he himself does not believe in order to be contradicted." Tired of the shopworn platitudes of Wilhelmian politics, his restless intellect strove to grasp the full complexity of each question. "Only in really severe crises does he cease to accompany his actions with complaints." Indeed, Bethmann seemed to thrive on adversity: "If he is told bad news, he becomes tough and tenacious. But otherwise he makes such a pitiful face—he doesn't even notice it himself." [5]

Revealing Bethmann the man as well as the public figure, Riezler's penetrating characterization not only captures his enigmatic personality but also his anachronistic political style. More a cabinet diplomatist and bureaucratic administrator than a dynamic mass leader, the chancellor lacked charisma and political intuition, for which he compensated with brilliant analysis, accomplished tactics, and a passionate commitment to long-range goals. His assistant was continually struck by "his great mind and his inability to cope with the routine of power. He radiates respect, not fear, and strangely enough, no warmth and friendship." Neither inspiring a devoted following nor amassing a party by patronage, and rejecting the tempting but irresponsible appeal to chauvinism, Bethmann addressed himself to the nation's best minds and instincts in striving for a lasting consensus. In contrast to more politically adept contemporaries, the chancellor knew that neither Machiavellian intrigues nor technical finesse, but a clear grasp of the basic needs of the majority of the people—which at times contradicted their immediate wishes—was the essence of statecraft. But in spite of this disdain for petty politicking and diplomatic finagling, Bethmann possessed a considerable instinct for political power, which made him outlast in office such rivals as Tirpitz, Falkenhayn, Bülow, Dallwitz, and Loebell. Nevertheless, he was beset by one other dangerous weakness besides his incapacity for mass interest politics: "The chancellor has absolutely no talent for getting along with the military, for impressing them and for getting information from them." Although he was continually advanced in the Prussian reserves due to William II's insistence that a chancellor must have a respectable military rank, Bethmann abhorred the fist-thumping of the officer corps; but his respect for their technical expertise made him hesitate to interfere in areas not his own. Despite his "personal difficulties, his handicaps in dealing with people," the chancellor's entourage agreed that "he is by far the best, possesses the greatest perspective, enthusiasm, intelligence, and culture, and especially political judgment." [6]

In contrast to his earlier cheerfulness, Bethmann viewed Germany's general political situation in early June 1914 "not at all optimistically." Apparently the Liman von Sanders affair and the lack of assurance of British neutrality in a future Balkan conflict "did not fail to have an impact upon the chancellor," Lerchenfeld reported with some concern. Because of traditional British enmity against the strongest continental power, Bethmann expected to find London "on the side of our enemies" and predicted, "the war of the future will not be concluded as rapidly as in 1870 because of the armies of millions." Although it was reassuring "that France [did] not want war" despite the reintroduction of three-year military service, the chancellor thought "Russia more dangerous. There the Pan-Slav dream could so turn their heads that they might do something stupid some day." In spite of his fear of growing Russian armaments, which necessitated hundreds of millions of additional expenditures in Germany, Bethmann agreed with Lerchenfeld that the hour for a preemptive strike had passed in 1905: "The kaiser did not want [a preventive war then] and will not lead one" in the future. In contrast to a widespread misconception of the Right, which "expected a war to turn domestic politics in a conservative direction," the chancellor anticipated "that a world war with its un-foreseeable consequences will greatly strengthen the power of social democracy, since it preaches peace and will topple many a throne." While irritated by the Socialist refusal to join in the *Kaiserhoch* (hail to the kaiser), Bethmann did not provoke a conflict over this issue to allow the gradual domestication of Bebel's party to con-tinue, but his lingering resentment of the Zabern vote of no-confi-dence colored his remarks "that he would not have considered it a special misfortune if [some other] question had necessitated the dis-solution of the Reichstag." To escape rising internal opposition to his moderate Weltpolitik and postpone a British military commit-ment to the Franco-Russian alliance, Bethmann warned Lichnowsky in mid-June: "It is obvious that increased activity of the German chauvinists and arms fanatics would hinder Anglo-German coopera-tion as much as an ambiguous position of the English cabinet secretly favoring Russia and France." Despite the initialing of the Bagdad, Congo, and Angola accords, he feared that the conclu-sion of an Anglo-Russian naval agreement would "have produced unforeseeable consequences because of the nervous tension in which Europe has found itself for the last years." Although he faced in-creasing difficulties both at home and abroad, Bethmann stubbornly clung to the leitmotiv of his foreign policy, "the idea of a common mission of England and Germany to assure peace." [7]

The desired clarification of Anglo-German relations was abruptly cut short by Princip's shots at Sarajevo. "The Archduke Inheritor [Francis Ferdinand] and his wife have just become the victims of a revolver assassination," a terse telegram informed William II on June 28, 1914. "The dynasty of Hapsburg Lorraine really is a house of Atreus, stumbling from catastrophe to catastrophe," Foreign Sec-retary Jagow wrote after his return to Berlin. "The political effects are difficult to foresee, because too little is known about the new successor. The old emperor's life is ebbing and his will power and resolution, never very strong, are exhausted—and the heir is very young." Whatever the diplomatic repercussions, the domestic con-sequences were clear: "Meanwhile the empire dissolves more and more, losing coherence and prestige internally and externally. A strong hand is needed to gather the reins; but will the young prince possess it?" As a sincere monarchist revolted by the heinous crime, Bethmann agreed that a fundamental blow had been struck against

Austria and that Serbia had to bear the onus of an "undeniable moral co-responsibility." But though "he looked very serious," Admiral Müller did "not believe that he feared already at that time that Sarajevo could be the cause of the great war." [8]

Although the gravity of the threat to Austria's existence was immediately clear, the initial response of the German government was hesitant, groping, and generally peaceful. To his predecessor Bülow, the chancellor admitted the "undeniable existence of unfounded nervousness in the whole world," but insisted on the necessity for a "calming policy." Indeed, "the crime of Sarajevo was reprehensible, but politically it would have the positive result of thoroughly disgusting leading Russian circles, and especially the tsar, with the Serbs." On June 29, Bethmann attempted to disabuse the Austrophobe and often amateurish Count Lichnowsky of his all too sanguine picture of the international situation. "The chancellor replied that he could not share my optimistic views. The Russian armaments, concerning which the General Staff had sent him a full report, were assuming proportions that could not but cause uneasiness in Germany." Aside from sharing his concern about the strategic railroads, the scheduled addition of some 900,000 men to the Russian army, and the anticipated difficulties in negotiating the trade treaty, Bethmann told the ambassador that, "according to secret and reliable reports he had received, a naval agreement between Russia and England was being drawn up," in which "English freight steamers were to transport Russian troops to the coast of Pomerania." This instruction to warn Grey against aligning himself openly with the Entente in case of a Balkan confrontation did not yet reveal which policy Bethmann would follow. Hence Saxonian ambassador Lichtenau could report that "here as everywhere there is agreement on the loathsomeness of the crime, but it is believed that no negative consequences for Europe will ensue." [9]

A first straw in the wind, indicating Bethmann's eventual course, was the chancellor's recommendation against the kaiser's planned funeral visit to Vienna on July 2. "This trip was not an act of state or of political necessity, but solely a voluntary show of friendliness going beyond the demands of etiquette," Bethmann persuaded William II. "Apparently the crime of Sarajevo is based upon a widespread conspiracy, and it is well known that assassinations have a suggestive effect upon criminal elements." A second step toward clarifying the ultimate policy was Zimmermann's strongly worded advice to the Serbian chargé that "Serbia should not leave anything undone in order to punish those guilty of the plot," since "given the storm of disapproval which the deed of Sarajevo has provoked in Austria, one cannot predict what will happen if the Serbian government does not fulfill its duty." Most importantly, when Ambassador Heinrich von Tschirschky—in agreement with Bethmann's initial impulse—"used every opportunity to warn [Berchtold] emphatically and seriously against overly hasty steps," William II exploded: "Who has empowered him to do that? This is very stupid! It does not concern him at all, since it is only Austria's business how it wants to react." To this reprimand he added the histrionic demand, "The Serbs have to be straightened out *and soon!*" Upon hearing of the royal displeasure, the aging ambassador assured Emperor Francis Joseph "that Germany would firmly back Austria, if its vital interests were imperiled." Even before the momentous decision for unequivocal endorsement of Viennese action had been formally made, the mood in the German capital began to change in favor of a stronger stand.[10]

"Although he hesitated initially, the chancellor now accepts the view" that Germany must "support Austria with all means," Badensian chargé Koester described Bethmann's reversal. No evidence has survived regarding the arguments and counterarguments in the informal consultations between William II and his top civilian and military advisors during the first sultry July days of 1914. Only the configuration of forces is clear. In retrospect, Bethmann "admitted that our military men were fully convinced that now they could *still* come out of a war victoriously; but in a few years, ca. 1916, after the completion of the Russian railroads, [this would] no longer be so. Of course this influenced our treatment of the Serbian question." In early July 1914 the army leadership and the General Staff clearly advocated preventive war, although the navy brass, unsure of the battle fleet, counseled peace. Under this pressure from his generals William II, frightened and angered by Serbian insolence, abandoned his previously pacifistic stand and favored some strong, dramatic action, thus removing an important obstacle to war. Within the Foreign Office some diplomats, like the tough [*nassforsch*] undersecretary Zimmermann, also leaned toward a militant stand, thinking it "extraordinarily desirable that Austria rap Serbia's knuckles with a few army corps." Others, like British specialist Wilhelm von Stumm, doubted the likelihood of English involvement, later admitting: "I made an error in 1914 and counseled Bethmann mistakenly." Beyond the Wilhelmstrasse loomed the increasingly chauvinist majority of the Reichstag and the nationalist press who, except for the Social Democrats, "fell more and more under the spell of imperialism and thereby pushed . . . Germany over the precipice, often thinking the idea of a world war too preposterous to come true." Although banking, shipping, and commercial circles generally abhorred the disruption of war, heavy-industrial interests as well as agrarian groups stood to gain from wartime production and had long supported chauvinist agitation. But most importantly, the growing frustration of moderate opinion with his limited Weltpolitik contributed to Bethmann's conviction that "Germany had no options left." [11]

When William II recalled Bethmann from Hohenfinow to act upon Francis Joseph's appeal, transmitted by Count Hoyos, the die had already been cast. Briefing the departing Lichnowsky on Hoyos's bellicose statements, Zimmermann "seemed to think if war was now after all inevitable for us in consequence of the unfriendly attitude of Russia, it would perhaps be better to have it now rather than later." During the late afternoon of July 5, Bethmann and Zimmermann went to the Neues Palais, and found William II surrounded by Adjutant General Plessen, Chief of the Military Cabinet Lyncker, and Minister of War Falkenhayn. Although the kaiser knew that Vienna intended "to confront Belgrade with the demand for most thorough satisfaction and to march its troops into Serbia if it remained unfulfilled," in these informal discussions "the opinion prevailed that the Austrians should move, *the sooner the better,* and that the Russians—although friends of Serbia—will not intervene." The chancellor's description of the ensuing conference between the kaiser and his political advisors is characteristically terse: "The emperor declared he could not deceive himself about the gravity and danger in which Pan-Serbian propaganda has placed Austria. But it would not be up to us to advise our ally how to react to the bloodbath of Sarajevo. Vienna herself had to decide that." Not merely a justification but also a coherent plan for diplomatic action, the argument continued: "We should abstain from direct influence and advice, since we should work with all our means toward the goal of not letting the Austro-Serbian quarrel become an international conflict. But Emperor Francis Joseph should know that we would not desert Austria-Hungary in this serious hour." Not sentimentality "but our own vital interests demand the preservation of Austria. It seemed desirable to him to draw Bulgaria in [to the alliance] as long as that would not alienate Rumania." Since it was based largely on his own and Zimmermann's ideas, Bethmann agreed with William's analysis, only recording, "these opinions of the emperor coincided with my own." Without hesitation, Germany had agreed to support the Austrian goal of "eliminating Serbia, the focus of Pan-Slavist agitation, as political factor from the Balkans." [12]

Predicated upon the belief that England's leaning toward the Entente, "a question of life and death for Germany," made the preservation of Austria as Great Power of cardinal importance, this unconditional German commitment was more than a blank check. Although the "chancellor, who was also in Potsdam, seems to believe as little as I [Minister of War Falkenhayn] that the Austrian government is serious about its recently more forceful language," the decision of July 5 represented a decisive break with Bethmann's previous course of restraint. The following morning the chancellor gave the senile Szögyény one of the most momentous assurances in European history. "Concerning Austria's relations with Serbia, the German government's position is that we must judge what has to be done to clarify the relationship; in this undertaking we can count safely on Germany's support of the monarchy as ally and friend—whatever our decision might be." Bethmann himself explained his dramatic about-face: "Although he had always advised us to get along with Serbia, after the recent events he understood that this was well nigh impossible." While the Austrian ambassador, who was bellicosely inclined, editorialized: "In the further course of the conversation I realized that the chancellor, like his imperial master, considers our immediate intervention against Serbia the most radical and the best solution to our difficulties in the Balkans." To his own representatives Bethmann stressed, rather, the diplomatic offensive in the Balkans and the establishment of a dam against Pan-Slavism, of which the Austrian punishment of Serbia—to be decided in Vienna, not Berlin—would only be one part. The chancellor rationalized in a vein contrary to the tenor of the alliance with Rumania, "H.M. understands that Emperor Francis Joseph considers reconciliation with Serbia impossible, and attempts to counteract the dangers threatening his house and empire from Serbia through an alliance with Bulgaria." Neither "intending to unleash a European conflict nor necessarily bringing it about," this diplomatic strategy seized upon the Sarajevo incident to break the tightening vise of encirclement through a fundamental realignment of Balkan powers. By the adherence of Bulgaria to the Triple Alliance, the addition of Turkey, and the strengthening of dynastic ties with Rumania and Greece, Serbia would be isolated politically and militarily and the Bagdad railway rest secure. The emperor ostentatiously embarked on his northern cruise, Berlin was deserted by high officials, and no noticeable military preparations were begun; but the fundamental step had been taken. Now Europe had to suffer the "consequences of the situation which results from the expected Austrian march into Serbia." [13]

Beyond the crucial decisions, official documents contain no clue that explains Bethmann's diplomatic reversal. When the *Frankfurter Zeitung* predicted on July 9 that Vienna's "diplomatic and political action" against Belgrade would "probably be executed in *short swift strokes,*" the chancellor commented cryptically, "Very good." Only the Riezler diary echoed "the melancholy and restraint in people and landscape" surrounding the chancellor's resolve. Under a starry sky on the veranda in Hohenfinow, Bethmann unburdened his soul: "The secret news which he lets me know conveys a shattering impression. He regards the Anglo-Russian negotiations for a naval agreement and a landing in Pomerania very seriously as last link in a chain. Lichnowsky [is] much too credulous, and could easily be duped by the British." Aside from this impasse in Anglo-German relations, the chancellor feared "Russia's quickly growing military might; after the completion of the strategic [railroads] in Poland our situation [will be] untenable." At the same time "Austria [grows] weaker and more immobile; its subversion from the north and southeast is very far advanced. At any rate [it is] incapable of going to war as our ally for the German interest. The Entente knows that we are consequently completely paralyzed." The failure of Tirpitz's naval attempt and the blockage of Bethmann's economic effort to achieve Germany's metamorphosis from a continental into a world power, called for "grave decisions. The assassination of Francis Ferdinand. Official Serbia incriminated. Austria wants to pull itself together; Francis Joseph's mission to the emperor with an inquiry about the casus foederis" confronted Berlin with "our old dilemma at every Austrian action in the Balkans. If we encourage them, they say we pushed them into it; if we discourage them, they say we left them in the lurch. Then they will throw themselves into the open arms of the Western powers and we shall lose our last powerful ally." In comparison, "this time it is worse than in 1912, because this time Austria is on the defensive against Serbo-Russian intrigues." Even during the initial decisions Bethmann was fully conscious of running a grave risk: "An action against Serbia can lead to world war." [14]

In contrast to the aggressive self-confidence of Wilhelmian officers and businessmen, Bethmann exhibited great reluctance to embark upon this perilous course. "The chancellor expects from a war, however it ends, a revolution of all existing order." Sensing the political and social calcification of the empire, the chancellor sighed, "everything has become so very old." Hence he irately rejected Heydebrand's hope that "a war would strengthen the patriarchal spirit as nonsense," seeing only "hubris and thick fog over the nation, indeed, all over Europe." Similarly, "the chancellor [was] very pessimistic about the spiritual situation in Germany," and deplored the emergence of mass society in all its crassness as "wretched decline of the political surface. Individuals as such are becoming smaller and smaller, and nothing great and true is being said anywhere." Because of his cultural pessimism regarding Germany's intellectual stagnation in the shallow formalism of Wilhelmian arts and letters, Bethmann blamed "the failure on the intelligentsia and the professors." In contrast, "the future belongs to Russia, which grows and weighs upon us as an increasingly terrifying nightmare." Unable to overcome the intellectual malaise of a pretentious idealism prostituted by the cult of force, the chancellor served an antiquated sociopolitical order because he himself was too much a part of the old system. Hence Bethmann fatalistically decided to try to reverse the diplomatic, political, and cultural deterioration of Germany in one bold stroke. Even after the fateful choice, he hoped: "Perhaps the old emperor will not decide [upon action] after all. . . . If war comes from the east, so that we have to fight for Austria-Hungary and not Austria-Hungary for us, we have a chance of winning." Revealing the ambiguities of the blank check, the chancellor would be content with a peaceful victory: "If war does not break out, if the tsar is unwilling, or alarmed France counsels peace, we still have the prospect of splitting the Entente." [15]

Instead of waiting for a diplomatic defeat, the erosion of Germany's position in the Balkans, and the loss of its last dependable ally, Bethmann Hollweg embarked upon a policy of calculated risk. Under the pressure of a military clamoring for preventive war, a bellicose emperor, a swelling imperialist public, and Viennese claims that "this was the last moment to restore Austrian authority in the South-Slav world," the chancellor decided on a diplomatic offensive which, as in the confrontations of 1908, 1911, and 1913, would test the Entente's will to war. "If the [opportunity] was not to be lost irrevocably, it had to be grasped firmly and quickly," he later stated with surprising candor. "War against Serbia was thereby possible and probable. We have not excluded it in our instructions but neither have we demanded it nor forced it upon them." The diplomatic-military strategy could produce three distinct results. First, a localized Balkan war, resulting in a diplomatic triumph, a realignment of the Balkan states, and a resounding defeat for the Triple Entente. Equally likely seemed a continental war, engulfing Russia, France, Germany, and Austria. In such a conflict, Germany stood a good chance of winning and of breaking the iron ring of encirclement. Although not to be undertaken lightly, such a continental war might ease the Russian pressure from the east, Germanize Alsace-Lorraine once and for all, revitalize Austria, and remove the roadblocks to economic expansion. Only the last alternative, a worldwide struggle, was fraught with serious dangers, since the entry of Great Britain or that of any other non-European power might upset the carefully calculated odds. The young Liberal Imperialist Riezler stood more fully behind the gamble than the scrupulous Bethmann: "Our position is desperate. If war should come and the veils fall, the whole nation will follow, driven by need and danger. Victory and liberation. The chancellor thinks I am too young not to succumb to the fascination of the unknown, the lure of the new, the great movement. For him this action is a *leap into the dark* and, as such, the *most serious duty*" (my italics). His grim resolution to face even extreme consequences, directed toward the maintenance of Germany's continental position and secondarily toward its Balkan interests, constituted only an indirect grasp for world power by breaking the psychological grip of the Entente and opening the path to peaceful economic Weltpolitik.[16]

After the fateful decision of July 5, Bethmann's chief concern became the smooth execution of the diplomatic offensive in the Balkans. Four days later, Bethmann explained his strategy to Vice-

Chancellor Delbrück: "In case of warlike complications between Austria and Serbia, he and Jagow believed that it would be possible to localize the conflagration." To a question about economic preparedness he replied, "It would not be permissible to take any measure from our side which could be interpreted as preparation for a coming war." Since this diplomatic position rested on maintaining the appearance of Austrian independence, the focus of decisions now shifted to Vienna, where the chief of staff, the foreign minister, and the Hungarian prime minister debated which measures should be taken against the Serbian threat. "In Austria there seem to be differences between Berchtold and Count Stephan von Tisza over the method" of punishment, Riezler recorded on July 11. "It is hardly possible to guide their hand from Berlin. Apparently they want a short ultimatum and in case of Serbian rejection, intervention. They seem to need an eternity to mobilize. Sixteen days says [Conrad von] Hoetzendorff. This is very dangerous," since Bethmann's scenario relied upon a "rapid fait accompli and afterwards friendliness toward the Entente, then the shock will be weathered. The Serbian intrigues must be exposed with solid and overwhelming evidence which cannot be questioned." Although the chancellor, vacationing in Hohenfinow, remained in touch with Austrian intentions, he did not intervene until his return to the Wilhelmstrasse during the critical phase of the confrontation.[17]

Despite the assurance of unconditional German support, the Austrian statesmen still controlled their own actions. "Berchtold debates the timing, whether before or after Poincaré's visit to Petersburg. Better before, because then there is a greater chance that France, suddenly frightened by the specter of war, will counsel peace in Russia," Riezler wishfully reflected upon the Hofburg's hesitations on July 14: "Austria has decided on this course today, but the Hungarian harvest must be gathered first." The Wilhelmstrasse and especially the two ambassadors, Tschirschky and Szögyény, repeatedly urged Berchtold to take speedy action lest Europe intervene in the Austro-Serbian quarrel. "As before our standpoint is that Austria should under no circumstances give in and we let it understand that we will endorse and support its measures toward Serbia." Such pressure strengthened the war party in Vienna; but the slowness of Tisza's conversion to war, the Ballplatz's bungling preparation of the crime dossier, and Conrad's halting military preparations undermined Bethmann's rationale. At the same time, Triple Alliance

partner Italy was "flirting with Russia. It wants Trentino as price
. . . probably even for neutrality. But we cannot inform it beforehand because it will betray everything in Petersburg," Riezler pondered. "We have no choice but to act very confident in Rome. It
is important that Italy believe so much in our victory that it prefers to counsel peace in Paris and Petersburg and gives the Entente
no cause to hope for its help." To strengthen the probability "that
no European power wants to unleash a grand continental war" over
Serbia, Foreign Secretary Jagow affirmed the previous decisions
upon his return from his honeymoon and developed the slogan,
"Under all circumstances, we want the conflict to be localized." [18]

"The chancellor is resolute and silent," determined to do everything in his power to make the strategy of localization succeed. Admitting to the Alsatian state secretary, Roedern, "that the present
European situation is not free from dangers," Bethmann stressed
that "it is imperative to isolate an Austro-Serbian conflict, should
one arise." To prevent the crisis from boiling over, "I have ordered
that any press polemic with France be stopped if possible during the
next weeks, and I must ask you to do the same in Strasbourg." The
hope of a diplomatic victory without a European war speaks clearly
from his conclusion: "If we succeed not only in keeping France itself quiet but also in having it plead for peace in Petersburg, this turn
of events will weaken the Franco-Russian alliance." In the same
vein, Bethmann protested to the emperor that Crown Prince William, "surrounded by completely Pan-German and utterly uneducated officers, has again sent several belligerent telegrams to Pan-
German speakers and writers." Enraged, the chancellor had his
political advisor, Jasper Freiherr von Maltzahn, reprimanded and
asked the kaiser to keep his son from engaging in such "public displays which, after all that has transpired, would be considered
planned provocation by our enemies while it is, according to Y.M.'s
orders, our task to localize the Austro-Serbian conflict. The solution
of this problem is so difficult that even a minor incident can tip the
scales." Similarly, the government press studiously avoided mention
of any German provocation.[19]

Disclaiming any public responsibility for the Austrian démarche
in Belgrade, Bethmann later insisted that "we . . . did not participate in working out the ultimatum, to say nothing of making it
sharper or even dictating it." Nevertheless, Zimmermann informed
Admiral Capelle on July 13 that Vienna intended to insist on "1. A

proclamation by King Peter to his people, calling for a repudiation of the Pan-Serbian agitation. 2. The participation of high Austrian officials in the investigation of the assassination. 3. The dismissal and punishment of all officers and bureaucrats, whose complicity in it is established." More importantly, a circular signed by the chancellor eight days later argued that rejection of the "fair and moderate" Austrian demands would leave Vienna no alternative but to "force their acceptance through strong pressure or military means if need be." But late in the evening of July 22, before the transmission of the ultimatum to Serbia, Bethmann referred to "the wording of the Austrian note, which is, so far, still unknown to me." On this basis, he later explained, "I considered the ultimatum, after I saw it, to be too sharp, and my subsequent policy has fully taken this judgment into account." By keeping Germany out of the actual formulation of the ultimatum to maintain the flimsy pretense of noninvolvement, the chancellor identified himself with the essence of the Austrian note and sacrificed any chance to moderate its flagrant form. Even if Zimmermann, who knew that it was "sharper than usually assumed" hoped that "first general negotiations will begin," there was no escape from the fact that "we have unequivocally assured our support." [20]

On the eve of the Austrian ultimatum, Bethmann pensively reviewed the entire course of his foreign policy: "Did it have to go this far? With his thorough self-criticism, the chancellor reflects about possible mistakes of his own." The key question was, "Should he have insisted upon his offered and rejected resignation when the kaiser decided in favor of Tirpitz in the question of the three battle cruisers in 1912?" But the consequence was clear: "Then Tirpitz or some other politician of his stripe would have become chancellor," and the crisis would have come earlier. "Many say the admiral prevents reconciliation with England only in order to achieve it himself as chancellor. But he will not succeed, because nobody trusts him." Riezler thus puzzled over the inherent contradiction between the German naval program and the political ambitions of its creator. "He is a great organizational talent and a political child, but very adept in machinations and profoundly false." Tellingly, he added, "For Tirpitz the navy is an end in itself." But beyond personal rivalry Bethmann sensed a structural limitation. "Because of the independent policy of the navy it is impossible to conduct a foreign policy with even tolerable support of the press." In a startling insight that reflected his mentor's feelings, Riezler added that any statesman advocating a more moderate course, like the cession of Tsingtao to Japan, "would be torn apart by the press jackals of the navy and would have emperor, nation, and Reichstag against him." The ill-fated heritage of Bülow's "earlier mistakes, the . . . Turkophile policy [directed] against Russia, Morocco against France, and the navy against England, aggravating all and being in everyone's way without hurting anyone enough," was produced by German "planlessness and the need for small prestigious successes seeking to please any trend in public opinion." The chancellor and his assistant were especially bitter about the " 'national' parties who, by clamoring for a [stronger] foreign policy try to shore up and expand their partisan position." This oppressive awareness of domestic pressures that clashed fundamentally with his own desire for peaceful development, reinforced the chancellor's bitter resolve.[21]

When, still in Hohenfinow, Bethmann pondered the diplomatic implications of his decision, he was morbidly fascinated by "Russia's growing demands and incredible dynamism. In a few years they cannot be fended off any longer, especially if the present European constellation continues." To escape the net, which was partially of his own making, Bethmann asked himself "if and how the entire present alliance system might be toppled and changed. But will that be possible? Only if Russia realizes that it has to reach an understanding with us because the Western powers did not back it to the hilt in the Serbian quarrel." But such an eventuality was unlikely, since "it must follow Pan-Slavism, if only for domestic reasons, as counterpoint to the revolutionary currents." The news from Vienna that "because of pressure from Hungary, which wants no increase in Slavic power, the Austrians have decided not to strive for territorial gain in Serbia," was reassuring, as this declaration opened the possibility of "deflecting the Russians from mobilization—onto the path of negotiations." Nevertheless, Riezler disgustedly saw this action as "typical of the entire misery of Austrian policy, which does not want to part with its inherited world power aspirations but is incapable of acting even [in a spirit of] resigned self-preservation." And exposing the fundamental absurdity of the German commitment, he added, "We shall eternally hobble after this weak state and use our youthful power to retard its decline." Because of such resentment, Sazonov's words, "*Si l'Allemagne lâche l'Autriche, je lâcherai immédiatement après la France,*" seemed attractive to the chancellor. "A lasting agreement with Russia would be preferable to an understanding with England. [But] the difficulties are probably even greater, since Russia is far more exacting." The alternative of sacrificing Vienna to a Russo-German accord was discarded as quickly as it had arisen, since Berlin would then have to face the Slavic tide alone. "We must maintain Austria proper. If Russia arouses the South Slavs, we will be lost." Nevertheless, the hope of resurrecting the Three Emperors' alliance died hard: "If the Serbian quarrel passes without Russian mobilization and consequently without war, we might safely come to an understanding with Petersburg, disappointed in the Western powers, since Austria would already be satisfied." [22]

When the pending ultimatum made at least local war likely, internal tactical considerations occupied Bethmann for the first time during the crisis. "How shall the Social Democrats be treated in case of war?" Riezler asked rhetorically. The chancellor intended to draw the single largest party, still vacillating between a pacifist and a patriotic posture, into the Prussian fold by "insuring himself immediately of their views, by negotiating with them in person, and by requiring guarantees from the military against the stupidities of Red-baiters in uniform." In a quickly scheduled conference in the Prussian ministry of war, Vice-Chancellor Delbrück forced a moratorium on the planned arrests of Socialists, Poles, Danes, and Alsatians—a decision that made their later partial loyalty possible. But the generals "apparently will refuse to let martial law and its implementation be wrested from their control," pleading "mobilizations, transports, and secrets." A week earlier Bethmann had argued that military jurisdiction over the empire would have fatal consequences for "unity, depth, and strength of patriotic sentiments," but his initiative was thwarted and the antiquated state of siege law continued in force and later became the legal foundation of the military quasi dictatorship. Now the chancellor set his domestic leitmotiv, "Emphasize the defensive war." Although this slogan was expedient in rallying the dissident elements of German society, Bethmann sincerely believed "if war were to break out, it would come through Russian mobilization, *ab irato,* i.e. before possible negotiations. Then one could hardly talk any longer, because in that case we would have to strike immediately in order to have any chance of winning at all." [23]

The pace of events began to quicken on July 25. "For the last days the chancellor has almost always been on the phone. Apparently [there are] preparations for all eventualities, conferences with the military about which nothing is being said," Riezler jotted down. "The merchant marine is warned. [Director of the Reichsbank] Havenstein [has begun] the financial mobilization. So far nothing could be done out in the open." Nevertheless there was "great commotion." The chancellor unquestionably agreed that "the Austrian note is clumsy, much too long. The first telegrams on the reception of the Viennese démarche by the Great Powers are coming in." It was time for Bethmann to return to Berlin and take charge during the critical phase of the confrontation. "What does fate will?" Riezler speculated. "Alas, fate is blind, unconscious, and tangled in accidents. Whoever dares to seize it holds it." And he added with a sigh often echoed by the chancellor: "This damnably confused modern world has become so complex that it can neither be grasped nor predicted. There are too many factors at once." [24]

In the train back to the capital, the troubled chancellor glanced at "the first telegrams on the effect [of the ultimatum] in Paris, Petersburg, London and Rome. Not unfavorable. It is crucial that Sazonov, though angry, has avoided committing himself. Paris is aghast [at] England's cold shoulder: an Austro-Serbian conflict does not concern me. Italy blackmails." Apparently Vienna and Rome "have not yet agreed. Everything depends upon whether Petersburg mobilizes immediately and is encouraged or discouraged by the West. As always, the chancellor is skeptical about favorable impressions," because of the war party in Russia. In a long discussion about the "German people, its future, its virtues and weaknesses," Bethmann pessimistically "sees a fate greater than human power hanging over Europe and our nation." In Berlin the streets were in turmoil and crowds milled Unter den Linden "awaiting Serbia's answer. The people have not yet quite awakened from the dream of peace, which seems still natural to them, and are incredulous, surprised, and curious." Bethmann's dark forebodings were brushed aside by the reaction of the masses: "At first the chancellor thought only young men would delight in the opportunity for ruckus and excitement and parade their curiosity. But the crowds grew and grew, the songs rang truer, the chancellor was finally deeply moved, touched, and heartened, since similar news poured in from all corners of the empire." Riezler sensed "an immense if undirected drive for action in the people, a longing for great movement, for supporting a noble cause, for showing one's valor." A shy and retiring man, Bethmann was gratified by this spontaneous wave of sympathy, which seemed to vindicate his perilous course. "Since the . . . answer of the Serbian government does not suffice for the Austrian demands, the ambassador, Baron Giesl, has left Belgrade," he cabled William II late in the evening. But he added hopefully that "in Paris and London we are working for the localization of the conflict." Would his calculated risk succeed? [25]

The threat of the third Balkan war in three years made William II override Bethmann's urgent advice and order the German fleet to return. Since he feared another Copenhagen or Port Arthur, the kaiser angrily dismissed his "civilian chancellor's" plea not to provoke an already vacillating tsar, "As long as Russia does not commit a hostile act, I believe that our stand, directed towards *localization,* must *remain peaceful,* too." Shielding the planned Austrian attack on Serbia, Bethmann stressed to Pourtalès that "the preservation of European peace solely depends upon Russia," because of Austria's territorial *désintéressement.* While emphasizing in Vienna the need for an understanding with Italy to "keep Rome in the Dreibund," the chancellor used the first rumors of preparations for Russian mobilization to warn bluntly in London: "Should they be confirmed, we would be forced to take countermeasures against our will. Even today we try to localize the conflict and keep peace in Europe." By direct pressure in Petersburg and by persuasion of Russia's allies, Bethmann hoped to prevent military preparations, since he feared that his generals would force his hand: "Mobilization would mean war and would have to be directed against Russia and France simultaneously, since we know the French obligations towards Russia." On the same day the chancellor proposed to William II that the necessary bills be introduced in the Federal Council, since "a check of the mobilization procedures has shown that it is advisable that the laws to be passed in case of mobilization be prepared so far ahead that they can be presented for decision to the Reichstag immediately after the proclamation." Although on July 26 the prevailing tenor of diplomatic exchanges was still peaceful, growing suspense made Bethmann reiterate the thesis of Russian responsibility. "Only compelled [by dire necessity] will we unleash the sword, but then with the clear conscience that we bear no guilt for the nameless misfortune which war must bring to Europe's peoples." [26]

On the day of the Austrian decision for a punitive expedition into Serbia, "all news points toward war. Apparently there are heavy struggles over mobilization in Petersburg," Riezler noted hastily. Bethmann resolutely clung to the strategy of localization: "We cannot negotiate on the conflict between Austria and Serbia, but perhaps between Austria and Russia." Intent on a decisive Austrian victory and curiously insensitive to the crucial nature of Britain's attitude, the chancellor rejected Grey's conference proposal and pointed toward the possibility of "a direct understanding between Russia and Vienna." Although initially "our attempt to localize the Austro-Serbian conflict was no foolish idea," the essential precondition of the chancellor's plan, Grey's disinterest in the Balkan quarrel, was beginning to erode dangerously. "England's language has changed—apparently London has suddenly realized that the Entente will be torn apart if it is too lukewarm toward Russia. Lichnowsky has completely lost his composure." Now one of Riezler's theoretical possibilities for war was rapidly turning into inescapable reality: "The danger [is] that France and England will commit their support to Russia in order not to alienate it, perhaps without really believing that for us mobilization means war, thinking of it as a bluff which they answer with a counterbluff." But the chancellor was still optimistic in his briefing for the indignant William II, who resented Bethmann's suggestion that, to avoid incendiary demonstrations, he should not appear in Berlin. According to Admiral Müller, "the tendency of our policy is calmness, let Russia put itself in the wrong—but if it has to be, not to shy away from war." In order not to affront Grey and to "look like we are forced into war," Bethmann now transmitted the British plea for negotiations without declaration of war to Vienna, although the conciliatory Serbian answer heightened the German dilemma of diplomatically shielding Vienna's punitive strike without losing British neutrality. There was "immense commotion in the Wilhelmstrasse. Nobody sleeps. I [Riezler] see the chancellor only for seconds. He is completely changed, has not a minute to ponder, and is fresh, active, lively and without anxiety." [27]

When Austria finally crossed the threshold of war on July 28, after half a century of peace, both William II and Bethmann Hollweg, impressed by the adept Serbian reply, became disgusted with Vienna. "This Austrian ambiguity is unbearable. They refuse to inform us of their program, saying *expressis verbis* that the ideas of Count Hoyos for partitioning Serbia are purely private; in Petersburg, they are like lambs, thinking no evil; and in London their embassy boasts about doling out Serbian territories to Bulgaria and Albania," the chancellor scribbled on the margin of a Lichnowsky telegram. Claiming "we are far from seeing the Austro-Serbian conflict as a trial of strength between the two European power blocs," he emphasized that "the declaration of war changes nothing" in German efforts to bring about a meeting of minds between Petersburg and Vienna. Simultaneously he empowered Wangenheim to conclude an alliance with Turkey on the condition that, "should Russia actively participate in the war and thereby the casus foederis arise for Germany toward Austria, it will also apply to Turkey." Nevertheless he warned Tschirschky that because "of the completely negative attitude of the Austrian government we must count upon a gradual reversal of public opinion all over Europe." He should impress upon Berchtold the necessity for negotiating with Russia on the basis of William II's "Halt in Belgrade scheme." Ultimately, he preferred "a modus that allows the realization of the Austrian goal to crush the backbone of greater Serbian propaganda without simultaneously unleashing a world war" and, should war become unavoidable, that at least improved the conditions under which it might be fought. Late in the same evening, a weary Bethmann attempted to persuade Sir Edward Goschen of the same scheme, warning that Russian mobilization might prevent the sole workable remedy, direct Austro-Russian talks, and emphasizing in parting, "War between the Great Powers must be avoided." [28]

Domestically as well as diplomatically, the hour of truth for Bethmann's strategy was inexorably approaching. "The Social Democratic demonstration for peace would be fatal." Because of massive spontaneous protests against the approaching war all over Europe, there was reason to believe that "the Socialists would not fight; of course, there are generals who want to meddle immediately and shoot 'in order to teach the Reds a lesson.' For the first day of mobilization all Social Democratic leaders are scheduled to be arrested." But against military objections, Bethmann succeeded in preventing such a psychological blunder. "Thank God, the chancellor has finally stepped in firmly. Moreover the Social Democrats are being implored from all sides," Riezler sighed in relief. More concretely, "the chancellor secretly negotiated with Albert Südekum and, as Loebell's deputy, William Drews with Hugo Haase." In an unprecedented move, Bethmann drew a leading—if revisionist—Socialist into his confidence with a candid assessment of the international situation. Honoring this gesture, Südekum answered for his party, "Your Excellency's step of directly informing us at this critical juncture has met with full sympathy," and offered the cooperation of the Socialist press with the governmental line. Since Bethmann guaranteed that there would be no detentions, the revisionist leader promised in return "that no action whatsoever (general or partial strike, sabotage, etc.) was planned or need be feared—especially because of our desire to serve peace." Now the chancellor's refusal to proscribe socialism and his increasing cooperation in specific measures were beginning to pay dividends. But because of the need for Socialist support, Bethmann had to exhort the emperor, "In all events Russia must ruthlessly be put into the wrong." [29]

The full effect of the Austrian declaration of war was only felt on July 29, the critical day for the chancellor's calculated risk. Growing more and more impatient to release the Prussian juggernaut, Moltke urged, "For our intended military measures in case of war, it is imperative to find out as soon as possible if France and Russia are willing to run the risk of war with Germany." The Saxon military attaché observed laconically, "It is undoubtedly clear that the chief of general staff favors war while the chancellor holds back." As a small but ill-timed concession, Bethmann sent warnings to Schoen and Pourtalès "that a further continuation of Russian mobilization measures would force us to mobilize and then a European war could hardly be avoided." In a crown council held at Potsdam in the afternoon, Falkenhayn and Moltke pressed for the declaration of "threatening danger of war," which authorized military preparations without technically being mobilization. Because of the chancellor's "very optimistic opinions about the preservation of peace among the Great Powers," only the troops in the staging areas were called back into the garrisons, and nothing was decided "which could be considered a measure based on political tension." Since he could give no clear answer about the likelihood of English intervention due to Zimmermann's and Jagow's contradictory opinions, Bethmann under this military pressure agreed to a premature test of British neutrality, a dangerous concession that went beyond his initial rationale.[30]

Because he was unable to derive a clear picture of London's intentions from the conflicting reports of Lichnowsky, Albert

Ballin, and Prince Heinrich, the chancellor proposed to Goschen, a formula reminiscent of the Haldane negotiations of 1912. "We can assure the English cabinet—*presupposing its neutrality*—that even in case of a victorious war, we will seek no territorial aggrandizement in Europe at the cost of France." To assuage Whitehall's fear of a fundamental shift in the continental balance of power, the chancellor declared that he would respect Dutch territorial integrity, although he refused to commit himself regarding the fate of the French colonies. "Assuming that Belgium does not take sides against us," he would guarantee its boundaries, but added ominously, "We do not know what countermeasures French actions in a possible war might force us to take." His studied silence regarding Belgian sovereignty implicitly revealed the threat to its neutrality contained in Moltke's strategy of outflanking the French, following the ill-fated Schlieffen Plan. But if England assured its "neutral position in the present conflict," his most cherished goal, the chancellor would propose "a general neutrality agreement in the future," the reward for which—stricken on William's opposition—would be a naval agreement. On reading this "infamous offer," the Germanophobe Sir Eyre Crowe noted sarcastically, "the only comment that need be made on these astounding proposals is that they reflect discredit on the statesman who makes them." Though consistent with his earlier policy, Bethmann's precipitous and ill-considered initiative was a desperate attempt to buy off British intervention with the crude promise of the territorial status quo ante in Western Europe. British love for Berlin did not increase at gunpoint, and Jagow sourly conceded to Goschen the next morning that, had Lichnowsky's warning of Grey's intention to keep his hands free arrived some hours earlier, Bethmann would not have committed this blunder.[31]

While military pressure for mobilization and the threat of British involvement seriously imperiled localization, Austrian unwillingness to negotiate with Russia and Italy threatened the Central Powers' moral position. Unless Berchtold made quick concessions, the weary chancellor feared, "we cannot continue to mediate in Petersburg and will be completely dragged in by Vienna. That I do not want, even at the risk of being accused of cowardice." To the Wilhelmstrasse "it was clear from the very beginning that Italy will not go along. They turn and twist the alliance treaty and [Foreign Minister] San Giuliano claims not to have been informed in time." Unconcerned about Rome's support for the Triple Alliance, "the

Austrians (bureaucrats gone mad, stubborn and dumb) string them along instead of offering them the Trentino in one gesture." The Foreign Office agreed "that if they had not procrastinated so long in their dealings with Italy or with the Serbian action, everything could have ended in a diplomatic victory." Revealing the chancellor's calculation, Riezler concluded his indictment of Viennese carelessness: "The Austrian action had to follow immediately after the murder, in the shadow of the crime, not as premeditated act, nor as long-prepared humiliation." Ironically, through stubbornness and misplaced pride, the benefactor of the calculated risk hastened its failure.[32]

Hopes for peace among the Great Powers received another severe blow when "the first news of Russian [partial] mobilization arrived. Now we had to work at top speed. Five days in a row and to five or six o'clock in the morning," Riezler noted in retrospect. The key diplomatic question now became "to what extent Germany should meet the British proposal for mediation." In order to "halt the catastrophe or to put Russia into the wrong at any rate, we must emphatically demand that Vienna begin conversations" with Petersburg, an exasperated Bethmann pleaded in a cadence of ever stronger late-night telegrams. Lichnowsky's warning that England could not remain neutral in a conflict between Austria and Russia, and Grey's hint at guarantees for Austrian security as basis for negotiations, spurred Bethmann to urge the "acceptance of mediation under the indicated honorable conditions." The chancellor's growing apprehension culminated in the historic words, "We are certainly ready to fulfill our obligations as ally, but we clearly refuse to be drawn lightly into a world conflagration by Vienna without consideration of our proposals." Württembergian ambassador Varnbüler summarized the impending collapse of German strategy: "The chancellor still believes in the possibility of a peaceful solution. But the reins are already markedly slipping from the hands of diplomacy into those of the war department." [33]

Although the thirtieth of July offered a respite to the harried chancellor, it only postponed the inevitable denouement. Since Bethmann was now convinced "that England will very rapidly enter the war on the side of the Franco-Russian alliance," everything depended upon the result of German representations in Vienna. More and more desperate, the chancellor strongly urged William

II to continue his correspondence with Nicholas II, and instructed Lichnowsky to have Grey force his proposal upon Russia and prevent the deployment of tsarist troops at the Austrian frontier. At the same time Moltke increased his pressure for German mobilization, jeopardizing the chancellor's plan "to act in such a manner that Russia will appear as the guilty party," in the tradition of the Ems dispatch. Bethmann briefed the ambassadors of the German states on the gravity of the crisis: "We have accepted the role of a mediator and it must quickly be brought to a positive or negative result, because the more time passes, the more Russia and France will gain advantages in their military preparations." Caught in the vise of military insistence on mobilization and Austrian reluctance to compromise, Bethmann grew despondent and admitted that "he himself could not predict the outcome of the decision in the Ballplatz." Convinced that he had done his utmost, he pleaded with Lerchenfeld: "Last evening I most energetically declared to the Viennese cabinet that Germany will not swim in Austria's wake in the Balkans. Should Vienna reply affirmatively, I still do not despair for peace." But the chancellor was too realistic to underestimate the danger. "Sad to say, through quasi-elemental forces and the persistent poisoning of relations among the cabinets a war desired by no one might be unleashed." [34]

In an attempt to defend his strategy, Bethmann claimed to the Prussian Ministry of State in late afternoon: *"Germany and England have undertaken all steps to avoid a European war."* Rejecting threatening military measures, since "one could not embark simultaneously on political and military actions, Bethmann demanded postponement of mobilization until *"the démarche in Vienna is concluded."* Although "we have lost control and the landslide has begun," he nevertheless insisted, "As a political leader I am not abandoning my hope and my attempts to keep peace as long as my steps in Vienna have not yet been rejected." More than ever before he hoped that the Ballplatz would accept Grey's mediation, but despite urgent long-distance phone calls Berchtold refused to negotiate. For the last time Bethmann emphatically instructed Tschirschky that Austria should accept the British proposal, "which maintains its position in every way," lest the odium of world war fall upon Germany. But now the chancellor could no longer hold the bellicose military and vocal chauvinist opinion in check, and upon the first rumors of general Russian mobilization he cancelled his last desperate warning in Vienna. When the military demanded a deadline for the decision about mobilization, a resigned Bethmann could do nothing but set it at noon on July 31. Goschen hardly understood the full significance of the chancellor's admission "that he was pressing the button as hard as he could and that he was not sure whether [the] length to which he had gone in giving moderating advice to Vienna had not precipitated matters rather than otherwise." [35]

By the time the news of the Russian general mobilization was confirmed on the morning of July 31, there was no turning back. "Strange that the unscrupulousness of the Russian grand dukes decided the issue in the enemy camp," Riezler mused four weeks later. "Perhaps they lied to the tsar that Germany had already mobilized. At any rate they wildly exaggerated Russian strength, since they earn millions from war supplies." Reflecting what soon was to become the official German version of events, that Russia had crudely ruptured the negotiations "whose beginning was a diplomatic victory for England," Riezler noted a strange irony in Berlin's last advice to Vienna that "the responsibility for a world war cannot be accepted because of such a small difference." In deep sorrow he contrasted the "chancellor's moral scruples" with the "hypocrisy and coldness of British policy," which had officially refused Bethmann's bid for neutrality during the same morning. At noon Bethmann could no longer hold out against Moltke's demand for mobilization and telephoned William II for authorization to proclaim the condition of impending war [*drohende Kriegsgefahr*]. An unauthorized telegram from the German chief of staff to his Austrian counterpart, General Conrad, had already snuffed out the last hope for moderation in Vienna. Military necessity took over: "Through the Russian measures we have been forced to proclaim the condition of approaching war, which does not yet mean mobilization." Goschen correctly observed that "the chancellor will only conduct war if he is forced to do so." Because of his miscalculations regarding British neutrality, Austrian stubbornness, Russian mobilization, and the bellicosity of his own general staff, Bethmann could no longer escape the logical consequence of the initial risk. "Mobilization must follow, unless Russia ceases any military action against us and Austria within twelve hours and makes a binding declaration to that effect." Since the chancellor bowed to the imperatives of the Schlieffen Plan, the mechanism of military preparation automatically meant war: "Even if a more rational opinion prevailed in Petersburg, we could not wait passively while Russian mobilization was going full speed ahead so that we would be completely behind militarily in case of war." Faulty brinkmanship had tied Bethmann's hands. The ultimata were on their way.[36]

The rest was anticlimactic. Bethmann and the Foreign Office went through the motions of last-minute compromise; but they were directed more toward a closing of ranks at home than toward peace abroad. A curious reversal had taken place. What had begun as a diplomatic offensive with limited aims had passed beyond the bounds of politics into the realm of the military. Not personal weakness, but the hallowed Kommandogewalt reduced the chancellor to the position of being only one of several advisors to the emperor. Moreover, the social structure and political culture of Wilhelmian Germany drowned Bethmann's voice of restraint. In the Bundesrat the chancellor had to admit the bankruptcy of his scheme of splitting the Entente through local Balkan war. "On the basis of my explanations I hope that the council is convinced that Germany worked until the last minute for the maintenance of peace. But we cannot bear Russia's provocation, if we do not want to abdicate as a Great Power in Europe." Upon Bethmann's momentous request that war be authorized should Russia not back down, Bavarian ambassador Lerchenfeld laconically answered, "I agree." [37]

Since the Russian answer had not yet arrived by midafternoon of August 1, Bethmann assented only "after long struggle" to German mobilization. But when a Lichnowsky telegram suddenly held out the hope for British neutrality if France were not attacked, Moltke's entire strategy collapsed, since the discarding of plans for an eastern deployment in April 1913 had rendered war against Russia alone technically impossible. For a fleeting moment Bethmann's calculation appeared to be victorious, "the Triple Alliance ruptured," and world war avoided. But when it became clear that this hope rested on a misunderstanding of the ambassador, gloom returned to the deliberations in the Berlin palace. Now Bethmann could only attempt to prepare for the inevitable diplomatically, by procuring new allies like Turkey and Bulgaria and neutralizing former partners like Italy and Rumania, as well as smaller sympathetic powers such as Sweden. Far into the early morning an incoherent debate between diplomats and generals about the advisability, necessity, and forms of the declaration of war to Russia revealed the fundamental irrationality of decision-making in the Wilhelmian government. Clinging to the realization "that according to international law we must have proof" of war, Bethmann rejected the military desire "to proclaim war not from government to government but from army to army." On the one hand Moltke "did not want any mobilization in which our troops limited themselves to deployment on our borders, but immediate attack," while Falkenhayn and Tirpitz denounced a "declaration of war to Russia as a *political* mistake, not because they thought war could still be avoided . . . but because they feared its negative diplomatic effects." Having brought the country to the brink of disaster, the generals shrank from the political consequences, utterly ignorant of international and domestic repercussions. "I must have a declaration of war against Russia immediately," Bethmann persevered, "since otherwise I cannot pull the Socialists along." But this technical victory over the generals could not gloss over the "general impression: utter confusion of the political leadership. The chancellor has completely lost the reins." [38]

The disintegration of Bethmann's diplomatic strategy continued at an increasing pace during August 2 and 3. Having never decisively objected to "the military's adherence to the Schlieffen Plan" because "offense in the East and defense in the West would have implied the admission that we expected at best a draw," the chancellor rationalized, "With such a slogan no army and no nation could be led into a struggle for their existence." Because of this abdication of responsibility Bethmann had to preside over the liquidation of his British policy as well. Reluctantly he accepted Moltke's argument that "there was no alternative . . . to the march through Belgium" and only insisted that "without a declaration of war to France he could not transmit the ultimatum for Belgium." While the generals wanted to reveal their hand as late as possible to make the coup on Liège succeed, Bethmann knew that the violation of Belgian neutrality would draw the British into the war. Up to this time "the decisions of the army and navy still depended upon the progress of diplomatic negotiations," Lerchenfeld observed sagaciously, but "from here on we can count on military considerations alone being decisive." Moving into the leadership vacuum created by the chancellor's scruples, Moltke sent the Foreign Office a long and detailed memorandum with his wishes for diplomatic preparation of the war. In the early afternoon of August 3, Bethmann took the next inescapable step. Justifying his action by citing French border violations, largely imagined, he telegraphed Schoen in Paris: "France has thereby put herself into a state of war with us." The continental conflagration was complete. But the chancellor feared that escalation would continue. Pleading "military necessity," he attempted to make Grey understand that "wedged in between East and West, we have to use any means to defend ourselves." The anticipated rupture of Belgian neutrality was "no purposeful violation of international law, but the action of a man struggling for his life." Soon the uncertainty in Berlin—"whether we have bought British neutrality by guaranteeing Belgian territory" and the French channel coast—would be dispelled, and only Bethmann's plea remain: "When the iron dice begin to roll, may God help us." [39]

The fiasco of the chancellor's policy in the July crisis was complete when Sir Edward Goschen requested his passport on August 4. Exclaiming repeatedly, "Oh, this is too terrible!" the deeply agitated ambassador inquired whether Bethmann could promise compliance with the British ultimatum. The chancellor reminded him that the foremost goal of his chancellorship had been the establishment of closer relations with England, and reviewed all the phases of the tortuous negotiations, the abortive Haldane mission, and the hopeful compromises. "All these attempts on which, as he well knew, I had worked incessantly were wrested from me. And by whom? by England. And why? because of Belgian neutrality! Could this neutrality, which we violated only out of necessity, fighting for our very existence and with the express assurance that we would repay any damage, that we would not touch the integrity of Belgium in any manner, if Belgium let us march through," he queried dramatically, "could this neutrality and the way in which it was threatened really provide the reason for a world war? Compared to the disaster of a world war, did not the significance of this neutrality dwindle into a scrap of paper?" But such entreaties colored by remorse came too late. Bethmann could no longer reverse the wheel of history, but could only plead: "It was a crime that Russia forced war upon us while we were still negotiating between Vienna and Petersburg, and Russia's and France's war against Germany was enough of a disaster. But this war turned into an unlimited world catastrophe only through England's participation." With the fury of betrayed confidence, the chancellor charged: "It was in London's hand to curb French revanchism and Pan-Slav chauvinism. It has not done so, but has, rather, repeatedly egged them on. And now England has actively helped them. Germany, the emperor, and the government were peace-loving; that, the ambassador knew as well as I. We entered the war with a clear conscience, but England's responsibility was monumental." These reproaches marked not only the collapse of a policy but also of a friendship; both men were deeply moved, and Sir Edward burst into tears. After a few minutes the British ambassador regained his composure and left the chancellery. There was nothing more to say. Now the guns had to speak.[40]

Only in one respect did Bethmann's fears prove unfounded. Although his calculated brinkmanship had failed in diplomacy as well as in foreign opinion, the German people responded to what their chancellor called a defensive war against Russia with great enthusiasm ("The mood is splendid"). Admiral Müller noted with satisfaction in his diary, "The government has shown a fortunate hand in making us appear innocent." During the August days the air along Unter den Linden vibrated with patriotic exultation: "The incomparable storm unleashed in the people has swept before it all doubting, halfhearted, and fearful minds. The foreigners I observed had tears in their eyes. The skeptical statesmen were surprised by the nation," Riezler jotted down excitedly. In contrast to disappointment in England coupled with the unwanted war against Russia and France, this unexpected rallying of the people was heartening to the chancellor. "I found Bethmann himself larger than life in the certainty of his good conscience and the greatness of the tasks confronting him," his cousin recalled. The great emotional upsurge of the masses, milling about the Wilhelmstrasse singing *"Heil Dir im Siegerkranz,"* allowed the chancellor to silence his scruples with patriotic oratory: "Should all our attempts [for peace] be in vain, should the sword be forced into our hand, we shall go into the field of battle with a clear conscience and the knowledge that we did not desire this war." In inimitable Wilhelmian style he added threateningly: "In this grave hour, I remind you of the exhortation of Prince Frederick Charles to the men of Brandenburg: 'Let your hearts beat unto the Lord and your fists upon your enemy.' " [41]

Despite his regret ("it is a misfortune that I could not prevent the war"), Bethmann prepared for the inevitable on the home front with much energy. "Now we must muster all our strength to win it," he confided to Wahnschaffe. Although the Reichstag had no formal power over war and peace, the chancellor needed its approval for war credits and economic measures of mobilization. To turn the hastily called session into a show of unity rather than of partisan bickering, he invited all major party leaders to Wilhelmstrasse 77 to brief them on the situation and to plot parliamentary strategy. Bethmann looked old and gray when he joined the meeting. In "clear and simple, serious and dignified words," he presented the case for preventive defense against Russian attack, interrupting himself occasionally to elaborate in more detail what he could not say in public, "growing so agitated that he banged both fists upon the table. His voice sank to a whisper when he said 'my conscience is clear.'" Bethmann's personal honesty, the tradition of enmity to tsarism, and the pervasiveness of revisionism combined in the heated discussions of the Socialist Reichstag faction to tip the scales toward acceptance of war credits. Although a passionate minority, gathered around Karl Liebknecht, denounced the conflict as an imperialist struggle, the argument in favor of "the necessity of a modus vivendi with the monarchy" in order to channel the surge of democratic patriotism won the day, by a vote of 78-14. Bethmann's long-standing desire to nationalize socialism had been fufilled. But the chancellor's second wish for dissolution of the Reichstag for the duration of the conflict was modified by liberal insistence on the mobilization of public opinion and advice, and instead of being dissolved, parliament postponed itself from session to session. Nevertheless, the representatives "believed that the need of the moment had to override otherwise important constitutional reservations" and declared that the Reichstag would be willing to pass a "general enabling act" empowering the government to take all economic war measures deemed necessary with the consent of the Bundesrat and subject only to parliamentary review. This unprecedented self-emasculation of the Reichstag, hastily worked into a bank-and-check law, was the logical culmination of Bethmann's policy of "standing above the parties," and established a dangerous precedent for 1933.[42]

The pageantry of August 4, one of the most rousing days of Wilhelmian Germany, was merely the outward confirmation of previous decisions. In the parliamentary reception in the White Ballroom of the Schloss, the Second Empire displayed all the military pomp, the dazzling wealth, the stiff elegance of a moribund society. When William II uttered, "we are not driven by lust to conquer," and concluded his apologia with the emotional words, "I do not know parties any more, only Germans," the dissension and hatred inherited from Bismarck seemed to have vanished. The spontaneous handshakes between the party leaders and the emperor symbolized the Burgfrieden, a self-imposed moratorium on politics. "Russia has hurled the torch into our house!" Bethmann thundered to an enthusiastic Reichstag, "We now act out of self-defense (lively assent); and necessity knows no law!" But despite the intoxication of such patriotic rhetoric, the chancellor soberly admitted that the march into Belgium was "contrary to international law." Strategic imperatives, the threat of a French sweep through Belgium, a fatal turning of the German flank, forced him reluctantly to violate Belgian neutrality. "The injustice—I say it openly—the injustice we commit thereby, shall be righted as soon as our military goal has been reached," Bethmann explained to shouts of bravo—although this statement was to provide much ammunition for his domestic and foreign enemies. "Whoever is threatened as we are, whoever defends his highest good, can only think of how to fight his way through (continuous rousing applause and clapping in the whole house and the galleries)." These honest words, the unanimity of the vote, and the roaring cheer for "kaiser, folk, and fatherland" drowned out all protest, and the "Reichstag session [left] an immense impression. The uncontrived but profound effect of Bethmann's seriousness; the deep moral anguish from which every decision flows; precisely that has called forth the best qualities of our inexhaustible people." [43]

The elated "spirit of 1914" projected "the dazzling image of a domestically reunited nation capable of strong political action." Riezler mused about the strangeness of the human soul: "All pettiness and emptiness seem to have vanished and even Bassermann appeared uplifted and filled by something." Psychologically, it was "of course only like a storm, clearing the air—and when it dies down again all the vermin come out of hiding—lukewarmness and depravity will reappear in state and individual." But the heady brew of oratory and emotion had welded the nation into one united force, unknown since 1870. "Despite all shudders of sympathy [for the dying] we felt a singing and ringing in our souls," Friedrich Meinecke sensed an exultation comparable to that surrounding the Wars of Liberation: "In us and around us we feel this time of German *Erhebung*" united in the resolve to "become a world people of power and spirit." Repressing all doubts about German complicity in the catastrophe, the mood of the August days struck a responsive chord in the chancellor's heart, because it seemed to herald an inner regeneration toward greater freedom and participation and toward a strengthening of the monarchical ideal. This passionate illusion of national unity and purity appeared to ring in a new era of Borusso-German history—the transition from liberation and unification to world power. Bruno Frank spoke for a whole generation, regardless of political and religious creed, social status and wealth:

> Frohlockt, ihr Freunde, dass wir leben
> Und dass wir jung sind und gelenk.
> Nie hat es solch ein Jahr gegeben,
> Und nie war Jugend solch Geschenk! *

Decades of Treitschke's teachings, Wagner's dramatizations, and Chamberlain's fantasies now exacted a willing blood toll:

> Vielleicht war Schönes noch auf Erden
> Für seine Augen auferbaut,—
> Das Grösste, das ihm konnte werden,
> Dies stolze Jahr hat er geschaut.†

In the feverish August of 1914, war was not man's ultimate horror but a passionate, prized—if deadly—embrace.[44]

"For five years I have worked and hoped that this insane war could be avoided. This work and hope have shattered in my hands," a chastened Bethmann confided to a close friend. He attempted to silence his persistent self-doubts ("But I feel innocent of the streams of blood which now flow"). Nevertheless the chancellor rejected the explanation "of the coincidence of unfortunate circumstances which unleashed the war" because "it is not true." Rather he stressed three distinct but related developments: "The imperialism, nationalism,

---

* Rejoice, my friends, that we are living
That we are young and, ah, so swift.
No previous year saw such a singing,
And never was youth such a gift!

† Perhaps more precious things on earth
Were destined to have been—
But that which is of highest worth
This proud year he has seen.

and economic materialism, which during the last generation determined the outlines of every nation's policy, set goals which could only be pursued at the cost of a general conflagration." Beyond the general consideration that "world imperialism would have triumphed even without our help," Bethmann was willing to recognize some of the peculiar effects of German Weltpolitik: "We were severely handicapped because of 1870–71 and our geographical position in the middle. Since the coronation of the emperor we have often done the opposite of that which would have lightened our burden." Conscious that Germany had become "partially with but largely without its own guilt, the object of revenge and envy of other great powers," he argued, "It remains highly questionable whether with reasonable actions we could have prevented the natural French, Russian, and British antagonisms from uniting against us." In Bethmann's mind, forced to relativize his own contribution to the war, "the two lines of general and particular [causes] are so much entangled that one cannot say on which side there was more driving power." Yet he could not entirely refute the Socialist claim that it was "the responsibility of the governments that no peaceful solution was found in July 1914." Despite his later overriding compulsion to exculpate his own actions, his personal probity forced Bethmann to come close to admitting his own failures: "We have all heaped guilt upon ourselves, but only universal and common guilt has brought about the world catastrophe." [45]

The crucial decision of July 5–6 was not the cold-blooded implementation of a war plan drawn up but postponed in December of 1912, but a tenuous compromise between two conflicting views. Led by the shocked emperor and a trigger-happy general staff, spurred on by a vocally chauvinist public opinion and the imperialist Reichstag majority, supported by the reactionary alliance of heavy industry and landed agrarian interests, the war party in Berlin seized upon the crime to force Bethmann to abandon his moderate Weltpolitik and to embark upon unabashed military imperialism. In an intellectual climate steeped in the Borussian historians, nurtured on the legend of the misunderstood Bismarck's fist-thumping realist politics, and shaped by the propaganda of imperialist mass-interest organizations, war became not only a legitimate extension of politics but an ennobling deed. While the navy leadership and the Liberal Imperialists in diplomacy, business, and education hesitated, only the socialist and radical masses, who were pressing for social reform and democratization of the antiquated sociopolitical structure of the empire, resolutely rejected preventive war and refused to march on behalf of the mirage of world power. For pacifist intellectuals the assassination of Francis Ferdinand, although morally reprehensible, was a result of the repressive anti-Slav policies of the Hapsburg Empire, which should be punished within the existing legal and diplomatic framework. The common ground between the hard and soft views of the crisis was the resolve to shore up Austria by a diplomatic offensive in the Balkans. While the military hoped that the carte blanche would lead to war, Bethmann and the Wilhelmstrasse were striving for a diplomatic triumph through localization. A diagonal of the opposing domestic forces, Bethmann's strategy of the calculated risk attempted to plot a cautious, and at the same time daring, middle course between provocation and pacifism. Nevertheless, by endorsing a punitive campaign against Serbia, which conjured up the possibility of a continental conflict, the chancellor, now urged on by many former advocates of restraint, decisively departed from his previous moderate course—and sowed the seeds of world war.[46]

If Bethmann acquiesced in the compromise and if for three weeks Berlin seemingly spoke with a single voice, the precarious agreement on the third Balkan war was shattered by forces largely beyond individual control. The chancellor never tired of repeating that "the Russian provocateurs desired and forced through war in 1914, and both powers allied with Russia lacked the will and strength to restrain it from this path." Indeed, the precipitous *general* mobilization in Petersburg made war inevitable, since the German military could not tolerate the condition of armed peace, and since it rebuffed the tentative Viennese feelers in the Russian capital. As important was the Austrians' refusal to comply with Bethmann's urgent requests that they accept British mediation or negotiate directly in Petersburg on the basis of seizing a Faustpfand in Serbia. Not only the original tardiness in reaching a decision and the procrastination with the ultimatum—its clumsy wording and other technical mistakes—had precipitated the continental war, but also Berchtold's obsessive fear that he could be cheated out of a military triumph if the European Concert were allowed to intervene. Graver yet was the chancellor's miscalculation of the likelihood of British intervention, because of his fluctuation between hope and despair. In retrospect Bethmann blamed "England's refusal of any firm commitment because of its fear of thereby alienating Paris and Petersburg which indicated approval and ultimately acceptance of the aggressive tendencies of the Franco-Russian alliance. On the other hand, our so-called naval policy, whose appetite could only be curbed through the demands of our army," was equally responsible. The last and most significant reason for Bethmann's failure was his underestimation of the pressure of the military and the war party on his own decisions. Contributing heavily to the initial resolve, the generals forced their timetable on the chancellor in the critical stages of the confrontation, overrode his pleas for mediation in Vienna, and precipitated the entrance of Britain into the conflict. "Bitter as they have become, these decisions had to be made, since the judgment of the highest military authority indicated that our lack of initiative would have sealed our fate from the beginning," Bethmann attempted to justify the abandonment of his initial strategy. The ambiguity of the original compromise carried Germany to the brink, transferred the final decisions to the military, threw Bethmann and the Wilhelmstrasse into confusion, and assured war with France, Russia, and England.[47]

For Bethmann localization was an act of desperation—a necessary risk to preserve the continental basis of Weltpolitik. "The policy of the German Empire is directed toward emerging from the crisis with a gain in prestige, but toward maintaining world peace." Psychologically and propagandistically, the German stand was indeed *defensive*. But the means that were adopted—the diplomatic offensive in the Balkans, the encouragement of Austrian war against Serbia, the effort to prevent the involvement of the Great Powers, and the attempt to split the Entente—were *offensive*. The central paradox of Bethmann's policy in the July crisis was this contradiction between his claim of defending a disintegrating ally, and the dynamism of Germany's imperialist thrust, which transformed the Balkan quarrel into "a question of dominance in Europe." A diplomatic victory of the Dreibund would help to establish German hegemony on the continent and remove obstacles to economic expansion in Afro-Asia, thereby transforming it into a world or super power. And yet Jagow sincerely believed, "Imperialist goals such as world domination were far from our minds." Subjectively, Bethmann, under domestic pressure for a forceful removal of the increasing hindrances to Weltpolitik, decided upon brinkmanship, which had been so successful in 1908, 1911, and 1913.

Among the probable outcomes of the crisis, he preferred diplomatic victory through local war, was willing to gamble on continental war, but abhorred world war, since he believed "should England enter the war against us, may God help us!" But objectively, the concept of limited war proved elusive, drawing Germany deeper and deeper into the vortex; after a generation of rampant imperialism the risk could no longer be calculated in terms of cabinet diplomacy. Moreover, the unbridled chauvinism of Wilhelmian elites, the "signs of [Germany's] general posture," as well as "the Pan-German agitation" destroyed the credibility of Bethmann's attempt to reap a diplomatic triumph short of general war. "What frightens England," Count Alexander Benckendorff reported perceptively, "is less Austrian hegemony in the Balkans than German hegemony in the world." Although to many non-German contemporaries and later historians the conflict unleashed in August 1914 was the culmination of those grandiose struggles for the dominance of Europe, the statesman largely responsible for the holocaust thought of himself as "thoroughly peaceful and deplored the war as a heavy fate." [48]

"I am no war chancellor!" Bethmann protested in deep anguish to Jagow when the bloodshed had become inescapable. "By God, we did not want this war," he repeated again and again to his moderate supporters at home and abroad. Though exaggerated, these recurrent claims contain a kernel of truth regarding the larger war, because the chancellor was drawn into the maelstrom of imperialism not as a rabid Pan-German expansionist but as a traditional nationalist attracted to liberal imperialism. Far from a scheming Machiavellian who concealed the truth about himself, his nation, and history, Bethmann, though he tried to minimize his mistakes, also wrestled constantly with his failures. "The chancellor is the only one who has gained new stature during the crisis. I have learned to revere him because of his conduct, so self-effacing, self-denying, and unostentatious," Riezler marveled. "How silently he bears the burden of having to lead the German people into war." The shadow of this responsibility, not legal but political and thereby moral, pursued Bethmann to his deathbed. During the height of the fighting he said disarmingly to the liberal journalist, Theodor Wolff: "When assessing the responsibility for this war—we have to confess honestly that we bear a share of the guilt. If I said this thought oppresses me, I would say too little—this thought never leaves me. I live in it." [49]

CHAPTER 7

Visions of Greater Germany

"War! War! The people have arisen—as if they had not existed before and now suddenly are there, powerful and moving. Everyone crawls out of his corner, seemingly in the greatest confusion, and yet in the most purposeful order: Millions have already marched across the Rhine."—In these words the chancellor's assistant marveled at the popular response to the emperor's call to arms. "Most striking are the people themselves and their silent and unquestioning loyalty. All rejoice in living devoted to a great cause." Nevertheless, apprehension dampened this exhilaration: "Everyone holds his breath but no one doubts, no one thinks for a moment what a gamble war is, and especially this war. Faith in God or irresponsibility, trust or delusion—it is all the same, only through such elation can we hope to win." Swept along by *furor teutonicus*, Bethmann sought to spur on his countrymen: "No German will let Bismarck's work be destroyed. Enemies rage around the empire, but we shall beat them." He invoked the Iron Chancellor's memory: "He has taught us fear only before God, rage against our foe, belief in our people. Thus we shall fight, win, and live for kaiser and Reich." Destined to be betrayed by years of slaughter, the enthusiastic patriotism aroused by the chancellor's appeal fulfilled "a deep psychological need of the people." After a century of peace Mars ruled again.[1]

The joyful confidence of August 1914 soon transformed self-defense into a struggle for the positive aim of aggrandizement. "We all felt that we were irresistibly outgrowing the saturated life of a continental great power," Friedrich Meinecke wrote in an attempt to explain the psychological motivation for the reversal from resistance against attack to desire for victory. The outbreak of fighting offered such traditional advocates of expansion as the Pan-Germans, naval, army, and colonial leagues, the HTK and anti-Socialist societies a welcome opportunity to realize their annexationist dreams. Calling for compensations for *"the incredible sacrifices exacted by the fatherland,"* Pan-German General Keim demanded a peace in which "the hammer of Thor is thrown far enough that those who are now after our lives will *be forced* to keep peace for generations." Moreover, the moderate elements that had hitherto followed Bethmann's economic imperialism joined the clamor for "defending our future as *Weltvolk*." The industrial barons hoped to secure raw materials and captive markets; landowners looked to the fertile expanses of the East for space to settle in; traders and shipowners claimed channel ports, coaling stations, freedom of the seas, and colonial open door; financiers and rentiers gloated at the prospect of a large indemnity; professors and schoolteachers thought it their scholarly duty to reestablish the frontiers of the Holy Roman Empire; and nationalist intellectuals frothed about German *Kulturmission*. Although a few islands of sanity remained, such as the Socialist movement and bourgeois pacifism, every social group, even the proletariat, was tainted by the hubris of self-aggrandizement. Centered around the symbolic goals of sea power and French *minette,* the dream of Central Europe, the slogan Berlin-Bagdad, the colonial scheme of Central Africa, and the legendary *Drang nach Osten,* this wave of collective hysteria, unprecedented in German history, coalesced in one ominous vision of Greater Germany. By a curious reversal the idealism of self-defense turned into lust for conquest.[2]

Among these conflicting pressures, Bethmann Hollweg groped for a coherent program which might justify the outbreak of the war and provide a blueprint for future peace. "Our nation is splendid and *cannot* perish. Much suffering, perhaps the hardest [trial] is still before us," he warned his friend Oettingen against over-estimating the early successes of the German arms. "The public's optimism is healthy but premature." He urged him to "help maintain the moral fiber of the nation. We shall need it." Although the chancellor knew that "the policy of a great empire cannot be directed according to the recipe of a few hotheads," he shared the universal belief in a German victory. "I want to emphasize from the beginning," he said, in an attempt to quell critics, "that probably nobody is more imbued than I with the necessity of concluding this war, fought with such sacrifices of life and property, with a settlement which is advantageous in every respect for kaiser and empire." But Bethmann could not yield to the ever-increasing pressures for a government commitment to annexations, because "the fortune of war will hardly allow turning the defensive struggle into a war of conquest." Moreover, the domestic precondition for the fighting, Socialist acceptance of the war and the precarious Burgfrieden, forced him to maintain the fiction of self-defense and to subsume his own aims under that limited concept. Caught between the millstones of the rampant annexationism of Wilhelmian elites and the latent pacifism of the masses, Bethmann could but strive for a tortuous middle course. Before the emergence of a radical antiwar movement in 1917, the war aims debate was not a battle between the alternatives of expansionism or peace but rather an internecine struggle between the moderate and extremist versions of a victorious *pax Germanica.*[3]

To tumble the Russian colossus, Bethmann and the Foreign Office unleashed a series of diplomatic measures in early August 1914, in which means and ends of fighting coalesced. Following a suggestion by Moltke and the precedent established by Bismarck, the Wilhelmstrasse proposed creating a belt of buffer states to absorb the pressure from the tsarist empire and revolutionizing natives throughout the French and British empires wherever they were willing to overthrow their colonial masters. Inspired not by ideology but by military need, these plots for insurrection revealed a high continuity with earlier economic penetration and soon tended to become goals in their own right. Although the chancellor did not initiate this policy himself, he supervised it "with the mien of a conspirator," and took personal interest in the "liberation and safety of the nations under the tsarist yoke," calling for a "rollback of Russian despotism toward Moscow." Baltic barons, Finns, Ukrainians, Russian Jews, and the Caucasian nationalities were courted avidly by German propaganda in highly secret, expensive, and often illusory missions. Similarly, to spark a Polish uprising against Russia, Bethmann had a Polish archbishop appointed to the vacant seat of Poznan, supplied the military with instructions not to alienate the Poles, and prepared inflammatory appeals to the population to throw off the tsarist yoke. When the former consul-general in Warsaw, Freiherr von Rechenberg, suggested the Austro-Polish solution to Wahnschaffe in mid-August, Bethmann's domestic advisor was less than enthusiastic ("We hardly intend to make territorial gains in the East"). Hence Bethmann cautioned against Austrian proposals for a renewed partition of Poland: "We cannot divide the bear's skin before we have slain it." Nevertheless, the separation of

Poland and the Baltic states from Russia became the Central Powers' main eastern war aim, and the *cordon sanitaire* one of World War I's chief diplomatic results.[4]

With respect to the West, Bethmann's British illusions died hard. "England holds back in order not to encourage the extension of the war. It would be most desirable to act likewise in order to make it possible for England to bring about peace," the chancellor confided to Admiral Pohl in early August. For a fleeting moment the harried Bethmann, toying with the creation of a western "cultural bloc," fantasized that "a German-British-French grouping would be the best guarantee against the dangers threatening European civilization from the barbaric colossus." Concerned more about Germany's continental position than world naval power, the chancellor initially considered the struggle against Russia as primary and hoped for a quick victory in France. Hence he was willing to spare French susceptibilities, to offer reasonable terms, perhaps even an eternal alliance within a German system, and demanded that in the occupation administration of the Lorraine ore mines "the sanctity of private property must be respected." But the stubbornness of French resistance as well as the landing of British forces in Belgium soon demonstrated that "we should not underestimate England's tenacity, but rather appraise it very highly." In late August, "in a very serious, almost depressed mood," Bethmann agreed with Tirpitz "that everything we could do to weaken the British would be highly important." While the chancellor had consciously entered the war as a struggle for continental supremacy against Russia, the dynamics of Germany's imperialism paradoxically transformed it into a worldwide confrontation with the Western powers, in which "the possibility of a sophisticated *Kontinentalsperre* after victory over France and Belgium" became an important instrument as well as an aim.[5]

After he moved with the Grosse Hauptquartier to Coblenz in mid-August, Bethmann was daily besieged by the military to formulate clearcut goals. Due to the mental habits of Prussian militarism, communications between political and military leaders were notoriously poor: "It is impossible to find out anything about the fighting: the generals, tight-lipped, promise that they will make sure the diplomats stick it out." Jagow and the Foreign Office staff did not provide the necessary counterweight to the generals, since "the diplomats never go beyond the limits of their routine—as if there were only ministers and all the others were dead pieces to be moved on the chessboard." A major source of irritation was the future of Poland, beyond its separation from Russia. While Vienna preferred to establish a conservative Austrian administration, to annex or if necessary partition it, the chancellor's entourage urged: "We can accept only a free Poland. Here, too, nothing has been prepared . . . the question contains untold difficulties and is now completely off the track." Another cause of friction was the "military raging against the Schleswig Danes, although Denmark is our only supply country." In the same mood the generals, lacking any self-restraint, demanded an immense indemnity of 480 million Marks from the conquered province of Flanders: "They have no idea of modern monetary exchange and believe that they will find all the gold of the Belgian bank in Brussels." Bethmann therefore decided, "With the exception of Antwerp, cut off by the army corps, Belgium shall be treated as a conquered nation to be fully utilized with all of its resources by the army directly for the relief of our own country." The chancellor sought to mark out an independent area for a civil administration and called the vice-chairman of the Deutsche Bank, Karl Helfferich, to GHQ (General Headquarters) to mitigate the inordinate demands of the military for Belgian "contributions." Although not yet specifying their aims beyond a decisive victory over all enemies, the generals in their reactions to the Polish, Danish, and Belgian questions demonstrated a fatal propensity toward territorial annexation and crude repression. "You can well imagine," Riezler informed Hammann in late August, "that due to the galloping rabies of the soldiers, the strongest currents here are for completely impossible outright annexation." [6]

While the generals were breaking their promise that "we do not want to take one village from the French," the desire for territorial gains also infected the crowned heads of the empire. "The kaiser had already said that Belgium must be annexed," but Bethmann "initially let him talk and then only afterwards put the flea in his ear that there were so many Catholics there," an offensive prospect to a Hohenzollern. During his visit to GHQ on August 26, Bavarian King Ludwig impressed upon the "tired and preoccupied chancellor" the necessity for dividing Alsace-Lorraine after the war, and claimed a share for Bavaria. Irritated by the untimely request, Bethmann politely admitted the shipwreck of his constitutional reform for the Reichsland but promised only "that any one-sided enlargement of Prussia would run counter to the federal character of the empire." In Ludwig's proposal for the annexation of Belgium, Bethmann encountered the first formal claim of a member state of the empire for inclusion in the eventual division of the spoils. Posing already as victors, the monarchs of the Reich in their greed for enlarging their domains raised grave "difficulties for concluding peace." Until 1917 the partition of Alsace-Lorraine remained the pathological focus of the war aims demands of the Federal States.[7]

More influential than the states were the German industrialists who united to lobby for the expansion of German power. One faction comprising coal and steel (Thyssen, Stinnes, Kirdorf, Röchling, and sometimes Krupp through Hugenberg), partially also chemicals (Duisberg), and smaller, independent businesses (Stresemann), as well as the large estates of East Elbia (Rösicke, Wangenheim), called for extensive annexations. Speaking for these interests, deputy Erzberger demanded in early September that Bethmann "use the consequences of victory in such a manner that *Germany's military dominance on the continent is secured for all time, that the German people look forward to at least one hundred years of undisturbed peaceful development.*" Concretely, this would mean the elimination of Belgium as a threat, strategic border rectifications toward France, the independence of the non-Russian nationalities, and the creation of Mitteleuropa and Mittelafrika. Toning down his first draft answer that "the goal of this war must be, aside from the military security of Germany, the consideration of economic possibilities," the chancellor replied: "Under any circumstances we have to persevere until Germany's future is completely secure. Even if all the possibilities have to be taken into account the eventual decisions still depend on further developments." Nevertheless, he did not turn a deaf ear to demands for the annexation of the iron-ore deposits of Longwy-Briey, the seizure of the Belgian mines, plants, and ports, and for a merciless economic war against England: "Russia must cede to us the Baltic provinces, perhaps parts of Poland and the Donbas with Odessa, the Crimea as well as territory around the Black Sea with the Caucasus, so that we can reach Asia Minor and Persia by land." Although he never identified completely with such heavy industrial claims, Bethmann adopted the annexation of the French ore mines as his own demand, adding: "The proposal that we have to advance the Alsatian frontiers westward . . . agrees with my own thoughts." In the view of this most aggressive section of German industry, never completely disowned by the chancellor, the war was Germany's rendezvous with destiny, a chance to become a major world power.[8]

The Liberal Imperialist industrials differed not so much in final aims as in means. Light industry (Rathenau, Siemens), the banks (Gwinner, Warburg, Bleichröder), and the large shipping lines (Ballin, Holtzendorff) admired not Russian despotism but Britain's indirect rule and tended to agree more with progressive bureaucrats and intellectuals than with reactionary robber barons. Meeting for the first time in early September as what was to become Delbrück's influential *Mittwochabend,* the heterogeneous group listened to Gwinner's reasoned rejection of "a blind policy of annexations" and his plea for "the necessity of establishing Germany's economic predominance." The mercurial Walther Rathenau, who best represented their ideas of veiled hegemony, proposed to Bethmann "a customs union between Germany, Austria-Hungary, Belgium, and France," based "on the assumption that we cannot expect a decisive victory over England." Germany should strive only for those goals which would procure the means for the continuation of the struggle: "The final aim is a constellation that alone can produce future balance in Europe: Mitteleuropa united under German leadership, strengthened politically and economically against England and America on one side and against Russia on the other. We will, of course, have to sacrifice territorial gains in France and lower the war contribution." Not through annexations and indemnities, but through its economic potential in the form of a customs union, would Germany achieve victory and dominance over Europe. Since the chancellor instinctively preferred nonviolent solutions, he encouraged Rathenau's planning, although Vice-Chancellor Delbrück commented acidly that his "memorandum [did] not contain a single new idea," but rather threatened the social basis of Prussia by endangering German agriculture.[9]

During the initial weeks of the war the Prussian bureaucracy developed its own idea about the shape of peace. Chief of the Imperial Chancellery Wahnschaffe, a conservative landowner in Upper Silesia, began to think about agrarian settlement in an eastern frontier strip to re-Germanize the Slavic border. Instructed by the chancellor to gather material on the "extent of the iron-ore deposits in Briey and in French Lorraine, as well as on the size of the present German financial interests in them," Vice-Chancellor Delbrück studied economic questions such as the "amount of indemnity which France and Belgium would be able to pay." Since territorial annexations in Europe were unlikely because of England's stubborn resistance, Colonial Secretary Solf proposed the creation of a giant Central Africa out of the Portuguese colonies, the Belgian Congo, and French Central African possessions. "Generally, I agree with you completely: as little as possible in Europe because too many foreigners will only weaken the Reich. But for *you* I would like to gain a large empire," Foreign Secretary Jagow responded: *"Meo voto,* the war will have been conducted in vain if we do not succeed in moving the Russian colossus eastward and [in creating] buffer states in between." In GHQ "the plans regarding the prize of victory are already beginning," Riezler noted in mid-August. "Jagow wants to divide Belgium. We have studied the map today." The foreign secretary proposed "a corridor to Antwerp and the Walloon remainder as a small and weak state, preferably not allied to France. On the other hand, western Prussian administrators echoed the sentiments of leading Rhenish industrialist Mallinckrodt, who preferred indirect dependence: "Any inclusion of continental Belgian territory will produce graver difficulties than those previously encountered in the Reichsland, East Prussia, and Schleswig." To Alsatian stadtholder Dallwitz, who championed border rectifications in France, Bethmann replied, "I also think that we should possess the western slopes of the Vosges to have a better strategic position toward France." But the milder annexationism of the Prussian bureaucracy did not suffice to stem "the military resolve to make Belgium disappear." Bethmann had to confess that he could "no longer succeed in maintaining it. Hence division between Holland, France, and ourselves." [10]

Although the chancellor thought it "impossible to make decisions since we are only at the beginning and cannot yet dictate peace to anyone," he correctly foresaw the "development of a greedy nationalism that wants to annex half the world." Late in August the presidium of the Pan-German League ratified the first war aims manifesto, which was circulated widely despite censorship, thereby providing the polemic foundation of the war aims movement. Calling for all possible annexations from Longwy and Briey to northern France, Belgium, and large colonies, for the expulsion of native populations from the territories to be incorporated, as well as Congress Poland plus the Ukraine for Austria, this Pan-German memorandum, together with the even more fantastic Eastern demands formulated by Stinnes, marked the beginning of rampant annexationism. To counteract this "reported hydra of Pan-German annexationist fury," Bethmann had Riezler write to press-chief Hammann that, although nothing definite had been established, "the completely burnt-down country cannot be reconstructed in its old form; perhaps we must lay hands on Antwerp—in short everything is still in flux. The same is true of Poland." Yet Pan-German daydreams for France were out of the question. *"The purpose of the war is to secure ourselves for the foreseeable future by weakening our opponents in East and West."* But despite public sentiment, "this must not necessarily be done through annexations. They can become the source of weakness. The reduction of our enemies' power can be economic and financial—through trade treaties, etc." Working against annexationism through "thoughtful people, perhaps professors," Wahnschaffe talked to sympathetic National Liberal deputy Schiffer "about the danger of too high-flung expectations about the territorial results of war." He offered to help but replied skeptically, "the slogan 'England must be crushed' dominates the discussions to an unexpected degree." Even before Bethmann had formulated his own program, he attempted to curb the excesses of public opinion, lest they once again force his hand.[11]

A last significant influence on the chancellor's war aims emanated from his personal assistant, Kurt Riezler. As early as August 21, he noted "tonight [we had] a long conversation about Poland and the possibility of a loose affiliation of other states with the Reich—a middle European system of differential customs. Greater Germany with Belgium, Holland, and Poland as closer, Austria as wider, protected allies." Rejecting crude annexationism, Riezler preferred a system of indirect rule and "always preached the construction of vassal states." Criticizing the chancellor's suggestion of dividing Belgium between Germany and France, since then the latter would be stronger than before, he suggested "letting Belgium, without Liège, survive as German protectorate; a piece of Limburg has to go to Holland, the southern corner to Luxembourg and Prussia, French Flanders to Belgium, and Belgium has to be chained loosely to Germany through an alliance." Projecting a daring yet tempered Machiavellianism, Riezler countered Jagow's and Stumm's criticism by stressing "the need to find a form of loose affiliation, if alone because of Holland, which we can only get if we respect its freedom.

Here, too, offensive and defensive alliance, perhaps colonial reciprocity, economic advantages for the Dutch, etc." Because of the prospect of protracted war with England, Riezler insisted: "A large economic system in Mitteleuropa must be crystallized around us, complemented by a loose federation with ironclad alliances. That is the chief goal." In the first days of September his persistent efforts at persuasion were beginning to bear fruit. "Officially, the Belgian question is still unsolved. But the chancellor seems to lean toward the solution supported by me, that Belgium losing only Liège, but not annexed, together with French Flanders, will become an economic ally and a military protectorate (right of occupation of the ports). [It] will be kept in our power against England but must outwardly continue to exist." [12]

When GHQ were transferred to Luxembourg in early September, the chancellor drove through one of the chief prizes of the war, the rich ore-fields of Longwy and Briey: "Beautiful clear sun. No walls remain standing in the fortification surrounding the square city on the hill." Riezler captured the contrast between destruction and scarcely disturbed nature. "In Longwy (?) franc-tireurs were shooting, the villages burnt with only women and children left, the battlefields strewn with French clothing." Man's self-destructiveness invited dark thoughts: "The people today do not have a single idea corresponding to the greatness of the times. If Europe does not find a permanent form of community now, it will perish." The generals' "blind belief in the steam roller, their completely outdated annexationism, their hair-raising economic mistakes," and their strategic blunders made the chancellor "experience serious days." Moreover, "despite all losses" the French armies were still physically and psychologically unbroken, Bethmann confided realistically to Loebell at the height of the struggle at the Marne. "Since the day before yesterday, a murderous battle has begun on the whole front. Now God will help us, hopefully also in East Prussia where the decision is near." On the fateful September 9, Valentini pessimistically noted in his diary: "The mood is gloomy, since the situation is critical in East and West." [13]

While Germany's military fate hung in the balance, Bethmann concretized his war aims in the September Program. Partly typed, partly handwritten by Riezler, this "preliminary note on the guidelines of our policy at the conclusion of peace which I [B.H.] have had prepared here" formulated the chancellor's goals in a coherent blueprint for a Greater Germany and combined elements of all major demands. Although Bethmann "curiously always [listened] on this question" without displaying much initiative of his own, he initialed the draft produced by his assistant and therefore took responsibility for its ideas. The intent expressed in the covering letter to Vice-Chancellor Delbrück was "to prepare the clarification of the individual problems so that it will be possible to find the right response quickly—in case of eventual peace preliminaries—and to create the right basis for the difficult later elaboration in brief formulas," should Britain's determination make a rapid peace unlikely. Since the proposed restructuring of the central European economy would prompt interest groups to do everything to prejudice the outcome, they were to be "consulted as late and as little as possible," and the direction of the planning was to lie in Delbrück's hands. "We have spoken about the economic program of a middle European customs union shortly after the outbreak of the war and have been able to state agreement in principle." In conclusion, Bethmann attempted to torpedo bureaucratically the emperor's fantastic proposal of military colonies on the French border and reminded the vice-chancellor "especially that the French government must agree to turn the iron-works over to German possession when ceding the ore-basin of the Lorraine." [14]

In a curious extension of defense, the actual program proclaimed as the general purpose of the war "the safeguarding of the German Empire for the foreseeable future in East and West. Hence, France must be so weakened that it cannot rise again as a great power. Russia must be pushed back from the German frontier as far as possible and its rule over the non-Russian vassal peoples must be broken." Because the military situation in the East was still unresolved, the bulk of the program dealt with the West. Regarding France, the military would have to decide whether the cession of Belfort, the western slope of the Vosges, the coast from Dunkirk to Boulogne, and the razing of the fortresses should be demanded. "At any rate the iron basin of Briey must be ceded, since it is necessary for our industrial ore supply." Moreover, a preferential trade treaty, making France "our export land", and an indemnity large enough to preclude armaments for the next two decades would have to be imposed. Belgium would fare worse. The annexation of Liège and Verviers by Prussia, and possibly also Antwerp with a corridor, would be necessary. "Even if it continues to be outwardly independent, all of Belgium must sink to the level of a vassal state. It will have to grant the right of occupation of any militarily important harbor, put its coast at the disposal of our navy, and economically become a German province." In exchange for its subjection, such a rump-Belgium would be compensated by French Flanders with Dunkirk, Calais, and Boulogne. Little Luxembourg would receive the Belgian province bearing that same name and be incorporated once again into the empire. In terms of nonterritorial gains, "the formation of an economic organization of Mitteleuropa through mutual customs agreements would be reached, including France, Belgium, Holland, Denmark, Austria, Poland, and perhaps Italy, Sweden, and Norway." Lacking any central political organization and resting formally on equality of membership, this new customs union would "stabilize German economic predominance over Central Europe." Similarly, German colonies should be welded into a large, more defensible Mittelafrika. An appendix outlined measures against Holland, leaving it "externally independent, but essentially subject to us." [15]

Still intoxicated by victory, Bethmann approved this awesome plan as preparation for the eventual conditions of peace. This bold and ruthless attempt to reshape the realities of the European system by creating a firm continental base for German world power drew a chilling diagonal between the various pressures for and against German war aims. Yielding to military demands for border rectifications and the channel ports, the desire of heavy industry to broaden the narrow raw material base, pressure from light industry for economic hegemony, bureaucratic plans for the subjection of Belgium and a central African empire, and agrarian calls for a rollback of Russia, the September Program incorporated something of all the traditional targets of Wilhelmian expansion. Furthermore, as a war measure against invincible Albion, it contained the grandiose design for indirect dominance, Rathenau's and Riezler's scheme of Mitteleuropa. Once it had become clear "that England [would] persevere" in the war, the only path to victory was the forging "of a European blockade until this and the effect of our machinations in India, Afghanistan, etc. are felt." Although the idea had already exerted much magnetism in the mid-nineteenth century as a solution to the traditional Austro-Prussian dualism, Bethmann embraced a central European customs union as a moderate path to German hegemony, still justifiable as expanded self-defense. As the imperialist counterpart, Riezler envisaged "taking the British naval bases and [creating] a kind of Hanseatic Empire," with the slogan of "Trade supported by militarism." But, ironically, while Bethmann sketched the grim outlines of a German peace, there were "heavy thunderclouds, fighting everywhere, and the French [were] still resisting desperately." It became clear that "in the West the encirclement has failed." The collapse of the Schlieffen Plan rendered all further war aims deliberations ultimately academic.[16]

Although the chancellor personally supported the idea of Mittel-europa, the generals, Foreign Office, and domestic administration were less than enthusiastic about its implications. *"The concept of the purely military celebrates orgies here,"* Riezler sketched the mood in GHQ. "Today the politicizing officers on the General Staff went back as far as Ariovist to support the expulsion of the Belgian population." Similarly Jagow, with his "nakedly Prussian mind [possessing] much judgment and even cleverness but no system, no great perspective," looked askance at such a novel scheme. The chancellor's assistant was furious about "Jagow's hogwash: he doesn't understand the first thing about it and raises the most superficial objections out of profound ignorance and in immense agrarian fear" of Hungarian competition with the Junkers of East Elbia. The Prussian bureaucracy, led by Delbrück, also resented the "newness of the surprising plans" of a middle European economic union and cautioned that this goal might conflict with territorial annexations and create "strong domestic political difficulties." Warning that a "customs union" comprising most of Europe would mean "a break with our economic policy and the beginning of a decrease in our tariffs," Delbrück nevertheless accepted the necessity of Mitteleuropa in this "struggle for the dominance of the world market" and suggested a customs alliance based on mutual preference to be achieved with a liberal parliamentary majority. Undaunted, Bethmann ordered a study of the "different possibilities for a more or less closed economic union of Central Europe," although he knew that such a revolution in international relations "could only be reached in a dictated peace under pressure of political superiority." Despite all objections, "we must maintain the basic idea and strive for unified minimal duties of the economic bloc toward other countries and for low preferential tariffs for the exchange of goods, at least for a list containing our chief export items." While Riezler was charged with preparation in GHQ, the vice-chancellor set up a coordinating office in the Imperial Department of the Interior under Freiherr von Rechenberg, thus absorbing the elaboration of war aims into the governmental structure. Despite Bethmann's initial commitment, German goals continued to fluctuate and evolve in response to diverse pressures, justifying his claim that he had "no plans but only ad hoc ideas which could be influenced through changes in the fortune of arms." [17]

The German defeat at the Marne confronted Bethmann with the unanswerable question: "What will happen if the advance grinds to a halt in the West?" Forced to "decide against whom we are actually waging this war," Bethmann agonized, "The tragedy is that there is no natural price of victory except for economic gain, and that neither the Polish nor the Belgian problem has a solution." Impressed with one of Paul Déroulède's *chansons de guerre,* the chancellor "admired the [French] *feu sacré* and the power of hatred. It is completely impossible to crush this nation through anything but economic" defeat. In terms of rational policy, Riezler suggested "treating with France *sur le dos du Belge,*—one half of Belgium for Briey and the colonies, and tacit cooperation against England to be introduced by great cultural fanfares." Since separate peace required a reduction of German aims, Bethmann repeated insistently, "Think of a solution for the Belgian problem"; but his otherwise so imaginative assistant could propose nothing better than a "military protectorate." The fate of Poland was equally vexing. Either it would "fall to the Austrians after the transitional stage of complete liberation under German protection" or "the inevitable disintegration of Austria" would render such a course impossible. Since Belgium and Poland, possessing such strong identities, could not simply be annexed, Bethmann saw Mitteleuropa as the only alternative. "Narrow is the path of a potential German rise to world domination: different possibilities around us, i.e. in the northwest and southeast, a system of small states [must be created] whose freedom is guaranteed by the empire," Riezler speculated. "But that can be done only with a light touch. Talk of liberty, small measures. That would guarantee our economic predominance in Europe." There was only one catch for Wilhelmian Germany in this course: "It would be feasible if we had political talent, but we don't." [18]

The inconclusive race to the sea forced Bethmann to retreat somewhat from the all too sanguine September Program. "Actually, it is impossible to foresee what course events will take. Probably we will be limited in the choice of alternatives at the peace table and must at any rate work for the establishment of a stable order." Revealing his uncertainty, he confessed to Weizsäcker: "It is an unenviable task to plot in advance all conceivable eventualities which will solely depend on our military situation at the conclusion of peace." On the other hand, he was not discouraged too easily by Austrian defeats: "First of all they will have to drive us out of our occupied territories [Faustpfand] in Belgium and France, and we should not overestimate the Russians." Nevertheless the chancellor was having second thoughts about Belgium: "In the beginning I mouthed the phrase about a half-sovereign tributary state. Now I consider this utopian, even if we had already shot the bear. A state like Egypt in continental Europe is not possible after all." To prepare for its future partition with France, Holland, and Luxembourg, Germany should only "annex whatever the soldiers and sailors absolutely demand and what even a reasonable man cannot deny to unreasonable Germans. But as little as possible." At most he would take Antwerp with a corridor and Seebrugge plus economic prerogatives, as well as Briey and the western slope of the Vosges." In the interest of a "peace guaranteeing German security, the goals should not only be measured according to what is obtainable but also what is really useful to us." Especially before any decisive military successes, Pan-German vistas were "utopias." But even in the case of victory, Bethmann was convinced "that the annexation of greater territories with partially undesirable, e.g. Walloon, populations would mean an enormous weakening of Germany." Although he rejected annexationist excesses, the chancellor still "seriously considered the establishment of Germany on the North Sea coast, Belgian dependence in some form, and the creation of close economic ties to that country." [19]

To gain greater flexibility in planning, Bethmann enjoined Undersecretary Zimmermann, "It will be necessary in time to prepare the different possibilities offering themselves for the solution of the Belgian question in case of decisive victory." A tributary state that did not discredit Germany politically while providing economic penetration and military control would be most desirable. Sketching to Delbrück the economic implications of a possible peace, he ordered him to consult the great banks, including Mendelssohn, Bleichröder, and Warburg, to establish realistic indemnities. "Commercially we will have to attempt to create replacements in France and Russia for the losses threatening us on the world market as a consequence of the war." This would entail the cession of Briey, a new trade treaty with Russia, and some customs arrangement opening up the British colonies. Perhaps the seizure of allied economic rights and concessions in the Far East could also be demanded, and most-favored-nation treatment claimed from Russia and France. To take into account the changing military situation, Bethmann instructed Delbrück in mid-November to investigate the Briey question "in such a manner that on the one hand a desirable maximum will be designated and on the other hand a minimum determined that must serve as the yardstick of the attainable." Since Colonial Secretary Solf had already called for the creation of a greater Central Africa, Bethmann had only to request the navy's demands from Tirpitz, concentrating on Belgium and the channel coast to make his staggering list complete. Nevertheless, a note of caution informed the chancellor's second answer to Dallwitz regarding border rectifications in the West: "For the time being it appears to be still somewhat early for such considerations, but one must attempt to gain clarity about certain goals even if their attainment is not yet assured." [20]

Because of the fluctuating fortunes of arms and the need for domestic unity, Bethmann attempted to exclude the issue of war aims from domestic politics. In mid-October the chancellor succeeded in obtaining William II's approval of a set of press guidelines which forbade "open or concealed criticism" of the government, thereby preventing public discussion of annexationist goals through censorship. In the same vein he instructed the Prussian ministry of state that it would be "premature to speak about the conditions for peace. Victory would have to be won first. Our demands would depend upon our military strength." More realistic than the public, who were unaware of the magnitude of the debacle at the Marne, Bethmann did "not believe that we could gain a peace which would allow us to dispose of the world. Even if we succeeded only in proving that an immense coalition like the present one cannot overcome us, this would guarantee our security for the future." In his first wartime Reichstag speech in early December, Bethmann ambiguously called for "a glorious, happy peace" to please all parties. "We shall persevere until we are sure that no one will dare to disturb our peace, a peace in which we want to unfold and develop German culture and German power—as a free people!" he thundered among "stormy, long-lasting bravos and applause on all sides of the house and in the galleries." Vague enough to placate even the pacifist Socialists and to allow for moderate annexations, this equivocation nevertheless failed to convince the growing war aims movement. Hence the chancellor hinted in private that "the goal of this war . . . is not the restoration of the European balance of power, but precisely its final elimination . . . and the foundation of German preeminence in Europe." While he attempted to head off growing discontent with his official position of moderation by indicating that he, too, believed in some expansion of German power, Bethmann continued his policy of noncommitment in order not to lose the support of the masses. "As you emphasize yourself, the prize of victory for which we fight is neither won nor certain," he replied coldly to Pan-German leader Class. "Hence it would be premature to discuss the alternatives. Moreover, I believe that we can better serve the common cause if you postpone your propaganda until the time when one can clearly see what we can demand and achieve." [21]

The flexibility of the formula of "guarantees and securities" did not prevent agitation but rather encouraged it. Among the first to claim their share were the federal states for whom Hertling demanded partition of Alsace-Lorraine: "Concerning Belgium, Bethmann maintained that annexation was presently *not* desired," but suggested a customs union, the expropriation of the state railroads, and the administration of the port of Antwerp. "Touching upon the incorporation of French territory, he spoke of frontier rectification and a corner of Briey." In the East Bethmann did "not consider incorporating the German-Russian provinces [Baltic] but a border adjustment in which a narrow strip of land, falling to Prussia, should be evacuated by the Russians"—an echo of Wahnschaffe's dream of peasant settlement. Even more rapacious were the representatives of the war committee of German industry, Gustav Stresemann and Heinrich Rötger, who although moving toward the overthrow of the chancellor, were still willing to press their demands upon him in person. Pointing to the military stalemate, Bethmann maintained that it was premature to "settle on anything like a program" but promised, "We shall make ourselves at home in Poland until we can conclude a separate peace with Russia, as I hope, or peace with all of our opponents." Attempting to reassure the expansionist spokesmen that he would never accept a settlement that was just an armistice, he added, "France must be completely wrestled to the ground." Stresemann concluded that "generally our opinions did not differ fundamentally"; but the chancellor escaped without committing himself to specific annexations. "My chief task is to render the coalition of the three Great Powers impossible for the future," Bethmann summarized, "to conclude a peace which will last at least fifty years . . . and to attempt to bury the century-old quarrels between France and us." Through such studied vagueness and ambiguous promises, the chancellor tenaciously occupied the ground between the proponents of an annexationist or a renunciationist peace.[22]

Not only expediency but also personal conviction made Bethmann ask whether a middle line regarding Belgium and other war aims was possible. In Riezler's judgment, "he has more desire for power than the clever skeptics in the Foreign Office, but in the depth of his soul, he has inherited the preconceptions of an earlier, smaller Germany." The chancellor wanted to keep his options open because "the military situation is favorable but unclear and undecided," as he wrote to a friend shortly before Christmas. "The excessive peace demands are, thank God, gradually shrinking because of the seriousness of the times." In the same vein, he complained to an old collaborator: "The people expect too much and you want our goals unchangeably proclaimed soon. But to me it seems blasphemous to force the hand of providence." A psychological substitute for victory, the vision of a "German empire as master of the continent and the world by depossessing England, annexing Belgium, northern and eastern France, and the Baltic states and Poland would be a dream—and since unrealistic, perhaps not even a beautiful one." Often the hyperpatriotism of politicians at home demanded more than the men in the trenches: "You will not accuse me of defeatism. But serious, victory-conscious soldiers today think that defense against this overpowering coalition would already be enough. If God gives us more, we shall accept it gladly, but we cannot count on it." Because of his growing doubt about a decisive triumph, Bethmann resented annexationist pressure from the Right and refused to lift the censor's ban against Heinrich Class's Pan-German memorandum, which circulated illicitly. Comparing the duty of the citizen to that of the soldier, the chancellor insisted "that every patriot . . . must be asked to subordinate his personal views about the future to the great needs of the present and must not engage in agitation as long as it is considered by those responsible as harmful to the general goal of the war." Convinced as he was that it was "useless to discuss the distribution of the fruits of victory before we have won it," Bethmann used the Burgfrieden to prevent premature and divisive debates.[23]

The upsurge of annexationist propaganda, which succeeded in circumventing all official prohibitions, confronted Bethmann with a vexing choice. "The mood here is quite indescribable. Most politicians are not only confident but even arrogant. The former we need, the latter seems bad," he wrote, groping for an effective response. "I cannot work against that. The psyche of our people has been so poisoned through boasting that it would probably turn fearful if one were to forbid it to brag," he ruminated. "Premature disclosures [about the military situation] can destroy the confidence we need" for victory. Irritated by a manifesto of six leading industrial organizations for the opening of the war aims debate, he scribbled in the margin: "I cannot enlighten the petitioners about the military position. Either they accuse me of defeatism, or they become frightened. We need neither. Only military events themselves can gradually sober them." To Bundesrat suggestions that he launch a countercampaign for moderate goals, Bethmann replied that "he would rather let the facts speak for themselves than hand out a possibly misunderstood slogan." Leery of undermining the confidence necessary for German victory, the chancellor relied on the sobering effect of military events and evaded any clearcut commitment in order not to abdicate his freedom of decision. But this refusal to puncture the optimistic balloons of military war reporting, which fed imperial visions at home, ultimately strengthened the chauvinists' hand.[24]

To combat the war aims movement, the chancellor employed a mixture of promises and calls for restraint. Since self-defense did not constitute "an adequate goal," he promised the visibly disappointed members of the Federal Council securities in Belgium, moderate boundary rectifications in the East and West, an indemnity, and a colonial empire in Africa to "insure that the sacrifices of this war were not in vain." [25] Similarly, in a long letter to Conservative leader Count Kuno von Westarp, he sought to counter the misrepresentations of National Liberal spokesman Ernst Hirsch: "In fact I have said that in case of peace offers from our enemies, the army and the navy have to decide if we can continue to fight. More-over, I told him that the army and navy would have to be heard first regarding the demands necessary for strategic reasons." But in terms of principle he added, "These ordinary functions of military leader-ship do not limit the equally natural role of the guiding statesman." Although economic subjection of Belgium would be the absolute minimum, "I have no doubt that the annexationist demands cham-pioned by him, including northern France and the Verdun-Belfort border together with the Czenstochova-Lake Peipus line, lie beyond practical discussion for me." Even in case of utter defeat of the enemy, Bethmann predicted "that against the proponents of these ideas I shall force through a *policy of relative moderation in the Bismarck spirit* and I would heartily welcome such a fight" (my italics). To placate the Conservatives, he promised that Belgium had to be "rendered harmless for us" through "military, political, and economic guarantees which would prevent it from becoming a future steppingstone for the Entente." Moreover, he pleaded with Hirsch himself, "It seems to me the duty of those circles who could or should be aware of the necessities of foreign policy to counter uneasiness rather than to promote it" and to follow the "utterly un-mistakable" lead of the government.[26]

Bethmann's appeals to personal decency, coupled with vague prom-ises, could not prevent the formation of the *Kriegszielbewegung* (war aims movement) in the spring of 1915. "I am accused of not yet having annexed Belgium and northern France . . . by Pan-Germans, navy, and H.M.," he complained. The frustration of the military stalemate, the impact of chauvinist articles, pamphlets, and books, as well as crass economic self-interest coalesced in a war aims movement of unprecedented magnitude, which was united in the resolve to force the chancellor into a stronger stand. The Conserva-tives, National Liberals, and Catholics all agreed on the "permanent possession of Belgium," the need for French coal and iron, and the annexation of as much land as possible in Russia, "certainly expecting the chancellor to show full cooperation with those wishes." Characteristically, the Right "hoped that the discussion about war aims would later have a salutary effect upon domestic policy" by creating a bourgeois front against liberalization and a renunciationist peace. The public spearhead of the movement, the *Sechsereingabe*—signed by the leading agricultural groups, *Bund der Landwirte*,

Deutscher Bauernbund, and *Christliche Deutsche Bauernvereine,* the industrial organizations, *Centralverband Deutscher Industrieller* and *Bund der Industriellen,* as well as the *Reichsdeutscher Mittel-standsverband* speaking for middle-class interests—demanded "no premature, weak peace!" Aside from security, a colonial empire "which fully statisfies our manifold economic interests," and adequate indemnity, the pressure groups, which represented nearly the entire business community, called for the exploitation of Belgium, the annexation of northern France, the incorporation of agricultural territory in the East in order to preserve the social balance of the empire, and large border rectifications toward Russia. The equally notorious manifesto signed by 1,341 intellectuals and professors, organized by the chauvinist historian Dietrich Schäfer, desired "certainly not world domination, but full world power corresponding to the greatness of our cultural, economic, and military might." With their slogan—directly aimed at Bethmann—*"No cultural policy without Machtpolitik!"* Wilhelmian imperialism reached the zenith of its illusory hubris.[27]

Resistance against this massive annexationist pressure was nearly impossible for Bethmann, since the small number of 141 signatures on the moderate counterpetition of Delbrück-Dernburg revealed that the overwhelming majority of Wilhelmian elites clamored for substantial conquest. "No man alone can turn the rudder and steer the ship against storm and waves; at most he can trim the sails to the wind," Riezler metaphorically described the chancellor's impotence. In this kind of situation "politics is the art of doing evil and achieving good." Now more than ever, the statesman's task was to "be wise enough to understand the complexities and to lead the evil spirits through evil to good." To forestall further agitation, Bethmann confidentially briefed the party leaders of the Right on May 13 on his relatively modest goals, which were reminiscent of the September Program. "We have not directed our policy toward unleashing a war in order to annex territories," he cautioned, but promised— "if the military situation allows it—to make Belgium innocuous, to prevent it from becoming a military, economic, and political dependency of England and France," i.e. to make it a German vassal. The cession of Liège, control of the fortifications, railroads, and the port of Antwerp, the establishment of a customs union, German law, social legislation, and a campaign against French influence, as well as the annexation of Briey and a better frontier in the Vosges were his most optimistic western aims. Toward Russia some limited border rectifications would be necessary, while the fate of the colonies depended upon England's power at peacetime. Bidding for continued support of the Right with these sweeping assurances, Bethmann implored the parliamentarians, "Public dicussion of the Belgian problem is undesirable, especially because of Holland." Despite Bassermann's, Spahn's, and Westarp's insistence on sizable gains, Bethmann maintained, "we must remain a homogeneous national state," and refused to disown the Socialists' interpretations of his moderation. But since the chancellor tended more toward "the Europeanization of our will to power . . . the middle European empire of the German nation," the chauvinists naturally continued to mistrust his personal commitment to annexations.[28]

When the representatives of the six leading industrial organizations, including Alfred Hugenberg, Conrad Freiherr von Wangenheim, Gustav Rösicke, Hirsch, and Stresemann, met with the chancellor four days later, Bethmann was more cautious and noncommital. Receiving them cordially as "testimony to our agreement on the final aim: unanimity in the struggle," he nevertheless justified his prohibition against debate by citing Italy's threatening entry into the war and the possibility of other severe setbacks. "From the first I have publicly proclaimed as goal: Germany must be strengthened so that our neighbors cannot make war on us without our consent." Although he preferred some degree of Belgian dependence, the chancellor stressed that the complexity of coalition warfare might necessitate separate peace with one of the enemies, and then conditions would have to be reduced "to free our rear." Assuring the industrialists, "I shall call upon your proffered help when the time comes," he warned against the danger of unrestrained discussion for the Burgfrieden. "It is our duty to stand together even if not every wish can be fulfilled." Not annexationist clamor but the fortune of arms would decide the outcome: "Russia is of prime importance; with Belgium [we can] hopefully form a lasting relationship." In an even less conciliatory tone, he reprimanded General Gebsattel by denouncing Pan-German agitation, which fanned "popular unrest about the unfounded and unproven defeatism and cowardice of the government" and thus hastened the very revolution that these "truly monarchist circles are warning against." Rejecting "this minority attempt to enforce their own will on the man called by the crown to direct the policy of the empire," Bethmann attempted to

stand firm against the wave of hysteria. Nevertheless, in late May
the chancellor was forced to promise to an enthusiastic Reichstag,
"The greater the danger . . . the more we must persevere until we
have created and won all possible real guarantees and securities, so
that none of our enemies—alone or united—will dare risk another
trial of arms against us." [29]

Since "the Pan-Germans, etc., [sensed] clearly that world hegemony [was] traditionally unsympathetic to the chancellor and Jagow," the public campaign for annexations continued unabated.
"The people have an enormous drive toward power," Riezler observed in midsummer 1915. An anonymous poet captured the popular mood in his call for action:

> Welcher Preis dem Vaterlande?
> "Halt!" des Reiches Kanzler spricht.
> "Vieles habe ich zu bedenken.
> Ruhe ist jetzt Bürgerflicht!"
>
> Und er wechselt neue Noten
> Und er weiss, dass nichts er will
> Wie er priestert, wie er poltert!
> Rings die Feldgrauen ernst und still.
>
> Was an uns, es ist geschehen.
> Kanzler jetzt tritt Du hervor!
> Politik ist Deine Sache
> Denke, was das Volk verlor!*

Invoking the dead warriors to ask "German people! Where is your
reward?" the writer explained rhetorically, "Shall we remain what we

---

* What will be our prize of glory?
But the chancellor cries out: "Stop!
There is much to be considered,
Quiet is now the citizen's job!"

Forever he's exchanging memos
Knowing that he has no will.
He pontificates and blusters
To the soldiers gray and still.

We have done our sacred duty,
Chancellor, now it is your move:
Politics is your department, but
Bethink how much the people lose!

were? Shall we go home with an angry heart?" and bitterly added
an imagined enemy taunt:

> Mit den Waffen mögt Ihr siegen
> Aber nicht in—Politik!
>
> Wehe Kaiser! Argem Schelme
> Reichest Du den Kanzlerstab!
> Emsig schaufeln Totengräber
> An des deutschen Reiches Grab! *

Painfully aware "that wide popular circles champion utopian plans
and exaggerated hopes," Bethmann warned Hertling, "if we proposed such extensive goals, the war would be prolonged indef-
nitely." [30]

As a counterweight to the pressures of the annexationist movement, Bethmann intensified his contacts with the Social Democrats.
In mid-March 1915 he assured party leadership that "I do not think
at all about realizing" the insane goals of the Pan-Germans, only
hinting at economic advantages in Belgium and boundary rectifications toward France. In mid-July Bethmann had a long and probing
conversation with one of the leading revisionists, Eduard David:
"We sit on the beautiful terrace toward the park. I am surprised
by his personally relaxed and outwardly rustic manner," the visitor
noted in his diary. "He does not want to annex Belgium [but
prefers] strategic corrections of the Belgian, French, and Russian
frontiers." Disappointed by the chancellor's pessimism about victory
over tsarism, David warned that the Party had to maintain its antiannexationist stand in principle; "otherwise we drive the people
into opposition." But he thought "that on the basis of economic
[dominance] we can come to a meeting of minds" and held out
Socialist support for moderate and indirect annexationism "if the
great domestic concessions come," such as Prussian electoral reform.
Partly because of such hints, Bethmann speeded preparations for
suffrage liberalization and had Wahnschaffe assure the Socialists
"that the chancellor does *not* share the view of the Six Associations,

*You may win in bloody battle
But never in—diplomacy!

Woe to our kaiser! A poor soul
The chancellor's staff you gave!
Busy undertakers' shovel
On the German Empire's grave!

petition." Nevertheless, when he showed as little inclination to move toward the Left as toward the Right in the fall of 1915, "the danger of the threatening Reichstag split" and the "utter failure of the *Neuorientierung* (new policy)" strained the support of the majority Socialists. Because of the socioeconomic limits of the chancellor's power, David disgustedly concluded, "He shows no resolution." [31]

Although his bid to remove the National Liberals from the ranks of the annexationists on the basis of Bassermann's personal indiscretion failed, the chancellor maintained, in the face of rising parliamentary opposition, "The discussion of the war aims is not yet possible." Invoking Bismarckian precedent to the party leaders, by stressing the danger to domestic unity, he merely promised, "After the sacrifices in life and property, we will not leave the war as we have entered it," implying that Germany must be "stronger, mightier, and freer." But when the stream of propaganda turned into a veritable flood, Bethmann swallowed his "great reluctance to discuss the possibility of the annexation of Russian territory" and spoke out more clearly in the Reichstag "in order to solidify his position toward the Right." Calling for the freedom of the seas, the liberation of the non-Russian nationalities in the Baltic and Poland, and the abrogation of the balance of power, he took an important step toward abandoning his studious neutrality: "Something new must arise! If Europe is to find tranquility at all, this can only be achieved through a *strong* and *untouchable Germany*," he exclaimed to the cheering Reichstag. Since the attempts of pacifist organizations such as *Bund Neues Vaterland* to create a climate for a status quo peace were unsuccessful, Bethmann's refusal to disown the annexationists forced him to retreat step by step into a stronger public advocacy of vindictive war aims.[32]

The creation of "Mitteleuropa, politically and economically our world-political task," appealed to Bethmann as an escape from the domestic and military contradictions of the German situation. Because of the military's "policy of Germanizing" Belgium and Poland, the chancellor cautioned Chief of Staff Falkenhayn that "from the standpoint of our general political interest I must emphatically reject the idea of annexing the Russian Baltic provinces," since this would make indirect dominance over a peaceful postwar Europe impossible. When Italy's entry into the war made Falkenhayn suddenly jump on the Mitteleuropa bandwagon, the chancellor grew suspicious, since the chief of staff would "accept a military convention only when the alliance was legally enlarged and anchored." Although he considered the suggestion "not stupid but probably only said for effect," Bethmann, in an object lesson in diplomacy, replied "that our military situation cannot be improved through a policy of strengthened alliances," as long as nobody new was willing to sign. Moreover, the diplomats were convinced, "One cannot create a new order in Europe out of thin air—but it is necessary to plant the seed so that it may grow without war." Only a "middle European imperialism with a light touch could succeed, not Falkenhayn's murky Napoleonic ideas." Thus throwing cold water upon the chief of staff's sanguine hopes for Central Europe as a miracle weapon, Bethmann seized upon the growing technical criticism in economic and governmental circles against the idea of a customs union and concluded that, at most, a revision of trade treaties could be realized. The cause of disagreement between military and civilian leadership was not so much the final goal, as Falkenhayn's insistence that "we should not only rule everything de facto but also de jure, i.e. in pronounced legal form." But this was absurd "since Austria is no petty principality. The only thing we can do and must do is to create such a constellation at the [conclusion of] peace that everything will be channeled into a European direction," Riezler observed. Falkenhayn's ideas smacked of "absolute rule of force . . . and that is impossible." [33]

In the fall of 1915, the chancellor diplomatically launched his own scheme for indirect hegemony over Central Europe. "Among the leaders of the old Germany, who grew up in the atmosphere of '70 and '80 and for whom a German world empire is an unthinkable self-contradiction, Bethmann is the only one capable of learning from events," Riezler observed perceptively. "Fortunately, the chancellor believes we should first reestablish our relationship to Austria economically and politically and only then discuss the Polish question." Because of his concern over the growing domination of the Magyar and Slavic elements within the Hapsburg monarchy, Bethmann proposed to Stephan Freiherr von Burian "a preferential system of tariffs" in order to leave the door open for later middle European unification. Since Germany would accept the Austro-Polish solution only if Vienna joined an economic and eventually political union, the Austrian foreign minister agreed in principle, coining the formula *Anschluss aber ohne Ausschluss* ("Inclusion without

Exclusiveness"). Explaining the advantages of "a customs agreement based upon mutual preferences," Bethmann stressed to his fellow ministers: "This would create a solid and indestructible economic nucleus around which other states on the continent could later crystallize, providing a necessary counterweight against England, Russia, and the transatlantic powers." Although he was willing to use Germany's full military weight, the chancellor strove for a negotiated *Mitteleuropa* in contrast to a forced *Diktat,* since only a voluntary agreement could be lasting. To the Bundesrat he explained: "It must be a vital task of German policy to deepen and affirm the relationship with Austria. The political formula for this would have to be greater cooperation of both armies, and economic equalization of tariffs on the basis of reciprocal preference." [34]

Continuing his balancing act between annexationism and defeatism, Bethmann attempted to head off the formulation of a publicly committed *Kriegszielmehrheit* (war aims majority) in the Reichstag. Already in midsummer of 1915, the National Liberals had endorsed a peace "which while extending our frontiers in East, West, and overseas, secures us militarily, politically, and economically, against a renewed assault and is worth the incredible sacrifices made hitherto by the German people." In early October the Conservative Reichstag caucus called for guaranteeing German national security in the East and for a lasting peace "based on the territorial expansion necessary for this purpose." Because of Matthias Erzberger's moderating influence, the Center Party resolution later the same month demanded only "increased protection of our country in East and West," as well as "lasting assurances for the economic needs of our growing population." Despite the chancellor's warning to "weigh every word," Free Conservatives and Progressives also committed themselves to annexationist stands in early December, making the front of bourgeois parties complete. [35]

When increasing opposition within their own party forced the Socialists to announce a peace interpellation, the Burgfrieden, always more illusion than reality, was in grave jeopardy. Admitting that "whoever does not look for peace and only thinks about the continuation of war must have a heart of stone," Bethmann attempted to prevent a show of disunity which could be interpreted abroad as growing weakness: "The [peace] conditions will be determined by our strength and by negotiations with our enemies. If I put my trumps on the table now I have lost the game," he argued cogently but without regard for the war-weary masses. "We cannot proclaim no annexations, status quo. Then they will say: we are through. I repeat: We need a sign of strength and unity in a form which reinforces the enemy's desire for peace." Although formal agreement on his policy had now become impossible, he nevertheless pleaded for a "common goal . . . an early, victorious, and honorable peace." When Phillip Scheidemann charged that government mistakes had turned the mood of the workers from exultation to despair, Bethmann replied emotionally: "We are defending hearth and home. When we have repulsed our enemies it will be our duty to obtain a peace that will curb the Entente intention to encircle and overrun us in the future." Unable to prevent the Socialist interpellation, since he could make no substantive concessions, the chancellor strove to render its form innocuous, repeating insistently, "We *must* stand together." When the party leaders of the Right threatened a concerted response to Scheidemann, Bethmann countered, "We must stage the Reichstag correctly and distribute the roles right." There could be no question about "unity against the enemy's intent to destroy us" but "beyond this, differences of opinion" had become unavoidable.[36]

Despite the chancellor's pleas, the Reichstag session of December 9, 1915, witnessed the first major clash between the champions of annexation and the spokesmen for peace. Stressing his firm confidence in the military situation and domestic morale, Bethmann vowed: "We will resolutely continue to fight this war, imposed upon us by our enemies, in order to achieve what Germany's future demands from us." But in response to growing pacifist sentiment Scheidemann demanded emphatically, "When the government has the opportunity to conclude a peace which secures German political independence, the integrity of the empire, and the freedom of economic development, then we insist that it conclude this peace." Bethmann replied by painting a grim picture of Allied war aims that would culminate in the destruction of Germany, claiming that the war of attrition would not wear down the country and that any offer had to come from the enemy. "This does not mean we want to extend the war unnecessarily even for one day and win this or any other Faustpfand," he countered Liebknecht's passionate accusation, "Plans of conquest!" Warning that German demands would increase the longer the war lasted, the chancellor promised to take the "avenues of attack" from the enemy: "We must secure ourselves against aggression politically and militarily as well as economically in terms of possibilities for growth (Bravo!). What is essential for this *must* be reached (renewed Bravo)." His strong appeal to the loyalty of the annexationists was balanced by a similar gesture to the Socialists: "For the German government this war has remained what it was from the beginning . . . a war of defense of the German people." Despite the chancellor's warning "not to irritate the Socialists," the bourgeois parties responded with a unanimous declaration that during peace negotiations "Germany's military, economic, financial, and political interests must be safeguarded in their entirety with all means, including necessary territorial annexations." The chancellor's hands were now doubly tied.[37]

Vexed by the Right's mixture of patriotism and self-interest, Bethmann exposed the irrationality of the annexationist fever in a long letter to Valentini: "In rash underestimation of our foes, everyone thought the end of the war near, the enemy beaten, and believed he could revise the map of Europe according to his whim." Socialist defeatism was not the cause of annexationism, as Conservatives claimed, but rather "the less hopes for a quick and decisive victory were fulfilled, the more our chauvinists believed they had to prove their bravery and loyalty by proposing the most power-hungry war aims and smearing everybody who refused to follow their lead as subversive weaklings." The very boundlessness of the demands immediately produced a reaction on the part of moderates in *all* parties, "who did not consider it unpatriotic to take into account political realities and to scrutinize the usefulness of the demanded annexations." Since military censorship suppressed their views more vigorously than those of the Right, and since they lacked the support of the imperialist press and mass organizations, their voice was more indistinct. "The Socialists' peaceful attitude, opposed to unlimited annexation, gave the Conservatives, the industrially dependent National Liberals, and part of the Center a welcome pretext for resurrecting the old front against the Reds as a requirement for patriotism." Even if the policy of "encouraging chauvinist tendencies and chimeras of world-domination" might once have been necessary for the creation of a navy on a par with England's, "it cannot be continued after the war." Pleading for a widening of the social basis of the Wilhelmian Empire to include the workers, the chancellor closed this outburst with the avowal, "A government which again conducts a policy of deceit will lead the people into the abyss." [38]

During the third year of the murderous struggle Bethmann stoically continued to espouse moderate war aims despite increasing criticism from both political extremes. While Karl Liebknecht and a growing band of followers denounced the chancellor as puppet of the monopolies, the Prussian Conservatives of the Upper House made another attempt to prod him into a more annexationist stand in January 1916, warning: "Our domestic situation will only remain tolerable if we gain a peace that fulfills our national aspirations and brings a sufficient indemnity." Yet Bethmann refused to be intimidated by demands for "the reshaping of Europe through Napoleonic decisions." Riezler often sympathized with "the people's understandable longing for action, movement, and a creative genius." In many ways "our bureaucratic apparatus with its slow understanding and relearning, together with the hesitant, deliberative chancellor—all that does not fit into our time." Nevertheless, the chancellor's assistant knew of no positive answer to the question, "Could a demonic will shape the nucleus of a United States of Europe out of the present crisis?" About only one thing was he sure: "This horrible stagnation. Gas pains. It is disgusting that the government always appears in a negative light. Thereby everyone becomes unsure and the doubters, in need of a banner, follow the Pan-Germans." Bethmann's studious silence and public equivocation made it seem "that the government strives for less than the moderates. That helps the Pan-Germans." There was no easy solution to the fundamental paradox that the overwhelming majority of elites were rabidly annexationist, while the masses increasingly craved peace. By political need and personal conviction the chancellor sought to plot a middle course. "It is difficult, if not impossible, to demand and push through a policy in opposition to the dominant will of the people. But this must be, because it is Germany's only path to greatness." [39]

In a revealing letter to the leading Bismarck scholar of the age, Erich Marcks, Bethmann claimed he was only following the Iron Chancellor's inspiration. "I have done everything to hold down the agitation of the Right," he pleaded for understanding, but "it refused to die, although . . . it called up opposition of the masses for whom the war was and is self-defense." To satisfy popular desire for a goal, "I have thrown into the ring the idea of Mitteleuropa which will determine our future. I have pointed to the great tasks in the East." But publicly, "I could not go beyond the safeguarding of our frontiers, . . . beyond the elimination of the staging areas in Belgium and Poland." Moreover, "I have hinted at the inclusion of Belgium and Poland in our sphere in Mitteleuropa, truly no petty aim." Not only the fluctuating fortune of battle but the imperatives of domestic unity made this a mandatory course: "Open debate would split the nation internally and endanger eventual success by the fixation of aims, which can prove mistaken and impossible at any time in such an unprecedented war." In this remarkable analysis Bethmann, as practicing statesman, showed more insight into the policies of his famous predecessor than had Bismarck's leading contemporary biographer:

> I believe he would have turned his famous riding boots first against the political agitators who, greater in words than in thought, wanted to force him to unfurl banners which he might have had to pull down again at any time . . . he would have maintained the thesis of self-defense which is the deepest truth; even in his public appearances he would only have followed the dictates of foreign policy. In his secret actions, I believe he would have set as his goal: laying a foundation for a strong center as focus for European development, a center that protects them but does not rape them. He would have kept open and prepared the different ways to such great ends with a hand of incomparable mastery and subtlety, as long as it remained uncertain which of them would be passable, and would have finally entered upon it with the faith that moves mountains.

Self-consciously, Bethmann strove to follow the tradition of the Iron Chancellor. "Had Bismarck, at the founding of the German Empire, acted according to the formula of those who see in him only Machiavelli—he would never have created the empire but would have attempted to enlarge Prussia by absorbing the South German states and thus delivered it to a Franco-South German-Austrian coalition." But the rampant imperialism of Wilhelmian elites could no longer be curbed by realistic moderation; it was closer to the evil spirit of another chancellor of a future Reich of even more terrifying magnitude.[40]

Undaunted, Bethmann continued to propagate his limited Realpolitik to diplomats, generals, and party leaders. Calling upon the

leading journalists "to use their immense influence" for the restoration of domestic unity, he sketched relatively moderate aims:
"Elimination of the avenues of attack, Poland and Belgium—better
boundaries on the other sides. Freedom of economic development—
in all directions, also across the seas. Truly no small thing. Establishment of an untouchably strong Germany in the middle of Europe—
around which all weaker states can cluster. That means not more
and not less than a Europe organized by Germany." True to his
tactic of small concessions to the Right while maintaining the fiction
of a defensive war, the chancellor discussed the fate of Poland,
Lithuania, and Latvia in the Reichstag in April. "History does not
recognize the status quo ante after such immense events," he said,
adding, "the postwar Belgium will no longer be the same." Although
he remained vague about the legal form of these territories, he implied the creation of a series of buffer states in the East and some
administrative measures in favor of Flemish autonomy. Despite his
increasing public commitment to specific goals, Bethmann knew that
"Belgium, colonies, *and* a large indemnity will be impossible," since
Germany would not be able to choose among a whole variety of alternatives at the peace table but rather would have to take what it could
get. "All we have now are certain proposals, since their practical
implementation and the choice of means depend upon the further
progress of the war." To the Bundesrat he hinted "that at the beginning we played with the idea of expropriating greater areas and
expelling their inhabitants," a reference to Hatakist settlement
dreams, but "at closer inspection this procedure appeared utterly
impractical." While not denying his resolution to make Germany
more secure and powerful in the future, he stressed to a moderate
supporter "that I have never succumbed to the pressure of preferring
annexations to self-defense." Instinctive realism as well as the knowledge that his power rested upon the precarious support of the
Scheidemann Socialists, prevented the chancellor from succumbing
completely to the war aims movement. At most he could publicly
endorse the formula: "Defense is no feeble goal exhausting itself in
the maintenance of the status quo." [41]

Afraid that "the number of moderate voices would be in the minority and the impression of war-weariness increase" should the war
aims debate be opened, Bethmann stubbornly refused the lifting of
censorship. "It does not seem right to propose aims when we are
trying to save our skins," he argued with the Conservative leaders of

the Prussian Landtag. "If we are strong enough when peace comes we shall reap great rewards. But our strength will not increase by proclaiming large goals." Although the Pan-German agitation had spread to include submarine warfare and domestic reform, the chancellor considered it irresponsible to solidify his position by championing annexationist aims: "We cannot put ourselves on the same level with France, England, and Italy." In contrast to the military, who were confident that government endorsement of conquests would raise flagging morale, Bethmann believed that "if we claimed as much [as the annexationists] we would find ourselves opposed to the broad masses fighting for the fatherland, and not for such a policy of expansion." [42] But the government-sponsored moderate countermovement, Deutscher Nationalausschuss, launched with much fanfare in the summer of 1916, did not succeed in rallying the public around "a middle line regarding the war aims," since at the last minute Bethmann refused permission for a massive enlightenment campaign regarding Germany's goals. Although he incessantly "struggled against all political and military chauvinism," the chancellor was psychologically incapable of using the weapons of mass society for his moderate ends, a failure through which he abandoned the field to the extremists. When the third OHL insisted on propaganda support for the Hindenburg Program, claiming that the chancellor's neutrality and aloofness had failed to create "that degree of domestic unity which we need," Bethmann could no longer resist. On November 26 the chief of the war press office, Major Nicolai, opened the floodgates of war aims agitation. The chancellor, bowing to the demigods, ratified the decision by arguing that the discussion would contribute "to a strengthened unity of national will." A major component of Bethmann's war aims policy had collapsed.[43]

Although annexationist hysteria was reaching new heights, Bethmann continued to hope that his limited aims would prevail by offering peace after the victory over Rumania. "That will be something, when Ludendorff is forced to understand that peace will be splendid if we finish plus minus nothing in the West, if Poland is freed, and we receive Suwalki and a few colonies," Riezler pondered the fresh dilemma. Indirect hegemony "might have been possible with Falkenhayn but never with Paul von Hindenburg and Erich Ludendorff. The chancellor says they will save the present for us but they mortgage the future heavily—under Falkenhayn the present was lost and thereby also the future." When Burian confronted Bethmann with extensive demands which put the burden of a compromise peace on German shoulders while reserving considerable gains for Austria in the Balkans, he had to stop hedging and commit himself. "Even today he could not draw up a list of peace conditions because in this coalition war it would require a thick book, while he had to limit himself to short sentences." In order to maintain some flexibility in the negotiations the chancellor proposed goals that, although more moderate than the chauvinist demands, still bore a striking resemblance to the September Program:

1. France: exchange of part of Briey for several villages in Alsace-Lorraine; colonial understanding

2. Belgium: restoration of the kingdom, cession of Liège, economic arrangements

3. Russia: cession of parts of Estonia and Lithuania; Polish independence

4. Colonies: loss of Tsingtao and the Pacific Isles; a compact Mittelafrika

5. Indemnity in case of economic concessions; trade treaties with France, Russia, and England

"To be candid, peace on that basis would be meager, but it would not disappoint him gravely. . . . If we show to the world that we cannot be conquered, that our development cannot be halted, that we have defended the achievements of 1870 successfully, we should be grateful to God," he concluded emphatically to the Prussian Ministry of State. "To reach more would of course be desirable, but since the military and economic prospects are so unsure, we must take this step if we have the opportunity to conclude an honorable and secure peace." There was only one striking omission: no overt mention of Mitteleuropa.[44]

Although still extensive, this program proposed aims which, if further reduced by negotiation, contained the outlines of a compromise peace favorable to the Central Powers. A combined list, swelled by Burian's Balkan demands, gained the approval of the Supreme Command after considerable expansion in detail, such as the addition of Luxembourg to the empire and an indemnity for the *Auslandsdeutschen* (German citizens abroad). Refusing to include a

Belgian contribution which "would immediately bring negotiations to a halt," the chancellor submitted eight points, also comprising a trade treaty with Russia, to the emperor on November 7. Although somewhat expanded by Ludendorff, these conditions nevertheless contained only minimal territorial annexations (undefined in the East while specifying Longwy-Briey in the West) and on balance represented the chancellor's design for indirect hegemony. Nevertheless, Bethmann did not consider even these aims inviolable, since he "assured [Burian] in strict secrecy [that he was willing] to sacrifice" territorial gains in France and Belgium in order to secure advantages in the East. Hence he agreed only "academically" to the Austrian demand for a binding war aims program. "If specific conditions were explicitly announced [in the peace note], and thereby the maximum demands of the Central Powers put on paper, the public would all too easily view them as minimal demands, through which not only our enemy's willingness to negotiate would become questionable but we would also be deprived of any flexibility from the outset." Bethmann sought to postpone any secret commitment by drawing Turkey and Bulgaria into internal discussion, and finally in mid-December he agreed to a promise of Austrian territorial integrity without binding legal force. His reluctance sprang from his willingness to accept minimal gains. "If the Entente came tomorrow and made the following offer, if they said: Not destruction, only restore Serbia and Belgium," he asked rhetorically, "would I then be able to say no apodictically?" [45]

Outflanked by Bethmann's limited annexationism, the Supreme Command nevertheless quickly reasserted itself with more extensive demands. "Today large maps with the eastern and western war aims of the OHL arrived together with a priceless letter," Riezler noted angrily. In the West, these aims, "based on the *present military situation*" called for the annexation of Longwy-Briey, the related Belgian mines, the Meuse crossings at Liège, of Luxembourg surrounded by German territory, the reduction of Belgium to a complete vassal state, the occupation of a naval base, and all border rectification toward France exclusively in Germany's favor. "In the East they are simply fantastic. Grodno, Vilna, Lemza, Bialystock, Brest Litovsk to be German, and a large stretch reaching southward around Poland, and in the West and North another fat slice taken from Poland." When the navy similarly called for the possession of "the Belgian and Estonian coast" as well as numerous overseas coaling stations, it was clear "that the high brass has not the vaguest idea that we can reach only one-twentieth of these aims because of our military situation and the dead weight of our allies." To Bethmann the blindness of the generals was stupefying. "I foresee terrible clashes if they still don't understand that we cannot dictate as long as the enemy is not beaten and that hardly anybody can decide while negotiating on the basis of the present situation who is strongest or least weakened." [46]

Although a formal war aims conference reached some measure of agreement regarding the fate of Belgium, "sharp disagreements regarding eastern goals—besides Estonia and Lithuania Hindenburg wants to have Brest-Litovsk and Bjelowitsch for *Prussia*—were not discussed in detail as premature." Claiming that he still regarded the November 1916 agreement binding, Bethman cautioned: "Since politics will always remain the art of the possible, nobody can foresee today if we shall reach all the goals we have set for ourselves." Intent on offering a cheap peace to any enemy that deserted the Entente "to split the coalition," the chancellor relied on the normal process of negotiations where maxima would slowly be reduced to minima for eventual compromise: "The more I consider the gain of these territories one of our most important war aims for which we have to strive with all our energy, the less I can assume the responsibility of proclaiming the realization as conditio sine qua non for the conclusion of peace." Nevertheless, his draft program of early January and the later instruction to Count Johann Bernstorff revealed the strong hand of the military, since it called for a strategic frontier against Russia, Polish independence, colonial restitution, border rectificaton of Belgium subject to guarantees, economic and financial equalization of burdens, compensation to private citizens, and freedom of trade and of the seas.[47]

While the war aims movement was supported by the annexationism of the military, the growing desire for peace on the part of the masses jeopardized Bethmann's moderate expansionism from the Left in the first months of 1917. "The chancellor's policy of leading the German Empire into European imperialism by grouping the heart of the continent around our silent leadership (Austria, Poland, Belgium) has slowly moved forward for some time," Riezler reflected. But the more visible Bethmann's attempt to win the masses for a measured Machtpolitik became, "the more it was apparent that the whole structure of the state, the intellectual habits of its elites, as well as their economic interests, oppose it." When the Right's fear that the chancellor's annexationism was tempered by his dependence on the Left erupted in a virulent attack by Heydebrand, the chancellor retorted that he still "thought it too early for myself to enter such debates." Instead, he merely called for the stretchable formula of a "lasting peace which compensates us for all wrong suffered and which secures a strong Germany's existence and future." The Right fumed, especially in the press, and the Left applauded when Bethmann castigated "empty phrases, boasting, and self-exaggeration," arguing that "such a policy of strength . . . can only be conducted if the political rights of the entire nation in all its strata, even in the broad masses, allow completely equal and joyful participation in the work of the State (Bravo!)." Because of unrelenting annexationist pressure, Bethmann was slowly veering toward internal reform. Despite the vocal fronde, "the policy of the chancellor can be successful as long as the domestic situation does not become catastrophic through Ludendorff's stupidities and blind commandeering." Although the obstacles to indirect hegemony were growing daily, "all can go well," Riezler hoped, "if our position at the peace table is strong enough to lay the outward foundations of a grander policy." [48]

In March Austrian separate peace feelers ("because the monarchy was at the end of its power") compelled Bethmann to take another step toward formalizing a detailed German war aims program. With some misgivings, he approved Viennese advances toward France, adding, "One could at any rate talk about exchanging the ore deposits of Longwy-Briey for parts of Lorraine or Alsace as a minimum." Adding "I have repeatedly declared in public that we do not want to annex Belgium but we must obtain some guarantees from that country," he suggested trade possibilities in Antwerp, railroad community, inclusion in a customs union, etc., since it was his "personal belief" that the annexation of Liège and the Flanders coast, demanded by army and navy, was illusory. While the chancellor was willing to countenance a partial give-and-take in the West "as long as Germany was not beaten in the East, it could only be a matter of 'how much we keep' and at worst a return to the status quo ante." More concretely, he renounced any claims to Polish territory and replied to Czernin's direct question about his intentions for Estonia: "I don't know yet. But if peace with Russia depended upon the return of Estonia we would probably give it up." To keep Austria in the alliance, Bethmann reluctantly agreed to a protocol promise of territorial integrity for the Hapsburg monarchy as a minimal program, and to a use of the *Faustpfänder* in proportion to mutual effort as maximal solution—for Germany directed toward Poland and the Baltic, for Austria toward Rumania. Although Bethmann was willing to forgo large annexations in order to end the carnage, his freedom to make concessions was severely limited by the power of the military and annexationist Reichstag majority.[49]

When the outbreak of the Russian Revolution raised the hope of a breach in the united enemy front, Bethmann attempted to "build golden bridges to the first opponent ready for peace." Increasing Austrian weakness and growing war-weariness at home forced the chancellor to find a formula that would bring the Provisional Government to the negotiating table while allowing for some border rectifications and the creation of dependent buffer states. Since the OHL vetoed the Socialist slogan of "no annexations, no indemnities," he called in the Reichstag for a peace "based on an honorable foundation for all parties" and elaborated in the *NAZ*: In December 1916 "Germany and her allies declared that they were ready for a peace that secures the existence, honor, and free development of their peoples." Striving for "a reasonable middle way between the extremes," Bethmann proposed that the Left should be told that only a settlement "which guaranteed the security of Germany's vital interests would be acceptable" while the Right needed to be convinced that, because of the stalemate, Germany could "not dictate conditions according to our wishes." In a war aims conference of the Prussian ministers in mid-April, Bethmann therefore stressed the need for a reasonable peace, for he was afraid that with Alexander Kerensky the Socialist formula would prevail making it "impossible to measure border rectifications with a Russian yardstick." Since German annexation of the Baltic shore would only insure permanent Russian hostility, the state ministry agreed on a program of "annexing only the militarily necessary, then [creating an] autonomous demilitarized belt," i.e. system of satellite states. Under the domestic threat of a Socialist "declaration synonymous with the Russian one, despite all of [Riezler's] vain attempts at persuasion," the chancellor embarked upon the policy of autonomy, which formalized indirect hegemony. Hence in the abortive *pourparlers* he instructed his negotiators to avoid the repulsive terms *annexations* and *border rectifications* to "make it possible for the Russians to renounce Courland and Lithuania by dressing them up as independent states, with domestic self-government, but tied to us militarily, politically, and economically." [50]

In the notorious Kreuznach Conference of late April, the Supreme Command finally succeeded in forcing its terms upon the reluctant chancellor. When the OHL first attempted to tie his hands, Bethmann balked, since "the splitting of the present coalition of our enemies and their conversion to our side in the future" would be endangered by annexationist inflexibility. But since the kaiser preemptorily ordered him to sit down with the military, Admiral Müller "read on the faces of the chancellor and Arthur Zimmermann the thought: It doesn't matter if we set maximum goals. It will happen differently anyway." While following the outline of the earlier war aims exchanges, the Kreuznach protocol breathed a spirit of virulent annexationism, perverting Bethmann's limited and indirect goals "by utter lack of measure in East and West." In the East:

1. Estonia and Lithuania must be won for the German Empire up to the line indicated by the OHL. . . . In the South the OHL will limit itself to the line Bialystok-Njemen. . . .

2. The delineation of the German border toward Poland depends upon the future relationship of Poland to the empire [but should include the Narev line and the Germanization of a border strip].

3. [Austria would have to cede East Galicia and be compensated in Rumania while Serbia] will be linked to it as South Slave state. [Bulgaria should return to the 1913 frontier in the Dobrudja while German oil interests in Rumania were to be secured.]

In the West:

1. Belgium remains in existence and will be taken under German military control until it is politically and economically ready for a defensive and offensive alliance with Germany [the time to be determined by the latter. Liège, the Flemish coast, and Bruges] are negotiable demands for peace with England. [The right of occupation, control of the railroads, and further territorial concessions were also included.]

2. The cession of the southern tip of Belgium (around Arlon) is demanded by the OHL for war-economical reasons on the assumption that there are ore deposits. [Luxembourg should become a member of the empire.]

3. The ore and coal basin of Longwy-Briey must be won for for Germany [and smaller strategic border rectifications on the rest of the French frontier were necessary].

4. At most single border points . . . can be considered for cession to France in order not to let peace fail for this reason.

Although excluding such old expansionist aims as Mittelafrika, Mitteleuropa, indemnities, etc., the Kreuznach protocol was the highwater mark of official German annexationism, as the chancellor's objections failed to modify its hubris.[51]

Riezler lamented the victory of outright annexation, military securities, and economic exploitation: "The *Grosse Politik* which we should conduct is ruined." "It is a miracle that Germany does not perish because of its fantastic kaiser, the prejudice of the court, the psychosis of the intellectuals, and especially the blindness of the Herr Generals and the popular belief that they understand everything." Since he had attempted to build a consensus along a middle line, on the continuum from renunciation to outright annexation, Bethmann added an emphatic reservation to the record: "I consider the agreed peace conditions attainable only if we can *dictate* the peace. Solely under this precondition have I assented." He suspected that Ludendorff "hoped to overthrow me because of disagreement about war aims, which would be easy right now, or thought he could pin me down so that I could not negotiate on a cheaper basis (peace offer of December 12)." To the harried chancellor "resignation over such fantasies would be ridiculous. Moreover, I will naturally not be bound by the protocol." Characteristically, he concluded the note: "If somewhere and somehow peace possibilities arise, I shall pursue them." Subjectively, Bethmann sincerely disassociated himself from the excessive demands of the military, which substituted crude outright domination for his more finespun design of indirect hegemony. To the Bundesrat, the chancellor reiterated that he had agreed to the Kreuznach protocol only "presupposing that we can dictate the peace. . . . If Russia does not agree to absolutely everything, then peace shall not fail because of it." Bethmann could console himself only with the hope that the negotiations, once begun, would help his moderate diagonal to prevail because of the popular cry to end the killing and the utter impossibility of reaching such annexationist goals.[52]

In the time borrowed by his assent to the Kreuznach program, Bethmann scored one last impressive parliamentary victory for his middle course, when the Conservatives insisted upon a war aims interpellation proposed but dropped by the Socialists. "Completely surprised," the chancellor pleaded with the leaders of the middle parties to avoid excited debates which would divide the country further, rebuff enemy peace feelers, and complicate possible negotiations. "As little as I [agree] with the war aims published today" (in a massive manifesto of the annexationists in the Reichstag), "so little am I [in accord] with Scheidemann." To the representatives of the states he "sharply deplored impatience about clear goals. Conservatives and Social Democrats have put me into a difficult situation." Although he would have liked "to shake Scheidemann off" because of William II's fears, the chancellor could not veer to the Right because Austria had accepted the Socialist peace formula and because the annexationist declaration was "too far-reaching and too deceitful toward the East." *Pro internum,* Bethmann considered "securing East Prussia extraordinarily important" and establishing Lithuania and Courland as dependent duchies "quite advantageous," but promised he would "not let [peace] fail because of territorial gains." [53]

When replying to Scheidemann's and Rösicke's attacks on his vacillation, Bethmann gave the most compelling and memorable speech since his inauguration. To the thunderous applause of the middle, Bethmann again publicly rejected the establishment of a concrete catalogue of war aims as "inimical to the national interest." Refusing to proclaim a program of annexations as well as to adopt the formula "no annexations, no indemnities," he asked for Reichstag sympathy "for the restraint which I must exercise." On the positive side, he sketched as his goal an agreement with Russia "founded upon mutual honest understanding, excluding any idea of rape, and leaving no sting, no trace of resentment." The Austrian ambassador concluded from this: "No one anywhere should doubt that the German government is immediately ready for peace toward Russia without making it dependent upon territorial annexations." Since only Conservatives and Social Democrats rejected the chancellor's plea for unity, "it became clear that Bethmann's moderate policy [had] the backing of an unconditional majority in the Reichstag." The formation of this "bloc of the middle" supporting the chancellor's war aims was one of his supreme accomplishments, as it meant the realization of a long-standing dream, parliamentary support for his policy. And yet it was a hollow triumph because it rested largely upon his misleading claim, "I find myself *in full agreement with the OHL.*" [54]

In early summer of 1917 the prospect of another winter of war, partially brought on by Germany's ambiguous but annexationist aims, triggered the fatal crisis of confidence in Bethmann. To prevent a collapse he pleaded with Ludendorff: "The question of war aims should never become a matter in which different parts of the country are played against each other according to their political orientation, appealing to military versus political authorities." The chancellor bitterly sought to keep the OHL from joining hands with his parliamentary enemies: "The prospects of a dictated peace are so nebulous and have receded to such a distance that the illusion of a fat peace must lead to new and great disappointments on the long and heavy road ahead." But he warned in vain: "Should the people believe that we are turning down possibilities for peace because of the present unattainability of war aims, untold consequences for morale will follow." Now the Left, hitherto his bulwark, deserted the chancellor because his compromises with the military and the war aims movement seemed to prolong the killing in the trenches and the suffering at home. "Our position is clear: we conduct a defensive war. We have said the Russian formula does not hinder an agreement." Bethmann wearily tried to restore the Socialists' faith in his moderation: "I have never thought of the annexation of Belgium; I have never spoken of territorial gains in France," he pathetically pleaded. "We must persevere without hesitation; every sign of weakness, every failure of nerve is only grist for the mill of our enemies." Toward the Right, which was disappointed in his scruples against annexations, the chancellor stressed the prospects in the East, and concluded in wounded pride: "I am criticized for lacking clarity in my war aims. Are our enemies any clearer? I have said in our peace offer that we want to sit down and negotiate a peace of reconciliation."

But the voice that had carried the national consensus for so long went unheard. "He fails completely. Everything was in vain," a leading revisionist wrote, reflecting parliamentary disillusionment. Nevertheless, only the military ultimatum to the kaiser prompted by the "disagreement between the chancellor and the OHL regarding the war aims," finally brought Bethmann down. "The chancellor is apparently resolved to take peace without annexations, if he cannot get it otherwise," Valentini concluded sagaciously, "while the OHL refuses to go that far and demands strategic securities." Postponing external peace, the war aims struggle in the end destroyed internal unity as well.[55]

In the Bismarckian tradition, Bethmann's war aims policy strove to follow a middle line between unbridled annexationism and advocacy of a status quo peace. While the radical Left attacked him as annexationist "to an extreme and that was Germany's disaster," the volkish Right denounced him as a *Flaumacher,* defeatist anglophile, and "grave-digger of the empire." Personally convinced that there were no natural goals for the Central Powers beyond a general strengthening of their continental position against attack and freedom for economic expansion overseas, the chancellor stubbornly refused to commit himself publicly in order to maintain the unity of purpose of 1914. Structurally, the paradoxical double majority of annexationist elites and increasingly pacifist masses left Bethmann no alternative but a cautious opportunism, "wanting to take what we can according to the military situation but resolved not to continue the war indefinitely should the opportunity arise for the conclusion of a modest peace." Because he "would have provoked the massive opposition of the great majority of the Reichstag, of the military as well as the kaiser," the chancellor could not openly embrace a renunciationist settlement, while the "strong war-weariness" of the workers compelled him "never to set his war aims too high." However, "the public mood which desires so much and cannot be overlooked" forced him into a series of increasingly stronger public and private statements. The immense popularity of Hindenburg and Ludendorff made it impossible for him not to agree to the Kreuznach protocol, although he belittled it as temporary internal understanding: "It was the basis neither for further decisions about the conduct of the war nor for a renewed peace offer." But when the Russian Revolution increased the pressure from the Left, Bethmann grew willing "to seize every opportunity for peace" even if he had "to sacrifice a larger or smaller part of the conquered territory." Since

"I consider present [annexationist] agitation harmful for domestic and foreign policy," he continued to hope "for the voice of reason, the weight of all honest and sensible spirits, when the time comes." [56]

To reconcile the clash of reactionary and progressive visions of a Greater Germany with the exigencies of diplomatic and military reality, Bethmann embarked upon a grandiose design for the restructuring of Europe. "There is but one solution, a United States of Mitteleuropa, including Poland, supported by the working masses and an international movement, overcoming all the small nationalisms. There lies the future—and there war itself points the way," Riezler speculated rhapsodically. "Everywhere a fearful [Götter-] dämmerung of nationalism will come, and Germany alone can replace it." In a breath-taking metamorphosis, he added, "without Prussia's and *Kleindeutschland*'s transcendence, *Grossdeutschland* cannot arise." More sober than his fanciful assistant, Bethmann seized upon the idea of a central European economic union which, by securing the substance but not the form of German domination, had some chance of being accepted by an only partially defeated enemy. Mitteleuropa alone could reconcile the domestic conflict between the territorial demands of the war aims movement and the limits of what the Socialists might construe as enlarged self-defense. Even if the final result resembled that desired by the annexationist mob, the particular form of autonomy contained the possibility of evolution toward a Europe gravitating around Berlin out of self-interest rather than naked compulsion. Although under military and chauvinist pressure it might be in danger of becoming Hitler's bloody Fortress Europe, the ambiguous concept of indirect domination might, at Socialist and Progressive insistence, be transformed into a renewed *Zollverein* or Common Market. Diplomatically torpedoed by the Austrians and internally sabotaged by the bureaucracy and interest groups, the dream of a united central Europe was nevertheless the persistent leitmotiv of Bethmann's war aims policy.[57]

In contrast to the unrestrained annexationism of the military and the majority of Wilhelmian elites, Bethmann championed a more moderate expansionist Realpolitik. Ethically the chancellor's personal goals did not differ significantly from those of other contemporary European statesmen. For Clemenceau, Lloyd George, Sonnino, and Sazonov, in binding international agreements as well as in the final Treaty of Versailles, espoused aims which meant either the destruction or the weakening of the Central Powers. In an age of

extravagant and widespread imperialism Bethmann sought to practice the Iron Chancellor's limited Machtpolitik, even if this meant
"keeping a group of madmen on the road to reason or, if that is impossible, taking the least idiotic way and acting as if it were the path
of rationality." But because his pursuit of the "national interest"
rested on military power, the chancellor was always vulnerable to
pressures from "the chauvinists in heavy industry who would like to
eliminate their Belgian competition," the Supreme Command, and
"the educated world, as well as the Pan-Germans." Since the Left,
tarnished by the majority Socialists' veiled annexationism, failed to
provide a sufficient counterweight to all these pressures, Bethmann
could not deny "that the wild demands of our annexationists bear
part of the responsibility for the protraction of the war." Although
always aware that "a clear and open announcement of the restoration
of Belgium would have taken the wind out of the sails of the enemies'
chauvinists," the chancellor defended his own failure to steer against
the current and create a large moderate countermovement with the
unanswerable question: "Can one *in politics* call something objectively right which is impossible? I believe not." Because of Bethmann's infection with the milder variety of annexationist mania,
World War I, begun in ambiguity, turned into a paradox: "Self-
defense against the present France; a preventive war against the
future Russia—and as such too late; and a struggle with England
for world domination." [58]

CHAPTER 8

The Impossible Quest

The restoration of peace through victory in battle or negotiation with the foe was the supreme test of statesmanship during World War I. Here military, diplomatic, and domestic pressures converged in an attempt to shape a settlement guaranteeing those goals which had motivated the original decision to go to war. The failure of the Wilhelmstrasse's calculated risk initially gave primacy to the generals, who in energetic simplicity sought to cut the gordian knot by force. In the race with the Entente for drawing neutrals into the conflict by promising ever larger conquests, which hampered eventual agreement, diplomacy was an extension of military strategy and the dispirited Foreign Office largely did the bidding of the OHL. Only the soldiers' failure to defeat the Entente militarily gradually returned priority to a political solution of the conflict, which developed momentum toward ever higher levels of escalation and finally culminated in total war. The repeated clashes between sword scepter involved, not so much the desirability of peace as such, but rather the kind of settlement, be it triumph, compromise, or subjection. The basis for a truce was frightfully hard to find, because a general solution was possible only as Diktat by either side, since neither coalition was willing to return to the status quo ante without at least a slight increase in power tipping the balance in its favor. To overcome the diplomatic deadlock growing out of the stalemate in the trenches, Germany could choose between two alternative courses of action: separate peace or national-social revolution. Achieving the primary diplomatic aim—the breakup of the hostile alliance either by buying off one enemy with diplomatic concessions or by undermining his will to fight from within—both strategies would insure at least a partial victory on one front and would thereby justify the sacrifices of blood. But in many ways separate peace and revolutionization were mutually exclusive, since—before the Bolshevik seizure of power—no government was willing to negotiate while it was the object of massive subversion. Coming from a traditional statesman of a conservative power, Bethmann's halfhearted attempts to create a national or social uprising behind the Entente front remained ideologically unconvincing, and because of his limited personal commitment met with little success. At the same time agreement with one opposition state proved elusive because the cohesion of coalitions was guaranteed by annexationist war aims, spelled out in binding international agreements, which promised each allied belligerent a larger share of the spoils than the Central Powers could offer.

Domestically, the German chancellor also faced great difficulties in his tireless pursuit of peace. The shaky consensus built on the diagonals of defensive war threatened to erode at any moment because of the war aims agitation of the Right and the pacifist propaganda of the Left. As early as April 1915 he complained: "On one side a certain war-weariness is growing. On the other side, illusory hubris about the war aims abounds. Hence the inner unity which we so emphatically need does not exist." The psychological mobilization characteristic of mass warfare left "none of the mobility and flexibility of the cabinet policy of previous coalition wars." Spawning goals insisting on the total destruction of some and the severe mutilation of other enemy powers, "the machine of belligerent passion, created for victory and endowed with ever greater might, forced the policy of the states to continue in its initial direction." As complement to his support for a stronger Germany, directed toward the elites, Bethmann sought to placate the longing for peace of the masses by protesting, "no one yearns more than I do for a speedy end." His personal sincerity was so successful in maintaining the loyalty of the Left, the precondition for Socialist cooperation in the war effort, that Scheidemann testified afterward that "his every sentence was inspired by a deep desire and a strong will for peace." However, not only the war-weariness of the workers but also the inferiority of the Central Powers' economic and manpower resources dictated that "we are interested in shortening and our opponents in lengthening the war." Since the diplomats could not win at the conference table what the generals failed to obtain on the battlefield, Bethmann tirelessly strove to consolidate Germany's military advantage into a negotiated but limited victory, embodying those war aims which could be subsumed under an expanded version of self-defense. Afraid that the Central Powers would not achieve a general triumph of arms, the chancellor was convinced that a favorable draw could only be secured by negotiated agreement, because if war were allowed to play itself out, it would probably end in German defeat. Not so much for moral as for these power-political reasons, Bethmann became the German statesman most dedicated to ending the senseless killing. "What a marvelous people, but what a fate God has bestowed upon us!" he reflected in late August 1914. "He can and will not abandon us!" [1]

In the wake of the outbreak of fighting, the German chancellor confronted "a number of vexing foreign political problems." Since, in spite of "all our remonstrations Austria has seriously affronted Italy with its negative and formalist attitude," Bethmann pleaded for a Viennese "promise of compensations" in order to bribe Rome into continuing neutrality. Similarly, he "warmly recommended Rumanian wishes for a minority statute in Transylvania and boundary rectifications in the Bukovina" to the Ballplatz, because "our whole Turkish combination will collapse if the Rumanians join the other side." While Germany's two previous allies were embracing precarious neutrality, the military's hope for the aid of other smaller powers such as Greece, Sweden, and Switzerland was bitterly disappointed despite Germanophile monarchs or governments. Although apparently on the verge of concluding an alliance with the Central Powers, Bulgaria, anxious to join only the winner, and for a high price, suddenly cooled and protracted negotiations for a year. Although he had initially warned Wangenheim to commit Germany only if "Turkey either can or will undertake some action against Russia worthy of the name," Bethmann nevertheless now pressed for immediate Ottoman intervention regardless of the cost. While the Balkan coalition against Russia failed to materialize, "the Japanese ultimatum arrived." A desperate "proposal of neutralization [of Kiao-Tchao] to America" aborted because Woodrow Wilson and William Jennings Bryan "lack any sense for the world political interests of the U.S." Therefore, the embattled empires were faced with the hostility of another Great Power. Since the king of Spain refused the bait of Gibraltar, "Portugal will declare war" with the sole consolation that "this is very good for a peace (*sur le dos du Portugal*) with England." In the initial diplomatic scramble, Berlin, most feared on the continent, clearly came out second best.[2]

Germany's professed desire for peace was first tested by an American offer of mediation in September. Bethmann coolly replied to Gerard that the recent agreement of the Entente to conclude only a common peace rendered negotiations premature. "England has declared on various occasions that it will wage a *guerre à l'outrance,* hoping for success in a lengthy conflict." Hence the enemy coalition had to make the first move. He formulated what was to remain his policy throughout his term in office: "We can only accept a peace that really promises to last and protects us from new aggression." Any other course would be understood abroad as weakness because German armies were deep in hostile territory, and "having sacrificed so much, the nation demands guarantees of security and tranquility." Since the waves of patriotic annexationism were rising, Undersecretary of State Zimmermann added that "in the interest of its own survival, the government could not dare accept the well-meant initiative." Although intent on "avoiding the appearance of favoring in principle an unlimited continuation of the war," Bethmann feared the danger of an international conference in which the Central Powers would clearly be outvoted. As a *Realpolitiker* suspicious of the "notorious world-reforming tendencies of Bryan and Wilson," the chancellor rejected a status quo ante settlement, since "if the luck of arms is favorable to us, we will hardly be able to renounce every prize of victory." [3]

The slow realization "that our advance in France will finally grind to a halt" short of complete victory, posed the "question of whether it is possible to made a deal with Paris and then decide against whom the war ought to be directed. Perhaps it would be easiest to make peace with Russia first, when it is beaten in Galicia. But then the Turkish combination, so necessary against England, will fail." In the traditional German dilemma between a western and eastern orientation, Bethmann and his entourage initially leaned toward "attempting to come to an agreement with France, already now suspicious of Russia," since a partition of Belgium might cement such a reversal of alliances. But when the Austrians suffered a major defeat at Ivangorod, the shoe was suddenly on the other foot: "The heart of the Viennese will drop into their pants—probably they will want to sue for peace. The main danger is that they will receive tolerable conditions from Russia through France and England and that Petersburg will throw itself upon us with all of its might." But Austrian defection could also be turned to advantage: "Since Vienna will certainly give up, we must ask ourselves if we should try to reach a settlement with Russia." When Riezler discussed it "at length with the chancellor," they found "no method for initiating such a

course [which is] difficult, even dangerous, because it is very hard to
judge the intentions of the enemy." In the first months of the war
Bethmann found it difficult to develop a clearcut political strategy.
One day the Wilhelmstrasse was convinced that "the possibility of
an understanding exists with Russia alone—but not with France
as long as there is no change of cabinet," while on the next, a settlement with Paris seemed "the best solution," since "in the foreseeable
future the French will not fight again, regardless of how harsh
the peace, as long as it is not dishonorable." Though willing to accept an offer from either direction, cultural preference and his own
prewar policy made the chancellor look more longingly toward the
West.[4]

If the enemy coalition could not be broken by a quick victory,
the balance might still be tipped in favor of the Central Powers by
drawing other states such as the Ottoman Empire into the conflict.
Although intent upon exorcising "the *cauchemar des coalitions*"
after the war, and despite his doubts about the military value of the
Turkish alliance, Bethmann was no longer satisfied with Constantinople's neutrality and pressed for the Porte's rapid participation in
the fighting. Endorsing the daring *Goeben* and *Breslau* escape into
the Straits, approving the Turkish demand for financial assistance,
and exhorting Wangenheim, Liman, and Souchon to overcome the
last hesitations of the Porte, the chancellor grasped at any diplomatic straw that might ensure victory. "Now the guns will speak in
the Black Sea. Will Italy remain neutral?" Riezler speculated in late
October. "The Turkish fleet left with the order to pick a fight with
the Russian navy." Berlin feared that the scheme might backfire.
"The arms must go off by themselves. If the provocation is too
strong, the Turks will put the blame on us." Even when the dice had
fallen Bethmann was still in the dark: "The cannons in the Black
Sea have been fired. We know nothing more precise." Because of
the slow progress of the attacks on the western front, which raised
the danger that "we have lost the war, if we cannot spare any troops
in the West," the Ottoman card was doubly important. "Through
Turkey's economic and political threat to England's colonies and
trade through submarines, etc., we could still win." But even the
proclamation of a Moslem holy war turned into a deceptive fata
morgana, since the "sick man of Europe" needed more military and
economic aid than he could give in return, and because the Arabs,
resentful of Ottoman domination, failed to rise against the West.

"Perhaps it is necessary to change the tactic." Bethmann's intimates pondered: "Defend and attempt to remain unbroken. If we then have the longer breath we could still win." [5]

The growing military stalemate, disappointing all hopes for a swift and decisive campaign, restored priority to a political solution to the conflict. "Events have developed quite differently from what we expected in the beginning," Bethmann admitted to a friend. "The result seems to be that the *spirit* of attack, which, thank God, dominates our army more than that of our enemies, has lost nothing of its value, but modern weapons technology has given defense a much higher importance than before. If the foe cannot be overrun with superior force, success can only be won with great patience." From a six-weeks outing, the war had turned into a desperate global struggle of attrition. "If we hold our line in France with slow progress on the right flank, if we prevent the occupation of large territories by the Russians" (Bethmann firmly believed in both), "then we might have the opportunity of weakening England through naval actions and increasing troubles in Africa, Afghanistan, and India. Here lies the decision at the moment." The prospect of a lengthy coalition war made a diplomatic resolution doubly difficult. "France is entirely dependent upon England in its decisions. Primarily for that reason no desire for peace is evident there." The German "retreat at the Marne" and the inconclusive battles in Poland destroyed the initial chance for a separate peace with the hereditary enemy. "Perhaps we deceive ourselves least, if we assume that their defensive power is still unbroken, but that they can hardly mount a large offensive any longer, except under English pressure." Bethmann candidly admitted, "I presently do not see any possibility of splitting the enemy coalition." But there was one slight hope. "The tsar is very peace-loving—as far as his person is concerned—but powerless." Although he had no ready-made answer, "my confidence in a favorable outcome remains unshaken, no matter how gigantic our task. But how everything shall fall into place is still in the dark." [6]

Surprisingly enough, the first call for peace came not from the enemy but from Chief of Staff Falkenhayn. Although he had grandiloquently announced that "even if we perish through this war, it was fun anyway," in early November he approached Bethmann "every day asking for a cease-fire because of gigantic losses in the West and lack of ammunition." [7] Seeking to gain clarity about the diplomatic consequences of the chief of staff's declaration, "We cannot win on all three sides," Bethmann reasoned, "I must also doubt that the military prostration of our enemies is still possible as long as the Triple Entente holds together." Decisive victory could be won only against one of the major enemies. "For the price of leaving everything toward Russia pretty much as it was before the war we could create the conditions which we desire in the West. Thereby the Triple Entente would be defeated." Were Petersburg to hold out, "war would only end because of general exhaustion without clear military defeat." A settlement on the basis of the status quo ante, though "not without peaceful consequences favorable for future growth, would be considered by the people as quite insufficient reward for such immense sacrifices." To secure at least a partial victory despite the stalemate, Bethmann instructed the Foreign Office: "I cannot completely escape the persistent pressure of General Falkenhayn for separate peace with Russia. At least the possibilities for it must be explored thoroughly." Though the prospects were none too favorable, the chancellor was willing to pursue this possibility, presupposing that Germany would not take the first step, since "our initiative, if unsuccessful, would be construed as a sign of weakness by the entire Entente and would smother possible French leanings toward peace." Preferring a western settlement, Bethmann was nevertheless reluctantly moving toward exploring the chances for an eastern peace, since to maintain Socialist support he had to leave no stone unturned.[8]

When "Russia . . . approached us through councillor Hans Niels Andersen, the King of Denmark, and the tsar's mother who feared revolution against her son," the chancellor did not have to make the first unpleasant move. Anderson was a valuable channel of communication between the belligerents, since as a neutral he possessed easy access to the leading statesmen in London, Petersburg, and Berlin. Although "the emperor is in an expansive Christmas mood and the military entourage preaches peace with Russia," Bethmann shrewdly agreed with his assistant in interpreting the "feeler as a sign that Russia is weakening and England afraid of the collapse of French morale. If we now make peace, we will have to repeat this war in a decade, alone, under unfavorable circumstances." Irrespective of Zimmermann's detailed warning against the dire consequences of a Russian deal for the Central Powers' eastern and Balkan ambitions, Bethmann, complaining about "the distrust of the diplomats and the misery with Falkenhayn," accepted the formula: "Considering the royal author, I gladly receive the mediation and reply according to its content." Intending to postpone any substantive response until after victory in the East, he elaborated, "Germany conducts a defensive war and therefore is ready to examine any peace proposals which secure it full compensation and security against a renewed attack by three enemies." Not wanting to rebuff the Danish king and yet "unsure of what and who is behind this offer," Bethmann swallowed his misgivings and asked Berchtold to approve a favorable reply. For an independent military opinion he visited "Hindenburg, who despairs of a decisive military victory against the Russians, telling him to accept if Russia offers peace." But Bethmann remained skeptical about the success of the Andersen mission, although he maintained that "we must primarily desire to break up the Entente, i.e. separate peace with one of our enemies, namely Russia." [9]

Toward the end of 1914, Bethmann considered the "military situation favorable, but unclear and undecided. Hence the attitude of Italy, Rumania, and Japan [?] is uncertain, perhaps threatening. Desires for peace are not yet visible in any of our enemies." Hence a papal peace message failed to meet with any positive response. "We answered the soundings of the Vatican in a friendly manner, because we did not want to foil the initiative through our resistance in order to let the onus fall upon our enemies." Bethmann rather encouraged Jagow's attempts to "spin threads to [former Russian minister] Count Sergei Witte, via Belli and Robby Mendelsson." The prospect seemed brighter because Witte's star was once again rising and "there are small signs of war-weariness in Petrograd, but nothing decisive yet." In Paris, "militarism, aggressive spirit, and confidence reign, whipped up by the government and England. The army is still quite firm." Undismayed, Bethmann ideologically preferred a western settlement, "We have no interest in the destruction of France and could grant an honorable peace for an indemnity and part of the colonies, i.e. the Congo." In the same mood, the chancellor welcomed Ballin's report from the Danish mediator that Grey "was willing to make peace today rather than tomorrow. The difficulty [is] Belgium." But since "at the moment the military decision lies in the East," he hoped for "a victory over Petersburg through the new army corps, before Italy and Rumania enter the fray" in order to prevent Austrian separate peace. Believing that "splitting Russia from the coalition is most desirable for us; England seems least prepared to yield," the chancellor anxiously awaited news from Andersen regarding sentiment in Petersburg. "The Danish king has written to the tsar. Russia is said to be angry at England and to desire peace." Refusing to go as far as his advisors, who called for "the slow dismantling of our eastern position, first Turkey and then Austria," as bribe to the tsar, Bethmann nevertheless hinted to Scavenius that "our conditions will not be severe, entailing only small concessions to guard our eastern frontier (but not Warsaw) as well as financial and trade agreements. We wish to live in lasting peace with Russia." [10]

Although Bethmann hoped that "things [were] moving toward peace," because there was no prospect of decisive victory on either front, his soundings toward Russia were unsuccessful. "Andersen returned from Petersburg. What he reports is in complete contradiction to everything we have heard so far. No word of peace. Witte without influence. The tsar and Sazonov confident of victory. Hence nothing can be done"—unless Italy called a peace conference to save European civilization. Riezler did not believe the amateur diplomat "brings anything. Andersen acted so much like a pacifist that everybody dropped him" in Petersburg. Indeed, since the Danish shipping magnate's connections were worse than in London, the substance of his report was discouraging. "The tsar rejected decisively the idea of separate peace, but he is peaceful and will not refuse to discuss a settlement through the king of Denmark." Confident of his military strength, Nicholas II left only the narrowest of cracks open. Bethmann replied that Germany was the attacked party and could therefore not take the first step: "Our untold sacrifices cannot have been made in vain; we would only conclude a peace that permanently secures us against the repetition of such aggression." Although the chancellor had been skeptical from the beginning, he was clearly disappointed. "You know about the success of the Andersen mission," he informed Karl Georg von Treutler. "Presently we possess many dead-pledges [Faustpfänder]. Our enemies have enough money to redeem them at an acceptable price. But I fear our situation will deteriorate with every month of fighting, not to mention the additional billions which we will then have to raise." Riezler sagaciously predicted, "when peace negotiations begin—all will be bluff. And the chancellor will have to adopt an uncongenial method." Appalled by the difficulties of a political settlement and the hubris of military and public opinion, Bethmann complained to his intimate, "Nobody in GHQ thinks the war through to its logical conclusion." [11]

A new ray of hope appeared in March 1915 with Colonel Edward House, who had been touring European capitals to sound out the prospects for compromise. Although Wilson's suggestion "took as a basis a more or less defeated Germany," Bethmann gladly welcomed the American envoy as a possible bridge to England. Warmly received in the Wilhelmstrasse, the colonel "felt the presence of Bismarck in the surroundings. . . . The chancellor came immediately and was exceedingly cordial and delightful." Bethmann perused Wilson's message "slowly and with more care than any one has yet done. He said it was fine and he appreciated the President's motives and wished I would tell him so." Like Jagow several days earlier, he approved in principle the suggestion of safeguarding the freedom of the seas beyond the London declaration, and promised equal concessions from Germany if the American president were willing to enforce this principle against the British. "The chancellor spoke of my plan as being the first thread to be thrown across the chasm which would eventually have to be bridged. He was enthusiastic over the suggestion and bade me Godspeed, asking me to keep him informed." House summed up his impressions in his diary: "He was courteous and he was kind and he impressed me as being one of the best types of German I have met. If he had as much authority as the British Prime Minister, the war would not have occurred." Although the colonel fervently hoped for an end to the fighting, he was realistic enough to admit to Bethmann that "the time for peace had not yet come. France is quite truculent and England somewhat less so." [12]

Since "peace feelers are nowhere in sight," Bethmann now preoccupied himself with the threat of Italy and Rumania entering the war. From the beginning he had resented the "pride, stubbornness, and stupidity, as if sent by the gods" with which Vienna had refused the necessary territorial concessions in the Trentino, Valona, and Bessarabia to Rome and Bucharest to safeguard their precarious neutrality. In Berlin "everyone wants to replace [Ambassador] Flotow with Bülow. . . . He is completely stereotyped and clinically vain, I am supposed to agitate with the chancellor, but the latter refuses, since Bülow would only work for the crown prince in Rome until he could appear as the savior of the fatherland," Riezler noted. But because of the counterargument, "he would destroy himself there," Bethmann recommended his ambitious predecessor to William II in order to prevent the charge of selfish motives on his part, although he knew that "one does not trust him, not even in Italy." On the positive side, "the Pope has tremendous fear of Italy's abandoning nonintervention," because it would reopen the troublesome Vatican question, and "therefore he wants to help us buy its neutrality." But the mission of Count Wedel to Vienna "in order to press for cession" of the Trentino was hampered by Bethmann's concern that "Austria would make separate peace out of fear of Italy and Rumania," threatening military collapse. Hence everything depended on "soundly defeating the Russians through the use of a new corps before the Italians and Rumanians attack." The chancellor used all diplomatic means at his disposal, such as the mission of a German cardinal "in order to impress the Vatican with the need for sacrificing the Trentino," and Center Party leader Erzberger to make contacts with the powerful ex-premier, Giovanni Giolitti. "The affair is bad because of the distrust of both parties," Riezler reflected on the difficulties of reaching a settlement. "The Trentino is the strategic key. Who possesses it can blackmail or resist." [13]

Caught between Italian avarice, Austrian recalcitrance, and Bulgarian intrigues, Bethmann was "utterly downcast" and nearly despaired of a solution. "Under no circumstances does Vienna intend to cede the Trentino. They cannot do so because of public opinion," which forced Berchtold to resign when he became too conciliatory. His successor, Stephan Burian, remarked coolly that "even if Italy marched it would not mean the end of the Danube monarchy." Bethmann's advisors were so embittered that they speculated about separate peace with Russia on the basis of a "Hapsburg collapse, if Hungary remains intact and Austria proper and Bohemia would loosely be allied to us." When the Austrians maintained that "the emperor will not go along, everything has been tried: the Pope has written; Mrs. Schratt [an old flame of Francis Joseph] has been set in motion," Count Thun remarked "it would be much easier for the emperor if we also carried part of the sacrifice," hinting at "Silesia, 30,000 souls in the Leobschütz district." Although "the chancellor apparently does not want to accept the Silesian cession [and] Jagow thinks the Austrians will cave in anyway," Bethmann was finally persuaded because of the "colossal danger." Falkenhayn, "who is now so strong that he has to be consulted in everything, also assented," and the Prussian Ministry of State ratified the unprecedented offer of compensation in Upper Silesia for Austrian concessions in the interest of common victory. "Great concern over Italy; Burian is dilatory. The chancellor thereupon cabled that he should assent quickly; otherwise he would ask for an audience with the old emperor." Finally this massive threat and growing Hungarian fear of Rumania were beginning to tell; Burian authorized Austrian Ambassador Macchio to offer part of the Trentino in Rome. "The chancellor is quite happy. This time the pressure was too strong for him not to feel joy in the resolution." But Bülow's tactic added to the strains in the alliance and "the Austrians demanded a high price for the Trentino, in Sosnowiec, and a loan." [14]

"The chancellor is in quite good spirits—despite or because of the not very hopeful situation," Riezler noted ironically. When the size of the Italian claims for "Görz, Grodiska, the Dalmatian islands, the Trentino to Klausen, and the independence of Trieste, to be put into effect immediately," became known in Berlin, there was utter "despair and anger." But, "the chancellor and Stumm still do not consider the matter lost. Partially a bluff. We know that the Italians will be able to be talked down." Upset because "Germany could perhaps still win decisively . . . if Italy, Rumania, etc. are kept out," Riezler suspected "that Italy has in its pocket considerable concessions by France, such as Corsica and Tunis, in order to attack" and feared that "it is resolved on war." Despite rumors about the signature of the London protocol, the chancellor "is in good humor and wants to pressure Austria into coming into an agreement with Italy *à tout prix*." Disregarding this urgent advice, "the Austrian answer is the most inflexible imaginable, always repeating the word *unacceptable*, while Burian is reported to have hinted that this would not be his last word. How maladroit!" Riezler's fear that our "Balkan edifice, which was always somewhat a house of cards, will collapse," proved only too correct. "Since the cabinet wants war, afraid of the rabble and intending to ride the bull market to the destruction of Austria," the long "struggle over compensations and Vienna's fluctuation between overconfidence and dejection" ultimately was in vain. "The hope that the Ballplatz concessions are so great that the cabinet will no longer dare to justify the war publicly," as well as the appearance of Giolitti as savior, the fall of the ministry, and the good prospects, evaporated when "Italy decided [for war] against all reason. A horrible spectacle: the terrorism of d'Annunzio and the mob." Although Bethmann had used every pressure to prompt Viennese sacrifices, the bait proved too small for Roman *sacro egoismo*.[15]

The Italian entry into the war had grave diplomatic and domestic repercussions. "A Rumanian attack against us and a separate peace by Turkey would cause unbearable unrest at home over the conduct of our foreign policy." Only new military successes in the East and Viennese concessions in Transylvania could keep Bucharest from following Rome's lead. To the disappointed party leaders, the chancellor pleaded that Austrian "concessions went to the limit of the possible" and that it was "not the maladroitness of the Central Powers' diplomacy, but the previous agreement with the Entente" which had wrecked the negotiations. Cleverly using an optimistic telegram of Chief of Staff Falkenhayn, he reiterated what he had already said earlier, "Even if Italy enters the war, I shall not despair." To the Bundesrat he stressed that Germany would only break relations with Rome and not declare war to avoid Italians troops on the Western Front. In the cheering Reichstag he denounced "the breach of faith of the Italian government," retraced the negotiations and the Austrian concessions, and concluded with the vow, "I am confident that united we will be victorious despite a world of enemies!" But aside from the impressive "simplicity and nobility of Bethmann's performance" in parliament, this "great success of his personality helps the statesman little since the people are immoderate, calling for a shark." Bourgeois and nationalist circles entertained "great doubts about our foreign policy and talked of a collapse without parallel," since many could "not suppress the fear that a storm is brewing in the Balkans if we do not soon win convincingly in Galicia." [16]

The question "Why don't we make peace?" weighed heavier on Bethmann's shoulders the longer the war continued. "We can only bring the war to a happy conclusion if we not only beat our enemies militarily but also force them to give up the struggle psychologically." This was easier said than done, as "there is no trace of war-weariness in Russia and absolute confidence in victory grows daily in France." Similarly, "after the formation of the new coalition ministry in England chances of achieving an acceptable settlement are minimal." Knowing "we shall not get peace with Russia as long as the Balkans are insecure and the Western Powers can legitimately promise the opening of the Straits," Bethmann assured Count Stephan Tisza that he was willing "to offer Russia equitable terms . . . taking the natural conditions of its survival into full account while maintaining our neighborly rights," i.e. economic advantages and a narrow frontier strip. Hence the chancellor "made it known in St. Petersburg through a [confidential] channel that Turkey would be prepared to grant certain prerogatives concerning free passage through the Straits with our mediation." Nevertheless, he had to admit that "experts on Russia and travelers from there disagree on the meaning" of the internal struggles. "At any rate one cannot consider them decisive for peace in the near future." But because "I presently see no other alternative for the conclusion of the war than Russian submission, I consider it our task to work toward this goal militarily and politically." [17]

Although sensing a "change of mood toward Germany," in early summer, Andersen reported that "the tsar and his advisors did not think of separate peace; they do not feel defeated and envisage even the fall of Warsaw with confidence." The reasons were simple: "Ruling circles in Petersburg hope that the Straits will soon be opened and that they will receive all necessary material by this route. As long as the Dardanelles have not been secured permanently, as long as Russia is not convinced that it will only receive passage through the Straits from us, the tsarist empire will not be ready for peace. Moreover, the tsar will be unfavorable to a separate peace in order not to break his word." Riezler saw a different reason for Russian obstinancy: "They cannot conclude peace for fear of the returning army—especially since the Liberals favor the continuation of the war, hoping to achieve a parliamentary regime, under the pretext of persevering." In the West, the French "still do not want to quit until we have finally been beaten." When London similarly showed no willingness to compromise, the bitter consequence became inescapable, "we have to face another winter campaign." Since "our enemies are not ready for the conclusion of peace," Bethmann warned the party leaders to expect "the war to last a long time." Although intent on "not prejudicing" a settlement with Petersburg after the failure of the Andersen mission, the chancellor in August 1915 made the first commitment in the Reichstag to the liberation of Poland by calling for "a rollback of the Muscovite Empire to the East and the separation of its western provinces." [18]

"Since the war rumbles on, and I still see no exit from it," Bethmann sought to tip the military balance by drawing Bulgaria into
the struggle. When Rumania proved too coy for German wooing,
Berlin and Vienna concentrated their attentions on Sofia, the strategic key to the Balkans, which was still smarting from its recent
defeat ("If the Balkan puzzle is solved all other opponents will
crumble"). In midsummer 1915, "Falkenhayn can no longer deny
that the whole war depends upon Constantinople and therefore is
slowly being pushed into negotiations for a military convention by
Bulgaria's eagerness." Although the price was the restoration of
Greater Bulgaria, Bethmann was willing to pay it—ready to spread
the war in order to end it. "But one cannot believe King Ferdinand
until they have actually marched," Riezler cautioned. "The Balkans
face another explosion—one never knows in what direction the
powder keg will blow up." Despite William II's dynastic preference
for Greece, the Wilhelmstrasse believed "that we must choose Bulgaria." When "Sofia's mobilization made a profound impression on
the Entente, most of all on Rome, of course," the Wilhelmstrasse
attempted to induce Serbia to make peace, promising part of Albania and the inclusion of Greece in "a new Balkan alliance under
German patronage." Confidently the chancellor reported to the
party leaders: "If we succeed in [subduing] Serbia and in securing
Constantinople, perhaps this will decisively change the course of
the war. The reversal must come from Russia." [19]

"On the train I had a long discussion with the chancellor about
peace possibilities," Riezler noted early in the second war winter.
"Italy is beginning to sway. In France Sembat is supposed to have
said he would wait for the result of the present offensive; if it brings
no real success, he would initiate a peace policy." Nevertheless,
blind hatred on all sides and unwillingness to settle for a draw made
all optimism premature. Although Bethmann agreed with Hertling
that "it would certainly be valuable to find out the position of the
Belgian king regarding possible negotiations on the future of Belgium," the clandestine meetings between Bavarian Count Törring
and Professor Waxweiler reached no result. The far-reaching German demand "that Belgium will be on our side and that it will
seek our military protection" prevented King Albert, who desired
genuine neutrality, from accepting the proffered hand. Since peace
with France "would be unthinkable without the return of Alsace-

Lorraine," talks with the Radical Socialists in Switzerland remained abortive. Because both sides realized that by "suggesting a compromise, our gains will be minimal," no one was willing to take the first step. The chancellor did not believe that "England and France will lean toward peace. Their manner of solving domestic problems betrays energy and firm resolve." Although he now hoped that the breaking point would first be reached in the East, he had to confess: "Russia remains a riddle. My news is uncertain, changing, and contradictory." Strongly disappointed by an appeal of the Socialists championing the war, he repeated Podbielski's dictum, *"Dat Proffezeien have ick nich jelernt."* Riezler, too, found "no signs of peace . . . except for some voices of reason in England. France and Russia swim in the tide of hatred they have unleashed." Hence the Foreign Office stepped up its efforts to foment national and social revolution within enemy countries by supporting such dubious figures as the Russian Socialist, Parvus Helphand.[20]

Vocalizing the growing pacifism of the starving masses, the Social Democratic interpellation in December 1915 forced Bethmann to take a public stand. "The soundings that we made in the spring and summer were rebuked by Russia officially and unofficially," he briefed the party leaders on his unsuccessful efforts. "There is no prospect of peace with Russia." The situation was hardly better in the West: "Of course large segments in France desire peace, but many say that right now it would be unfortunate and a crime against their future." In England, some circles were beginning to doubt the war as a business proposition, though the trend was still far from persuasive. "Whoever thinks not of peace and only of continuing the war must have a heart of stone," Bethmann exclaimed. But in a veiled reference to his war aims he stressed that not any peace would do. It should prevent the recurrence of attack. "We cannot announce: no annexations, status quo. Then they will say that we are finished. I repeat: We need a show of strength and unity in a manner that will increase their desire for peace." To counter the effect of the "irresponsible Socialist" initiative on popular morale, Bethmann polemicized against the vindictiveness of the enemy: "As long as this mixture of guilt and ignorance dominates the hostile leaders and the spirit of their peoples, any peace offer from our side would be a stupidity (hear! hear! on the right) which would not shorten, but prolong the carnage (lively applause)." But as a concession to the Left he added: "Should our enemies come with offers corresponding to the dignity and security of Germany, we are always ready to discuss them." Despite such strong words, "the fear that peace was being postponed because of too high demands" began to restrict the chancellor's freedom of decision, already imperiled by the opposite rumor that "he did not ask for enough." [21]

Because of this pressure from the Left, Bethmann wondered if victory over Serbia were not the right moment "to send out peace feelers *from our side.*" Hoping for a settlement by next summer, the chancellor anxiously focused on the East: "The difficulty lies in judging Russia: great desire for peace, but even greater fear of revolution." Nevertheless, he hoped that "in such internal turmoil the country will be unable to develop the necessary power of organization and thereby give us the chance to split the enemy coalition." But if the killing were likely to continue for more than one year, "we must strive to bring movement into the stagnant positions. If it is militarily impossible, it must be done politically." Since "we will not receive peace offers from one . . . or all of our enemies in the foreseeable future," Bethmann saw as "the only way out the strengthening of the peace movement in England so that we can, at the right moment, talk peace without giving the impression of weakness to our enemies." Technically, "an offer of preliminary talks for the fall of 1916 is quite a good idea—it is difficult to reject, since, except for England, no state can say openly that it is too early." Even at a rebuff, the discussion would have begun and a diplomatic solution would be closer. A German initiative would also silence the ever-louder public clamor for the ultimate weapon: "The problem is to free submarine warfare from American restrictions. Perhaps through a peace offer and preliminary negotiations on October 1 with Wilson. If accepted, we will not need the submarines," Riezler speculated. "If rejected, we can perhaps use them without war with America." Already at its inception what was to become the Central Powers' peace move implied the threat of escalation.[22]

In early 1916 the second visit of Colonel House to Berlin offered a new chance not to have "to ask for peace" but rather, as Bethmann preferred, to "begin talking about peace." Because Wilson's envoy had moved further toward a pro-Entente stand, the chancellor earnestly stressed that he was the only statesman of the belligerents "who had spoken out for peace, but he could not understand why there was no receptive echo anywhere. He deplored the war and its ghastly consequences, and declared that guilt did not lie upon his soul."

When House countered that this desire to end the war was merely intended "to cash in" on Germany's victories, Bethmann disagreed: "We went over this ground again and again, he maintaining that he did not understand why the Allies were so stubborn, and I [House] on the other hand explaining the real situation." The practical difficulty was that Germany "would make demands on the basis of the present military situation which the Entente could not fulfill because it was not defeated." To the chancellor's hint "that Germany would be willing to evacuate both France and Belgium" for an indemnity, the president's intimate replied, "That the Allies would not consider for a moment." Bethmann could only sigh "that it had been the dream of his life to bring Great Britain, Germany, and America together," and he hoped "that even now this might be brought about." Disgusted with his lack of success in persuading the chancellor to accept his own interventionist version of the war, House sarcastically noted: "The beer did not apparently affect him, for his brain was as befuddled at the beginning as it was at the end. Into such hands the destinies of the people are placed." The second trip of the colonel had revealed that the chasm separating the belligerents remained too deep to be bridged, and that the war would have to run its course. When House suggested a further visit in May of 1916, "he was told he would be welcome but the German people would only accept Wilson's official mediation if he had at least obtained something from England." As a truly disinterested mediator, the American president would have to procure concessions from the other side as well.[23]

"I would gladly be prepared to conclude a separate peace with any of our large neighbors," Bethmann answered the crown prince in the spring of 1916, when the latter voiced conservative hatred of England and called for a deal with Russia. "However . . . there is not the least indication that official Petersburg is presently ready for peace under any circumstances." If there were exaggerated fears of German war aims circulating abroad, "the boundless demands of our Pan-German press must bear the chief blame." Similarly, the chancellor protested to the Prussian minister of the interior, who was impatient with the war: "Had it solely depended upon our willingness for separate peace with our adversaries, it would long have been concluded. I completely agree with your excellency that this would be the most desirable way out of the tumult." But Bethmann knew he would have to sacrifice Germany's position in the

Baltic or the Balkans for Russian friendship. Although Swedish mediation through minister Wallenberg might be attractive, it necessitated concessions which would "only be bearable for us, if we forever sold our souls to the Russians. I consider such a Russo-German marriage a mirage. It would spell servitude for us." Despite the continuation of contacts with the French opposition through Switzerland, with the tsarist government through the Scandinavian courts, and with the British through occasional intellectuals, peace was no closer at the end of the second year of the war. Because they were unwilling to return to the status quo, both sides refused to compromise. "The will to fight is apparently unbroken in Russia," Bethmann briefed the Bundesrat. "In France there seems to be some uncertainty. There a peace movement might coalesce first. England is completely obstinate. In Italy there is discontent with the situation." [24]

Convinced that "we should conclude peace with Japan as soon as possible," Bethmann encouraged coal baron Stinnes's negotiations with Baron Ushida in Stockholm as a prelude to separate peace with Russia. Initially Riezler was optimistic: "These yellow chaps deal with delightful brutality. . . . They offer pressure for peace on Petersburg in return for the cession of Tsingtao and the Pacific Islands. They shall get it in case of success." But "nobody knows if they shall be content with such gains." The chancellor's prime objective was that "Japan *immediately* entice Russia into *serious* negotiations," but according to ambassador Lucius the Japanese were only interested in "pressure for general peace" while increasing their own possessions. Hopes soon turned to gloom: "The Japanese thing is over. They answered, 'It is impossible to reach a separate peace.'" With elegant duplicity, "they simultaneously made all the discussions known to Russia and the others, as appears from intercepted chiffres. Hence nothing can be done at present." The failure of the Japanese feelers, coupled with "the Russian victory over Austria and its profound impact on morale" made it clear that "presently nothing can be gained from new soundings." Nevertheless, Bethmann attempted to reassure the kaiser and the public: "Our efforts continue and we do not want to abandon the hope that one day the official terrain in Petersburg will be more favorable and the desired result can be obtained." But the impression that Germany could have peace from the Western Powers if "the chancellor declares the restoration of Belgium," which he refused because of "domestic difficulties," undermined the trust of the pacifist Left.[25]

The Russian victory in the Brusilov offensive made "Rumania sway. [Prime minister] Bratianu has probably made a deal with the Entente, according to the intercepted telegrams of Teschen. Does the king know of it?" Riezler asked in August 1916. From the beginning of the war, Bethmann had been troubled by "Austria's utter lack of flexibility, stubbornness, and pride" in refusing territorial concessions in Transylvania as compensation for King Carol's neutrality. To win "the footrace with the Entente powers," Berlin had even toyed with the idea of "forcing Rumania through an ultimatum," but because of Bucharest's instability, the chancellor had to be content with some grain and other supplies. The magnitude of the Austrian collapse hastened "Bratianu's defection to the Entente" and the pro-German king, faced with Francophile public opinion, entered the war reluctantly ("Everything is now in vain"). The frustrated Bethmann was "surprised only by the personal infidelity of the king and the date of the attack." The chancellor explained the tangled events to the party leaders: Because military preparations were still incomplete, "Russia held back, while England and France pushed on," threatening "Rome and Bucharest that they would abandon them and make peace." The simultaneous Italian declaration of war seemed to portend "a grand plan of the Entente to attack on all fronts." In the Bundesrat, Bethmann called the situation "the most serious yet since the first days of the conflict" and asked for a declaration of war against Italy and Rumania. Rather than pursuing separate peace from a position of strength, Germany once more had to struggle for its very survival: "Everything now depends upon Rumania. If we suceed in beating Bucharest, all will end tolerably. Perhaps more quickly than we imagine today." [26]

"Since the self-confidence of our enemies has grown, our outstretched hand would be rebuffed with more derision than before"— thus Bethmann defended his failure to produce peace or diplomatic victory. "Indeed, we must divide the Entente coalition." Countering Bassermann's renewed charges of diplomatic incompetence, he stressed his "willingness to meet Russia halfway. We promised the Straits with Turkish agreement. Through neutrals we have worked hard in Petersburg, but were rejected with mockery." But since it seemed unlikely that "Russia would last a third winter," suggestions for separate peace might soon fall on more receptive ears. To the nationalist allegation of favoring a western settlement Bethmann replied: "We are not in the happy position of being able to choose. If the opportunity for peace arises anywhere we are duty bound to seize it." For the public record he reiterated in the Reichstag that, since the struggle was a defensive war for Germany, "we could as the first and only ones declare our *readiness for peace negotiations.*" Afraid that "we must clearly envisage a third winter campaign and accustom the nation to this thought," the chancellor welcomed Swedish (Stinnes-Kolyshko) and Bulgarian (King Ferdinand) mediation with the Stuermer cabinet. Because of the Protopopov-Warburg conversations "thinking there is some chance for negotiations with Russia at the beginning of winter," Bethmann agonized about declaring Polish independence, and only after Hindenburg's insistence did he put his scruples aside.[27]

In early winter 1916 General Mackensen's spectacular victory over Rumania suddenly created the military basis for "a direct offer of peace negotiations through the neutrals," long planned by Bethmann: "It may be a great coup or a great mistake." The chancellor endorsed Austrian Foreign Minister Burian's and Progressive deputy Haussmann's proposals for a peace move, "corresponding to my ideas in many points," because "our military situation excludes any thought of weakness." Since all attempts at a settlement with one of the belligerents had proved barren so far, he was now willing to seize "the psychological moment" in order to launch a general initiative to end the war. "Through the officially pronounced word *peace* I intend to strengthen the ardent desire of all peoples for an end to the horrible struggle in order more or less to compel the enemy governments to accept our proposal and enter into negotiations." Technically, the Central Powers would approach all major enemies through the good offices of the European neutrals, the U.S.A., and the Pope. In preparation, Bethmann, in a speech which David called "good and highly important," declared his willingness *"to enter into a League of Nations at any time; yes, lead an organization which curbs those disturbing peace."* But despite Burian's urgent appeals for a binding war aims agreement, the chancellor refused to tie his hands in order not to lose flexibility and discourage separate peace by publishing too frightening a list of demands: "When we sit together at the negotiating table we shall set forth our conditions." After the chancellor had convinced William II and had overridden last-minute objections of the OHL, the stage was set for "the great démarche." [28]

The motives behind Bethmann's peace offer were a mixture of high-mindedness and expediency. The chancellor sincerely reiterated to his friends "that he would definitely seize the first opportunity for a favorable peace, even if there were much public outcry against him." He was not speaking rhetorically to the Bundesrat when he insisted, "we do not want to prolong the war one day more than necessary because of wild annexations," adding, "If we offer the chance for peace to return, our conscience will be clear before God and our nation." Bethmann's conviction that he had "a moral duty" to end the fighting was reinforced by political reasons. "It has been the chancellor's nightmare, expressed time and again in the last one-and-a-half years," Riezler noted perceptively, "that the governments will no longer be able to stop the war, which will finally be concluded by the people, and we will be ruined since we are the most cosmopolitan, idealistic, and yielding." A realistic appraisal of the military situation complemented this fear of revolution: "Our situation is such that we must make peace as soon as possible, as long as we are still victors." Despite the defeat of Rumania, Bethmann thought "that our condition and that of our allies did not inspire confidence that the continuation of the war into the next year would create more favorable circumstances than now." Despite the Right's growing accusations of personal weakness, the chancellor was willing to settle for "the general status quo ante," convinced that "we already have won the war, if we succeed in resuming our economic development." Although he still hoped for a favorable settlement, Bethmann, in his peace move, implicitly admitted that he was willing to accept a *partie remise*.[29]

In statements to the Bundesrat, briefings of the party leaders, and confidential expositions to the Prussian Ministry of State, the chancellor developed his internal and external objectives. This step "will demonstrate to the German people that the government does not merely drift with events, but that it takes the initiative for peace negotiations at the present moment," thus proving its pacifism to the war-weary masses. Intended to show "that it is not our fault if the war continues," the démarche, even if it failed, would spur the people "to fight on to the last breath." Similarly, Bethmann stressed to Haussmann, "According to human foresight this step will be very useful, politically and morally, presupposing that public opinion, including [that of] the Social Democrats, will remain firm and quiet at possible countermoves of the enemies." While restoring a semblance of Burgfrieden at home, the peace offer would also counteract the galloping disintegration of morale in the Hapsburg monarchy ("We are forced to take this step for Austria's sake, too"). Moreover, "our initiative will increase the desire for peace that exists among a great part of the enemy nations," he predicted optimistically. The strain of the war of attrition was cracking the monolithic unity of the Entente: "If our enemies reject our peace offer their governments will not be strengthened at home but weakened. I would also assume that it will give us the opportunity to take those measures according to the axiom *divide et impera* that have hitherto been tried unsuccessfully." Separate peace might yet be brought in through the back-door of general peace. As a last dividend, "we can expect a good impression on the neutrals." To the chancellor's way of thinking, Germany stood to lose nothing and to gain everything.[30]

Because of massive pressure from the emperor, the military, and the Reichstag majority for unrestricted submarine warfare, the peace initiative was Bethmann's last alternative to further escalation. Although he knew that Wilson's mediation "would have had many advantages," he feared that the opportunity might pass unused, since "we have no means at our disposal to influence the decisions of the president in regard to the crucial timing of his action." Uncertainty as to whether "Wilson is at all willing to undertake such a step" during his reelection campaign, because of continuing friction over the submarine issue as well as general suspicion of Washington's motives, persuaded Bethmann to proceed on his own initiative. "It cannot be questioned that if our offer is refused, public clamor for a ruthless use of all means of war will grow more forceful." The chancellor knew that only the beginning of negotiations could prevent further escalation. "I am convinced that a peace proposal launched by us and refused by our enemies will markedly improve our position in the U-boat question vis-à-vis the U.S. and European neutrals and will allow a substantial increase of submarine warfare above the present level." The argument that "it will considerably better the chances of our submarines" convinced the conservative and nationalist opposition to go reluctantly along, especially when Bethmann reiterated that "all important authorities here [i.e. the OHL] and our allies are in agreement that this step is possible and necessary." Despite his skeptical prediction that "refusal is more likely than acceptance," the chancellor united all the discordant forces of Wilhelmian Germany in his effort to reach a tolerable peace, since "I consider myself bound by my conscience to take an action in which I can still place hope." [31]

Unfortunately, the final wording of the German note owed more to Ludendorff's insistence on a victorious stance than to Bethmann's desire for conciliation. "Based on the consciousness of their military and economic strength, prepared to continue the struggle to the last man if need be (bravo on the right) but simultaneously inspired by the desire of preventing further bloodshed (bravo on the left) and of ending the horrors of the war, the four allied governments propose to enter into peace negotiations immediately," the chancellor announced to the cheering Reichstag on December 12, 1916. "The proposals which they bring to these negotiations, directed toward securing the existence, honor, and future development of their peoples, constitute, according to their conviction, a proper basis for the conclusion of a durable peace."

This proclamation was a high point in Bethmann's policy of the diagonal, since the resolve to fight on was welcomed by the Right while the Left rejoiced about the willingness to halt the carnage. "The chancellor is now very strong. The impact of the démarche as well as the speech was immense," Riezler jotted down the following day. "All reasonable men are convinced that it is a fortunate stroke of policy. I also believe he is killing many birds with one stone at home and abroad. It could be parried well, but it is more probable that the surprised and domestically embarrassed enemies cannot unite on anything intelligent—France will attempt to refuse it quickly before it becomes public knowledge. But slowly the move will have its impact." The chancellor was satisfied. "I, too, believe that our action is having a good effect at home. Even the press is quite reasonable, with the exception of the *Pommersche Tagespost* and the *Berliner Neueste Nachrichten*," he confided to Loebell. "About the foreign reaction, I know nothing more than the papers." But even if diplomatic success was doubtful, the Social Democrats, his chief internal target, hailed the peace move as "a great, bold policy" and predicted "good consequences whatever the answer." [32]

"The situation is completely dominated by the peace offer," Riezler noted in late 1916. "Much, perhaps everything, depends on the [Entente's] answer." Initially, Bethmann was moderately optimistic about "the further progress of the peace move"; he asked Hindenburg for possible armistice conditions, Vienna for diplomatic support, and public opinion for firmness and quietness. But when the Entente denounced the German move as *"une manoeuvre de guerre,"* he was stunned, since he had hoped for a reply which, though critical, would still allow talks to begin. "Through the refusal of our peace proposal, pretending it is dishonest and unimportant, and through the declaration of willingness to conclude a peace based on reparation, restitution, and guarantees, the Entente attempts to blame us for continuing the war." Riezler considered the reply "a strange document. Harsh, but not from strength, a rough rebuff and at the same time cautious about their own public but not about peace conditions." Not only the kaiser but Bethmann "was upset by the answer," and the general impulse was to "respond strongly and firmly so that the others get frightened at their own courage and regret having refused." Now lacking political ammunition against the "heavy intrigues" of the military, he was unable to prevent a martial "order of the day" calling for renewed vigilance. But in conference with the new Austrian foreign minister, Czernin, he pleaded for an answer "which without giving the impression that we are pursuing the others would not completely slam the door to peace." [33]

The Entente's rejection of Bethmann's initiative did not snuff out all hopes for peace, because in late December President Wilson sought to realize his messianic dream by mediating between both camps. Following a policy of "two irons in the fire," Bethmann had initially encouraged American action as bar against further submarine crises and as prelude to general peace, as long as the belligerents were left to arrive at their own terms, unlike at the peace of Portsmouth. Weary and discouraged, the chancellor had repeatedly complained to the American chargé that "Germany had been ready for peace for a year and was therefore not guilty of the continued slaughter." But exposing the domestic pressures under which he labored, he added ominously, "If his suggestion that Germany wanted peace should be continually ignored, Germany would be forced in self-defense to adopt harsh measures, but this would not be Germany's fault." Similarly, he stressed to the journalist William B. Hale, "It is always our wish to resume our work for peace as soon as possible." Nevertheless the Wilhelmstrasse was deeply ambivalent toward American mediation (fearing that cultural and economic ties as well as political self-interest were pulling the United

States toward the Entente) and therefore blew hot and cold when confronted with the prospect of Wilson's action. Convinced that *"America did not want to let us end the war victoriously,"* the chancellor nevertheless welcomed the U.S. initiative as "a wise and high-minded action" which might be more successful in Allied capitals than his own move. Caught between the substantive American desire to publish German peace conditions and the objective likelihood that their necessary modesty would provoke a storm from the war aims movement, Bethmann chose to procrastinate and to await the reaction of the Entente before even communicating the Central Power's demands confidentially to Washington. Although, in Zimmermann's words, Germany beat Wilson to the punch with its own offer, the chancellor was nevertheless willing to pursue American mediation to see where it might lead, when his hand, as in July 1914, was once again forced by the generals.[34]

Impatient with the slow workings of diplomacy and even more distrustful of Wilson's initiative than the Wilhelmstrasse, the OHL made its decisive bid for the unleashing of the U-boats in January 1917. "Because of the failure of our peace initiative the OHL wants to be certain that we do not leave any weapons unused," the chancellor candidly informed the Federal Council. Since victory on land had become impossible but "the navy . . . unanimously claimed that with sizable U-boat forces it could make England sue for peace even before the new harvest," Bethmann could no longer hold out against the resumption of unrestricted submarine warfare. The purpose of his peace offer was deflected into a justification for escalation. "The peace note had a positive effect: it was necessary because popular morale had begun to deteriorate," the chancellor argued before the Prussian cabinet. As he considered the Entente peace conditions completely unacceptable, Bethmann only feebly welcomed Wilson's last-minute "démarche to show confidence and communicate the terms." Coinciding with the announcement of renewed U-boat warfare, the chancellor's instruction detailing the German conditions came too late. "The *fatum* dominating everything suggests that Wilson might really intend to pressure the others and has the power to do so. That would be one hundred times better than submarine warfare," Riezler speculated disconsolately. Within one month the chancellor had traveled from the guarded optimism of the peace offer to the grave apprehensions of the submarine decision: "We have signed a paper not knowing if it contains an inherited million or our death sentence. William the Very Great or William the Last?" [35]

A result of unrestricted submarine warfare and "the immense Mexico blunder" of Zimmermann, America's entry into the war lessened prospects for peace and undercut the chancellor's credibility with the Left. The mobilization of neutrals in Latin America and Asia widened the conflict and strengthened the Entente's will for victory.[36] Moreover, U.S. participation seriously strained the Dual Alliance, since, "despairing of victory, Austria [began] flirting with France and England. Ominous situation." Insufficiently informed about the Parma-Sixtus negotiations, Bethmann nevertheless assured Czernin that "he did not at all want to avoid a dialogue with France, and welcomed the feeler toward Austria; but he had to insist that the trustworthy mediator designated by the Hapsburg monarchy remain completely passive, not prejudicing the future in any way." Fearing that Vienna's "legitimate separate peace" efforts might lead to Austrian surrender, the chancellor reluctantly agreed to the establishment of a channel of communication with the Western Powers, in the hope "that talks between *responsible individuals* . . . will result." American intervention also had a negative effect on feelers to France and Belgium through the King of Spain, making Bethmann question whether "we can consider the Marquis de Villalobar the right mediator." Chauvinistic mass emotions reached new heights with the widening and intensification of the war. "Cabinet diplomacy possessed opportunity for reason," Riezler mused. "I fear Europe will go utterly bankrupt because of modern political techniques and their consequences." [37]

Gloom turned to joy in Berlin when the news of the March uprising in Petersburg arrived: "Now naturally hopes are flying high because of Russia. . . . According to all indications a revolutionary government cannot wage such a complicated war." Since Germany might soon follow the Russian example and Austria threatened to break the alliance, Bethmann had no choice but "to use the Russian Revolution to obtain peace. We must side with freedom in Russia and declare not only our general readiness for peace but for an honorable settlement." Afraid that if the governments were incapable of ending the carnage the people might impose an "international peace of socialism," the chancellor promised in the Reichstag, "We shall keep following the principle of not meddling in the affairs of other countries." To ringing cheers from the Left he continued, "We desire nothing but to live soon in harmony with Russia again, in a peace which is built on an honorable basis for all parties." Despite this invitation to the Provisional Government, he was privately skeptical: "The news from Russia varies. In this war human reason has often been mistaken. My hope that [liberal foreign minister] Miliukov will initiate negotiations to save himself from an anarchist-socialist revolution rests on shaky ground," he wrote to a friend. "I fear that the eventual rule of [socialist deputy] Chkeidze will lead not to peace but to the continuation of the war, and will threaten to revolutionize the world." By mid-April this pessimism had solidified: "The Russian Revolution is going the wrong way for us. To be true, it will sap the Russian army's fighting power for the next weeks, but I fear that it will not lead to peace," since "Miliukov is utterly bent on war and seems to be gaining greater influence over Kerensky and Chkeidze." In the chancellor's mind "everything depends upon the attitude of the Russian army, which is obscure and contradictory at present. Of course we are seizing every opportunity to use the Russian situation to make peace, but we cannot entertain any definite hopes in this regard." [38]

"The manner of dealing with the Russian Revolution and the question of an offer of a limited armistice" provoked long discussions between the chancellor and his advisors regarding the old dilemma of separate peace versus further revolution. Were Germany to propose a cease-fire, the *muzhiks* might desert en masse, thereby increasing the internal chaos in the tsarist empire. But since the Provisional Government appeared resolved to maintain its alliance with the Entente, Bethmann approved the passage of Lenin and other emigrés in the "sealed train" to Petrograd, although he feared that the Bolsheviks were more interested in "revolutionizing us than in peace." By the time he reported to William II that he had gotten "in touch with the Russian political exiles in Switzerland as far as seemed safe for us, to arrange for their return to their fatherland," Lenin had already crossed the empire's frontiers. A masterstroke of unsentimental cynicism, this fanning of the revolutionary flames was to turn against Germany within the year and consume the last remnant of domestic unity.[39]

Although he did not take the first step toward the Provisional Government, Bethmann, willing to proceed on the diplomatic level as well, considered its halfhearted declaration of war an "indirect peace offer." Hence he procured full negotiating powers from the kaiser and replied with the promise of honorable peace in the *NAZ,* despite his doubts "that Prince Lvov, even in case of honest intentions, will be able to enter into successful negotiations with us." Intent on "bringing about a favorable negotiated peace before America's entry can become effective," Bethmann encouraged Erzberger's talks with Kolyshko and the mediation efforts of Swiss Bundesrat Hoffmann, as well as several other private feelers. To counter Czernin's defeatist memorandum, he stressed that presently "peace could only be gained through 'submission to our enemies' will' " and nothing more could be done than to "observe and support the process of development and disintegration in Russia." Therefore, "future Russian attempts at separate peace must be treated without undue haste but so that they lead to actual negotiations" which might ultimately become the "prelude to general peace." [40]

Bethmann's receptive passivity seemed vindicated when a telegram of General Eichhorn reported the arrival of Russian emissaries in late April. "That does not mean immediate peace, rather the beginning of negotiations. It is much more pleasant than the international," Riezler speculated. "The reports from the Russian army are such that one cannot imagine how they could resist the offer of an armistice." Considering it his "first task to use the political conditions in Russia to gain peace," Bethmann personally was ready to accept the Socialist formula "No annexations, no indemnities," although he thought some "territorial enlargement desirable." Hence he assured the Austrians "that despite necessary frontier rectifications we shall not let negotiations with Russia, if they are possible, fail because of the desire for annexations," and insisted on not mentioning annexations and boundary rectifications in his instructions, preferring the slogan of autonomy. To facilitate the talks of the hand-picked delegation of Colonel Winterfeld-Menkin of the OHL, Friedrich Rosenberg from the Foreign Office, and Eduard David of the majority Socialists, the chancellor promised in the Reichstag: "If Russia wants to spare its sons further bloodshed, if it abandons all plans for brutal annexations, if it wants to create a *lasting relationship of peaceful coexistence with us*—yes, gentlemen, then it goes without saying that we share this wish (Bravo in Center, National Liberals, Progressive, and German caucus)." But this "attempt to reach a cease-fire with the Russians" was premature, as the bourgeois Provisional Government was unwilling to reconcile itself to the independence of Poland, Courland, and Lithuania, and bury its dreams of a Slavic Constantinople, therefore refusing to come to the conference table. In June, Riezler noted dejectedly, "In Russia, chaos and no chance for peace." [41]

"A last way out, a peace possibility which could be imposed on the kaiser" materialized when the Vatican, in whose "just and impartial spirit" the chancellor trusted unshakably, offered its services. Since, at the front he had "constantly encountered the wish for a rapid peace" and since he could "hardly count on submarine warfare forcing England to capitulate in the near future" because *"time was running against us,"* Bethmann cordially welcomed Nuncio Pacelli on June 26. The formality of the papal envoy's questions led the chancellor to believe he confronted a major peace initiative of Benedict XV, undertaken in the justified hope of Entente cooperation. Embracing the principle of arms limitation and international arbitration, Bethmann *"clearly renounced Belgian"* domination, only cautioning that "it would not be in keeping with the full independence" which he was now willing to restore "if Belgium became dependent on England and France, since they would abuse their rule to Germany's disadvantage." Although the dreams of the September Program still echoed faintly in this conditional promise, it heralded a significant and substantial departure from the previous insistence on "real guarantees" of German influence, and for the first time opened the possibility of true Belgian neutrality. Regarding Alsace-Lorraine, he added in a similar spirit of conciliation that "if the German government were ready to make *territorial concessions to France* by saying that *peace will not fail on this issue,* and if France would accept this, an agreement could be worked out in the form of certain *mutual border rectifications.*" This hint at a compromise over the ill-fated legacy of 1870 was a promising step forward. The chancellor received the distinct feeling that "the Nuncio considered his declaration suitable to furthering peace substantially"—a conclusion confirmed by Lerchenfeld: "Eugenio Pacelli has made a good impression and has, as he tells me, a favorable opinion of the chancellor." After years of futile clandestine efforts for peace, Europe had some cause for hope, as Bethmann's concessions made negotiations a realistic possibility. [42]

In cruel irony, at a moment when he thought himself on the threshold of an acceptable compromise, Bethmann was felled by the Reichstag Peace Resolution, which expressed the masses' fervent desire for an end to the killing and their disappointment with his timid peace policy. Because of the failure of the Stockholm conference, the majority Socialists argued that "great steps internally and toward peace are necessary, to avert collapse," since they feared the growing echo of the Spartacist slogan "Peace, freedom, and bread." When Bethmann only replied, "We must work for peace, but are not furthering it if we shout for it," and went on to appeal for patience, "since peace cannot be brought about by general formulas," the Left, hitherto his strongest support, began to see him as the chief obstacle to peace. The chancellor's warning, "Do you gentlemen sincerely believe that we can lure a dog away from the fire with a new peace offer?" failed to convince Social Democrats, Progressives, and the Center Party of his personal commitment to a peace of reconciliation. "Erzberger's idea, which he privately told me," Lerchenfeld reported, "is that peace cannot be reached on the basis of the chancellor's policy." Bethmann's failure to inform the pacifist Left sufficiently for fear of provoking the wrath of the annexationist Right now exacted its price. By putting pressure on the Reischstag, the growing antiwar movement sought to force the chancellor's hand toward peace or, should he not comply, intended to overthrow him.

Public desire for "determined moves instead of this halfheartedness," revealing a deep crisis of confidence in the chancellor, inspired the ambitious Center Party leader to suggest a Reichstag initiative to end the carnage. Largely unaware of the fine threads of secret diplomacy, the Center-Left parties and press organs responded enthusiastically, demanding that "the government must publicly accept the common declaration about the peace aims in clear and unmistakable words as its own *program*." Since cabinet diplomacy had proven unable to bring peace, the German parliament, in an unprecedented move, assumed the power to declare that "it *strives for a peace of understanding and lasting reconciliation among nations.*" Although Bethmann had been personally and politically evolving toward this formula, his cautious feelers, intent on a favorable draw, appeared to a public disillusioned with submarine warfare as prolongation of the war. Anticipating a sellout of the bloody spoils of battle at the conference table, the OHL—for precisely the opposite reason—spread the rumor, credulously believed by many, that "Bethmann is not the man to conclude peace." By July 1917, the chancellor's unceasing quest for a lasting "negotiated peace" accepting the status quo if necessary and including some gains if possible, contributed centrally to his fall: it neither satisfied the claim of the Left for an immediate and unconditional cease-fire nor the dreams of the Right for a Greater Germany.[43]

"Was I really equivocal, was I swayed by considerations of party favor?" the ex-chancellor reflected on the apparent contradictions of his peace policy after his resignation. "Our peace move of December 12 was only a logical step in my previous direction, and as much as one may attack its form, it unmistakably declared our readiness for a negotiated settlement in principle." Since the failure of the Schlieffen Plan at the Marne, Bethmann had been fundamentally convinced that "Our position at the conclusion of peace will not be such that we can freely choose among a number of different alternatives, but we will have to try to obtain as much as we can." Hence he emphatically rejected any public commitment to specific aims: "For his person, he embraces the standpoint that God directs history and it would be blasphemy to indicate beforehand the price one intended to demand, since it depended upon providence and not our power." Concretely, the chancellor hoped in sanguine moments "to maintain the occupied areas under Germany's leadership with as much self-government as possible—Belgium under its own crown and probably also Poland—but make them militarily and economically dependent." Considering them provinces once belonging to the Holy Roman Empire, Bethmann argued that "the take-over of all areas in question should occur in a greater German spirit" as a national task, while military and economic formulas depended upon the fate of arms at the conclusion of peace. Reflecting the reality of German dominance over Mitteleuropa, these objectives were unacceptable to the Entente because they implied the acknowledgment of partial defeat. Nevertheless, since the chancellor continued to reduce his terms during spring and summer of 1917, they need not have prevented the beginning of compromise negotiations, *if* the Western Powers had been willing to settle for the status quo ante. But although the chorus of peace demands was swelling in London, Paris, Rome, and Petrograd, and although "the enemy statesmen knew generally that the German government was ready to negotiate, they did not in the least hint at a similar readiness." Even if Bethmann's indictment was colored by the bitterness of the collapse, the failure of his numerous peace feelers during the first three years of the war demonstrated convincingly that, contrary to the opinion of his leftist critics, the Entente was unwilling to accept anything short of outright victory. In Bethmann's mind even a partie remise would have meant the triumph of a moderately strengthened Germany.[44]

The futility of Bethmann's untiring pursuit of a favorable compromise was largely due to the domestic obstacles in his path. "The chancellor must force the emperor and the OHL to . . . admit that the war has not been won. These idiots will say that he is caving in but they will not have concrete arguments against him," Riezler reflected on the domestic obstacles. "He must raise the people from the newspaper clichés to the level of facts. . . . They are all insane." The mass hysteria whipped up by zealous propaganda and the depth of popular suffering demanded a smashing victory and could not readily be channeled into pacifism without creating mass depression and strengthening the enemy resolve to fight. "During my time in office, I would have encountered the decisive opposition of the great majority of the Reichstag, the military authorities, and the emperor," with a public renunciation of annexations and a clear commitment to the restoration of the status quo. In Bethmann's mind the war continued to rage not so much because of his unwillingness to promise the rehabilitation of Belgium but because "both sides [lacked] ultimate honesty" about their mutually exclusive aims. "This determination of policy in a people's war, and the compulsive effect of the unleashed forces of war limited the possibilities of all peace efforts, nipped them in the bud, and sealed their fate." Only the immense sacrifices, the hunger, disease, and despair of three war years gradually broke the grip of the imperialist madness. But once begun, this psychological reversal was so profound and overwhelming that it required the immediate cessation of hostilities and rejected the patient diplomatic bargaining proposed by the chancellor. Not until the early summer of 1917 were the domestic preconditions fulfilled for a meaningful peace move, since the peace resolution provided a parliamentary base, papal mediation offered a channel, and the West's war-weariness—heightened by submarine warfare—promised success. At the very moment when Bethmann's strategy appeared vindicated, "the majority of this [Reichstag] majority believed it to be high time and its principal task to eliminate me." [45]

Diplomatic difficulties were equally decisive in condemning Bethmann's quest. Negotiating through semiofficial and private channels was exasperating, since the enthusiasm of amateur diplomats for peace often raised false hopes and communicated erroneous terms. "I more and more come to regard Andersen's tact and *judicium* as problematic," Bethmann criticized one of the most prominent mediators. After Jagow's ouster, his instrument, the Foreign Office, was in "a terrible condition, due to Zimmerman's heavy-handedness and the skeptical resignation of others." Moreover, at no time during his tenure did he face Entente statesmen who prized peace above the destruction of the Central Powers' militarism, the restoration of Belgium, the *desannexion* of Alsace-Lorraine, the occupation of the Straits, the liberation of *Italia irredenta,* or the division of Germany's colonial empire. The failure of the chancellor's efforts to initiate negotiations revealed that the enemy coalition would rather continue the war than accept a Germany that controlled Central Europe, either indirectly or through negotiations reduced to its prewar level of power. Hence Bethmann replied to Delbrück's criticism "that the establishment of peace through Wilson's mediation depended upon our will" by pointing to "the Entente's resolution to fight as the primary hindrance." Although the first Russian Revolution momentarily raised hopes in Berlin, the Wilhelmstrasse soon found out that "it is difficult to conclude peace with democracies, especially revolutionary ones," since the Provisional Government was unwilling to disavow tsarist expanionist aims. Because of the unattainability of general peace, the chancellor unceasingly probed all major hostile belligerents for signs of desires for separate peace. Able to generate some support from the Right as well as the Left, this strategy was the diplomatic counterpart to his domestic diagonals. Directed at a negotiated peace short of total victory, Bethmann's scheme aimed at German preponderance on the continent but ultimately collapsed because of the insufficiency of German military and economic power. Though more realistic than the vindictiveness of the Right or the sentimental pacifism of the Left, the chancellor's design foundered on the rock of illusion that Europe would accept even a moderately strengthened Germany. When, after his fall, "the pressure of the masses was becoming ever more decisive for ending" the continuing struggle, Bethmann comforted himself with the thought, "Perhaps I was not so completely mistaken in shaping my policy accordingly from the beginning." [46]

CHAPTER 9

The Ultimate Weapon

"Our troops have performed miracles in this first part of the war. But grave, perhaps the most serious, trials still confront us." Bethmann reflected on the fighting with sober confidence: "I was profoundly moved by what I saw on the battlefield. Bismarck said in 1866: 'Our boys are delightful [*zum küssen*].' I can only repeat that." Despite his pride in "such united heroism, unparalleled in world history," the chancellor was not blind to the human sacrifice involved. "When I come to the front and see the decimated ranks of our men in gray . . . walk into the slaughter at Ypres, my heart throbs with pain. But I must not and cannot let my feelings speak." Sympathizing with a friend's "bitter and heavy sacrifice for the fatherland," he could not foresee that soon his first-born son would be mortally wounded in Russian Poland while on cavalry patrol. "I cannot speak out during these horrible and great times. All feeling is petrified." He poured out his grief in the words, "My son could and had to die the most noble death given to man. . . . The loneliness which the past year imposed upon me has grown heavier yet." He sought to console himself: "I must be silent here. One man has no right to complain in view of the hecatombs of the nation. And yet it is bloody difficult for me to accept that a second dear one, who was mine, is now no longer." And so, although he admired the sacrificial idealism of Langemarck and hoped to see the dead immortalized by victory, Bethmann, too, had to pay the personal price. Hence the chancellor approached the crucial strategic decisions with a somber sense of responsibility and weighed human suffering against potential military gain.[1]

In his attempt to practice Karl von Clausewitz's paradox of the primacy of politics in the conduct of war, Bethmann was forced to relive the struggle that had taken place between Moltke and Bismarck in the Franco-Prussian War. "The soldiers are horribly secretive. Frictions arise in a thousand details." Riezler "told the chancellor of his fear that the generals consider war as an end in itself and conduct it for art's sake" rather than for political ends. Bethmann's personal lack of talent for getting along with the military increased "the generals' desire to extend their power into the political realm" and to arrogate control of the empire's destiny to themselves. "If Germany believes that I lead the army, it is mistaken. I drink tea and cut wood, go for walks, and then find out from time to time what has been decided, just as the generals please," William II resentfully confessed his failure as supreme warlord. The personality clashes between civil and military leaders and within the Supreme Command were deeply rooted in the advocacy of contradictory strategies, predicated upon differing priorities of goals and means, which often overshadowed the fundamental purpose of victory. The conflict was acted out before a participating audience drunk with militarism, whose belligerent hysteria rode roughshod over bureaucratic caution and Socialist pacifism, and whose war aims bore no relation to the drastic inferiority of Central Powers' resources as compared to those of the more populous and industrialized enemy coalition. These internecine quarrels of the Wilhelmian leadership culminated in the protracted struggle over the ultimate weapon, submarine warfare, for it symbolized the OHL's attempt to establish a quasi dictatorship and ultimately precipitated defeat through American participation. The stage on which this epic unfolded, the GHQ, was therefore "dominated by tension and polluted by disputes, rivalries, and optimistic or pessimistic illusions." [2]

Ironically, Bethmann first clashed not with the generals but with Admiral Tirpitz, who insisted on the futile defense of Tsingtao and called for a dreadnought offensive to break British naval supremacy. The chancellor's circle denounced him as "the lord of lies" and "*l'homme nefaste* with his battle fleet. If we only had light cruisers today instead of these huge useless crates! The emperor's battleship parades are his fault." At the core of the disagreement lay a difference of priorities between the navy, "waging war only on England," and the Wilhelmstrasse, preoccupied with the Russian steamroller—between the admiral's desire for seeing his *Flottenpolitik* vindicated by a naval victory, and the chancellor's insistence on "the fleet in being" as a bargaining point for peace with Britain insuring future overseas development. Again and again Bethmann stressed to William II, "*we should maintain the navy until the conclusion of peace;* it should not be endangered." A suspicious Riezler predicted that if the chancellor would call the admiral's bluff and "said use it, Tirpitz would immediately back down." Since he had opposed the building of cruisers and submarines suited for commercial warfare, Tirpitz, "always saving his skin," hoped for a major naval engagement to preclude any possibility of reconciliation with his archenemy, England. But Bethmann's cautious argument against staking everything on a victory at sea over Britain prevailed, and William II's first order to the fleet authorized defensive use of light forces to wear down English power and, only then, a decisive battle. Riezler noted triumphantly: "The emperor understood that no new dreadnoughts are to be built." [3]

On land the failure of the Schlieffen Plan necessitated a radical restructuring of the army leadership and a profound reappraisal of Germany's strategic position. "We are presently living through serious days. Despite all losses the French armies are still strong and capable of taking the offensive," Bethmann wrote to Berlin in early September 1914. Hoping for a miracle in East Prussia, he continued: "The unfortunate tactics of [General von] Prittwitz have brought untold sufferings to the poor province." Although Hindenburg's victory at Tannenberg blunted the Russian thrust, "in the West the encirclement failed. [General] Joffre is not maladroit. There is horrible fighting going on." [4] When the full extent of strategic mistakes leading to the withdrawal from the Marne became clear on September 14, and the younger Moltke collapsed, William II, himself psychologically crushed, proved incapable of directing the war. Valentini noted "great commotion . . . Moltke —Falkenhayn; [chief of the military cabinet] Lyncker splendid. Moltke's breakdown. Falkenhayn takes over the direction of the general staff." The early setbacks brought to power those generals with whom Bethmann was to wrestle during his entire term of office. The chancellor remained studiously optimistic: "During the last few weeks events have progressed more slowly than expected in the beginning and hoped for at home. Nevertheless, one can say that the actual situation does not allow us to be disappointed." Since in the age of barbed wire and the machine gun defense proved superior to offense, *Durchhalten,* perseverance alone could win the protracted struggle of attrition. "Although I am easily inclined to look at the dark side of things, I carry my head high," he sought to reassure Hammann. Partial victory in the West had brought sufficient spoils, and although "the Austrians are doing badly, they are not doing as badly as people think. If they hold Cracow and Przemysl defensively, things might yet work out." There was still hope for a breakthrough in Flanders, but it was clear that "if it fails and we have no troops to spare in the West, we have lost the war." Hence, after November 1914 the chancellor expected at best a partial success. Riezler mused dejectedly: "All that comes from the battle of the Marne. Had we won that, everything would have been possible." [5]

Although Falkenhayn was "very shrewd, quite captivating if he wants, strong-willed, with a talent for organization, and not without genius"—all traits which compensated for his "self-indulgence, tactlessness, lack of education, and frivolousness"—the new chief of staff could only formalize the strategy of attrition. "The enormous losses of the struggle for Ypres [created] general nervousness because of the danger of our bleeding white. The generals are for it as a question of honor. But it is politically insane." After their initial blunders, Bethmann grew more and more distrustful of the military, who seemed more preoccupied with winning battles than the war. "Finally events proved the chancellor right, who had advised the soldiers two weeks ago to break off the engagement and to throw everything available to the East," Riezler noted in late November. "Nothing has been gained, and in the East two additional corps would have been decisive—now they are being sent, hopefully not too late." When the temporary chief of staff's nerves failed and he demanded an immediate armistice or separate peace, "the chancellor railed against the liars Tirpitz and Falkenhayn who only think of themselves," jeopardizing the country's future to spread their own glory. In personal terms, Riezler saw a strange contradiction between the "congenital pessimist" and "cold-blooded dilettante in the Supreme Command," and the "chancellor's heavy nature, so immensely superior in judgment, spirit, and education, always groping at first but finally equally sure of himself and correct, without ever saying anything for effect, like the former." Indeed, "both must boundlessly loathe the other's mentality. When recounting some really stupid and thoughtless proposal of Falkenhayn's, the chancellor asks with his touching modesty, 'I don't know, am I completely blind, etc.?'" Their dispute over assigning top priority to the eastern front, and the "grave responsibility of forcing him to persevere" in the war against Russia, made Bethmann receptive to the "ubiquitous call: Falkenhayn must go. He is generally [considered] an unscrupulous gambler." When his assistant warned him that "H.M. has to understand that in the Falkenhayn question his throne is at stake," the chancellor "listened, rose, paced the floor, and only replied yes, he knew—this man had to go." [6]

Realizing that "the personality question is intimately tied to the general conduct of the war," Bethmann asked Hindenburg for a professional opinion on the chief of staff's costly blunders. The hero of the Masurian Lakes was "very skeptical about Falkenhayn. Everyone says that he has no reputation left in the army. The chancellor seems resolved to do something about him, even go to the emperor." Although Bethmann understood that "there will be a rude awakening and a witch-hunt if excessive hopes are disappointed, and everything would be all right if people had confidence in the military leadership," he was confronted with a delicate task, since the emperor genuinely liked Falkenhayn and resented civilian interference in his Kommandogewalt. While Bethmann was attempting to line up Adjutant General Hans von Plessen and Lyncker, the general "strengthened his position through the publication of his [permanent] appointment as chief of staff, which makes a bad impression everywhere." The dilemma of whether "the fresh reserves should be thrown into Russia in spite of the slim hope of forcing Petersburg to make peace, i.e. gambling on its moral disintegration," or should be employed in a further fruitless offensive in the West, prompted Bethmann to act. "Today the great personnel question will be presented to H.M.," Riezler noted on January 2, 1915. "General Marschall (military cabinet) and Lyncker fight like lions for Falkenhayn, whom they invented." Bethmann adroitly presented the matter to William II as a question of "accumulation of offices," since Falkenhayn was also Prussian minister of war. The emperor could not deny the justice of the chancellor's charge but refused to drop his chief of staff, who "enjoyed his full confidence. He would never put Ludendorff in his place, . . . a dubious character corroded by ambition." Although predicting that "military history will one day judge that Falkenhayn always left the initiative to the enemy" and deploring his "character flaw of personal ambition," Bethmann did not stake his office on the general's removal, since he also feared Ludendorff's intrigues. "The change of leadership is blocked. The emperor is opposed. He does not comprehend its demoralizing effect on the people," Riezler noted dejectedly, but added, "It will be brought up again." [7]

When Falkenhayn dispatched his rival Ludendorff to serve in a newly formed Carpathian army designed to stiffen Austrian resistance, Moltke and Hindenburg offered their resignations to force William II's hand. The chancellor once again "was quite wrought up over the conflict between Hindenburg and Falkenhayn." Valentini sensed "a severe crisis." Indeed, Hindenburg wrote an "astonishing letter" to the emperor demanding "the return of Ludendorff and the rescinding of the appointment of the chief of staff because of the incompatibility of this post with the Ministry of War in one person. The former was granted, and the latter in the form of the appointment of a new minister of war," Falkenhayn's trusted follower, Wild von Hohenborn; but he himself remained. The involvement of the empress as well as the threats of the generals made William II explode with rage, and only Bethmann's warning that "I could not bear the responsibility for the political situation" if the field marshal were fired, prevented Hindenburg's dismissal. Now Falkenhayn's position was firmer than before. After investigating whether the chief of staff's Carpathian strategy was designed to discredit his rival Ludendorff, Riezler "warned everybody that they should not attack Falkenhayn so indiscriminately since this only strengthens him." Hindenburg's irresponsible intervention ruptured Bethmann's finely spun threads. The chancellor had to continue working with a man "whose competence should not be underestimated, even if his character could not be valued equally highly." The abortive effort to remove the chief of staff left a legacy of suspicion between the Wilhelmstrasse and the second OHL and intensified the rivalry between Falkenhayn and Ludendorff.[8]

Although he protested, "I want to keep from interfering and meddling in military operations," Bethmann considered it his "right and duty to criticize military measures which, according to his opinion, exert an injurious influence on the political situation." Among the numerous disagreements regarding major (East vs. West priority) or minor (amphibious landing in Riga) strategic issues, one question above all troubled the German leadership: the freeing of a supply line to Turkey. Because it involved the arteries of the tsarist and British empires in the Straits of Constantinople and the Suez Canal, Bulgaria's and Rumania's choice of alliances, as well as pivotal grain and crude oil supplies from Bessarabia, Bethmann continually advocated the occupation of the northeastern corner of Serbia in order to gain control of the Danube. "Now the military have finally come around to understanding the importance of the northeastern tip of Serbia," Riezler exclaimed prematurely in March 1915; "It is the sole means of drawing Rumania and Bulgaria in and of really harming Russia." To the chancellor's constant entreaties, Falkenhayn replied that he had no troops to spare, since he "preferred a concentric advance on Warsaw" in order to beat the Russians. "Unfortunately, I still have not yet been able to push through the munitions transports to Turkey," Bethmann sighed to Weizsäcker. "Luckily, today calmer news followed the alarming reports of lack of ammunition on Gallipoli." In midsummer 1915 Riezler sought to convince the chancellor: "The emperor and Falkenhayn must understand that Bulgaria is the key, that peace is impossible as long as the Russians and the French still hope for the Balkans." At last public opinion and diplomatic pressure from the Allies finally persuaded Falkenhayn to "undertake this action as soon as it is militarily feasible and that he is making preparations" such as freeing enough forces for a campaign in the fall of 1915. After a crushing victory over hapless Serbia, the Central Powers' Balkan flank stood secure. Although the chancellor attempted to participate in the shaping of German strategy, the fundamental decisions of the war of attrition were made by the generals, with little regard for their political implications and results.[9]

"I cannot say anything about GHQ, it would be indiscreet. But once in a while I sigh: It makes me cry," Bethmann wailed in disgust over the military's hold on the kaiser. Although he had "grown white and quite serious," William II was incapable of reconciling political with military demands, since after September 1914 he was "a broken man, wallowing in the image of Germany as armed camp with his life's goal—peace—in shambles. The crown prince is an utterly lost cause. There is no hero among the generals, only the beauty of collective competence." Bethmann's strongest support came from civil cabinet chief Valentini who "makes an excellent, concrete, reasonable impression, firm and honest, with a refreshing sense of humor and much understanding for the domestic situation and for the great trust of the masses in the chancellor's course." Since Ambassador Treutler, the chancellor's official representative in GHQ, "defends his policy sincerely but probably too weakly and too unimpressively," military ideas constantly surrounded the emperor, and Falkenhayn was able to create "an enormous position and can do anything with the kaiser, who has a mystical relationship with his chief of general staff. But he interferes as little with him as with the chancellor in politics—always maintaining that *he* directs the war." To the parties of the Right, dissatisfied with Bethmann's halfhearted pursuit of war aims, his quest for peace, and reluctance to use all weapons against the enemy, Falkenhayn appeared as the ideal strong man who, in contrast to Tirpitz and Bülow, possessed the emperor's full confidence. "The chancellor asks whether Falkenhayn would be a greater evil as chief of staff than as chancellor, speaks of his duty to resign, etc." Bethmann confessed despondently: "You know yourself I lack the energy and levity to be able to put down fellows like Bassermann. I can work neither with the [National Liberals] nor with the Conservatives." One of the closest collaborators of the chief of staff analyzed the conflict: "Where should trust come from if Bethmann sees in Falkenhayn a rival for the chancellorship—and correctly so! How shall this heavy-blooded, thoroughly honest, and scrupulous man find a common ground with this adroit, unscrupled rascal?" Wild added revealingly: "Falkenhayn is and remains a believer in the political and military generalissimo; moreover, he has quite a lordly nature and possesses the ear of the kaiser, who always prefers to side with the soldiers against the diplomats. So Bethmann has a hard task." Even if he sincerely tried to overlook the personal and political rivalry, the chancellor found himself forced to warn time and again. "Although Falkenhayn's merits are recognized more and more, he is trusted nowhere, he will never be able to get rid of Ypres, and cannot convince the public that envy of Hindenburg does not dictate his military decisions." [10]

If lack of expertise and the militarism of Wilhelmian elites kept him from having a decisive voice in land warfare, Bethmann proved as "tenacious as old shoe leather" on the even more important issue of the submarines. Because of the U9's sinking of three British cruisers in the Channel and the English imposition of a tight blockade around the landlocked Central Powers, Admiral Pohl implored the chancellor to "use sharper means of commercial warfare," i.e. a counterblockade "of the hostile coast through U-boats." Bethmann was immediately conscious of the potential risk: "I still think the dangers considerable; perhaps the planned blockade should only be undertaken if it forces England to make peace, and when our military situation in East and West is favorable while Britain's colonies are threatened seriously; or if, on the other hand, such a blockade is our last resource in extremis." Although aware that "the torpedoing of neutral ships cannot be completely reconciled with the general rules of international law" Bethmann, enraged by British starvation policy, endorsed "those measures of warfare which seem most appropriate to the enemy's defeat and the rapid conclusion of the war." Hence, his misgivings were not based on sentimental humanitarianism but on military expediency. The chancellor hesitated to unleash an untried weapon because the disadvantages of neutral reaction might outweigh the benefits of damage to England. Although he discounted the eventuality of an American declaration of war because of "a lack of armed forces," he knew of the dangers of an official trade boycott, cutting Germany "entirely off from all supplies and aiding England's plan of a complete commercial blockade." Italy's precarious balance might tip toward intervention, pulling Rumania along. Scandinavia, Holland, and the other continental neutrals would no longer be able to trade with Berlin, while Germany alone would have to feed all of Belgium. "Measures like a submarine blockade, which are certain to have a negative effect on the attitude of the neutrals and our supplies, can only be undertaken without dangerous consequences when our military situation is so secure that the issue is beyond doubt and the danger of the neutrals joining our enemies can be ruled out." [11]

Since the admiralty continued to press for unrestricted submarine warfare as "one of the most effective means of reaching our war aims toward England," Bethmann sought a decision by William II on January 7, 1915. "Pohl advanced his proposals with more pathos than skill," observed naval cabinet chief Müller. "Then the chancellor quietly and ably presented his point of view that the general political situation—the complete insecurity of the neutrals, the failure of the Austrians and the Turks—presently allowed neither a submarine blockade nor Zeppelin raids on residential London." [12] In the end, "coached by Müller, the kaiser opted for postponement. Only when the military situation leans more in our favor" could such grave risks be run. But the responsibility for not using a potentially decisive weapon rested heavily on Bethmann. No one could deny the "technical difficulties. At night the blockade is completely ineffective, actually a bluff; the scare will be over in a week," and British commerce continue undeterred. Despite such doubts, the chancellor became more and more defensive. "In public Tirpitz agitates for [U-boat warfare] so that he can say the Foreign Office has refused." Bethmann also fumed about the admiral's sensational promise to American journalist Karl von Wiegand: "England wants to starve us; we can play the same game, bottle her up and destroy any ship trying to run the blockade." Because of frustration with restraints on the battlefield, this bold submarine threat captured the public imagination, was generally praised by the German press, and called forth a series of manifestos: "Wide circles of the population consider it an economic and military necessity to use all possible means in order to foil by retaliation the plan of starving Germany, contrary to international law." But, unconvinced of the certainty of success, Bethmann thought it imperative "to wait for a great victory on land before taking a step which could provide Italy with a pretext for declaring war." [13]

In the preparatory conference with Pohl, Falkenhayn, Zimmermann, and Delbrück, in the first days of February, the chancellor found the military and civilian leaders deeply divided. According to Zimmermann's later recollections, Bethmann protested that the number of available craft, a mere twenty, was insufficient for an effective blockade and that additional neutrals, especially Italy, might enter the war. But Admiral Pohl's overly sanguine promise that England would be weakened and subjugated in a short time prevailed over Falkenhayn's scruples regarding the feeding of Belgium, although no formal decision was made. Undersecretary Zimmermann, who had received the impression from the American ambassador that Washington would content itself with paper protests, and the dynamic secretary of the treasury Helfferich, who was optimistic about the possible economic consequences of an interdiction of British trade, counseled the chancellor to override his diplomatic concerns. Similarly, the "public did not understand [Bethmann's] negative attitude, rumoring that he prevented submarine warfare for love of England." The rising National Liberal parliamentarian Gustav Stresemann wrote to a friend that Erzberger, Westarp, and Heydebrand, as well as his own party, had brought severe pressure to bear on the reluctant chancellor in favor of a submarine counterblockade. His humanitarian scruples against killing women and children were counterbalanced by British starvation measures ("the most barbaric kind of warfare"), since they stretched the definition of contraband beyond recognition by including foodstuffs. But while Bethmann still wrestled with himself, Admiral Pohl "extracted without my [the chancellor's] consent the decisive imperial order after a general discussion with myself and the other authorities in question and implemented it in such a

manner that intervention after the fact was made impossible for me."
Encouraged by the navy brass in Wilhelmshaven, the "old salt"
bowled over William II and released the imperial decision to the
press, thereby outmaneuvering the hesitant chancellor. On February 4 the seas around Great Britain were declared a *Kriegsgebiet*
(war zone) and all neutral shipping warned to keep away as errors
might be unavoidable. Clairvoyantly, Valentini deplored "this maladroit blockade declaration against England. . . . *Dies nefastus!*"
Bethmann, who "under the pressure of the Tirpitz-inspired agitation" had acquiesced in the admiralty's coup, appeared to his assistant as "a strange man. He has the intellect but not the drive for
power. He always has to be pushed forward and edged on." [14]

The diplomatic repercussions of the war-zone declaration exceeded
Bethmann's fears. President Wilson warned emphatically that he
"would be constrained to hold the Imperial German Government
to a strict accountability for such acts of their naval authority," and
Bülow cautioned from Rome that an incident could well push Italy
over the brink. In a dramatic confrontation between the civil willingness to grant and the naval refusal to make concessions, the chief of
staff proved decisive: "Falkenhayn considered the first American
note a threat to fight, said it would be our economic doom, and was
ready to give in completely." Since "Tirpitz is through with the
kaiser, who is sick of lying," Riezler could note gleefully, "with
courage, determination, and energy the chancellor has obtained
from the kaiser a polite but firm answer." In substance reflecting
the Foreign Office's desire for conciliation but in tone echoing the
martial confidence of the navy, the German reply offered "to abstain
from all violence to American merchant vessels when they are
recognizable as such," and promised the cessation of submarine
warfare if Wilson could force England to adhere to the Declaration
of London.

When Secretary of State Bryan took up the latter hint and proposed a modus vivendi based on admission of foodstuffs in exchange for abandonment of the U-boat campaign, another crisis arose
in Berlin. Fearful for a weapon introduced with so much fanfare, and
which was already limited by William's insistence on sparing
American and Italian ships, the navy brass unanimously protested
against the Wilhelmstrasse's desire to accept the U.S. proposal, provided it also included raw materials. After a long and heated debate
in which Tirpitz warned against the "practical cessation" of U-boat

warfare and Bethmann countered that "the odium of a British refusal would improve our position toward the neutrals," the wavering emperor finally came down on the chancellor's side. But Bethmann's victory remained hollow, when Grey, sneering at the cessation of U-boat attacks as an inadequate quid pro quo, refused to lift the stranglehold of the blockade. "America cannot get herself to do anything against England," Riezler wrote, regretting the evaporation of all hope for successful Wilsonian mediation. "The United States of America would be able to play an influential role if imaginative and strong men stood at its helm," Bethmann disappointedly informed the Bundesrat, and continued, "That is not the case. The American politicians limit themselves to paper protests even against Japan so that their businessmen may enrich themselves." [15]

The "growing number of neutral ships falling victim to submarine warfare" prompted Bethmann to protest once again to the admiralty, lest an incident "cause serious complications and drive the [uncommitted] powers into the camp of our enemies." In cruel irony, one day after the chancellor's refusal of responsibility for the consequences and his demand for guarantees of safety of neutral shipping, a German submarine torpedoed the pride of the Cunard Line, the *Lusitania,* sending 1,198 passengers and sailors to a watery grave. Sparking a nearly unanimous revulsion of American public opinion against Teutonic brutality, despite the ship's partial cargo of contraband ammunition, the incident strengthened Anglophile influence in Washington and heightened the danger of U.S. participation in the war unless submarine warfare was substantially modified. Although William II "failed to grasp the seriousness of the situation," Müller extracted "the half-concession . . . that the opinion of the chancellor must be respected" and curtly ordered the chief of the admiralty "to avoid the sinking of neutrals in the near future. It is better to let an enemy ship pass than to destroy a nonbelligerent." Preoccupied with the impending entry of Italy into the war, and reassured by Count Bernstorff's calming reports, Bethmann decided to ride out the storm and to treat dilatorily the American protest against these "acts, so absolutely contrary to the rules, the practices, and the spirit of modern warfare." Bryan's demand for a German disavowal, for reparation, and for taking "immediate steps to prevent the reoccurrence" of such incidents, and his appeal to "indisputable rights," left little room for compromise. To smooth the domestic waves before the necessary showdown with the navy, the chancellor reassurred the parliamentary leaders: "Do not get excited! The final wording is being worked out with the help of the navy." Much depended upon the actual facts of the case and whether or not the *Lusitania* was a British auxiliary cruiser, as the admiralty claimed. "Perhaps, therefore, not a note but an exchange of notes, of course not asking for forgiveness but defending our point of view. This is also the emperor's wish." Indeed, the German reply emphasized the martial nature of the *Lusitania* (claiming that there were guns on deck—a fact later disproved in court) and asked the American government to reassess its position on the basis of this additional evidence. But while stressing the "principle of defending ourselves with every means at our disposal," Foreign Secretary Jagow hinted strongly that this was only the beginning of "further conversation." [16]

With tactical adroitness, Bethmann sought to insure Falkenhayn's support by convincing him that "the United States are close to breaking off relations." His warning that he "could no longer guarantee the attitude of the neutrals if the submarine war continues in its present form" persuaded the chief of staff, although the admiralty claimed that "the chancellor will have to take the full responsibility" for the necessary cessation of *all* submarine attacks. "The repeated sinking of neutral ships has gotten on the nerves of the chancellor; he finally went to the emperor to get the necessary order for the navy; the kaiser commanded [the admirals] Tirpitz and Bachmann to appear but of course they say that such restrictions render U-boat warfare ineffective," Riezler chronicled. The trial of strength resulted in a victory for Bethmann, since together with Müller he was empowered to frame a new instruction that stressed the sparing of neutral shipping. To cement his advantage the chancellor quickly demanded "that already during the negotiations with America submarines should not attack passenger liners. After long disputation with the navy, which always claims that everything is technically impossible, the kaiser decided in the chancellor's favor." Riezler was pleased by the outcome: "Thereupon Tirpitz and Bachmann offered their resignations. Counseled by Müller, the kaiser refused them very emphatically [as infringements on his] Kommandogewalt." Despite mounting criticism of "the imperial order to put down the sword in the middle of a war," Bethmann prevailed through Falkenhayn's support. Unwilling to abandon an effective weapon, he was equally opposed to bringing further neutrals into the struggle on the other side. Hence the chancellor forced a compromise that allowed submarine warfare as long as it respected non-belligerent shipping.[17]

The second American *Lusitania* note, adopted over Bryan's resignation, endangered Bethmann's careful middle course by demanding the virtually complete cessation of U-boat attacks. Wilson's appeal to "the sacred rights of humanity," allowing U.S. citizens to travel on passenger liners of the belligerents thus preventing their attack by German submarines, caused grave consternation in Berlin. "Jagow, supported by all the diplomats, maintains that it is no bluff this time. . . . At any rate a rupture of relations would exert such a suggestive power on the remaining neutrals as to endanger Holland and prevent Rumania's entry on our side," Riezler pondered. "Hence the navy has to give in" even if there was reason to fear "that public opinion will be outraged in that case." Indeed, "the naval opposition has alerted the domestic enemies of the chancellor to the dangers of the cessation of submarine warfare." But despite the submarine psychosis expressed in a petition of the six industrial organizations that were demanding, *"Germany must not abandon the sharpest weapon* at its disposal," the chancellor found support for a conciliatory course in the army leadership. Convinced by Bernstorff's emissary, Meyer-Gerhard, that Americans would have to be allowed to travel on enemy liners, Bethmann attempted to persuade the chief of the admiralty that "concessions must be made, since aside from the legal issue it was also a question of power." Otherwise war with America would be inevitable, "which we cannot survive even according to the opinion of the OHL," he agonized. "But the concessions are not supposed to reduce the effectiveness of submarine warfare. That almost requires squaring the circle."

Intent on avoiding a break with Washington, Bethmann sought a compromise without "granting all American demands that would amount to a suspension of U-boat warfare for which I cannot bear the responsibility." Since "my communication with our embassy is very irregular," it was next to impossible to gauge correctly what might suffice to placate Wilson. After days of intense discussions with diplomats, admirals, business leaders, and even the American ambassador, Bethmann resolved "to cut the knot, even if the navy does not agree . . . since the decision was ultimately his to make." Following a suggestion made by James Gerard in the belief that Washington was intent on a workable compromise, and unaware of Robert

Lansing's *non possumus* ("we do not feel that the principles upon which this government stands can be properly made the subject of preliminary negotiations"), the German answer reiterated the right of retaliation but offered unmolested voyage for regular shipping as well as recognizable U.S. liners, negotiations about further neutral passenger steamers, and the addition of four *enemy* liners to create enough passenger space. Short of abandoning submarine warfare entirely, Bethmann could force no greater concessions.[18]

The third *Lusitania* note, which warned that further sinkings would be construed as "deliberately unfriendly" acts, renewed the furor in Berlin: "People and court are angry about America—this naturally also works against the chancellor. But once more he has succeeded in smoothing things over with H.M." As domestic reasons prevented Bethmann from accepting Wilson's demands, he followed Bernstorff's "advice perhaps not to answer at all." But Lansing's call for "the practical cooperation of the Imperial Government" to restore the freedom of the seas, struck a sympathetic chord with Secretary of the Treasury Helfferich, who argued for conducting submarine warfare according to the *Prisenordnung* (naval prize law) and using America to break the British blockade stranglehold. Although Tirpitz, who was convinced that "our defeat is in the American interest," objected vigorously, "the chancellor subscribes to Helfferich's argument. . . . Either war will end on the continent through the exhaustion of the Russians," rendering the blowing up of a few freighters more or less irrelevant, "or war does not end and then we cannot throw away the hope for freedom of trade on the basis of the London declaration—since, on this ground, we could hold out indefinitely."

While Bethmann was moving toward "asking the American government to renew negotiations with England in order to return the sea war to the basis of the London declaration," the sinking of the British liner *Arabic* once more posed the fundamental issue of the goals of submarine warfare. Protesting angrily, "under no condition can we let a situation continue to exist" in which the question of war and peace depended upon the whim of one U-boat commander, he now pressed for a new instruction, limiting attacks on *all* passenger liners to cruiser warfare. After obtaining a preliminary order to that effect, "the chancellor [went] to Pless. Great fracas against the navy because of the *Arabic*." Bethmann's patience had worn thin: "Even if it might be possible to avert the worst, I cannot continue to walk on a volcano. I must have security for my policy," he demanded agitatedly; but the admiralty would not yield. In the decisive conference with William II, the navy refused to make concessions and Bethmann felt betrayed, complaining of having been "surrounded from all sides . . . but unlike the Russians he would not capitulate" without obtaining new orders. Only because of Falkenhayn's advice did the kaiser decide against Tirpitz in the end. Riezler ruminated: "We must declare that we will not torpedo liners without warning. That will be difficult for the German people, but through censorship we [can] suppress all criticism." [19]

Despite Bethmann's initial victory in imperial councils, the issue was far from settled, when "Tirpitz submitted his resignation because he lost in the struggle over our American policy." Although he detested the "unreliability and intrigues of his colleague," the chancellor could not press his advantage, since Erzberger was correct in warning him against a Tirpitz crisis, because of the admiral's "great popularity in the Reichstag and [with the] general public." Therefore "his resignation was struck down as an inadmissible complaint against the chancellor. Now we have to work in order to make the compromise understandable" to the people, Riezler noted with relief. But although the Grand Admiral ostensibly continued in office, the emperor, enraged by his habitual insubordination, excluded him from any influence on sea warfare. "Meanwhile [Chief of the Admiralty Staff] Bachmann has been replaced by Henning von Holtzendorff. . . . His appointment is a triumph for the chancellor"; the new admiralty head possessed more political understanding than his predecessor. In order to "assuage the discontent of parts of public opinion" over the defeat of their idol, Bethmann stressed to the parliamentary leaders that the Grand Admiral's competency had merely been redrawn and that "Tirpitz has not been eliminated" from decisions.[20]

"This tension with America is awful, yet I hope to overcome it. Only death is cheap," Bethmann unburdened himself to a friend. But Washington was not placated by Bernstorff's assurance that commanders were under strict orders to spare liners. Even without Wilson's massive threat to break relations, Bethmann knew that "repetition of the *Arabic* incident means war," and with the cooperation of Holtzendorff, who temporarily suspended submarine attacks in general, he was resolved to do everything in his power to appease the American government. But when Bernstorff exceeded his orders and expressed regret, disavowed the guilty commander, and promised an indemnity, the chancellor asked in angry surprise, "Does that agree with the instruction?" Afraid of offending the new admiralty chief, "who apparently seemed ready to reform U-boat warfare radically," Jagow softened the final wording to read that the captain had been "notified" accordingly, and that reparation would be paid solely "out of friendly consideration." Although Wilson's pressure had led to a complete return to cruiser warfare ordered voluntarily by the admiralty on September 18, Berlin's hopes for equally effective American action against British violations of international law were to be bitterly disappointed.[21]

When reflecting on the fluctuations of warfare in late 1915, Bethmann refused to make predictions: "The most miraculous feature of this war is the immense power of the people. Nowhere is there a single man who has destiny in his hands." Despite the "incredibly slow tempo of the war," Riezler found "the chancellor in [a state of] remarkable equanimity and tenacity." In order not to extend the bloodshed unnecessarily, Bethmann "continued to do heated battle with the navy. Tirpitz agitates for U-boat war as an end in itself, even if we thereby drive America into the enemy camp. I consider that insane and I have prevented it," he confided to Oettingen. In the first showdown the chancellor had prevailed because he could reply to his navalist critics with Falkenhayn's formula, "At present I cannot countenance a war with America." After the entry of Bulgaria and the resulting Balkan victories, however, the acute crisis on land had passed. "We can continue the war for a long time!" the Prussian minister of war stated confidently, claiming that German resources would last defensively until the next winter. But the chief of staff admitted offensive impotence: "He has no assurance for ending the war before winter, no military means [to achieve it], since any breakthrough in the West is doubtful and, even if successful, it might not prostrate France." Riezler reported Falkenhayn's reversal: "He called Tirpitz and Holtzendorff to find out about the possible effectiveness of submarine warfare. Tirpitz said that if we began immediately, he was sure that within a few months England would be forced to its knees. Holtzendorff replied that the political side did not concern him and we could also begin in March; but then, due to technical improvements, England would be ripe for peace through actual damage and terror [undergone] in four to eight months." The noose was tightening around Bethmann's neck.[22]

Confronted with military unanimity and the increasingly powerful agitation for submarine warfare of the Right Reichstag majority, Bethmann began to doubt his own judgment. Characteristically he temporized. "The chancellor has expressed his misgivings, but has not taken any definite stand. He has . . . spoken clearly and convincingly. He believes Falkenhayn has admitted military bankruptcy and therefore considers it a *coup de désespoir*," Riezler recorded Bethmann's ruminations. "When we do that, England can only give in when it absolutely has to. Then any concession would be an admission of lost naval supremacy and political suicide." Moreover, he feared "a rupture of relations with America, and the alienation of all neutrals. If we lost we would be beaten to death like a mad dog." Falkenhayn's claim, "Without it, peace is unthinkable," could not be denied, but unrestricted submarine warfare would also kill all chances for compromise and severely strain the alliance of the Central Powers. To the sympathetic chief of the naval cabinet, Müller, Bethmann "spoke very seriously about the grave decision regarding stepped-up submarine attacks, which might result in a kind of crusade against Germany, anathematized by the entire civilized world." Since it was, in effect, "a second decision for war," the chancellor, who had been burned once before, recoiled from taking the risk: "Our military situation was not so bad that we had to make such a desperate move. He vented much ill-feeling against the 'gambler' Falkenhayn." As a decisive step toward total war Bethmann considered "submarine warfare the ultima ratio; such a challenge would mean *finis Germaniae* in case of failure." On the other hand, because, if the admiralty's facts were right, unrestricted submarine warfare was *the* miracle weapon, Bethmann attempted to clarify his thinking in a long memorandum. Ready to resign if overridden, he stated that "if *certainty* for the defeat of England exists, we have to dare it." But he quickly added, "Nobody can give such *assurance* and it remains a throw of the dice with Germany's existence at stake." Since to obtain effective American measures against British violations of international law appeared to him "a hopeless undertaking," peace would have to be attempted directly with England, even if it were then very meager. But he feared the "enormous danger" that the submarine and war aims movements might first force the country "into a submarine war—regardless of who was chancellor." Faced with immense pressures for a decision that might seal Germany's doom, Bethmann frantically sought a way out.[23]

Convinced that unrestricted submarine warfare would "so diminish English tonnage that it would be forced to beg for peace" within six months, the admiralty and the chief of staff urgently pleaded with William II. "The decision is getting very difficult for H.M. It is hard for him to refuse the military something which it considers the last resort," Riezler observed of the power struggle. "In the end I believe that H.M. will follow the chancellor. Despite everything, he is very cautious and responsible." When the kaiser nevertheless began to cave in and ordered Bethmann to begin diplomatic preparations for resuming submarine warfare on March 1, the chancellor declared to Holtzendorff, "Presently I could not assume the responsibility for a U-boat war, which must lead to a break with America." Since parliamentary, industrial, and press agitation were weakening his hold on William II, Bethmann agreed to seek a diplomatic compromise, allowing the "conduct not of completely unrestrained but of increased submarine attacks." He refused to go further since, even if the navy could sink four million tons within six months, it was unlikely that England could be *forced* to come to terms. "The chancellor has not yet made up his mind. It is a grave risk and yet promises a considerable chance of success." His assistant pondered the "immense difficulty of correctly judging the general military situation." But whatever his personal doubts, Bethmann asked William II to "avoid any firm decision," since he could not bear the responsibility for "provoking" a war with the United States. Alone the chancellor could only fight the navy to a standoff, and in early February a memorandum was drawn up and delivered to the neutrals, justifying the resumption of stepped-up submarine warfare with the arming of enemy merchantmen.[24]

This compromise was short-lived, since the threat of resumed U-boat attacks effectively scuttled the *Lusitania* settlement with Washington while whetting the appetite of the navalists in Berlin. Lansing's unequivocal demand not only for an indemnity but for "recognition of the illegality of our action" created "great uproar over America" in the Wilhelmstrasse. "Intent on avoiding a break with the U.S.A. as long as honor permits and the U-boat weapon is not taken from us," Bethmann was willing to go to the limit to appease Wilson. The effect of the chancellor's admission of German liability for reparations and his warning that anything further would be an "impossible humiliation" was destroyed by the admiralty's concurrent "attempt to step up [attacks] with American consent." Unconvinced by Bethmann's argument that "we can act in no other way than to treat the armed merchant vessels as men of war," Washington allowed the *Lusitania* case to lapse and contented itself with paper protests when the chancellor obtained orders against sinking armed passenger ships. "At home the Conservatives have attacked and agitated greatly against the chancellor. They have revolted on the submarine question in the Budget Commission of the Landtag," Riezler recorded angrily. Bethmann's plea that he was not opposed to the U-boats on principle and that morale would suffer if the Reichstag "demands submarine warfare and it does not happen," convinced few deputies. "Naval propagandists whisper into the ear of all domestic enemies of the chancellor that we could wrestle England down, if we only wanted to—but courage is lacking; utterly false numbers are being bandied about, such as that six weeks of submarine warfare would suffice." Discontent and frustration erupted when "the National Liberal and industrial agitators pulled along the gullibles, attacked in the Commission, and passed a resolution" in favor of unlimited U-boat attacks. Hiding behind the Kommandogewalt and claiming that the conduct of the war was not subject to parliamentary control, "the chancellor replied that as soon as he was convinced that England could be forced to its knees, he, too, would order unrestricted submarine warfare; for the time being he did not believe this was so." Although the parliamentary challenge in the Prussian Lower House was defeated by a ringing denunciation in the *NAZ*, it revealed the weakness of a government torn by disagreements and inner doubts.[25]

"Because of Falkenhayn's and Holtzendorff's position, not to speak of public opinion, it will be impossible to chain the U-boats" permanently, Bethmann reflected. Wavering between "undeclared commercial war" that would spare American ships and British liners, and "a proclamation in which everything is spelled out," the chancellor groped for some way to conciliate the military and the chauvinist public without drawing America into the conflict. After much agonizing, Bethmann rejected the naval point of view in another memorandum. Because of the effectiveness of new defense weapons, the increase in shipping, and German keels in neutral ports, the claimed four million decrease in British tonnage would not be even half reached ("The entire calculation of British shipping losses rests on shaky ground"). Hence the expected sinkings "will certainly hurt England, but not until fall will they render the continuation of the war impossible and thereby force her to make peace." In contrast to the attitude of the submarine claque, Bethmann did not underestimate the significance of American entry into the war, predicting that the enemy would gain "immense moral support," that Britain would no longer have to respect any limits in its blockade, that the confidence of the German allies would wane, and that the perseverance of the Left at home would be seriously undermined. "Although American armed help will have to be considered of little military value," the prospect of unlimited financial aid, further war material, and hundreds of thousands of sporty volunteers was frightening. Rumania and other neutrals like Holland and Denmark would probably enter the enemy coalition. "The question of whether we will be able to continue the war under these worsening circumstances to a victorious end must be negated after reasonable consideration." Bethmann did not mince words in denouncing this "game of *va banque* whose stakes will be our existence as a Great Power and our entire national future, while our chances of winning . . . are quite uncertain." Separate peace would then become illusory. Only cruiser warfare on all seas, mine-laying on the enemy coast, unrestricted attacks on armed enemy shipping, as well as on unarmed hostile freighters in the war zone, could take place without causing a break. To achieve victory, submarine warfare had to be limited. But Bethmann failed to answer the question: "How will the emperor decide? Should the chancellor then resign or not?" [26]

Contrary to his reputation for weakness, Bethmann did stand up to the military in the decisive confrontation in early March. Although "the chancellor is being attacked from all sides" by Conservatives, National Liberals, Center Party, and other bourgeois parliamentarians, by Pan-Germans, industrial organizations, and the majority of the professional intelligentsia, he refused to buckle under. But he was not alone in resisting this "orgy of ruthless force, sweeping the people." The Foreign Office, supported by Bernstorff and Richard von Kühlmann, predicted disaster; the Bundesrat saw grave dangers; the Austrian ambassador refused to conspire against the chancellor; and the Reichstag Left together with the Liberal Imperialists opposed the risk.[27]

Since, "in the bottom of his heart, H.M. does not want unrestricted submarine warfare and expects as well as abhors a break with America," the chancellor boldly called for a crown council. On the eve of the crucial decision Bethmann was "very nervous, smoked countless cigarettes, moved from chair to chair, but was also firmly resolved to avoid a rupture with America and equally determined to leave his office if the decision were negative." In Charleville, to his pleasant suprise, "the emperor said . . . that he completely endorsed [his] memorandum and did not think of risking war with America—the chancellor should not be afraid, he would tell the others that." On March 4 Bethmann, Falkenhayn, Holtzendorff, and the three cabinet chiefs struggled fiercely for William's consent: "The chancellor made a big speech with utmost energy, portraying the danger to the throne and dynasty, etc." Typically, he "used Frederick the Greak and the Seven Years War" to show "that despite the desperate plight, despite the impossibility of defeating even one enemy, he finally reached a peace which created Prussia's position as Great Power." Over Falkenhayn's and Holtzendorff's objections, "the emperor resolved on a temporary postponement to the first of April to try to get around American [objections]—but there is no doubt that he will decide in the same manner in April, i.e. against unrestricted submarine warfare, as long as the chancellor does not endorse the risk freely." Although no formal resumé was drawn up to spare Falkenhayn, "whom William fears," and "the cute old walrus" Holtzendorff, the result was a vindication for Bethmann. "On the following day, Sunday, [the kaiser] came to the chancellor after church to thank him for his firmness, which had made a difficult situation so much easier for him." Riezler was astounded that against heaviest odds "the chancellor has succeeded in pushing the matter through in greatest harmony with William II without making it a cabinet question. That is very important." [28]

The chancellor's victory remained incomplete as long as the tumor of navalism which poisoned the body politic had not been removed. Political instinct, the prodding of his advisors (Wahnschaffe, Jagow, and Hammann), as well as the uniqueness of the opportunity, encouraged Bethmann to force the issue of Admiral Tirpitz's dismissal. "The stupid agitation of the press, the brouhaha whipped up by the Imperial Navy Office, and the near unanimous unleashing of wild demands" for unrestricted submarine warfare "enraged the emperor," who loathed having his hand forced by an irresponsible public. "In a sharply worded cabinet order, Tirpitz is commanded to turn over to Holtzendorff the appropriate section of the RMA (Reichsmarineamt)" responsible for propaganda. The admiral's deft playing with press, parliamentary, and organizational pressures finally backfired, but he escaped for a last time when he proved that censorship in naval matters was already under the formal control of the admiralty staff. However, because of rumors of a chancellor crisis, inspired by his rival, Bethmann grew "more and more determined to eliminate Tirpitz, who creates difficulties for him at every turn." Fortunately, "Tirpitz had someone make an absolutely misleading declaration in the Bundesrat about the existing number of submarines, counting all boats under construction and those not ready for years to come." Since Captain Löhlein failed to indicate the date of completion, the size of probable losses, etc., the figure of 203 submarines gave the erroneous impression that Germany could strangle England at will. "Now we all wait to see whether Tirpitz will submit his resignation on receipt of the sharply worded cabinet order or whether his reply will create a pretext for his dismissal." Jubilantly, Riezler noted on March 10: "Waiting was worth it. Tirpitz has answered . . . that he is ill and has turned over his office to Admiral Wilhelm Büchsel. He will be told that this is *regrettable* but that his resignation is expected."

Finally the personal dualism between aggressive navalism and liberal economic imperialism had been resolved. The new man, Admiral Capelle, lacked Tirpitz's imagination and power. "It is Bethmann's gravest mistake that he did not fight this through years ago. Now the last of those responsible for Germany's prestige policy in the first decade of the twentieth century is gone." Not even a belated offer of resignation by Chief of Staff Falkenhayn could turn the tide. When imperial resentment against the navy's attempt "to prejudice the decisions of the highest Kommandogewalt and the supreme political leadership by making them clash with popular feeling" offered Bethmann a chance to eliminate the *Nebenregierung* which had ruined his prewar foreign policy, the chancellor struck ruthlessly and successfully.[29]

The dismissal of the symbol of German navalism created an "incredible atmosphere in Berlin. The public is white-hot because of Tirpitz and their betrayed hope in the U-boats." To calm the outcry Bethmann explained to the press that "cool and sober calculation" of the chances of submarine warfare dictated caution and that the propaganda campaign "has done immense harm to the fatherland. I hope that, aware of your grave responsibility, you will be ready to direct public opinion into saner channels." To the party leaders he similarly stressed that he, too, believed "we have a *sharp* weapon" but that a "blockade of England cannot succeed with the present number or with the expected increase until fall." The Left and the Center agreed with Bethmann ("I cannot let decisions be forced upon me for which I cannot bear the responsibility"). But the Right, notably the Conservatives Wangenheim and Hugenberg, the National Liberals Fuhrmann and Bassermann, and the war aims movement led by Dietrich Schäfer, started a petition drive with the slogan "Rather war with America than starvation" and called "the resignation of Tirpitz as serious as Bismarck's fall." To solidify his support Bethmann defended himself before the Prussian Ministry of State by repeating William II's vow, "I won't be so stupid as to get America on my back by this attempt!" In the same vein he emphasized to the Bundesrat, "As long as it cannot be proven that England must capitulate . . . it is a *va banque* gamble for which I will not be responsible." [30]

Only after a severe struggle did Bethmann manage to deflect Conservative and National Liberal Reichstag resolutions in favor of unrestricted submarine warfare into the secrecy of the Budget Committee by using the Socialist threat of counter-resolutions for peace. Provoked by Bassermann's critique, a "tense, tired, and nervous" chancellor whose hair had turned white and whose face was lined with deep furrows, retorted: "In this most cruel war of history any means of shortening it is the most humane. We will act accordingly. . . . But I do not believe that England can be crushed through it." Although Scheidemann, Payer, and Erzberger criticized the U-boat psychosis, the chancellor was nevertheless forced to promise that attacks "will resume as soon as I am persuaded that they will not lead to a rupture with the U.S.," thus obtaining the Right's consent to a Center Party compromise resolution: "Since the submarine has proven an effective weapon . . . the Reichstag expresses its conviction that all our military means must be employed . . . and the necessary freedom for the use of this weapon, while respecting the justified interests of the neutrals, must be obtained . . . in future negotiations with foreign states." Bethmann weathered the severe parliamentary challenge only with great effort, and the depth of discontent, focusing on the submarine as a symbol for peace and victory, limited his options in the future.[31]

Officially, "the submarine question is dead—but it continues surreptitiously," since relations with America "can take a turn for the worse at any moment [and] Falkenhayn continues to probe." By allowing the sinking of armed enemy freighters, Bethmann had preserved the semblance of unity in the Reichstag. ("We recognize the justified neutral interests in world traffic. But we expect . . . the recognition of our right, yes, duty, to use all means of retaliation against enemy starvation measures contrary not only to international law but to simple humanity.") Unfortunately, the chancellor's principle of compromise was shipwrecked by the practical impossibility of a middle course. When it became clear that a German submarine had sunk the French liner *Sussex,* President Wilson sent a "very unfriendly note," fatally resembling an ultimatum, to Berlin: "Unless the Imperial Government should now immediately declare and effect the abandonment of its present methods of submarine warfare . . . the U.S. can have no choice but to sever diplomatic relations . . . altogether." Despite this undisguised threat, Bethmann feared he "could not back down in front of America," since he despaired of convincing the German public of the necessity of complete surrender. The alternatives were clear. Either Germany "must strive to calm American apprehension about new incidents and turn it against British breaches of international law by leaving the U-boats at home," or it had to make "war on the U.S. and sink at least three times as many ships as are torpedoed at present." For three days Bethmann wavered. But after Ambassador Gerard implored him to compromise, he reassured Burian "that I am doing my utmost to avoid a rupture with America." On April 27 he informed Holtzendorff and Falkenhayn that the "tenor of the American note and the reports of Count Bernstorff left no doubt that only through a concession in the conduct of submarine warfare could a break with Washington be avoided." As Riezler noted, "In the final analysis the German Empire must not perish because of the interests of the U-boats commanders," even if cruiser warfare was growing increasingly dangerous.[32]

The sinking of the *Sussex* forced Bethmann to demand a complete return to legal warfare in order "to make a clean slate with America." In the last days of April and early March the events of the previous crisis were replayed mechanically, but with one important difference: "The chief of staff, completely intransigent, demands unrestricted submarine warfare, maintaining he cannot win any longer and a war of exhaustion will be certain otherwise." Perhaps seeking to shift the blame for the failure of his "bleeding white" strategy, Falkenhayn convinced the emperor: "You now face the alternative—either Verdun or submarine warfare." The chancellor speculated: "The generals are basically still imbued with the spirit of the battle of the Marne; they believe a war can only be ended militarily. Since they see no means for achieving that, they say either U-boats or defeat." Enraged by this new ultimatum issued by the chief of staff, the retired Tirpitz, and the chief of the high seas fleet, Bethmann countered: "That is not our situation—if we succeed in keeping America out forever, nobody can wrest victory from us." Falkenhayn's attempt "either to get rid of the responsibility for Verdun or to overthrow the chancellor and gamble on unrestricted submarine warfare," thereby becoming Germany's savior, came dangerously close to succeeding, because Bethmann, weary from his incessant struggles with the military and chauvinist elites, was on the verge of resigning. To Valentini, he seemed like "a broken man, incapable of dealing with the immensely difficult situation." But at the height of the crisis, Admiral Holtzendorff surprisingly saved the day by adapting the navy's wishes to Bethmann's political views: "Submarine warfare against England can only remain successful as long as America stays out—and besides, a pause is desirable for technical reasons." On May 1, "refusing a common audience, the emperor accepted [Bethmann's] draft reply, which had been improved and unified after much reworking." Angered about being bypassed in the final decision, Falkenhayn submitted his resignation the next morning—a tactical blunder since the kaiser had already signed the order. His request was denied; the chief of staff "gave in and had a tolerable conversation with the chancellor." Although not the strong man in the public mind, Bethmann, "never a personal or political opportunist, ultimately makes the right decisions and implements them with cunning. . . . A strange man. Since the war has become so oppressively slow, and the most daring show moments of weakness, he, grim in good times, has grown beyond other men." [33]

The *Sussex* pledge to conduct U-boat attacks according to the laws of cruiser warfare was Bethmann's most important submarine victory. But it rested upon shaky foundations. "With public opinion everything went very well. Most of those who yesterday clamored loudest for unlimited use have now grown afraid." With surprising unanimity, the press accepted Zimmermann's explanations at face value. The Bundesrat approved the chancellor's reasoning that Wilson could not break with Germany unless he really desired war, because the concession was so large. Most astonishingly of all, in the Reichstag "commission even Bassermann reversed himself," and except for the "stubborn Conservatives" all parties endorsed the chancellor's caution. But as Bethmann warned Gerard, German renunciation of the submarine weapon depended upon American enforcement of the Declaration of London vis-à-vis Great Britain. When the ambassador excused himself with the typical metaphor, "if someone murdered my sister I would probably pursue him first in preference to a small boy who had stepped on my flower beds," the chancellor emphasized that "a serious situation would arise for President Wilson too, if America did nothing against England." When Lansing refused to acknowledge any connection between German concessions and American actions, the *Kölnische Zeitung* warned that "in this event we would be confronted by a new situation and would regain freedom of decision."

Because submarine agitation in Germany continued unabated, Bethmann knew that only a positive alternative, such as an armistice, could permanently ban the danger of further escalation. "The desire for peace is great and our economic difficulties will assume catastrophic proportions if the harvest fails. If we are convinced that submarine warfare cannot defeat England then we must seize every opportunity for a settlement." Hence the chancellor intensified feelers and welcomed American mediation. But continuing navy pressure and the disputed victory of Jutland necessitated "another submarine decision. Time flies. It is still impossible because of the developments in France, the unstable military situation, and Wilson's extrication from Mexico." When the issue of interdicting cross-channel supplies arose in August, the chancellor again succeeded in postponing a decision by pointing to the unsettled fate of German arms. To the party leaders and the Bundesrat he pleaded that further U-boat agitation, opposed by the OHL, could only weaken morale. To his intimates, Bethmann often sighed: "The submarines will pursue me to the grave. It will always remain the great riddle: what would have happened if they had been unleashed ruthlessly? But since one cannot make the experiment, nothing will help." [34]

When the kaiser finally "began to doubt Falkenhayn's character" because of the futility of Verdun, Bethmann set out once more to remove the chief of staff in June 1916. The Austrian disaster in

Galicia posed the question, "Would not a unified local command in the East have been able to recognize and prevent this development which seems to have surprised everyone?" He complained to Valentini: "The whole world knows that we have the right men in Hindenburg and Ludendorff. Nobody understands why we only use their military abilities in such a limited way. . . . The situation is too serious and is becoming even more so by the month. Hindenburg must receive supreme command over the entire German forces in the East." Unwilling to risk the same frontal assault on the Kommandogewalt which had misfired in January 1915, Bethmann first sought to persuade the emperor's military entourage, Plessen and Lyncker. "The name Hindenburg is a horror to our enemies, electrifies our army and people who have boundless trust in him. Even if we should lose a battle . . . led by Hindenburg our nation would accept it as well as any peace, covered by his name"—thus Bethmann paid eloquent tribute to the Hindenburg myth. But "all attempts to overthrow Falkenhayn have failed," Riezler noted dejectedly at the end of June. "To be sure he wobbles, but H.M. does not want the whole eastern front to be turned over to Hindenburg. If the chancellor demanded it from the emperor all would be spoiled and Falkenhayn strengthened." When Lyncker attempted to broach the command question, William II, in clairvoyant rage, replied, "This means abdication and my replacement by Hindenburg as tribune of the people!" But he did agree to propose the change to Vienna. Since the insulted Conrad von Hoetzendorff adamantly refused the change, the kaiser, "half mad" with responsibility and "beside himself, decided *against* conferring the command on Hindenburg." As a scapegoat, the chancellor's representative at GHQ, Karl von Treutler, one of the strongest voices against unrestricted submarine warfare, was banished from the imperial entourage. "The beautiful plan is shipwrecked and Falkhenhayn has won." [35]

"Dejected and desperate" about the failure of his effort to unseat the chief of staff, Bethmann queried: "Can one continue to keep on working, seeing how the country steers toward disaster, not because of objective necessity but out of personality clashes? Does this not make me guilty?" Valentini's reassurance that national interest demanded his staying on gave him the necessary strength to implore GHQ by a steady stream of telegrams that "a new Austrian defeat . . . will have critical domestic repercussions unless the Hindenburg factor is soon used fully." None too choosy in his means of overthrowing Falkenhayn, Bethmann received unexpected assistance from the collapse of the German offensive at Verdun, the Allied attacks at the Somme, and Hungarian opposition leader Count Andrassy's warning that only Hindenburg's appointment could stave off the collapse of the Hapsburg monarchy. Since "I see that we run the danger of steering into disaster, my responsibility forces me to act, and widest circles—even high officers—hourly expect me to move." Bethmann swallowed his fear "that I will probably spoil everything by intervening myself" and seized upon the Hungarian cry for help as occasion to confront William II directly. "The kaiser is slowly becoming more favorable, but Falkenhayn always finds new twists for foiling everything. Hindenburg and Ludendorff are too clumsy and give the opposition one pretext after another." On July 26 in Pless, Bethmann cornered the emperor and demanded that "he make Hindenburg supreme commander of the entire eastern front, emphasizing . . . that the Hohenzollern dynasty was at stake. He could conclude a disappointing peace with Hindenburg, but never without him." When Falkenhayn returned with yet another Austrian refusal, "excited resentment spread against him" in GHQ. "The chancellor is furious and speaks very seriously with H.M., leaving nothing unsaid." Since Falkenhayn, "affronted, and sporting a toothache," refused to participate, the kaiser himself had to press the "appointment of Hindenburg as a demand of popular psychology" on the reluctant Archduke Charles. Only after hours of exasperating negotiations could Valentini note joyfully: "Everything is arranged: The Austrians accept Hindenburg's supreme command, including [General] Linsingen, and even offer the Böhm-Ermolli corps." With the help of the cabinet chiefs, Bethmann's massive pressure had resulted in a half-victory. But William II, instinctively recoiling from the ruthless Ludendorff, sighed: "I am spared nothing! Now I am asked to do the impossible!" [36]

The compromise of extending *Oberost*'s sphere of command from Riga to Tarnopol collapsed when Austrian demands for new reserves clashed with the chief of staff's attempt to turn disaster into victory at Verdun. On August 21 Bethmann rushed to Charleville to "settle differences between Falkenhayn and Hindenburg in favor of the latter, and perhaps remove the chief of staff. But his position is quite firm although the whole general staff has admitted that he deployed [troops] falsely—he is only kept in power by Marschall and the weak [Colonel] Tappen." To Prussian Minister of War Wild the chancellor "enumerated with surprising assurance all of Falkenhayn's strategic 'mistakes' and maintained that he had repeatedly received the distinct impression from high military circles . . . that he did not possess the confidence of the army." But Wild protested, and as long as the Emperor's military advisors were unwilling to force the issue a disgusted chancellor had "to return without accomplishing his main goal." Nevertheless, Falkenhayn's days were numbered, since Rumania's intervention "finally ripened the fruit of our long efforts—everybody says thank God," as Riezler noted in relief. When Bethmann telegraphed the news of the Rumanian and Italian declarations of war to GHQ, "H.M. was severely depressed and full of dangerous thoughts. General excitement." The chancellor's telephone call on August 28 was hardly necessary to prod "Lyncker and Plessen [into] suggesting Falkenhayn's resignation to H.M." Wild found William II "deeply shaken, but nevertheless resolved to put Hindenburg in Falkenhayn's place." According to Bethmann's explanation to Müller, the chief of staff resigned because he did not want to share power with Hindenburg: "The kaiser has only one counselor and that is the chief of staff. If the emperor insisted on having Hindenburg come, he [Falkenhayn] had to go!" Thereupon came the reply: "Please do so!" Bethmann's long struggle with Falkenhayn had ended successfully. "The nation is relieved by Hindenburg's appointment, the chancellor's hand in it, and his good relations with the field marshal." Bethmann also was overjoyed. "The change was a battle. But I feel firmly confident, despite the great seriousness of the general situation." [37]

Beyond the inevitable conflict of offices, mentalities, and personalities there were grave political reasons for the chancellor's insistence on Falkenhayn's fall. "It is impossible to maintain morale if the chief of staff is pessimistic and, as a gambler, always says we have no chance but to risk this or that, while the political leader is honest enough not to exaggerate the positive aspects of the situation." Aside from the chief of staff's reputed aspirations to the chancellorship, his tactical blunders forced Bethmann to act. "From the beginning of the war all our strategic decisions were based upon false factual assumptions, and we have not yet learned from our mistakes." Instead of planning for a war of attrition and seeking a decision in the East where mobile warfare still seemed possible, Falkenhayn had gambled on ever new breakthroughs in the West, most notably in Verdun. Bethmann's anguish at such senseless slaughter was summed up in his question, "Where does incompetence end and crime begin?" Undeniably Falkenhayn had lost the confidence of the army, the press, and the parliamentarians, except for the chancellor fronde. Moreover, Bethmann intended "to rob the navy of its strongest pillar of support in the submarine question" and generally to reassert control over the political purpose of the war. On the other hand, the case for Germany's most popular soldier, Hindenburg, was exceedingly persuasive. Determined not to yield to the most exorbitant war aims demands, intent on stifling the cries for the miracle weapon, and "needing support against the agitation" of the fronde, the chancellor sought to strengthen his own power by appointing the victor of Tannenberg. So far, cooperation between Oberost and the Wilhelmstrasse had been exemplary, since both were united in opposition to GHQ. The solidity and probity of the gray Hindenburg seemed to provide reassurance against the Caesarean ambitions of his unstable chief of staff, Ludendorff. But by relying on the "military genius of Hindenburg" Bethmann made the costliest error in judgment of his entire political career. Like Goethe's sorcerer's apprentice: "Die ich rief, die Geister,/Werd' ich nun nicht los." [38]

Bethmann's "great delight about Hindenburg's character" soon evaporated when it became clear that the third OHL "only supports the chancellor as long as the latter pursues a strong policy and a victorious peace." Ludendorff's "lack of political gifts, complete primitivism, and old-Prussian directness" reduced politics to a simple contest of wills. Shaken by the fall of his chief of staff, "the kaiser has completely fled into the shadow of the two soldiers—without volition of his own he swims in their wake." This psychological abdication spelled danger for Bethmann, since "Ludendorff, possessing the energy of a genius and perhaps great strategical gifts, if he had free reign would shortly push Germany into the abyss." Outwardly the more impressive of the pair, "Hindenburg signs everything. The chancellor and Wahnschaffe were . . . in Pless in order to remedy the situation—both are supposed to have been quite outspoken, and the generals have promised to improve." But Riezler noted skeptically: "Will it help? Ludendorff is too uneducated and, like all soldiers, lacks any respect for the complexity of politics." In total contrast to the Nietzschean quartermaster general, Bethmann did not convey "the impression that a definite will to act dominates him, but rather the sober weighing of advantages and disadvantages." Buoyed by his immense popularity and egged on by emissaries of the Right, Ludendorff gradually began to reject the chancellor's influence over basic strategic decisions and to intervene in politics; the clash of personalities and styles became one of substance as well. In early December 1916 Bethmann admitted that a moderate "policy is impossible with the military," since the OHL "is incapable of doing anything in agreement with the people, always wants to dot the *i*'s, and insecurely brags of its power, supposedly to maintain authority." Although Bethmann strove to coexist with the mercurial Dioscuri for the sake of the country, clashes over the tightening of the Austrian alliance, the resignation of Foreign Secretary Jagow, the need for the restoration of Poland, and the repressiveness of the Auxiliary Service Law grew more intense with each repetition. "Either out of conviction or disloyalty [Ludendorff] disagrees with the kaiser and his entire manner of proceeding in the Civilian Service question; his excited telegrams flogging Helfferich like a lame carriage-horse are incredible, and quite unbearable." Instead of reaffirming the chancellor's control, the appointment of the third OHL represented a decisive step toward total war and the militarization of German life.[39]

The crucial issue of the civil-military struggle was the resumption of unrestricted submarine warfare, the key to Germany's military fate. "After Rumania's entry, the U-boat question trembled once more on the razor's edge as the sole but weak possibility of a decisive success," Riezler commented. Because of popular belief in this miracle weapon, "an inner logic lies in this cruel tragedy that it, too, must be tried some day." Nevertheless, before the Bundesrat and party leaders Bethmann reiterated that the political consequences would be "worse today than last fall." For the moment the appointment of the Dioscuri offered a respite. "The opposition desires a rapprochement, since it understands that it cannot attack head on in the submarine question as long as the chancellor acts in unison with Hindenburg; moreover, it knows that U-boat warfare will be waged if the OHL admits its military feasibility." Hence Bethmann countered the navy's argument that "only ruthless submarine warfare leads to peace" with the claim that "the OHL's estimate of our military situation must be decisive," since he was confident that Ludendorff would counsel postponement because of the crisis in the Balkans. In spite of the new OHL, the old pattern soon revived, since naval authorities, industrial leaders, and right-wing parliamentarians clamored for action, and as long as Wilson failed to mediate, Bethmann had no counterargument. "The chancellor is appalled that Hindenburg ordered the chief of the admiralty staff (von Throta) to report and was persuaded by him in favor of unrestricted submarine warfare," Müller noted ominously. But due to the strains of the Rumanian campaign, moderation prevailed once more. "The [OHL] sympathizes with [unlimited U-boat attacks] in principle but considers the military situation too unclear to run the risk of a break with America and its consequences *at present."* When in early October the navy attempted to sway William II directly, Bethmann irately demanded a general conference, knowing that the kaiser preferred to sound out America first about peace, even if his own memorandum for Gerard was a diplomatic impossibility. But the chancellor was now on the defensive when he claimed, against Ludendorff's encroachments, that the submarine question affected foreign policy, "for which I have to bear the sole and nontransferable constitutional responsibility." [40]

By October 1916, Bethmann's opposing voice was beginning to ring less convincingly because his position in parliament and public was rapidly deteriorating. The chancellor's bold refusal to gamble on the U-boats was grist for the mill of the Pan-Germans, Conservatives, National Liberals, East Elbian agrarians, heavy industrialists, and chauvinist intellectuals, who comprised an ever-multiplying fronde. Unwittingly, he himself gave the starting signal in the Reichstag: "A German statesman, gentlemen, who shies away from any weapon, useful against the enemy and capable of shortening the war, *such a statesman deserves to be hanged!"* In a stormy session of the Budget Committee, the Conservatives and most National Liberals attempted to force a plenum debate on the submarine issue, to discredit Bethmann and capitalize on popular frustration with the unending suffering and deceived hopes for victory. The chancellor's plea that "my position toward submarine warfare is not a matter of principle; when the means suffice for a quick victory it will be waged, otherwise not," met with little sympathy. Only his declaration that Hindenburg "considers it a grave mistake to make submarine warfare a matter of partisan politics," and his warning that general discussion would "harm Germany's foreign policy," convinced the majority to avoid "the impossible situation" of discrediting Bethmann completely in the eyes of America and his own people. Center Party leader Erzberger suggested a compromise resolution stressing the chancellor's responsibility but adding that the OHL's views "have to be nearly decisive. . . . If Hindenburg resolves upon ruthless submarine warfare . . . no chancellor can take a different position." This Center Party defection to the ranks of the U-boat enthusiasts drastically undercut Bethmann's parliamentary position. It was of little consequence that his promise—"we shall wage submarine war when we can—or when we have to"—and Hindenburg's declaration against further agitation left a mass meeting of Schäfer's annexationist committee without ammunition to launch a nationwide U-boat campaign.[41]

The only escape from the increasing pressures for escalation was a peace move either by Germany itself or by the leading neutral power, the United States. Unsure of the timing of Wilson's mediation, which he had earlier helped to invite, and unable to wait until the American president had weathered his reelection campaign, Bethmann in the late fall resolved on independent action. As a precondition, the chancellor begged the navy to cease underwater attacks, which had resumed in mid-October, emphasizing that "under all circumstances a conflict with America must be avoided until the peace démarche, planned either by ourselves or Wilson, has taken place." It took great pressure to extract a restrictive order from Holtzendorff, and OHL sabotage of the German peace offer was only overcome by Zimmermann's dangerous argument that "intensified submarine war toward America would certainly be facilitated if we could refer to such a peace action." The derisory response of the Entente to Bethmann's desperation move left the chancellor with few arguments to fight the military, because German distrust of the motives of Wilson's mediation would not let the Foreign Office explore the American initiative fully as a channel to peace. Welcoming Washington's effort to bring the belligerents to the conference table, Bethmann, fearful that Wilson would attempt to influence the actual terms of the settlement in favor of the Entente, hesitated to inform Bernstorff of the German conditions for peace. But in his impatience with the time-consuming exchange of notes, Admiral Holtzendorff announced ominously that he would seek the emperor's decision even if he had to circumvent the chancellor: "Since I do not believe in a quick effect of the beautiful peace gesture, I am totally committed to the use of our crucial weapon—unrestricted submarine warfare." This naval challenge signaled the beginning of a race between peace and the expansion of war. The die was cast when the allies scornfully refused the Central Powers' offer and Bethmann could not follow his impulse and pursue the American lead. He had been strong enough to force a peace move, but against the overwhelming majority of his country's elites he was incapable of compelling a settlement that might not even return the status quo. "Under these circumstances the demands for submarine warfare as the only effective way to peace could no longer be countered with real prospects for negotiations." [42]

Co-responsible for the chancellor's failure to obtain peace, the generals immediately called for the intensification of submarine warfare. "Ludendorff has had another seizure and is sending wild telegrams because he has been left without supervision for ten days." Riezler complained that military cooperation with the civil authorities was "getting worse all the time." Prodded by the admiralty, his own staff, and politicians on the Right, Ludendorff, helpless "before the incredible complexity of these questions, says America does not count," or more graphically, *"Ich pfeife auf Amerika."* His blunt demand that "now submarine warfare must begin with all sharpness" did not answer the larger question, "Will we be able to obtain better conditions from an England subdued by submarines if we have to sue a fighting America for peace at the same time?" Unable to resist the most popular figure in Germany because of the pro-submarine Reichstag majority, Bethmann reluctantly suggested "that first the question of torpedoing armed enemy freighters must be cleared up with America," and asked for time until the Entente had responded to the German peace move. "When our military situation allows us to be certain that we can keep the neutrals from intervening . . . and when you can convince me that the advantages of completely ruthless submarine warfare are greater than the disadvantages of America's addition to our enemies, I shall be ready to consider the question of unlimited U-boat attacks." Despite this hint, Ludendorff, in a fit of rage, refused to include the anti-U-boat Helfferich in a preliminary conference. Gravely affronted by this snub, the chancellor complained to Valentini: "I have never attempted to circumvent the OHL in the submarine question. But in the present circumstances, it could not order unrestricted submarine warfare unilaterally." Involving the withdrawal of assurances to America, "it is a political act for which I bear the exclusive constitutional responsibility." Despite his burning resentment, Bethmann felt compelled to compromise and approve that "the resumption of torpedoing armed merchantmen will be communicated to America." With youthful enthusiasm, Riezler believed "it is good that we have done so before the Entente answer to Wilson—because it would be too late, should it be mild. And once the armed [ships] are included we can sharpen [the campaign] further under water." [43]

"The unanswerable question of fate, Peace or submarines?" rested heavily on Bethmann's stooped shoulders, since another "half or full year of war might bring down our enemies but will certainly exhaust us as well." Riezler noted in surprise, "Now a secret emissary from the navy staff . . . reveals to the chancellor the game of cat-and-mouse being played by the admiralty, saying that it is impossible to discriminate between armed and unarmed vessels from a submerged submarine, that therefore errors are unavoidable, i.e. soon even unarmed (N.B. of course also neutral) ships will be hit." As in February 1915, Bethmann was duped by the navy, which had intended an unrestricted campaign all along without informing the chancellor and giving him a chance to devise a counterstrategy. On January 6, Bethmann was confronted with Holtzendorff's massive memorandum arguing that the bad Entente harvest, the increased number of submarines (over two hundred), and the anticipated British shipping losses of near 40 percent pointed to the inescapable conclusion that "under present conditions we can force England to make peace within five months," provided that "all ships are free to be sunk." Wrestling with his conscience for an answer, the chancellor left no clue to his thoughts in this decisive week. But his intimates pondered: "If one could trust the navy, ruthless U-boat warfare would be splendid, under present circumstances. The public asks: "Will it come? If not, will there be a crisis?" It is difficult to refuse it completely. But in the last analysis one could stand all this clamor if the kaiser's nerves would hold." The military consequences were impossible to predict. "It is quite revolting that cruiser warfare is now doing so well [sinking ca. 400,000 tons per month] and has always been rejected and ridiculed as an unmilitary imposition." As on the land, war on the sea was becoming an end in itself. Wilson's previous notes had left no doubt that the consequence of escalation would be American participation. But having compromised in late December, Bethmann had no options left, no points to concede. This time it would be all or nothing. [44]

"The decision has been made; it was already made when the chancellor arrived" in Pless on a dreary January 9, 1917, for the crucial crown council. On the previous evening the kaiser, "with unexpected suddenness, convinced himself that unrestricted submarine warfare was imperative and declared himself decisively in its favor, even should the chancellor refuse." By telephone a converted Müller fought to calm the "excited and depressed" Bethmann, who sensed what was coming. The next morning the chief of the naval cabinet met the chancellor at the train to emphasize that "for the past two years he had always taken a moderate position and now under the changed circumstances considered ruthless submarine warfare necessary and promising." Ill with "a cold and pessimistic about the very difficult situation," Bethmann denounced unlimited U-boat attacks as "the last card," but conceded, "When the military authorities consider submarine warfare essential, I am not in a position to object." Whether he had resigned himself to the inevitable before leaving Berlin, or whether the blustering self-confidence of the generals and the defection of William II and moderates like Müller determined his resolve, will never be known. Confronted by "the emperor, Hindenburg, and Ludendorff strongly supporting the step and arguing that otherwise only defense is possible, i.e. deterioration is to be expected in 1917," Bethmann no longer held out. In the decisive conference with William II in the late afternoon, the chancellor did not use Helfferich's last-minute countermemorandum, nor did he invoke the continuing peace negotiations with Wilson, because he realized that if he forced the kaiser to choose between himself and Hindenburg, William "would decide against the chancellor." Touching rather upon the expected response of the neutrals, he stressed that although war with America would be certain the others might not follow suit, and concluded: "Given the chiefs of general and admiral staffs' analysis of the situation, he (the chancellor) could not oppose unrestricted submarine warfare. That means not endorsement but acquiescence in a fait accompli." With the psychotic haste of a man incapable of decision, William II signed the order, snorting, "By God, this man still has scruples." Privately, Bethmann deplored the kaiser's "great damage to the dynasty" through his "vanity and chauvinism," sighing, "Yes, I had to give in to military considerations." The end would come only after further losses, and peace would be very modest. His friend Valentini sagaciously predicted that the chancellor's surrender meant *"finis Germaniae."* [45]

"The chancellor said yes. His personal position is favorable since he has always said no only temporarily and he himself pointed out the growing reasons in its favor." Riezler recorded the fatal step: "But he has not agreed with a light heart. Despite all promises of the navy it remains a leap into the dark." Nevertheless, it was a relief that the two-and-a-half-year struggle had ended. "In the future, the German people will be free of the horrible question: What would have happened with ruthless submarine warfare?" Bethmann had been caught in a horrible dilemma ("One cannot believe the navy and one cannot refuse to believe them"). His assistant reasoned: "He had to go along even if he did not want to do it. After the kaiser and Hindenburg were committed it was inevitable, and the situation in 1917 was different from 1916. . . . He could have resigned but then neither at home nor abroad would anyone have believed in success, his dismissal would have encouraged Social Democrats and neutrals to resist, and everything would have been ruined." But by acquiescing and remaining in office, Bethmann became guilty of complicity. "Now nobody must get out, the chancellor must lead in putting up a good front, since he alone can carry along the masses, who believe that he does not undertake it lightheartedly and without justified hope." Although not preventing "a nervous breakdown" Bethmann's concept of duty, the central ethos of the Prussian bureaucracy, forced him to cover the decision with his name and stay on. "If I resign now, the emperor will say, 'The chancellor is deserting me in this critical hour.' Then I have to remain and the situation is worse than before," he tried to persuade himself. "For a long time I, too, considered a middle course possible," he explained to Weizsäcker. "The navy expects only unrestricted submarine warfare to produce a decisive success. Therefore I ultimately consider it preferable, despite all its great danger." The iron logic of total war had won. [46]

"Nobody thanks the chancellor for the decision. If it succeeds, Tirpitz will be acclaimed as the savior; if it fails, the same man who was accused of sparing the enemy will be damned because he has lent his name to it," Riezler predicted perceptively. "I, too, was beset by feelings similar to those of July 1914. Perhaps even more intense," Bethmann rationalized his surrender to the Prussian

Ministry of State and Bundesrat. "I could not take the responsibility for this No!" Despite his claim that "the prospects of success were never so bright as now," his colleagues in the ministry and state governments went along only reluctantly. "The National Liberal and Conservative agitators are in seventh heaven. When I informed Bassermann confidentially, his heart visibly dropped from his decorated hero's chest into his quaking pants because of the American danger," Bethmann described the parliamentary reaction. "Payer and his friends will go along. The Socialists are shaken but will comply, emphasizing that it is only possible for them if I do not resign. . . . But we are still not yet in the clear, because Wilson will certainly come with another peace initiative." [47]

With the help of Czernin's complaints about "being placed into a politically intolerable position by the navy" and Wilson's magnanimous "peace without victory" speech, the chancellor, in a last feverish effort, sought to delay the unleasing of the submarines and thereby to postpone the threatening rupture. But "nothing could be changed because the boats are already on their way," and Bethmann, "greatly distressed" by the lost chance for peace and by Bernstorff's warnings, could only insist on the futile gesture of communicating his terms to the American president. The chancellor knew all too well that his request to Wilson to continue working for peace was doomed to fail. His public vow—*"We must, therefore we can!"*—could hardly drown out the lurking fear. "It is a strange irony of fate that this great, strong man, so serious, cautious, and warm-hearted, must conduct and defend the most daredevil policy—that he, intent on the best for Germany, must let himself be used to keep the masses, the only great and admirable thing today, behind Ludendorff's and Tirpitz's policy," his assistant pondered. "May it be otherwise and the submarines successful." [48]

"Now everything depends upon at least introducing [submarine warfare] cleverly," Riezler suggested. "We must give an incentive to the English peace movement, which grows stronger every day, and to the Americans—then God be with us and *vogue les sous-marins!*" Arguing that the failure of American efforts to force British compliance with international law had "created a *new situation,* which forces Germany to make *new decisions,*" the German note left little room for negotiation, since the claim *"the U-boat creates its own law"* convinced only the Central Powers. Afraid of a rupture,

Bethmann told Gerard that "the Allies had refused to make peace when Germany wanted to and that [the] president had Germany's terms and so there was nothing left to do but use all means at hand." On both sides of the Atlantic "it was too late" for compromise. Failing to understand the complexity of German politics and outraged by the apparent duplicity of the chancellor's decision, Wilson persuaded Congress to break relations with Germany and recalled his singularly ineffective ambassador. When this news arrived in Berlin, Bethmann drafted a circular in which he said, "I believe that Wilson sincerely works for peace, albeit in a sense favorable to the Entente." But the monstrous enemy war aims, directed toward "the despoliation of Germany, the shattering of Austria-Hungary, and the destruction of European Turkey," necessitated the use of all weapons regardless of cost.

"I cannot yet predict how America will act in the future," the chancellor reflected in mid-February. "Together with some other straws in the wind, Wilson's continuing desire not to break with Austria speaks for the fact that he does not want war. Should this be true, we will do nothing to provoke a conflict." But despite Swiss suggestions that some token concession might encourage renewed negotiations, the chancellor's hands were tied: "Measures which mean the cessation of submarine warfare seem to me impossible," since German hesitation would push the other neutrals into the hostile camp. "Moreover, I do not want to deny that so far the success of submarine warfare has surpassed my expectations, even if one cannot yet judge conclusively." To reassure himself he argued: "On the whole my confidence is growing steadily, as well as my conviction that we could not have acted differently. This is true not so much because our situation on land, though serious, is tolerable but because in general the war is nearing its end and I believe that in that stage of development the advantages of submarine warfare outweigh its disadvantages. *Quod deus bene vertat!*" [49]

In his desperate attempt to keep the neutrals from joining the enemy camp, Bethmann was more successful with Germany's European neighbors than with the United States. "The submarine war is going better than the enemies expect," Riezler noted confidently. "Daily we count the tonnage sunk. Heavens be thanked that the navy seems to keep its promises. The nightmare of distrust is slowly dissolving." Because of Bernstorff's cables "that the country is

peaceful and Wilson will protract the matter in its present state,"
Zimmermann unrealistically insisted upon the resumption of relations before secret negotiations could begin in order to stabilize nonintervention. To pull along the weary masses and to undercut the
chauvinist fronde, Bethmann feigned confidence in the Reichstag.
Criticizing the American president for allowing "the delivery of
weapons and war material" to the Entente, for "not preventing"
England's hunger blockade, and for applying a double standard to
German violations of international law, the chancellor "deplored
the rupture with a nation destined by its history to stand not against
but with us for common ideals. Since our honest peace offer has
met only with the ridicule of our enemies, we cannot go back any
more, only forward!" With the exception of the radical Left, all
parties and the overwhelming majority of the press welcomed this
exhortation of the will to victory.

Finally Zimmermann's "incredible blunder with Mexico" pushed
America over the brink of armed neutrality into war. "It would
have been better . . . to leave this small help unused and to let
the Americans wage war against a blank wall with all the resistance
in their own country," Riezler noted angrily. "This is the work
of [councilor] Kemnitz, the fantastic idiot, and Zimmermann and
Stumm have approved it; the skeptical Jagow would never have
missed the boat like such a dilettante." Hoping against hope, Bethmann seized upon Bernstorff's optimistic report that "Wilson and
too many Americans do not want to fight." But the admiralty and
William II vetoed the suggestion to "overlook American freighters
for a while and eliminate all pretext: 'Now the time has passed for
negotiating with America! If Wilson wants war he must bring it
about and then shall have it!' " When Wilson's missionary call, "The
world must be made safe for democracy," swept Congress into the
bloody struggle, Bethmann's halfhearted efforts to prevent the consequences of the January decisions were proven vain. He could
only note tersely, "These are critical times." [50]

The American entry turned the war into a race between the
collapse of tsarist Russia and the growing effectiveness of U.S. intervention. "Our chances center solely around submarine warfare,
whose timing and success remain completely uncertain." Although
the immediate military impact was slight, American participation
vitiated the chance for separate peace created by the Russian Revolution. "We should not entertain any definite hopes in this regard. The
U.S. declaration of war and our recent defeat at Arras have an espe-

cially unfavorable effect at the present moment," Bethmann cautioned Hertling. "The navy is quite content with the successes of submarine warfare. But it is still too early to judge its results." Although attempting to maintain a grim cheerfulness, Bethmann began to share his assistant's reservations: "Despite all enthusiasm and propaganda, the effectiveness of the U-boats is apparently not increasing but rather decreasing. Thereby time is running against us once again. America!—If that is so the war cannot be ended, let alone won." In spite of record loss figures, "the neutrals undobutedly continue their voyages undeterred." By mid-April Bethmann admitted to Müller his disappointment in the political result of the submarine war: "Thanks to the Russian Revolution we would probably today be closer to peace without submarine war." But publicly he maintained: "I place my hope upon our finishing the war before American help arrives." When the British succeeded in "getting through a convoy of sixty-nine grain ships," while German weapons, munitions, and nutrition were deteriorating, the chancellor warned the OHL of an impending collapse in morale. "The expectation for the quick and decisive effect of submarine warfare has been recognized as exaggerated. Hereby the widely spread hope for ending the war before fall . . . has vanished." In the face of mounting public criticism, he refused to abandon hope: "Neither I nor the navy have argued that we can force the enemies to capitulate through submarine warfare, only to come to terms. But they must not believe that we are collapsing. They must know that our breath is longer." However, undermined as it was by his own personal doubts, the chancellor's attempt to stem the crisis of confidence in the U-boats failed to convince the Reichstag. Having sacrificed his own better judgment and used his integrity to defend a step about which he had the gravest reservations, Bethmann became the scapegoat for the failure of the ultimate weapon to perform the expected miracle.[51]

Bethmann's surrender on the submarine question did not succeed in placating the power-hungry generals. "The military dictatorship is getting worse and worse," his assistant noted the ascendancy of the OHL. But by attempting to prevent the "ruin of Germany by the complete insanity and most grandiose ignorance" of the generals, Bethmann denied himself the satisfaction of protest and became an accomplice in deceiving the people. Despite the chancellor's *sacrificium intellectus,* Ludendorff continually "demanded Bethmann's dismissal," and only Valentini's stubborn defense that he alone possessed the political prestige to keep the Left and the Allies loyal to the war effort prevented his ouster. The real issues underlying "the unhealable split, aggravated by calumny," involved war aims, separate peace, strategic priorities, domestic reform, and such subordinate points as the fate of Alsace-Lorraine. "The utterly naïve Ludendorff, imbued with dictatorial instincts and believing in the miraculous power of the will, characteristically falls for all suggestions" of the reactionary fronde, which represented an alliance of heavy industrialists, agrarians, Pan-Germans, and chauvinist intellectuals. Intent on preserving the primacy of politics, Bethmann incessantly struggled against the general's "Caesarean ambitions and intention to militarize the entire state." Although he abdicated his supreme control by yielding on the submarine issue, the chancellor nevertheless succeeded in preserving a semblance of domestic independence and some degree of veto power over the conduct of the war. But his concessions to militarism drastically undercut the credibility of his policy with his moderate and progressive supporters in the Reichstag, and also among the workers and some segments of the elites. Hence, when he was on the verge of creating a solid parliamentary majority on the Left independent of the cowed kaiser, and of gaining a platform for reasserting his authority over the soldiers in the peace resolution, Ludendorff knew that the ultimate test had come. Gambling on the Reichstag's loss of faith in the chancellor, the generals "half used parliament, half [let] it act" to fell Bethmann in a preventive coup. When William II, under the threat of the Dioscuri's resignation, chose the myth of victory over the bridle of reason, the military quasi dictatorship, acclaimed by both public and press, became complete.[52]

In the epic struggle between the civilian chancellor, who employed war as a means to a limited end, and the generals, who were fighting for fighting's sake and for boundless aims, the latter had triumphed disastrously. Bethmann's defeats in office, and his fall, signified the victory of the all-consuming demon of total war. In this conflict, which involved political goals as well as military measures, submarine warfare became the central symbol of the primacy of politics or militarism. "After the evident fiasco of U-boat war it is tempting to accuse me of weakness because I did not prevent it," the chancellor wrote, in a painful attempt to assess his own co-responsibility. "But in order to white-wash himself, everyone forgets that submarine warfare was passionately demanded not only by the emperor and Hindenburg-Ludendorff but also by the great majority of the Reichstag—from the Right into the ranks of the Progressives—almost by the entire press, by the military authorities of the old bureaucratic state, and also by those representatives of the people who want to and should determine policy in the new system of the *Volksstaat.*" Resolutely opposed only by the Socialists, the unleashing of the U-boats was therefore Bethmann's most democratic decision. Domestically, "a struggle against the OHL and the Reichstag possessed no chance of success and could never have been waged," since the chancellor would immediately have been dismissed by William II.

In his tireless pursuit of a middle course between complete abandonment of submarine attacks and unrestricted U-boat war, the chancellor found little encouragement from Washington. Despite his sincere commitment to neutrality, President Wilson, ill-informed about the dynamics of German domestic politics, would not do the one thing that Bethmann needed in order to curb the military: take effective measures against English breaches of international law. Hence more so even than on the question of war aims and peace moves, the chancellor was caught between the militarism of the Wilhelmian elites and the uncomprehending self-righteousness of the chief remaining neutral power. Bethmann felt he could not wager on American impartiality, since culturally and economically the U.S. was deeply committed to the cause of the Entente and shared its fear of the establishment of a stronger Germany. The chancellor faced a "depressing sight: Germany stumbling along the edge of the precipice, desiring nothing more passionately than to fling herself into the abyss." When Bethmann finally capitulated, he incurred the grave "historical guilt of permitting in Germany's most fatal question that which he knew to be wrong." Another man would have resigned to salvage his conscience. But once having accepted the hazardous ambiguity of the calculated risk, he was trapped by his initial complicity. Nevertheless, the chief responsibility for the decision must be sought in the "grave hallucinatory disease," as Bethmann described the intellectual heritage and social environment that bred Wilhelmian militarism. "The history of this U-boat war, the ultimate lie, must reveal the lack of education, the military stupidity, and the rottenness of the whole chauvinist ruling class" of Imperial Germany.[53]

CHAPTER 10

Toward New Departures

The exhilarating spirit of 1914 seemed to herald a national "rebirth through war." All shackles of regional prejudice, religious discord, and class antagonism vanished and strife-torn Germany stood united in self-defense. "Although we have to struggle against East and West with all our might and our sons and brothers are risking their lives for us, we feel a singing and rejoicing in our souls," Friedrich Meinecke wrote, celebrating the emotional upsurge of "our holy war." Symbolized by William's handshake with the party leaders in the memorable Reichstag session of August 4, a compelling urge toward unity swept before it all fearful doubts of the Progressive and Socialist Left. "In the entire nation there were no longer any particularists, no Guelphs, Poles and Alsatians, no aristocrats and plebeians, no ultramontanists and anti-Semites, no imperialists and socialists . . . nothing but Germans." Despite the massive peace demonstrations of the last days of July, not only the nationalist bourgeoisie, the Junkers and peasants, but also the internationalist workers, spurred by the revisionists, rallied around the flag to prove, in Karl Broeger's words, that Germany's "poorest son is also its truest." Although some sober minds foresaw the years of bloodshed and privation, most in a paroxysm of patriotic sentiment, abandoned themselves to the intoxicating mania of war. Bismarckian unification, having truncated both the greater and democratic German traditions, stood vindicated in this hour of nationalist revival. Profoundly touched, Bethmann said to Riezler, "Our common effort is a new and powerful drama, much greater than in 1813." [1]

"At all costs we must maintain the great [rejuvenation] which this war brings to our people," the chancellor vowed, determined to build his domestic policy on this overpowering psychological reality. "No frost shall fall upon this springtime of our nation as long as we mortals can prevent it." Viewing the disappearance of internal divisions as the culmination of his effort to reconcile the bourgeois parties and nationalize socialism, Bethmann understood the truce within the beleaguered fortress, the Burgfrieden, not only as a necessary expedient, but as a positive goal. "Unity must be preserved above all. Greatest care should be taken in the treatment of the Social Democrats, Poles, Danes, and the press," he exhorted the Prussian Ministry of State, implying that generosity rather than compulsion would win the loyalty of those groups. To minimize economic dislocation, workers should not be locked out, the food supply of the population had to be assured, and the unemployed supported publicly. Bethmann sought to persuade his reluctant colleagues to adopt a more liberal attitude: "Even if it is doubtful whether the Socialists have taken their present position for tactical or ethical reasons, we must consider the facts." The cessation of partisan strife allowed the chancellor to launch a bureaucratic consensus policy pursuing those goals around which all factions could unite and thereby cure the malaise of Wilhelmian interest struggles. Although this "program of informal trust," in Naumann's phrase, was primarily directed toward ensuring the chancellor's freedom of decision, it was predicated on the realization that in peace the old divisiveness should not return. As in 1813 and 1870, the voluntary support of the people for the state implied greater liberalization as price of victory. In Bethmann's mind the moratorium on politics for the duration of the struggle carried the obligation of postwar reform.[2]

All patriotic rhetoric to the contrary, the Burgfrieden suffered from severe contradictions from the very beginning, since political differences between regions, religions, and classes had not been resolved, only suspended. In the hectic preparations for the passage of the first war credits, all parties agreed that "criticism must be silent during the fighting, not only because it is worthless but also because it is harmful, especially if it is justified." Nevertheless, the Reichstag's agreement to temporary adjournment rather than dissolution revealed that parliament was unwilling to abandon all control to the bureaucracy and the military. The Right saw the closing of ranks as a success of national *Sammlung* in the tradition of the Iron Chancellor and intended to use the opportunity to crush socialism and halt the erosion of Junker and grand industrial privileges. "Imperial Adjutant Caprivi calls Frank's death a trick of the Socialists! Plessen also warns against reconciliation with them," Riezler noted disgustedly. "But the emperor, genuinely moved by working-class support, has forbidden voicing such ideas." One of Heydebrand's associates feared that if the Socialists "become completely nationalized, the radical Left will be greatly strengthened." On the other hand the Progressives, and more so the revisionist Socialists, perceived their support for the war effort and conversion from enemies to partners of the state as their historic chance to transform the Hohenzollern monarchy into a social empire: "Now we have a common ground for influence during and after the war. We do not want to be left out again." On August 28, Eduard David asked Vice-Chancellor Delbrück unequivocally: "What will the people receive for their incredible sacrifices . . . ?" hinting that "there is only one reward which is great enough, a democratic reform of the Prussian suffrage." Although the secretary of the interior refused to commit the government, he could not deny the logic that "electoral reform offered generously and quickly . . . would make possible the evolution of our party toward national democracy." Even during the first month of the fighting the basic dichotomy of Wilhelmian politics reasserted itself.[3]

"Today the chancellor [talked] for a long time about the new course of our domestic policy. Completely without prejudices, opposed to all caste spirit," Riezler noted in late September. Emotionally, Bethmann had convinced himself that "the barriers must fall; after the war a new time will begin [since] class differences have dwindled as never before." Since prewar principles could no longer be binding, the chancellor agreed with Delbrück that a middle European order could not be implemented with the Right but rather with the Socialists, at any rate only through a Liberal majority. Hence Bethmann urged the vice-chancellor: "We must attempt, in every possible way, to seize this unique opportunity to give our Social Democracy a national and monarchist foundation." It followed that "this effort, if the Socialists give us a chance, must lead to a *Neuorientierung* (new orientation) of our whole domestic policy." Convinced that only reform could carry the national consensus into peacetime, the chancellor nevertheless set severe limits: "The leaders of the Social Democrats must be aware that the empire, and especially the Prussian state, will never allow the erosion of the firm ground of true loyalty upon which they have grown, and the system which the Socialists have hitherto branded as militarism." Reconciliation would have to come on Prussian terms. "When the German Left is willing to accept our system of defense, a new direction of our policy will be possible." In order not to disrupt the precarious harmony, Bethmann, in a typical compromise, approved Delbrück's formula that the necessary reforms would have to wait until the end of the war. "If such concessions must and should be made, they ought to be given as a reward afterwards and not as a premium beforehand. The less they are demanded publicly, the easier it will be to grant them." Hence the vice-chancellor promised the Landtag leaders that the spirit of August 1914 "will exert an essential influence upon all of our domestic policies and will cause a reorientation in several areas," even if it had to be postponed in order not to "sow seeds of discord among the parties." [4]

To begin "the impossible task of pouring the old Germany into a new mold," Bethmann discussed the necessary changes with his close associates in late September. Delbrück, Wahnschaffe, and Riezler suggested using the anticipated indemnity to establish state monopolies, "as the way to the state of the future." Despite massive rightist attacks on government socialism, the chancellor "resolved not to conduct a conservative policy after the war under any circumstances, perhaps to resign over the question of Prussian suffrage and provoke a [constitutional] conflict." His advisors strengthened him in this conviction by warning that revolution threatened if the war ended in reaction: "He admitted as much with the old saying that so far we have governed conservatively in form and liberally in substance, and that it should be just the opposite" from now on. [5]

Emerging from these conversations, Riezler's October memorandum on the goals of the Neuorientierung departed from the premise, "The war, however it ends, will create a new domestic situation for the empire." Since, for the first time, the broad masses showed themselves willing to accept and support the monarchy, the government should seize the opportunity to "win wider circles of the people for the state or to hold those newly converted through this great movement." Although broader participation was now desirable, the state will "have to grow organically, without cataclysm, leaving its inner essence intact." Concretely, "since the non-German subjects of the Prussian king have loyally participated in the common cause . . . the discriminatory laws in general, including the Jesuit law, will have to be abolished." Because "Prussia has made great moral conquests in the rest of Germany" and Alsace-Lorraine proved itself secure, "this situation should be used for the strength-

ening and solidifying of the entire empire." Intent on completing
Bismarck's work of external unification by overcoming his legacy
of internal strife, Riezler warned, "Without new practical tasks, the
nation will quickly sink back into the old morass of partisan
politics." [6]

The specific reform proposals of the October Memorandum enumerated the unfinished business of the Wilhelmian state from a
liberal-conservative point of view. "The final settlement of the
imperial finances and financial relations between the empire and
member states can only be achieved with state monopolies," a step
toward state socialism, as suggested by Rathenau. "Prussia [needs]
the construction of the Mittellandkanal, the reclamation of the
deserts and swamps, and internal colonization," the former an old
demand of liberal industrial and commercial circles, and the latter,
one of Bethmann's favorite projects since his days as Landrat in
Freienwalde. Because the empire was not a truly national state, the
policy toward non-German minorities had to be reformed "more on
the basis of identification with the state than with nationality, and
the discriminatory laws should be lifted if possible." To produce
cadres for the administration of the worldwide colonies, Riezler
proposed: "The necessary enlargement of political education must be
supported by the state through more teaching of politics in the
universities, perhaps through the foundation of a political academy
for higher officials and officers." Closer to the chancellor's own
previous concerns as administrator, "the training of the higher
bureaucracy is to be opened to wider classes as a matter of principle,"
in order to break the aristocracy's and haute bourgeoisie's hold on
officialdom. For more flexible economic support of Weltpolitik the
stock exchange should be reorganized, along the lines of Helfferich's
ideas: "Should the war end successfully, the Berlin bourse will become the heir of the city of London as long as this does not adversely
affect the health of our economy." The domestic counterpart of the
September Program, this collection of recommendations from the
chancellor and his circle called for breaking the remnants of feudal
prerogatives and for sharing power not only with the *Gross-* but also
the *Kleinbürgertum* and the workers' elite. [7]

The central issues of this blueprint for reform were the revision
of Prussian suffrage and the transformation of the labor movement.
Reflecting the failure of the chancellor's effort in 1910, the memorandum proposed only "secret and direct voting, keeping the

remaining features of the existing system." Not even the half-hearted rationalization "that an ideal suffrage does not exist and a fundamental revision of the whole electoral system, a task which must be left for the future, cannot be accomplished overnight," could gloss over the insufficiency of this recommendation. But "there is no doubt that the common danger has turned the German working class in favor of the fatherland. This is perhaps the last opportunity for winning them not only for the nation but also for the state." Although the victoriously returning worker-soldiers would not listen to revolutionary rhetoric, "they will remain workers. The government will have to attempt not to treat the labor movement as treasonable, to gain the cooperation of its mainstay, the unions, and to offer no pretext to the dogmatic old Socialists, opposed to the system, for leading the workers against the state once again." Bethmann thought it mandatory for "the government to unfurl the flag of domestic unity, strengthen the state, and broaden its foundation." Practically, the cabinet "will have to try and get the parties of the middle to agree to this program, perhaps by bringing individual leaders into the government," if necessary at the risk of dissolving the Reichstag. Though considerably less than demanded by the Left, the October Memorandum nevertheless envisaged a gradual evolution to a bourgeois and increasingly parliamentary empire, positively incorporating the Socialists. Bethmann had come far from the stand-pattism of the Prussian minister of the interior of 1905, and had turned into a sincere reforming conservative, seeking to preserve what he prized of Prussian traditions by rejuvenating them.[8]

Because "the great and serious enthusiasm of the little people and the nation at large" contrasted with an appalling "lack of nerve, defeatism, etc. in the upper strata," Bethmann resolved to make the second wartime Reichstag session a convincing demonstration of national unity. "This unanimity will facilitate victory as well as the solution of our domestic problems," he explained to the Prussian ministers, "since a country which bears the immense sacrifices of the war with such greatness and agreement cannot be torn asunder again by a return to party conflicts." On "his knees," the chancellor begged the Socialists not to issue a separate pacifist declaration; but even a promise of Prussian electoral reform did not satisfy the radicals and only succeeded in softening the wording of the Socialist call for peace. When the Progressive Haussmann proposed a vote of "confidence in government," Bassermann uttered, "that would top it all, confidence in this government!"; and the bourgeois parties framed a firm counterproclamation calling for "a peace commensurate with the sacrifices." Despite these reemerging differences, Bethmann spoke energetically, interrupted by hearty applause: "As if by magic the barriers which divided the members of our nation for a bleak and stagnant time and which we had erected against one another in misunderstanding, envy, and distrust have fallen." Affirming that a new order would arise after the war, the chancellor concluded, "It is liberating that all this refuse and waste has been swept away, that a man is a man, one equal to another, joining hands for a united, sacred cause." Although war credits passed overwhelmingly against Liebknecht's lone voice of dissent, Center deputy Adolf Groeber in the Finance Committee demanded the immediate abolition of all Exceptional Laws, while other parties complained about the heavy hand of military censorship. But Delbrück's second promise of a "new orientation of all domestic policy" was well received: "The Reichstag was good. The great wave devoured the dirty slime of a few vain politicians." Bethmann wrote to a friend, "Perhaps I stressed idealism too much. But we cannot do without it." [9]

Convinced of the "need to save this wartime exultation for the new Germany," Bethmann asked Loebell to begin preparations for a Prussian suffrage reform, since minor concessions like the sale of Socialist publications on government property and the admission of Socialist party members to the bureaucracy were but palliatives. Because "the future must be different from the past," the question of "a change of electoral system must be thoroughly considered and prepared so rapidly that the government will be able to introduce a bill in the Landtag as soon as the war ends." In a memorandum, Geheimrat Meister therefore argued for "the abandonment of three-class suffrage and the transition to general, secret, and direct elections, with votes graduated according to a plural system." But when Loebell wanted to obtain William II's approval for negotiations with the parties of the Right, Bethmann hesitated, unsure whether such a limited reform would suffice. Authorizing only further internal preparations, Bethmann justified his reluctance: "As long as the military situation and the political conditions dependent on it remain so unclear, H.M. will not be inclined to make a decision in a question which has received new importance through this war." [10]

The personal and political obstacles to any substantial broadening of the vote could only be overcome by strong leadership. "I have told the chancellor that he should not be misled by the gibberish of Bassermann and Co., especially not by the incorrigibility of our parliamentarians. The people below are capable of everything, full of desire for a better, ideal Germany, if they are called upon and the politicians thrown out," Riezler argued. "Bethmann must become the trumpeter of the future." Since bourgeois and conservative parliamentarians in Prussia opposed any change, Bethmann found "idealism only among the Socialists. . . . He sat there and played solitaire. The kaiser would not endorse the domestic policy necessary after the war." Hence the chancellor shrank from his assistant's advice to "step before the nation and set forth these principles . . . the idea will never perish and the people will eventually find their way." [11]

The gradual erosion of the Burgfrieden in the spring of 1915 forced Bethmann to find ways of reconciling the demands of the growing war aims movement with the increasing calls for peace. "In a lengthy war we will have difficulties with the Social Democrats," Riezler predicted. At the same time, "the Right is completely bereft of sense, dominated by the phraseology of power—Westarp madly scolds the chancellor, Wangenheim makes speeches, and Heydebrand declares, when asked, that Egypt has to be returned to Turkey even if the war lasts two years longer. The Left is growing more and more suspicious of annexations." The complexity of his parliamentary position limited Bethmann's freedom of choice. "If he speaks pessimistically—Conservatives and National Liberals will overthrow him with the kaiser by claiming that he is undermining morale." But silence in the face of the chorus of Pan-German demands would lose the confidence of the Socialists. "He does not want to remove censorship, primarily in order not to unleash Pan-German annexationist furor. Their sharp opposition creates many difficulties for him. . . . He considers a good relationship with us [the Socialists] very important." [12]

Since the Reichstag was too unwieldy and the Budget Committee, often attended by over one hundred deputies, too large for secrecy, the chancellor instituted a series of informal "leadership conferences" with the representatives of all parties to map out strategy before each session. Although often less effective than he desired, these frequent briefings of parliamentary leaders became Bethmann's chief instrument for explaining his personal views and for achieving some measure of agreement on tactics as well as fundamental policy. Serving equally to restrain the Socialists from premature peace proposals, as in March 1915, or to dampen the excessive annexationism of the Right, as in the meetings in May, these discussions, growing out of "the Reichstag's wish" for better information, became the most important link between chancellor and parliament.[13]

Since he was acutely aware of the "difficulty of preventing a collapse of morale because of the masses' desire for peace and the long duration of the war," Bethmann sought closer contact with the Socialists. Although he had attempted to buy off the annexationists with halfhearted promises of a greater Germany, he denounced the Pan-German goals as "nonsense. I will never pursue them," in order to convince Scheidemann that he was genuinely striving to end the war. "Yesterday the labor leaders visited Bethmann. The president of the woodworkers' union has lost his only son at Ypres," Riezler recorded. "Impressed with their idealism, the chancellor concluded: 'I hope that all this blood has not been shed in vain and that we will understand each other better in years to come.' One should have seen how the eyes of the visitors sparkled at this promise." Though sincerely convinced that "the future lies with such men," the chancellor hoped that he could postpone the implementation of the promised reforms until after the conclusion of peace in order not to jeopardize the Burgfrieden. While Erzberger and Stresemann clamored for parliamentary state secretaries to increase annexationist influence on the government, the Socialists warned that promises might no longer suffice and that they might refuse war credits. "Prussian electoral reform [is the crucial] factor for morale during the war . . . and the precondition for positive development" of the Socialist Party, the revisionist leader David cautioned the chancellor. Visibly impressed, Bethmann "declared that he would bring electoral reform, but not Reichstag suffrage." When David responded that too little given too late "would be received with ridicule and do more harm than good," he replied, "And what if the Socialists do not agree even then!?" Although there was no assurance, David thought that a far-reaching proposal would "carry weight and be of continuing importance for our inner development." Through these conversations the chancellor began to understand that inaction rather than reform endangered domestic unity.[14]

In late spring of 1915 the Prussian bureaucracy produced a new memorandum on broadening the suffrage. Convinced that some changes had to be made in order to "silence the agitation even if not all wishes can be fulfilled," councilor Berger, one of Loebell's conservative associates, emphasized that—in contrast to 1910—"an unbending will to success must be present, even if the Lower House has to be dissolved." The Ministry of the Interior argued: "The revision of the suffrage must allow the National Liberals, the Center Party, and the Conservatives to agree;" and the Progressives should be drawn in if possible, while "one can hardly count on the Socialists, since their constitutional ideas deviate too far from the path to which the government feels bound." Although the chancellor hesitated, William II "voiced his agreement on almost every page and commented with 'yes' on the remark that electoral reform was an inevitable national demand at the end of the war." Based on Loebell's June 26 votum, the draft of September 3 "proposed a direct and secret ballot, and instead of three-class division, a moderately graduated plural suffrage, taking into account age, family, residence, independent business, and taxation." This proposal sought to reform the electoral system in an antiplutocratic direction without destroying the conservative-agrarian majority, considered a necessary counterweight to the egalitarian Reichstag. Another similar memorandum "gained the kaiser's full assent," while Bethmann added reluctantly: "I consider the proposed principles of the reform, direct, secret, and plural suffrage mandatory and correct."

Nevertheless, "the chancellor suffers from strong electoral pains. About Loebell's plural suffrage proposal he says that it will be odious not for the minister of the interior but for him to defend votes based on taxation to the returning soldiers," Riezler noted. "The chancellor is disgusted with the airs of a Bassermann, Westarp, etc., surprised about the idealistic strength of the lower classes, and does not know how the new Germany of power and finance will find harmony with Goethe." Pondering Meinecke's dilemma of cosmopolitanism versus nationalism, Bethmann "says he cannot find the future in Thyssen, Stinnes, etc.—nor in the present frame of mind of the *Krautjunker*. Either cultural development has bypassed the Hohenzollerns or spiritual decline is having a rapid effect on them." [15]

Loebell's orthodox and Bethmann's liberal conservatism were the two major domestic alternatives for the German government during the war. In the winter of 1915, in a long report to the emperor, the Prussian minister of the interior claimed that domestic unity, a result of the "will to greatness and national glory" was threatened by the Left and, though necessary, reforms had to be strictly limited. Perceptively and persuasively, the chancellor criticized this majority view of the Prussian ministry: "It was not national ambition that united the people at the declaration of war," but the sincere feeling of self-defense. "The assertion of the memorandum, that the boundless annexationist plans of heavy industry were provoked by Socialist defeatism, is false," since already before any leftist calls for peace "I received dozens of petitions demanding a greater Germany." In response, "in almost all parties level-headed men who do not consider it unpatriotic to take political realities into account, stood up" and, although muffled by "chauvinistically minded military censorship," they, not the Pan-German warmongers, represented the country's best interests. The Right was using annexationist and submarine agitation merely as a flimsy pretext for the resumption of Red-baiting. Although the Left passionately called for peace, "on the whole today even the Socialists want to serve the fatherland and cooperate actively in its affairs." Here Bethmann differed in principle from the minister of the interior: "I do not consider this a passing wartime mood, but an ideal to which the best men in the party had already quietly aspired before the war and which has come about now." Seeing it as his task to strengthen this trend, the chancellor denounced any return to an anti-Socialist policy as "a fatal mistake" because the consequence might well be revolution.[16]

Predicting widespread postwar criticism of all existing conditions, Bethmann pleaded for reform before it was too late. "We can and will surmount all these dangers when the immense domestic challenge finds a nation which, though divided into parties and following different paths, in the final analysis strives for a common goal." Obsessed with making newly found unity the foundation of a healthier postwar politics, the chancellor knew it would be a "hard and sober task." The Social Democrats and the Progressives had changed for the better: "In their own way, but equal in results, both these parties have thrown overboard most of their negative doctrinaire ballast and joyfully participate in the life of the state." While the Center Party continued its amphibian existence between chauvinism and moderation, the Conservatives and National Liberals had failed "to rejuvenate themselves." Although he could not blame the former for clinging to the past, the latter had missed their historic chance to lead the transformation of the state: "Bereft of leadership and dependent upon the subsidies of the antilabor industrialists, they do the opposite and seek their salvation in the same hollow demagogical nationalism with which they covered their nakedness before 1914." This sterile reaction could be pardoned "if this war were to become the gateway to our world hegemony, but in reality it is only an element of disappointed discontent." Warning unequivocally that "a policy of encouraging chauvinist tendencies . . . cannot be continued in peacetime," Bethmann concluded: "Despite all marvelous deeds of the army, the slowness of the war's decision should not obscure the fact that this struggle is a catastrophe which must create new bases for human life, if the future is not to be hopeless." [17]

When the "nervous direction" of the Wilhelmstrasse and the increasing animosity between the annexationists and pacifists made the December 1915 Reichstag session an embarrassing display of disunity, the chancellor could no longer put off concrete measures. Scheidemann's emphatic demand for electoral reform lest the radicals gain control of the Socialist Party, and Hermann Pachnicke's warning that the Progressives were planning a suffrage interpellation, convinced Bethmann to act; but the necessity for dissolving the Landtag to ensure success limited him to a declaration in the *Thronrede*. "In the last weeks we have tinkered with a suffrage pronouncement. My idea of announcing the matter so clearly that there is no way out immediately convinced the chancellor," Riezler noted optimistically. But because of the opposition of a large group in the Prussian cabinet, Bethmann had to struggle hard to produce "agreement that the government must offer a new suffrage bill after the war." Insisting that "it will become necessary for the ministry to take a stand" in favor of liberalization as "beacon of light of our policy for broad classes of the population," Bethmann vetoed Loebell's suggestion of a separate notice in the *NAZ*. Schorlemer, Trott, and Lentze rejected any commitment of the crown, recalling the fiasco of 1908, and only Sydow and Beseler followed Helfferich's argument that "with a negative attitude all of our efforts towards the Social Democrats would be in vain." Overruling the objection of the crown prince by stressing the inevitability of reform, "more dignified if granted without threat and pressure," Bethmann informed Heydebrand, "who kept his composure, although it was quite a bitter pill" to swallow. On January 13, 1916, the chancellor announced in the Lower House: "The spirit of mutual trust and understanding will . . . permeate our public institutions and find living expression in our administration, legislation, and in the formation of the bases of popular representation in the legislative bodies." This open commitment to including suffrage reform in the Neuorientierung was greeted with satisfaction by Progressives and Socialists, and with unconcealed horror by the Right, who considered the three-class system "almost ideally suited" to Prussia and was hardly reassured by Loebell's promise in the Landtag that its implementation would have to wait until the end of the war.[18]

Lofty proclamations, however, could not ease the growing hunger of the masses, heat their freezing homes, and restore their faith in victory. "We find ourselves in such a novel situation that all tried means and ideals fail. Perhaps even caution, tenacity, and deliberation—Bethmann's best traits—will be of no avail," Riezler ruminated. "I have growing misgivings about the superb chancellor. He lacks demonic action, and these times cry out for it. Many others unconsciously feel the same way." When the Socialist leaders like David emphasized the danger of a decline in morale because of the "grave mistakes in food policy" and "the utter failure of reform," Bethmann found little to reply. "The question of provisions is serious, but we *must* overcome it," he implored Haussmann. Although only indirectly involved, the chancellor supported the establishment of price ceilings, the rationing of commodities like butter and fats, as well as state control over distribution, against the opposition of agricultural minister Schorlemer, who was more responsive to the producers' interests represented by the *Bund der Landwirte* and the *Landwirtschaftsrat* (agrarian pressure groups). "I know well that some circles suffer gravely. It is our task to distribute the food correctly," he stressed to the party leaders, claiming that there was enough for everyone if only dealt out properly. Although he publicly countered "all unjustified accusations maligning the attitude of agriculture," the chancellor reassured Socialist and trade-union members that "the correct distribution of these supplies at just prices, available also to the less well-off part of the population is the [essential] task that must be solved." Because of the need for working-class support for the war effort, Bethmann approved the appointment of Adolf Batocki as food dictator "capable of acting quickly and decisively," in cutting through the snarls of bureaucratic red tape. Although this administrative reorganization, as well as the whole system of *Zwangswirtschaft* (government control), could not create grain where there was none, the imperative of "maintaining popular morale under all circumstances" forced Bethmann to engage in a food policy that favored the consumer and alienated agrarian support.[19]

When in the submarine struggle of the spring of 1916 domestic "tensions [were] coming to a head everywhere," Bethmann "upbraided the journalists and then the party leaders who were full of rage" at Tirpitz's dismissal. "It helped considerably. The Center is still avoiding idiocies," Riezler noted, "but things are reaching such a point that National Liberals and Conservatives act as chauvinistic parties, which will destroy them after the war." The parliamentary challenge of the Right pushed Bethmann further to the Left. The Socialists "publicly attempt to occupy the same ground as the government in advocating a reasonable policy and branding the National Liberals and Conservatives as the reactionary fronde that they are." In strange irony, the Socialists criticized the Right for hoping "to capitalize on the longing for peace with their agitation and undermining the foundation of the state, i.e. public confidence." At the height of the U-boat crisis, the radical Socialists publicly rejected war credits and constituted themselves as a separate Reichstag faction, a schism branded by Friedrich Ebert as "not only a breach of discipline but also an act of *incredible treachery*." In stormy sessions of the Budget Committee Bethmann sought to restore unity by denouncing submarine warfare while holding out the hope for sizable war aims and by stressing his desire for peace while calling for perseverance. "The domestic effect was surprisingly good, and the foreign response none too bad," Riezler noted. But despite censorship and government propaganda "a quarrel over the ideas of 1914 slowly begins to dawn." Bethmann was even more candid: "The Conservatives' and National Liberals' agitation for submarine warfare proves that one can hardly talk of a Burgfrieden any longer." [20]

To strengthen collaborationist sentiment among the Social Democrats by fulfilling a long-standing wish of the trade unions, Bethmann broke with the principle of postponing reform and suggested
the revision of the associations law. He proposed that "under certain
conditions labor unions will no longer be treated as political parties,"
and argued in the Prussian Ministry of State that "it will hardly
be possible to keep the revisionist wing on its present course, unless
we allow some of its domestic aims to succeed." Intending to lift the
ban against political agitation for professional ends while maintaining the "protection of youth" as well as the odious language
paragraph, Bethmann believed that "the division of the Socialists
will continue; if the government does not use its influence to encourage a favorable development within the party, it incurs a grave
guilt." The conservative ministers retorted that any liberalization
would be a grave danger to the social basis of the monarchy. "It is undeniable that the government has hitherto considered the free unions
as organizations that must be fought." The chancellor thought it
imperative to "abandon this position. . . . One should not be too
petty in measuring the concessions. It is most important to grant
them greater freedom." When Socialist deputies like Wolfgang
Heine asked for the inclusion of agricultural and railroad workers,
the chancellor, though insisting on a strike ban, yielded, convinced
that the unions had "become necessary and useful members of our
economic life and have proven themselves such during the war."
A sizable reform "would enable the government to oppose the
pressure for further change more resolutely on the basis of concessions regarding the right of coalition." Despite the protests of the
conservative ministers Loebell, Schorlemer, Trott, Wild, and Lentze
and a flaming denunciation of the Landwirtschaftsrat, the chancellor's commitment carried the associations law through the Reichstag:
"People's wars necessarily lead to the fulfillment of political wishes
for broad lower classes." Bethmann invoked the precedent of the
Stein-Hardenberg reforms: "Whenever reform comes in time and
by the free will of the ruler, it strengthens the monarchy." [21]

Bethmann's hope that the progressive majority that had voted
for the revision of the associations law might become a permanent
bloc favoring peace and reform was quickly disappointed. The retirement of the ailing Delbrück and Helfferich's consequent appointment as vice-chancellor was an indirect setback to change because
"as a South German and bourgeois, he is inclined not to alienate the

Right," and his banker's past made him less sensitive to social justice than his predecessor. When the chancellor denounced the hysterical attack of the fronde as piracy of public opinion, he was disappointed by "the incredible maladroitness of the Socialists, who although touched by his warm words about the people . . . rejected the budget and made propagandist speeches." On the other hand, Center Party deputy Erzberger rebuffed his overture to enter a moderate reform coalition in exchange for the abolition of the anti-Jesuit law, because his political friends still harbored annexationist and submarine dreams. "Full of passion and prophecy" and with "a burning faith in the people," the chancellor spoke to his intimates "about the *cauchemar* of revolution after the war weighing upon him" and predicted "incredible demands by the returning soldiers and disillusionment about the peace." Because of their irresponsible factionalism, "the parties must be totally transformed and the public spirit reformed completely. If not, Germany will perish. It is impossible to change East Elbia—it must be broken or vanish." To the sympathetic Friedrich Meinecke, Bethmann complained about "the spread of the Pan-German chauvinist attitude among the intelligentsia" and the parties. "On the other hand in the rising and culture-hungry strata of the unions he saw something really new, still unformed and fermenting, which would have the greatest importance for our intellectual and political life." [22]

Although the appointment of the third OHL silenced the chauvinist critics of Rumanian intervention, the plebiscitary military authority, which had previously endorsed the chancellor's consensus politics, soon became the major obstacle to gradual reform. To reaffirm popular faith in victory, the demigods insisted on opening war aims discussions, and redefined the Burgfrieden to allow for patriotic i.e. annexationist, demands while branding agitation for a moderate peace as defeatism. In pursuit of its vast strategic aims in East *and* West, the third OHL demanded the mobilization of all material and human resources in a gigantic step toward total war. Inspired partially by the profit desires of heavy industry and the counterrevolutionary dreams of Colonel Bauer, the Supreme Command intended to go far beyond the newly created WUMBA (Weapons and Munitions Procurement Agency) to increase the output of war machinery dramatically. On September 13 Ludendorff brusquely demanded from the chancellor the extension of the draft to include all men between sixteen and fifty, the enforced registration of all workers—including the wounded, women, students, and those unfit for combat—in order to use them more efficiently for war production. *"Every day is important.* The necessary measures must be taken *immediately."* Miffed by such rudeness, Bethmann responded that the military aspects of the matter had to be decided by the OHL alone but the general economic and political effects should be discussed together. Basing his arguments on a countermemorandum by Helfferich, the chancellor sarcastically warned against "ill-conceived measures which would create a near-fatal disturbance in our economic body whose breathing and working cannot be completely replaced by administrative fiat." Germany had almost no unused labor left. Perhaps all public building could be halted, the wounded returned to action more quickly, seventeen- and eighteen-year-olds drafted, and the upper age limit raised to fifty. To subject female labor to military conscription would "raise the gravest economic, moral, and social objections." [23]

Temporarily rebuffed, the High Command shifted its demands to the creation of a supreme war office empowered to organize the gigantic mobilization. Since it required only an imperial order, the establishment of a *Kriegsamt* coordinating the war ministries of the states, the KEA (War Food Office), WUMBA, KRA (Raw Materials Section), and the commanding generals was proposed by General Groener to the astounded Bethmann on October 14, 1916. Realizing the drastic political implications of militarizing the entire economy, the chancellor "wants neither forced labor nor the elimination of freedom of movement." Nevertheless, he could not object to the administrative reorganization, as long as it formally remained under the control of the Prussian Ministry of War and did not establish a military dictatorship in domestic affairs. In a compromise move, Bethmann accepted a supreme war office with "improved organization," i.e. under the war minister, except for food questions under the KEA; its head could issue decrees binding on the commanding generals while receiving its own instructions from the OHL. This solution appealed to Ludendorff, since it respected constitutional appearances while giving him the substance of power when Wild von Hohenborn resigned, because he intended to be *"a responsible minister of war,"* not a rubber stamp for the Dioscuri.

This temporary unanimity was shattered when, in a near ultimatum, the quartermaster general threatened to extend conscription to all men and women between fifteen and sixty despite the chancellor's clear warning that any compulsory regimentation of labor "would meet the sharpest resistance" from the Reichstag. In a hurried conference in GHQ, Bethmann argued for voluntary mobilization of the necessary labor, but Groener stressed lack of time, the need for more workers, and the possibility of replacing conscripts with women, students, and old men. "It is not yet clear which path we can generally follow; the field marshall's plan seems impracticable at present," the chancellor informed Wahnschaffe, adding "somehow we must step in and organize it." Due to Bethmann's resistance, military duty was becoming the less odious national service.[24]

When the Prussian Ministry of State debated the *Vaterländische Hilfsdienst* (national service), Groener, though persuasive and conciliatory, received little support from the ministers, since Helfferich and Sydow strongly objected to compulsion and regimentation. Nevertheless, the chancellor's conclusion, which noted "agreement that some form of auxiliary service duty must be proclaimed," indicated that the cabinet recognized the need for decisive action, only preferring a Bundesrat proclamation to the complications of a Reichstag bill. Although Bethmann retorted angrily, "nothing will bring a more annoying failure than an impractically and superficially worked-out draft," William II, prodded by Ludendorff, "ordered the immediate and speedy introduction of the labor bill in the Reichstag." In the preparatory discussions with industrialists, labor leaders, and parliamentarians, Helfferich proved less responsive to Reichstag wishes for some control and union demands for parity than Groener who, under OHL pressure for quick success, was willing to make sacrifices. Nevertheless, the vice-chancellor succeeded in appending a series of guidelines stipulating the establishment of determination (closure of factories), draft (conscription of manpower), and arbitration (complaint review) committees. After a lengthy cabinet discussion about the feasibility of including union representatives, Bethmann noted general "agreement on the necessity of the law," and the slightly amended version was sent to the Bundesrat. When the OHL impatiently demanded action rather than further deliberation, the chancellor angrily pointed to the parliamentary obstacles yet to be overcome: "I cannot accept the responsibility for the consequences of the hopeless attempt to railroad the bill through." [25]

In the Reichstag the fate of the Auxiliary Service Law bore out the chancellor's dire predictions. Provoked by Stein's haughty speech and exacerbated by Helfferich's inflexibility, the Budget Committee added the phrase, "general regulations need the consent of a committee of fifteen appointed by the Reichstag out of its own members," i.e. the formalization of parliamentary co-control.[26] Moreover, the Socialist caucus demanded "the introduction of guarantees for the protection of workers," Carl Legien insisted on the election of labor representatives, freedom of coalition, and the slashing of war profits, while bourgeois deputies called for safeguards against arbitrary shutdowns and compensation for the owners. In the Prussian Ministry of State, Bethmann supported the establishment of a special committee which would keep the *Hauptausschuss* from "developing into a Comité de Salut Public" while Helfferich managed to prevent higher taxation of war profits by allowing workers to move for important reasons such as better wages elsewhere. On November 29, Bethmann exhorted the Reichstag: "This task can only succeed if it is not based on compulsion but on the free consent of our nation, if industry and agriculture, if workers and entrepreneurs, and especially their proven organizations dedicate and devote themselves voluntarily." Although the Prussian ministers almost unanimously opposed the further committee modifications safeguarding the right of association, they reluctantly agreed with the chancellor's recommendation, "We cannot let the bill fail because of its great national importance." When the Socialists decided that recognition of unions as equal partner was a sufficient gain, Bethmann, relieved, cabled William II: "The auxiliary law has just been accepted by a 235:19:8 vote." By his farsighted acceptance of the parliamentary transformation of the bill, Bethmann had turned a law designed to militarize German life into a moderate success for his new course, since he was convinced "that the political Neuorientierung necessitated by the war rendered the introduction of obligatory workers' committees and arbitration boards at the conclusion of peace inescapable." [27]

Nonetheless, the economic and political effects of the Auxiliary Service Law were nothing short of disastrous. "Domestically there are severe transportation crises and growing plans for a military dictatorship. This is caused by the dilettantism of the colossal Hindenburg Program, compulsively grafted upon the economy, a plan that can only be achieved in this magnitude at the expense of other equally vital projects," Riezler acidly voiced sentiments of the chancellor's circle. Since Groener had made pessimistic predictions to be proven right in any eventuality, Bethmann became the scapegoat for the failure of the Hindenburg program due to the popular belief that "civilians are naturally more stupid than anyone in uniform." But he rejected the blame: "It would be impossible to abolish the law or to remove or limit the rights given to the workers according to the wishes of certain employers from heavy industry. The consequences would be unpredictable." To accomplish the "task of strengthening the patriotic and reasonable elements of labor," the "price of certain sacrifices" had to be paid.[28] Because of this and other disagreements, the third OHL more and more became "the battering ram" of the "long and bitter campaign against the chancellor . . . ultimately rooted in domestic reasons." Socially accessible to parliamentarians of the Right like Westarp and Stresemann as well as industrial leaders like Röchling and Krupp, Hindenburg and Ludendorff, in their self-consciously nonpolitical, patriotic stance, opposed any major reforms. Although the chancellor insisted that political responsibility was his alone and denounced the "appeal to military authority as the central tactic of his opponents," he was pushed more and more on the defensive against the quasi dictatorship of the generals.[29]

"While I had to press forward in Prussia, I was forced to restrain the democratic parties in the empire from making stormy demands," Bethmann described the parliamentary polarization of early 1917. "My most important duty was the preservation of the crown's leadership in order to guard it against the fate so dangerous to all monarchies. Inevitable reforms, if too long delayed and finally forced through, irredeemably weaken the royal principle instead of strengthening it." But the deprivations of the turnip winter and the fuel and transportation crisis could no longer be neutralized by administrative measures such as the appointment of Michaelis as Prussian commissioner for nutrition. Riezler deplored that "the domestic situation is damnably difficult. Everything must be done in order to hold the Social Democrats. The prochancellor faction stands on shaky ground," since the radicals expressed the aspirations of the starving masses more convincingly. "Because everybody believes that we are nearing the end, internal struggles are becoming hotter by the day. The present ruling classes feel economically and politically threatened by the government's co-operation with the Socialists," since they were too blind to see that precisely this moderate progressivism safeguarded the crown. When, in a move to appease the Right, Bethmann allowed the introduction of a new *Fideikommiss* (entail) law, guaranteed by Loebell to arouse no opposition, the Socialists and Progressives raged against this resurrection of feudalism in a portent of things to come.[30]

Although Riezler's attempt "to induce Schiedemann to say something in favor of the monarchy . . . misfired," Bethmann felt compelled to renew his commitment to the Neuorientierung in the Reichstag: "This is not a beautiful word! I believe I am using it for the first time today and it easily gives the wrong impression. As if we could decide whether we want it or not! No, gentlemen, the new time with a rejuvenated people is here" already. To the warm applause of the Left he promised the preservation of this spirit of national unity "into peacetime, if channels are created in which it can work freely and gladly." Partially a result of the Neuorientierung, "the enormous political landslide triggered by the Socialists' transformation into potential partners" for the government offered Bethmann for the first time a realistic "possibility of creating a Left coalition." But the cabinet, torn between reforming and stand-pat conservatives, lacked cohesion since Minister of Agriculture Schorlemer publicly quarreled with Prussian Food Commissioner Michaelis and Imperial Nutrition Head Batocki.[31]

"The programmatic speeches of Count Yorck and [Leo von] Buch in the Upper House," denouncing Reichstag suffrage and rejecting an increase in living expenses for the Landtag deputies, provoked such an outcry that the usually self-possessed National Liberal leader Friedberg warned, "We shall unleash a movement to reform the *Herrenhaus!*" Counseled by Erhard Deutelmoser, Wahnschaffe, and Riezler "to speak clearly and energetically," the chancellor agreed "that we are in the middle of a still unrecognized domestic crisis." Rising to the occasion, "he did so splendidly, speaking without notes, passionately—yes with a *feu sacré*, with great feeling and 'a fervent love' for the people." Convinced that "this war will and must lead to a *transformation of our political life* in important aspects, despite all opposition," he called into the agitated diet:

"The royal government has repeatedly and unmistakably declared that it will propose a reform of the Prussian suffrage." Although still preferring implementation after the end of the war, he vowed to fight for political equality: "I want these ideals. I shall put them into practice! (bravo!) I shall give everything for them (renewed lively assent!)." Conservative taunts made Bethmann thunder like an angry prophet: "Woe unto the statesman who does not recognize the signs of the times; woe unto the statesman who believes that after an incomparable catastrophe . . . he can simply resume where he left off, that he can pour new wine into old skins without their bursting! Woe unto the statesman!" The "success was immense. Finally we have a program," Riezler rejoiced, and Haussmann saw "the great Bethmann speech as a historical event for our domestic policy." [32]

"It is a strange coincidence. The chancellor spoke on Wednesday; Thursday morning the first news of the victory of the revolution in Petersburg arrived," Riezler mused on March 18. "One day later he could no longer have done it; then it would have been called weakness." Though timely, the mere promise of reform now no longer sufficed, since the shock waves of the Russian upheaval turned distant hopes into direct demands. "Through the Russian Revolution . . . the Social Democrats caught a whiff of red air—and on the 18th and 19th brewed up a revolutionary storm in the *Vorwärts,* threatening by implication." Hearing that Bethmann intended to revise the Prussian suffrage with the help of the Left if it would vote the necessary taxes, Scheidemann, in a controversial article, "Time for Action," called for immediate change, warning that the kaiser might be compelled to follow his cousin the tsar. "This has had bad effects on the military—and the *Kreuzzeitung* takes advantage of it by circling around the throne hyperpatriotically." Although William II congratuated Bethmann on his timely and courageous speech, "the imperial generals are also affronted and shake their heads. At home the mood continues to be serious and precarious." Hence, in negotiating with the Socialist leaders, Bethmann claimed "he could not push through electoral reform in Prussia during the war" and "demanded a conversion to the monarchy" first. But hunger, strikes, the party schism, and a long tradition of revolutionary rhetoric made the Social Democrats impervious to government persuasion. "At the other extreme, the conservative generals howl with rage, accusing the chancellor of increasing the appetite [of the reformers] and doing nothing against the so-called glorification of the Russian Revolution." Although he lectured the crown prince that any support of the fallen monarchy would be "a grave political error" and cautioned War Minister Stein "to avoid nervousness and fear in all orders, especially those concerning censorship," the chancellor faced a "very precarious situation in the Reichstag: Electoral reform now or later?"[33]

To prepare the ground with William II, Bethmann warned: "It would be quite dangerous to brand the democraic demands, the inevitable consequence of this war, as antimonarchist according to previous practice and recognize only conservatives as reliable supporters of the throne. . . . A reactionary military dictatorship would have catastrophic results." But while the chancellor was urging timely concessions, the speeches of the arch-conservative Junkers, Erwin von Kleist and Count Albecht von Roon in the Upper House sparked a parliamentary explosion which revolutionized party alignment in the Reichstag. When Spahn (Center), Noske (Socialist) and Müller-Meiningen (Progressive) demanded concrete proof of the Neuorientierung, the hitherto chauvinistic Stresemann sensationally reversed himself: "We do not have to wait with reform until the end of the war." In order not to let "the driftwood swim over to the Left, otherwise we will lose the next election," and because reform "becomes more and more expensive," the leader of the annexationist wing of the National Liberals called for the appointment of a constitutional commission. Confronted with a resolute reform majority in the Reichstag, while under ever heavier attacks from the OHL, Bethmann sought to parry the thrust by promising the immediate "lifting of the anti-Polish laws, division of the mammoth parliamentary districts, and repeal of the anti-Jesuit law." Expecting the frenzied resistance of moribund Prussia and only halfhearted cooperation from the bourgeois factions in the Landtag, the chancellor cautioned, "As long as I cannot convince myself—*and until this moment I have been unable to do so*—that the *immediate* beginning of this reform would serve the interests of our country, I have to wait until I have reached this conviction." This all too cautious speech, seeking to reestablish some contact with the Conservatives, decisively disappointed the Left without regaining the support of the Right. In an unprecedented move, the Reichstag passed a resolution creating a constitutional committee (*Verfassungsausschuss*) by a vote of 227 to 33.[34]

"The Russian Revolution is making people in Berlin very nervous," Bethmann reflected on his failure to calm the waves. "More than the Social Democrats, the Progressives, and the National Liberals increase the existing difficulties with impetuous pressure." The parliamentary Easter recess offered a tactical reprieve to the crown to prepare a dramatic initiative. Together with the American declaration of war, President Wilson demanded the overthrow of "the irresponsible autocratic government of Imperial Germany," and Austrian Foreign Minister Czernin warned, "If the war is not over in three months, the people will terminate it without the governments." To avert the worst, Bethmann called together his trusted domestic advisors, Helfferich, Count Roedern and, for the absent Loebell, his undersecretary Drews, in the evening of March 31: "Great commotion," Riezler recorded. "It was decided to announce a reform of the suffrage and of the Upper House at once. This is right. It must be done as rapidly as possible—events apparently call for quick action—an element of haste has entered the deliberations." Though not without regret, Bethmann, "forced into new decisions" now abandoned his previous insistence on postponement and some graduated suffrage short of true equality. Although he had at one time favored Loebell's plural voting system, "the cataclysmic transformations of this war have made the imperative of resolute support for the monarchy by all, even the most extreme, means, a matter of such firm inner conviction, that I consider concessions demanded by this purpose not as sacrifices but as the result of compelling raison d'état." The force of circumstances had converted Bethmann to insist on Reichstag suffrage in Prussia. Riezler suggested a careful course: "First the kaiser and then the Ministry of State. Perhaps then some ministers will resign, which would be just as well." [35]

Spurred on by the "strange fears about the condition of Germany" in the capital, Bethmann traveled to GHQ on April 1 to obtain the emperor's agreement to a "proclamation without making any specific suggestions about its content." Aware of the hostility of the military entourage to any change, the chancellor "only asked for . . . imperial approval to discuss the content of the announcement with the Ministry of State and to envisage especially a reform of the Upper House." As he reported to Riezler, "at first the emperor hesitated but afterwards he quite agreed to make a declaration about the Prussian suffrage on Easter Sunday—tomorrow the Ministry of

State will meet to decide." An eloquent letter from the food dictator, Batocki, also suggesting immediate royal intervention, finally
convinced William II that "the people should be reassured in a
liberal direction as soon as possible." On the margin of the letter
the kaiser scribbled: "The crown must speak at Easter. After Easter
too late." Encouraged by a warning of the Bavarian Minister of
War that some action was necessary to restore popular morale, Bethmann replied immediately: "According to my personal opinion, the
rescript must announce equal suffrage. Vague assurances would
only exacerbate the quarrel without satisfying anybody." To neutralize Ludendorff's resistance, he added, "The opinions of the
military must not be decisive under any circumstances, because I
convince myself more with every day that the intended step is
utterly essential for the support of the monarchy."

On his return to the Wilhelmstrasse, Bethmann, with the help of
Helfferich and Wahnschaffe, drafted an imperial message with the
intent "of widening the forms of our constitutional life in order
to create room for the free and joyful participation of all members
of our nation." Specifically, the original version promised the fulfillment of the demands of the new age: the transformation of the
army into a true people's force, the immediate beginning of the
reforms, equality of suffrage, the renovation of the Upper House
as a first chamber representing all German elites, the abolition of
the exceptional laws, the revision of the Polish policy, the improvement of workers' and servants' rights, the streamlining of the judiciary, and the liberalization of local self-administration. This was a
sweeping program for a revolution from above.[36]

In the Prussian Ministry of State on April 5, Bethmann passionately pleaded for reform in order to preserve the monarchy.
Since plural voting was inequitable "from moral and ethical considerations," the chancellor thought it "necessary to settle the electoral question once and for all." Because the failure of peace and
increasing starvation had turned the war into a race for the survival
of the monarchy, "the government must lead with an energetic
hand, otherwise it will lose the reins. Now a positive goal must be
set and this can be nothing but the promise of universal, equal, and
direct suffrage." At the same time "a reform of the Upper Chamber
is also mandatory," in order to transform it into a constructively
conservative counterweight against the egalitarian lower house.
Since the war had swelled the democratic tide, one could no longer

oppose it, but only channel the flood "so that the state suffers as little as possible. This can be achieved most securely if the monarchy makes itself truly popular" by becoming social and parliamentary. Summoning the arguments of Old Prussia, Loebell nevertheless countered "that grave doubts remain about such a step." The federal structure of the empire would force all other states to follow suit; the Junkers, industrialists, and bureaucrats of the Wilhelmian elite would be alienated from the throne and the promise of equal votes would unleash a merciless struggle for power. Since Trott, Schorlemer, Stein, and Lentze were willing to resign in protest, the minister of the interior suggested as compromise his plural suffrage proposal, to be adopted with the support of the parties of the Right. Because Vice-President Breitenbach, Sydow, Beseler, and the state secretaries Helfferich and Roedern who urged drastic action formed only a majority of one, Bethmann warned emphatically: "Until now I have conducted a policy which maintained the support of the great masses and I believe I have been successful in this. . . . Should you presently embark upon the opposite course, I will be impossible as chancellor." Struggling against centuries of Borussian traditions, he concluded: "In 1866 Bismarck put the proclamation of universal suffrage into the scales of fate to create the German Reich. Today this action is perhaps necessary to preserve Prussia and the Empire." [37]

Propelled by the parties of the Left, the Neuorientierung confronted Bethmann with a decision which might determine the survival of Hohenzollern Prussia. Though favoring a rejuvenation of the monarchy as long as it did not transfer real power, William II exclaimed at the chancellor's far-reaching proposals: "He did not speak to me about the Reichstag ballot!" Swayed by the conservative members of the cabinet, Valentini sent repeated warning telegrams to the chancellor, asking "must we commit ourselves now to equal suffrage?" When consulted, Ludendorff completely rejected [the idea], wanted only a strong government, then everything would be fine." Since "I could not yet bring the kaiser to a quick decision for equal suffrage," Bethmann knew that the only alternative, "the formation of a new cabinet with this program, . . . was excluded. My own resignation would not have resolved the crisis." The practical difficulty of imposing a voting system demanded by the Left Reichstag majority *against* the Right Landtag majority could not simply be dismissed. In the cabinet session of April 6, Bethmann therefore decided on a compromise: "The principal difference from the first draft [of the proclamation] is that the bill shall only be introduced after the war and that it will not announce equal suffrage but only demand negatively the elimination of the three-class system." While some of the liberal ministers regretted this step backward, the conservative bloc quickly assented, since the new version struck the detailed enumeration of specific reforms substituting the bland promise, "I am resolved to develop further our domestic, economic, political, and social life as rapidly as possible." Riezler deplored the emasculation of the reform: "Unfortunately, the unequivocal announcement of equal suffrage was cut because the ministers feared that the bourgeois parties would prove intractable; the Bund der Landwirte would mount a great campaign against the cities which would have dangerous repercussions for our food supply—hence it is presently impossible." Although, "if the war lasts long we will have to grant it anyway," the chancellor could console himself, "More could not be achieved at this moment, either with H.M. or with the Ministry of State." [38]

The psychological effect of this "imperial Easter egg for the people" was initially positive despite its ambiguity. "The *Lokalanzeiger,* which is slipping more and more under the domination of heavy industry, has kicked me several times like a jackass, and Georg Bernhard will probably also grumble," Bethmann explained to Valentini. "But the papers influencing the great masses, the *Vorwärts, Volkszeitung, Berliner Morgenpost,* etc., are favorable." The conservative press, though critical, promised constructive cooperation, and the Socialist Party sheets professed satisfaction and optimism. But "we are not yet on dry land. Only if our situation develops favorably in the next two, at most three months, and justifies hopes for a quick peace will the *Osterbotschaft* survive," Bethmann cautioned. "The prospects for this are uncertain and bleak." To prepare the ground for more far-reaching steps in the future, he protested, "In the long run it means an unbearable burden on the kaiser's shoulders if, in the most important political questions, the generals closest to him pull the other way." Though admitting in a sentence later stricken from the letter that "much that is valuable will be shattered," Bethmann reiterated to Breitenbach, "After the proclamation I have become more and more convinced that it was absolutely necessary and right." To Bavarian Prime Minister Hertling, he justified this step: "Any review of the problem of

Prussian electoral reform is unpleasant. As always in big political questions, omissions are punished most heavily." Having learned from his defeat in 1910, Bethmann now endorsed the principle that "after the experience of this war the perpetuation of the struggle for electoral reform must be prevented, and only a monarchy which is popular in the best sense of the word will survive." [39]

In mid-April the "impending strike of the metal workers in Berlin against the cutting of the bread ration" revealed that the Osterbotschaft would not suffice to stem the radicalization of the Left. When the food allowance was reduced to even less than half the medically established minimum daily requirement, and the foundation of the Independent Socialist Party (USPD) with the Spartacists as radical wing provided the political spark, hundreds of thousands of workers struck, protesting for "food, freedom, and peace." Because the government needed "the Social Democrats domestically and abroad at every turn," it was essential "to grant Prussian electoral reform immediately in order to steal the enemy's thunder, since [Wilson] threatens to offer the Germans peace without the Hohenzollerns." But when the Socialist Party committee called for the "immediate abolition of all inequality of rights" as well as for a peace of "no annexations and no indemnities" Hindenburg angrily demanded the dismissal of the chancellor on the grounds that he was "incapable of mastering the Socialists" and imposed the utterly fantastic Kreuznach program on Bethmann. As the commanding general of Berlin professed himself powerless to repress the demonstrations and walkouts by force, the chancellor sought to calm the workers in long top-level sessions and individual conversations with the "imperial" Socialists. While promising minor improvements in food supply and setting up a workers' advisory committee, Bethmann, in a firm circular to the state governments, sought to appease the Right: "Whoever dishonorably and disloyally attacks our brave warriors from the rear in this sacred struggle steps outside the national community and shall be struck down with the full force of the law." Because of this mixture of conciliation and coercion, "the first of May passed peacefully. But everything is exceedingly precarious and the Socialists are quite afraid—secretly they ask for the strongest measures against the USPD." [40]

"The constitutional committee can become unpleasant. The childish idea that the parliamentary system can be introduced through legal paragraphs finds enthusiastic advocates, especially among the National Liberals." This prediction turned out to be truer than imagined when Bethmann's suggested sacrifices, the division of the large Reichstag districts, the abolition of the anti-Jesuit law, and the notorious language paragraph merely whetted parliamentary appetites. "The chancellor hesitates too much domestically—probably because H.M. does not see very well and the military entourage is blind," wrote Riezler. He feared the desertion of the Left: "Every day Theodor Wolff calls for a parliamentary regime and the Socialists make trouble with their renunciationist formulas." Although the "demand to make elected representatives [ministers] means a complete overthrow of the imperial constitution and is practically impossible," Bethmann, conscious that "the government and the monarchy . . . need a stronger and broader base which they can achieve through the participation of Reichstag spokesmen," now "decided still to propose to H.M. the appointment of party leaders to several ministries during the summer."

Not a formally responsible cabinet, as demanded by the Verfassungsausschuss, but a coalition ministry made up of prominent deputies, this solution went far to satisfy National Liberal desires, and was approved by Valentini as well. But when the committee challenged the imperial prerogative to appoint officers by demanding Reichstag review of commissions, "the Emperor became furious . . . ; the chancellor's position is severely shaken" since "Old Prussia rears its head—the Left no longer wants to wait." Although with Wahnschaffe's and Helfferich's aid Bethmann convinced the parties "that they [could not] commit any further follies related to the Kommandogewalt," William, inspired by the military, raged against the so-called parliamentary system: *"The Easter Message will be implemented—after the war—under no circumstances shall I go further!"* The Reichstag's rash attack on the military basis of Hohenzollern power provoked the OHL, seriously antagonized the kaiser, and jeopardized the entire Neuorientierung. Only massive pressure on the parliamentary committee to postpone decisions and a Bundesrat vote not to accept any reduction of states' rights temporarily halted the erosion of Bethmann's power.[41]

Prospects for further reform were dim, as long as the "kaiser [vacillated], torn by Left and Right, afraid of Ludendorff and angry at the Reichstag over interfering with his Kommandogewalt." Since action was impossible, Riezler counseled Bethmann to speak energetically against the Right in parliament, but "unfortunately he has been tired, angry, and quietist during the last few days." On May 15 contradictory Conservative and Socialist war aims interpellations gave the chancellor the platform for his last oratorial triumph. While Roesicke demanded a clear endorsement of a "national peace," and Scheidemann threatened revolution if the war were continued for the sake of annexation, Bethmann steered between the extremes: "Gentlemen, I am not in any party's camp, neither the Left's nor yours (turned to the Right)—no certainly not, and I am glad of it (stormy applause and cheers). If I am under some spell, it is the spell of the German people, a people whom I alone have to serve." This plea for a negotiated peace and moderate liberalization "solidified the domestic front" under a parliamentary majority extending from the Social Democrats to the National Liberals and gave Bethmann breathing room for the duration of the Reichstag adjournment, until early July. Since the revolution in Petrograd the chancellor had been on the defensive. The fundamental dilemma of his consensus politics reasserted itself more dramatically during each crisis. "All of Germany seems to divide into two parts." No longer content with promises, the Left "presses for a coalition ministry of parliamentarians," but the "dumb soldiers believe the war is decisively won . . . and Ernst Reventlow performs a danse macabre on the crumbling boards of a hollow world." Hoping for a policy that would combine "power and freedom," Riezler despaired. "That the chancellor cannot do, partly because he lacks confidence, partly because he must take the ruling insanity into account." [42]

Within the government, the center of resistance to reform was Prussian Minister of the Interior Friedrich von Loebell. A former collaborator of Bülow and an intimate of Conservative and National Liberal leaders, he clashed with the chancellor over the degree of change necessary. On May 19, Riezler noted angrily: "Loebell has stitched together a suffrage proposal with the Landtag. If the parties agree and publish the result, the chancellor, who has not yet gotten the emperor on his side, will be faced with an impossible situation." His assistant felt: "It is his own fault. He understood all of this, he knew Loebell; why did he not prepare and get rid of him in time?" To redeem his tactical error, Bethmann protested to Valentini: "Neither I nor the Ministry of State was informed about this proposal. . . . For the time being I consider the draft inacceptable."

To Loebell's "great surprise, the chancellor was extremely dissatisfied with this maneuver and predicted difficulties with the Reichstag," since any agreement among the Center-Right parties in Prussia would be rejected by the more radical Center-Left majority in the empire. But when, on May 23, the conservative bloc of ministers refused to disavow Loebell's work, Bethmann feigned agreement, only cautioning, "I cannot yet judge if the proposal endorsed by the parties can form the basis for government action." However, "convinced that only equal suffrage would be possible after this war," he adroitly instructed Loebell "to inform the parties" that the cabinet did not consider itself bound by his commitments. Although the minister of the interior and the Landtag parties continued to negotiate on this basis, the chancellor had succeeded in gracefully burying plural suffrage.[43]

To counter "the ever stronger attacks of the Right, sure of Ludendorff's covert sympathy," Bethmann made one last attempt to convince the OHL of the necessity of thorough reform. Any steps forward, like the "dismissal of the most decrepit Prussian ministers and the announcement of equal suffrage," were unattainable as long as "the various specimens of the county insane asylum, the generals, blinded by the gods . . . effectively bombard the kaiser with reactionary propaganda—raising the specter of a Scheidemann peace while stubbornly believing in the subjection of England by submarine warfare." But through Colonel Bauer connected with Schäfer, Stresemann, the industrialist Röchling, and other members of the fronde, the generals rebuffed Bethmann's soundings of their attitude toward liberalization conducted by Secretary of the Treasury Count Roedern. In a long letter of June 25, Bethmann went the extra mile to assure "the unanimous cooperation of all decisive authorities." Warning against the impending collapse of morale, he pleaded for realistic moderation in assessing Germany's military chances and war aims: "The widespread and persistent impression that the opponents of the new course enjoy strong, perhaps decisive, support [in the OHL] contributes an element of growing unrest to the domestic scene, increases radical demands, and weakens our hand." But in a brusque conversation with Wahnschaffe, Ludendorff denounced the Easter Message as "a kowtow to the Russian Revolution," deplored Bethmann's responsibility for the Verfassungsausschuss and the strikes, and concluded: "We cannot support the chancellor!" According to Bavarian Colonel Mertz of the GHQ, "the

hatred against Bethmann is so deep that it knows no limits. . . .
The reason is simple. The arch-conservative Borussian circles find
their political skins floating down the river because Bethmann
wants a radical reform of Old Prussia with its constitution, a travesty of political morality." Despite all claims to the contrary, "the
actual cause of the OHL's desire to overthrow [the chancellor] lies
in domestic politics." [44]

By midsummer 1917, Bethmann realized that "the situation will
become untenable if nothing is done domestically, unless there are
signs of peace in July or August." According to the Austrian
chargé, "even the Left [was] beginning to grow tired of the chancellor," since it was getting impatient with mere promises of peace
and reform. Although refuted in an officious *NAZ* article, Wilson's
attempts to use the threat of democratization against William II
were beginning to tell. Czernin's dire predictions about Austria's
waning strength spread like wildfire in parliamentary circles, and
intermittent strikes in the Ruhr basin revealed widespread discontent. In a provocative article, the *Nationalliberale Correspondenz*
warned that liberal support for a Left-Center bloc "does not at all
mean a life and death pledge in favor of the government," while
Progressives and Socialists publicly committed themselves to demands for immediate reforms. When reporting to the chancellor
about the Stockholm conference, Philip Scheidemann left nothing
unsaid to dramatize the domestic effects of disappointed hopes for
peace and food. Bethmann "agreed with almost all points," only
adding, "if you could only name one French Socialist who thinks
as you do . . . my position would be much better in every respect."
David similarly "voiced a very pessimistic attitude and demanded
a clear conversion to the Russian [peace] platform and domestic
action" in favor of Reichstag suffrage. Visibly impressed, Bethmann
asked for a memorandum that he could use in his coming struggle
in the GHQ. Because of the deterioration of nutrition, the lack of
reform, the loss of faith in victory, the disappointment in ruthless
submarine warfare, and the example of the Russian Revolution,
the Socialist leaders warned that "the inner power of resistance of
our nation is coming to an end." The approaching fourth war
winter made "peace without annexations and indemnities . . . and
a liberal reform of domestic conditions" imperative. Since the approaching Reichstag session threatened to expose "this severe crisis

of morale," the chancellor saw that the hour of decision had come.[45]

While he was in Pless to discuss the papal mediation, Bethmann resolved to force the issue. For two hours he passionately urged William II to embrace reform. Justifying the Easter Message as a result of the moral renewal of the people, he warned: "So far only promises have been made. The nation calls for immediate fulfillment." Shortsighted Conservative opposition had focused "popular pressure on two grievances: Prussian electoral reform and increased parliamentary participation in government." Heeding the imperial *Non possumus!* Bethmann hoped to "renew popular confidence without rapid suffrage liberalization and to maintain the crown's lead" by suggesting an alternative move: "To maintain the unity of the nation and the state and to keep events from becoming critical, it will be necessary and useful to call a few deputies to high office, not as representatives of their parties but as qualified personalities." When the chancellor returned "completely exhausted and without result," his bold initiative seemed to have been fruitless. Thoughts of resignation flashed through his mind, but "the prospects of peace opened by Nuncio Pacelli and the domestic reforms initiated by me made a change of chancellors just before the reconvening of the Reichstag in July undesirable, especially since I knew that our allies possessed considerable confidence in me." Although Hindenburg also threatened to step down, the chancellor on his own authority informed Payer and Center and National Liberal leaders "that the kaiser has assented to my proposal of filling several important government positions with spokesmen of the parties." [46]

Since "almost all regions of the empire and their representatives were in deep depression" the Reichstag session beginning in early July promised to be stormy. In preparatory discussions, Scheidemann, afraid of being outflanked by the USPD, demanded a negotiated peace and electoral reform as preconditions for passing the war credits, and even threatened the ouster of the chancellor. But since the Progressives rejected the imposition of equal suffrage on Prussia by imperial decree, Bethmann hoped to save the day by "exuding confidence" to the party leaders on July 2. Stressing that Hindenburg was "fully satisfied with the military situation," and that peace could not be reached with empty formulas because the Entente was uncompromising, he demanded: "We must persevere without wavering. Any vacillation, any nervousness is only grist for the mill of our enemies." But his emphasis on the success of submarine warfare and his plea, "We must show nerves of steel," had no effect on the excited deputies. "The public mood is ugly," Reichstag president Kämpf countered. "Austria will not hold out, the food situation [is critical], and it is rumored that the navy doubts the effectiveness of the U-boat attacks." When Bethmann replied that Vienna was crying louder than necessary, Erzberger skeptically remarked: "I gather a new winter campaign from the chancellor. That explains the pessimism. We must do everything to keep morale up." Since only the Conservatives dissented from this gloomy view, Bethmann's show of optimism only accelerated the erosion of confidence in his leadership. "He has failed completely. Everything in vain. Apparently he has not made any decisive proposals in GHQ," David noted in bitter disappointment. "He is an indecisive bureaucratic *Kleber* (hanger-on)." In the Ministry of State, Bethmann blamed Pan-German excesses and cautioned that unless the government fulfilled the domestic demands the morale crisis could not be stopped. "It is undeniable that even those parties which reject imperial intervention in a state constitution—with the sole exception of the Conservatives—exhibit an ever increasing desire for quick implementation of practical measures of reform." [47]

Since Bethmann refused to speak in the Constitutional or Budget Committee in order to save his reassurances for the entire Reichstag, the hurried succession of meetings after July 3 did little to restore parliamentary confidence in his leadership. Although a cabinet promise to partition the mammoth Reichstag districts took the wind out of the Verfassungsausschuss's sails, Helfferich, Zimmermann, and Capelle failed to refute deputy Hoch's charge: "Confidence in the government has gone. Hope is dead, and it cannot be resurrected. The German people feel themselves deserted by everyone, by the government and by the parties." Deeply agitated, Bethmann confided to Valentini: "Never before have I seen the Reichstag in such a nervous and volatile mood. The daily news of food riots and strikes has an enormous effect." Although the Socialist threat of bloody revolution during a fourth war winter was exaggerated, "the Progressives and National Liberals press so strongly for an immediate start of electoral reform that I cannot yet predict how the next days will pass in the Reichstag." In order to mend the broken spirit of unity, Bethmann suggested that the kaiser receive the party leaders, including the Socialists, during his coming sojourn in Ber-

lin: "A renewal of August 4 would have a deep impact if it expressed
the emperor's warm feeling for the sufferings of the people, his
readiness for peace, his dislike for annexationist schemes, and his
firm confidence in the victorious outcome of our just, defensive
struggle." He added, "Since electoral reform cannot be accomplished
immediately and the government cannot passively observe the
threatening developments of the public mood, only the rejuvenation
of the government with new men remains; but it will probably soon
have to be followed by a declaration about a revision of the suffrage."
Reopening this touchy question, Bethmann demanded that "the
kaiser must reserve full freedom of action for himself and his government. Should any other policy be immutably decreed for the
duration of the war, I could no longer bear the responsibility for
the conduct of affairs." Even before the Left had pointed the gun
at his head, the chancellor staked his office on electoral reform.[48]

Matthias Erzberger's dramatic exposure of the failure of submarine warfare on July 6 created "a completely new parliamentary
and political situation." His call for a peace resolution of the Reichstag, because *"I do not believe that we can obtain a better settlement
at the end of another year,"* signaled the conversion of the Center
Party to peace and reform and pulled the divided National Liberals
along into an interparty steering committee, established by the new
Center-Left majority. Since Socialist and Progressive caucuses on
the previous evening had favored making parliamentarization a
condition for the passing of war credits, the first session of this *Interfraktionelle Ausschuss* (IFA) debated whether or not to force Bethmann to take some action to assure Prussian electoral reform. As an
alternative to using compulsion or persuasion on the reluctant
Landtag, the reformist leaders charged Progressive deputy Payer
with asking the chancellor for a declaration in favor of equal suffrage
to concretize the vague promise of the Easter Message. Still unsure
of overcoming William's and the OHL's resistance, Bethmann answered: "You should not doubt that I take into full account the
decision of these four parties, i.e. the great Reichstag majority. But
you cannot expect an immediate reply, which I am unable to give
before the decision of the State Ministry and His Majesty." Nevertheless, "the necessity of clarifying the issue before the Reichstag
disbanded again" could no longer be denied, since Eugen Schiffer
made it clear that the National Liberals were convinced that other-

wise "a change of personnel [was] necessary" in the Wilhelmstrasse. In a long and heated conversation with a delegation of Socialist leaders the same evening, "the chancellor said that in general he was very favorable toward free suffrage in Prussia and that he would take his position accordingly." For the first time in the war Bethmann faced a solid majority that favored reform, but it insisted that "the initiative must come from the Reichstag." [49]

Now Bethmann confronted the delicate task of complying with the parliamentary will for action without affronting the emperor, who alone could grant the necessary changes. To resolidify his public position, the chancellor sternly rejected Erzberger's charges in the Budget Committee: "Although I am confident, I am convinced of the seriousness of our situation; but the graver the times, the brighter our courage must shine." Because his private assurances of reform and the National Liberal disagreement on priorities with the interparty committee eased some of the immediate pressure, Bethmann described the situation as "quite grave but not incurable" to the returned William II. When, on the morning of July 8, the chancellor pressed for further concessions, the emperor, "still in favor of plural suffrage" and opposed to the imposition of the Reichstag ballot on the member states, agreed to call a crown council. In a preliminary session of the Prussian cabinet, the chancellor attempted to convert the conservative ministers: "No solution but equal suffrage can be proposed now or after the war," as plural voting would only restore the odious three-class system in a different guise. "The situation is critical and public morale is presently quite low" because of widespread starvation and disappointed hopes for peace. The warnings of liberal monarchist intellectuals such as Delbrück, Meinecke, and Harnack, that the war should appear as a "struggle between capitalist imperialism and a socially progressive Germany," indicated that something had to be done before it was too late. "Hence I consider it imperative for the State Ministry to decide in favor of equal suffrage and to publicize this decision in some manner." Since the parliamentary crisis had not converted any of the opponents of the Easter Message, and he possessed only a majority of one, Bethmann avoided a vote and insisted on "being free to choose according to H.M.'s decision." [50]

On the morning before the crucial crown council, Stresemann, in the Budget Committee, viciously charged the chancellor with weakness, incompetence, and unfitness for making peace: "In this

hour of grave crisis, must we not make parliament responsible?"
Warning that western parliamentarianism was incompatible with
the federal character of the empire, Bethmann characteristically
replied, "I favor the establishment of closer and stronger ties between government and parliament, appropriate to our constitution, with the intent of leading not to formal Reichstag responsibility but to actual participation." Impressed with the impatience
of the bourgeois parties, the chancellor spoke more passionately
and compellingly to his ministerial colleagues: "I have become
convinced that to avoid great upheavals in the state we can introduce only equal suffrage after the war." To sway the vacillating
emperor he added: "Not for a moment do I deny the gravity of
such a step, but I ask myself whether it is wise to oppose the natural consequence of this struggle of nations." Although there was
"no absolutely just electoral law" taking into account understanding
and responsibility, the chancellor wanted "to avoid glaring injustice
at all costs" and counseled: "H.M. still is free to grant equal suffrage
to the people on his own initiative, and to do so now is my most
humble suggestion." Loebell's counterattack, which appealed to
Prussian tradition in favor of plural voting, failed to persuade because Helfferich vividly retorted that in the present mood of the
Reichstag such a move would be preposterous. Although the five
Prussian ministers still resisted Sydow's warning, *"bis dat qui cito
dat,"* they were joined only by Postmaster General Kraetke, while
the state secretaries Zimmermann, Capelle, Solf, and Lisco supported
reform. Bethmann warned emphatically that, without change, deep
and disastrous conflicts would arise, since "the present government is
not strong enough to continue working with parliament without
equal suffrage." In spite of the force and clarity of the arguments
for action, the emperor nevertheless once more postponed the decision until he could consult the crown prince.[51]

In the end, Bethmann won the constitutional struggle. After a
sleepless night because the empress had made him a scene, William
II conferred with Loebell, Eulenburg, Valentini, and finally also
with his chancellor. "According to one opinion, the proclamation
of equal suffrage means *finis Borussiae;* according to the opposite
contention, not to do so signifies the probable loss of the war and
thereby the demise of Germany and Prussia," the kaiser restated
the dilemma. Although he welcomed the participation of the imperial heir, Bethmann opposed the consultation of Landtag deputies

"as an act unworthy of the crown." He could bear the "undermining of [his] position through the opposition of the Conservatives, Pan-Germans, National Liberals, and especially through the widely known enmity of the OHL," but the collapse of his support in the Center-Left made him "ask H.M. to consider if it would not be better to change chancellors." In a dramatic plea for a democratic and social empire, Bethmann added that "any chancellor has to demand equal suffrage and the inclusion of the parliamentarians in the government," which William *"explicitly recognized."* Because he was not demanding reform to save his office—as Loebell alleged —the emperor was visibly moved, sighing afterward to Valentini, "And I am supposed to drop this man who is head and shoulders above all the others?" That same afternoon William II drafted an executive order for equal suffrage and opted for a constitutional monarchy. Later in the evening, Bethmann informed Spahn, Payer, Ebert, and Schiffer that "the kaiser is ready to move," hinting strongly *"that the demand for a free voting system would be fulfilled"* and parliamentary leaders called into the government. The next morning, Bethmann received the long-expected telephone call from the imperial palace: "The crown prince, like he [William II], is convinced that I have to stay and equal suffrage must be conceded." Though angered by the misleading insinuation that the kaiser authorized the change, since "my resignation at present would be dangerous, especially considering our allies," the chancellor could rejoice in the success of reform.[52]

When Bethmann announced the imperial decision for equal suffrage and parliamentarization to the saddened ministers on July 11, Loebell, Lentze, Schorlemer, Trott, and Stein tendered their resignations "to lighten the difficult task of reconstructing the cabinet." Stressing that he, too, had offered to step down, Bethmann concluded, "H.M. has decided against it; I shall continue to bear this burden . . . as long as my strength lasts, my eyes steadfastly focused on the serious dangers facing the fatherland, hoping that the measures presently necessary will be of lasting profit to the crown and the nation." To ease the transition into parliamentary government, Vice-Chancellor Helfferich and other imperial state secretaries also offered their positions and conducted lengthy negotiations with representatives of the new majority parties about the exact constitutional arrangements. Suggesting the appointment of party leaders as imperial state secretaries, and the creation of a War Council consisting of five representatives of the great parties, five members of the Bundesrat, and five state secretaries—i.e. a partial coalition ministry—Roedern and Wahnschaffe gave "the impression that Bethmann and Helfferich certainly believe they will remain in office." When in the late evening the text of the imperial rescript arrived in the chancellery, Bethmann quickly informed parliamentarians and press of the kaiser's order "that the bill regarding the reform of the electoral system of the Lower House, to be introduced into the Landtag . . . must be based on equal suffrage" and be presented "early enough so that the next elections can be conducted according to the new system." The officious *NAZ* commented sanctimoniously, "A step of decisive importance for Prussia and Germany was taken by H.M.'s signature of the pronouncement." [53]

The clamor and confusion of the struggle over the peace resolution robbed the imperial declaration of any lasting public impact. "The papers of the Left considered it a significant step in the right direction," only, like the *Vorwärts* and the *Berliner Tageblatt,* they asked for complete parliamentarization as well. "The Conservative press contended, on the contrary, that the rescript meant the destruction of Old Prussia"; the *Kreuzzeitung* denounced the proclamation as a trick of the chancellor to continue in office, while the *Alldeutsche Blätter* raged: "Disaster is inevitable, *if Bethmann Hollweg is permitted to continue in the chancellorship which he has used for eight years to the detriment and downfall of the German people."* The reaction of moderate editors was hardly more encouraging: though the *Germania* noted a reconsolidation of the chancellor's position, other Catholic and most National Liberal organs denounced the proclamation as too early and too much or as too little and too late. Instead of serving as a platform for the emerging Center-Left coalition, the promise of electoral reform ironically hastened the collapse of parliamentary confidence in Bethmann. Considering "equal suffrage a misfortune," the Right, spurred on by Stresemann's personal enmity, demanded Bethmann's head in ringing resolutions; while the Left, disappointed with the slowness of change, failed to defend him and agreed with Erzberger's charge that "Bethmann misses every opportunity and thereby prevents peace." In theory mortal enemies, the contradictory progressive and reactionary majorities, anchored by an ambivalent Center, joined hands to oust a chancellor who refused to satisfy either fully. By forcing the fall of a man rather than a revision of structure and policy, the victorious Reichstag ultimately defeated itself and cemented the plebiscitary quasi dictatorship of the OHL.[54]

"I am falling not because of real policy differences, but because of personal agitation and intrigues," Bethmann concluded, seeking to vindicate the sincerity of his commitment to reform. Nonetheless, his conversion to making the Neuorientierung more than an ideological defense of the Burgfrieden had been painfully slow. With Riezler, he rejected the western idea of "practical freedom, no regimentation, as few factual concessions of the individual to the state as possible, personal independence, liberty through equality as formulated in the French Revolution." Like Hans Castorp in the *Magic Mountain,* he groped for an intellectual counterpoint to the ideas of 1789. "The best suggestion is Fichte's: Self-realization through the state," in a formula of "freedom through order, the state as a supra-individual organic" whole. Despite his recurring doubts of "whether the transition to equal suffrage will not destroy our highest and truest values" and his incessant questioning "of whether the leap which we are about to make is not too great and too abrupt," Bethmann found no German alternative to parliamentary government. "The decisive consideration for me was and is that any suffrage which does not offer political rights to the masses to the same degree as the duties demanded by this war will clash with the justified desire for a government embodying the will of the people." In his political testament he reiterated: "Even today I do not doubt for one moment the necessity and the correctness of my decision." Despite the irresolvable Rousseauean dilemma "that the true *volonté générale* cannot be grasped or that even equal suffrage does not securely guarantee its expression," the war made Bethmann regard equality of the vote "not as a theory, but as an ethical postulate which is stronger than any justified objection." Although parliamentarization was basically incompatible with the Bismarckian constitution, "the desire that the personal composition of the government express the will of the people manifest in parliament is such a naturally necessary result . . . of the war that it cannot be refused in the long run." Though gradual, Bethmann's transformation from a bureaucratic conservative into an advocate of reform in order to conserve, was genuine.[55]

The only partial success of the chancellor's reordering of priorities in favor of liberalization revealed the severe limitation of his

cautious and piecemeal approach to change. Bethmann often reiterated the structural necessities underlying his middle course. "I
believe that this line must be a diagonal, which is difficult for the
leading statesman, because he then becomes—to speak with Bismarck—an owl upon whom the crows swoop down from Left and
Right." Although he correctly understood that the forced unanimity
of the Burgfrieden required a positive goal such as the Neuorientierung rather than censorship and repression, the chancellor hesitated and temporized in fighting for the constitutional and social
reformation of Wilhelmian politics. Despite his "heroic and martyr-
like struggle against extremism" and his "amazing tenacity and
sobriety," Bethmann was "without boldness and belief in power."
Intellectually and politically sympathetic to Leftist demands for reform, as minister-president of Prussia the chancellor feared Conservative, OHL, court, and bureaucratic resistance to any substantive change that threatened to transfer economic, political, or cultural power to the lower middle class or proletarian elite. Bethmann's
vision of completing the Iron Chancellor's external unification by
reconciling Catholic, Socialist, Radical, and non-German citizens to
the empire through making the state more responsive to their religious, social, constitutional, and national desires, failed to maintain the unity of purpose of August 1914 because, by yielding to
the reform pressure of the Left, the Neuorientierung precipitated
the desperate resistance of dying Prussia. On the other hand, the
chancellor's hesitant gradualism did not suffice to channel the turbulent waters of reform into the quiet stream of parliamentarianism.
A reforming conservative, he ultimately failed to conserve because
he was unable to reform. Bethmann's socially and psychologically
conditioned failure of creative leadership, which merely responded
to the diagonals of power without bending them to his constructive
will, blocked the path to the constitutional evolution of the Wilhelmian Empire. When both extremes joined hands to overthrow the
chancellor in July of 1917, "the German revolution had begun,
aided but not desired by the army leaders, and even by the conservatively inspired heir to the throne." [56]

CHAPTER 11

The Clash of Diagonals

"The present party alignment and our constitutional structure force [me] to rely basically on a policy of diagonals," Bethmann rationalized his style of bureaucratic consensus leadership. "But even the diagonal is a straight line, and I believe I have followed it." In order to act in what he considered the national interest, free from parliamentary pressures, the chancellor ardently hoped "that recognition of practical necessities will overcome the rule of slogans and will thereby prepare the ground for a policy which, regardless of necessary partisan differences, makes the collaboration of all bourgeois parties possible." In such a Sammlung of the moderate elements of Wilhelmian political life (excluding the Socialists), Bethmann sought "to build a bridge between the National Liberals and the Conservatives, so as not to fall under the exclusive domination of the Center." This rapprochement foundered repeatedly on "Bassermann's unreliability and radicalism and the 'little one's' [Heydebrand's] untractable dictatorial strain." National Liberal "political ignorance . . . , desire for parliamentary rule, and unscrupulous exploitation of every serious national crisis for partisan purposes" were aggravated by the Conservatives' tendency "to abandon traditions strongly rooted in the countryside," and "to destroy their long-standing special relationship with the government." Since the only viable alternative, the inclusion of the Social Democrats in a Left-Center coalition, was rendered impossible by the Right's control of the Prussian Landtag, Bethmann, before 1914, failed to establish a firm parliamentary base for a foreign policy of liberal imperialism and a domestic program of gradual reform. Although he knew that "any chancellor only too easily invites the charge of trimming with the wind," he had to rely on shifting parliamentary majorities.[1]

The outbreak of the war offered Bethmann the chance to realize his domestic aim of overcoming the divisiveness of Wilhelmian interest politics. "If the Conservatives demand special consideration from the government, they themselves must show it first," he noted angrily during the July crisis. "Whoever, as in 1909, Morocco, and 1913, not only fails to spare the cabinet, but directly attacks it in an hour of need, and whoever, alleging that the regime does not sufficiently defend public authority, undermines it as the Conservatives ceaselessly do, has lost his right to a special position." Bethmann's psychological break with the Conservatives coincided with a fundamental revision of his attitude toward the Social Democrats. While previously he had hardly disguised his hostility despite limited legislative cooperation and had covered for Police Chief Jagow's "energetic actions" to suppress peace demonstrations, the chancellor viewed his bargain with Albert Südekum as a historic chance to pull the Socialists into the Prusso-German state. Since "a strong majority of the Socialist caucus worked zealously toward making August 4, 1914, a turning point for the party," by concluding peace with the monarchy, Bethmann could launch the Burgfrieden, based on the equal cooperation of all parties. Annoyed by the Right's warning that the social and political opening to the Left "must not lead to the abandonment of the bases of our state and community life," Bethmann countered: "That is an utterly stupid phrase. The Conservatives have for instance maintained before the war that the trade unions undermined this foundation. By and large their work has proven quite positive for the state." When skeptical officials only reluctantly agreed to concessions, Wahnschaffe, the chancellor's closest domestic advisor, counseled, "Presently the imperative of national unity must be uppermost in our minds, and for that we need the Socialists." The voluntary suspension of party politics created a vacuum in which Bethmann could lead unchallenged with the bureaucratic measures he preferred to the irrational emotionalism of mass appeals.[2]

In practice, Bethmann's consensus policy rested not so much on the spirit of August 1914 as on the antiquated state-of-siege law of 1851. Over the chancellor's warning that "its possible military usefulness cannot equal the harm it can do in political and ideological terms," the transfer of executive authority to some twenty generals commanding the army corps districts was retained unchanged. According to a memorandum of the chancellery, Bethmann's responsibility did *not* extend to "the measures taken by the military commanders according to wartime law, since these are an outflow of the Kommandogewalt, for which they are not constitutionally liable."

Though a procedural safeguard granted power only "in so far as the welfare and safety of the fatherland imperatively demand," the commanding generals suspended large parts of the Prussian and other state constitutions, establishing a military quasi dictatorship outside of parliamentary control. By serving as basis for curtailing the rights of free speech, assembly, and strike, Paragraph Nine, which dealt with the maintenance of public safety, created a series of petty army fiefdoms removed from the chancellor's authority, since the generals often failed to comply with the directives of the Prussian minister of war. Only when harassment under the *Belagerungs-zustand* (martial law) became a major source of Reichstag discontent, did Bethmann, to "satisfy a pressing need," approve the reduction of penalties from imprisonment to fines. But since he did not dare to challenge the military source of the emperor's power, the chancellor was largely at the mercy of the district commanders, whose views clashed with his moderately progressive policy.[3]

The most contested aspect of martial law was the direction of censorship. As soon as late August Bethmann telegraphed to the Wilhelmstrasse: "The chief of staff agrees that a premature proclamation in the press of definite demands as victory prizes must be prevented and has sent orders accordingly. Hence where oral influence fails, censorship must be used against excessively annexationist articles." Since "public opinion must show greatest patience and be prepared for long fighting, heavy sacrifices, and potential setbacks, despite justified confidence in a rapid and victorious end," Bethmann warned the Foreign Office: "Especially any discussion of possible land conquests, be it in Europe or in colonies, is completely out of place. Security against further wars in the forseeable future must be the first goal. The press must be tuned to this note." To assure that the censors would intervene against war aims agitation as enthusiastically as against defeatism, Riezler drafted a series of guidelines branding "any doubt about the national spirit and determination of any man, party, or paper [as] illegal, since it limits the impression of German unity and energy." The Wilhelmstrasse's principles culminated in the demand: "The foreign policy firmly directed by the chancellor in agreement with H.M. must not be disturbed in this critical time" by unwarranted criticism. Although the proposed penalties were stricken, the wording modified, and the document sent out as a circular of the war ministry, these guidelines institutionalized the Burgfrieden by outlawing dissent from either side.

But the press attempted to circumvent such political restrictions wherever and whenever possible, and the commanding generals, who were sympathetic to the arguments of the Right, censored more drastically the "unpatriotic subversion" of the Left. "Old Kessel, supreme commander of Brandenburg, bade me come," Riezler recorded one of many clashes. "He is so sad because he is supposed to reprimand the 'national' papers—he calls those of the Right national; the others are the democratic ones and only pretend. I attempted, certainly without lasting success, to explain the tactical necessity" of justice toward both sides. One of the chief means of control, censorship, soon lost much of its effectiveness for the government because of its military tinge.[4]

Aware that the "control of the news and the prevention of undesired opinions must be complemented by the propagation and direction of correct attitudes," Bethmann also launched a positive information policy. Through the official *Norddeutsche Allgemeine Zeitung,* the officious Wolff-Telegraph service, the placing of articles in friendly papers such as the *Kölnische Zeitung* and through conversations with trusted journalists such as August Stein, Theodor Wolff, Eugen Zimmermann, Otto Hoetzsch, and others, the Foreign Office sought to create a public climate favorable to government policy.[5] More formally, he authorized the establishment of bi- and tri-weekly press briefings "in order to give the Berlin representatives of the papers information in as manageable a form as possible and present guidelines in certain questions." Directed by an officer of the deputy general staff, these meetings served as channels of communication for regular, confidential, and secret news and as sounding boards for the response of the media to official policy.[6]

But the incredible maze of competing bureaucratic organs dealing with public opinion, only loosely coordinated by Director Hammann in the Foreign Office, prevented the formulation of a unified policy and vitiated most efforts at control. When the Prussian Ministry of the Interior sought to consolidate domestic propaganda, Bethmann rejected this proposal and insisted that "unified cooperation with the press office of the Wilhelmstrasse, i.e. the chancellor and minister president, be assured under all circumstances." Moreover, the chancellor, afraid of a precipitous collapse of morale if the full truth of the German defeat at the Marne were known, shrank from exposing the falsehood of military denials of any setback or retreat. "Premature hints can only paralyze the very confidence that we need. It seems to me that the gravity and the danger of the times are beginning to make themselves felt. We can probably wait and see." This decision that "enlightenment can only take place gradually and through military events themselves," and the paternalistic and restrictive press policy of the government, contributed heavily to a credibility gap. Bethmann's fear that moderation would lose against the annexationist or pacifist extremes in the free competition of opinions, robbed him of his potentially strongest weapon—appeals to the majority of German citizens, who continued to support him even after the elites had turned away.[7]

Forced underground, extremist agitation developed new ammunition, techniques, and organizations after the outbreak of the war. Disappointment in the failure of expected victory inspired Conservative deputy Maltzahn to complain about Bethmann's leadership to the crown prince, alleging "that in Berlin everyone is against him." Suspecting that the agrarians were behind this plot, the chancellor angrily telegraphed to the Wilhelmstrasse: "Undoubtedly, Conservative intrigues against myself and Delbrück for general political reasons are the cause." Temporarily concealed in the national revival, the enmity of the Right resurfaced when Bethmann, who soberly realized the limitations of German military power, refused to turn the defensive war into a struggle for conquest. "Bülow sits in Berlin and agitates. Together with Tirpitz he is the main villain. Now he looks for a conference where he hopes to rescue the fatherland." Sent to Berlin in early November to gather information on popular morale and intrigues, Riezler was appalled by the nervousness of the ruling circles and the personal slander against Bethmann. "Tirpitz lurks everywhere and spreads a colossal slime" by demanding an armistice to engage in a new naval race against England. "He agitates tirelessly against the chancellor: The same people who started the war unprepared should end it." Uneasiness in the capital centered on Bülow's mission to Rome to keep Italy out: "He is a complete stereotype and pathologically vain." Even after Bethmann had agreed to send his predecessor to the Quirinal, "a circle of Conservatives propagates the rumor that the kaiser is making the generals nervous by intervening everywhere, and at the same time they praise the crown prince to the skies." Although still largely gossip, allegations about the collapse of German diplomacy and resentment against the first assurances about a Neuorientierung provided a core of grievances for the formation of a chancellor fronde obsessed with "overthrowing this destroyer of our nation." Predicting a Conservative complaint to the kaiser about Falkenhayn and Delbrück, Bethmann sighed: "Apparently these people have no understanding of the treasonous nature of their agitation in this serious time." [8]

After initial suppression, the revolutionary and pacifist Left also reemerged as a vocal critic of government policy. The Socialist minority, which had acquiesced in the first vote for war credits only because of the tradition of party unity and discipline, disassociated itself more and more clearly from the progovernment majority in the winter of 1914, since it considered "this war not as defensive but as imperialist in its causes and goals!" Annexationist agitation spurred the establishment of an antiwar movement in a curious dialectic of political extremes. When, in an "intercepted wire message from the Eiffel Tower, Liebknecht [declared that] the entire Socialist Party in Germany opposed the war," the chancellor's advisors considered energetic measures imperative, such as "his expulsion by the Socialists, drafting him into the army, and putting him in a hospital for observation." While Bethmann refused to violate Liebknecht's parliamentary immunity through arrest, Commander Kessel rudely retorted: "We are at war now! Please take that into account and do not make difficulties for me with parliamentary scruples." In the margin of a Riezler memorandum carefully suggesting steps to "put the chief agitators of the intransigent group under lock and key for investigation," Bethmann commented, "Südekum has told me . . . that under any circumstances they will kick Liebknecht out of the party." In order to ensure that the collaborationists would gain a majority in case of a schism, the government could "only intervene if assured of the tacit approval of the right wing." Hence Bethmann rejected the "revival of Redbaiting" suggested by the Conservatives, and "Liebknecht, whom Kessel wanted to arrest at any cost, will not be arrested but drafted," since, as Wahnschaffe remarked, "Liebknecht as soldier is ridiculous but as martyr, dangerous." Insistent on suppressing the "systematic distribution of pamphlets by the opposition wing of the Socialist Party," the chancellor instructed the minister of the interior, "It seems necessary to me to use all means to restrict and prevent this propaganda." To strengthen the revisionists, Bethmann at the same time piloted through the reefs of censorship progovernment books by

Anton Fendrich, and provided collaborators such as Heine and Südekum with opportunities to broadcast their views.[9]

The emergence of a mass annexationist movement in the spring of 1915 broadened the popular base of the chancellor's right-wing opponents, so dangerous because they appealed to the nationalist predilections of the Prussian elites and the emperor. The veritable flood of memoranda and resolutions calling for large territorial annexations, heavy indemnities, and in general a vindictive peace stemmed from "the lack of trust of the energetic people in the will of the chancellor," whom they sought either to pressure into a stronger stand or to replace by a more forceful man. To a friend Bethmann complained: "Here in Berlin people exhaust themselves in intrigues and political pettifogging. A pitiful sight in this great time." Since Erzberger refused to commit the Center to a frontal assault upon the chancellor, the fronde could only engineer the formulation of the war aims demands of German industry and of the Center-Right parties as independent but simultaneous pressure-group actions. After the attempt to placate him in person misfired, Bethmann stressed to the National-Liberal Hirsch the duty of German elites "to acknowledge those reasons which force the government to be reticent rather than to attack its unambiguous pronouncements with secondary pretexts such as the alleged inequality of censorship." Through far-reaching intimations to the party leaders and industrialists that "the situation has changed through the war," making some extension of German power necessary, the chancellor only temporarily assuaged the suspicions of the Right at the risk of jeopardizing the confidence of the Left.[10]

Confronted with such massive propaganda, Bethmann saw no alternative but to "forbid the distribution of war aims memoranda, demanding annexations in the West as far as the Somme and in the East as far as Lake Peipus." Leaving no doubt that "the propagation of your ideas is highly undesirable at the moment," the chancellor approved the confiscation of Pan-German leader Class's annexationist brochure as "necessary for the protection of important imperial interests connected with the conduct of the war."[11] In a passage struck from the final reprimand of General Gebsattel, Bethmann similarly argued: "No man, not even the chairman of the Pan-German League, has the right to accuse the government of renouncing our conquests if his suspicion is based only on hearsay and the fact that the government still prevents public discussion of war aims for reason of defense and foreign policy." But censorship and repression fed the rumor mill with absurd claims. "I have never told anyone that we will return Belgium," he angrily noted. "This allegation of Strantz [a conservative publicist] is therefore a bold-faced lie." In such cases the chancellor was not above using pressure on the war ministry to reprimand the culprit. Despite the open sympathy of some commanding generals for the annexationist fronde, Bethmann faced the mounting pressure with equanimity, reassuring Hertling: "The intrigues and agitation of certain circles are unpleasant enough but they can be borne if need be," as long as he was sure of the support of the member states.[12] Time and again he intervened with Kessel to censor Reventlow's "whipping up and martialling of public opinion," to lift restrictions against moderate supporters such as Eugen Zimmermann, and to justify the temporary suspension of the *Vorwärts* with the claim, "We are constantly striving for all possible equity in the handling of censorship." But even a new imperial order charging the commanding generals with careful respect of the central guidelines and the establishment of a war press office "to maintain public confidence in the government and the OHL" brought little improvement, since its capable head, Deutelmoser, could not propagandistically create unity of purpose where there was none.[13]

To steer the National Liberals into more moderate waters, Bethmann sought to discredit the excessive annexationism of the party leadership. "Bassermann's telegram to Buhl (Deidesheim) was intercepted," Riezler jotted excitedly in his diary in midsummer 1915. Since Hammann's "impossible draft" of an imperial proclamation for the first anniversary of the outbreak of the war ("sounding like a confession of collapse") had leaked out, the National Liberal leader telegraphed to a South German party member: *"Der Lange* plans a pronouncement against annexations for the first of August. Take immediate steps against it in Munich." When Riezler brought the deciphered message to the chancellor, "we were overjoyed. Bassermann is like a conceited bubble, bursting when pricked." Repelled by the "idiotic blindness of National Liberal" chauvinism, the chancellor "resolved to press his advantage to the utmost. An amusing scene [followed] with the National Liberal leaders minus Bassermann, whom he had ordered to report to rub their noses in the telegram." The carefully selected Friedberg, Krause, Schönaich-

Carolath, Vogel, Kahl, Schiffer, and Jungk, predominantly moderate and progovernment, listened sheepishly to Bethmann's warning, "If you want war, you shall have it!" As Bassermann's incitement of the Bavarian king against imperial policy was indefensible, Friedberg assured Bethmann that a recent party resolution in Cologne had not been intended as criticism of the government, and Kahl went even further, protesting his complete confidence. But on Stresemann's promptings, the Central presidium of the party, over the sole objections of Schiffer and Jungk, vindicated Bassermann's conduct; and the latter, adding insult to injury, condemned the chancellor as "a man torn by doubts" who should be pressured into a martial stand. Bethmann's bid to recapture the allegiance of the professional and commercial elites of Germany misfired, as they were still blinded by the tinsel glitter of Bülow's Weltpolitik. But when briefing the leaders of the other parties, the chancellor exploited the incident, "forcing himself to speak honestly and firmly. The inflated zeroes like Bassermann are a strange spectacle." As the Pan-German wing of the National Liberals continued to agitate against him, Bethmann confided his revulsion to a friend: "Time and again I am startled by how much personal ambition, intrigue, and deceit abounds in our highest political circles." [14]

Since despite continuing public polarization the Burgfrieden still shielded Bethmann from direct assault,[15] "in the spring of 1916 . . . the focus of the agitation and opposition shifted from war aims to the submarine," the miracle weapon that promised swift victory. The policy struggle within the government provided the domestic foes of the chancellor with authoritative grounds for attacking him in Landtag sessions, in U-boat petitions, and in a stream of newspaper articles and broadsides. Riezler shuddered: "As the great slogans of 'shining armor,' the naval parades, the chauvinist agitation and intrigues of Tirpitz, and Bülow's penchant for phrases undermined our policy before the war, it would now be logical for Germany to perish because of the blind and ruthless plottings of Tirpitz's circle and the utter insanity of those wanting to force submarine warfare." Emphatically imploring Falkenhayn that "unscrupulous articles," if published without restriction, could only create "a deep depression, paralyzing the will to fight," Bethmann succeeded in having the submarine question reclassified as a "purely military matter" for censorship purposes. But when he insulted the popular Admiral Tirpitz into resignation, because of the independent press policy of the Naval Office, the chancellor was greeted with such a storm of abuse that he was forced to lecture the editors: "In politics there are things which one does but does not *say*. Force must be used where necessary, but one should not speak about power at every opportunity." Riezler amusedly observed, "The present excitement against the chancellor is said to be much worse than that of the Berlin citizenry against Bismarck during the constitutional conflict—if speech were unrestricted, hundreds of thousands would spontaneously demonstrate in front of the chancellor's palais." In contrast to the alarmist report of the chief of the Berlin police, Bethmann maintained that discontent chiefly "infected only intellectual circles fanned by skillful propaganda, since the government cannot oppose such charges with convincing reasons in public," but that the excitement had not yet penetrated into the masses and "it seems that my windows will not be broken for the time being." By plainly warning the party leaders in private and public against the dangers of further agitation, Bethmann succeeded in restoring a semblance of calm, but this time the disagreement had been more basic, the struggle harder, and the opponents more numerous.[16]

The continued "raging of the press" against his moderate war aims and submarine policy reinforced Bethmann's conviction that free discussion would only force him to adopt a less responsible course. "The most dangerous agitation comes from heavy industry. But the academic intelligentsia has also gone mad," he complained. "The terrorism is so great that one cannot get any reasonable pen to write or any Conservative or National Liberal sheet to accept sensible articles." To a Conservative critic he explained that the fault lay not with him: "Our conferences have impressed a large number of German papers. The majority of the sheets—here Berlin gives a misleading impression—does not at all oppose my policy, and many organs of the Free Conservatives, the Center, the National Liberals, and not the Progressives alone, raise their voices in support." Protesting his willingness to come to an understanding with his publicist opponents, he stressed: "Personal animosity, always attributed to me but foreign to my nature, will certainly not prevent such a rapprochement when I am convinced that they are willing for the sake of the fatherland." Skeptical about "reversing [the deterioration] of public morale by a lessening of restrictions," the chancellor rejected Loebell's suggestion of freeing war aims discussion as "utterly impossible," and warned that "one should not expect anything miraculous" from such a measure. He merely authorized general discussions about the basic goals outlined in his last Reichstag speech as long as they contained no specific demands. When Falken-hayn replied to a petition of the Imperial Press Association for the lifting of all prohibitions without consultation, Bethmann angrily protested against "constructing a contradiction between political and military censorship" in order to accept the latter and reject the former. Therefore he answered the editors' complaint curtly: "To my regret I cannot promise to lift the ban against the discussion of the so-called war aims, but I concur in the desire that this area of censorship be implemented more mildly." [17]

Halfhearted repression spawned a series of widely circulated, privately printed broadsides opposing the chancellor, which culminated in the notorious pamphlet by *Generallandschaftsdirektor* Kapp. "In the most loyal and patriotic classes the present censorship policy has created the impression of serving not the fatherland but its leaders by protecting them against criticism aroused by their political and economic attitudes." The conservative official charged that "before, at the outbreak of and during the war, our political leadership was not equal to its task, and it utterly lacks political instinct." Dramatically he demanded, "Anybody who has committed as many mistakes as the chancellor (trust in England, scrap of paper, etc.) should resign voluntarily." In a comprehensive bill of nationalist complaints, Kapp assailed his formal superior for failing to pursue unrestricted submarine warfare. "What can America do to us, if it really breaks with us?" he asked in profound ignorance. "We need positive guarantees for our future development as a world power. . . . That is precisely what the chancellor does not want," he continued, harping on the annexationist theme. Appealing to the economic self-interest of the Junkers, Kapp violently denounced price ceilings: "In order to flatter the masses, he brings us . . . to the brink of starvation with his mistaken measures." To this list he added "renunciation of victory over England" as Bethmann's cardinal sin. Universal suffrage, the specter of the Neuorientierung, would be the death knell of Old Prussia: "Hence it is the right and the duty of every German to break the oppressive silence before it is too late." When Bethmann reprimanded the unruly East Prussian bureaucrat, Kapp demanded satisfaction, but because he was not an officer, the chancellor's second, Minister Trott, was able to refuse the ludicrous demand. After acrimonious correspondence and heated discussions about the legality and political wisdom of drastic punishment, Schorlemer finally insisted, "The manner in which Kapp . . . has dragged the dispute on to the personal level is a violation of official discipline which cannot be tolerated." But because of Conservative counterpressure, Kapp was only refused reappointment when his term expired. In this and similar incidents Bethmann was unable to enforce his policy even within the Prussian bureaucracy.[18]

The National Liberal case in the campaign of vilification was formulated by Franz Sontag, a leading Pan-German journalist, under the pseudonym "Junius Alter." Because he felt the chancellor's policy led to an "ochlocratic flood" through the broadening of suffrage, "the destruction of the economic pillars of empire and nation," the propagation of "decadence in philosophy, literature, and art," and the coming of a second Punic War, he implored the people to use their "sacred right to petition the crown during this grave crisis for the removal of a statesman who has achieved such horrible successes and will do even more damage should he remain." The anti-Semitic publisher and subsequent patron of Hitler, J. F. Lehmann, suggested an even more drastic remedy: "We should leave judgment to God, although I would not criticize anyone who shot down a man who is destroying his people." In three scurrilous volumes the volkish publicist, Hans von Liebig, attempted the same task in print by meticulously comparing the incompetent B[ethmann]-system with the foresight of the A[lldeutsche]-system: "Should the war end according to the chancellor's ideas it would mean the eclipse of the German Empire and the destruction of the German people," through a cheap peace and the influx of "the eternal Jew" and the nefarious Jesuit. Repeatedly searched out, arrested, and put under correspondence surveillance, Liebig still succeeded in publishing the first two parts of his pseudoscholarly indictment, but the third was confiscated when it reached the bindery. When Conservative deputy Graefe was caught distributing the chemist's rantings in the trenches, Bethmann complained about "the intolerable situation that Pan-German propaganda against H.M. and his government finds its way into the army without the intervention of the responsible authorities." Although too irresponsible to be taken seriously, the pamphlets of Class, Pudor, Hirsch, Zeppelin, and Bacmeister did eventually weaken public confidence in the government.[19]

By midsummer of 1916 "a powerful and widespread movement coalesced, directed toward the *overthrow* of the present chancellor, Bethmann Hollweg, and his replacement by a 'man with a strong hand.' " In a penetrating analysis, the Bavarian minister of war observed that "many Pan-Germans admit openly that they work with all means toward the chancellor's fall," since they considered his foreign and domestic policy too weak. *"Landed interest,* especially in East Elbia . . . seems to prefer the extension of the frontiers toward the East, while *heavy industry* . . . desires especially the annexation of Belgium, the French mining areas, control over the mouth of the Rhine, and the subjection of England." But both groups were divided between those "trying to make him accept their war aims through *influence"* and those "openly working for the chancellor's fall." The Conservative Party opposed Bethmann "for *domestic reasons"* and hoped for his ouster under the pretext of war aims or peace questions, although because of traditional governmentalism the party disagreed about the manner of hastening this end. "The attitude of the *Center* in the empire is split" between Pan-German sympathizers of the agrarian wing and moderates in the urban and industrial segments of the party.[20]

"Among the *Liberals,* as a mixed party, all directions are represented." While business spokesmen and imperialist ideologues Fuhrmann, Stresemann, Brandenburg, and Schifferer were among Bethmann's most vehement foes, a sizeable segment of the party press and the commerical and financial bourgeoisie, who stood to lose much from an indefinite continuation of the war, "express their confidence in the chancellor." Among the *Progressives* and *majority Socialists* who represented the democratic and radical segments of the middle class and proletariat, only a few opposed the chancellor, while "the *Socialist minority* naturally rejects Bethmann as a matter of principle." To coordinate these diverse discontented groups, the Treitschke student, Dietrich Schäfer, founded the *Unabhängige Ausschuss für einen Deutschen Frieden,* financed by industry and led by chauvinist intellectuals. Controlling over twenty of the large circulation dailies, this cartel of nationalist agitation attempted to capture the allegiance of the Wilhelmian power structure and to mount a counterrevolutionary mass movement against the consensus policy of the chancellor.[21]

Because the scurrilous attacks of the fronde jeopardized his goal that "inner peace must remain the holy legacy of this struggle,"

Bethmann "suddenly decided to bang his fist on the table in the Reichstag." Furiously, he exploded against the underground pamphlets of Sontag and Kapp: "The pirates of public opinion often abuse the banner of patriotism. (Very Good!) They want to attack me under this flag as traitor to the great and strong traditions in which the old parties of this house take justifiable pride. And to prove this they reiterate that I court the Socialists and favor the defeatists." To the deafening applause of the Center-Left parties and the galleries, Bethmann, in a second speech, dismissed the apologetic efforts of Bassermann and Westarp: "Call me optimistic, but I hope that after the war, the conflict that pleases no one among us, the contradiction between *national* and *antinational* parties will have disappeared." All moderates were "touched by this speech. Everyone rejoiced and the Conservatives sat like blocks of ice." Although Bethmann received declarations of support from all corners of the empire, this bold stroke deepened the enmity of the Right. "After the speech, the Conservative Party had to emphasize that its fundamental opposition to the republican, antimonarchical, ochlocratic ideas and the goal of the class struggle which the Socialists like Scheidemann and company continue to profess, cannot be ignored," Count Westarp stubbornly maintained. Similarly, Bassermann reiterated: "One can charge the Pan-Germans with an exaggeration of national feeling, but in their struggle they have often foreseen the course of events more clearly than the Wilhelmstrasse," which he accused of "lacking the necessary energy." Bethmann alone had learned from the war: "It is not I who have invented the opposition between national and antinational [parties] but the Pan-German, Conservative, and National Liberal press," in order to denounce "all others—myself included—who have different views as unpatriotic." [22]

Following Payer's advice that "the government should, without abandoning its position above the parties, fight all excesses," [23] Bethmann attacked the "widely spread and dangerous distrust" which "slowly undermines state and moral authority" on three fronts. In a blistering letter to Kessel, he called for stringent censorship measures against the U-boat agitation. "Since the government is condemned to silence, the proponents of ruthless submarine warfare continue with numerous pamphlets to spread allegations which will have a poisonous effect, since they cannot be contradicted in public."

To set an example, and "perhaps destroy the entire nest of snakes," Bethmann, in a purposefully rude letter to Capelle, branded the rumor-mongering of Admiral Thomsen as "dangerous to the state and unbecoming to an officer," and demanded that "wherever such frivolous machinations appear, they be suppressed with a firm hand." [24] On the positive side, Bethmann reassured Hertling, "I have ordered the military as well as the Prussian civil authorities to launch extensive and persuasive propaganda in order to show the people what is at stake for each individual." Beginning in late August, a series of ministerial deputy conferences in the chancellery discussed measures for improving public morale, but only agreed to the creation of an official newsletter called *Deutsche Kriegsnachrichten.*[25]

Since Bethmann thought private propaganda more effective, he approved the formation of the *Deutsche Nationalausschuss,* "as phalanx of reason," in an attempt to create a mass basis for his policy in the moderate and progressive *Besitz-* and *Bildungsbürgertum* beyond traditional party lines. "I am especially pleased that it sees its main task in cultivating unity domestically and resolution abroad." To one of its leading speakers, he privately wrote, "I owe you heartfelt gratitude for . . . having evoked in such impressive words the spirit of unity and trust against the confused voices which carried odious agitation among the people." But, like all other bureaucratic efforts to sponsor moderate movements, the committee, racked by disagreements between intellectuals and industrialists, was a complete failure, because Bethmann, by refusing permission to discuss war aims in its first countrywide meeting, robbed it of its most effective cause. Hence he confided to Treutler: "No matter how busily we work on organizing the reasonable people, the Conservatives retain the support of heavy industry, army, Pan-Germans, and a great number of unscrupulous agitators and gossips. To be sure, with the general public they will have little success, but they will continue to undermine and spread distrust." [26]

Because the Conservatives constituted the core of the opposition, Bethmann was apprehensive about the mission of his brother-in-law, Count Kessel, to affect a rapprochement between the party and the emperor: "The Conservatives have no intention of changing the personal and practical objectives of their policy. My fall is and remains their first and foremost aim." The kaiser's pardon for past obstruction would "make the gentlemen who had boxed themselves

in and therefore felt deserted, ride quite high again, encourage them
to new machinations, and the result would be a further deterioration of our domestic situation," without bringing about the victory
of the governmental wing of the party. Hence Bethmann toned
down his answer to Kessel, warning that "the unbending opposition
of the Conservatives against the government, previously apparent
only against Bismarck, is a grave liability to the country in present
and future." Further irresponsible agitation could only "drive the
ship of state into more democratic waters than the government itself
desires." Since merely "renouncing . . . the present form of opposition will not suffice," the chancellor proposed a modus vivendi, "in
which the Conservatives, regardless of their irreconcilable differences, change their attitude toward the government so as not to endanger its authority at home and abroad." Although William II
welcomed the official apologies of the party for failing to support his
policies, he pointedly asked that "the Conservatives stop criticizing
decisions" for which he alone was responsible. Although he was convinced that "the Conservatives, propelled by Bassermann, will despite Heydebrand's moderate speech drift more and more into fundamental hostility and cover their intrigues with self-righteous smiles,"
Bethmann made one further effort to turn the party into loyal opposition. In a conversation with Westarp "he belabored the point
that the Conservatives opposed him in order to overthrow him,"
although they disagreed in degree rather than in kind. But by late
1916 the gulf between reformist and reactionary conservatism had
become too wide to be bridged.[27]

The chancellor's most effective but ultimately fatal move to restore public confidence was the appointment of Hindenburg and
Ludendorff to the OHL in order to utilize their enormous popularity. "Despite Rumania, a great burden has been lifted from our
shoulders by the change of personnel in the general staff," Riezler
confided to a leading industrialist. "I hope that the present good
personal and practical cooperation between chancellor and OHL
will exert a beneficial influence on our disgusting domestic quarrels."
In the submarine struggles in the Hauptausschuss, as well as in correspondence with his supporters, Bethmann, though claiming not to
hide behind the military, played this card to the fullest: "One would
be completely justified in saying that in all great questions affecting
the conduct of the war, the Supreme Command and the political
leadership act in closest consultation and harmony." Indeed, Basser-

mann considered "the situation damnably difficult," since "we can and should not rage against the Supreme Command," and by OHL fiat the fronde was forced to call off a major new prosubmarine campaign. But the Hindenburg myth of total victory soon developed its own dynamism, pushing the government toward the domestic and foreign goals of the Right, thereby threatening to provoke revolution. "The political elite is totally incapable of understanding this point, except for a few like Valentini. The kaiser seems to sense it, the generals do not comprehend it. The chancellor knows what might happen." When Bethmann appealed for "sharp measures of censorship against the *Pommersche Tagespost* and the *Goslarer Zeitung*," since "otherwise we will face further excesses of the press," the OHL coldly refused to use its powers, thereby leaving him to the Pan-German wolves. The chancellor's argument that "it is the common interest of the political as well as military leadership of the empire to oppose all attempts to endanger the inner unity of the nation," convinced Ludendorff as little as Wahnschaffe's repeated pleas that, for parity's sake, censorship also had to repress the Right. Although cooperation with Falkenhayn had been troubled, collaboration with the third OHL, which owed its appointment to Bethmann, soon became impossible and Kreuznach itself gradually turned into the headquarters of the fronde.[28]

"To improve our public morale," Ludendorff, in early November 1916, demanded "the freeing of the war aims debate in as wide limits as possible." Unsure of being able to marshal a large following for his pragmatic moderation, Bethmann was concerned that in this case "we must also envisage a more or less open development of the pacifist tendencies and their domestic and foreign repercussions." Since in spite of "all censorship pressures, all reminders, and all propaganda, the necessary degree of internal unity could not be reached," Deutelmoser argued that only free debate between the advocates of annexation and renunciation could "prepare national consciousness correctly for peace." When the Foreign Office, the Imperial Secretariat of the Interior, and the Prussian Ministry of the Interior joined the clamor of the parties and the press for liberalization of censorship, the isolated chancellor reluctantly reversed his stand: "After consideration of all pros and cons . . . I, too, consider the lifting of the present prohibition mandatory," as long as the order "contains some controls against excessive pacifist tendencies" without suppressing all voices for a modest peace.[29]

To prevent "a heightened division of public opinion and an increase in dangerous domestic strife," Bethmann suggested that "the government influence the process of discussion through information, moderation, and direction from the beginning." Stating in a stern circular that "any government measure to influence public opinion in war aims questions is interdicted unless it has been expressedly approved by me," he created a special war aims bureau in the news section of the Foreign Office. To divert parliamentary criticism to the military, the chancellor also proposed the establishment of a central control office to supervise and receive complaints regarding censorship and other decisions of the commanding generals based on the state-of-siege law. In preparation for active leadership of public opinion, Bethmann authorized a major reorganization of the Foreign Office's press section, rejected Ludendorff's suggestion of consolidating propaganda in the chancellery, and put the capable Deutelmoser in charge. In the press briefing that announced the lifting of restrictions, the new press chief stressed that domestic unity "cannot be maintained on the basis of plans for conquest but only by firm faith in the justice of our cause and the duties following therefrom." No longer able to shield his bureaucratic middle course through censorship, Bethmann was thrown into the propaganda struggle for the allegiance of German elites and masses, a task for which he was singularly ill-equipped.[30]

When the chancellor's effort at positive leadership by proposing peace failed in the first days of 1917, and unrestricted submarine warfare was resumed, the domestic agitation redoubled. "The craziest rumors circulate," Riezler noted disgustedly. "The whole fronde seems to fear that the war will end before they have succeeded in overthrowing the chancellor. Now they have nothing else to complain about, do not know where to start, and are getting wilder and more frustrated." At the other extreme, the Socialist majority, though reluctantly agreeing, "maintains its grave reservations about U-boat warfare and rejects any responsibility for it," while the radical minority was openly proclaiming its intention of leaving the party. At the same time "the Conservatives fear for their control of Prussia; with their ideology of the Prussian territorial state narrowly linked to the *Ostmark*-policy, they feel that a liberal solution of the Polish question will subvert Prussian ideals, already tainted by Conservative demagoguery." The fronde was largely financed by "heavy industry [pursuing] a primitive uneducated policy of power, force, and domination, thinking of nothing beyond an increase in industrial might in the West and control of ruined Belgian industry." If the Conservatives' mental set was the authoritarian patriarchalism of the manor, "the alpha and omega of the [robber-barons'] policy is the relationship to the Socialists. This explains all their fears and all their opposition." Such influential papers as the *"Lokalanzeiger* and the *Vossische Zeitung* are completely in the hands of Hugenberg, Stinnes, and Hirsch," who mounted a hate campaign of Northcliffian proportions: "The mob of the Pan-German sheets and the fronde work systematically . . . ; actual power would long have passed into their hands if the government were not independent." Faced with this growing polarization of public opinion and repeated military interference, "Deutelmoser fails completely in theory and in practice." The chancellor was rapidly on the way to becoming "a smoke screen for conflicting interests." [31]

In late February 1917, the anti-Bethmann campaign developed an even more brazen strategy. "On the 25th the frondeurs will meet at the Adlon. The former Jesuit Hoensbroech, Admiral Knorr, and Emil Kirdorf issued the invitations; they plan to debate all day long" how best to overthrow the chancellor. Through a stroke of luck, the government intercepted "the material and will publish it the same day." Riezler gloated, "Thank God they are so stupid." The summons to the clandestine meeting reverberated with outraged indignation: "The present chancellor is not man enough to stand at the helm of the empire during the final struggle for its survival and even less capable of conducting the peace negotiations, especially if the war does not end with a complete victory." The resumption of unrestricted submarine warfare, the renunciation of Belgium, and the impending break with America made it "more than ever our patriotic duty to demand the dismissal of Bethmann Hollweg." The familiar list of the chancellor's sins, covering all his major policies, prefaced a draft petition of the Reichstag: *"Your Majesty will deign to order that diplomacy shall not spoil what our soldiers have conquered by blood and sword."*

If a parliamentary vote of no confidence were to fail, Hoensbroech suggested as alternative a flattering letter to Ludendorff expressing "the German people's boundless confidence in the OHL," and planting a dangerous seed: "If the emperor has to choose between Hindenburg and Bethmann, the latter's removal will be certain." In the actual meeting, attended by some fifty politicians, industrialists, and publicists of the Right, the speakers Duisberg, Knorr, and Hoensbroech criticized Bethmann's weakness, pacifism, reform leanings, and lack of enthusiasm for large annexations. When a "charming article in the *Vorwärts*" revealed Duisberg's claim of acting in Ludendorff's name, William II was "quite embittered about this 'treasonous' agitation against the chancellor, which he considered a violation of the monarchical prerogative to choose his ministers." Since the OHL would not publicly disavow the meeting, Bethmann could use the incident only to improve his parliamentary position. "Great coup with the Adlon Conference like a flare over a night patrol—everybody hides in a grenade hole. Haussmann made a very clever speech, based on my hints," Riezler jotted into his diary. The Progressive leader's revelations in the Reichstag caused a profound sensation, forced Westarp, Fuhrmann, and Schäfer to disassociate themselves from the conference, and revolted moderate and even conservative circles because of the crudeness of the frondeurs' methods.[32]

Since "the attacks of the Pan-Germans . . . strengthen the trust of the masses," Bethmann knew his diagonals were secure as long as the fronde did not receive the open backing of Germany's most popular soldier, Hindenburg. But the man behind the myth, "Ludendorff, characteristically blessed with naïveté, dictatorial instincts, and faith in the effectiveness of the will, is easily misled by the suggestions of the Conservatives and heavy industrialists. The former scream because of the disloyalty and unreliability of the Poles, the latter because of the ingratitude and lack of patriotism of the workers; both are one-fifth right and four-fifths wrong. Hence they are forging an alliance with Ludendorff, who is presently our most indispensable and therefore most powerful man." In close touch with leading fronde figures, Colonel Bauer, the OHL's top domestic advisor, exposed in three memoranda Bethmann's failure to "direct all resources toward the war," his passive acceptance of "the deterioration of German loyalty, morale, and duty" and his "squandering of our reputation abroad." Specifically, Bauer claimed that "Bethmann has long ago lost the favor of the *staatserhaltende* circles by his kowtowing to the parties opposed to a strong monarchy (Jewish liberalism and social democracy) and because of his unfortunate hand in foreign policy." Predicting the doom of the dynasty and thereby of Germany's international power, he attacked the Neuorientierung as effeminate: "History teaches time and again that *yielding* to the popular will leads to certain disaster, since it only makes the people involuntary tools of fanatics who abuse their power." In a curious mixture of traditional conservative and revolutionary volkish ideas, Bauer demanded a political strong man: "We need firm and resolute *Führen* and insight. The present government has neither the mind nor the body for such tasks." Despite William II's warning to Hindenburg not "to let himself be abused by all kinds of people who feel the periodic urge to act as saviors of the fatherland," the third OHL inexorably drifted into open conflict with the chancellor because its unbending will to victory clashed with his more realistic desire for negotiated peace.[33]

Instead of miraculously saving the House of Brandenburg as during the Seven Years War, the Russian February Revolution hastened the chronic erosion of public confidence in the government. There were spontaneous "strikes here and there and the Left increased its demands" for bread, peace, and reform. In the first week of April the Socialist opposition groups formed their own independent party in Gotha spurred on by Spartacist radicals in "fundamental opposition to the ruling system, to the war policy of the government and to the course of the nominal party swimming in the chancellor's wake." On the other hand, the imperial promise of electoral reform and the separate peace efforts with Russia provoked "paroxysms of the Right. The Pan-Germans [pass an annexationist] resolution—they hope that the war will continue because of the stubbornness of our enemies." In order "to overthrow Bethmann at the last moment since he will be invincible with the Neuorientierung when he makes peace," the OHL insisted on the suppression of news from Moscow to counteract dangers stemming from the Russian Revolution. "Hindenburg answered coolly and naively that in 1830 and 1863 the revolutionary bacillus from the East had been stopped by a cordon against Poland. Today a buffer would be far stronger!" But Bethmann objected that excessive severity would only give "the impression of weakness and insecurity," and his advice prevailed in the establishment of new censorship guidelines, which allowed free discussion and prohibited only "articles which point out . . . that here circumstances are ripening for a similar upheaval." [34]

The frustration of three years of inconclusive warfare was becoming unbearable and the policy of diagonals, once a unifying force, began to divide the nation deeply. "The press rages from Right to Left, especially the former, without leadership, without tactics, in blind anger, destroying everything that has so far escaped unharmed." Riezler complained, "I can hardly fend off nameless despair—if the chancellor did not carry on in heroic solitude, one would have to run away." By May 1917 "the mood had worsened in the chancellor's disfavor" in all political circles. Although William II's personal dependence on Bethmann kept him in power, the hostility of the fronde continued unabated, the enmity of the generals grew despite his war aims surrender, and his last oratorical triumph in the Reichstag gravely disappointed the Left because he did not unconditionally embrace peace. Riezler deplored "the utter lack of restraint. Raging of the yellow press. . . . In the GHQ everybody swears there will be peace in June. Nobody knows why. They probably only assume it. They have still not yet understood the war." The soldiers' refusal to admit the gravity of the German situation prevented the chancellor from publicly deflating exaggerated hopes and undermined his efforts to stem unjustified pessimism.[35]

A captured French circular, a "priceless document and indirectly the gravest accusation against Pan-Germans, Conservatives, etc." exposed the corrosion of public credibility, accomplished by this poisonous dialectic of the extremes. Though heterogeneous, the fronde had but one aim, that of "submitting the government to their will and of pushing German nationalism to an extreme." In the unlikely event of Bethmann's reconciliation with the Right, the opposition of the Left "would be even more dangerous for the dynasty and the chancellor." In effect the pacifist revolutionaries "are an ally of the Pan-German fronde, give it its fulcrum, and maintain the equilibrium between the two great contrary powers in Germany, the parties of the *Übermensch* and *Untermensch*." Because of this polarization, the French observer concluded optimistically "that Germany is an enemy destroying itself internally, and therefore condemned to ultimate catastrophe." In early June the diagonals were still functioning, "since the vehement attacks of the Right . . . keep the Left from pressing further forward." But Riezler worried, "In July the Reichstag reconvenes and the constitutional committee will resume its sessions, needing a success. What then?" [36]

Erzberger's sensational attack on the government in the Budget Committee on July 6 completed the collapse of public and parliamentary confidence in Bethmann. Since he was convinced that "a peace resolution and the ouster of the chancellor were imperative," the Center Party deputy had disregarded Bethmann's warning, "It is our common duty, demanded by country and people, to attempt, with all seriousness and confidence, to raise morale and to restore unity." Austrian Foreign Minister Czernin's revelation of the impending doom of the Danubian monarchy, and Bauer's confidential admission of the limits of German resources, spurred the ambitious Erzberger to charge "that our calculations concerning submarine warfare have proven false." In a dramatic conversion from his erstwhile annexationism, he proposed, "We must provide a platform which will make peace possible this year," by drawing up a Reichstag resolution reaffirming the purely defensive purpose of the war. Hushing the shouts of surprise and approval, Ebert suspended the committee meeting, since "we have reached the critical point in our proceedings." Totally "unprepared for Erzberger's coup," Bethmann asked, "Why had he sprung this speech on him 'like Ziethen's ambush' without informing him or any other cabinet member beforehand?" Erzberger's excuse, that "he had previously announced, in the presence of witnesses, his intention to oppose the government energetically" and that he only wanted to "create a large majority for me with this action," failed to placate the chancellor's wrath over this betrayal by one of his closest parliamentary confidantes. The nervous tone of the press, Stresemann's demand for "a change of personnel" as price for Liberal participation in the interparty committee, and David's halfhearted defense left no doubt that Bethmann faced the most severe crisis of his tenure.[37]

Disturbed but not desperate, Bethmann sought to restore his hold on the emerging peace and reform coalition by assuring the Center deputy Spahn, the National Liberal leader Schiffer, and Progressive parliamentarian Payer that he was fighting for new concessions in Prussian suffrage reform. In response to the wish of a Socialist deputation for the acceptance of the Russian peace formula, he stressed, "Time and again I have emphasized the defensive character of the war, indicating as its sole purpose the safeguarding of our existence and our future development." Warning that "unilateral renunciation will get us nowhere," the chancellor added: "I cannot ignore the other parties when attempting to make Socialist support of my policy possible. Otherwise we will have chaos." Despite this reaffirmation of the diagonals, Scheidemann maintained in the Socialist caucus "that Bethmann is quite in agreement with us regarding the *term annexations.*" In the Budget Committee, the chancellor, "stooped, his forehead deeply furrowed," sought to accept the substance of the Left initiative while rejecting its form in order not to provide the OHL with a pretext for intervention. Although from the beginning of the war he had favored a negotiated settlement, Bethmann considered another peace move "absolutely wrong and detrimental in our present situation," since "we would be refused with the same derision as before and even the Russian government would join the chorus of abuse." Because "the people need encouragement, not further depression," he proposed as an alternative that "the Reichstag agree in saying we do not fight for the sake of conquest; we defend home and hearth; we are today as ready as we were in December to sit down with our enemies at any time and discuss peace on such a basis." Although the Independent Socialist, Dittmann, branded this transformation of the resolution as rejection, the chancellor concluded, "Neither the reception of my speech nor my conversations with the party leaders led me to believe that I faced a hopeless situation." Indeed the interparty committee agreed on a less radical text and deputized Payer to present it to the chancellor.[38]

To prevent the consolidation of Bethmann's position, the third OHL now intervened personally on July 7. Since "'there [was] no longer a majority which [supported] the chancellor's policy," Ludendorff seized upon the parliamentary crisis to proclaim, "It is high time for the chancellor to disappear." Pronouncing his "gravest misgivings" about the proposed Reichstag resolution, Hindenburg peremptorily demanded that William II "instruct the government to prevent such a declaration." But Bethmann adroitly intercepted William II on his return from Vienna and argued that he was already working against too defeatist a text. "I consider dragging the field marshal and the quartermaster-general into the Reichstag confusion dangerous, and oppose it." The same evening, Valentini reported the confrontation: "His Majesty received the field marshal and General Ludendorff this afternoon and listened to their military report, but when General Ludendorff wanted to discuss the situation in the Reichstag, he forbade him fairly harshly to meddle in politics, hinting that the gentlemen would have been better advised not to have hurried their trip to Berlin so much; here his political advisers would restore order themselves." Although William II had rejected the military's coup de main, Ludendorff, before his departure, spread the rumor through Stresemann that Bethmann had prevented his meeting with the Reichstag leaders. Since the OHL refused to disown this dangerous lie, "the resentment against the chancellor increased considerably. . . . Even his loyal partisans were losing their faith in him." [39]

Although the crisis of confidence seriously undermined his position, it took a masterful intrigue to bring Bethmann down. The OHL's political henchman, Colonel Bauer, remained in Berlin to plot with Erzberger and Stresemann how to "commit the parties to opposing the Bethmann government regardless of any concessions and to change the peace resolution while preventing its passage." United only in their hatred of Bethmann, the conspirators differed fundamentally in their political aims. Convinced that "his policy led the country from disaster to disaster" and that he opposed a Ludendorff peace, Stresemann, though favoring parliamentarization, still believed in submarine warfare and remained skeptical of the peace resolution. Erzberger, who emphatically demanded Bethmann's resignation, desired a compromise peace and democratization, since he was appalled by the failure of the U-boat campaign. The coordinator of the scheme, Bauer, who was influenced by volkish and anti-Semitic ideas, rejected both points of view and agreed ideologically with "Heydebrand, Westarp, Hugenberg, and Röchling," whose aid he enlisted for his designs. He did not even refuse to mobilize his political archenemies, the Socialists, through Colonel Haeften. "As if on signal, all sheets hostile to the chancellor unleashed a formal witch hunt" against Bethmann, who was defenseless since any mention of the OHL's role in the political crisis was prevented by censorship. When, in the IFA, National Liberal Richthoven declared that his party "will only go along if a change in the system takes place at the same time," and Erzberger repeated the rumor that Bethmann had misinformed the kaiser, David noted "great indignation, and [general] resolve to render this man harmless." On the morning of July 9, Stresemann rose in the Hauptausschuss to deliver the fatal blow. Certain of the support of a massive Center-Right majority, he left nothing unsaid in denouncing Bethmann's bankruptcy: "When a parliamentary speech suffices to cause a crisis like the present one, it is clear that government policy has collapsed." To capture the Left, Stresemann added the novel charge: "The chancellor is by trade unfit. No one is more poorly equipped to conduct peace negotiations, both with America and Russia." As if by magic, he implied, Bethmann's removal would end the bloodshed and bring a victorious peace.[40]

To this opportunistic tirade Bethmann replied with the fervor of patriotic responsibility. "I shall not make the situation more difficult. My person does not matter when the well-being of the fatherland is at stake"; he offered to vacate his office if the Reichstag majority so desired. Rebutting one by one the Right's objections to his policy toward Switzerland, Greece, Russia, Poland, Belgium, and Germany's allies, the chancellor answered proudly: "You charge that I have developed no program at home or abroad. . . . I contend that my policy has followed the same course since the outbreak of the war." He had never opposed submarine warfare as a matter of principle, but as soon as the military situation promised success, "I proceeded to carry it out." Dispelling the myth that he had jealously shielded the emperor from the public, Bethmann boldly hinted at the true reason—the Supreme Command, responsible also for the Polish proclamation and the deportation of the Belgian workers: "Gentlemen, I must urgently warn you against drawing the OHL into domestic politics."

Although the deadening fog of suspicion spread by the fronde dimmed his voice, the chancellor tenaciously defended his "policy of the diagonals" as the sole course capable of reconciling the contradictory demands of the war aims and electoral reform majorities that comprised Wilhelmian politics. He clung to his vision of achieving a freer and more powerful Germany through persistent moderation and reiterated with sober optimism, "Do not formulate a weak declaration, forgive me the word, if you agree on something." Intent on maximizing enemy willingness to negotiate, he elaborated in response to interjections, "No, not a Pan-German resolution, absolutely no boasting in any way!" To disarm Erzberger's charge that "I am so compromised that I am incapable of making peace," he concluded movingly, "I personally mean nothing, the fatherland everything." Though it did not convert those conspirators who were unwilling to listen, this dignified speech enheartened the chancellor's moderate followers and reconsolidated his position despite the hysterical chorus of the chauvinist press. "The chancellor crisis has been overcome," Valentini rejoiced, and Hohenlohe received the distinct "impression that the kaiser is firmly committed to retaining the chancellor." [41]

The positive resolution of the peace issue was complicated by the unexpected defection of many of Bethmann's sincerest supporters in the moderate Center and Left. The agitation of the fronde neutralized the effect of the imperial grant of equal suffrage in Prussia which, though welcomed by many, failed to restore the Reichstag's confidence in the chancellor. Afraid of damaging the papal peace feeler by premature disclosure, the chancellor could not go far enough in unconditionally accepting the peace resolution because of the resistance of the OHL and conservative ministers. Due to his insistence, the interparty committee's formula, "the Reichstag desires a peace of understanding and lasting reconciliation between nations," was modified by Helfferich and Wahnschaffe to include the promise that Germany would, in case of enemy rejection, "stand together as one man, persevere and fight resolutely until its and its allies' rights to live and develop are guaranteed." Confronted with this text, Hindenburg irately telephoned William II that "if the final sentence remained unchanged, the offensive and defensive power of the army would be undermined." While the chancellor's effort to produce a version acceptable to the generals alienated his moderate supporters, the OHL made it known in the Reichstag that "if Bethmann remains, we will lose the war," and Ludendorff "will resign if the chancellor stays on." Lerchenfeld reported pessimistically: "The general confusion is getting worse and worse. Almost all papers demand or predict his resignation." Even such former allies as Ballin and Rathenau urged his retirement, the five reactionary ministers made his ouster a condition of reform, and prominent Progressive papers such as the *Frankfurter Zeitung* and the *Berliner Tageblatt* called for a changing of the guard. Within the Center Party, the parliamentary key, Spahn and Fehrenbach managed to fight the frondeurs to a standoff: "The chancellor shall not be pushed out as long as he is no hindrance to peace." Hence William II could still telephone the Austrian ambassador on the evening of July 11 that the "chancellor crisis has been overcome" through suffrage reform.[42]

Now the fronde played its strongest trump. Intercepting the chauvinist crown prince immediately after his arrival in Berlin, Prussian Minister of War Stein and Colonel Bauer played on his revulsion toward "Bethmann's incredible domestic policy." Persuaded by his father that Bethmann's fall would be detrimental, Prince Wilhelm concluded a temporary armistice with the chancellor, criticizing his policy to his face but agreeing to his continuation in office as "a bad temporary solution." But under the promptings of deputy Maltzahn, he invited Bethmann's most influential enemies, Westarp, Stresemann, Erzberger, Mertin, and David, to discuss the advisability of a change of leadership. Except in the case of the loyal Progressive deputy Payer, who maintained "he had no reason for a *revirement* and a leap into uncertainty," Bauer had done his homework well. Slightly embarrassed by the shadiness of the proceedings, Count Westarp objected to democratization and the peace resolution and thought Bethmann "utterly unfit for the chancellorship." The industrial lobbyist, Stresemann, was even more outspoken: "My party considers a change of chancellors the most urgent imperative [since] he has let quite a dangerous mood develop in the people. Nobody has confidence in him and in his government." Rightist parliamentarian Mertin rejected the peace resolution and emphasized, "we do not believe that he is capable of continuing to govern effectively." The instigator of the crisis, Erzberger, called "cooperation impossible" for reasons diametrically opposed to those of the OHL: "Bethmann must go—he is an obstacle to peace, he misses the right moment for everything and it will not get better, only worse." Instead of supporting the man who had done more than anyone to strengthen the revisionists, David took a Pilatian stand—"If the chancellor subscribes to our program, we have no reasons to demand his fall"—but he denounced the "government's lack of direction [and] the obsolescence of our system." However, when ambassadors Hohenlohe and Rizoff warned that any change would severely disturb the alliance, the crown prince once more yielded, telling Valentini that the chancellor should remain in office faute de mieux.[43]

On July 12, the diagonals which Bethmann had balanced so skillfully for eight years collided in a final violent clash. Using Ludendorff's warning that "if the chancellor remains, we will lose the war even if we win ourselves to death," Stresemann succeeded in committing the National Liberals to oppose him. "Against three votes it was finally resolved that Prince Carolath should declare to Valentini that the crisis could only be overcome if the chancellor went." Based on this precedent, Erzberger used the Socialist demand for the resignation of Capelle and Zimmermann to unite the peace and annexation wings of his party when Spahn physically collapsed: "The Center caucus considers Bethmann's continuation in office as a severe hindrance to peace and hence sees no reason to support him further." While this hostile Center-Right majority was forming in the Reichstag, Bethmann's passionate debate with William II over the peace resolution was interrupted by Lyncker's ominous words, "Kreuznach has telephoned that Hindenburg's and Ludendorff's letters of resignation are on their way." Warned by Stresemann that their bluff was about to be called in the Reichstag, the generals thundered. "It is impossible for me to collaborate with the chancellor in a manner necessary for the benefit of our country," since "his beliefs and deeds [are] a serious danger for throne and fatherland." To underscore the unprecedented ultimatum, Colonel Marschall added, "Ludendorff has stated he will not give in, but he insists on his demand under any circumstances." Chagrined by "this act unprecedented in Prussian history," William and his entourage urged the crown prince to "talk them out of their intention" and, still undecided, ordered the generals to report to Berlin. But the situation was beyond repair, since "letting Hindenburg and Ludendorff go in order to hold the chancellor means the loss of the war." Amidst this frantic confusion, Bethmann decided on the ultimate self-sacrifice: "I said to H.M.: 'Of course the resignation of Hindenburg and Ludendorff is out of the question' and took my leave." Valentini noted dejectedly: "Hindenburg-Ludendorff are threatening to resign! The chancellor has decided to go." [44]

On his return to the Wilhelmstrasse, a distraught Bethmann suggested to Payer that "the members of the parties concerned deal with Hindenburg and Ludendorff directly" in order to arrive at an acceptable text of the peace resolution. "My hint fell on fertile ground," he wrote to William II in renewed hope; "I would most humbly like to ask Y.M. to be received before the field marshal." In desperation William II jotted on the margin, "All this is impossible if we want Hindenburg to stay." Upon hearing of the resolutions of the Center and the National Liberals and the mood of the Conservatives, Bethmann sent the loyal Wahnschaffe to Count Hertling "to prepare him indirectly for the possibility of having to take over the chancellorship." After a soul-searching discussion with Valentini, the chancellor drafted his letter of resignation on the morning of July 13: "The general situation of the Reichstag has, as I cannot deny, developed in such a manner that a future solution can only be achieved if Y.M. has the grace to relieve me of my office." To spare the emperor, "who had de facto abdicated, Bethmann did not mention the true reason, Ludendorff's blackmail," and recommended Count Hertling as his successor, "since he will receive the immediate trust of our allies." William II already held this letter in his hands when the crown prince brought written confirmation of the party declarations against Bethmann and peremptorily demanded that "the chancellor must resign now." To the surprised Hindenburg and Ludendorff, the kaiser nervously glossed over his capitulation: "What do you want? The chancellor is long gone!" This tawdry comedy of errors, which made the unknown but energetic food administrator, Michaelis, interim successor at Plessen's suggestion, revealed that immaturity and ambition had betrayed the parliamentarians into playing the military's game. With a blindness shared by a majority of Wilhelmian elites, the crown prince rejoiced, "This is the happiest day of my life." [45]

"If the combined efforts of both extremes have now made it impossible for me to continue my work, I leave my office with the conviction that my policy will not have to fear the verdict of history," Bethmann proudly reflected upon his fall. Although he seemed "self-possessed and apparently much relieved, the chancellor was outraged about Hindenburg and Ludendorff, who had put a pistol to the kaiser's head with their offer to resign." Admiral Müller found him pessimistic about the future, predicting further declarations of war, grave domestic struggles, and "frequent changes of chancellors." In response to William II's ritualistic gratitude and Lerchenfeld's warm eulogy, Bethmann modestly restated his reforming conservative creed: "It is our present and future task to create, upon this [constitutional] foundation, space for all national forces . . . striving for sunlight and for conscious participation in our political life." Contemplating the larger causes of his overthrow, he placed the prime "responsibility on those authorities who are all-powerful with us and who time and again have sought to derail" his policies—i.e. the OHL and the fronde. When Naumann charged that he should have created a progressive parliamentary majority for himself, he replied that the annexationist prosubmarine bloc had dominated the Reichstag until June 1917, and argued that doing their imperialistic bidding would have been the quickest road to disaster. "At last during the July crisis a majority coalesced with which I could have worked *politically,* not because I had changed from Saul to Paul but because the Center Party decided to drop its annexationist dreams and its deep-rooted fear of liberal domestic evolution." But the impatience of the Left was as instrumental in crossing the diagonals as the intransigence of the Right: "It was not I who refused the establishment of a parliamentary majority but, on the contrary, the first possible Reichstag majority refused me." [46]

The last Great Power statesman co-responsible for the war to fall, was "the loyal servant of his emperor, the good and too honest philosopher Hohenfinow," as sailor Stumpf called him. Count Westarp observed that "Bethmann was ousted because his methods failed and he let the reins slip out of his hands." His bureaucratic consensus policy, so effective in the first months of the struggle, was gradually eroded because the clandestine agitation of the fronde and the peace propaganda of the Radical Left in the long run could not be suppressed by censorship. When the third OHL insisted on freeing discussion on war aims, the chancellor, a master at analysis and cabinet negotiation, failed in the task of creating a popular basis for his moderate aims; and although he retained the respect of the less imperialistic segment of the elites and of a substantial majority of the common people until the end, he proved incapable of leading the Reichstag beyond the careful balancing of the pressures from Right and Left. The defeat of the Old Politics, represented by Bethmann, coincided with a "change of generations in the Reichstag." The chancellor's skill within the inner corridors of power was no match for the opportunistic, emotional mass appeals of Stresemann and Erzberger. Dictated by the sociopolitical structure of the empire, the diagonal in the parallelogram between annexation and self-defense, repression and liberalization, was deflected by the Supreme Command's attempt to tip the balance to the Right or, failing that, to exploit public resentment against such compromise leadership. "The OHL, hostile to a peace of understanding, called upon the parties *favoring* such a peace in order to overthrow the chancellor," and after his fall acquiesced "in a resolution which it had before denounced as detrimental to the fighting power of the army." Unable to bridge the structural chasm of Wilhelmian politics through gradual reform, the chancellor fell before the combined vengeance of the dissatisfied extremes, thus hastening the dangerous polarization of

German politics into social-revolutionary-democratic and reactionary-imperialistic-authoritarian camps. Bethmann himself dimly realized that the catastrophic consequences of this disintegration of the political middle transcended his personal fate: "In the eight days since the Erzberger initiative in the Hauptausschuss, the German Empire has been shaken to the very depths of its foundation." [47]

CHAPTER 12

The Sage of Hohenfinow

The fall from power was both a liberation and a bereavement for Bethmann. Though he claimed, "I can leave my office calmly and proudly," with an unshaken faith in the future of the German people, he was repelled by the utterly disgraceful manner of his overthrow: "I depart without bitterness, but pained at the spectacle that my country has recently presented to the pleased enemy." Since it was clear to him that he could no longer serve his nation because of the enmity of the OHL, Bethmann almost welcomed his ouster: "If the change of chancellors means a step toward peace, then I shall gladly . . . put my own head on the block." Although he could reassure himself that the structural constraints of Wilhelmian politics forced "things [to] continue along the lines of my policies at home and abroad," the psychological adjustment for the fallen statesman was difficult.[1]

Disgusted with "the undignified form" of his ouster, Bethmann faced the personal consequences with quiet serenity. "At first I was glad to have regained my freedom and to be relieved of a situation which had become unbearable long ago." But in the long run he keenly suffered from "no longer being able to carry on the fight" himself. To his collaborator Eisendecher he poured out his heart: "I have had to find my way in many respects. The sudden rupture of all old friendships is part of what was most difficult." Reemerging out of "a kind of stupor, because the accustomed whip does not drive me forward," he gradually sought to "hammer together a new life." The practical tasks of moving his papers and possessions to Hohenfinow and of reassuming responsibility for his estate helped to ease the transition. "In the Bavarian mountains I have rediscovered my old passion for hunting, which the Wilhelmstrasse had almost extinguished in me." He lyrically described the enchanting scenery and the balmful solitude. "But I will need many long days like these in order to become myself again." The eight trying years of his chancellorship had taken a heavy toll.[2]

Withdrawn to his quiet estate overlooking the Oder valley, Bethmann now strove to become what his critics had always accused him of being—the philosopher of Hohenfinow. To those officials who were not afraid to seek out a fallen man, those parliamentary leaders who had not disavowed him, those journalists curious for a glimpse behind the scenes, and those historians eager for a statesman's recollections, the ex-chancellor related "the entire story of his dismissal and the generals' ultimatum." But soon time thinned the ranks of the visitors, and Bethmann began to complain that his "ignorance of political affairs [was increasing] arithmetically," since, in contrast to Bülow, he did not want to pursue people himself. Although "growing outward and inner isolation" brought him the leisure to indulge in his intellectual and musical interests and to reflect upon his past and future, Bethmann found "the purely contemplative life meager. Unfortunately, I do not yet understand how to create a counterweight in agricultural work." Having shaped events for more than a decade, the elder statesman only reluctantly contented himself with philosophic reflection.[3]

Although he continued to search for "some relationship to public life, which I do not want to forgo," the ex-chancellor scrupulously shunned the Bismarckian precedent of angry interference, "because in Germany a dismantled and superfluous statesman had better shut up." He believed that the time had not yet come to speak out publicly, but he nevertheless continued "to follow political events with unchanged interest and—I must emphasize—utterly without bitterness." Afraid that "in the last three months much political capital [had] been wasted" by his faltering successor Michaelis, the ex-chancellor welcoming Hertling's appointment but predicted "a provisional settlement to the taste of Theodor Wolff, who believes frequent cabinet changes to be a hallmark of parliamentary government which could become critical because of our complete lack of papabiles." Riezler surmised that "they would have called Bethmann again had they not been afraid of Ludendorff"; but the ex-chancellor, considering himself "only a spectator," never sought to regain the burden of office. Deeply troubled about the lack of progress of Prussian electoral reform, he fulminated against both "the praetorians and the *crapule*," and denounced the "capital crimes of the Conservatives" as harshly as "the rule of the extremists" of the Left: "But perhaps that is a historical necessity because of the grave malaise of the nation and the state. May God turn all well. Our people still deserve it." [4]

Not content with being a Cassandra, Bethmann sought privately to encourage those political leaders who were fighing for his moderate course of peace and reform. "I beseech you to hold out," he implored Valentini, for "it would be an incalculable misfortune if your clear voice of reason were silenced and our emperor lost this support." Approving the appointment of parliamentary state secretaries, since "it has long been my conviction that this was a necessary development," he predicted that the Right's intransigence, which had sown the wind, would soon be reaping the storm.[5] Although his influence in the capital was waning, the ex-chancellor was encouraged by a speech of the South German Liberal, Prince Max von Baden, which "expressed in almost classical form what I believed in and struggled for." Thanking him for appealing to reason against insanity and to morality against deception, Bethmann argued: "These forces have made Germany what it is today, and during the last generation they have run the risk of being falsified by parvenu imperialism." The line of development from Luther and Goethe to Bismarck did not have to end "in those goals which the luminaries of Pan-Germanism have graced with their name."

In what was to become his political testament, Bethmann denounced imperialism and reaffirmed his basic philosophy of gradualism. Peace and reform were mandatory lest revolution and defeat engulf the country. "We can only do justice to the new tasks, which like all great things contain grave dangers, if we courageously strip ourselves of illusions and recognize the reality of [popular] power in this chaos. Only in this way can we avoid catastrophe and save as much of the old for the new as possible." The ex-chancellor pleaded for a reinvigorated reforming conservatism: "This immense revolution cannot end, the nations cannot be 'absolved' by God or the world from their crimes until mankind decides to turn its back upon the conditions that caused this war and puts something new in their place." The "all-consuming struggle between the two centers of power," military and civilian, had to be overcome by parliamentarization, while rampant imperialism had to be curbed by expanding government beyond the discredited elites. "I do not want to say it is the height of wisdom to establish a full-fledged democratic regime here according to foreign blueprints. But we must recognize the great trend which, written in bloody letters, determines history and act in such a way that the flood will not wash us away." In this clearest statement of his beliefs addressed to his last successor-to-be, Bethmann called for drastic change to preserve what he considered the best in the Prussian and German traditions.[6]

Considering German claims to Courland and Lithuania "a terribly dangerous gamble and deception, not worth staking our existence upon," Bethmann intervened in the struggle over Brest Litovsk to plead moderation. "Never have I presented to the OHL —either the present or an earlier one—a general war aims program whose achievement prolonged the war," he informed Chancellor Hertling of the purpose of his peace policy. "I have always emphasized the necessity of grasping any opportunity for beginning negotiations in order to obtain whatever the military-political situation allowed and whatever was recognized as useful for the country." Only general outlines had been sketched, such as the restoration of the colonies, the elimination of Belgium as enemy glacis, the possible acquisition of Longwy-Briey, the independence of Poland, the improvement of Prussia's strategic frontiers with minimal annexations, and perhaps the formation of Courland and Lithuania as buffer states. The infamous Kreuznach program had been forced upon him as *"military necessity"* by imperial order, and represented "only a preliminary internal agreement binding neither in international nor domestic law." Although the OHL had prevented the acceptance of the "no annexations" formula, his commitment to a compromise peace in the Reichstag "created a completely new situation," leaving his successors free to pursue moderate goals.[7]

But his warning that "we must not spoil the chance for a Russian peace" lest the masses take things into their own hands, was even less effective than his restraint in office. In the internal conflict over the terms of Brest, Cabinet Chief Valentini, Bethmann's last link to the emperor, fell beneath the onslaught of "chauvinistic and reactionary forces. It was understandable that this pack devoured me, the old sinner! But you . . . ?" Since the annexationism of the settlement went far beyond the ex-chancellor's desires, he was vexed by the imprudence of such lack of measure, and though suspending judgment on specific issues like the advance into the Baltic provinces, he concluded: "Our eastern policy seems to me to be *very* risky for the future." Since "the quixotic whims and bloody dilettantism of the OHL" prevailed, Bethmann began to despair of winning the war and to predict "a great *ruere in servitium*." The Pan-Germans' resumption of irresponsible criticism of such a Diktat proved to him "that they still enjoy powerful backing and that disunity and self-deception continue, which must lead to a catastrophe." [8]

Unable to reverse Imperial Germany's suicidal course, Bethmann could only passively observe the disintegration of a system that he had struggled to preserve. "The compass needle is in great confusion. The heavens will us ill. Almost uninterruptedly it has rained on the freshly cut barley. This is a symbol of the great flood rising to our necks." In late spring of 1918 he noted dejectedly, "Everything now depends on the offensive—should it be completely successful, military dictatorship is inevitable and will be welcomed by the people—should it fail, a severe crisis of morale will ensue which none of the present rulers will survive peacefully." Fearing that this gigantic military fling would eliminate all room for compromise, push Wilson more firmly into the arms of the Entente, and fail to bring "not tactical or strategic but political" success, the ex-chancellor glumly predicted, "In short, a Bolshevik peace will become more probable." Similarly, "the Reichstag's incapacity for bringing about orderly change" heightened his apprehensions, since the chauvinistic speeches of Stresemann, the crown prince, and the field marshal "drive the masses to act for themselves and to force war policy into the channels of peace." [9]

Since Ludendorff's last gamble could not pierce the Allied lines, time had run out on the Wilhelmian Empire: "Apparently the front is not holding any longer and the soldiers have lost their nerve. Now peace must be concluded at breakneck speed and an armistice reached immediately." Although the OHL's sudden reversal silenced the noisy opposition of the Pan-Germans and the Fatherland Party, Bethmann, doubtful that this would suffice to overcome Entente suspicion, suggested appealing to Ludendorff's vanity and talking him into heading a popular movement for peace. When the military failure of nerve triggered Count Hertling's resignation, the ex-chancellor's name suddenly reappeared in the gossip of Berlin cafes. "Of course [Bethmann] would be best, because of his savoir-faire, his authority and power. Potential negotiators trust him and the Entente believes that he can hold the German people together." But Bethmann "refused and when I [Riezler] recently hinted at this possibility, he protested in honest anger against it. The old phalanx of his enemies rages at the mere mention of his name." Already "having tasted the cup of bitterness," the ex-chancellor fatalistically recoiled from "taking over the present mess . . . concluding a bad peace, or letting the waves close over the drowning empire and being unable to save it." Rather, he suggested that "only someone who has personal contact with the Reichstag and is not suspect to its majority" could inform the kaiser of the magnitude of the impending disaster. This resignation betrayed his conviction that the inevitable had to take its course.[10]

When Prince Max von Baden's belated efforts at reform failed to restore morale, Bethmann saw his direst predictions of defeat and revolution become reality. "Now the crisis is upon us. Long, long have I foreseen this disaster. But that it would be *this* bitter!" Domestically "the upheaval was inescapable." Prepared gradually during the war years, the empire would be able to adapt; but Prussia, fossilized by the obscurantism of the Conservatives, would fare worse: "Radical change will come too suddenly; parliament and legislation will function but the administration will not follow. And that will prompt horrible convulsions in the military-bureaucratic state." [11] In November Riezler stoically chronicled the Hohenzollern doom: "It is all over. Workers' and soldiers' councils are springing up everywhere, forming more or less Bolshevik republics. Berlin has fallen like a ripe fruit. The troops are fraternizing with the revolutionaries." For the former chancellor the revolution was overshadowed by the fear "that peace will be dictated by the phrase *Germaniam esse delendam.* Wilson's great words are only humbug and intended to hide the rawest power politics behind hypocrisy." Gloomily, Bethmann predicted the apocalypse to come one generation later: "Their *ultimate goal* remains our annihilation so that in West and Southeast the French, at the coast the British, and to the Elbe the Russians, Poles, and Czechs can take our place." [12]

Not only "our enemies' orgies of imperialism, but our own lack of dignity" tormented the ex-chancellor after the military and political *Zusammenbruch* (collapse). In his darkest moments he was close to believing "that our people are incapable of resisting the elemental forces which, like nature, play ruthlessly with men, but time and again my love and faith in our nation keep me from accepting such a fate." Since the old had been outdated too long, "the fall of the ancien regime is almost petty compared to the world historical tragedy of the destruction of a country" by the vengeful victors. Sympathetic to some of the ideals of the new, he was confident that "despite some operatic traits the revolution can do much good." Believing that the "habit of order and industry is deeply" ingrained in the people, he "did not consider the domestic dangers as grave as the foreign ones. Among the latter I also count Spartacism." Because a truly just League of Nations could only have been born in a stalemate, he now predicted "a sham league, built upon imperialist excesses and excluding us from the circle of world powers." All his political work lay in shambles. "The blood and death in which the idealism of these four years ends corrodes my soul." [13]

The shock of "the tumbling of thrones, and the fall of empires," shattered Bethmann's universe and forced him to examine his own contribution to the disaster. The magnitude of the diplomatic and domestic collapse "leaves me only a weak hope. Political passivity is enormous and the decline into democratic pseudoeducation appalling." As a critical and well-wishing observer of the nascent Weimar Republic, he encouraged younger parliamentary leaders like Conrad Haussmann: "Happy are those who can participate in reconstruction. Living in seclusion I can only nourish hope." But despite his refusal to become actively involved because of his monarchist commitment, the ex-chancellor, intent on preserving the continuity of conservative traditions across the chasm, sought to convince his former supporters not to abandon the state to the Left but to stabilize it by cooperation: "The present passivity of the bourgeois parties brings us closer and closer to the danger of a complete victory of the Socialists, busily working in the countryside." [14]

While he was trying to cope with the disasters of the present, the shadow of the past relentlessly pursued the ex-chancellor. "Our horrible calamity strongly suggests [my guilt], and it is child's play to prove that any other course would have been right. But here correctness [of action] and responsibility are confused," he pondered. Following his ouster and increasingly after November 1918, Bethmann attempted to explain his policies in a steady stream of lettters and personal conversations. When a right-wing periodical accused him of sabotaging military preparedness, he called the charge "the most amazing piece of nonsense I have ever seen. . . . Hatred against me becomes so red-hot that it does not shrink from the most absurd slanders." Especially to sympathetic observers like Hans

Delbrück and Friedrich Naumann, he denied that his diagonals were "the same as double-dealing and the wish to offend no party." Thorough in self-examination, the ex-chancellor was nevertheless incapable of admitting the central reason for his political failure, and gradually he began to construct a system of rationalizations to explain his course.[15]

The impending verdict of Versailles prodded Bethmann to defend his, and thereby the Second Empire's, policies in print. "Public self-incrimination and the search for a Jonah" made him "fear that the victim cannot beg the hunters and masochists to put down their spears and whips." But he cordially welcomed Friedrich Thimme's suggestion to edit his *Kriegsreden* in order to counter the most blatant historical falsifications and to prove his essential moderation. "You judge the goals of my war and domestic policies so accurately that I can wish for no better interpreter," the ex-chancellor assured the liberal-conservative historian and publicist. "The nearly classical form of Horst Kohl's edition of Bismarck's speeches" was Bethmann's ideal, since by reproducing all interruptions, cheers, and boos they were vivid, immediate, and not "a collection of sermons." Although preparations for the volume, containing also some of the more important Hauptausschuss addresses, had almost been completed in the last summer of the war, the collapse of the empire postponed its release until mid-1919. "I have read your precise and sovereign interpretation with the greatest attention [and am gratified] that you were able to follow my general judgment in all essential questions," he wrote, thanking Thimme for his extensive historical-critical introduction and his notes describing press reaction. Seeking to lay the groundwork for "a more unbiased and just appreciation of this much misunderstood chancellor," the subsequent editor of *Die Grosse Politik* defended Bethmann's middle course as measured power politics against attacks from both extremes: "May our enemies press the martyr crown of thorns upon Bethmann's head: All the more certainly history will do him full justice."[16]

The publication of the wartime speeches was "but a weak substitute for the personal recollections" of the ex-chancellor. "I still have not yet abandoned my hope that he will begin them," Wahnschaffe wondered. "At present it is difficult for him, because sorrow for our fatherland weighs heavily upon him and he is afraid of being too pessimistic. Nevertheless I do not doubt that he will feel compelled to leave some justification." Instead of collaborating with a historian, Bethmann asked a former assistant in the Wilhelm-strasse, *Legationsrat* Heilbron, to prepare "springboards" on the basis of the official files, from which he could compose more freely. With customary thoroughness, the ex-chancellor went to work and asked Jagow for help: "It would be of great value if I could discuss with you what I intend to publish." The "quick criticism" of his former collaborators speeded the work along, and in the spring of 1919 Bethmann could inform Thimme "in *strictest confidence* that I hope to be able to have my reminiscences, 'considerations about the world war,' so far covering the period up to its outbreak, appear in about six weeks." Although he openly confessed, "I have not yet regained my balance since the publication of the peace conditions," he nevertheless "attempted to take as unpolemical a stance as possible" and to write with statesmanlike detachment. An outline of his own decisions and positions in the first five years of his chancellorship, tempered by the bitterness of their failure, the first volume of his *Betrachtungen* stressed the peacefulness and progressiveness of his policies while slighting the fundamental structural obstacles they had to confront. Never denying his responsibility for war and defeat, but only asking respect for his motives, Bethmann sought to shape a tradition of limited Machtpolitik. "Even those who were unable to prevent the catastrophe may still hope that the spirit which made our people heroic will not die but will one day lead us out of the night of domestic and foreign disaster into the shining light." Revealing his practical purpose, the former chancellor gave one member of the German peace delegation "the proofs of my memoirs . . . to read in order to understand my basic goals when negotiating at Versailles." [17]

"I doubt that my book will have a salutary effect in the foreseeable future," Bethmann accurately predicted the intensely partisan reaction to his first volume. "Certainly not in this country; perhaps at some later time in America." The reason was "that I am still too close to the events to be able to write something which will impress the people who think differently, and my pen is not persuasive enough." Led by the rantings of the volkish fringe, the former elites poured out their hatred for the "Destroyer of the Empire" (*Reichsverderber*): "The war had to be lost with a chancellor like him." In Heydebrand's words, "despite his noble character and high intellectual gifts, Bethmann as chancellor was a national disaster." Still under the annexationist spell, Stresemann attacked him: "Bethmann was not a genius, especially since his false orientation and his lack of political instinct were compounded by his resignation, his shying away from a fight." Center Party reviewers deplored that "events were stronger than this man . . . who honestly strove to accomplish his tasks but whose forces were too weak and whose personality condemned him to failure." Prussian intellectuals spread the myth of his weakness: "History . . . judges according to actions and successes; it will deal roughly with Bismarck's epigone despite all the touching explanations of his book." Only a few voices in the moderate Center and Left, the core of the Weimar coalition, saw him as a "representative of what is best in Germany," praised his "strong domestic acumen" and his moral earnestness: "Even if Bethmann was no great statesman, the German people must not be ashamed of this man's proud germanity, honest dedication, and passionate good will." Coming full circle, the extreme Left denounced him as a reactionary whose diplomatic naïveté made him stumble into war: "More fatal yet and fraught with dangerous consequences was Bethmann's eastern annexationism, which, slamming the door to peace, inexorably had to—and did—lead Germany into the abyss." [18]

To provide less ammunition for the Diktat of Versailles, the ex-chancellor branded criticism of his own policies as traitorous support of the war-guilt lie. "Putting the burden of responsibility on our shoulders means to declare the enemies guiltless, who for decades pursued plans realizable only in warlike explosion," he refuted Kurt Eisner's sensationalist indictment, based on Bavarian documents.[19] "The Old Regime should have a central clearing office where a common effort can be undertaken." Bethmann consciously sought to prevent an incriminatory memorandum of the German delegation at the peace conference. Though largely successful in this instance, he failed to influence the oppressive peace: "Now everything must perish in the nameless calamity. There remains nothing but silence." [20] Nevertheless, the struggle for Clio's verdict continued, and Bethmann was appalled that Falkenhayn's and Ludendorff's reminiscences failed even to allude to their strong differences. Suspecting a "previous agreement . . . to create a closed phalanx against me," he concluded, "Any guilt of the soldiers must be denied, everything dumped on me." [21]

The ex-chancellor was even more shocked by the "abundant contradictions, lies, and self-congratulations" of Tirpitz's memoirs, but decided to hold his fire since *"at present* little can be gained from revelations and counterattacks unless they are of a scandalous nature." But in an attempt to present his version, Bethmann encouraged the publication of the Pohl diaries, of Müller's critical rebuttals, as well as the release of the political recollections of Jagow, Helfferich, and Hammann.[22] Nevertheless, in several unpublished draft pamphlets he dissected the risk theory, based on the erroneous premise "that our relations . . . with England improved the stronger our navy become." While the hopeless spiral of the naval race, not the largely fictitious "trade rivalry" "provoked a cold war with England" and ultimately hastened "Britain's decision not to remain aloof from a European war but to use it for our subjection," the naval legislation, "a political mistake, possessed the tactical advantage of justifying every new naval expense." Because of high-minded disdain for responding in kind to the generals' and admiral's "personal hatred and untruths," Bethmann, despite his private criticisms, failed to provide an authoritative antidote to the aberrations of naval imperialism, that clearest expression of the illusions of Wilhelmian Weltpolitik.[23]

"Hope for a future revision of the Treaty of Versailles" inspired the ex-chancellor's refutations of German responsibility for the war as well as the critique of popular militarism in the Reichstag inquiry into the causes of the collapse. Resenting the charge stemming from Gooss's disclosures of the Viennese archives, that Berlin gave Austria too much of a free hand, Bethmann pointed to the critic's "failure to mention that England and France did not effectively hold back Russian warmongers." To counteract the misleading impression of one of the editors of the German diplomatic documents, "[Professor] Schücking, who supposedly believes that we wanted a preventive war," the ex-chancellor stressed that French and Russian policies, directed toward Alsace-Lorraine and Constantinople, were at least co-responsible. "Otherwise the Austrian confrontation with Serbia, executed through diplomacy or war, would never have resulted in world war." [24] In the crowded room of the investigating committee, the gray and stooped Bethmann pleaded eloquently: "Not only in words but in deeds have I consciously struggled against letting my freedom of decision be curtailed by uncontrollable passions and emotions." Since any peace and reform policy "did not have a majority in parliament and in public opinion until July 1917," he could not absolve Reichstag and press from hastening submarine warfare. But decisive was "the *soldiers' claim to dictatorship based upon their aspiration to make the final decisions in all pivotal questions, supported by the people at large.*" Although intended merely as self-justification, this indictment of military bonapartism prompted one observer to applaud Bethmann's "superior awareness, making him the sole statesman among politicians." [25]

Instead of clarifying the responsibility of the military and chauvinist elites for defeat and revolution, the Reichstag hearings, by launching the stab-in-the-back legend, became as the springboard for antidemocratic counterattack. "The five weeks during which I was forced to do battle with the U.A. in Berlin were sickening," Bethmann complained. "Reality was even more grotesque than the papers described." The half-investigation, half-trial provided little insight at the price of "an exhibition whose lack of dignity could hardly be topped. Helfferich's explosions nearly succeeded in giving the discredited *Untersuchungsausschuss* a new lease on life." Even more distressing than the radicals' "incredible maladroitness mixed with perfidy" was the "debut of the two dioscuric generals. Their political ignorance made me wince, as when a preacher stumbles in his sermon. Again the field marshal was a puppet in the hand of his assistant, who radiated superiority, lack of discipline, and duplicity." Nevertheless, "the incredible actions of the commission produced the misleading and hence dangerous result that the old regime closed ranks," and Bethmann merely "hinted at the dualism of the two supreme powers" in his subsequent testimony. Offended by the self-incrimination of the Left, the ex-chancellor considered it "impossible to have it out before the commission" and concluded, "the more vulgar the committee became, the more one needed to preserve quiet dignity oneself." Bethmann wailed: "Where will all of this lead . . . ? The destruction of all morality—international, national, and private—is what pains me most. I have abandoned my hope that the basis of the new world order and the future of our country will be a great inspiring ideal." Agreeing with Oswald Spengler's mystifications despite reservations in detail, he feared: "The West is . . . slowly declining. Petty and trivial will be all that comes." [26]

In late 1919 Karl Kautsky's "untrue denunciations from the German archives" forced Bethmann to testify to the Inquiry Committee on his policy in the July crisis. To put the emperor's impulsive and often outrageous marginalia into perspective, the ex-chancellor protested in the *Tägliche Rundschau* "against the publication of marginal notes which did not initiate political actions and *did not form any part of official policy.*" On account of the Socialists' pamphlet assigning sole guilt to Germany, Bethmann called for "the exclusion of Herr Kautsky from the deliberations" of the Commission because of "the legal untenability of a situation where witnesses are forced to reveal facts under oath for which they may be prosecuted legally or morally in the future." Although the attempt predictably misfired, it "made the chairman more thoughtful" and led to the request of written testimony. In a long memorandum, the ex-chancellor defined the "maintenance of Austria-Hungary's position as a Great Power" as a Bismarckian axiom without alternative. The assassination of Francis Ferdinand was "such a crushing blow to Austrian authority [that it] demanded an immediate resolute response. We agreed with this interpretation of the situation, leaving the choice of means to our ally, neither excluding war with Serbia expressly . . . nor demanding it or driving Vienna into it." Admitting the failure of his calculated risk, Bethmann nevertheless justified it as Great Power practice: "Perhaps pacifists may theoretically condemn our acceptance of war with Serbia as a solution to the Austro-Serbian quarrel, but those governments, denying their own history, whose statesmen signed the Treaty of Versailles, cannot band it as a crime." Directed against domestic criticism and foreign vindictiveness, his apology, though surprisingly candid, lacked ultimate clarity.[27] Similarly, Bethmann's revelations of German separate peace moves in 1915 and 1917 convinced few of his public critics.[28]

The Erzberger trial once more forced the ex-chancellor to take a public stand. When Helfferich's successor as minister of finance sued the flamboyant financier for slander (e.g. the pamphlet *Erzberger Must Go!*), the conservative bias of court and press turned the litigation into a travesty, with the plaintiff Erzberger on the defensive against Helfferich's anti-Republican sallies. Though disgusted with the vulgarity of his former vice-chancellor's performance, Bethmann charged that the Center Party leader had misrepresented several of their conversations: "Despite the anxious mood which had arisen in the previous days, I was completely and utterly surprised by Erzberger's démarche of July 6," 1917, which launched the Reichstag peace resolution. The parliamentarian's claim that his action "had intended to form a sound majority basis for Bethmann's policy" was accepted neither by the chancellor nor by the jury. When Stresemann testified that Erzberger had boasted, "it was my purpose to overthrow the chancellor," the Center Party leader's duplicity toward Bethmann could no longer be denied. Moreover, the ex-chancellor publicly destroyed the legend that he had prevented the Supreme Command from meeting with the parliamentary leaders, which Erzberger and the fronde had used so successfully against him. Helfferich's defense, based on the claim of "conscious untruth," was accepted by the court and the libel case dismissed. Bethmann, despite the temptation to avenge his betrayal, had mixed feelings about this outcome: "Heaven be thanked that the Erzberger case is coming to an end. Did Helfferich and the district attorneys not go too far?" Similarly, when in the spring of 1920 one of his most ardent enemies, Landschaftsdirektor Kapp, sought to restore monarchial law and order by putsching, Bethmann did not rally to the standard because he became more and more convinced that "we stand at the threshold of a new era of democracy." [29]

In growing inner and outward isolation, Bethmann prepared the final statement of his political legacy, the second volume of his memoirs. "I have not been able to begin serious work on it partly because of the commission of inquiry and partly because I have not yet achieved the necessary distance." To find the right tone between polemics and recriminations was difficult. "Since I do not have to and cannot give a history of the war, but can only comment on it, I need a measure of inner freedom which I cannot yet attain. It has even diminished in the last months," he sighed to a friend. Considering "personal feuds among those responsible with the express goal of shifting the blame to others undignified and unsuited for serving the renascence of our people," the ex-chancellor strove for a stance that would inspire a moderate and rational reform-conservatism: "Of course in my second volume I shall have to touch upon many points; but here, as in the first part, I shall attempt to be unpolemical." [30]

When his dwindling energies rendered progress more and more difficult, Bethmann hired the young historian, Peter Rassow, to help him sift through the massive documentation and prepare a draft. "For months I have been sitting intensively at work, but I am advancing only slowly. I am no writer and the topic is damnably difficult. Now the summer has almost passed without having had any effect on me." As he wrestled with the problem of characterizing William II, he asked Valentini for advice: "I do not have to tell you what motives inspired my manuscript. What I say between the lines will probably be incomprehensible to the average reader . . . I believe I have spoken only the truth." Because of uncompromising self-criticism, he had to confess late in 1920: "Despite most strenuous labors, no progress with my book. You do not know how it is when spirit and ink fail—and on top of this the pain over past and future, all the more intense the less I can act." Published posthumously by his son Felix, the second part of the *Betrachtungen* attempted to clear the German name from the shame of Versailles, explicate the concepts behind his policies, and tackle the elusive question of guilt. Inspired by the "wish to preserve for peacetime something of the spirit in which Germany grew without an admixture of imperialism, annexationism, and any other -ism," the chancellor's justification remained fragmentary, not only because of its factual incompleteness, but because it was an attempt to reverse in print what could no longer be changed in fact. Characterized by the same restraint and high-mindedness as the first volume, the final part of the *Reflections* was a passionate indictment of the blindness of fate.[31]

"Outward circumstances here were tolerable," Bethmann described his retirement in Hohenfinow during his waning years. "Actually, life has continued in its old tracks." Although the internal and external future of the Republic remained dark, he consoled himself that "my children are fine. Felix is studying economics and agriculture in Berlin. The Zechs [his son-in-law] in Munich have lived through difficult times. I gratefully experience what has remained of the joy of living." Old friendships, his love of music, and extensive reading in Goethe sustained him. "Actually, I keep on trying to raise my spirits with such pursuits," he confessed. The years of responsibility and the bitterness of defeat had left their mark. "This whole summer I was in poor health spiritually and psychologically. Perhaps the physical machine did not want to go on." Estate and village were slowly emerging from the postwar chaos. "Work has improved and become more regular, but the stealing and loafing is still the same. The crop was tolerable, but I am pessimistic for the next year [since] the barley had not yet begun to grow when the frost came." Despite his love of hunting and the prospects of improvement, such as a new barn and new workers' quarters, a Junker existence failed to satisfy Bethmann's deeper needs. "I live alone and almost completely at the writing desk." Remembrances of the past often darkened a present which seemed hostile and bleak. "Spiritual ties of friendship recreating what has been, are, in our difficult times, a precious good, making the pressures of today bearable." But the outward rhythm of life and such tasks as the dedication of a war memorial in Hohenfinow kept the aging statesman from losing himself completely in the political battles of yesteryear. "I delight in your poems every time I take them into hand," he thanked Oettingen. "I still have to read your Goethe. When I finally have completed the damned book, I shall attempt to become a human being again." [32]

In order to be able to live with his share of the responsibility for war, defeat, and revolution, Bethmann struggled toward a quiet stoicism. "When I think back about many events, before and during the war —about the mood of the centennial in 1913, about the war aims conference of Kreuznach on April 23, 1917—then I am overcome by the feeling that our emperor had many traits that oppressed us like a nightmare," he confessed to Valentini in December 1920. "Then the nagging question returns why this burden, which we clearly recognized as such, was not removed in time?" But even with hindsight he found no better solution because of the hubris of William and the German elite. In order to bear these times, "firm despair now seems to be the sole stance for anyone restricted to passive contemplation." Although occasionally "I have angered myself into hopeless pessimism," Bethmann refused to "make diagnoses; the world has turned into a giant insane asylum and one cannot tell whether most of the inmates are curable or not." Similarly, he admitted to Oettingen: "My son-in-law told me the other day he was 'often without hope.' Perhaps that is the attitude one needs." Although "the population was *very* slowly recovering from its revolutionary binge," the chancellor was pessimistic about Germany's prospects as a power: "I do not believe that we are finished intellectuallly. But politically we will always remain fools. Hence the Entente will reach its goal of finally eliminating us as a political factor. . . . In the inescapable world conflicts of the future we will often be and remain the universal whipping boy." Despite his dire predictions, Bethmann affected the air of a none too discontented country squire in his New Year's wish to an old friend:

"May it bring back the healthy optimism which has always characterized you." [33]

In the closing days of 1920 Bethmann succumbed in the gallant struggle against himself. A virulent pneumonia racked his weakened body and the ex-chancellor died, scarcely sixty-four years old. "In the last months he had looked into the future with somewhat greater hope," his son informed a close friend. "Many events had restored his faith in mankind. Hence, retrospectively, one can find his death fortunate." Friedrich Thimme noted: "High personal regard, warming his reserved and lonely nature, and the noisy hatred of his many detractors follow him into the grave." The empty pathos of the public condolences contrasted with the heartfelt eulogy of pastor Passow: "We will not fail to treasure his memory as a man who, despite the deep tragedy that he experienced, was one of the greatest, noblest, and best," a seer among the blind. Those who "followed the bier in the melancholy dusk of a dark winter afternoon" to its resting-place under the shadow of the ancient church steeple "were filled with the painful recognition: he died too early for Germany and himself." With touching simplicity, a *Volksdichter* captured the affection of the people in the crude lines [34] that could no longer reach Bethmann alive:

> Ob heute Deine Sterne sanken
> Dein Volk wird Deiner Treue danken:
> Kanzler a.D. und Philosoph
> Wir grüssen Dich auf Deinem Hof.
>   Gehab Dich wohl auf Hohenfinow! *

Official Germany, however, greeted the fifth chancellor's death with almost unanimous derision. "Herr von Bethmann's chief guilt for our defeat lies not in his foreign policy mistakes, but in his failure as *Führer* of his nation in its struggle." The chancellor's old enemies on the respectable as well as the volkish Right charged him with "weakness" and ranted against the "Bethmann system, infecting our public life" and characterized by "acceptance of a weak government and currying the favor of foreigners." The National Liberals

---

* Although your stars have dipped today
Our people will your faith repay:
Retired chancellor and sage
We greet you on your manorage.
Farewell on Hohenfinow!

and the educated bourgeoisie belittled his memory, scoffing, "his life was always ruled by others" and joined the clamor for a new Bismarck: "Such a man had to be *harmful* and *could never* achieve anything good." Only his former allies in the Center and moderate Left saw him as a statesman "who loved truth and honesty, not usually found in corridors of power." Although recognizing "something of a great man in him" because of his political ideals, the supporters of the Republic deplored "his fatal faculty for adapting to every situation and thereby failing the future; of recognizing right and doing wrong; of hearing the voice of reason and letting it be smothered by strong men, and of noting his protest in the files." Good intentions were not enough for the majority Socialists: "Bethmann's name will be tied to the most fateful and trying time in our history . . . but the people must finally learn that they will not be saved by a *strong man*," only by themselves. To the Communist Left the chancellor appeared "a hero of halfheartedness," the "prototype of the late Wilhelmian era, the passive wrongdoer, who took the responsibility for the mass carnage upon himself, attempting to cover this incredible crime with a philosophical and moral mantle. When world history tore it from him, he stood there, naked and bare, and we beheld a helpless, thin, poor man, attempting to defend himself in stutters." [35]

But "hatred betrays recognition," as Riezler correctly observed. "Small men, petty men, are not hated." For the close circle of his former collaborators, the public verdict that "the German Empire hammered together by Bismarck's art of statesmanship was shattered by Bethmann" went wide of the mark. They knew him "in close conversation, ponderous and full of scruples in the good days, powerful and resolute in times of crisis, as long as he could act. They saw him as sovereign chairman of momentous and decisive counsels. They often viewed him as a master of parliamentary speech in Reichstag, Landtag." To his friends, he was "deeply venerable in the dignity of his grief while our country's misfortune revealed and elevated so much baseness and, together with outward power, so much of inner value was lost." Hence the personal probity of Bethmann's political intent lived on in a circle of former intimates who met to commemorate the chancellor for almost two decades after his death. The moderate leaders of the fallen empire respected his memory as that of a "highly gifted, widely read and idealistic man, free of ambition and other low motives, only desirous to put into practice what he had recognized as right for the welfare of the state and the German people." But this "uncommonly developed consciousness of duty and responsibility" failed, not only in his lifetime but also posthumously, to inspire a political tradition. Defeated by those forces that eventually triumphed in the Third Reich, Bethmann himself traveled only halfway to the Weimar Republic. The political consequences of the failure of his reforming conservatism prevented the integrity and moderation of his Machtpolitik from serving as a symbolic example. But in the half-century after his death, Germany all too often lacked Bethmann's most admirable trait: "the striving for realistic policy without misreading the facts and without nebulous goals." [36]

CHAPTER 13

The Narrow Path of Reason

Midway in history between Bismarck and Hitler, Theobald von Bethmann Hollweg wrestled with German destiny for one decisive decade. Although he lacked their demonic greatness, this enigmatic statesman was nevertheless "the last imperial chancellor who actually governed," since his three successors were only makeshift and stop-gap appointees. Behind William II's colorful show of personal rule, it was Bethmann who shaped the crucial decisions in peace and war. Hence the political intentions and actions of the fifth chancellor were central links in the fatal chain of events leading to the self-destruction of the Second Reich. At the beginning of his chancellor-ship, Imperial Germany stood at the apex of its power, seemingly free to choose between naval imperialism coupled with domestic repression and peaceful economic expansion complemented by gradual reform. By the end of his tenure engulfed in one of the bloodiest struggles of history, the Prusso-German state tottered toward defeat and revolution, deaf to its chancellor's voice of restraint. Because of this extraordinary reversal of fortunes, Bethmann and his collaborators appeared as "the exponents of decline" to contemporaries, who concluded that "a high degree of responsibility for our catastrophe must be attributed to him." But liberal observers wondered if his sin were not one of omission rather than of commission. In the last analysis, it was not the fifth chancellor's moderately progressive aims and limited power politics but the chauvinist hubris of Wilhelmian elites which sealed "the entire immense tragedy of the Bismarckian Empire."[1]

In the heyday of imperialism, Bethmann was a strikingly untimely chancellor. Although the psychological recesses of his mind remain mysterious, his public "stance fitted the political style of Wilhelmine Germany like a fist into an eye." Lacking charm, he appeared "a sober and ponderous pedant as well as a trustworthy man who, after struggling for a conviction, clung to it with stubborn integrity. At the same time, he was a courtier, thoroughly skilled in the small arts necessary to maintain oneself on the slippery royal parquet." Because of his popular image as "doubter, seeker, and agonizer," he was generally respected for his "deep honesty and ethical scruples." To sympathetic minds he possessed much "of the wisdom, understanding, foresight, and sense of responsibility of a true statesman, combined with an enormous capacity for work." In his independence of public opinion and his grasp of the substance of political needs, Bethmann was "a master, an unusual talent, rich in ideas and solutions, perspicacious regarding situations and men, and clever enough to be cunning without deception." A paradoxical blend of reluctance and resolve, the fifth chancellor excelled, not in dynamic activism, but in "defensive energy." Although his alleged weaknesses were his actual strengths, his admirable characteristics ultimately contributed to his downfall. Denounced as weak-willed in his pursuit of world power, Bethmann succumbed because he was not ruthless enough to make his moderate realism prevail against the imperialist mania. In this way, "the hesitation of his nature attuned to compromise became a misfortune for crown and country." [2]

At first largely conventional, Bethmann's political credo grew with his experience of the chancellorship into a sharp awareness of the illusions of Wilhelmian Weltpolitik. "He was one of those conservative Prussian officials who were not fettered by prejudice and possessed a mind open to new solutions as well as the strength and resources to carry them out." The perceptive Ernst Troeltsch called him "the kind of British Tory who accommodates himself to changing times and defuses social tensions by making sacrifices in the interest of the whole." Uncritically subscribing to the Bismarckian tradition, the fifth chancellor set out to transcend it by completing diplomatic unification and reconciling all internal political forces to the Prusso-German state. His reform proposals sprang from the Burkean conviction that to preserve its heritage Imperial Germany had to rejuvenate itself—that evolution was the best antidote to revolution. Unprepared for the intricate chessboard of Great Power diplomacy and not immune to committing faux pas, Bethmann nevertheless grasped the fundamental imperative of foreign policy: Compromise between competing interests rather than bluffing brinkmanship promised lasting satisfaction and stability. When he deviated from such restrained Realpolitik, as in his miscalculated risk of the July crisis and in his vision of Greater Germany in the

form of an economically dependent Mitteleuropa, his defensive aims
were opposed by the rest of Europe as aggressive threats. Realizing
that as a statesman he could not prevent change only channel it,
Bethmann, in the decisive phase of the war, opted for negotiated
peace and domestic liberalization but proved incapable of forcing
the irreversible final step. Although it motivated his constant struggle against chauvinist excesses, his political philosophy provided no
constructive alternative to brutally simplistic Machtpolitik or
western plebiscitarian imperialism, since it shared many of the basic
misconceptions of its ardent domestic and foreign antagonists. Not
without justification could the radicals charge, "His opposition to
the Pan-German warmongers did not flow from a rejection of imperialist policy in principle," only from a difference in degree.[3]

Striving for a course between the extremes, Bethmann's political
methods failed to sober Imperial Germany's intoxication with
Weltmacht. A master at patient bargaining in the inner corridors
of power and at swaying the impulsive kaiser, the fifth chancellor,
because of his suspicion of irrational mass appeals, "neither could
nor would manipulate public opinion or rely on it." Since he lacked
a majority base in the Reichstag because of constitutional tradition,
imperial hostility to parliamentarization, and the political immaturity of bourgeois parties, Bethmann was "time and again forced
to resort to a diagonal policy" of compromising between the conflicting demands of Right and Left. Such bureaucratic consensus
leadership lacked charismatic inspiration and failed to generate any
powerful popular movement for its support, thereby leaving the
government at the mercy of competing interest groups. "His
greatest mistake was not to draw the people openly into his confidence but to depend on the support of the crown, which was misled
by other advisors."[4] Though sometimes responsive to the pressure
for peace and reform, Bethmann's diagonals more often yielded to
the clamor for war and repression. In the balance, such defeats as the
naval race, the miscarriage of justice at Zabern, the military resolution of the July crisis, the proclamation of war aims, the unleashing
of submarine warfare, and the oppressive exploitation of Mitteleuropa outweighed his successes in providing a constitution for
Alsace-Lorraine, nationalizing socialism, launching the German
peace offer, and forcing the promise of Prussian suffrage reform. In
retrospect the ex-chancellor grudgingly admitted to himself that his
struggle against the OHL, the fronde, the imperial entourage, and

the chauvinist majority of Wilhelmian elites had not been resolute enough—that, afraid of the creative leap into parliamentary government, he had gambled away what he had sought to preserve. Incapable of permanently committing the Second Reich to peace and reform, Bethmann's halting implementation of his progressive conservatism proved too weak a prescription to arrest the fatal illness of Imperial Germany, for the remedy itself contained large amounts of the disease.

The defeat of evolution and the triumph of war were not primarily due to a default of individual leadership but to the blind hubris of the Wilhelmian age. The breath-taking dynamism of the second phase of industrialization that made Berlin the economic fulcrum of Central Europe, created an imposing array of physical power that pushed Germany beyond the limits of a saturated and landlocked continental state. This expansion of productive forces, moreover, deepened the structural dichotomy of Prusso-German society, in which a class-conscious proletariat confronted a semi-feudal ruling class, blending the surviving aristocracy with the new prerogatives of *Bildung* and *Besitz*. Thereby, political conflicts turned into interest struggles that left little room for compromise, since the independent bourgeoisie, crushed between capital and labor, could no longer mediate, while the growing white-collar salariat dependent upon industry, and the declining elements of the old middle class provided the popular base for chauvinist appeals. Hampered by constitutional irrationality, parliamentary ambition, and royal irresponsibility, the fragmented system of politics only succeeded in transforming the Catholic *Reichsfeinde* into imperial standard-bearers but continued to exclude the Socialist Party and unions, as well as the non-German minorities. Rather than easing the painful transition to a high industrial mass society, the overwhelming majority of elites were gripped by the ideological fever of imperialism, which infected the lower middle class as well as large numbers of workers and became the fashionable creed of a generation of intellectuals.

A travesty of the Iron Chancellor's politics of realism, Wilhelmian Weltpolitik combined the worst elements of Pan-German chauvinism, Tirpitzian navalism, and Wagnerian anti-Semitism in an explosive complex of defensive inferiority and aggressive superiority. Lacking a firm tradition of pragmatic restraint abroad and gradualist reform at home, the Second Reich became one of the chief sources of international instability; as a latecomer it challenged the established distribution of colonial spoils in order to deflect its social conflicts abroad. But the increasing success of Socialist propaganda among the working classes and the spread of democratic ideas among segments of the bourgeoisie combined into a massive opposition to militant expansion, and divided Germany into two warring nations incapable of lasting consensus. Only temporarily successful in the enforced Burgfrieden, Bethmann's attempt to bridge this chasm by a liberal imperialism was doomed because of the structural and ideological incompatibility of the movements it sought to combine. Incapable of reforming itself and not content with its share of the globe, Imperial Germany was not killed by defeat from the outside or revolution from the inside; it committed suicide.[5]

The impact of Bethmann's failure transcended his personal fate. As a type, the fifth chancellor represented the Old Politics, which played an intricate game for limited ends with limited means, but could not control the psychological, economic, and military forces unleashed by the modern age. From the Stein-Hardenberg reforms to Goerdeler's resistance against Hitler, too many German statesmen understood politics as administrative reconciliation of divergent demands rather than as public debate and struggle. Though in breadth of vision the chancellor clearly transcended the bureaucratic stereotype, he administered power rather than shaped events. His penchant for trying to impose unity from above by suppressing conflict between differing groups only aggravated the discord between reaction and reform and eroded the legitimacy of the Bismarckian Reich. In the last analysis, the enigma surrounding the Bethmann administration arose less as a result of his self-effacing personality than as a result of a system of government that persisted in substituting obedience to authority for participatory consensus.

Because of the impotence of this tradition during World War I, Bethmann's chancellorship served as matrix both for the Weimar Republic and the Third Reich. The blockage of gradual evolution, the discrediting of compromise and reasoned Realpolitik, the polarization of the body politic into revolutionary and reactionary camps, ruptured political continuity and opened the door to the violent oscillation of extremes. Though his social and constitutional reforms prepared for the bloodless transition of power to the Republic's first Socialist government, Bethmann also anticipated the inhuman designs of the Nazi ideologues in the deportation of Belgian slave labor and the encouragement of volkish settlement in the East. Most of his personal and political adherents became reluctant *Vernunftrepublikaner* and, if not emotionally at home in Weimar, were willing to work toward stabilizing the given state. On the other hand, the Pan-German fronde as well as the respectable opposition of the Right assumed the leadership of the antirepublican forces, and some, like Ludendorff, went so far as to embrace the new Führer, who self-consciously styled himself as Bethmann's antithesis. Similarly, the radical Left, acidly scornful of the ineffectiveness and deceptiveness of gradualism, longed for another kind of totalitarian solution, which was equally repugnant to the fifth chancellor. Although other contemporaries stood more convincingly for the peaceful evolutionary alternative, Bethmann's defeat, occurring at a critical time and in a strategic place, exemplified the catastrophic role of Germany's political middle in the first half of the present century.[6]

Since he "suffered and grew under the weight of fate," Theobald von Bethmann Hollweg possessed "not historical, but human greatness." Although he ultimately did not succeed in curbing and transforming Wilhelmian power, the fifth chancellor had struggled manfully not to let the country stray from the narrow path of reason. Despite his instinctive traditionalism, he had painfully realized that Fichte's first dictum, "Love of fatherland must itself govern the state and be the supreme, final, and absolute authority," had to be subordinated to his second imperative that "freedom, including liberty in the activities of external life, is the soil in which higher culture germinates." Despite his justifications of the German case, Bethmann possessed a deep respect for natural and international law, a profound belief in the community of nations, and a clear understanding that one country's gain was limited by the rights of other countries. Rejecting the tradition from Machiavelli to Treitschke that "the purpose of the state is the increase of its power," so often used as justification for the desire for world domination, he rather agreed with the antiannexationist warnings of his teacher Wach: "Since states have sprung from the individual history of peoples rather than from forceful conquest, they have the right to defend themselves but not the license to destroy other nations in order to increase their domains. . . . There cannot be a moral war of aggrandizement and annihilation." But despite his acute sense of responsibility for power Bethmann, as chancellor, time and again felt compelled to override his individual ethical judgment for the sake of raison d'état, thereby incurring a grave sense of personal guilt for the collective transgressions of his country. Rather than a moral absolutist, he was, in Max Weber's dichotomy, a *Verantwortungsethiker,* always conscious of the consequences of his acts or his omissions. Hence he was deeply troubled by the irresolvable tension between ethical impulse and political necessity.[7]

Yet Bethmann's conscience was most heavily burdened by those crucial decisions forced upon him by Wilhelmian hubris against his considered diplomatic or domestic judgment. He would have willingly borne his moral shortcomings, trusting in divine forgiveness, if like the Iron Chancellor he could have looked back on his political work with satisfaction. But he was continually tormented by his feeling of co-responsibility for the disintegration of Imperial Germany since, though clearly seeing the abyss, he had not succeeded in preventing the fatal plunge. In this dual ethical and political failure, the enigmatic and antiheroic chancellor was both accomplice to and victim of the self-destruction of the Second Reich. As Treutler observed in bitter irony: "He perished because of the shadow cast by the light" of his integrity. The price of his defeat in subordinating power to critical and moral reason was first his inner peace, then his family, and in the end his own life. His personal decline was a symbolic counterpoint to the national calamity. Although inclined to view his defeat fatalistically as the result of overpowering forces, the fifth chancellor did not console himself by blaming the impotence of individual man. His belief in human control over destiny fostered an acute feeling of accountability. Thus, his inability to shape events forced him to confront the existential anguish of *la condition humaine.* "When observing in his last years how the graying man passionately debated his nation's destiny under his high old linden trees—himself only a gnarled figure, swinging his walking stick—how he reasoned about the link between guilt and fate," Riezler pondered Bethmann's part in the German tragedy: "a verse of Hölderlin's crossed my mind":

> Would surging hearts rise upward, foaming into soul,
> Were they not dashed upon the silent cliff of fate? [8]

Mitteleuropa: The Cases of Belgium and Poland

The scheme of a middle-European order, "economically and politically our world historical task," appealed to Bethmann as a constructive solution to the century-old problem of strengthening Germany's position in Europe. It was a multiple compromise between the pathological "greed for land, Belgium, Belgrade, and God knows what more" of the war aims movement, as well as the concept of indirect rule suggested by the Liberal Imperialists. Attractive to the kaiser's racism, the military's security consciousness, the business community's interest in markets, and the educated elite's sense of *Kulturmission,* Central Europe became Bethmann's deus ex machina, reconciling the conflicting domestic and diplomatic pressures for a *pax Germanica.* Moreover, by returning to a Bismarckian tradition, such a quasi-federal system assured Berlin primacy on the continent while meeting the demand for restitution of all conquered territories and for liberation of the subject nationalities championed by the radical Left and the neutrals. The chancellor and a "tiny minority of moderates" strove to group Europe around Berlin through voluntary political and economic self-interest in order to achieve the substance of German dominance without its repressive form. But the contradiction between military and economic needs that resulted in harsh exploitation, and the political imperative of creating sympathetic satellites, bedeviled the vision of indirect hegemony from the beginning. Only the effects of German policy toward Belgium and Poland would demonstrate whether the chancellor's attempt to reconcile force and freedom in a German peace would win the allegiance of non-German nations or be rejected as suppression.[1]

The bloody German victories in Flanders Fields left Belgium at Berlin's mercy and presented Bethmann with difficult decisions regarding the future relationship between the two countries. Pressured by William II, the annexationist public, and the generals to "make Belgium disappear," the chancellor initially vacillated between the Foreign Office's advice for "a partition between France, Holland, and ourselves," and the moderates' counsel to "establish a vassal state." When the hope for French separate peace faded with the defeat at the Marne, he began to lean toward a protectorate, involving certain strategic cessions, military control, political as well as economic dependence, but not its complete destruction. To combat the "utterly outdated annexationist ideas of the military and their appalling economic mistakes," the chancellor created "a civil administration under the military governor-general" that was instructed to treat Belgium as a conquered nation, supply the army of occupation, and provide material aid to Germany. Even if the territory was treated as a unit, the order to the *Zivilverwaltung* breathed a spirit of ruthless domination, insisting that "the restless industrial population endangering our supply routes" be moved to Antwerp. Although the civil administration was granted authority over finances, courts, police, local government, and traffic, and eventually included a representative of the Foreign Office, all political decisions were reserved for the governor-general, who was directly responsible to the emperor. Led by General Goltz until December 1914, General Bissing until April 1917, and then by General Falkenhausen, this dualistic military-civilian bureaucracy soon developed its own impetus toward annexation by administration.[2]

Although a few moderates argued that "Belgium ought to be governed with a light hand," official blunders, military vindictiveness, and annexationist proclamations alienated the population. At the fall of Antwerp the emperor's vow, "this city must remain German and the diplomats will be hanged if they don't see to that," was only a mild indication of the *furor teutonicus*. The bloody repression of the franc-tireurs "will never be forgotten. A cavalry officer told of the executions in the small towns, all men from sixteen to sixty, thousands shot in rows on the meadows, every tenth one step forward. The women had to bury them." Coupled with these atrocities were heavy economic burdens. "The generals knew nothing of modesty; today they announced the figures for the Belgian indemnity; they want to raise 480 million in the province of Flanders," while also suggesting the expulsion of the native inhabitants. The physical destruction was severe: "I shall never forget the drive from Brussels to Antwerp, the shell-torn villages, the trampled tomato fields full of dead cows, the ransacked stores, and the grenades in the wonderful cathedral of Mechlin." Compounded by the "bureaucratic weaknesses" of the chief of the civil administration, Maximilian von Sandt, this suffering produced a deep hatred for the German conquerors, and inspired the protests of the historian Henri Pirenne and Cardinal Primate Mercier. "Belgium is a horrible problem which cannot be solved cleanly," Bethmann confided to a friend. Therefore, "We can only search for the least offensive solution." [3]

The stalemate in the trenches made the chancellor retreat from the idea of a half sovereign protectorate: "The right of military occupation would . . . conjure up massacres," and "we cannot close our eyes to the realization that the annexation of large territories with undesirable Walloon populations would weaken Germany enormously." Although seriously considering "a German foothold on the North Sea coast, some degree of military dominance as well as close economic ties," Bethmann now attempted to find a way toward a middle course of dependence coupled with autonomy for Belgium. Despite the mounting stream of annexationist propaganda, the chancellor sought to solve "the Belgian question so as not to hinder the development [of Mitteleuropa], but advance it." Hence he opposed "the tendency toward Germanizing in Belgium and Poland" and attempted to keep "Bissing within political limits" while ignoring "the old jackass, the king of Bavaria [who] topped it all with his speech about the annexation of the mouth of the Rhine." Although he shared the desire that Belgium should never again "become a battering ram of the Entente," Bethmann remained skeptical regarding Bissing's demands that "Germany would have to keep all of Belgium in its hands." Demanding economic and military prerogatives, the chancellor nevertheless was fundamentally convinced that "our future relationship with Belgium has to be based on a free economic community of interests," just as were dealings with smaller neighbors in general. The intention of Bethmann's Belgian policy was "to control, but to let live." [4]

The chancellor's concept of indirect hegemony was continually threatened by the military's naïve demands for "the reduction of the Belgian army to a police force and the right of occupation in the fortresses and on the coast." Such ironclad guarantees were inacceptable to King Albert since they would have reduced the country to a German province. Different concepts clashed: "All that necessitates a complete rule of force—in order to avoid constant friction, troubles, and the continuation of latent war, one would have to control everything, but that is impossible." A second challenge to Bethmann's policy arose from the Rhine-Ruhr industrialists' foundation of the *Industriebureau* in Brussels, ostensibly to aid the economic administration but practically to gain a lion's share of the profits and to eliminate their former competitors. Only after direct intervention by the chancellor was the economic bureaucracy reorganized to exclude the influence of the factory-owners. However, the economic advisory committee, controlled by heavy industry, continued to further the expropriation of private property, forced trusteeship administration, etc., combining private enrichment with professions of patriotism. Despite his opposition to the blatantly self-serving methods of the coal and steel tycoons, Bethmann agreed with the aim of rendering Belgium "harmless, at any rate economically dependent," and authorized the elaboration of a draft treaty "assimilating Belgium to the German customs area and securing the empire's dominant influence in the economic realm." But among the minimal and maximal goals outlined by Foreign Office representative Baron Oskar von der Lancken, he clearly preferred the former, which renounced annexation and repudiated force.[5]

Afraid that he "could not dispose of Belgium at will at the peace conference," Bethmann sought to link the countries politically. "It will be useful to support, visibly, if possible, the Flemish cultural movement in Belgium," he instructed Sandt as early as September 1914. "Independent of the question of the later territorial fate of Belgium, our interests seem to demand that the German Empire gain and secure the position of a natural protector and a reliable friend with a strong part of the Belgian population." Since the Flemings could be expected to view Germany favorably if they owed their freedom to Berlin, the chancellor instructed Bissing: "Aside from gradual approaches to the intellectual and spiritual leaders of the movement, the most extensive propagation of the Flemish language (not giving German a superior place . . .) seems especially important, as well as the transformation of the University of Ghent into a purely Flemish institution and the establishment of a press connection with Holland." Although Bissing preferred a "quieter, purely practical and realistic approach" to the "fantastic castles in the air" of the young Flemings, Bethmann urged the establishment of a Flemish advisory committee to the governor-general, since "appearing as their benefactor can only help us during and after the war." Rejecting the chimera of a kingdom of Flanders, the chancellor stressed that "the negotiations about Belgium will be considerably facilitated if we can point to a strong, existing national Flemish movement which of its own accord opposes the government in Le Havre and its collaborators." In early 1916 Bethmann considered the moment opportune to encourage the formation of a Flemish front through common cultural demands, to be granted by the German administration, and suggested the foundation of a Flemish national council which would slowly assume a political character.[6]

Despite the reluctance of prominent Belgians to collaborate and the outcry of the Walloon intelligentsia, Bethmann began to consider an "administrative separation," i.e. the creation of separate Flemish and Walloon provinces. Since the military also called for "a better kind of dominion after the English pattern," and no one in the Reichstag "demanded the annexation of Belgium any longer," Bethmann in early 1917 telegraphed to William II: "A decisive strengthening of the Flemings, toward which Governor-General Bissing and I have been working for two years, seems to me the best political guarantee of influencing our future relationship to Brussels." Captivated by young Flemish circles in touch with the Pan-Germans, the kaiser enthusiastically ordered "Sandt, so far the chief hindrance, to carry out administrative division." In March 1917 Bethmann received a deputation of the *Raad van de Vlaanderen,* calling for Flemish autonomy within the Belgian state: "Today God makes it possible that in this bloody struggle, Germans and Flemings become aware that in fighting the advancing French, common paths must lead to common goals." The chancellor promised that "as soon as possible the linguistic boundary must become the border between two administrative districts, united under the authority of the governor-general, but otherwise separate." Lastly, he assured the Flemish representatives that "during the peace negotiations and afterwards, the German Empire will do everything that will serve to advance and safeguard the free development of the Flemish nation." [7]

Any positive echo was, however, vitiated by the deportation of Belgian workers. To mobilize non-German laborers more effectively in order to fulfill the exaggerated aims of the Hindenburg program, Governor-General Bissing forced "unemployed and work-shy" laborers to accept employment in Germany "voluntarily" or by sentence. Not disagreeing with the fundamental rationale and unwilling to fight the ever stronger Ludendorff over this "secondary" issue, Bethmann only protested the "abuses in its execution," which clearly violated international law: "I could not have said anything against the OHL's principle that we needed workers in order to execute the Hindenburg program." Although the deportations brought little economic gain, the chancellor acquiesced in them until the outcry of international opinion and the Left finally compelled him to act against this iniquity. After he had investigated the "harm done to our cause through the manner in which the Belgian workers were enlisted," Bethmann reassured Hertling that he had "attempted to pressure the appropriate military authorities for the correction of the worst abuses. These efforts have been successful in so far as no further workers will be deported from Belgium to Germany by force and all those unjustly evicted will be returned." But because of his declining power, the deportations continued in a somewhat less inhumane form.[8]

Bethmann's general aim of establishing indirect hegemony by appealing to political and economic self-interest in Belgium was distorted by a combination of bureaucratic, economic, and military acts of repression. His championship of an indigenous Flemish nationalism appeared not as a grant of self-determination to a suppressed minority but as a brutal expedient of *divide et impera!* Although the chancellor's moderate conception of German domination revealed more political realism than Ludendorff's annexationist fantasies, the domestic constellation of power prevented its execution in a manner acceptable to Belgium. Hence the result was not voluntary association but its exact opposite, stronger hatred against Germany.[9]

If Belgium was the diplomatic and strategic key to western Europe, Poland became the focus of the German struggle with Russia. In the West, Berlin could dispose of the occupied territories alone, but in the East it faced a formidable competitor in its Austrian ally. Because of the Germanizing legacy of the *Polenpolitik* and *Ansiedlungspolitik,* the Prussian Poles and the majority of Russian subjects (except for part of the Jewish community) looked rather toward the Hapsburg monarchy, where the administration of Galicia was almost completely in Polish hands. In Germany the same phalanx of interest groups that clamored for the annexation of Antwerp demanded the incorporation of the largely agrarian lands of Congress Poland to strengthen the social basis of Junker conservatism. Realizing that "we can only live with a free Poland," Bethmann personally favored a more moderate course, since he understood the strength of the

Polish revival. In August 1914, before German policy could be formulated, Berchtold approached him, "wanting to establish as conservative an administration as possible. Of course they intend to annex the whole mess, or partition it and give us a piece on this side of the Vistula." Riezler feared that "once the Polish question is solved the Austrian way, it will be exceedingly difficult to undo." Because there was no alternative that was not fraught with serious drawbacks, Jagow ordered the question to be treated "dilatorily" and Bethmann agreed, "At the present stage of the war, this problem is hardly pressing." [10]

Throughout the first two years of the war Bethmann vacillated regarding Poland. Since "the majority of the Polish population and its leading elements remain passive toward us," the chancellor hesitated to commit himself: "The present state of the war does not allow any prediction about Poland's fate at the conclusion of peace." In general "there is no solution to the Polish problem which would be favorable and safe for us." To obtain the overriding aim of separate peace with Russia, Germany should "return Poland to Petersburg, except for strategic frontier rectifications that are absolutely necessary for us." In case of victory allowing "the rollback of the Russian danger to the East as far as possible," Poland would either "be established as independent state and attached to Germany through alliance and military convention, or united with Galicia, or at least with its Polish part, to [form] an autonomous kingdom of Poland under the Hapsburg crown. The eventuality of dividing Congress Poland between Germany and Austria is not to be considered at present," since a fourth partition would arouse the undying hostility of the Poles. "At any rate our interest demands that we do not make enemies out of the Poles." Since "only a friendly Poland [would] be a steadfast breakwater against the Pan-Slav flood," everything should be avoided which would "irritate the Poles *unnecessarily*. Especially no attempts at Germanizing, no unessential contributions." In concession to annexationist pressure, volkish settlement dreams, and military arguments, the chancellor agreed to the incorporation of a frontier strip including as little as 175,000 or as much as three million Poles. Although objecting to a definite commitment to liberation, in order not to destroy the chance for separate peace with Russia, Bethmann sought to "find ways not to appear as oppressors," indicating that he was moving toward the reestablishment of a Polish state.[11]

In January 1915 Bethmann pushed through the establishment of a civil administration, creating a dualistic bureaucracy subordinate both to the Eastern Supreme Command and the Secretary of the Interior. After the capture of Warsaw in late summer, the "exceptionally intelligent and understanding" General Beseler was appointed governor-general and, despite some frictions, cooperated well with the head of the civil administration, Wolfgang von Kries, since both favored a paternalistic but not vindictive regime. Because of Viennese pressure, Congress Poland was divided into Austrian and German administrative spheres under the condition that "this territorial arrangement shall not prejudice the future discussions regarding the peace treaty." Sent to Warsaw to prevent mistakes of the "stupid *miles,*" Riezler encountered a conflict between military behavior as conquerors and political intent to win Polish sympathies by the appointment of Prince Lubomirski as city president of the capital. Otherwise "everything went well, even the eviction of the legionaries, who gathered from all corners the first day . . . crying for their leader Jozef Pilsudski." The passivist majority of the population preferred neutrality, believing that "the Polish fate would be determined by the Great Powers at the peace table, depending upon the outcome of the fighting." The chancellor's emissary concluded his report: "Our men have the order not to act as if in enemy territory, and to be as careful as possible. They will be mild in fact, yet harsh in form, gruff and benevolent as they are. . . . But will that work?" [12]

Jagow's indecision regarding the fate of Poland encouraged the "alternative of uniting Congress Poland with Galicia (perhaps excluding the Ruthenian part) into one kingdom which would be incorporated into the Hapsburg Empire." Fearing for the fate of the German element in Austria and economic interests in Poland, Bethmann "voiced his gravest doubts" about Burian's proposed "subdualism" and therefore could "only hypothetically take these suggestions *ad referendum.*" Riezler was more explicit: "Austria has lost all power to attract. For economic reasons alone such a creation would long for [Russia] and be anti-German if only because it can never forgive the new partition—cession of the Narev-Warthe line —since we then must Germanize there." When the chancellor's intimate proposed "a protectorate with a constitution giving power to the landed nobility, a German prince as Grand Duke of Warsaw, a military convention, no freedom of movement, a customs union, and no territorial cessions except those to Vienna," Foreign Secretary Jagow argued for "the affiliation of Poland to Austria as the least unfavorable solution for us, provided the necessary economic and military demands are met." According to Riezler, "Jagow wants to give it to Austria *à tout prix:* For God's sake no Poles—meaning primarily no Jews!" Only reluctantly accepting the foreign secretary's rationale, Bethmann intended to use Warsaw to force Vienna into Mitteleuropa: "Then we have to bind Austria economically and militarily to such a degree that it cannot escape and that Poland cannot lean toward Russia." In November 1915 Bethmann assented to the Austro-Polish solution as a quid pro quo for a renegotiation of the alliance on all levels, to which the Austrian foreign minister agreed only provisionally. Since "too much German blood has been spilled in the conquest of Poland for Germany to disinterest itself in the future of that country entirely," the chancellor insisted on strategic frontier rectifications (not a fourth partition), economic prerogatives, etc.[13]

The obstacles facing a genuinely liberal policy were immense. In yet another visit to Warsaw, Riezler was struck by "the hopeless difference of mentality of both peoples . . . and the excessiveness of Polish nationalism, celebrating the capture of the old Polish city, Vilna, by exhibiting maps with the old frontiers, including Poznan and Danzig." Since only a small group of activists favored collaboration, the blunders of heavy-handed administrators struck him with "the hopelessness of the questions of political detail and more so of the entire problem." Governor-General Beseler was "intelligent but weak, afraid, and suspicious. The important things are the minor issues which his staff decides without showing them to him. The chief of his entourage, a General Esch, is the prototype of a dumb soldier, outraged that the people here speak Polish, the theaters perform in Polish, etc." The Hakatist military, "not making war upon Russia but on the civil administration," and "the absolute maverick and crank, George Cleinow in the press office," vitiated all efforts of "the competent civil administration" to foster pro-German sentiment by such measures as the opening of a Polish university in Warsaw. "The terrible cancer of the political soldiers," forbidding, e.g. the celebrations of the 1830 anti-Russian uprising, was compounded by Austrian propaganda and sabotage: "Even without the involvement of both governments Germany and Austria are wrestling for the allegiance of Poland in the hearts and minds of the people." When Beseler was called to Berlin to report on the problems, "it is the same old story, he speaks very well and acts as if everything were perfect," but he was not impressed by the chancellor's belief in "the necessity of friendliness toward the Polish liberation movement." [14]

In early 1916 a mixture of annexationist and Liberal Imperialist pressures prompted Bethmann to reverse his acquiescence in the Austro-Polish solution. With rare unanimity, the rivals Falkenhayn and Ludendorff called for "a more or less independent state under German control," since "from the military standpoint [they] could no longer recommend leaving Poland to Austria-Hungary." Similarly, the *Ostmarkenverein,* the robber barons and magnates of Silesia, chauvinist intellectuals, and spokesmen of the Left demanded the restoration of Poland, disagreeing only about the degree of its dependence on Germany. From Warsaw, Bethmann's cousin Gerhard von Mutius, his friend Hutten-Czapski, and Riezler exhorted the chancellor: "It is best to force the issue immediately, [by granting] independence, including Congress Poland in the German confederation with a special position; declaring war against Russia; conscription, flags, patriotic noise, etc." Beseler's plea "that this irritating and dangerous agitation be terminated as soon as possible by a thorough confrontation with Vienna" reinforced the chancellor's growing resolution. It would be most "effective if a positive program for a German alliance were proposed by the Poles," along the following lines: "Only ceding the smallest possible frontier strip in West and North, necessary for Germany, undivided Congress Poland will become a state, economically and militarily included in the German Confederation, but for the rest self-governing [compensated] if possible by the inclusion of the purely Polish territories between Grodno and Brest Litovsk." In the same vein Bethmann wrote to Hindenburg: "The foundation of a Polish state closely tied to Germany is for us the most useful alternative and we should strive for it." [15]

Once resolved to restore an autonomous Poland dependent upon Berlin, Bethmann confronted Burian, who "had boasted of bringing Warsaw back to Vienna in his suitcase. Of course, they have asked for everything. We based our case on a national Poland with autonomy and declared only that their solution was absolutely inacceptable to us." Although the chancellor's resistance destroyed the Austro-Polish solution for the time being, he refrained from dictating his terms, offering, through Jagow, the Stanislas crown to Archduke Karl Stephan and the annexation of some frontier districts. In midsummer 1916 the Brusssilov offensive and the threat of a Russian "Polonophile proclamation . . . legally reaffirming their promise of autonomy," forced Burian "to agree to Polish independence, but he demands conditions which are four-fifths inacceptable," such as the exclusion of any frontier rectifications and Austro-German equality of political and economic influence. Backed by lengthy memoranda of Beseler and Kries that now supported autonomy without reservations, Bethmann sought to widen the provisional Austrian agreement in further discussions: "Now Burian has accepted the formation of a Polish state which should be tied firmly to Germany by a military convention." But despite this decisive step forward, the form of economic association, the territorial boundaries, and the Austrian administrative condominium were not clarified, and its actual constitution was postponed until after the peace. "If the Polish foundation succeeds," Riezler speculated, "together with a declaration of war on Russia and conscription, we can hold the front even if Austria collapses and perhaps achieve a tolerable peace over the corpse of our Allies." Despite the Prussian Ministry of State's notable lack of enthusiasm about creating an independent buffer state, Bethmann obtained its approval for the restoration of Poland as "the smallest evil." [16]

Although Bethmann intended to let the Polish problem ripen slowly, his hand was forced in early fall of 1916 by the Supreme Command's demand for Polish troops: "The Pole is a good soldier. If Austria collapses, we have to tap new sources of manpower." Because recruitment would be more successful for a future Polish army, the form of the Polish state had to be determined first: "We cannot digest the Poles," he told the Bundesrat, "hence we can only create an independent buffer state that must remain under German influence. The new state shall be Polish and not be Germanized, but the Polish army will be bound to the German army by a convention." Convinced by Governor-General Beseler that "with a proclamation we will easily get 80,000 to 100,000 men," the third OHL accepted the necessity of Polish autonomy and persuaded William II as well. Since "the military use of Polish manpower presupposes the amalgamation of administration," Bethmann suggested to Burian as a face-saving device "their unification on the principle of equality." In order not "to let the favorable moment to draw Poland to our side slip by," the chancellor overcame his scruples: "If these [military reasons] demand it, the political ones have to be overridden." Hence, he left the mercurial Ludendorff the lead in the final conference with the Austrians and, over Burian's resistance, a new compromise emerged. The military organization of the proposed state would be in German hands, while the two government-generals were to continue to exist, to be merged at some unspecified date. "Soon a proclamation will be issued in which, in the name of both emperors, the Poles will be promised the establishment of an independent kingdom after the peace, comprising the conquered Polish territories; immediately thereafter the recruitment of volunteers and the establishment of Polish legions in the occupied territory will begin." [17]

After the basic decision had been reached, Bethmann hesitated once more in order not to destroy the flickering hope for separate peace with Russia. Afraid of alienating the new cabinet in Petersburg by restoring Polish independence, he asked for a postponement of action: "Should it become apparent . . . that separate peace with Russia lies beyond the realm of the attainable, there will be no more obstacles." But domestic hindrances emerged as well when the Conservatives, Free Conservatives, and National Liberals adopted strong resolutions to prevent Polish independence, denouncing it as a "grave danger to the *Ostmarken.*" In reply, Bethmann called "an autonomous state an enormous advantage to Germany." Better than annexation was "making this neighbor a member of our corporation. Alone we are no longer the equal of Russia. We must create a firm block in Europe." To break Prussian resistance, Bethmann stressed "the need, the absolute necessity of organizing the military potential of Poland" as a "political imperative" supported by the OHL. In the Ministry of State, discussions were even more stormy, since Minister of the Interior Loebell raised "grave objections" regarding the security of Prussia's Polish provinces and future relations with Russia. In two long sessions, opinions by the supporters of the Prussian tradition of subjection confronted the advocates of indirect hegemony. Ultimately, Bethmann's reference to military necessity, and the warning that "he believed that he could not bear the responsibility for conjuring up a catastrophe next spring by refusing the manifesto," won the day. What had begun as part of a liberal middle European scheme was now concluded through the pressure of the generals.[18]

On October 28, 1916, "after untold difficulties, and shaking with fear, the Polish deputation arrived from Warsaw," led by Professor Brudzinski. Pleading for "the creation of a strong Polish state, capable of broad development and guaranteeing equality to all its citizens," the delegates demanded the appointment of a regent, the merger of the two occupation zones, the establishment of a council of state, and the formation of an army from the nucleus of the legions. "Soberly, energetically, and only declaring the foundation of a state," Bethmann answered: "Both united empires . . . are willing to establish a Polish state under a king with a Polish army in firm association with both powers—especially in military aspects—a state within whose boundaries the Polish desire for a nationally and culturally independent life will be guaranteed." Despite the outward impressiveness of the ceremonies, Riezler observed, "Never has such an act beeen proclaimed with as little faith and so reluctantly." Typically, the OHL refused to include the word *independent* in the promise of establishing "a Polish state," which enraged Bethmann: "If we want to achieve a military success with the manifesto . . . we cannot hamper it from the outset by a wording that arouses suspicion instead of enthusiasm." Nevertheless, the November 5 proclamation, read by Beseler with great fervor to a multitude of Warsaw dignitaries, promised an "independent state with hereditary monarchy and constitutional government," including its own army. "The great western neighbors of the kingdom of Poland will gladly see a free and happy state, proud of its national existence, rise and flourish on their eastern borders." Welcomed only by a minority of educated and often titled activists, greeted with a mixture of hope and suspicion by the vast majority of the population, and virulently opposed by the pro-Entente intelligentsia, this ambiguous declaration marked the rebirth of the Polish state.[19]

The contradictory motives that prompted Bethmann's support of Polish autonomy colored his justifications to press, Bundesrat, and Prussian parties. Knowing it was based not so much on love or respect for Polish nationalism, he considered the revival of Germany's eastern neighbor "a power political fact with which we have to reckon." Although he knew "no complete and ideal solution to the Polish question," the chancellor championed the buffer-state concept because he considered it "a great advantage if we should succeed in severing Poland from Russia and in barring the latter's *Drang nach Westen* by advancing the former's frontier." Economic interests were best safeguarded if the country was independent of

Vienna and Petersburg, but incorporation into Prussia was impossible because of the Junker abhorrence of an increase in the Slavic and Jewish populations. Although the Bismarckian injunction against Polish Russophilia convinced him that complete independence was too dangerous, Bethmann saw the war as a chance to "orient the Poles to the West" and include them in his middle European scheme. In Riezler's words, "Poland is the sole case where we can create and prove the form of a culturally free protectorate, so important for the German future." Compared to this political rationale, the issue of military volunteers played merely a tactical role in temporarily swaying the OHL and in determining the timing of the proclamation. Only liberal administration in Warsaw and Poznan could make autonomy a political success. "Now that the matter has come this far, we are only going halfway." Riezler warned, "Unless we go all the way, it will be a complete mistake." [20]

The first crucial test of German intentions was the issue of the oath for the future Polish army. Seeking to control Poland militarily and thereby to abolish the condominium with Vienna, the OHL demanded that the legions be sworn in on "the German emperor as commander-in-chief," while the political leaders, appalled by such psychological ignorance, insisted on the Polish king, without any direct mention of Austrian and German monarchs. "It is a completely secondary question of form," Riezler fumed, "but Ludendorff capriciously calls for an oath to the emperor, which neither the Poles want to swear nor the Austrians to concede." The recruitment of volunteers was an unmitigated fiasco, since the German cause was unattractive as long as "we build them up as allies with our right hand, and skin them with our left like absolute enemies." Disturbed that "failure in this question . . . means our abdication as *Weltvolk*," Riezler concluded that the fundamental obstacle to substantive Polish independence was "the insane spirit called Prussia. These people are incapable of going beyond the small military state and its aspirations." Nevertheless, after almost half a year of bickering, the legions under Austrian command were—due to Polish pressure —transferred to Beseler as the kernel of a future national army. But by then the cynical instrumentalism of the German high command had ruined the political appeal to Polish patriots, and the desired army never materialized. [21]

The revision of Prussian Polish policy was a similar stumbling block. Although Bethmann knew that "any Hakatist policy" had become impossible lest Poznan become a Polish irredenta, Prussian Minister of the Interior Loebell provoked a fierce dispute with Wojciech Korfanty in the Landtag: "The expected tumult arose because the Poles did not want to let the opportunity slip by to poison everything." Fearing a loss of support because of the proclamation, the National Democrats needed an incident, since "they want to prevent reconciliation. Now the German parties who have the same aim possess the desired ammunition." Nevertheless, the domestic price for the restoration of Poland had to be paid in the form of ending the traditional discrimination. After long preparations, Berlin "attempted to influence the Korfanty circle through Warsaw to obtain a pledge of allegiance from Prince Janusz Radziwill in the Upper House in order to answer with the renunciation of the expropriations law." Over Loebell's resistance, Bethmann moved to eliminate the most hated provisions and symbols of Polish inferiority: "In order to quiet the Prussian Poles, two members of the Council of State, Roskoworsky and Pomorsky . . . talked persuasively to the Poznan Poles and have gotten far enough with the old Radziwill that he wants to declare Polish loyalty to Prussia in the House of Lords—then the expropriation and the language paragraph can be rescinded and we will be one step further." These legislative changes were undertaken because of Bethmann's conviction that he could "not lead a policy of constant repression," but they were too little and too late to halt the growing alienation of the Prussian Poles, for so long second-class citizens of the empire.[22]

The most important test of Bethmann's Polish policy was the formation of organs of the new state and the degree of popular support they might command. "In Poland itself everything is half-baked, since in every decision Berlin, Vienna, Warsaw, Lublin, and even the GHQs at Pless and Teschen participate"—nothing could be done. Despite Count Czernin's pronounced opposition to any administrative merger, Beseler, with Bethmann's approval, established a Council of State as first organ of the nascent Poland, in January 1917. Primarily consisting of large landowners and educated burghers, with a sprinkling of peasants and clerics from the Right, it proved a capable spokesman for Polish interests. Riezler was continually amazed about this "strange foundation of a state. Once born, the improbable child continues to live, even grows and cries, nobody believes it is alive or will be able to live, including myself—and yet it prospers." But in the eyes of the majority passivists, the *Staatsrat* could only legitimize itself independent from Germany's heavy hand, while any gestures of defiance raised Prussian opposition and pushed "the Polish cart further in the mud." Quietism reigned in the Foreign Office. The chancellor "is in the throes of doubt" when the threat of resignation of the Council of State over the question of a king produced a new crisis. Although in late June 1917 the chancellor and William II agreed to Beseler's suggestion for "the slow but continued evolution of the political institutions of the kingdom of Poland," the regency issue remained open until the July crisis. As one of his last political victories, Bethmann obtained the kaiser's agreement to the future appointment of an interrex.[23]

This final triumph, like the entire Polish policy, remained sterile. The contradiction between the political need for "a policy which will bring us peaceful relations with our Polish neighbor," and the OHL's desire for military expansion and repression was too great to be reconciled by a policy of indirect hegemony. Conceived as the least offensive alternative, the reconstitution of a Polish state, dependent upon Berlin, was also a matter of conviction for the chancellor. Having developed from a nationalist supporter of Bismarckian and Bülowian repression to a champion of coexistence before the war, Bethmann sincerely believed: "The most bearable solution for us— there was no good one—was an independent Poland so closely tied to us that the full development of our economic relations would prevent the rise of a militarily or politically dangerous neighbor." The opposition of agrarian, industrialist, and chauvinist circles to Polish freedom prevented the liberal execution of this plan. Hence the pro-German minority in Poland was continually frustrated, and Pilsudski's resignation from the Council of State in midsummer of 1917 left Bethmann's middle course utterly discredited. Austrian resistance to a German solution helped to prevent a clear-cut and generous policy of the Central Powers because the con- soon turned into a contradominion. Despite the realization that the Polish problem could only be solved with Polish cooperation, Bethmann's attempt to find a compromise between Wilsonian self-determination and German military-economic exploitation foundered on the social and intellectual realities of Prussian power, which lay beyond his control.[24]

The failure of Bethmann's Mitteleuropa, directed toward indirect German hegemony, had far-reaching consequences. Unlike northeastern France and the Baltic territories, which were under the direct authority of the army and were therefore exploited ruthlessly, Belgium and Poland served as test cases for the German order in Europe. Limited by the need to maintain Socialist support, the chancellor's purpose was the reorganization of the continent around Berlin, not primarily through brute force or ironclad treaties, but through the natural weight of economic and political self-interest. But the execution of this plan bore more resemblance to ruthless suppression, imposed by military and economic needs and prompted by the rigid authoritarianism of Prussia coupled with a new German annexationist imperialism. In some instances, such as the deportation and the settlement schemes, Bethmann's policy even anticipated later volkish designs. If the substance of German domination promised advantages for some minorities like the Flemings, who were forgotten by Wilsonian promises, Berlin's actual use of the slogans of self-determination and autonomy betrayed crude self-interest to a greater degree than the appeals of the western powers. Even compared to the duplicity of the Bolsheviks' nationalities policy and the unctuous moral egotism of the democratic interventionists, Bethmann's new European order aroused little enthusiasm. Although he was capable of formulating a solution to the problem of Germany's preponderance on the continent both in terms of numbers and of material interests, the fifth chancellor lacked the power to enforce a liberal implementation, which alone might have won the support of the smaller states. Hence his vision of Mitteleuropa, one of the *idées fixes* of German foreign policy from Holy Roman Empire to Common Market, never became a reality.[25]

Notes

Chapter 1

1 Bethmann to Clemenceau, June 25, 1919, AA *Nachlass* Jagow. As early as Nov. 1917, in an interview with the *NAZ*, the former chancellor had expressed "the wish to help truth win out before a neutral high court to which all material from both sides should be submitted." When he went through with the offer, he expected severe criticism, but "I try not to think of the coming tempest when I am writing. I can never please everyone anyway." Bethmann to Jagow, Apr. 5, 1919.

2 Bethmann to Jagow, May 20, 30, 1919, AA *Nachlass* Jagow. On May 20 Bethmann requested Foreign Minister Brockdorff Rantzau to transmit his proposal to the Entente: "In terms of foreign policy it will do little good, since the answer will be derisory. But domestically it may strengthen our nerve." Bethmann to Delbrück, June 16, 1919, DSB *Nachlass* Delbrück.

3 Bethmann to Jagow, May 30, 1919, AA *Nachlass* Jagow. Since the cabinet construed Bethmann's offer as recognition of Allied jurisdiction, it refused to transmit the proposal. Bethmann initially did "not insist on the execution of his scheme but later disregarded the government's warning." Cf. also BA, R43 I/805, cited in Eberhard von Vietsch, *Bethmann Hollweg: Staatsmann zwischen Macht und Ethos* (Boppard, 1969), p. 287, with the misleading implication that Bethmann thereafter desisted from his project.

4 Bethmann to Jagow, June 28, 1919, AA *Nachlass* Jagow. Only moderates like Colonel Schwertfeger supported Bethmann's initiative, while the majority of the German press ridiculed the futility of the gesture. BA *Nachlass* Schwertfeger, Bethmann to Schwertfeger, July 5, 1919.

5 See Paul Mantoux, *Les Délibérations du conseil des quatre, 24 mars–28 juin 1919* (Paris, 1955), 2 : 562 f., for a transcript of the Big Five's discussions of Bethmann's suggestion. For Sir Maurice Hankey's protocol see National Archives, Washington, D.C., RG 256, American Commission to Negotiate Peace, vol. 323, June 28, 1919. Cf. also J. W. Bruegel, "Das Schicksal der Strafbestimmungen des Versailler Vertrags," *VJHfZG* 6 (1958) : 263–70.

6 Memorandum by Dr. Scott, communicated to British Delegate Mr. Hunt, July 4, 1919, NA, RG 256, vol. 323. Sir Maurice Hankey instructed the Commission on Responsibility "that the Allied and Associated Powers recognize the spirit in which the offer was made but . . . should not accept Herr Bethmann Hollweg's interpretation of the German constitution." Hankey to Dutasta, June 28, 1919.

7 Draft Reply to Bethmann Hollweg, drawn up by the Commission on Responsibility in its session of July 15, 1919, NA, RG 256, vol. 323.

8 U.S. Naval Communication Service. American Commission to Negotiate Peace, NA, RG 256, dispatch of August 1, 1919. Writing to Jagow on July 13, Bethmann was still completely in the dark: "About my extradition I know nothing beyond the newspapers" (AA *Nachlass* Jagow). Cf. also F. Dickmann, "Die Kriegsschuldfrage auf der Friedenskonferenz von Paris, 1919," *HZ* 197 (1963) : 1–101. For the entire complex see Arno J. Mayer, *Politics and Diplomacy of Peacemaking: Containment and Counterrevolution at Versailles, 1918–1919* (New York, 1967).

9 Obituary "Bethmann Hollweg," by the Independent Socialist paper *Die Freiheit*,

Jan. 3, 1921. "With the name Bethmann Hollweg history will forever link the millionfold curse that is connected with the world war."

10 J. W. Headlam, *The German Chancellor and the Outbreak of War* (London, 1917), and F. Passelecq, *The Sincere Chancellor* (London, 1917). Cf. also Paul L. Hervier, "Silhouettes allemandes: Le docteur Theobald von Bethmann Hollweg," *Nouvelle Revue* 21 (1915): 49 ff.

11 Anonymous, *Rufe aus dem Felde* (printed as manuscript, n.p., n.d.), Hoover Institution:

An den Kanzler

Weh Kanzler Du bist schlecht beraten!
Du ahnst des Volkes Sehnen nicht.
Wohl sprichst Du kühn von deutschen Taten
Und donnernd sich die Stimme bricht

Im hohen Raum am Königsplatze.
Doch donnern macht es nicht allein:
Es zeigt das Heer des Löwen Tatze,
Der Kanzler muss ein—Staatsmann sein!

12 Stanza of a poem signed by Rudolf Geett (?), sent by Oettingen to Bethmann on the day before his death, Dec. 30, 1920, to amuse him with its "naive loyalty." BA *Nachlass* Oettingen.

13 Gottlieb Egelhaaf, *Der fünfte Reichskanzler* (Stuttgart, 1916) issued in a field edition of the serial "Aufrechte Männer" as patriotic literature for the trenches.

14 Hermann Kötschke, *Unser Kanzler: Sein Leben und Wirken* (Berlin, 1916). Often overlooked, this early 160-page biographical essay comes closer to Bethmann's political intentions than many later monographs. "We must rally around Bethmann and help him with critical advice and all our power to succeed in securing a favorable and lasting peace and in strengthening the structure of the empire after the war!"

15 Fritz Hartung, "Bethmann Hollweg," *Deutsches Biographisches Jahrbuch für 1921* (Stuttgart, 1927), pp. 21–41, was chiefly responsible for turning the contemporary polemical stereotype of the "weak," philosophical Bethmann into respectable history.

16 "Zu Bethmann Hollwegs Gedächtnis," *Deutsche Politik* (1921), pp. 81 ff. Originally a supporter of the Burgfrieden (as coeditor of the collective volume *Vom inneren Frieden des deutschen Volkes* [Berlin, 1916]), Thimme supported Bethmann's reform conservatism, and in a series of dramatic articles broke with Heydebrand in the *Konservative Monatsschrift* over the liberalization of Prussian suffrage. Containing a sizable correspondence with Bethmann, partial research notes and excerpts from official documents, fragments of the chancellor's writings, and a voluminous exchange of letters with his former collaborators and relatives, the Thimme *Nachlass* is one of the chief sources for Bethmann studies. For Thimme's plans, see his letter to Zimmermann, Sept. (?), 1937, listing three projected volumes of a biography and his claim to Wahnschaffe, Mar. 23, 1928, that "my entire historical and political activity is directed toward the memory of our late chancellor." Although the biography was never written, due to his sudden death in a mountaineering accident, his edition of *Bethmann Hollwegs Kriegsreden* (Stuttgart, 1919), as well as the extensive notes to the concluding twenty-plus volumes of *Die Grosse Politik,* reveal his commitment to the limited Machtpolitik of the fifth chancellor, whom he saw in the lineage of the Prussian reformers. For

some of his prolific articles, see "Bethmann Hollweg als militärischer Kanzler," *BT*, Sept. 15, 1917; "Bethmann Hollweg und Bismarck," *Deutsche Politik*, nos. 4 and 5 (1917); "Bethmann Hollweg und die deutsche Wehrkraft," ibid., Sept. 7, 1917; "Zum Kanzlerwechsel," ibid. (1917), pp. 948–49; "Bethmann Hollweg und die deutsche Flotte," *BT*, June 1, 1918; "Zur Geschichte der Mission Lord Haldanes," *Deutsche Politik* (1918), pp. 759 ff.; "Bülow und Bethmann Hollweg," ibid. (1919), pp. 225 ff.; "Reichsleitung und Heeresleitung," ibid. (1919), pp. 489 ff.; "Das Problem der Obersten Seekriegsleitung," ibid. (1919), pp. 723 ff.; "Bethmann Hollweg und die Tirpitzsche Flottenpolitik," ibid. (1921), pp. 186 ff.; "Was Fürst Bülow im Sommer 1914 getan hätte," *BM* (1930), pp. 173 ff. Cf. also his rebuttal to Prince Bülow's memoirs, "Bülow und Bethmann Hollweg," pp. 194 ff., in the volume edited by him, *Front wider Bülow: Staatsmänner, Diplomaten und Forscher zu seinen Denkwürdigkeiten* (Munich, 1931).

17 Alfred Rosenberg, "Der Kanzler ohne Kopf: Ein trübes Kapitel deutscher Vergangenheit," *Der Hammer* 38 : 269 ff., reprinted in *Novemberköpfe* (Munich, 1938), which denounces Bethmann in the same breath as Walther Rathenau and Friedrich Ebert. In *Mein Kampf* (American ed. [Boston, 1943], pp. 275, 476–77), Hitler himself ridiculed "the helpless stammering of a Bethmann Hollweg" and blamed part of German unpreparedness for World War I on the fifth chancellor's "attitude and weakness, even more miserable, if possible" than that of the Reichstag.

18 Werner Frauendienst, "Bethmann Hollweg," *Neue deutsche Biographie* (Berlin, 1965), pp. 188 ff., and *Biographisches Jahrbuch*, pp. 68–69, written on the basis of a knowledge of the files of the DZA Po and Me, but still representing a traditionalist point of view.

19 The unpublished dissertation, under Otto Becker, of Brigitte (Barth) Haberland, "Die Innenpolitik des Reiches unter der Kanzlerschaft Bethmann Hollwegs, 1909–1914" (Kiel, 1950), and that of Rudolf Koschnitzke, "Die Innenpolitik des Reichskanzlers von Bethmann Hollweg" (Kiel, 1951), though short on primary documentation, began to move beyond the narrow personal focus.

20 Hans-Günther Zmarzlik's *Bethmann Hollweg als Reichskanzler, 1909–1914: Studien zu Möglichkeiten und Grenzen seiner innenpolitischen Machtstellung* (Düsseldorf, 1957), is actually an analysis of his position in the governmental hierarchy, the struggle over the inheritance tax, and the constitutional reform of Alsace-Lorraine. "The fact [is] that the state apparatus and the leading strata remained tied to conservative traditions, while in the empires a movement toward the Left arose, and political aims sharply opposed to conservatism assumed growing importance. . . . Could there be anything but halfheartedness in this situation?"

21 Fritz Fischer, *Griff nach der Weltmacht* (Düsseldorf, 1961; 3d rev. ed., 1964); translated and slightly abridged as *Germany's Aims in the First World War* (New York, 1967), pp. xxi ff. Cf. my discussion "Drive for Power," *The Progressive* (April 1968), pp. 44–45. The actual controversy was ignited two years before the book by Fischer's preliminary findings in "Deutsche Kriegsziele, Revolutionierung und Separatfrieden im Osten, 1914–1917," *HZ* 188 (1959) : 249–310, to which Hans Herzfeld bitterly responded, "Zur deutschen Politik im Ersten Weltkriege: Kontinuität oder permanente Krise," ibid. 191 (1960) : 67 ff., while Fischer replied, "Kontinuität des Irrtums. Zum Problem der deutschen Kriegszielpolitik im Ersten Weltkrieg," ibid., pp. 83 ff. In the third edition Fischer strengthened his thesis to stress "the fundamental unity and strength for annexation, including the kaiser, the civilian government, and the military leadership, as well as the majority of the Reichstag and the German press" (pp. 190–91). The concluding

quote stems from Hans Gatzke's new foreword to the paperback edition of his *Germany's Drive to the West* (Baltimore, 1950, 1966), in which he revised his previous image of Bethmann as reluctant imperialist and admitted that he "was more annexationist, and consistently so, than has hitherto been realized."

22 The most incisive summary is W. J. Mommsen's "The Debate on German War Aims," in the enlarged German paperback version of the *JCH 1*, no. 3 (1966) : 45–70. Cf. also E. W. Lynar, *Deutsche Kriegsziele, 1914–1918* (Berlin, 1964); K. Barthel, "Beobachtungen am Rande der Kriegszieldiskussion," *GWU* 16 (1965): 83 ff.; and James Joll, "The 1914 Debate Continues: Fritz Fischer and His Critics," *Past and Present* 34 (1966) : 101 ff. For the present state see Wolfgang Schieder, ed., *Erster Weltkrieg: Ursachen, Entstehung und Kriegsziele* (Cologne, 1969).

23 F. Klein, "Die Westdeutsche Geschichtsschreibung und die Ziele des deutschen Imperialismus im Ersten Weltkrieg," *ZfG* 10 (1962): 1808 ff.; W. Gutsche, "Erst Europa—und dann die Welt," ibid. 12 (1964): 745 ff.; and F. Klein, ed., *Politik im Krieg, 1914–1918: Studien zur Politik der deutschen herrschenden Klassen im ersten Weltkrieg* (Berlin, 1964), as well as the three-volume collective work, *Deutschland im Ersten Weltkrieg* (Berlin, 1968–70). Cf. also W. Gutsche, F. Klein, H. Kral, and J. Petzold, "Neue Forschungen zur Geschichte Deutschlands im ersten Weltkrieg," *Jahrbuch für Geschichte* (Berlin, 1967), 1 : 282 ff.

24 See Klaus Epstein's ambivalent discussion, "German War Aims in the First World War," *World Politics* 15 (1962) : 163 ff., which praises the importance of Fischer's breakthrough in the text while attacking the study in the footnotes for falling into the revisionist trap of "overemphasizing the aggressive character of German war aims."

25 The most rabid reactions came from Michael Freund, "Bethmann Hollweg, der Hitler des Jahres 1914," *FZ*, March 28, 1964; Erwin Hoelzle, "Griff nach der Weltmacht," *Das Historisch-Politische Buch* (1962), pp. 65 ff.; Giselher Wirsing, ". . . auch am ersten Weltkrieg schuld?" *Christ und Welt*, May 8, 1964. Cf. also Hans Herzfeld, "Literaturbericht," *GWU* 13 (1962): 246 ff., and "Die deutsche Kriegszielpolitik im Ersten Weltkrieg," *VJHfZG* 11 (1963) : 224 ff.; G. Ritter, "Griff Deutschland nach der Weltmacht? Zu Fritz Fischer's umstrittenem Werk über den ersten Weltkrieg," *Hannoversche Zeitung*, May 19, 1962; "Eine neue Kriegsschuldthese? Zu Fritz Fischer's Buch 'Griff nach der Weltmacht,'" *HZ* 194 (1962) : 646 ff., and "Zur Fischer Kontroverse," ibid. 200 (1965) : 783–84; L. Dehio, "Deutschlands Griff nach der Weltmacht? Zu Fritz Fischers Buch über den ersten Weltkrieg," *Der Monat* 161 (1962) : 65 ff.; Golo Mann, "Der Griff nach der Weltmacht," *Neue Züricher Zeitung*, Apr. 28, 1962; F. Epstein, "Die deutsche Ostpolitik im Ersten Weltkrieg," *JGOE* 10 (1962) : 381 ff.; and D. Mende, "Die nicht bewältigte Vergangenheit des ersten Weltkrieges," *Europa Archiv* (1963), 333 ff.

26 For some samples see F. Fischer, "Der erste Weltkrieg—ein historisches Tabu: Realpolitik oder Eroberungspolitik?—Das Rätsel Bethmann Hollweg," *Die Welt*, July 27, 1963; "Vom Zaun gebrochen—nicht hineingeschlittert: Deutschlands Schuld am Ausbruch des Ersten Weltkrieges," *Die Zeit*, Sept. 7, 1965; K. D. Erdmann, "Der Kanzler und der Krieg," ibid., Aug. 28, 1964; and "Bethmann Hollweg, Augstein und die Historikerzunft," ibid., Sept. 25, 1964; E. Zechlin, "Die Illusion vom begrenzten Krieg: Berlins Fehlkalkulation im Sommer 1914," ibid., Sept. 21, 1965. *Der Spiegel* serialized part of Fischer's book in 1964, in issues 21–23, and continued to report on the progress of the debate.

27 G. Ritter, preface to volume 3 of *Staatskunst und Kriegshandwerk: Das Problem des 'Militarismus' in Deutschland*, entitled *Die Tragödie der Staatskunst: Bethmann Hollweg als Kriegskanzler, 1914–1917* (Munich, 1964), and the difference in

tone to volume 2, *Die Hauptmächte Europas und das wilhelminische Reich, 1890–1914* (Munich, 1960). For his other contributions, see "Der Anteil des Militärs an der Kriegskatastrophe von 1914," *HZ* 193 (1961) : 72 ff.; "Bethmann Hollweg im Schlaglicht des deutschen Geschichtsrevisionismus," *Schweizer Monatshefte* 42 (1962–63) : 700 ff.; "Der Erste Weltkrieg: Studien zum deutschen Geschichtsbild," a series of radio lectures reprinted by the *Schriftenreihe der Bundeszentrale für politische Bildung*, no. 64 (1964); "Bethmann Hollweg und die Machtträume deutscher Patrioten im ersten Jahr des Weltkrieges," in P. Classen, ed., *Festschrift für Percy Ernst Schramm* (Wiesbaden, 1964); and the constant revisions of *Das deutsche Problem: Grundfragen deutschen Staatslebens gestern und heute* (Munich, 1962–). Cf. also Klaus Epstein's scathing review, "Gerhard Ritter and the First World War," in W. Laqueur and G. Mosse, eds., *Nineteenfourteen: The Coming of the First World War* (New York, 1966), paperbound edition of the *JCH* 1, no. 3 (1966) : 186 ff.

28 Egmont Zechlin, "Friedensbestrebungen und Revolutionierungsversuche," *Aus Politik und Zeitgeschichte* supplement to *Das Parlament*, nos. 20, 24, 25 (1961), nos. 20 and 23 (1963). For his other essays see "Das 'schlesische Angebot' und die italienische Kriegsgefahr, 1915," *GWU* 14 (1963) : 533 ff.; Probleme des Kriegskalküls und der Kriegsbeendigung im ersten Weltkrieg," ibid. 16 (1965) : 69 ff.; "Die türkischen Meerengen—ein Brennpunkt der Weltgeschichte," ibid. 17 (1966) : 1 ff.; and "Die 'Zentralorganisation für einen dauerhaften Frieden' und die Mittelmächte," *Jahrbuch für internationales Recht* 11 (1962) : 448 ff. Cf. also the change of view between his most closely reasoned contribution, "Deutschland zwischen Kabinettskrieg und Wirtschaftskrieg: Politik und Kriegsführung in den ersten Monaten des Weltkrieges 1914," *HZ* 199 (1964) : 347 ff. and the more recent articles, "Bethmann Hollweg, Kriegsrisiko und SPD 1914," *Der Monat*, Jan. 1966, pp. 17 ff. and "Motive und Taktik der Reichsleitung: Ein Nachtrag," ibid., Feb. 1966, pp. 91 ff.

29 Fischer's major rebuttals are his long essay, "Weltpolitik, Weltmachtstreben und deutsche Kriegsziele," *HZ* 199 (1964) : 265 ff., deploring the critics' "fascination with Bethmann's soul," and the slim book, *Weltmacht oder Niedergang: Deutschland im ersten Weltkrieg* (Frankfurt, 1965).

30 Karl Dietrich Erdmann, "Zur Beurteilung Bethmann Hollwegs," *GWU* 15 (1964) : 525 ff. He is currently preparing an edition of the disputed diary. For the views of the generation of younger scholars, see I. Geiss, *Julikrise und Kriegsausbruch, 1914*, 2 vols. (Hanover, 1963), translated as *July 1914* (London, 1969); his essay "The Outbreak of the First World War and German War Aims," *Nineteenfourteen*, pp. 71 ff.; and the collaborative volume with Hartmut Pogge-v. Strandmann, *Die Erforderlichkeit des Unmöglichen: Deutschland am Vorabend des ersten Weltkrieges* (Frankfurt, 1965). Compare K. H. Janssen, *Macht und Verblendung: Kriegszielpolitik der deutschen Bundesstaaten, 1914–1918* (Göttingen, 1963) and *Der Kanzler und der General: Die Führungskrise um Bethmann Hollweg und Falkenhayn, 1914–1916* (Göttingsen, 1967); as well as W. Steglich, *Bündnissicherung oder Verständigungsfrieden: Untersuchungen zu dem Friedensangebot der Mittelmächte vom 12. Dezember 1916* (Göttingen, 1958); *Die Friedenspolitik der Mittelmächte, 1917–1918* (Wiesbaden, 1964); and Andreas Hillgruber, "Riezlers Theorie des kalkulierten Risikos und Bethmann Hollwegs politische Konzeption in der Julikrise 1914," *HZ* 202 (1966) : 333 ff.

31 Fritz Fischer, *Der Krieg der Illusionen: Die deutsche Politik von 1911 bis 1914* (Düsseldorf, 1969). For a sample of reactions see K. H. Janssen, "Das Spiel mit dem Krieg," in *Die Zeit*, Oct. 17, 1969; R. Augstein, "Deutschlands Fahne am Bosporus," *Der Spiegel*, no. 48 (1969), pp. 87 ff.; Paul C. Martin, "Fritz Fischer und

sein Leisten: Führte eine Rezession in den Ersten Weltkrieg?" *Christ und Welt,* Jan. 23, 1970; Andreas Hillgruber's review in *MGM,* no. 2 (1970); Gerald Feldmann's discussion in the *JMH,* no. 2 (1971); Henry Cord Meyer's assessment in the *AHR,* no. 3 (1971); and my own, "World Power or Tragic Fate? The *Kriegsschuldfrage* as Historical Neurosis," *CEH* 5 (March, 1972).

32 Willibald Gutsche, "Die Beziehungen zwischen der Regierung Bethmann Hollweg und dem Monopolkapital in den ersten Monaten des ersten Weltkrieges," (MS Berlin, 1967). Cf. also "Bethmann Hollweg und die Politik der Neuorientierung: Zur innenpolitischen Strategie und Taktik der deutschen Reichsregierung während des ersten Weltkrieges," *ZfG* 13 (1965) : 209 ff.; "Das Kriegszielprogramm der Regierung von Bethmann Hollweg vom 9. September 1914," *Geschichtsunterricht und Staatsbürgerkunde* (1964), pp. 353 ff.; "Taktik oder Alternative? Zum Problem der Differenzierung innerhalb der herrschenden Klassen während des ersten Weltkrieges in Deutschland," ibid. (1965), pp. 189 ff.; "Die Auseinandersetzungen zwischen Falkenhayn und Bethmann Hollweg um das Kriegsziel 'Mitteleuropa' im Spätsommer 1915," *ZfMG* (1965), pp. 672 ff.; "Probleme der Erforschung des ersten Weltkrieges," ibid. (1965), pp. 65 ff.

33 Wolfgang J. Mommsen's *Habilitationsschrift,* "Die Aussenpolitik Bethmann Hollwegs als das Problem der politischen Führung 1909–1914," (MS Cologne, 1967) scheduled for publication (Munich, 1972). Cf. also his "Die Regierung Bethmann Hollweg und die öffentliche Meinung, 1914–1917," *VJHfZG* 17 (1969) : 117 ff.; "Die italienische Frage und die Politik des Reichskanzlers von Bethmann Hollweg, 1914–1915," *Quellen und Forschungen aus italienischen Archiven und Bibliotheken* 48 (168) : 282 ff.; "L'opinion allemande et la chute du gouvernement Bethmann Hollweg en juillet 1917," *Revue d'histoire moderne et contemporaine* (1968), pp. 39 ff.; and *Das Zeitalter des Imperialismus* (Frankfurt, 1968), as vol. 28 of the Fischer *Weltgeschichte.*

34 Fritz Stern, "Bethmann Hollweg und der Krieg: Die Grenzen der Verantwortung," *Recht und Staat in Geschichte und Gegenwart,* nos. 351/2 (1968), originally reprinted as "Bethmann Hollweg and the War: The Limits of Responsibility," in *The Responsibility of Power: Historical Essays in Honor of Hajo Holborn,* edited with L. Krieger (New York, 1967), and "Die Kunst das Böse zu tun: Ein Kriegskanzler gesehen von seinem Intimus," *Die Zeit,* Jan. 2, 1968.

35 Eberhard von Vietsch, *Bethmann Hollweg: Staatsmann zwischen Macht und Ethos* (Boppard, 1969). For his view of Wilhelmian Germany, see his *Wilhelm Solf: Botschafter zwischen den Zeiten* (Tübingen, 1961); *Gegen die Unvernunft: Der Briefwechsel zwischen Paul Graf Wolff Metternich und Willhelm Solff 1915–1918* (Bremen, 1964); and "Der Kriegsausbruch 1914: Im Lichte der neuesten Forschung," *GWU* 15 (1964) : 472 ff.

36 Bethmann to Oettingen, Aug. 31, 1901, BA *Nachlass* Oettingen.

37 James J. Sheehan, "Germany, 1890–1918: A Survey of Recent Research," *CEH* 1 (1968) : 345 ff. One cannot quarrel with his advice: "Hopefully such a recognition would lead students of wartime Germany away from the motives and morals of the individuals involved to a more careful analysis of the institutional and constitutional setting within which these men operated." For the most recent survey of the literature see Hans Herzfeld, "1862–1918," *GWU* 21 (1970) : 183 ff.

38 Klaus Hildebrand, *Bethmann Hollweg: Der Kanzler ohne Eigenschaften? Urteile der Geschichtsschreibung: Eine kritische Bibliographie* (Düsseldorf, 1970), is the best introduction into Bethmann research.

39 For some of the larger perspectives, cf. Hillgruber, *Deutschlands Rolle in der Vorgeschichte der beiden Weltkriege* (Göttingen, 1967); George W. F. Hallgarten, *Das Schicksal des Imperialismus im 20. Jahrhundert: Drei Abhandlungen über*

Kriegsursachen (Frankfurt, 1969); Ralf Dahrendorf, *Society and Democracy in Germany* (Munich, 1965; English ed., 1967); the provocative essays collected by Hans-Ulrich Wehler, *Moderne deutsche Sozialgeschichte* (Cologne, 1966); Michael Stürmer, ed., *Das kaiserliche Deutschland: Politik und Gesellschaft, 1870–1918* (Düsseldorf, 1970); G. Masur, *Prophets of Yesterday: Studies in European Culture 1890–1914* (New York, 1963); and F. Stern, *The Politics of Cultural Despair: A Study of the Rise of the Germanic Ideology* (Berkeley, 1961).

40 Bethmann to Oettingen, June 7, 1877, BA *Nachlass* Oettingen.

Chapter 2

1 Gerhard von Mutius, *Abgeschlossene Zeiten* (Herrmanstadt, 1926), pp. 189 ff.; *Der deutsche Herold* (1909), pp. 208, 223, 235; ibid. (1910), pp. 11, 62, 118; *Daheim*, vol. 41, no. 12, pp. 7–8; *Die Woche* (1909), no. 30, pp. 1268 ff. *Familiengeschichtliche Blätter* 10 : 188; ibid. 14 : 265; ibid. 15 : 137. When volkish critics alleged that his ancestry was part Jewish (e.g. *Weimarer, bisher. General-Taschenbuch des ges. Adels jüdischen Ursprungs*, 1915, p. 501), Bethmann refuted this insinuation in his correspondence with the writer Kekulé v. Stradonitz. Cf. his *Personalakten*, BA, R 43/I, and Kekulé's article in *Deutsche Graveur und Stempelzeitung*, no. 49 (1911), as well as the rebuttal of the *National Zeitung* of July 14, 1909.

2 Claus Helbing, *Die Bethmanns: Aus der Geschichte eines alten Handelshauses zu Frankfurt am Main* (Wiesbaden, 1948); Heinrich Pallmann, *Gedenkbuch der Familie Bethmann* (Frankfurt, 1896), and *Simon Moritz von Bethmann und seine Vorfahren* (Frankfurt, 1898). Cf. also Stricker's résumé in *Allgemeine Deutsche Biographie*, 2 : 574 ff.

3 Handwritten manuscript, "Die Hoffnung eines künftigen Lebens erwiesen an der Auferstehung Jesu" (dated 1796), which argues: "Man has the gift and the capacity for discriminating between truth and error. Since he could not have given that to himself, it probably derives from his creator, namely God." See also L. Beutin, "Das Bürgertum als Gesellschaftsstand im 19. Jahrhundert," *Blätter für deutsche Landesgeschichte* 90 (1953) : 132 ff.

4 Anonymous, *Verzeichnis der Nachkommen des Moritz August von Bethmann Hollweg und seiner Gemahlin geb. Gebser* (Görlitz, 1935). Cf. also Wach's lengthy eulogy in *Allgemeine Deutsche Biographie*, 12 : 762–73. A more immediate source is his autobiography, printed as manuscript in two volumes in Bonn (1876 and 1878) and entitled *Familiennachricht*, a detailed account of his personal, religious, and political development. Cf. also Leonore O'Boyle, "Klassische Bildung und soziale Struktur in Deutschland zwischen 1800 und 1848," *HZ* 207 (1968) : 105 ff.

5 For his political philosophy, see Fritz Fischer's older work, *Moritz August von Bethmann Hollweg und der Protestantismus* (Berlin, 1938), which skillfully places Moritz August "between orthodoxy—its alliance with the monarchy, the Junkers, the peasants and artisans—and the liberalism of the bourgeois and socialist world, caught in irreconcilable contradictions, since with the first he shares positive religion (and conservative principles), and with the latter the idea of freedom (religious as well as political)." This "blend of *Christianity and idealism*," typical of Moritz August's reforming judicial Protestantism, is further developed in Fischer's essay, "Der deutsche Protestantismus und die Politik im 19. Jahrhundert," *HZ* 171 : 473 ff. Cf. L. Cecil, "The Creation of Nobles in Prussia, 1871–1918," *AHR* 75 (1970) : 757 ff.

6 W. Schmidt, *Die Partei Bethmann Hollwegs und die Reaktion in Preussen* (Berlin, 1910); R. Müller, *Die Partei Bethmann Hollwegs und die orientalische Krisis,*

1853–1856 (Halle, 1926). See also A. von Mutius, ed., *Graf Albert Pourtalès, Ein preussisch-deutscher Staatsmann* (Berlin, 1923).

7   For his famous caveat against Bismarck, see the Friedrichsruh edition of *Bismarck's gesammelte Werke*, vol. 14/I, no. 504; Maximilian Harden, *Von Versailles nach Versailles* (Berlin, 1927), pp. 558–59; and most recently, E. von Vietsch, *Bethmann Hollweg*, pp. 21 ff., 317 ff. And for a summary of Moritz August's work on freedom, see *Familiennachricht*, 1 : 448 ff. Cf. also his main scholarly work, *Der Civilprozess des Gemeinen Rechts in geschichtlicher Entwicklung* (Bonn, 1863–74), vols. 1–4, and his essays "Zur Geschichte der Freiheit," *Protestantische Monatsblätter*, ed. H. Gelzer, vols. 9 and 10 (1857/58).

8   M. A. von Bethmann Holloweg, *Familiennachricht*, 1 : 326–30.

9   On Dec. 25, 1864, Felix von Bethmann Hollweg began to chronicle the history of his family and estate from the time of his marriage and the purchase of Hohenfinow: "This handsome book, a Christmas present from my parents, shall be used to record the daily events and the relations of my family to the estate of Hohenfinow." Continued—with some interruptions—until 1893 by Felix and carried on until 1904 by Theobald, it is the chief source of information about his parents and youth. The MS "Gutsbuch" is still in the family possession at Schloss Altenhof near Kiel.

10 Gerhard von Mutius, *Abgeschlossene Zeiten* (Herrmanstadt, 1926), pp. 189 ff.

11 The development of the estate of Hohenfinow since the Middle Ages is traced by its pastor, S. Passow, in *Ein märkischer Rittersitz*, 2 vols. (Leipzig, 1907). See also E. Kittel, *Die Erbhöfe und Güter des Barnim, 1608–1652* (Bernburg, 1837), pp. 45 ff. For Felix von Bethmann Hollweg's tenure as *Landrat*, cf. also PrGStA, Rep. 77, no. 5389.

12 Felix von Bethmann Hollweg, "Gutsbuch," pp. 16 ff., 22 ff., 34 ff., 47 ff., 55 ff., 59 ff., 66 ff., 90 ff. While ridiculing the reactionaries' "false idea of their position," Felix was equally caustic about the "foolish shibboleths of the democrats." During the Austro-Prussian war, he wrote, "We fight for our existence and for the future of Germany." But despite his success as Landrat and gentleman farmer, Felix never quite fit in with his reactionary neighbors. "Since I do not want to howl with the wolves, they do not consider me as fully belonging to them." Cf. K. G. Faber, "Realpolitik als Ideologie: Die Bedeutung des Jahres 1866 für das politische Denken in Deutschland," *HZ* 203 (1967): 1 ff., and Otto Pflanze, "Juridical and Political Responsibility in Nineteenth-Century Germany," in *Responsibility of Power*, pp. 162 ff.

13 Passow, *Rittersitz*, 1 : 274 ff.; Kötschke, *Reichskanzler*, pp. 11 ff.; H. Hensch, a journalistic description, Sept. 1, 1909, AA, Dld 122, no. 16, vol. 1; F. Meinecke, *Strassburg-Freiburg-Berlin* (Stuttgart, 1949), pp. 232 ff.; and Theodor Fontane, *Wanderungen durch die Mark Brandenburg* (Berlin, 1899), 2 : 47 ff.

14 Passow, *Rittersitz*, 1 : 276 ff.; balance sheet, added to the "Gutsbuch," pp. 135 ff. Of the 61,509 Mk income, 28,729 Mk were the average annual receipts from agriculture; the rest derived from subsidiary enterprises. Cf. also Hans Rosenberg's suggestive essay, "Die Pseudodemokratisierung der Rittergutsbesitzerklasse," and "Wirtschaftskonjunktur, Gesellschaft und Politik in Mitteleuropa, 1873–1896," in H. U. Wehler, ed., *Moderne deutsche Sozialgeschichte* (Cologne, 1966), pp. 225 ff., 287 ff. See also T. S. Hamerow, *The Social Foundations of German Unification, 1858–1871* (Princeton, 1969), 1 : 181 ff.

15 Bethmann to Oettingen, July 23, 1877; BA *Nachlass* Oettingen. His grandfather's death "challenges me to be independent and demands strength in order not to drift." Although Moritz August's direct and indirect influence on his nephew was considerable, it need not be exaggerated, as in Vietsch, *Bethmann*, p. 26.

16   Insert into the "Gutsbuch," Dec. 21, 1865. Bethmann to Oettingen, Dec. 8, 1877; BA *Nachlass* Oettingen. Cf. also "Gutsbuch," pp. 131 ff.

17   On June 8, 1908, Bethmann informed Oettingen of the death of his "dear old mother." "The clear and sober quietness with which she encountered death, the full transformation of her mind into peace, goodness, and love were touching." BA *Nachlass* Oettingen. The dearth of source material on Bethmann's early childhood precludes any tempting psychohistorical speculations. Cf. H. U. Wehler, "Zum Verhältnis von Geschichtswissenschaft und Psychoanalyse," *HZ* 208 (1969): 529 ff.

18   Felix von Bethmann Hollweg, "Gutsbuch," 26 ff., 39 ff., 61 ff., 63 ff., Cf. also Kötschke, *Reichskanzler*, pp. 14 ff.

19   Felix von Bethmann Hollweg, "Gutsbuch," pp. 70 ff., 78 ff. Kötschke, *Reichskanzler*, pp. 16 ff. For the whole problem of family and education, see Philippe Ariès, *Centuries of Childhood: A Social History of Family Life* (New York, 1962).

20   For a vivid description of Pforta during Bethmann's days, see his cousin Max von Mutius MS "Lebenserinnerungen, 1865–1918," pp. 40–51; BA *Nachlass* Mutius. He remembered the pupils as "quite common and uncouth." See also Bernhard Rogge, *Pförtnerleben* (Leipzig, 1923), and Vietsch, *Bethmann*, pp. 32 ff. Cf. also the brilliant sketch of Matthew Arnold, *Higher Schools and Universities in Germany* (London, 1882), pp. 120 ff.

21   Felix von Bethmann Hollweg, "Gutsbuch," pp. 80–81, 83 ff., 100–01.

22   Unfortunately, Bethmann's letters to Lamprecht are no longer extant, according to Dr. U. Lewalt, who is currently preparing a Lamprecht biography. See her essay, "Karl Lamprecht," in Max Braubach, ed., *Bonner Gelehrte: Beiträge zur Geschichte der Wissenschaften in Bonn* (Bonn, 1968) pp. 230–53.

23   Kötschke, *Reichskanzler*, pp. 16 ff.; Sydow, MS "Lebenserinnerungen," p. 346; BA *Nachlass* Sydow. One of his classmates, Friedrich Zimmer, reminisced in 1909 in *Die Woche*, pp. 1269–71: "If we had been asked 'Which of you will become chancellor one day?' I believe we would have answered unanimously–'If anybody, Bethmann will.' "

24   Bethmann to Oettingen, May 25, June 23, 1876, Apr. 30, Nov. 23, 1877, Feb. 1878; BA *Nachlass* Oettingen. "The many disappointments" in his friendships and "all the petty annoyance with unfriendly teachers and the great questions of the golden section of spherical dimensions where in an infinity of imaginary numbers millions of cubic roots praise their creator," made Theobald look back to his days at Pforta with mixed emotions. For the intellectual atmosphere, see also Hajo Holborn, "Der deutsche Idealismus in sozialgeschichtlicher Bedeutung," *HZ* 174 : 359–84.

25   Bethmann to Oettingen, June 5, 1875; BA *Nachlass* Oettingen. The first letter to Wolfgang von Oettingen, three years his junior, was the beginning of the only surviving purely private correspondence of Bethmann that covers his entire life except for several major interruptions. Because of his literary and artistic interests and kindred idealistic spirit, Oettingen fulfilled Bethmann's need to share his intellectual enthusiasms, feelings, and moods. Independently wealthy, the talented Oettingen first became an art historian, then curator of the Goethe National Museum; but despite Bethmann's repeated efforts, he was denied a professorship. See Oettingen's extensive oeuvre, W. Kosch, *Deutsches Literarisches Lexikon* (Berlin, 1956, 3rd rev. ed.) p. 1934.

26   Bethmann to Oettingen, Jan. 8, May 25, July 7, 1876; BA *Nachlass Oettingen* (the Oettingen letters are listed in temporal sequence, *not* in order of their citation in the text). Bethmann resented the degrading routine of military service, which forced him "to be busy for the *whole* day with barracks and stable duty." Cf.

John Gillis's unpublished essay, "Youth and History: An Introduction" (Princeton, 1970).

27 Bethmann to Oettingen, May 25, 1876, Mar 3, and Nov. 23, 1877, BA *Nachlass* Oettingen. "A spark in a powder keg," David Friedrich Strauss's controversial *Der alte und der neue Glaube* (Berlin, 1872) rejected theology and philosophy in favor of positivism, or developing Christianity toward a secularized "humanism" of scientific inquiry, of poetry and music. Cf. Karl Löwith, *From Hegel to Nietzsche: The Revolution in Nineteenth-Century Thought* (Zurich, 1941). For Darwin's influence see J. Barzun, *Darwin, Marx, Wagner* (Garden City, N.Y., 1958), and for the influence of Haeckel's materialistic monism see H. G. Zmarzlik, "Der Sozialdarwinismus in Deutschland als geschichtliches Problem," *VJHfZG* 11 (1963) : 246 ff. For the relationship between cultural and personal crises see Sterling Fishman, "Suicide, Sex and the Discovery of German Adolescence," *History of Education Quarterly* 10 (1970): 170 ff.

28 Bethmann to Oettingen, July 17, 1876, Jan. 22, Feb. 17, and later the same month, as well as July 23, 1877. One stanza from his second poem expresses a typical mood:

> Kälter und kälter wirds mir im Herzen.
> Traurig blick in die Welt ich hinein.
> Bitter und bitterer werden die Schmerzen,
> Möchte wohl lieber im Grabe sein.

In less exalted moments Theobald knew: "I am too much subject to passing moods and I do not want to have them alone reflect my inner life." In another instance of self-analysis he added: "It is not sentimentality or complaining about the world's depravity which periodically make my head spin." On the contrary, "I basically love people very much and I know no greater pleasure than looking into the faces of strangers I meet or see on the street and guessing their character or frame of mind." BA *Nachlass* Oettingen.

29 Bethmann to Oettingen, Jan. 22, Apr. 30, June, July 23, Oct. 26, Nov. 10, 1877, Feb. 1878, Feb. 10, 1879, and Mar. 8, 1881, BA *Nachlass* Oettingen. The abstract vocabulary of his letters makes it nearly impossible to extract evidence of his actual sexual experiences, although it seems likely that he was initiated in *fin de siècle* bourgeois fa hion, i.e. in the bordello in Strasbourg, because of his reference to "knowing sensuality." Another characteristic refrain was, "A great passion could heal me, but I cannot sustain it," because of disappointments with previous "serpents nourished on my breast."

30 Bethmann to Oettingen, Mar. 3, June 7, Oct. 26, Nov. 10, Dec. 8, 1877, and Feb. 10, 1879, BA *Nachlass* Oettingen. For the religious element in his philosophical wanderings see his letter: "Unfortunately my beliefs have become damned threadbare, otherwise I would pray. . . . And *Wilhelm Meister*, just reread, spooks around in my head, so much so that I want to cry." Asking his friend for "a jolly good carnival devil," he sighed: "Of late the angels no longer want to have anything to do with me." Bethmann to Oettingen, late Feb. 1877, ibid. For the larger ramifications of his intellectual search see Carlton J. Hayes, *A Generation of Materialism, 1871–1890* (New York, 1941).

31 Bethmann to Oettingen, Jan. 18, June, July 23, Oct. 26, Nov. 10, 1877: "I shall always criticize myself and others. Hence you must not take it too seriously." Evidence of any formal influence of his university teachers is almost nonexistent. Cf. Kötschke, *Reichskanzler*, pp. 19 ff. and Vietsch, *Bethmann*, pp. 43 ff. With Wach, Bethmann continued to correspond during World War I, which testifies to a longstanding attachment. (Cf. Adolf Wach, "Staatsmoral und Politik," *Zwischen Krieg*

und Frieden [Leipzig, 1916], no. 39, a succinct summary of his legal credo.) For R. von Gneist cf. Heinrich Heffter, *Die deutsche Selbstverwaltung im 19. Jahrhundert: Geschichte der Ideen und Institutionen* (Stuttgart, 1950), pp. 372 ff., and Guido Ruggiero, *Geschichte des Liberalismus in Europa* (Berlin, 1930), pp. 240 ff. See also his late work, *Die nationale Rechtsidee von den Ständen und das preussische Dreiklassenwahlsystem* (Berlin, 1894), pp. 264–65.

32 Bethmann to Oettingen, Jan. 18, June, July 23, Oct. 26, Nov. 10, 23, Dec. 10, 1877, Jan. 15, June 30, 1878, BA *Nachlass* Oettingen. Reflecting the visual stereotype of the Central European Jewry, Bethmann's occasional anti-Semitic references were largely conventional expressions of disdain. Cf. G. Pulzer, *The Rise of Political Anti-Semitism in Germany and Austria-Hungary* (New York, 1964). Bethmann's reluctance for *Mengenumgang* betrays not so much social as cultural elitism. For Leipzig University cf. W. Bruchmüller, *Der Leipziger Student, 1409–1919* (Leipzig, 1909); Emil Friedberg, *Die Leipziger Juristenfakultät: Ihre Doktoren und ihr Heim* (Leipzig, 1909); and Franz Eulenburg, *Die Entwicklung der Universität Leipzig in den letzten hundert Jahren* (Leipzig, 1909).

33 Bethmann to Oettingen, Dec. 8, 1877, Jan. 15, Feb. 8., June 13, 1878, BA *Nachlass* Oettingen. Cf. also Vietsch, *Bethmann*, pp. 41 ff., 320–21, for the shortened text of the Rheineck confession, which deletes Theobald's typical neo-Romantic reveries.

34 Ibid. Theobald concluded the letter with a dash of self-irony: "Well, I shall be healed when I am again in hot and dusty Leipzig, since blood flows more slowly in the rough and sluggish East and my disgusting work will make me tired and reasonable. I have good resolutions and I intend to put them into practice." The Rheineck confession marks the end of Bethmann's intellectual crisis, when he began to succeed in his attempt to find a middle ground between the unsettling modern ideas current in some university circles and his traditional upbringing.

35 Bethmann to Oettingen, Nov. 16, Dec. 7, 1878, Jan. 19, 1879, BA *Nachlass* Oettingen. G. von Mutius, *Abgeschlossene Zeiten,* pp. 185 ff. "These lines breathe a certain boredom," he apologized to Oettingen. "I ask you not to reproach me for it; otherwise I shall become all too prosaic and bereft of passion. And passion was perhaps my best trait." In a similar vein he complained, "I have the feeling that I could accomplish something, but laziness and damned sensuality do not permit it." Cf. also Max Lenz, *Geschichte der königlichen Friedrich-Wilhelms-Universität zu Berlin* (Halle, 1910), vol. 2, pt. 2.

36 Bethmann to Oettingen, Feb. 10, May 27, June 18, Oct. 12, 1879, BA *Nachlass* Oettingen. Bethmann's dissertation did not survive the wars, although an entry into the *Doktorbuch* of the faculty of law at the University of Leipzig proves that he received his Dr. jur. degree on February 14, 1880. For a critical reappraisal of German universities, cf. Fritz K. Ringer, "Higher education in Germany in the nineteenth century," *JCH* (1967), pp. 123 ff., and *The German Mandarins: The German Academic Community, 1890–1933* (Cambridge, 1969).

37 Bethmann to Oettingen, July 22, Nov. 12, 1879, BA *Nachlass* Oettingen.

Chapter 3

1 Bethmann to Oettingen, Nov. 12, 1879, Aug. 21, 1880, Mar. 8, 1881, BA *Nachlass* Oettingen. Cf. also Hans Rosenberg, *Bureaucracy, Aristocracy, and Autocracy* (Cambridge, 1958); L. Muncy, *The Junker in the Prussian Administration under William II, 1888–1914* (Providence, 1944); R. Morsey, *Die oberste Reichsverwaltung unter Bismarck, 1867–1890* (Münster, 1957); and John R. Gillis, *The Prussian Bureaucracy in Crisis, 1840–1860* (Stanford, 1971). Hugo von Lerchenfeld, *Erinnerungen und Denkwürdigkeiten, 1843–1923* (Berlin, 1935), pp. 392–93.

2 C. Michaelis, *Für Staat und Volk* (Berlin, 1922), pp. 47 ff. Bethmann to Oettingen,
   Oct. 18, 1880, Mar. 8, 1881; BA *Nachlass* Oettingen. When Wolfgang von Oettingen inherited a castle on the Rhine, Theobald congratulated him enviously: "I
   have not experienced it myself, but knowing you are independent, not forced
   to milk the cow of state office, able to follow your inclinations and gifts and to
   surround your leisure with the stately spell of a knightly castle, this thought is
   too beautiful to keep a friend from congratulating you." Deploring the cultural
   limitations of Frankfurt/Oder, Bethmann wrote: "One does not sacrifice to the
   beaux-arts here. To be sure, there is much music, but what kind! And the
   theater is reputed to be bad."

3 The documents relating to Bethmann's state examinations and appointment as
   Landrat are in DZA Me, Rep. 77, Tit 183 d, no. 12, Vorakten no. 1, and his
   Personal Akten, Rep. 77, Tit 1159, as well as PrGStA, Rep. 90, no. 1034; Bethmann
   to Oettingen, Apr. 13, 1881; Dec. 1, 1885; BA *Nachlass* Oettingen. An interesting
   example of Bethmann's legal learning is his long explanation of the history of
   Notare, with suggestions for further reading to Oettingen on June 26, 1881. For
   the intricacies of Prussian administrative training, cf. H. Jacob, *German Administration since Bismarck: Central Authority versus Local Autonomy* (New
   Haven, 1963), pp. 48 ff. See also Felix von Bethmann Hollweg, "Gutsbuch," pp.
   96 ff., 105.

4 Bethmann to Oettingen, Dec. 1, 1885, Jan. 20, 1886; BA *Nachlass* Oettingen. After
   this date the correspondence lapses until Jan. 1901. The episode of Wilhelm II's
   first hunt is recounted in great detail by Felix von Bethmann Hollweg in the
   "Gutsbuch," pp. 99 ff. See also Wilhelm II, *Ereignisse und Gestalten, 1878–1918*
   (Berlin, 1922), pp. 105 ff.

5 Felix von Bethmann Hollweg, "Gutsbuch," pp. 100 ff. Ironically, the pattern of
   disgrace of the eldest son was repeated with Theobald's firstborn, August Friedrich, who reputedly accumulated large gambling debts before he was killed in
   World War I.

6 PrGStA, Rep. 77, no. 5389. Cf. also StAPo for files on Theobald's administration
   of Oberbarnim, such as Rep. 6C, no. 9, dealing with roads. Unfortunately, except
   for one further folder on schools and pastors, other documents relating to the
   Kreisverwaltung were destroyed during World War II. See also StAPo, Rep. 1,
   no. 931, and Graf Cuno Westarp, *Konservative Politik im letzten Jahrzehnt des
   Kaiserreiches* (Berlin, 1935), vol. 1, and Vietsch, *Bethmann*, pp. 51–52. For the importance of the Landrat after the administrative reforms of the 1870s, cf.
   R. M. Berdahl, "Conservative Politics and Aristocratic Landholders in Bismarckian Germany," *JMH* 44 (1972), pp. 1–20.

7 Bethmann to Oettingen, Jan. 20, 1886; BA *Nachlass* Oettingen. Felix von Bethmann Hollweg, "*Gutsbuch*," 103 ff., 107 ff. Gerhard von Mutius, *Abgeschlossene
   Zeiten*, pp. 189–90. *Grabrede* of Pastor Passow, Jan. 5, 1921, BA Coblenz, Kl. Erw.
   342–1. The Pfuels were old Brandenburg gentry, and Martha was to have become
   Hofdame for the empress before her marriage. Theodor Fontane, *Wanderungen*,
   2 : 495–506. For a female description of Martha von Pfuel cf. *Lettres de la Princesse Radziwill au Général de Robilant, 1889–1914* (Bologna, 1934), 4 : 86.

8 Felix von Bethmann Hollweg, "Gutsbuch," pp. 110 ff. *Stenographische Berichte
   des Reichstages*, 1890, vol. 1, p. 223. F. Specht and P. Schwabe, *Die Reichs-
   tagswahlen von 1867 bis 1903* (Berlin, 1904), pp. 77–81. Theobald von Bethmann
   Hollweg outpolled his nearest opponent by 1,401 votes, but since he had only one
   vote more than the required 50 percent of the entire votes cast, the election was
   contested and voided. From February to May 1890, Bethmann was a member of
   the Free Conservative faction of the Reichstag, but made no speeches. Cf. also
   Max Schwarz, *MdR: Biographiches Handbuch der Reichstage* (Hanover, 1965).

9 On May 27, 1890, Felix von Bethmann Hollweg wrote into the "Gutsbuch" an extensive summary of the Kaiser's explanations during his visit on May 8, 1890 (pp. 111 ff.). Cf. most recently, J. Alden Nichols, *Germany after Bismarck: The Caprivi Era, 1890–1894* (Harvard, 1958), pp. 12 ff. N. Rich and M. H. Fischer, eds., *The Holstein Papers* (Cambridge, 1963), and J. C. G. Röhl, "The Disintegration of the Kartell and the Politics of Bismarck's Fall From Power, 1887–1890," *HJ* 9 (1966) : 60 ff.

10 Felix von Bethmann Hollweg, "Gutsbuch," pp. 118 ff., 123 ff. Cf. also Erich Eyck, *Das Persönliche Regiment Wilhelms II* (Erlenbach-Zurich, 1948) and Fritz Hartung's critique, *Das Persönliche Regiment Kaiser Wilhelms II* (Berlin, 1952). See also W. Goetz, "Kaiser Wilhelm II und die deutsche Geschichtsdeutung," *HZ* 179 (1955) : 21–44. For a detailed reexamination cf. J. C. G. Röhl, *Germany without Bismarck: The Political Crisis of the Wilhelmian Empire, 1890–1900* (London, 1969).

11 Felix von Bethmann Hollweg, "Gutsbuch," p. 129. G. von Mutius, *Abgeschlossene Zeiten*, pp. 189–90. Kötschke, *Reichskanzler*, pp. 30–31.

12 For his promotions, cf. his *Personalakten*, DZA Me, Rep. 77, Tit 183d, no. 12 and *Vorakten*. The main evidence for his work as councilor is in substantive files in the StaPo, Rep. 1, nos. 626, 928 and 1,149. For his appointment in Bromberg see PrGStA, Rep. 90, no. 990 and DZA Me, Rep. 89H, Posen II, no. 20. See also Bogdan Hutten-Czapski, *Sechzig Jahre Politik und Gesellschaft* (Berlin, 1936), 1 : 361–62. For the administrative climate of the times, consult J. C. G. Röhl, "Higher Civil Servants in Germany, 1890–1900," *JCH*, no. 3 (1967): 101–122. See also John R. Gillis, "Aristocracy and Bureaucracy in Nineteenth Century Prussia," *Past and Present* 41 (1968) : 105 ff.

13 Joachim von Winterfeld-Menkin, *Jahreszeiten des Lebens* (Berlin, 1942), pp. 114 ff. Bethmann to Oettingen, Jan. 31, July 28, Aug. 31, 1901; BA *Nachlass* Oettingen. Theobald von Bethmann Hollweg, "Gutsbuch," pp. 131 ff.

14 Bethmann to German Ambassador Metternich, Aug. 16, 1904, quoted in Vietsch, *Bethmann*, p. 59. Winterfeld-Menkin, *Jahreszeiten*, pp. 112–13. Cf. F. W. von Loebell's MS "Erinnerungen," 2 : 84–85; BA *Nachlass* Loebell. The key documents on Bethmann's tenure as *Oberpräsident* are in the StAPo, Rep. 1, nos. 627, 1078, 1150 and 1180. Cf. also DZA Me, Rep. 77, Tit 4045, no. 2, vol. 1, Rep. 89 H, II Brandenburg, no. 2a and no. 3a. Cf. Hannelore Horn, *Der Kampf um den Bau des Mittellandkanals* (Cologne, 1964) and Gerhard Masur, *Imperial Berlin* (New York, 1971).

15 Bethmann to Oettingen, Jan. 31, July 28, Aug. 31, 1901; Dec. 24, 1903; Jan. 15, 18 and Feb. 11, 1905; BA *Nachlass* Oettingen. With a dash of self-irony Bethmann characterized his state of mind as "a head bewildered by too much business," and asked his artistic friend for advice on choosing a sculptor for a Paul Gerhardt monument: "I personally would prefer it if we could support a young artist aspiring to greatness."

16 Bethmann to Loebell, Oct. 12, 1904; BA *Nachlass* Loebell. R. Vierhaus, *Tagebuch der Baronin von Spitzemberg* (Göttingen, 1960), pp. 446 ff. Bethman to Oettingen, Apr. 18, 1905; BA *Nachlass* Oettingen. For his appointment as minister of the interior cf. Count Eulenburg to Bethmann, May 6, 1905 in his *Personalakten*, DZA Me, Rep. 77, Tit 183d, no. 12 and *Vorakten*, and for the files of the Prussian Ministry of the Interior generally, DZA Me, Rep. 77. Cf. also Bülow's patronizing comments in his *Denkwürdigkeiten* (Berlin, 1930), 2 : 181. For public reaction see "Der neue preussische Minister des Innen," *Illustrierte Zeitung*, Mar. 30, 1905.

17 Walter Rathenau, *Tagebuch, 1907–1922* (reedited by H. Pogge-v. Strandmann, Düsseldorf, 1967), p. 141. For Bethmann's role as minister see especially the minutes of the Prussian Ministry of State, i.e. the Prussian cabinet, in whose dis-

cussions he often participated; DZA Me, Rep. 90a B III 2b no. 6, vols. 150 ff. For his more important speeches see the *Stenographische Berichte* of the Lower House of the Prussian Landtag, 1st session (1905 ff.), columns 12,523 ff., 12,545; 2d session, columns 137 ff., 547 ff., 1,073 ff., 1,145–46, 1,273–74, 1,821–22, 2,148 ff., 353 ff., 3,739 ff., 5,456 ff.; 3d session, columns 399–400, 1,007 ff., 1,074 ff., 1,138–39. Cf. also Th. von Wilmowsky, "Erinnerungen" (printed as MS, 1951), p. 45, and E. Schiffer, "Um Bassermann und Bethmann," *Historisch Politisches Archiv* 1 (1930): 194–95.

18 DZA Po RdI, no. 15,671, clipping of *Deutsche Arbeitgeber Zeitung*, editorial Nov. 19, Bethmann Hollweg *vota* of Dec. 27, 1905, Jan. 18, Feb. 28, Oct. 22, 1906 and the discussion of the Prussian State Ministry of Nov. 10, 1906. Cf. also StAPo, Rep. 1, no. 1,150 for his administrative orders against Socialist agitators and Rep. 1, no. 1180 and PrGStA, Rep. 1139–40 for the *Wanderarbeiter* law, especially his *votum* of Mar. 18, 1906. See also Leo Stern, ed., *Die Auswirkungen der ersten Russischen Revolution von 1905–1907 auf Deutschland* (Berlin, 1955), II/I, pp. 84, 92, 137, 150, 156, 176, 204. Cf. Bethmann's answer to a Progressive interpellation in the Prussian House about the expulsion of Russian revolutionaries: "He had ordered that persons without an economically secure existence, without legitimate documents, or those politically suspicious be expelled immediately (applause)," although the measure would not be directed against the resident commercial Russian community. Schulthess's *GK* (1906), pp. 106–07.

19 Bethmann before the Prussian Lower House, *Stenographische Berichte*, Jan. 15, 1906. Cf. also his *vota* of Sept. 25, Oct. 23, 1905 and his large memorandum of Dec. 22, 1906 in PrGStA, Rep. 90, nos. 1612, 1613, 1614, 1568 and DZA Po, Rkz. nos. 999–1,000 ff. For Bethmann's role in the Polish question see also F. H. Gentzen, "Der Posener Schulstreik 1905–1907," *Jahrbuch für Geschichte der deutsch-slawischen Beziehungen* 2 (1958): 156–225; R. Korth, *Die preussische Schulpolitik und die polnischen Schulstreiks* (Marburg, 1963); and more generally, the unpublished dissertation of D. Keil, "Die preussisch-deutsche Polenfrage der Wilhelminischen Epoche vor 1914. Unter besonderer Berücksichtigung der Regierung Bethmann-Hollweg," (Tübingen, 1961). Cf. Hutten-Czapski, *Sechzig Jahre*, 2 : 55 ff.

20 DZA Po, RdI no. 15,685, Bethmann *vota* of Jan. 28, Mar. 13, June 19 and Oct. 15, 1906 and DZA Me, Rep. 77, Tit 496a, no. 177, vols. 1–2. Sessions of the Prussian Ministry of State, Mar. 3, 31, May 11, Dec. 17, 1906, DZA Me, Rep. 90a B III 2b no. 6, vols. 152–53. For his programmatic suffrage speech of Mar. 23 cf. Schulthess's *GK* (1906), pp. 68–72, and for his explanation of Apr. 2, 1906, see *Stenographische Berichte* (1906), columns 3,975 ff. Cf. also the scathing reception of the mini-reform by the Social Democrats: Paul Michaelis, *Von Bismarck zu Bethmann: Die Politik und Kultur Grosspreussens* (Leipzig, Berlin, 1911), pp. 46 ff.

21 Bethmann to Oettingen, Feb. 6, Apr. 4, 1906; BA *Nachlass* Oettingen. In the first letter, Bethmann complained: "I have been plagued by influenza and am extremely busy." In the second letter, describing his public debacle, Bethmann ended on a human note: "Tomorrow I shall escape all this mess. Day after tomorrow at this time I will be on the Gotthart Pass, in the evening in Genoa, and then for two weeks in Portofino close to St. Marguerita. My wife is recovering *slowly* but positively. The children are well!" Cf. also John L. Snell, "The World of German Democracy, 1789–1914," *The Historian* 31 (1969) : 521 ff.

22 DZA Po, Rkz. 1,070, memorandum of Mar. 2, 1907. His major memorandum on the necessity of electoral reform was Bethmann's first attempt to apply his private political insights to his office and to use the emergence of the Bülow bloc for an initiative toward reform in a manner reminiscent of David Friedrich Strauss's suggestions in *Der alte und der neue Glaube*, pp. 80 ff., and Rudolf Gneist's *Die nationale Rechtsidee*, pp. 257 ff.

23 G. D. Crothers, *The German Elections of 1907* (New York, 1941). Carl E. Schorske, *German Social Democracy, 1905–1917: The Development of the Great Schism* (Cambridge, 1955), pp. 59 ff. Karl Bachem, *Vorgeschichte, Geschichte und Politik der deutschen Zentrumspartei* (Cologne, 1930), 7 : 11 ff. Bethmann to Oettingen, Nov. 4, 1906; BA *Nachlass* Oettingen. Cf. also Peter-Christian Witt, *Die Finanzpolitik des deutschen Reiches von 1903 bis 1913* (Lübeck, 1970), pp. 152 ff.

24 Martin Schmidt, *Graf Posadowsky: Staatssekretär des Reichsschatzamtes und Reichsamts des Innern 1893–1907* (Halle, 1935), pp. 170 ff. Theodor Eschenburg, *Das Kaiserreich am Scheidewege* (Berlin, 1929), pp. 76–77. Grunelius to Podewils, June 24, Lerchenfeld to Podewils, June 28, July 1, 1907, cited in Peter Rassow and Karl E. Born, *Akten zur staatlichen Sozialpolitik in Deutschland 1890–1914* (Wiesbaden, 1959), pp. 264 ff. For the rumor of Bethmann as Bülow's successor see Hans von Tresckow, *Von Fürsten und anderen Sterblichen* (Berlin, 1922), pp. 165 f. Because of Bethmann's refusal to pass the list of homosexuals compiled during the Eulenburg scandal on to the emperor, since "I do not want to make that many people unhappy," the *Kriminalkommissar* considered him "too weak and well-meaning. As minister of the interior, as so-called police-minister, one has to be energetic and act, even if it means sacrifices." Cf. also J. Haller, *Aus dem Leben des Fürsten Philipp zu Eulenburg-Hertefeld* (Berlin, 1924), pp. 321 ff. For Bülow's posthumous revenge on his successor, cf. *Denkwürdigkeiten*, 2 : 300 ff.

25 Bethmann to Oettingen, July 26, 1907, BA *Nachlass* Oettingen. Vietsch, *Bethmann*, pp. 79–80. Session of the Prussian Ministry of State, June 25, 1907, DZA Me, Rep. 90a B III 2b no. 6, vol. 154. For the surprising appointment of Bethmann to the vice-chancellorship, overriding Rheinbaben's seniority, see his long letter to Moltke of June 25, 1907, reprinted in Hans Goldschmidt, *Das Reich und Preussen im Kampf um die Führung* (Berlin, 1931). See also the documents in his *Personalakten*, DZA Me, Rep. 77, Tit 184d, no. 12.

26 Richard Bahr, "Von Posadowsky zu Bethmann," in *Die Zukunft*, 67 (1907) : 265–73. Bülow to Holstein, Sept. 29, 1907, reprinted in N. Rich and M. H. Fisher, *The Holstein Papers* (Cambridge, 1963) 4 : 497. Bethmann to Oettingen, Nov. 6, 1907, BA *Nachlass* Oettingen. For Bethmann's views on federalism cf. Lerchenfeld's report to Podewils, July 1, 1907, and the subsequent dispatches of the Bavarian representatives in the Bundesrat, Rassow-Born, *Akten*, pp. 269 ff. Bethmann to Frau Boetticher, Sept. 15, 1907, BA *Nachlass* Boetticher. Kötschke, *Reichskanzler*, pp. 31–32 and Schulthess's *GK* (1907): 150, 154; cf. also *Soziale Praxis* 17 (1907), no. 11, and *Jahrbuch für Volks und Jugendpflege* (Leipzig, 1907), for Bethmann's views on *Sozialpolitik* and sport. For this problem see Klaus Saul, "Der Kampf um die Jugend zwischen Volksschule und Kaserne. Ein Beitrag zur 'Jugendpflege' im Wilhelminischen Reich, 1890–1914," *MGM* no. 2 (1971), pp. 97 ff.

27 For the files on Bethmann's tenure as state secretary of the interior see DZA Potsdam, Reichsamt des Innern, 1907–1909, passim. For his programmatic speech on *Sozialpolitik* cf. *Stenographische Berichte der Verhandlungen des Reichstags*, vol. 229, cols. 1, 956 ff. Cf. also Karl Erich Born, *Staat und Sozialpolitik seit Bismarcks Sturz: Ein Beitrag zur Geschichte der innenpolitischen Entwicklung des deutschen Reiches 1890–1914* (Wiesbaden, 1957), pp. 205 ff. An important milestone in Bethmann's political development was his realization that, since socialism could no longer be effectively combatted, it had to be won over to state and monarchy. According to Prussian Minister of War von Einem: "It had almost become an *idée fixe* with him that the Social Democrats were on the way to developing into a bourgeois and loyal party and that hence everything which might disturb this process had to be avoided." Karl von Einem, *Erinnerungen eines Soldaten 1853–1933* (Berlin, 1933), pp. 155 ff. However, the limits of his reform

conservatism are clear in his refusal to legislate against industrial black-listing of unruly workers, putting the blame on the "immense fluctuation" of labor due to agitation. Answer to a Center Party interpellation in the Reichstag, Jan. 29, 1909, Schulthess's *GK* (1909), pp. 47–48.

28   DZA Po, RdI, nos. 15,614 and 15,615; PrGStA, Rep. 90, nos. 2262 and 2263; *vota* of Mar. 19 and Sept. 11, 26, Oct. 14, 1907; and the discussion of the Prussian Ministry of State on Oct. 5, 1907, DZA Me, Rep. 90a B III 2b no. 6, vol. 155.

29   For the legislative fate of the associations law cf. the reports of Bavarian Ambassador Lerchenfeld and plenipotentiary Stössenreuther to Podewils, Nov. 13, 16, 18, 1907, Jan. 16, 22, 23, Feb. 5, 7, 28, Mar. 1, 2, 16, Apr. 8, 1908, Rassow-Born, *Akten,* pp. 273 ff. For Bethmann's claim that "he himself was the intellectual father of the [language] paragraph" in the Reichstag, see Schulthess's *GK* Dec. 9/11, 1907, p. 188 and Apr. 2/6, 1908, p. 839. Cf. also *Vorwärts, Kölnische Zeitung,* Nov. 26, 1907; *Bayrischer Kurier,* Nov. 28, 1907; *Neue Freie Volkszeitung,* Feb. 28, 1908. Cf. also Theodor Heuss' account, *Friedrich Naumann* (Stuttgart, 1937), pp. 253 ff.

30   DZA Po, Rkz, nos. 2,327 and 2,328; PrGStA, Rep. 90, nos. 1,220–1,230; *vota* of Mar. 5, June 27, Dec. 2, 1908, Feb. 22, 27, April 28, May 11 (1909) ff. Bethmann circulars to the federal states of Mar. 5, Oct. 15, 1908, in Rassow-Born, *Akten,* pp. 412 ff. Meetings of the Prussian Ministry of State, Jan. 6, Feb. 2, 1909 ff., DZA Po, Rep. 90a B III 2b no. 6, vol. 158. See also Bethmann's speech to the conference of social insurance representatives of Oct. 27, 1908, in Schulthess's *GK,* pp. 152–53. Cf. also H. Kaelble, *Industrielle Interessenpolitik in der Wilhelminischen Gesellschaft: CVDI 1895–1914* (Berlin, 1967), pp. 86–87.

31   DZA Po, RdI, no. 15,701, *vota* of Nov. 28, Dec. 28, 1907, June 22, July 6, 1908. Session of the Prussian Ministry of State, July 11, 1908, DZA Me, Rep. 90a B III 2b no. 6, vol. 157. Bethmann's speech in the Reichstag on Jan. 15, 1909. Schulthess's *GK* (1909), pp. 10–13. Cf. Lerchenfeld to Podewils, July 6, 1907; Draft of the State Secretariat of the Interior, Feb. 1, 1908; Bethmann circular July 14, 1908; Apr. 23, 1909; Nieser report, Oct. 21, 1908, reprinted in Rassow-Born, *Akten,* pp. 271 ff.

32   Bethmann to Oettingen, Aug. 8, 1908; BA *Nachlass* Oettingen. Despite Bethmann's attempts to persuade his colleagues "most insistently," his efforts on behalf of procuring a professorship for his respected friend Oettingen proved vain; Bethmann to Oettingen, Oct. 21, 1907, Sept. 18, 1909. Their relationship is summed up in a postcard from Bethmann, vacationing in Helgoland, to Oettingen on Aug. 7, 1907: "In raging storm and rain your song sounds joyful and refreshing," since the minister considered himself as "one of those troubled and weighed down by profession and duty who have the longing, if not always the ability, to liberate themselves from the chains of the unharmonious world surrounding them."

33   In a long marginal comment on Loebell's note of Sept. 6, 1907, Chancellor Bülow refused to choose between action and inaction: "Certainly we must proceed with great caution in the question of electoral reform. But above all we should not yet tie our hands." DZA Po, Rkz. nos. 1070 and 1071. For Bethmann's initiative, cf. his letter to Bülow of June 3, 1907, and his correspondence with conservative Prussian Minister of the Interior Moltke, Dec. 18, 1907, and the note of Jan. 10, 1908 in DZA Me, Rep. 77, Tit 496a, no. 179, vol. 1. For the debate in the Prussian Ministry of State on Jan. 2–3, 1908, cf. DZA Me, Rep. 90a B III 2b no. 6, vol. 156. Cf. also Witt, *Finanzpolitik,* pp. 190 ff, 237 ff.

34   Walter Goertlitz, ed., *Der Kaiser . . . : Aufzeichnungen des Chefs des Marinekabinetts Admiral Georg Alexander von Müller über die Ära Wilhelms II.* (Göttingen, 1965), pp. 69 ff. Count Szögyény to Foreign Minister Count Aerenthal, Oct. 28, Nov. 10, 18, 1908, HHStA, PA III, 167, varia. The most intimate account of the *Daily Telegraph* Affair is Bülow's MS typescript of over 250 pages, "Sedan's

Day Memorandum" finished in Nov. 1910, in which he concluded: "In the last analysis it was fortunate for country and crown that this happened." See especially pp. 55 ff. For the whole question, cf. also Wilhelm Schüssler, *Die Daily Telegraph Affaire: Fürst Bülow, Kaiser Wilhelm und die Krise des Zweiten Reiches* (Göttingen, 1952).

35 Bülow, "Sedan's Day Memorandum," pp. 112 ff. For the sessions of the Prussian Ministry of State, cf. DZA Me, Rep. 90a B III 2b no. 6, vol. 157. See also Bülow's version in his *Denkwürdigkeiten*, 3 : 350 ff. and the critique of Freiherr von Schoen: "Fürst Bülows Irrungen und Unwahrheiten," in Fr. Thimme, ed., *Front wider Bülow* (Munich 1931), pp. 76 ff. Cf. also O. Hammann, *Deutsche Weltpolitik 1890–1912* (Berlin, 1925), and Witt, *Finanzpolitik*, pp. 239 ff.

36 Bethmann's statement in the Reichstag, Dec. 2/3, 1908, Schulthess's *GK* (1908), pp. 234–35. Cf. also Vierhaus, *Spitzemberg Tagebuch*, pp. 467 ff.; Count Westarp, *Konservative Politik im letzten Jahrzehnt des Kaiserreiches* (Berlin, 1935), 1 : 37 ff.; Theodor Eschenburg, *Das Kaiserreich am Scheidewege*, pp. 152 ff.; and Ernst Deuerlein, *Der Bundesratsausschuss für Auswärtige Angelegenheiten 1870–1918* (Regensburg, 1955), pp. 259 ff.

37 Bülow, "Sedan's Day Memorandum," 3 ff.; Szögyény to Aerenthal, Nov. 25, Dec. 9, 1908, Mar. 3, 13, 31, 1909; HHStA, PA III, nos. 167 B and V. Cf. also Lerchenfeld's report to Podewils, Jan. 9, 1909 about the growing fronde against the chancellor, in Rassow-Born, *Akten*, pp. 401–02. For the Bosnian crisis cf. also W. L. Langer, "The 1908 Prelude to the World War," *Foreign Affairs* 7 (July 1929); H. Rothfels, "Studien zur Annexionskrise von 1908/09," *HZ* 147 (1933): 320 ff.; and B. Schmidt, *The Annexation of Bosnia 1908/09* (New York, 1937). The best account of the reform is by the former finance minister R. Sydow, "Fürst Bülow und die Reichsfinanzreform 1908/09," *Front wider Bülow*, pp. 105 ff.

38 Bülow carried his "Sedan's Day Memorandum" through the *Reichsfinanzreform* to his fall. Cf. also DZA Po, RdI no. 15,768 and PrGStA, Rep. 90, nos. 1342–45, Bülow *vota*, Dec. 31, 1907, Aug. 25, 1908, Bethmann *votum*, June 9, 1908, and the letter to Bassermann, Apr. 8, 1909, on the need to raise supplementary taxes replacing those voted down in the Reichstag. Cf. the discussion of the Prussian Ministry of State of June 14, 1908, in which Bethmann, in contrast to the chancellor, suggested that, "because of the great differences of the bloc parties, the Center Party, when treated carefully, would cooperate in the end anyway." DZA Me, Rep. 90a B III 2b no. 6, vol. 156. See also Szögyény to Aerenthal, Apr. 27, May 18, June 21, 25, July 6, 1909, HHStA, PA III, 167B. The best analysis of the interest-group struggles is P.-C. Witt, *Die Finanzpolitik des Deutschen Reiches von 1903 bis 1913*, pp. 199 ff.

39 Bülow, "Sedan's Day Memorandum," pp. 220 ff. Müller, *Der Kaiser*, pp. 77–78. Szögyény to Aerenthal, June 27, 29, 1909, HHStA, PA III, 167B. Karl Bachem, *Geschichte der Zentrumspartei*, 7 : 44 ff. Graf Westarp, *Konservative Politik*, 1 : 51 ff. Cf. also Eschenburg, *Das Kaiserreich am Scheidewege*, pp. 244 ff., 78 ff. For Bülow's war with the Center Party, cf. also Karl von Hertling, "Bülow, Hertling, Zentrum," in Thimme, ed., *Front wider Bülow*, p. 136 ff. There is no critical study of Bülow's chancellorship.

40 Bethmann to Wermuth, June 10, June 25, 1909, in Adolf Wermuth, *Ein Beamtenleben* (Berlin, 1922), pp. 268 ff. Szögyény to Aerenthal, July 6, 8, 1909, HHStA, PA III, 167B. Bethmann's statement in the Reichstag, July 10, 1909, Schulthess's *GK*, pp. 257 ff. Bethmann's acceptance of the Center-Conservative taxes paved the way for his subsequent appointment as chancellor. Cf. also Witt, *Finanzpolitik*, pp. 297 ff., and Loebell to Klitzing, June 19, to Valentini, June 19, to Dohna, June 27, and Bülow to William II, July 4, 10, 1909—all in DZA Po, Rkz. 213.

41 Szögyény to Aerenthal, July 8, 1909, HHStA, PA III, 167B. Bethmann to Wermuth, June 25, 1909, *Beamtenleben*, pp. 270 ff. For Freiherr von Rheinbaben and Bethmann's other rivals, cf. Otto Graf zu Stolberg-Wernigrode, *Die unentschiedene Generation: Deutschlands konservative Führungsschichten am Vorabend des Ersten Weltkrieges* (Munich, 1968), pp. 368 ff. Cf. also Botho von Wedel, "Diplomatisches und Persönliches," *Front wider Bülow*, pp. 345–46. For Monts see F. von Oppenheimer, "Botschafter Graf Monts," ibid., pp. 95 ff., and K. F. Nowak and F. Thimme, *Erinnerungen und Gedanken des Botschafters Anton Graf Monts* (Berlin, 1932), especially pp. 23 ff., 463 ff. Cf. also K. H. Janssen, ed., *Die graue Exzellenz: Aus den Papieren Karl Georg von Treutlers* (Berlin, 1971), pp. 171 ff.

42 Bernhard Schwertfeger, *Kaiser und Kabinettschef: Nach einigen Aufzeichnungen und dem Briefwechsel des Wirklichen Geheimen Rats Rudolf von Valentini* (Oldenburg, 1931), pp. 122 ff. See also F. Thimme's excerpts from the Valentini diary, entries for July 7 ff. 1909, BA *Nachlass* Thimme. Cf. Müller, *Der Kaiser*, pp. 68 ff. Szögyény to Aerenthal, July 20, 1909, HHStA, PA III, 167B. Bülow later denied that he had suggested Bethmann as his successor, but contemporary evidence as well as the meticulous critique of Hiller von Gaertringen, *Fürst Bülow's Denkwürdigkeiten* (Tübingen, 1956), pp. 38 ff., 213–254, have established it as a fact.

43 F. W. von Loebell, MS "Erinnerungen," 2 : 97 ff., 110 ff. Bethmann to William H. July 8, 1909, DZA Me, Rep. 89H, II Deutsches Reich 1. Bethmann to Eisendecher, July 20, 1909, AA *Nachlass* Eisendecher. Cf. also *Lettres de la Princesse Radziwill*, 4 : 80 ff. and Witt, *Finanzpolitik*, pp. 301 ff.

44 Szögyény to Aerenthal, July 20, 1909, HHStA, Pa III, 167B. Lerchenfeld to Podewils, July 14, 15, 1909, in Rassow-Born, *Akten*, pp. 404 ff., stressing that Bethmann had "accepted only reluctantly," and was not received "with trust by all parties," since they doubted his firmness. Bethmann declined to resurrect the bloc, but intended, "if possible, to draw the National Liberals into the new majority." Ambassador Hill to Washington, July 27, 1909, NA, U.S. Embassy in Berlin.

45 Ernst von Reventlow, "Unsere Aufgabe für die Zukunft," *AB*, July 17, 1909; *Die Grenzboten* (1909), pp. 192–95; "Bethmann Hollweg," *Konservative Monatsschrift* (1909/10), pp. 556 ff.; *Das Echo*, July, 1909; L. Sochaczewer, "Die Politik des fünften Kanzlers," *Blaubuch*, no. 46 (1909); *Die Woche*, no. 29 (1909), p. 1217; no. 30, pp. 1268 ff.; F. Naumann, "Der neue Kanzler," *Die Hilfe* no. 46 (1909), pp. 722 ff.; L. Hutter, "Der neue Kanzler," *Der März* (Aug., 1909), pp. 166 ff.; E. Francke, "Der neue Kanzler," *Die Illustrierte Zeitung* (July 29, 1909), pp. 258 ff. Max Maurenbrecher, "Regierungswechsel," *Sozialistische Monatshefte* 13 (1909) : 982–83 and *Die Neue Zeit* 27 (1909) : 561–564.

46 Octavio von Zedlitz und Neukirch, "Kanzlerpolitik," *Die Gegenwart*, no. 30 (1909). *Lettres de la Princesse Radziwill*, 4 : 85 ff., reiterating that Bethmann would only be an interim chancellor until William II found someone more to his liking. Vierhaus, *Spitzemberg*, pp. 497 ff. See also his cousin Helene Harrach's letter to Baroness von Spitzemberg, August 12, 1909: "I have unlimited confidence in his noble intentions, his great gifts, and his genuinely independent spirit. It is another question how far he will meet with success in solving so many—especially now —difficult tasks. If not, he will suffer for his principles as well as personally" (ibid.). Cf. Bülow, *Denkwürdigkeiten*, 2 : 511 ff. Cf. also the reputed comment of Graf Schlieffen, falsely attributed by Vietsch, *Bethmann*, p. 102 to Elard von Oldenburg-Januschau's *Erinnerungen* (Leipzig, 1936), p. 111—"I am curious how this man from Frankfurt will be able to take care of the German Empire."— actually in Generaloberst von Einem, *Kriegsminister unter Wilhelm II: Erinnerungen eines Soldaten 1853–1933* (Leipzig, 1933), p. 155.

Chapter 4

1 Szögyény to Aerenthal, July 19, Aug. 13, HHStA, PA III, 168. Cf. also Count Vitzthum's memorandum for the Saxon king, July 22, 1909: "From the viewpoint of the united governments the recent events must be deplored." For Bülow's version cf. his conversation with the Saxon minister on July 14, 1909, SHStA, AM no. 1,090. Cf. F. Stampfer, *Erfahrungen und Erlebnisse* (Cologne, 1957), p. 137, for Bethmann's characterization. The chancellor's speech to the Landwirtschaftsrat, Feb. 15, 1910 is in Schulthess's *GK* (1910), pp. 136 ff. Riezler diary, Feb. 2, 1910: "Bethmann's character reawakens my interest in my profession," since he felt "able to achieve something with factual arguments." Courtesy of Prof. K. D. Erdmann. Cf. also Bethmann to Lamprecht, Jan. 8, and to Breysig, Sept. 8, 1910: "I often feel that the basic task of a statesman is a certain listening to developments and an essential recognition of the depth and lasting direction of movements under an accidental and deceptive surface." AA, Dld 122, no. 6, vol. 8 and E. Vietsch, *Bethmann*, pp. 111–12.

2 The only full treatment of Bethmann's domestic politics before the war is B. Haberland's unpublished dissertation, "Die Innenpolitik des Reiches unter der Kanzlerschaft Bethmann Hollwegs 1909–1914" (Kiel, 1950). For a more trenchant analysis of Bethmann's constitutional role cf. H. G. Zmarzlik, *Bethmann Hollweg als Reichskanzler, 1909–1914*, pp. 9 ff.; S. Schöne, *Von der Reichskanzlei zum Bundeskanzleramt: Eine Untersuchung zum Problem der Führung und Koordination in der jüngeren deutschen Geschichte* (Berlin, 1968), pp. 18 ff.; and E. Deuerlein, *Deutsche Kanzler von Bismarck bis Hitler* (Munich, 1968), pp. 141 ff. For Martha von Bethmann Hollweg's exclamation cf. H. Grüber, *Erinnerungen aus sieben Jahrzehnten* (Kiel, 1968), pp. 35–36.

3 Bethmann to Weizsäcker, July 19, 1909, *Privatnachlass* Weizsäcker. Bethmann to Eisendecher, Sept. 16, 1909, June 2, 1913, AA *Nachlass* Eisendecher. Vierhaus, *Spitzemberg*, pp. 514–15, Martha von Bethmann Hollweg on the trying relationship to the emperor. Cf. also Admiral Müller, *Der Kaiser*, pp. 91 ff., and Szögyény to Aerenthal, Nov. 24, 1909, HHStA, PA III, 168. William II, *Ereignisse und Gestalten*, pp. 110 ff. For the limits of Bethmann's pliability cf. his conflict with the kaiser about an article in the *Daily Graphic*, where William had agreed with the assertion that "Germany is a patriotic land governed by fearful, meticulous bureaucrats, who hate doing anything and are only plagued by fearful, meticulous experts." DZA Me, Rep. 89H, II Deutsches Reich 1, vol. 2. Cf. also Count Stolberg-Wernigerode, *Die Unentschiedene Generation* (Munich, 1968), pp. 370 ff.

4 Bethmann to Weizsäcker, July 19, 1909, *Privatnachlass* Weizsäcker. Bethmann to Eisendecher, July 20, 1909, Jan. 28, 1910; AA *Nachlass* Eisendecher. Cf. also reports of Ambassadors Lerchenfeld, Salza, and Nieser to their foreign ministries, BHStA, MA III 268 7th f., SHStA, AM nos. 1090 ff., and GLAK 233, nos. 34,814 ff. Bethmann to the historian C. Bornhak, May 7, 1912; DZA Po, Rkz. 1601, no. 4. The federal component in the decision-making of the Second Empire has been consistently underestimated.

5 Bethmann to Wermuth, late Aug. 1910; Wermuth, *Beamtenleben*, p. 289. Note by Riezler in his diary, July 19, 1910; Cf. Admiral Tirpitz, *Der Aufbau der deutschen Weltmacht* (Stuttgart, 1924); E. Jäckh, *Kiderlen-Wächter der Staatsmann und Mensch*, 2 vols. (Berlin, 1925); C. von Delbrück, *Die wirtschaftliche Mobilmachung in Deutschland 1914* (Munich, 1924); A. von Mutius, "Aus dem Nachlass des ehemaligen Kaiserlichen Statthalters von Elsass-Lothringen, früheren preussi-

schen Ministers des Innern von Dallwitz," *Preussische Jahrbücher* 214 : 1–22, 147–66, 290–303; Wilhelm von Loebell, MS "Erinnerungen," BA *Nachlass* Loebell; B. Schwertfeger, ed., *Kaiser und Kabinettschef* (Oldenburg, 1931). See also Hans Goldschmidt, *Das Reich und Preussen im Kampf um die Führung* (Berlin, 1931) and Fritz Hartung, "Verantwortliche Regierungen, Kabinette und Nebenregierungen im konstitutionellen Preussen, 1848–1918," *Forschungen zur Brandenburgischen und Preussischen Geschichte* 44 (1932) : 1–45, 302–73.

6   Bethmann to Eisendecher, July 18, 1913; AA *Nachlass* Eisendecher. Bethmann to the Prussian Ministry of State, July 14, 1909, DZA Me, Rep. 90a B III 2b no. 6, vol. 158. Cf. W. Frauendienst, "Demokratisierung des deutschen Konstitutionalismus in der Zeit Wilhelms II," *Zeitschrift für gesamte Staatswissenschaft* (1957), pp. 721–46. For Bethmann's relationship to the Reichstag cf. the files in DZA Po, Rkz nos. 1,391–419. Cf. also Thomas Nipperdey, *Die Organisation der deutschen Parteien vor 1918* (Düsseldorf, 1961) and P. Molt, *Der Reichstag vor der improvisierten Revolution* (Cologne, 1963).

7   Bethmann to Eisendecher, July 20, 1909, AA *Nachlass* Eisendecher. Bethmann to the Prussian Ministry of State, July 14, 1909, DZA Me, Rep. 90a B III 2b no. 6, vol. 158. For his relationship to Bülow, cf. F. Thimme, "Bülow und Bethmann Hollweg," *Front wider*, pp. 194 ff. and Riezler in his diary, July 19, 1910: "Bülow is in Berlin, full of the 'most honest' praise for Bethmann. Serene and jovial, he makes behind his desk those speeches which he can no longer give in Parliament." Bethmann to the Reichstag, Dec. 9, 1909, Schulthess's *GK* (1909), pp. 350 ff. Cf. also Vierhaus, *Spitzemberg*, pp. 518 ff. for Paul Schwabach's gasp: "How can such a thoroughbred pull this heavy, mired cart out of the mud?"

8   For the resumption of the electoral reform, cf. DZA Po, Rkz. nos. 1,071 ff., 1,078, RdI, 15,685, 15,811, 15,925; DZA Me, Rep. 77, Tit 496a no. 179, vols. 3–4, Rep. 89 H, I Preussen, no. 1; AA Bonn, Preussen 3, no. 2, vols. 2 ff. Cf. also Lerchenfeld to Podewils, Feb. 21, 1910, BHStA MA III 2688 and Flotow to Aerenthal, Oct. 12, Nov. 9; Szögyény to Aerenthal Dec. 7, 1909; HHStA, PA III, 168. The draft proposal of Minister of the Interior Moltke of Nov. 7, 1909, is in DZA Po, Rkz. 1,071. Cf. also the extensive debates of the Prussian Ministry of State on Nov. 22, Dec. 21, 31, 1909, Jan. 22, 1910; DZA Me, Rep. 90a B III 2b no. 6, vols. 158–59. See also Bethmann's very conservative letter to Arnim-Züsedom, Oct. 2, 1909, DZA Po, Rkz. 1,071, as well as Bethmann to Eisendecher, Jan. 28, 1910; AA *Nachlass* Eisendecher. Bethmann to Cardinal Kopp, May 3, 1910, DZA Po, Rkz. 1,071. Except for the older dissertation by Hans Dietzel, *Die preussischen Wahlrechtsreformbestrebungen von der Oktroyierung des Dreiklassenwahlrechts bis zu Beginn des Weltkrieges* (Lechte, 1934), there is no satisfactory study of this crucial issue in the prewar years. Cf. also Count Cuno Westarp, *Konservative Politik*, 1 : 97 ff.

9   For the purpose of the reform, cf. the officious release of the *NAZ* on Feb. 4, 1910. Bethmann stated his tactical considerations in the Prussian Ministry of State, Dec. 21, 1909, Feb. 26, Mar. 7, 15, 1910, DZA Me, Rep. 90a B III 2b no. 6, vols. 158–59. For the Landtag session of Feb. 10 see Schulthess's *GK* (1910), pp. 110 ff., 126 ff., and Bethmann's statement in the Reichstag of Feb. 19, ibid., pp. 143 ff. For the effect of the speech, cf. Nieser to Karlsruhe, Mar. 13, 1910, GLAK no. 34,814 and Szögyény to Aerenthal, Jan. 18, Feb. 15, 1910, HHStA, PA III, 168. Cf. the Riezler diary, July 19, 1910, for the speech which Bülow claimed he would have given: "I shall not make an electoral reform against the party which has exhibited such courageous sacrifices, which had led the wars of liberation, and which is one of the pillars of the state. I shall make a reform only with the approval of this party."

10 Bethmann to the Ministry of State, Mar. 15, Apr. 18, 1910; DZA Me, Rep. 90a B

III 2b no. 6, vol. 159. Bethmann memorandum about the party constellation. Mar. 16, Bethmann to William II, Apr. 19, 27, 28, 1910, DZA Po, Rkz. 1,071. Szögyény to Aerenthal, Mar. 5, 12, 17, Apr. 26, 1910, HHStA, PA III, 168. Bethmann to Hutten-Czapski, Apr. 20, 1910, DZA Po *Nachlass* Hutten. For the larger political reasoning behind this attempt, cf. his letter to Schmoller of Apr. 9, 1910: "Our Prussian landed aristocracy is certainly not free of faults, but it provides impulses for army, administration, and self-government without which we cannot do in the present as little as in the past." Hence he intended not to break the backbone of conservatism, as was later alleged, "but to modernize it. Already our whole economic and political development guarantees that they will not gain a preponderant influence thereby." Cited in Zmarzlik, *Bethmann*, p. 44. For the role of the Center Party see also Karl Bachem, *Vorgeschichte*, 7 : 115 ff.; for the National Liberals cf. W. Gagel, *Die Wahlrechtsfrage in der Geschichte der deutschen liberalen Parteien, 1848–1918* (Düsseldorf, 1958); and for the Progressives, Th. Heuss, *Naumann*, pp. 282 ff.

11 Bethmann to Hutten-Czapski, Apr. 30, 1910, DZA Po *Nachlass* Hutten-Czapski. Bethmann to Ministry of State, May 24, 26, 1910, DZA Me, Rep. 90a B III 2b no. 6, vol. 159. Bethmann to William II, Apr. 19, 28, 1910, DZA Me, Rep. 89 H, I Preussen 1. William II to Bethmann, Apr. 19, 1910, DZA Po, Rkz. 1,071: "The Conservatives' actions are incomprehensible and deeply regrettable, because they reveal an incredible lack of political insight and have no concept of raison d'état." Cf. also ibid. Wahnschaffe to Hugenberg, Apr. 29, May 5, 1910, attempting to use economic leverage to produce an agreement between National Liberals and Conservatives.

12 Schulthess's *GK* (1910), pp. 282 ff. Bethmann to William II, May 27, and Valentini to Bethmann, May 28, 1910; DZA Po, Rkz. 1,071. Szögyény to Aerenthal, May 10, 24, 1910; HHStA, PA III, 168. Cf. also Nieser's reports of Apr. 30, May 15, and May 28, 1910, GLAK 34,814. Bülow to Bethmann, June 25, 1910; Bethmann to Bülow July 14, 1911, BA *Nachlass* Bülow. Bethmann to William II, Aug. 28, 1910, DZA Me, Rep. 89H, I Generalia 6. Despite the setback, Bethmann clung to his political ideas, claiming in a letter to Hans Delbrück of Sept. 3, 1910, that domestic politics would only be improved "when the hysterical nervousness and, in its wake, the unscrupled nihilism which has seized wide circles of the moderate press, and thereby also a great part of the people, are destroyed." In a revealing self-appraisal he continued, "Only then will the foundations have been laid upon which a *reasonably progressive* policy can build [my italics]." Cited in Zmarzlik, *Bethmann*, pp. 46–47. Cf. also Bethmann to Eickhoff, Sept. 27, 1910, DZA Po, Rkz. no. 1,391, and the sagacious comment of the Princess Radziwill: "Nobody is satisfied, not the people, not the parliamentarians who voted in the House. Necessarily one must come back to it and it will be too late to do any good." *Lettres de la Princesse Radziwill*, 4 : 111 ff.

13 Bethmann's extensive memorandum on Alsace-Lorraine, Dec. 16, 1908, is in DZA Po, Rkz. no. 153. Cf. also DZA Me, Rep. 89H, Elsass-Lothringen, no. 6. vol. 1 f. Bethmann in the Prussian Ministry of State, Oct. 11, 1909, DZA Me, Rep. 90a B III 2b no. 6, vol. 158. Bethmann's speech in the Reichstag, Dec. 13, 1909, Schulthess's *GK* (1909), pp. 388–89. For the sensitivity of the Alsatian issue, cf. also E. Klingenmann, "Der Reichskanzler und Elsass-Lothringen," in *AB*, Dec. 25, 1909. Cf. also Zmarzlik, *Bethmann*, 85 ff.; H. U. Wehler, "Elsass-Lothringen von 1870 bis 1918: Das 'Reichsland' als politisch-staatsrechtliches Problem des zweiten deutschen Kaiserreichs," *Zeitschrift für die Geschichte des Oberrheins* 109 (1961): 133–99, and Dan P. Silverman, "The Economic Consequences of Annexation: Alsace-Lorraine and Imperial Germany, 1871–1918," *CEH* 4 (1971) : 34 ff.

14   Bethmann to the Reichstag, Mar. 14, Dec. 10, 1910, Jan. 28, Mar. 23, May 23,
     1911, Schulthess's *GK* (1910), pp. 191 ff. (1911), pp. 13 ff. Bethmann to Wedel,
     Apr. 19, 1910, DZA Po, Rkz. 153. Discussion of Prussian Ministry of State, Oct. 21,
     1910, DZA Me, Rep. 90a B III 2b no. 6, vol. 159. William II's attitude to the
     proposed reform is clear from his marginalia to an article of the *Strassburger Post*,
     transmitted by Valentini to Bethmann on Apr. 25, 1910. The kaiser approved
     local self-government as "Very correct," but added to speculations about a repre-
     sentative body, "No Reichstag suffrage!" DZA Po, Rkz. no. 153.
15   Bethmann to the Prussian Ministry of State, Feb. 11, May 20, 30, 1911, DZA Me,
     Rep. 90a B III 2b no. 6, vol. 160. Bethmann to Wedel, Feb. 20, Apr. 1, May 10,
     July 4, 1911; Bethmann to William II, Mar. 9, May 10 and 19, 1911; Bethmann to
     Hertling, May 19, 1911, DZA Po, Rkz. no. 154. Cf. also the Riezler diary, Jan. 27,
     May 17, 1911, for the progress of the reform: "The government now faces the
     question of whether it should abandon the plural vote. Then the law would be
     accepted by Socialists, Progressives, and Center against the right National Liberals
     and both conservative parties." Typical of the Wilhelmian state, was Riezler's
     further comment: "This is impossible for the chancellor's position in Prussia. . . .
     The chancellor would be finished with the kaiser and in Prussia." The chan-
     cellor's assistant speculated that Bethmann's acceptance of equal suffrage meant
     "that the combination of the entire Reichstag against the Conservatives tempts
     Bethmann, who asserts that in the next six years we cannot govern conservatively
     and that we always have to hold back against the Right." Bethmann to Eisen-
     decher, June 4, 1911, AA *Nachlass* Eisendecher; Bethmann to Bülow, July 14, 1911,
     BA *Nachlass* Bülow; and Bethmann to the crown prince, May 10, 1912, DZA Po,
     Rkz. no. 155. Cf. also C. Westarp, *Konservative Politik*, 1 : 314 ff.; Bachem, *Vorge-
     schichte*, 7 : 144 ff.; Th. Heuss, *Naumann*, p. 284; H. U. Wehler, *Sozialdemokratie
     und Nationalstaat* (Würzburg, 1962), pp. 63 ff.
16   Bethmann in Prussian Ministry of State, July 23, 1909, Mar. 20, June 30, 1911,
     May 1, 1912, Jan. 7, Dec. 13, 1913, DZA Me, Rep. 90a B III 2b no. 6, vols. 158–62.
     Szögyény to Aerenthal, Aug. 3, 1909, Jan. 18, Aug. 15, 1910, July 17, 1912, Flotow
     to Berchtold, Sept. 9, 1913, Szögyény to Berchtold, June 17, 1914, HHStA, PA III,
     168–71. Bethmann in Landtag, Jan. 19, 1910, Schulthess's *GK* (1910), pp. 51 ff.,
     Bethmann to "Deutscher Tag," May 28, 1911, ibid. (1911), p. 117. For the Reich-
     stag's "no confidence" vote of 213 (Center, Socialists, Poles, and Alsatians) to 97
     (Conservatives and National Liberals), with 43 abstentions (of the Progressives),
     see ibid. (1913), p. 35. Bethmann to Valentini, Aug. 12, 1910, DZA Me *Nachlass*
     Valentini. Cf. Bethmann to Hutten-Czapski, Aug. 29, 1910. Cf. also DZA Po, Rkz.
     1,004; PrGStA, Rep. 90, nos. 1,614–15. The persistent attempts at *Besitzbefestigungs*-
     laws and administrative measures for the "strengthening of German influence," are
     in DZA Po, RdI 15,858 and PrGStA, Rep. 90, no. 1,568, finally rejected by
     Bethmann in a letter to Arnim of Oct. 5, 1909, since "I consider any special legis-
     lation for the eastern provinces questionable in principle." For the general com-
     plex see also D. Keil, "Polenfrage," pp. 325 ff. and A. Tims, *The HKT Society:
     Prussianizing German Poland* (New Haven, 1941).
17   Bethmann to Valentini, Aug. 12, 1910, DZA Me *Nachlass* Valentini; Bethmann to
     William II, Feb. 9, 1911, DZA Me, Rep. 89H, Reichssteuern 1, vol. 3, which al-
     ready suggests a *Vermögenszuwachssteuer* as socially more just and politically more
     expedient. Cf. also Wermuth, *Beamtenleben*, pp. 258 ff. For the specific documen-
     tation cf. DZA Me, Rep. 89H, 26, no. 1, vol. 2 ff. and DZA Po, Rkz. 1,251/1. For
     the general background cf. also the pro-Ludendorff account of Hans Herzfeld,
     Die deutsche Rüstungspolitik vor dem Weltkriege (Bonn, 1923); Gerhard Ritter,

Die Hauptmächte Europas und das wilhelminische Reich, 1890–1914 (Munich, 1960), pp. 148 ff., 272 ff; and P.-C. Witt, *Finanzpolitik*, pp. 361 ff.

18 Bethmann to Bülow, July 14, 1911, BA *Nachlass* Bülow. Bethmann to Loebell, Nov. 7, 1910, BA *Nachlass* Loebell. Bethmann to *Landwirtschaftsrat*, Feb. 16, 1910, Schulthess's *GK* (1910), pp. 136–37; Bethmann to *Handelstag*, Apr. 13, 1910, ibid. (1910), pp. 214–15; Bethmann to *Landwirtschaftsrat*, Feb. 15, 1911, ibid. (1911), p. 39; Bethmann to *Handelstag*, Feb. 19, 113, ibid. (1913), p. 81; Bethmann to *Landwirtschaftsrat*, Feb. 11, 1914, ibid. (1914), pp. 70–71; Bethmann to Hamburg Senate, Mar. 2, 1914, ibid. (1914), p. 111; Bethmann to Reichstag, Oct. 23, 1911; ibid. (1911), pp. 171 ff.; Oct. 25, 1912, ibid. (1912), pp. 219 ff.; Dec. 10, 1913, ibid. (1913), pp. 426 ff.; Jan. 13, 1914, ibid. (1914), pp. 15 ff. Bethmann to Prussian Ministry of State, July 13, Sept. 29, 1911, Sept. 24, 1912; DZA Me, Rep. 90a B III 2b no. 6, vols. 160–61. Cf. also H. Böhme, *Deutschlands Weg zur Grossmacht: Studien zum Verhältnis von Wirtschaft und Staat während der Reichsgründerzeit, 1848–1881* (Cologne, 1966) and F. Fischer, *Krieg der Illusionen*, pp. 348 ff. The whole area of the government's economic policy during the last decade of the Wilhelmian Empire deserves further investigation. For one limited aspect see Lothar Burchardt, *Friedenswirtschaft und Kriegsvorsorge: Deutschlands wirtschaftliche Rüstungsbestrebungen vor 1914* (Boppard, 1968).

19 Bethmann to Hutten-Czapski, Aug. 28, 1910, DZA Po *Nachlass* Hutten-Czapski; Bethmann to Loebell, Nov. 7, 1910, BA *Nachlass* Loebell; Bethmann to Eisendecher, Dec. 27, 1910, AA *Nachlass* Eisendecher. Cf. Riezler diary, Mar. 24, 1911. Cf. C. Westarp, *Konservative Politik*, 1 : 366 ff. Winterfeld-Menkin, *Jahreszeiten*, pp. 145 ff. See also the revealing Hermann von Dewitz, *Von Bismarck bis Bethmann: Innenpolitische Rückblicke eines Konservativen* (Berlin, 1918), and Heydebrand, "Beiträge zu einer Geschichte der konservativen Partei," *Konservative Monatsschrift* (1922), pp. 695 ff. Knowing that "no chancellor can weather the pronounced opposition of the Conservatives in the long run," or in another phrasing, "in this country a government supported only by the Left is ultimately impossible," Bethmann attempted to woo the Conservatives rather than to fight them, although he clashed with Heydebrand often enough in the Reichstag. "According to his entire character, he too belongs to his party, which in his opinion ought to be the main pillar of Prussia," Ambassador Szögyény analyzed; "Since the survival of the empire is only possible under strong Prussian leadership, he is greatly concerned about the future." Szögyény to Aerenthal, Oct. 11, Dec. 13, 1910, May 10, June 6, Nov. 30, 1911; HHStA, PA III, 168–69. Cf. also Westarp *Nachlass* in DZA Po, and with Freiherr Hiller von Gaertringen. For the role of agrarian interest groups within the Conservative Party, cf. H. J. Puhle, *Agrarische Interessenpolitik und preussischer Konservatismus im Wilhelmischen Reich* (Hanover, 1966), and Hans Booms, *Die deutsch-konservative Partei* (Düsseldorf, 1954).

20 There is no recent secondary study of the Free Conservatives. For some information see *Die Bürgerlichen Parteien in Deutschland* (Leipzig, 1970) and O. Stolberg-Wernigerode, *Unentschiedene Generation*, pp. 228 ff. Cf. also BA *Nachlass* von Kardorff. For the National Liberals see Bethmann to Eisendecher, Dec. 27, 1910, AA *Nachlass* Eisendecher. Riezler diary, Jan. 27, 1911. Despite his liberal leanings, Riezler was forced to admit Bethmann's criticism, adding, "They need a man who possesses sufficient authority and ruthlessness to keep all these petty bourgeois in line." Cf. the Schiffer *Nachlass* in the PrGStA, the Richthoven *Nachlass* in the BA, and the Hutten-Czapski *Nachlass* in the DZA Po. Cf. also Bassermann's "longing for a strong statesman" in his speech to the party caucus on Feb. 9, 1914,

in K. P. Reiss, *Von Bassermann zu Stresemann: Die Sitzungen des nationalliberalen Zentralvorstandes 1912–1917* (Düsseldorf, 1967). See also Eugen Schiffer, *Ein Leben für den Liberalismus* (Berlin, 1951), pp. 30 ff.; L. Maenner, *Prinz Heinrich zu Schönaich-Carolath: Ein Parlamentarisches Leben der wilhelminischen Zeit* (Stuttgart, 1931); and D. G. Warren, *The Red Kingdom of Saxony: Lobbying Grounds for Gustav Stresemann 1901–1909* (The Hague, 1964).

21 Bethmann to Eisendecher, Nov. 16, 1911, AA *Nachlass* Eisendecher. Bethmann to Hertling, Dec. 13, 1912, BHStA MA I 955. Bethmann to Prussian Ministry of State, Jan. 2, 1911, DZA Me, Rep. 90a B III 2b no. 6, vol. 160. Szögyény to Aerenthal, June 6, 7, 22, 1910. HHStA, PA III, 168. Bethmann to Reichstag, June 9, 1910, Schulthess's *GK* (1910), pp. 317–18. For the transformaton of the Center Party and the struggle between the Berlin and Cologne factions, cf. Bachem, *Vorgeschichte*, vols. 7 ff. For Hertling's relation to Bethmann, cf. his extensive correspondence with his son and wife in his *Nachlass*, BA, and his son's introduction to *Ein Jahr in der Reichskanzlei* (Munich, 1919). See also K. Epstein, *Matthias Erzberger und das Dilemma der deutschen Demokratie*, rev. ed. (Berlin, 1962). For the tactical considerations of the chancellery, cf. also Riezler diary, Feb. 5, 1911. Bethmann to the Reichstag, Mar. 7, 1911, Schulthess's *GK* (1911), pp. 63 ff. Bethmann to Eisendecher, Oct. 1, 1913, AA Bonn *Nachlass* Eisendecher.

22 Bethmann to Hutten-Czapski, Aug. 29, 1910, DZA Po *Nachlass* Hutten-Czapski. Riezler diary, Aug. 30, 1910: "The only chance is to stand on the Prussian leg and hold on." Bethmann in the Reichstag, Nov. 26, 1910, Schulthess's *GK* (1910), pp. 391–92. F. Naumann, "Der einsame Kanzler," *Die Hilfe*, no. 50 (1910): 789–90. Szögyény to Aerenthal, Aug. 27, 30, 1910, HHStA, PA III, 168. Cf. also the Naumann *Nachlass* in DZA Po, the Haussman papers in WHStA, and the Payer *Nachlass* in the BA, as well as Th. Heuss, *Naumann*, F. Payer, *Von Bethmann bis Ebert* (Frankfurt, 1923), and C. Haussmann, *Schlaglichter* (Frankfurt, 1924). See also Ludwig Elm, *Zwischen Fortschritt und Reaktion: Geschichte der liberalen Bourgeoisie in Deutschland 1893–1918* (Berlin, 1968) and P. Gilg, *Die Erneuerung des demokratischen Denkens im wilhelminischen Deutschland* (Wiesbaden, 1965).

23 Riezler diary, Apr. 8, May 17, 1911. The magnitude of the bureaucratic resistance to working with the Social Democrats is apparent in Riezler's remark regarding Alsace-Lorraine: "This time and on this question [collaboration] is impossible even if the plural votes are debatable." Bethmann in Prussian Ministry of State, Sept. 19, Nov. 7, 1910, DZA Me, Rep. 90a B III 2b no. 6, vol. 159. Bethmann in the Reichstag, Dec. 13, 1911, Schulthess's *GK* (1911), pp. 443–44. Bethmann to Bülow, July 14, 1911, BA *Nachlass* Bülow. Bethmann to Eisendecher, June 4, 1911, AA *Nachlass* Eisendecher. For Bethmann's relations to the Socialists, especially valuable is the *Nachlass* of the revisionist Albert Südekum, BA. See also E. Mathias and E. Pikart, *Die Reichstagsfraktion der deutschen Sozialdemokratie 1898 bis 1918* (Düsseldorf, 1966). H. J. Varain, *Freie Gewerkschaften, Sozialdemokratie und Staat* (Düsseldorf, 1956); Institut für Marxismus Leninismus beim ZK der SED, *Geschichte der Deutschen Arbeiterbewegung* (Berlin, 1966), vol. 2, and the forthcoming study by D. Groh, *Die 'vaterlandlosen Gesellen' und das Vaterland* (1972).

24 Bethmann to Eisendecher, Dec. 26, 1911, AA *Nachlass* Eisendecher. Bethmann to Oettingen, Dec. 17, 1912; BA *Nachlass* Oettingen. Bethmann to Kiderlen-Waechter, Jan. 2, 1912, KPs. *NAZ*, Jan. 2, 1911, Schulthess's *GK* (1911), p. 1. Memorandum to the officials' right of election, n.d. and Dallwitz instruction, Dec. 8, 1911, in PrGStA, Rep. 90, no. 307. See also J. Bertram, *Die Wahlen zum Deutschen Reichstag vom Jahre 1912: Parteien und Verbände in der Innenpolitik des Wilhelminischen Reiches* (Düsseldorf, 1964), pp. 120 ff. for further literature.

25 Bethmann to Schwerin-Löwitz, Jan. 17, 1912; PrGStA Rep. 90, no. 307. Szögyény,

to Aerenthal, Jan. 19, Feb. 10, 15, 1912; HHStA, PA III, 170. According to the
Austrian Ambassador, Bethmann did not view the outcome of the election tragically, since "In Germany there exists no parliamentary regime and, according to
the present constitution, it is equally impossible in the future." Bethmann in the
Reichstag, Feb. 16, 1912, Schulthess's *GK* (1912), pp. 36 ff. Bethmann attributed the
defeat of the Right to opposition to juster taxation, and the Socialist victory to
the radicalization of liberalism, but he claimed: "The great tasks do not lie in
the direction of democratizing the empire." Bethmann circular to the Prussian
ambassadors in Germany, Feb. 3, 1912, *Privatnachlass* Weizsäcker.

26 Admiral Tirpitz to Bethmann Hollweg, Aug. 30, 1911, *Der Aufbau der deutschen
Weltmacht*, pp. 207 ff. Lerchenfeld to Hertling, Nov. 9, 1911, BHStA MA III 2689.

27 Admiral Müller, *Der Kaiser*, pp. 89 ff., 95 ff. Widenmann reports to Tirpitz, Oct.
14, 28, 30; Metternich to Bethmann, Oct. 31; and William II's running marginalia,
such as "Nonsense . . . ! Incredible stuff . . . ! Chicken . . . ! Ridiculous . . . !
Gobbledygook . . . ! We have received a slap in the face and are supposed to
build no ships!!! Usual Metternich advice. Don't build in Germany, and England
will be in a good mood!" in Tirpitz, *Aufbau*, pp. 231 ff. Bethmann to Reichstag
about the prospects of disarmament, Mar. 30, 1911, Schulthess's *GK* (1911), pp.
89–90 and Bethmann to William II, Mar. 31, 1911: "Utopians will call the speech
brutal," BA, ARkz Bethmann Personalia 1. Cf. also the unpublished chapter of
his memoirs, "Flottenpolitik: Die Memoiren des Herrn von Tirpitz," BA Kl. Erw.
342. See E. Jäckh, *Kiderlen-Waechter*, 2 : 155. Metternich to Bethmann, Nov. 1,
1911, *GP*, vols. 28 ff. and Bethmann memorandum of conversation with Normann,
Oct. 19, 1911, in DZA Po, Rkz. 951/1. Müller to Valentini, Nov. 16, 1911, DZA
Me, Rep. 89H, 27, Marine, no. 3, vols. 2 ff. For the social roots of navalism cf.
E. Kehr, *Schlachtflottenbau und Parteipolitik, 1894–1901* (Berlin, 1930) and his
posthumous *Der Primat der Innenpolitik*, ed. H. U. Wehler (Berlin, 1965). For a
defense of the navy point of view see W. Hubatsch, *Die Ära Tirpitz: Studien zur
deutschen Marinepolitik, 1890–1918* (Göttingen, 1955). "Der Kulminationspunkt
der deutschen Marinepolitik im Jahre 1912," *HZ* 176 : 291–322 and "Zur Beurteilung von Tirpitz," *WaG* (1951), pp. 174–84. See also Jonathan Steinberg, *Yesterday's Deterrent–Tirpitz and the Birth of the German Battle Fleet* (London, 1965)
and "The Copenhagen Complex," *JCH*, 1, no. 3 (1966): 21 ff. The most incisive
study is Volker R. Berghahn, "Zu den Zielen des deutschen Flottenbaus unter
Wilhelm II," *HZ* 210 (1970): 34 ff. and *Der Tirpitz Plan* (Düsseldorf, 1971).

28 Heeringen to Bethmann, Nov. 19, 1911; Wermuth memorandum, Oct. 21, 1911;
Bethmann to Wermuth, Nov. 21, 22, 1911; Wermuth note and memorandum,
Dec. 8, 1911; Bethmann to Heeringen, Dec. 4, 25, 1912; Bethmann before the
Bundesrat, Dec. 15, 1912, all in DZA Po, Rkz. 951/1. Bethmann to Ministry of
state, Dec. 15, 1911, DZA Me, Rep. 90a B III 2b no. 6, 160 and Rep. 89H, 27 no. 3,
vol. 4. Bethmann to Valentini, Dec. 25, 1911; ibid. *Nachlass* Valentini. Bethmann
to Eisendecher, Dec. 26, 1911, AA *Nachlass* Eisendecher. Müller, *Der Kaiser*, pp.
105 ff. Cf. Ritter, *Staatskunst und Kriegshandwerk*, 2 : 209 ff.

29 Bethmann to Kiderlen-Waechter, Jan. 2, 1912, KPs. Cf. also the excerpts from the
Valentini diary for the spring of 1912: "Report to H.M. who is very agitated about
Bethmann." BA *Nachlass* Thimme. Nieser to Dusch, Dec. 15, 1912; Berckheim to
Dusch, Feb. 11, 1912: "Apparently the chancellor still vacillates." GLAK 233, no.
34,815. Cf. also Bethmann's note of thanks to Emil Ludwig for the latter's new Bismarck biography: "Just like last summer people are losing their heads again. So
far I have not yet done so. But it will be good to strengthen oneself with the
great man . . . !" Bethmann to William II, Jan. 13, 1912; DZA Me, Rep. 89 H, 26
Mil 1. Bethmann to Eisendecher, Feb. 22, 1912, AA *Nachlass* Eisendecher. Wermuth's

letter of resignation, Jan. 6, 1911; Bethmann to William II, Feb. 18, 1911, DZA Me, Rep. 89 H, II Reichssteuern I, vol. 4. Cf. also F. Fischer, _Der Krieg der Illusionen_, pp. 175 ff. and P.-C. Witt, _Finanzpolitik_, pp. 356–57.

30 For the Haldane Mission see H. J. Henning's unpublished dissertation, "Deutschlands Verhältnis zu England in Bethmann Hollwegs Aussenpolitik, 1909–1914," (Cologne, 1962). Cf. also Bethmann before the Prussian Ministry of State, Mar. 4, 1912: "It is impossible to foresee what the future holds. But I believe that war is not unavoidable as long as German policy is quiet and firm." DZA Me, Rep. 90a B III 2b, no. 6, vol. 161. Müller, _Der Kaiser_, pp. 116 ff. Tirpitz, _Der Aufbau_, pp. 317 ff. Jäckh, _Kiderlen-Waechter_ 2 : 158 ff. William II, _Ereignisse_, p. 132. Bethmann to William II, Mar. 6, 1912; William II to Bethmann, Mar. 7, 1912; Bethmann to Valentini, Mar. 8, 1912, DZA Me, Rep. 89H, II Reichssteuren 1, vol. 4. Szögyény to Aerenthal, Mar. 17, 22, 1912; Flotow to Berchtold, Apr. 21, 1912, HHStA, PA III, 170. See also Berckheim to Dusch, Feb. 22, Mar. 6, 1912, reporting Wermuth's telling admission: "I don't know whether I am hammer or anvil at present." GLAK 233, no. 34,815.

31 Lerchenfeld to Hertling, Mar. 7, 8, 24, 1912, BHStA MA I 955; Szögyény to Berchtold, Mar. 20, 1912, HHStA, PA III, 170. Muller, _Der Kaiser_, pp. 118 ff. Berckheim to Dusch, Mar. 23, 1912, GLAK 233, no. 34,815. Salza to Vitzthum, Apr. 18, 1912, SHStA AM 1,090. Kiderlen's warning that the new naval law "will make any political agreement with England impossible" turned out to be correct, and in this sense the chancellor's policy had indeed been defeated. But the one-sided stress on the failure of the Anglo-German negotiations (Vietsch, _Bethmann_, pp. 140–41) misses the significance of the shift of priorities from sea to land defense and the defeat of Tirpitz's attempt to develop the risk theory into secret parity.

32 Bethmann before Prussian Ministry of State, Mar. 21, Apr. 1, May 20, 1912, DZA Me, Rep. 90a B III 2b no. 6, vol. 161. Bethmann to the Bundesrat, Mar. 14, 1912; Bethmann to William II, Mar. 14, Apr. 20, May 22, 1912, DZA Po, Rkz. 951/1. Bethmann to William II, Mar. 17, July 9, 1912, DZA Me, Rep. 89H, II Reichssteuern 1, vol. 4. Wermuth, _Beamtenleben_, pp. 287–88. In his bitter critique of Tirpitz's memoirs, Bethmann called "Tirpitz's entire naval policy . . . a hopeless spiral without end. . . . Among the different factors, determining England's participation in the Russo-French alliance, German naval policy has always played a decisive role." MS in BA, Kl. Erw. 342. For the parliamentary situation following the passage of the arms bills, cf. Bethmann's dramatic clash with Scheidemann in the Reichstag, May 17, 1912, Schulthess's _GK_ (1912), pp. 152 ff. See also the debates over a possible suspension of the anti-Jesuit law on Apr. 26, Dec. 4, 1912, Apr. 16, 1913; ibid. (1912), pp. 127–28, 264 ff. (1913), 200 ff. Bethmann was upset about "this new battle cry of the Center Party. Apparently the Conservatives want to use the constellation to overthrow me." Bethmann to Eisendecher, Dec. 20, 1912, AA _Nachlass_ Eisendecher. Szögyény to Berchtold, Dec. 9, 1912, HHStA, PA III, 170, and Lerchenfeld to Hertling, Apr. 12, Nov. 8, 1912, and Hertling to Bethmann, Dec. 10, 1912, BHStA MA I 955.

33 Bethmann to Eisendecher, Dec. 20, 1912, Mar. 23, 1913, AA _Nachlass_ Eisendecher. Müller, _Der Kaiser_, pp. 124 ff. Bethmann to William II, Dec. 18, 1912, DZA Me, Rep. 89H, generalia 6. Bethmann to Hertling, Dec. 23, 1912, BHStA MA I 955. Cf. F. Fischer, _Der Krieg der Illusionen_, pp. 232 ff., who goes beyond J. C. G. Röhl, "Admiral Mueller and the approach of war," _HJ_ (1969), pp. 661 ff. in making the _Kriegsentschluss_ of Dec. 8, 1912, the keystone of his argument for the deliberate preparation and unleashing of a hegemonial war by Germany in 1914. It seems surprising that the otherwise so excellently informed Lerchenfeld and Berckheim, in contrast to the overeager military attachés, should not have known anything

about this momentous decision. Cf. Lerchenfeld to Hertling, Dec. 14, 1912, BHStA MA I 955 and Berckheim to Dusch, Dec. 8, 1912, GLAK 233, no. 34,815.

34 H. Herzfeld, *Die deutsche Rüstungspolitik*, pp. 47 ff. Bethmann to Hertling, Dec. 23, 1912, BHStA MA I 955: "Since the billion could not be raised through borrowing, something extraordinary had to be undertaken, and that itself produces novel side-effects." He justified the excessive brouhaha for the levy, "which goes, as you well know, 'against my grain.'" Cf. Zmarzlik, *Bethmann*, pp. 60 ff. and DZA Me, Rep. 89H, III Reichssteuern 1, vol. 4. Lerchenfeld to Hertling, July 7, 1913; Hertling memorandum of conversation with Bethmann, Apr. 21–24, 1913, BHStA MA I 955. Szögyény to Berchtold, Mar. 13, Apr. 7, May 6, July 1, 1913, HHStA, PA III, 170. For the Bundesrat difficulties cf. also Salza to Vitzthum, Oct. 10, 1913, SHStA AM 1090. See Bethmann to Vitzthum, Dec. 24, 1912 and Jan. 10, 1913, DZA Po Rkz. 215; Bethmann to Bassermann, May 10, 1913, DZA Po, Rkz. 216; and Bethmann to Oncken and Binding, Mar. 20, 1913, DZA Po, Rkz. 1252/1.

35 Bethmann before the Reichstag, Apr. 7, 9, 12, June 28, 1913; Schulthess's *GK* (1913), pp. 128 ff., 161–62, 184 ff., 274 ff. Bethmann to Eisendecher, June 2, 1913; AA *Nachlass* Eisendecher. Bethmann to Pourtalès, June 2, 1913, AA *Nachlass* Pourtalès. Bethmann to Oettingen, June 26, 1913, BA *Nachlass* Oettingen. Bethmann to the Prussian Ministry of State, Feb. 24, Mar. 4, 9, June 12, 1913; DZA Me, Rep. 90a B III 2b no. 6, vol. 162. Wolf protocols of Bethmann to Bundesrat, Mar. 2, 10/11, June 14/15, 1913, and Bethmann circular, June 14, 1913, DZA Po, Rkz. 215–16. Westarp, *Konservative Politik*, 1 : 250 ff. Cf. also Walter Wittwer, *Streit um Schicksalsfragen: Die deutsche Sozialdemokratie zu Krieg und Vaterlandsverteidigung, 1907–1914* (Berlin, 1964). See also G. Ritter, *Staatskunst und Kriegshandwerk* 2 : 280–81, and P.-C. Witt, *Finanzpolitik*, pp. 370 ff.

36 Bethmann to Eisendecher, June 2, 1913, AA *Nachlass* Eisendecher; Bethmann to Hans Delbrück, July 18, 1913, DSB *Nachlass* Delbrück. Once again, "unfortunately the Conservatives have underlined this increase of power [for the Reichstag] quite unequivocally." Bethmann to Hutten-Czapski, Aug. 6, 1913. DZA Po *Nachlass* Hutten-Czapski. Bethmann to Oettingen, June 23, 1913, BA *Nachlass* Oettingen. Gottlieb von Jagow, "Rücktrittsgedanken des Reichskanzlers von Bethmann Hollweg" (1913), in MS "Politische Aufsätze," AA *Nachlass* Jagow. Salza to Vitzthum, Apr. 5, 1913, SHStA, AM, 1,090.

37 Count Wedel to Bethman Hollweg, Nov. 25, 1912, with William II's marginalia, DZA Me, Rep. 89H, I Elsass-Lothringen, no. 6, vol. 1 ff. Count Wedel to Bethmann Hollweg, Nov. 16, 23, 29, 30, 1913; Bethmann to Treutler, Nov. 29: "At any rate I am getting the impression that the military has transgressed its authority." Bethmann to William II, Nov. 30, heavily edited to eliminate the Levy incident. Bethmann to Wedel, Dec. 1, 1913. Treutler to Bethmann, Dec. 1, 1913, all in DZA Po, Rkz. 170. For recent discussions summarizing the vast secondary literature cf. Zmarzlik, *Bethmann*, pp. 114 ff.; H. U. Wehler, "Der Fall Zabern: Rückblick auf eine Verfassungskrise des Wilhelmischen Reiches," *WaG* (1963): 27–46; and K. Stenkewitz, *Gegen Bajonett und Dividende: Die politische Krise in Deutschland am Vorabend des ersten Weltkrieges* (Berlin, 1960), pp. 125 ff.

38 Bethmann to Reichstag, Dec. 3, 4, 1913, Schulthess's *GK* (1913), pp. 377–401. Since only the Conservatives supported the chancellor halfheartedly, the second vote of no confidence in the history of the Bismarckian state was a clear 293 to 54, with 4 abstentions. Bethmann to William II, Dec. 3, 4, 1913; Wahnschaffe to Bethmann, Dec. 5, 1913; DZA Po, Rkz. 170. Cf. also Lerchenfeld's description, "This day was a dies nefastus for the chancellor and minister of war in the Reichstag." Although the Bavarian ambassador considered a "chancellor crisis" unlikely, Bethmann's

admission of transgression without immediate remedial action "must weaken his position." Lerchenfeld to Hertling, Dec. 3, 1913, BHStA MA I 955. Cf. Vierhaus, *Spitzemberg*, pp. 563 ff., and the clipping file of the Saxon government, SHStA, AM, no. 1,091, I for the public outcry. See also *Lettres de la Princesse Radziwill* 4 : 252 ff.

39   Bethmann to Oettingen, Dec. 15, 1913; BA *Nachlass* Oettingen. William's marginal comment on the report of the investigating officer, General Kühne, Dec. 2, 1913. Bethmann to William II, Dec. 5, 6, 1913. Wedel to Bethmann, Dec. 7, 1913. Bethmann to Wedel, Dec. 19, 23, 1913. Bethmann's endorsement of an article in *Die Schlesische Zeitung*, Dec. 19, 1913, with "very good." DZA Po, Rkz. 171. Szögyény to Berchtold, Dec. 2, 3, 16, 29, 1913, Jan. 23, 1914, HHStA, PA III, 171: "Since he has never thought of asking for his dismissal on this occasion there has been no chancellor crisis. Nevertheless, Bethmann is—as I am told by his close associates— quite distraught because of the recent events and fears that further successful conduct of affairs will be difficult in light of the hostile attitude of the House." Salza to Vitzhum, Jan. 1, 1914, SHStA, AM 1090. Bethmann in the Reichstag, Dec. 12, 1913, Jan. 23, 1914; Bethmann in the Landtag, Jan. 15, 1914, Schulthess's *GK* (1913), pp. 433 ff.; (1914), pp. 33 ff., 52 ff.

40   Hans von der Goltz to Bethmann, Jan 29, 1913, DZA Po, Rkz. 171. Bethmann to Reichstag, Dec. 10, 1913; Bethmann to Landtag, Jan. 13, 1914. Schulthess's *GK* (1913), pp. 427 ff.; (1914), pp. 15 ff. For the Braunschweig succession quarrel cf. Prussian Ministry of State, Oct. 16, 1913, DZA Me, Rep. 90a B III 2b no. 6, vol. 162. Bethmann proposal to Bundesrat, Oct. 16, 1913, Schulthess's *GK* (1913), pp. 338–39. Herzogin Viktoria Luise, *Ein Leben als Tochter des Kaisers* (Göttingen, 1965), pp. 87–88. The unresolved question of Prussian electoral reform troubled Bethmann, as when he asked Walther Rathenau "three times to sketch his ideas concerning electoral reform for him," in the summer of 1913. H. Pogge von Strandmann, ed., *Walther Rathenau Tagebuch 1907–1922* (Düsseldorf, 1967), pp. 169–70. But after Moltke's resignation, conservative Minister of the Interior Dallwitz and his successor Loebell adamantly rejected the reintroduction of reform proposals into the Landtag during their tenure. Dallwitz's note Mar. 26, 1912, DZA Me, Rep. 77, Tit 496a no. 179, vol. 4. Prussian Ministry of State, Apr. 20, 1912, Dec. 31, 1913, DZA Me, Rep. 90a B III 2b no. 6, vols. 161–62. See also Loebell's MS memoirs, 2 : 151 ff., and Lerchenfeld to Hertling, Jan. 3, 1914: "Bethmann assured me most emphatically that he is not anticipating a reform of the Prussian suffrage. In his opinion, this attempt would infuriate the Conservatives and worsen the situation." BHStA MA I 957a.

41   Szögyény to Berchtold, Jan. 23, 28, Apr. 8, HHStA, PA III, 171. Bethmann to Wedel, Jan. 5, Feb. 10, 1914; Bethmann to William II, Jan. 23, 1914; Bethmann to Heeringen, Feb. 8, 1914, DZA Po, Rkz. 171–72. Bethmann to Valentini, Mar. 30, 1914, DZA Me, Rep. 89H, I Elsass-Lothringen 5, vol. 2. Bethmann to Eisendecher, Feb. 19, Apr. 7, 1914, AA *Nachlass* Eisendecher. Bethmann in Prussian Ministry of State, Jan. 30, Feb. 3, Mar. 18, Apr. 29, 1914, DZA Me, Rep 90a B III 2b no. 6, vol. 163. Lerchenfeld to Hertling, Jan. 3, 21, Apr. 13, 1914. Just when the anxiety about the Zabern affair was beginning to die down "the *Preussen-Bund* calls the Reichstag a rat, defends the mendacious army and gets everyone up in arms again," Bethmann complained to the Bavarian ambassador. "The chancellor maintains that it was correct to given the Reichslande the kind of constitution they received." BHStA MA I 957a.

42   Bethmann to Eisendecher, Feb. 18, 1914, AA *Nachlass* Eisendecher. "They keep on inventing new chancellors here," Lerchenfeld reported on Jan. 21 and Feb. 28,

1914, from Berlin: "Tirpitz, Schorlemer, and Lichnowsky. But for the time being Bethmann's dismissal is unthinkable." BHStA MA I 957a. General Gebsattel's "Gedanken über einen notwendigen Fortschritt in der inneren Politik Deutschlands," (printed privately, 1913); Bethmann to crown prince, Nov. 15, 1913; William II (i.e. Valentini) to crown prince, n.d. (December, 1914), reprinted in H. Pogge-v. Strandmann, "Staatsstreichpläne, Alldeutsche und Bethmann Hollweg," in *Die Erforderlichkeit des Unmöglichen* (Frankfurt, 1965). For the thesis of the growing counterrevolution see also Stenkewitz, *Gegen Bajonett und Dividende*, pp. 290 ff.; G. Heidorn, *Monopole—Presse—Krieg* (Berlin, 1960), pp. 310 ff; and F. Fischer, *Der Krieg der Illusionen*, pp. 384 ff.

43 Salza to Vitzthum, Mar. 7, 1914, SHStA, AM 1,090. "The agrarian Conservative circles are working strongly for Bethmann's fall and . . . accuse him of being too weak to conclude the upcoming trade treaties in Germany's favor." Minister of Agriculture Schorlemer was the Conservative-Clerical candidate. "On the other side, Bethmann's position is threatened by the military and Tirpitz." Despite the growing fronde Salza nevertheless predicted: "Everything will remain the same although it is not quite certain yet." Feb. 13, Valentini diary, BA *Nachlass* Thimme. Bethmann to Eisendecher, Oct. 1, 1913, AA *Nachlass* Eisendecher. Wahnschaffe article, "Wilhelmstrasse 77," DZA Po, Rkz. no. 2,398. Bethmann to Bülow, June 5, 1914, BA *Nachlass* Bülow. Salza to Vitzthum, May 14, 1914, SHStA, AM 1090. Berckheim to Dusch, Feb. 2, 1914, GLAK 233, no. 34,815. Lerchenfeld to Ludwig and Hertling, May 15, June 4, 1914: "I found him worn but composed and erect, firmly resolved to complete his duty as before." BHStA MA III 2691/2 and MA I 957a.

44 Bethmann to Eisendecher, Apr. 25, Oct. 1, 1913, AA *Nachlass* Eisendecher. Wahnschaffe article, "Wilhelmstrasse 77," DZA Po, Rkz. no. 2398. Bethmann may have been contemplating some concessions to the Rightist pressure, but one can hardly speak of a "reversal of Bethmann's policy," like Pogge, "Alldeutsche," pp. 26 ff., but rather of a tenacious clinging to his middle way. While he apostrophied the "further extension of the *Fideikommisse* as one of the most important means of maintaining a vital landed property," he appointed the conciliatory Eisenhardt-Rothe successor to Schwarzkopf in Poznan, insisted on the nonapplication of the expropriation law and refused to step up the nationalities struggle in Schleswig-Holstein, DZA Me, Rep. 90a B III 2b no. 6, vol. 162, Prussian Ministry of State, Oct. 21, Dec. 13, 1913, June 10, 1914. Szögyény to Berchtold, June 17, 1914, HHStA, PA III, 171, and Hertling note Apr. 13, 1914, BHStA MA I 962.

45 Bethmann to Oettingen, Dec. 15, 1913, BA *Nachlass* Oettingen. For the interpretational problem cf. also J. Snell, "Imperial Germany's Tragic Era 1888–1918: Threshold to Democracy or Foreground to Nazism?" *JCEA* (1959), 380–395 (1960), pp. 57–75. For Bethmann's awareness of the domestic deadlock cf. also his conversation with Rathenau in early 1914: "He asked (perhaps somewhat rhetorically) if one should be consequential or opportunist toward the country. I answered: 'This polarity does not exhaust the question. Above all the nation demands a visible direction.' He should draw guidelines in a programmatic speech. Externally he considered it possible, but domestically it would be difficult, if not impossible. Then he talked about the Conservatives, principally about Heydebrand, who intends to destroy him." Pogge-v. Strandmann, *Rathenau Tagebuch* p. 182. Similarly, although haunted by the nightmare of war, Bethmann consistently dragged his feet regarding economic preparations for a possible conflict. Thus, although some beginnings had been made, the country was basically unprepared in July 1914, DZA Po Rkz. 1267/2 f and L. Burchardt, *Friedenswirt-*

schaft und Kriegsvorsorge, pp. 248 ff. Cf. also Bethmann to Frank, May 3, 1913: "We cannot remain strong without healthy social development." DZA Po Rkz. 1252.

Chapter 5

1 Carl Peters, *Zur Weltpolitik* (Berlin, 1912), pp. 37 ff., 159 ff. Although he believed "naked and brutal facts force the German empire to expand," Peters added realistically: "World policy is not identical with world conquest." Cf. also Hans-Ulrich Wehler, *Bismarck und der Imperialismus* (Cologne, 1969); Helmut Böhme, *Deutschlands Weg zur Grossmacht* (Cologne, 1966); A. S. Erusalimskii, *Vneshniaia politika i diplomatiia germanskogo imperialiszma v kontze XIX veka* (Moscow, 1953); Wolfgang J. Mommsen, *Das Zeitalter des Imperialismus* (Frankfurt, 1969); and Fritz Fischer, *Krieg der Illusionen: Die deutsche Politik von 1911 bis 1914* (Düsseldorf, 1969).

2 For the thesis of the apogee of German imperialism between 1898 and 1908 see Volker R. Berghahn, "Zu den Zielen des deutschen Flottenbaus unter Wilhelm II," *HZ* 210 (1970) : 34 ff. Cf. Norman Rich, *Friedrich von Holstein*, 2 vols. (Cambridge, 1965); Werner Frauendienst, ed., *Die Geheimen Papiere Friedrich von Holsteins*, 4 vols. (Göttingen, 1956–63); and William L. Langer, *The Diplomacy of Imperialism, 1890–1902*, 2d ed. (New York, 1960). For the Foreign Office's briefing paper on Anglo-German relations drafted by Bussche-Haddenhausen cf. AA, Dld 137, vol. 6 and *GP* 28 : 201 ff. See also Raymond James Sontag, *Germany and England: Background of Conflict 1848–1894* (New York, 1938), and Otto Hammann, *The World Policy of Germany, 1890–1912* (London, 1927).

3 Memoranda for Bethmann Hollweg concerning Russia (July 15), Austria-Hungary and Italy (July 16), and Turkey (July 17, 1909) in AA Bonn, Dld 137, vol. 6. Cf. also Erich Brandenburg, *Von Bismarck zum Weltkriege* (Berlin, 1924); Friedrich Haselmayr, *Diplomatische Geschichte des Zweiten Reichs von 1871 bis 1918* (Munich, 1954–), especially vols. 5 and 6; George W. F. Hallgarten, *Imperialismus vor 1914: Die sozialpolitischen Grundlagen der Aussenpolitik europäischer Grossmächte vor dem Ersten Weltkrieg*, 2d enlarged ed. (Munich, 1963); and Peter G. Thielen's bibliographical introduction "Die Aussenpolitik des Deutschen Reiches, 1890–1914," *WaG* 22 (1962) : 27–48.

4 Goschen to Grey, July 23, 1909; *BDs* 7 : 279 ff. Grey's dictum cited from Peter Hatton, "Britain and Germany 1914. The July Crisis and War Aims," *Past and Present* 36 (1967). For the diplomatic response to Bethmann's appointment, see the reports of the German ambassadors in AA, Dld 121 no. 16, vol. 1. For a virulent attack on Bethmann's policy revealing the fundamental Pan-German misunderstanding of his aims, cf. Count Ernst Reventlow, *Von Potsdam nach Doorn*, 5th ed. (Berlin, 1940). Cf. the liberal apology by Veit Valentin, *Deutschlands Aussenpolitik von Bismarcks Abgang bis zum Ende des Weltkrieges* (Berlin, 1921).

5 Szögyény to Aerenthal, Aug. 3, 1909, HHStA, PA III, 167 B. Long Aerenthal memorandum about his conversations in Berlin, Feb. 22–25, 1910, in *Oe-U* 2 : 724 ff. Jules Cambon to Doumerge, Jan. 28, 1914, *FDs*, 3d ser. 9 : 209 ff. Cf. also Cambon's telegram to Cruppi, Apr. 19/20, 1911, characterizing Bethmann as "completely preoccupied with following a policy of external economic expansion," in *FDs*, 2d ser. 13 : 462 ff. Bethmann to Eisendecher, July 22, 1912; AA *Nachlass* Eisendecher. The most sensitive analysis of the fifth chancellor's foreign policy is Wolfgang J. Mommsen's *Habilitationsschrift*, "Die Politik des Reichskanzlers von Bethmann Hollweg 1909–1914 als Problem der politischen Führung," (Cologne, 1967).

6 Aerenthal memorandum, Feb. 22–25, 1910, *Oe-U* 2 : 726–27. William II, *Ereignisse*

und Gestalten, pp. 103 ff. Wilhelm von Schoen, *Erlebtes* (Stuttgart, 1921) : 104 ff., calling his relations with the chancellor "harmonious and loyal." Ernst Jäckh, *Kiderlen-Waechter der Staatsmann und Mensch,* 2 vols. (Berlin, 1925) containing substantial inaccuracies compared with the surviving Kiderlen papers at the E. M. House collection, Yale University. From Kiderlen's July 9, 1909 letter: "Among all [the chancellor candidates] I would ultimately prefer Wedel or possibly Bethmann. Monts is reputed to have traveled to Berlin. This would be ridiculously simple," Jäckh, for example, reproduces only, "Among all I would ultimately prefer Wedel." Kiderlen Papers no. 26 and Jäckh, *Kiderlen* 2 : 31. Cf. Bethmann to Kiderlen, Aug. 26, 1912, in AA, Dld 122, no. 21. The reprimand for Tirpitz (drafted by a gleeful Kiderlen) is in Jäckh 2 : 153–54. For Bethmann's softening of the blow cf. Tirpitz, *Aufbau,* pp. 431 ff. Cf. also Goschen to Grey, July 3, 1910, quoting Bethmann: "It is I who direct the Foreign Affairs of the empire and as long as I hold my present office those under my orders will have to adapt their sentiments to mine." *BDs* 7 : 494.

7 Bethmann memorandum, Aug. 13, 1909, AA, England no. 78 no. 3 secr, vol. 1, also in *GP* 28 : 211 ff. Despite Fritz Klein's claim to the contrary, *GP* is remarkably accurate, given the anti-Versailles bias of its editors, when compared to the Foreign Office originals. Cf. Fritz Klein, "Über die Verfälschung der historischen Wahrheit in der Aktenpublikation 'Die Grosse Politik der Europäischen Kabinette 1871–1914,'" *ZfG* (1959) pp. 318 ff. Cambon to Cruppi, Apr. 19/20, 1911, *FDs,* 2d ser. 13 : 463 ff. There is at present no systematic analysis of the Reichstag's influence on German foreign policy before 1914, although W. J. Mommsen moves in this direction.

8 Kurt Koszyk, *Deutsche Pressepolitik im Ersten Weltkrieg* (Düsseldorf, 1968), pp. 17 ff. Cf. also Otto Hammann, *Bilder aus der letzten Kaiserzeit,* pp. 69 ff. American Ambassador Hill to Washington, Feb. 10, 1910, NA Reports from the German Embassy. Vierhaus, *Spitzemberg,* pp. 518–19. Szögyény to Aerenthal, Feb. 3, Mar. 20, 1910; HHStA, PA III, 168B. Cf. Bethmann's statement in the Reichstag: "Even if the economic value of the Mannesmann concession is quite high . . . it does not constitute a question of life and death for Germany." See also Heinrich Class, *Wider den Strom,* pp. 143 ff; *AB,* January 29, Feb. 12, and Mar. 19, 1910; and Alfred Kruck, *Geschichte des Alldeutschen Verbandes* (Wiesbaden, 1954), 54 ff.

9 Bethmann's programmatic memorandum on British policy, Aug. 13, 1909, with a table of comparative ship-building compiled by Admiral Tirpitz and a covering letter to Foreign Secretary Schoen, Aug. 14, 1909. Cf. also Bethmann to Tirpitz, Sept. 16, 1909. The originals relating to the Anglo-German rapprochement are in the AA, England no. 78, no. 3 secr., vols. 1 ff. and the printed versions in *GP* 28 : 211 ff. Cf. also Fritz Strigel, *Die deutsch-englischen Flottenverhandlungen in den Jahren 1909–1911 unter Bethmann Hollweg* (Lohr, 1935); Alexander Kessler, *Das deutsch-englische Verhältnis vom Amtsantritt Bethmann Hollwegs bis zur Haldane-Mission* (Erlangen, 1938); Hansjoachim Henning, *Deutschlands Verhältnis zu England in Bethmann Hollwegs Aussenpolitik 1909–1914* (Cologne, 1962), and Oswald Hauser, *Deutschland und der englisch-russische Gegensatz, 1900–1914* (Göttingen, 1958). Cf. also the brilliant but one-sided E. L. Woodward, *Great Britain and the German Navy* (London, 1935) and Jonathan Steinberg, *Yesterday's Deterrent—Tirpitz and the Birth of the German Battle Fleet* (London, 1965).

10 For Bethmann's correspondence with Kiderlen and the latter's influence on German British policy, cf. KPs nos. 62/63, substantially published in *GP,* vol. 28, and Jäckh 2 : 48 ff. Cf. Zimmermann to Kiderlen, Aug. 25, and Stemrich to Kiderlen, Oct. 6, 1909, ibid., pp. 33 ff. See also Goschen's correspondence with Grey and Hardinge, Aug. 21–Oct. 27, 1909, as well as King Edward's note: "This subject is

one of grave importance—but it is satisfactory that the first move comes fr[om] Germany—through the new Chancellor!" and the long marginalia by Crowe, Langley, and Hardinge. *BDs* 7 : 283 ff. See also Bethmann to William II, Oct. 5, Bethmann memorandum, Oct. 15, and Bethmann to Metternich, Oct. 27, 1909, *GP* 28 : 237 ff. Cf. also F. Meinecke, *Geschichte des deutsch-englischen Bündnisproblems 1890–1901* (Munich, 1927).

11 Bethmann memorandum, Oct. 15, Nov. 5, Nov. 6, 1909, *GP* 28 : 239 ff. Minutes to Crowe, Langley, Hardinge, and Grey on Nov. 8, Nov. 10, Goschen to Grey, Nov. 25, 1909, with marginalia by King Edward: "The proposed negotiations must obviously 'lie dormant' but there is no sign of the German naval program lying dormant . . ." *BDs* 7 : 309 ff. For the mixed feelings of the other powers cf. Osten-Sacken to Isvolsky, Nov. 12, 1909, *Isv* 1 : 165 ff.; and Szögyény to Aerenthal Sept. 14, Nov. 24, 1909: "Bethmann Hollweg recently assured me that he considered it one of his chief tasks to establish better relations between the Berlin and London cabinets. He did not underestimate the great difficulties which had to be overcome in this regard. At any rate he would strive for this goal with all his means." HHStA, PA III, 167B, 168B.

12 Bethmann to Metternich, Feb. 1, 21, Aug. 8, Bethmann to Foreign Office, Aug. 23, Bethmann to William II, Oct. 1, 1910, Bethmann memorandum, Apr. 5, Bethmann to William II, May 15, Bethmann to Tirpitz, June 11, 1911, etc. *GP* 28 : 282 ff. See also Goschen's correspondence with Whitehall Apr. 11, 1910–Nov. 3, 1911 *BDs* 7 : 454 ff. For the Bagdad question cf. the material in *GP* 28 : 589–90. See also Arthur J. Marder, *From the Dreadnought to Scapa Flow: The Road to War, 1904–1914* (London, 1961), pp. 173 ff. Bethmann to Eisendecher, Dec. 27, 1910, *AA Nachlass* Eisendecher. Cf. also Bethmann to Bülow, July 14, 1911: "We make slow but steady progress with England." Thimme, *Front wider*, pp. 198 ff.

13 The Potsdam agreement has generally been slighted by diplomatic historians. For the originals of Bethmann's memorandum and telegram to William II, Nov. 6, 1910 cf. AA Dld 131 secr., vols. 15 ff. and for the press reaction Dld 131, vols. 32 ff. See also Bethmann note, Sept. 15, 1909, Bethmann to William II, Jan. 2, 1910, *GP* 26, pt. 2 : 852–53; Bethmann note, Feb. 25, Bethmann to Pourtalès, Feb. 27, Bethmann to William II, Sept. 15, Bethmann to William II, Nov. 1, Bethmann to Pourtalès, Nov. 8, 15, 1910, *GP* 28, pt. 2 : 471 ff., 835 ff. Cf. also Serge Sazonov, *Fateful Years, 1909–1916* (New York, 1928), pp. 17–18. Hauser, *Deutschland*, pp. 127 ff. Cf. Kiderlen's sanguine comment: "Perhaps we stand before a turning point of our policy," KPs, no. 32.

14 For the Russian documents cf. Osten-Sacken to Sazonov, Nov. 11, 1910, *Isv*, 1 : 77 ff.; and the profuse assurances to French diplomats to quiet their suspicions, beginning with Cambon to Pichon, Nov. 9, 1910 *FDs*, 2d ser., vol. 13, pt. 2 : 22 ff. and Aerenthal to Bethmann, Dec. 6, 1910, *Oe-U* 3 :89 ff. Cf. also Szögyény to Aerenthal, Nov. 27, Dec. 7, 1910, HHStA, PA III, 168B.

15 Bethmann to Foreign Office, July 5, 6, memorandum by Bethmann, July 6, 1912, AA, Dld 131 secr. 17; Dld 131, 28–29; *GP* 31 : 436 ff. Bronewski to Sazonov, July 15, 1912, *RDs* 2 : 411 ff.; Sazonov to Benckendorff, July 8, 1912, *Isv* 2 : 177 ff. Bethmann to Eisendecher, July 22, 1912, AA *Nachlass* Eisendecher. See also Szögyény to Berchtold, July 2, 17, 1912, HHStA, PA III, 170B.

16 Bethmann to Reichstag, Dec. 9, 1909, Schulthess's *GK* (1909), pp. 350 ff. Bethmann's foreign policy speeches were usually terse and based upon extensive preparations within the Foreign Office. Nevertheless he occasionally drafted various versions himself when necessary. Together with their foreign echo they are in AA, Dld 122, no. 16, no. 1, vols. 1 ff.; *Die Post*, July 27, 1912, with long Bethmann marginalia. Although the chancellor was a copious reader of dispatches and

foreign newspapers, hardly ever did he more than underline specific passages or make a procedural suggestion, which reveals a higher degree of dependence on his advisors than in domestic affairs. Cf. his approval of Pourtalès's report of Nov. 25, 1909, arguing for *"cool reserve"* toward Russia ("Yes!") and his underscoring of an article of the *Berliner Lokalanzeiger,* Feb. 9, 1910, reprinting an interview with Isvolsky, and his comment, "Influence the press according to page three." AA, Dld 131, vols. 31, 32, 34. Cf. also his angry letter to Pourtalès, July 30, 1912, DZA Po *Nachlass* Pourtalès.

17 For the reports of his impressions cf. Bethmann to Eisendecher, July 22, Bethmann to Pourtalès, July 30, and Bethmann to Hutten-Czapski Aug. 7, 1912, DZA Po *Nachlass* Hutten-Czapski. Cf. also Rathenau's entry into his diary that "Bethmann only hopes for a modus vivendi" with Russia, Pogge, *Rathenau Tagebuch,* pp. 168 ff. in contrast to the popular anecdote of his unwillingness to plant trees in Hohenfinow because the Russians would be there in a few years anyway. Cf. Vietsch, *Bethmann,* p. 143. See also W. Zapaar, *Russia and Germany: A Century of Conflict* (Boston, 1965), pp. 35 ff.

18 Cambon to Pichon, Sept. 14, Oct. 17, 1909, Feb. 17, 1910, *FDs,* 2d ser., 12 : 454 ff. *Lettres de la Princesse Radziwill* 4 : 143 ff. Bethmann to Foreign Office, Sept. 26, Oct. 12, 1909, May 18, 1910, stressing "reserve but friendly consultation with France" as correct policy in Morocco, *GP* 29 : 25 ff. For Bismarck's decision cf. the debate between Walter Lipgens and Lothar Gall, "Bismarck, die öffentliche Meinung und die Annexion von Elsass und Lothringen 1870," *HZ* 199 (1964) : 31–112; "Zur Frage der Annexion von Elsass und Lothringen 1870," ibid. 206 (1968): 265–326 and "Bismarck und die Frage der Annexion 1870: Eine Erwiderung," ibid. 206 (1968), 586–617. See also E. N. Anderson, *The First Moroccan Crisis, 1904–1906* (New York, 1930) and Peter Rassow, "Schlieffen und Holstein," *HZ* 173 (1952). Cf. also Bethmann to the Reichstag, Mar. 16, Dec. 10, 13, 1910, AA, Dld 122, no. 16, no. 1, 2–3.

19 Goschen to Grey, Apr. 28, May 9, 1911, *BDs* 8 : 207 ff. For the correspondence relating to Kiderlen's appointment cf. Bethmann's letters of June 5, 21, and Kiderlen to Kypke, June 30, 1910, KPs, nos. 28–32. Cf. also Kiderlen to Kypke, August 7, 1910: "I get along with the chancellor very well, since he has realized that I lay it on the line." During his tenure the relationship deteriorated so much that the chancellor frequently complained about his stubbornness and a rupture seemed near. Vierhaus, *Spitzemberg,* p. 551. Szögyény to Berchtold, Jan. 15, 1913, *Oe-U* 5 : 454 ff. For the continuing debate about Kiderlen's stature, cf. Willy Andreas, "Kiderlen-Wächter, Randglossen zu seinem Nachlass," *HZ* 132 (1925) : 246 ff.; G. P. Gooch, *Studies in Diplomacy and Statecraft* (London, 1942); and Stolberg-Wernigerode, *Konservative,* pp. 379 ff.

20 The originals are in AA, Frankreich 102 secr., 5–6 and Frankreich 102, no. 8 secr., 1 ff. See also *GP* 29 : 79 ff. and *FDs,* 2d ser. 13 : 419 ff. Riezler Diary, May (?) 29, 1911. Although Riezler was not yet as close to Bethmann as during the war, his notes do reflect the feeling of the German chancellery. Cf. Lerchenfeld's revealing report to Hertling on May 4, of a conversation with Kiderlen, BHStA MA III 2689. Cf. also Berckheim to Marschall, May 10, "I have the feeling (on the basis of Kiderlen quotes) that we are firmly resolved to repair the mistakes of our Morocco policy at the right moment and expect positive results from a separate deal with France." GLAK 233, no. 34,814. Cf. also Fritz Hartung, "Die Morokkokrise des Jahres 1911," *Einzelschriften zur Politik und Geschichte* (Berlin, 1927), no. 19, and Joanne Stafford Mortimer, "Commercial Interests and German Diplomacy in the Agadir Crisis," *HJ* 10 (1967) : 440–56.

21 Lerchenfeld to Hertling, May 4, June 20, July 3, 1911, BHStA, MA III 2689. Cf.

also Szögyény to Aerenthal, June 2, 1911, HHStA, PA III, 169B. The Riezler diary, May 29, 1911, is hopeful that "the Spaniards intend to occupy Alcazar on the Tangiers-Fez road. Then the French can only get out with difficulty," and concerned that "H.M. may intervene and spoil everything." For Kiderlen's rationale see also Jäckh 2 : 122 ff. and *GP* 29 : 104 ff. Cambon to Cruppi, Apr. 19/20, 25, 28, June 11, 1911, *FDs*, 2d ser, 13 : 462 ff. See also G. A. Müller, *Der Kaiser*, pp. 85–86. Kiderlen's own Morocco documents are largely disappointing, *KPs*, nos. 67–68. Cf. also the opinion of the American chargé Laughlin that the warship was sent "to force new negotiations with Paris." Laughlin to Washington, July 13, 1911, NA, Dispatches of the German Embassy 1909–1912.

22 "The Foreign Office is not satisfied with the progress of the Morocco question," Lerchenfeld reported to Hertling on July 5, 1911, BHStA MA III 2689. Bethmann to Metternich, July 4, Bethmann to William II, July 3, 10, 15, 20, *GP* 29 : 163 ff. For Kiderlen's negotiations with the Pan-Germans cf. his letter to Kypke, Apr. 19, 1911, different in text from Jäckh 2 : 122. KPs 33. Cf. also H. Class, *Wider den Strom*, pp. 202 ff. and *AB*, June 10, 1911. Cf. Goschen to Grey, June 1, 1911, reporting Bethmann's facetious comment: "There is only one thing I can tell you, and that is that the situation in Morocco does not cause me the very slightest feeling of anxiety." But cf. the alarmist minutes of Crowe on July 3, July 18, and Nicolson of the same day, *BDs* 8 : 276 ff. For Lloyd George's Mansion House warning that England's interests as a great power had to be taken into account in any settlement, cf. Metternich to Bethmann, July 22, 1911, *GP* 29 : 206 ff. and Grey to Goschen, July 25, 1911, *BDs* 8 : 397 ff. Cf. Riezler Diary, July 29, 1911. "This time H.M. wil have to say yes and amen to everything. . . . If our policy is softened, the November storm [of the *Daily Telegraph* Affair] will return with renewed vengeance and the people will be wrathful in their disappointment. This time we must force our way through."

23 Riezler Diary, July 30, 1911: "Bethmann is not informed completely. Kiderlen lets nobody look into his cards and says the chancellor should find another [foreign minister] if he does not trust him." See also Vierhaus, *Spitzemberg*, pp. 521 ff. and *Lettres de la Princesse Radziwill* 4 : 155 ff. For Kiderlen's offers of resignation see Jäckh 2 : 128 ff. Bethmann answered on July 18, 1911: "It goes without saying that I shall defend your Morocco policy, which I have approved, to H.M. Your dismissal because of Morocco would also bring about my resignation." KPs no. 67. For William II's yielding see Müller, *Der Kaiser*, pp. 87 ff. Cf. also Saxon Ambassador Salza to Vitzthum, Sept. 1, 1911: "The pensive chancellor, who made a worn and tired impression, complained about the difficult and responsible times. . . . He did not look into the future optimistically, since it was too early to tell what it would bring, especially whether France would bargain on our terms." SHStA, AM 1,090. Cf. also Rathenau's notes on Bethmann's "liquidation policy" in Morocco: "It is somewhat for show. We cannot yield too much," which indicates that from the beginning the chancellor only strove for "compensation through territorial gain." July 23, Apr. 28, 1911. Pogge, *Rathenau Tagebuch*, pp. 147 ff.

24 Bethmann to Julius Bachem, Aug. 13, 1911: "The resolution of the Augustinus Verein . . . was a very praiseworthy support since the opinion that we should settle in South Morocco is spreading as political idiocy through the country and confuses heads." DZA Po, Rkz. 1391/2. Riezler Diary, Aug. 1, 9, 1911: "If war comes we fight against a foreign threat, if not, we remain in the Sus. And we will have obtained something which France and England together declared they could not bear. Then the spell is broken. Such a plan would gradually pull chancellor and kaiser in and create an ironclad case for war. This thesis seems correct but

unprovable." Cf. also Bethmann's confession to Oettingen that "in the daring trick," the gunboat would serve as object of attack to produce the casus foederis for Austria and Italy. Vietsch, *Bethmann*, p. 149. Cf. Aerenthal to Szögyény, July 4, 1911, *Oe-U* 3 : 267 ff. For the completion of the Morocco accords cf. Bethmann to William II, Oct. 11, Nov. 2, 1911, *GP* 29 : 397 ff. and Cambon to de Selves, Nov. 5, 1911, *FDs* 3d ser. 1 : 30 ff. See also Lerchenfeld to Hertling, Sept. 16, Nov. 9, 1911, BHStA MA III 2689.

25   Bethmann to Reichstag, Nov. 9, 1911, Schulthess's *GK* (1911), pp. 194 ff. For the preceding propadanda battle over Lindequist's resignation cf. ibid., pp. 182 ff. Cf. also AA, Dld 122, no. 16, no. 1, 4. P. Herre, *Kronprinz Wilhelm* (Munich, 1954), pp. 25 ff. Saxon Ambassador Salza concluded "that because of the crown prince's tensions with the emperor his demonstration considerably strengthened the position of the chancellor, as I in general do not believe in Bethmann's future resignation." Salza to Vitzthum, Nov. 11, 1911, SHStA, AM 1090. Cf. also American Ambassador Leishman: "Although not as great as the German public was led to believe would be insisted upon, the deeded territory should more than satisfy them, as everything the German government obtained can practically be regarded as clear gain, for if the French had not moved so rapidly and had acted in a more politic manner, the chances are that in the course of 8 or 10 years they would in the natural course of events have acquired full possession of Morocco, without a struggle and without compensations." Leishman to Washington, Nov. 7, 1911, NA, Dispatches of the German Embassy, 1909–1912.

26   Bethmann to Reichstag, Nov. 10, 1911, Schulthess's *GK* (1911), pp. 213 ff. Bethmann to Bülow, July 14, Nov. 21, 1911, Thimme, *Front*, p. 200: "The manner in which I have defended our agreements with France in the Reichstag should leave no doubt in public and parliament that in the treatment of the Morocco problem I have acted in accord with the principles of your policy." Cf. Bethmann to Loebell, Nov. 20, 1911, regarding the "sharp self-defense into which I was forced. You know me and understand that I do not like to speak in this tone, and all the less toward a Conservative." But he "was convinced . . . that my harsh language was necessary if the authority of the government was not to suffer irreparable harm." DZA Po, Rkz. 1391/5. Cf. Cambon to de Selves, Nov. 10, 1911, who claimed "on good authority that this speech which was much better received than the first, was concerted in Potsdam in the emperor's own cabinet." See also Goschen to Grey, Nov. 6, 11, 1911: "The balance of public opinion is unfavorable to the arrangement." *BDs* 8 : 658 ff.

27   Goschen to Grey, Nov. 16, 1911, *BDs* 8 : 693 ff. See also Lerchenfeld to Hertling, Nov. 9, 10: "As Bethmann told me himself the criticism of the leader of the Conservatives was not easy for him, if only because of concern for the coming elections. But . . . he believed that he owed it to his and the kaiser's dignity not to let Heydebrand's speech of the day before go without rejoinder." BHStA MA III 2689. Cf. Szögyény to Aerenthal, Nov. 17, 30, 1911, HHStA, PA III, 169V.

28   Bethmann to Eisendecher, Nov. 16, 1911, AA *Nachlass* Eisendecher, and his identical language to Weizsäcker, Nov. 16, 1911, *Privatnachlass* Weizsäcker: "The attacks in the Reichstag and in the public leave me cold. One may criticize details of the agreement. It is not without flaws." But war "for the fiction of the sovereignty of the Sultan of Morocco, for a piece of Sus or of Congo, for the Brothers Mannesmann?" Although he had supported Kiderlen's brinkmanship, "the thoughtless playing with war fills me with sorrow." Cf. also Goschen to Grey, Dec. 17, 1911, *BDs* 8 : 788 ff.

29   Bethmann to Eisendecher, Dec. 26, 1911, AA *Nachlass* Eisendecher. "The English parliamentary negotiations and the political sense which speaks from them awaken

my envy. I would like to present them to the kaiser but the popular mood is not right to listen to pro-German statements." Bethmann to Metternich, Nov. 22, Dec. 6, 14, 16, *GP* 31 : 31 ff. Goschen to Grey, Dec. 17, 1911, *BDs* 7 : 188–89. Cf. also E. Hartl, *Preussen-Deutchlands diplomatische Niederlagen und deren Folgen in der Geschichte: Eine historisch-politische Betrachtung zur Marokko Affaire und zur deutsch-englischen Spannung* (Leipzig, 1912).

30 Metternich to Bethmann, Dec. 18, 1911. Bethmann note with British memorandum, Jan. 29, Bethmann to Metternich, Jan. 30, Feb. 4; Metternich to Bethmann, Jan. 31, 1912; *GP* 31 : 80 ff. Grey to Bertie, Feb. 7, 1912, *BDs* 7 : 670 ff. For the originals relating to the Haldane Mission cf. AA, England no. 78, no. 3, vols. 10 ff. F. Thimme, "Zur Geschichte der Mission Lord Haldanes," *Deutsche Politik* (1919), pp. 759 ff. Cf. also A. Huldermann, *Albert Ballin* (Berlin, 1922), pp. 252 ff. L. Cecil, *Albert Ballin* (Princeton, 1967), pp. 182 ff. Cf. P. Graf Wolff-Metternich, "Meine Denkschrift über die Flottennovelle vom 10. 1. 1912," *Europäische Gespräche* 4 (1926) : 57 ff. and E. C. Helmreich, "Die Haldane Mission," *BM* 12 (1934) : 112 ff. For opposing views cf. F. Fischer, *Der Krieg*, pp. 182 ff. and W. J. Mommsen, "Die Politik," pp. 103 ff.

31 The German documents on the Haldane Mission are sketchy. Bethmann to Metternich, Feb. 8, William II to Bethmann, Feb. 9, Bethmann notes, Feb. 12, Bethmann to Metternich, Bethmann marginalia on Metternich report, Feb. 13, *GP* 31 : 109 ff. Cf. Haldane's more extensive diary, Feb. 10, with appendixes and long Crowe marginalia, Feb. 12, as well as Goschen's reports of Feb. 9 ff., *BDs* 7 : 670 ff., especially Goschen to Nicolson, Feb. 20, 1912: "If what has been suggested is carried out, the Germans get what under Grey's instructions I have been opposing for two years, namely a political understanding without a naval agreement. . . . That it was possible for Haldane to get more I do not believe, but I am not surprised that the emperor and the chancellor are 'in a good mood'!" Cf. also Tirpitz, *Der Aufbau*, pp. 280 ff. and Walther Hubatsch, *Die Ära Tirpitz: Studien zur deutschen Marinepolitik, 1899–1918* (Göttingen, 1955), p. 78 ff.; "Der Kulminationspunkt der deutschen Marinepolitik im Jahre 1912," *HZ* 176 (1953) : 291 ff.

32 Privately, Bethmann was less sanguine: "Confidentially the negotiations are much worse. Haldane has received a very bad impression of Tirpitz. It is impossible to tell what will come of it." G. A. Müller, *Der Kaiser*, pp. 112 ff. Bethmann to Eisendecher, Feb. 22, 1912, AA *Nachlass* Eisendecher. For the subsequent negotiations about a neutrality formula cf. Bethmann to Metternich, Feb. 24, Bethmann memoranda, Feb. 28, *GP* 31 : 132 ff. and Goschen to Nicolson, Mar. 15, *BDs* 7 : 716 ff. See also Woodward, *Great Britain*, pp. 323 ff. Cf. Szögyény to Aerenthal, Feb. 10, 15, 1912, HHStA, PA III, 170 B. Lerchenfeld to Hertling, Feb. 21, 1912, BHStA MA I 955: "At present London is still thinking about which of the German offers to accept and what to propose," Bethmann informed the Bavarian ambassador, who "gained the impression that a general agreement has failed."

33 William II to Metternich, Mar. 5, Bethmann to William II, Mar. 6, 1912, *GP* 31 : 156 ff. Bethmann to William II, Mar. 6, 1912, original in DZA Me, Rep. 89H, II Rst no. 1, vol. 3, printed by Jäckh 2 : 159 ff. Lerchenfeld to Hertling, Mar. 7, 1912, BHStA MA I 955. The Bavarian ambassador was aghast when "Kiderlen told me that the chancellor has just demanded his dismissal because of the naval question." Cf. also *Lettres de la Princesse Radziwill* 4 : 179 ff. Bethmann was reputed to have said during a reception, "I do not understand how Bülow could resist for eleven years against that kind of regime."

34 G. A. Müller, *Der Kaiser*, pp. 116 ff. Lerchenfeld to Hertling, Mar. 8, 13, 1912, BHStA MA I 955, reporting "the apparent end of the chancellor crisis." Because

William backed down the "chancellor did not insist on his dismissal . . . although he said yesterday to his intimates that he would remain under no circumstances." Szögyény to Aerenthal, Feb. 27, Mar. 17, 1912, HHStA, PA III, 170B. For Tirpitz's counterthreat cf. *Der Aufbau*, pp. 324 ff. Cf. Cabinet Chief Valentini's diary, Mar. 6 ff., with the exclamation, "Again Chancellor Tirpitz!" affirming the intervention of the empress with Bethmann; BA *Nachlass* Thimme. Berckheim to Dusch, Mar. 23, 1912, GLAK 233, 34,815. For a popular treatment of the cause of rivalry cf. Charles Sarolea, *The Anglo-German Problem* (London, 1912).

35 Bethmann memorandum, Mar. 8, 18, 21, Bethmann to William II, Mar. 12, 15, 17, Metternich to Bethmann, Mar. 29, 1912, *GP* 31 : 159 ff. Goschen to Nicolson, Mar. 15, 22, 29, and Asquith to Grey, Apr. 10, 1912, *BDs* 7 : 716 ff. Cf. also Bethmann's statements to Berckheim that "he, the chancellor, put the *main emphasis* upon reaching a *general political* understanding with England," because it alone would loosen the Entente, and if "it succeeded the entire political situation in Europe would be changed in our favor through one stroke." Berckheim to Dusch, Mar. 15, 1912, GLAK 233, 34,815. Cf. G. A. Müller, *Der Kaiser*, pp. 118–19. See also Paul Cambon to Poincaré, Feb. 23, Mar. 21, 1912, *FDs*, 3d ser. 2 : 82 ff.

36 Bethmann to Metternich, Apr. 3, 1912, *GP* 31 : 264 ff.; for the subsequent negotiations cf. *GP* 37, pt. 1, and *BDs* 10, pt. 2. The best source for the colonial talks are Richard von Kühlmann's *Erinnerungen* (Heidelberg, 1948), pp. 349 ff. Bethmann to Eisendecher, July 22, 1912, AA *Nachlass* Eisendecher. For the long-standing feud between the naval attaché and the ambassador cf. W. Widenmann, *Marineattaché an der kaiserlich-deutschen Botschaft* (Göttingen, 1952), pp. 274 ff., Alfred Vagts, *The Military Attaché* (Princeton, 1967) and William II's marginalia throughout *GP*, 31. Long destined for London, Metternich's successor, Marschall von Bieberstein, died before he could achieve any political impact. Bethmann favored the retired Admiral Eisendecher and preferred Wilhelm von Stumm as a "calm and conscientious worker who knows the true value of English 'assurances,'" but ultimately accepted "Prince Lichnowsky as suitable." Bethmann to William II, Oct. 3, 1912, DZA Me, Rep. 53J. Cf. Lichnowsky's reminiscences, *Heading for the Abyss* (New York, 1928), pp. 2–3. Cf. also Salza to Vitzthum, Apr. 18, 1912, SHStA, AM 1090.

37 Bethmann to Aerenthal, Dec. 23, 1910; *Oe-U* 2 : 120 ff. Bethmann to William II, Sept. 15, Pourtalès to Bethmann, Sept. 18, 1909, *GP* 26 : 852 ff. Bethmann to William II, Oct. 28, Nov. 3, 1909, Bethmann memorandum, Apr. 5, 1910, Bethmann to Tschirschky, May 21, 1910. Bethmann to Pourtalès, Feb. 27, 1910, *GP* 17, pt. 2 : 475 ff. For the originals on the Triple Alliance Cf. AA, Dld no. 128, no. 1, vols. 28 ff., Oesterreich no. 95, vols. 2 ff., Italien no. 82, vols. 2 ff. Cf. also Szögyény's private letters regarding the Austrian statemen's difficulties with Tschirschky, Jan. 3, 19, 1912, *Oe-U* 3 : 740 ff. See also Barrère to Pichon, Nov. 30, 1910, *FDs*, 2d ser., vol. 13. Sazonov to Isvolsky, July 8, 1912, *Isv* 2 : 177 ff. Oswald Henry Wedel, *Austro-German Diplomatic Relations, 1908–1914* (Stanford, 1932); L. Salvatorelli, *La Triplice Alleanza. Storia Diplomatica 1877–1912* (Milan, 1939); Fritz Fellner, *Der Dreibund: Europäische Diplomatie vor dem Ersten Weltkrieg* (Munich, 1960), and Helge Granfeld, *Der Dreibund nach dem Sturze Bismarcks* (Lund, 1964), vol. 2.

38 Bethmann to Aerenthal, Nov. 14, 1910, *GP* 27, pt. 1 : 382 ff. Bethmann to Tschirschky, Oct. 3; Bethmann to William II, Nov. 24, Dec. 11, 1911, *GP* 30, pt. 1 : 87 ff.; Bethmann note, Aug. 5, 1912, Bethmann to Jagow, Nov. 24, Bethmann to William II, Nov. 25, Bethmann to Tschirschky, Nov. 26, 1911, *GP* 30, pt. 2 : 448 ff. Bethmann to Hutten-Czapski, Aug. 7, 1912. For once "the kaiser was well and *calm.*" DZA Po *Nachlass* Hutten. For the premature renewal of the Dreibund cf.

AA, Dld 128, no. 1, vol. 32. Cf. also Szögyény to Berchtold, July 2, 1912, HHStA, PA III, 170B. Cf. also W. Kalbskopf, *Die Aussenpolitik der Mittelmächte im Tripoliskrieg und die letzte Dreibunderneuerung* (Erlangen, 1932).

39 Szögyény to Berchtold, July 30, 1912. Berchtold to the Joint Austro-Hungarian Council of Ministers, July 8/9, 1912. Berchtold notes of his conversations with Bethmann, Sept. 7/8, 1912, concluding that despite Bethmann's good will, his "obvious doubts about the dependability of the German alliance . . . could not be eliminated." *Oe-U* 4 : 254 ff. Jules Cambon to Poincaré, Sept. 19, 29, 1912, *FDs*, 3d ser. 3 : 304 ff. Sazonov report of his trip to England, France and Germany, Oct. 1912, *Isv* 2 : 289 ff. Bethmann to Foreign Office, Aug. 7, Bethmann to Kiderlen, Aug. 29, Bethmann to William II, Oct. 1, Kiderlen's memorandum of Sazonov's visit, Oct. 9, *GP* 33 : 43 ff. Granville to Nicolson, Oct. 18, Grey to Goschen, Oct. 25, 1912, *BDs* 9, pt. 2 : 36 ff. Kiderlen to Kühlmann, Oct. 20, William II's resumé of a conversation with Bethmann and Kiderlen, Nov. 11, 1912, *GP* 33 : 233 ff. Berchtold to Szögyény, Nov. 28, Szögyény to Berchtold, Oct. 11, Nov. 28, 1912, *Oe-U* 4 : 604 ff. Salza to Vitzthum, Nov. 5, 1912, SHStA, AM 1090. Cf. also Ernst Christian Helmreich, *The Diplomacy of the Balkan Wars, 1912–1913* (Cambridge, Mass., 1938) and Hugo Hantsch, *Leopold Graf Berchtold: Grandseigneur und Staatsmann,* 2 vols. (Graz, 1963).

40 Bethmann to Reichstag, Dec. 2, 4, 1912; AA, Dld 122, no. 16, no. 1, vol. 5. Grey to Bertie, Dec. 3, Grey to Goschen, Dec. 4, 1912, *BDs* 9, pt. 2 : 238 ff. Berckheim after a conversation with Stumm to Dusch, Dec. 8, 1912, stressing the uncertainty of the hope of keeping England from supporting Russia in case of conflict; GLAK, 233, 34,815. Lichnowsky to Bethmann, Dec. 3, 1912, first printed in Tirpitz, *Der Aufbau,* pp. 361 ff. and then in *GP* 39 : 119 ff. William memorandum to Kiderlen, Dec. 8, ibid., pp. 123 ff. Cf. J. C. G. Röhl's perceptive comparison between Goerlitz's published version of the G. A. Müller diary, *Der Kaiser,* pp. 124 ff. and the original in the Militärarchiv Freiburg, establishing significant variations, "Admiral von Mueller and the Approach of War, 1911–1914," *HJ* 12 (1969) : 651–73. For a critique of Fischer's thesis that the *Kriegsrat* was the turning point of German prewar policy, *Krieg der Illusionen,* pp. 231 ff., see W. J. Mommsen, "Die deutsche 'weltpolitik' und der Ersteweltkrieg," *Neue Politische Literatur* 16 (1971) : 482 ff.

41 G. A. Müller, *Der Kaiser,* pp. 125–26. Cf. also Müller's later addition: "I talked about it at that time with the wife of the chancellor. She declared that her husband would under no circumstances be willing to engage in war." Bethmann to Eisendecher, Dec. 20, 1912, AA *Nachlass* Eisendecher. See also William II's letter to Eisendecher of Dec. 12, and the ambassador's answers of Dec. 15 and 23, ibid. Cf. also Bethmann's pacific hopes expressed to Oettingen, Dec. 9, 1912, cited by E. Vietsch, *Bethmann,* p. 149.

42 For Leuckhart's report of Dec. 12 and Wenninger's report of Dec. 15, 1912, cf. Röhl, "Admiral von Mueller," pp. 662 ff. Bethmann memorandum, Dec. 14, 1912, *GP* 39 : 145 ff. Bethmann to Hertling, Dec. 23, 1912, hinting at the preparation of arms increases and stressing the tax difficulties, BHStA MA I 955. Lerchenfeld to Hertling, Dec. 14, 1912, ibid., and Berckheim to Dusch, Dec. 15, 1912, cited by Mommsen, "Die Politik," pp. 157–58. Bethmann memorandum, Dec. 20, 1912, 33 : 477. Bethmann memorandum regarding the *Kriegsrat,* without precise information other than William's order to the military: "Now start using the press!" Dec. 17, and his rebuttal to the kaiser, Dec. 18 and Dec. 31, 1912, *GP* 39 : 8 ff. and *GP* 33 : 102 ff. Goschen to Grey, Jan. 10, 1913, *BDs* 9, pt. 2 : 385–86. Cf. also Szögyény's report on the extent of the war scare in Berlin, Dec. 17, 1912, *Oe-U* 5 : 145 ff. Cf. also Bethmann to Binding and Oncken, Mar. 20, 1913, asking intellectuals "to participate in the coming struggles" for adequate armament. DZA Po, Rkz. 1252/1.

43 Bethmann to Eisendecher, Dec. 20, 1912, AA *Nachlass* Eisendecher. Szögyény to Berchtold, Jan. 3, 1913: "Not as chancellor but as friend I allow myself to tell you openly that your armaments contain the spark of a possible conflagration which we must prevent in the interest of all of Europe." Szögyény to Berchtold, Jan. 20, 30, *Oe-U* 5 : 299 ff. Cf. also Bethmann to the Bundesrat Mar. 2, 10, 1913: "I do not belong to those who consider a European war unavoidable," but admitting to "having lived through grave hours" recently, DZA Po, Rkz. 1252/1, 216. Bethmann to Berchtold, Feb. 10, 1912, cited by Hantsch, *Berchtold*, pp. 387–88. Bethmann note on Austrian armaments, Jan. 8, Bethmann to Tschirschky, Jan. 19, Bethmann marginalia to a Lichnowsky report, Jan. 20, Bethmann to Lichnowsky, Jan. 20, Bethmann memorandum, Jan. 25, Bethmann to Lichnowsky, Jan. 27, 30, 1912, *GP* 34 : 149 ff. Cf. also Edward C. Thaden, *Russia and the Balkan Alliance of 1912* (University Park, Pa., 1965).

44 Szögyény to Berchtold, July 6, Mar. 13, 25, Apr. 8, May 27, June 29, 1913. Berchtold to Jagow, Mar. 13, Berchtold to Szögyény, May 2, 1913, *Oe-U* 5 : 937 ff.; 6 : 50 ff. Jagow to Berchtold, Mar. 23, Bethmann to Treutler, Apr. 8, Zimmermann note of a conversation between Bethmann and Tschirschky, July 6, *GP* 34, pt. 2 : 548 ff. and 35 : 128 ff. Bethmann to Eisendecher, Mar. 23, 1913, AA *Nachlass* Eisendecher. Cf. Kiderlen's report to the Federal Commission of Foreign Affairs, Nov. 18, 1912, Jäckh 2 : 193 ff. For Jagow's appointment cf. also Szögyény to Berchtold, Jan. 15, Feb. 12, May 20, 1913, HHStA, PA III, 170B and V. Cf. also Lerchenfeld's judgment, "Jagow does not appear to possess the caliber of his predecessors" but "is certainly quite intelligent, calm, and reliable. . . . Without doubt he will conduct a factual and not a fantastic policy," in his letter to Hertling, Jan. 5, 1913, BHStA MA I 955. See also Berckheim to Dusch, Feb. 13, "we are, so to speak, with both hands holding back the Austrians by their coattails." GLAK 233, 34,815. Cf. also Gottlieb von Jagow, *Ursachen und Ausbruch des Weltkrieges* (Berlin, 1919) and his manuscript essays on various facets of his policy in his *Nachlass*, AA. For German economic interests in the Balkans cf. Fritz Fischer, "Weltpolitik, Weltmachtstreben und Deutsche Kriegsziele," *HZ* 199 (1964) : 265 ff., and L. Rathmann, *Berlin-Bagdad* (Berlin, 1962).

45 Bethmann to Eisendecher, June 2, 1913, AA *Nachlass* Eisendecher. The chancellor thanked his friend for his efforts to improve Anglo-German relations: "I beg you to continue to help. We shall finally reach our goal." Bethmann to Pourtalès, June 2, 1913, DZA Po *Nachlass* Hutten. Cf. also G. A. Müller, *Der Kaiser*, p. 128, and Herzogin Viktoria Louise, *Ein Leben als Tochter des Kaisers*, pp. 93 ff.

46 Bethmann to Foreign Office, Aug. 8, Zimmermann to Wedel, Oct. 16, 1913, *GP* 35 : 360 ff., *GP* 36, pt. 1 : 146–47. Berchtold to Szögyény, Aug. 1 (instruction and covering letter), Szögyény to Berchtold, Aug. 12, Protocol of joint Austro-Hungarian ministerial council, Oct. 3, 1913, Szögyény to Berchtold, Nov. 5, 7, 19, 1913, *Oe-U* 7 : 1 ff. Bethmann to Eisendecher, Oct. 1, 1913, AA *Nachlass* Eisendecher. Cf. also Hertling's notes of a conversation with Bethmann on Nov. 24, 1913, in which the chancellor was optimistic, stressing as his "main task the prevention of the partition of Asian Turkey." Relations with both Austria and Russia were satisfactory, and although Rumania seemed unreliable in peacetime it would clearly fight in case of a Russian attack. "He called the most valuable result the favorable development of our relations with England." BHStA MA I 962. Cf. also Helmreich, *The Diplomacy*, pp. 368 ff., 426 ff.

47 Bethmann to Eisendecher, Apr. 7, 1914, AA *Nachlass* Eisendecher. Bethmann memorandum, Nov. 13, Bethmann to Kokovtsev, Nov. 27, Bethmann to Lucius, Nov. 29, Bethmann to William II, Dec. 31, 1913, Bethmann marginalia on Pourtalès report, Jan. 14, Bethmann to Pourtalès, Jan. 15, 1914, *GP* 38 : 220 ff. For the originals cf.

AA, Dld 131, vols. 35 ff. Dld 131, secreta, vol. 17. Sazonov report to the tsar of his trip to Paris and Berlin, Nov. 6, 1913, Kokovtsev report, Nov. 19, 1913, *Ivs* 3 : 328 ff. Cambon to Pichon, Nov. 20, 30, 1913, *FDs*, 3d ser. 8 : 641 ff. Goschen to Nicolson, Dec. 12, *BDs* 10, pt. 1 : 376 ff. Cf. Ulrich Trumpener, "Liman von Sanders and the German-Ottoman Alliance," *JCH* 1 (1966) : 179–92. See also Hans Herzfeld, "Die Liman-Krise und die Politik der Grossmächte in der Jahreswende 1913–1914," *BM* 2 (1933) : 837 ff., 973 ff.

48 Bethmann to Eisendecher, Feb. 19, 1914, AA *Nachlass* Eisendecher. *Kölnische Zeitung*, Mar. 2, 1914: "Now they openly admit that Russia arms for war against Germany." Cf. Zimmermann's dementi to the editor of the *Hann. Anzeiger*, Mar. 3, and Pourtalès's private letter to Hammann, Mar. 5, claiming "the embassy had nothing to do with it." AA, Dld 131, vol. 35. See also Jagow's strongly worded warning in the Reichstag against further Russian polemics in May in a speech that Bethmann was to have given but could not because of the death of his wife. Schulthess's *GK* (1914), p. 282. Szögyény to Berchtold, May 13, 1914, noticing despite the foreign secretary's warm words a marked "emphasis on Germany's *own* rights." HHStA, PA III, 171B. For a chauvinist propaganda piece of the German Army League see H. Müller-Brandenburg, *Russland und wir: Volkswirtschaftliche, politische und militärische Schlaglicher* (Berlin, June 1914). Bethmann to Eisendecher, Apr. 7, 1914, AA *Nachlass* Eisendecher. Bethmann to Lichnowsky, Mar. 14, June 16, 1914, *GP* 39 : 558 ff. Cf. also Günther Heidorn, Monopole-Presse-Krieg: *Die Rolle der Presse bei der Vorbereitung des ersten Weltkriegs* (Berlin, 1960), and K.-D. Wernecke, *Der Wille zur Weltgeltung. Aussenpolitik und Öffentlichkeit in Deutschland am Vorabend des Ersten Weltkriegs* (Düsseldorf, 1969).

49 Bethmann to Tschirschky, Apr. 6, Bethmann to William II, Apr. 6, Bethmann note, May 8, Bethmann to Tschirschky, May 8, 1914, predicting "the complete collapse of the Dreibund and of our present political system" if Austria failed to be more conciliatory toward Italy on Balkan questions; *GP* 38 : 336 ff. Bethmann to Foreign Office, Apr. 16, 17, 21, 22, Bethmann to William II, June 15, Bethmann marginalia on Tschirschky telegram, June 29, *GP* 36, pt. 2 : 568 ff. Szögyény to Berchtold, Mar. 4, Apr. 18, 1914, *Oe-U* 7 : 1062 ff. See also Count Hertling's note of a conversation with Bethmann, Apr. 13, 1914, BHStA MA I 962. For the mood within the Austro-Hungarian monarchy, cf. Count Tizsa's memorandum of Mar. 15, *Oe-U* 7 : 974 ff., calling for "a far-seeing *politique de la longue main*" and the settlement of political differences with Germany. Cf. also F. Klein, "Die Rivalität zwischen Deutschland und Oesterreich-Ungarn in der Türkei am Vorabend des ersten Weltkrieges," *Politik im Krieg, 1914–1918* (Berlin, 1964), pp. 1 ff.

50 Bethmann to Eisendecher, Mar. 23, 1913, AA *Nachlass* Eisendecher. Goschen to Grey, Jan. 13, 1913, Granville to Nicolson, Oct. 18, 1912, reporting a private conversation with Bethmann, *BDs* 9, pt. 2 : 36 ff. Bethmann to William II, Feb. 8, 1914, *GP* 39 : 77–78. Tirpitz, *Der Aufbau*, pp. 406 ff.

51 Bethmann to Eisendecher, July 25, 1913, Feb. 19, Apr. 7, 1914. Kühlmann, *Erinnerungen*, pp. 363 ff. Lichnowsky, *Heading*, pp. 4 ff. For Bethmann's fluctuation between hope for British neutrality and fear of intervention in a Balkan conflict, see his later refutation of Tirpitz: "Despite the successful and precisely circumscribed agreements with England in the last years before the war, which appeared to the naval partisans only as expression of anglophile weakness, German policy never deceived itself about the firmness of the English position in the enemy camp." Bethmann MS, 12, BA, Kl. Erw. no. 342. For a concise account of the complex Bagdad negotiations cf. John G. Williamson, *Karl Helfferich, 1872–1924: Economist, Financier, Politician* (Princeton, 1971), pp. 91 ff.

52 Goschen to Grey, Mar. 29, Apr. 21, Grey to Goschen, Apr. 7, 1914, *BDs* 10, pt.

2 : 566 ff. Jagow to Lichnowsky, Feb. 26, 1914, Bethmann to Lichnowsky, Apr. 26, 1913, Lichnowsky to Bethmann, July 14, Zimmermann to Wedel, June 19, 1914, *GP* 37, pt. 1 : 102 ff. Bethmann to Lichnowsky, June 16, 1914, *GP* 39 : 628 ff. Anonymous (Hans Plehn, inspired by Kühlmann), *Deutsche Weltpolitik und kein Krieg!* (Berlin, 1913). Rejecting the irrational mood favoring preventive war (Bismarck's "suicide for fear of death") Plehn argued *"not war but diplomacy must be the means with which we conduct a successful and at the same time safe policy of expansion,"* preferably into Central Africa. Cf. also Peter Hatton, "Britain and Germany 1914: The July Crisis and War Aims," *Past and Present* 36 (1967) : 138 ff.

53 Kurt Riezler, *Die Erforderlichkeit des Unmöglichen: Prolegomena zu einer Theorie der Politik und zu anderen Theorien* (Munich, 1913). "The deepest, most general, and desperate task of today's German policy is to find a way between all necessities of external struggle and follow the path which is given in the ungraspable law of its folk-personality." J. J. Ruedorffer (pseud.), *Grundzüge der Weltpolitik in der Gegenwart* (Stuttgart, 1914), pp. 102 ff., 188 ff. "We must conduct a world policy. Economic expansion and the will of the people press outward. German policy must escape this vicious circle. It cannot opt for a purely continental policy. This task is the central problem of the foreign policy of the German Empire." Riezler's thesis that the tension between this dynamic vitalism and the need for a cautious and moderate policy was the dilemma of German Weltpolitik appears as a rationalization of Bethmann's concerns. Cf. Andreas Hillgruber, "Riezler's Theorie des kalkulierten Risikos und Bethmann Hollweg's politische Konzeption in der Julikrise 1914," *HZ* 202 (1966) : 333 ff., and I. Geiss's more aggressive interpretation, "Zur Beurteilung der deutschen Reichspolitik im ersten Weltkrieg," in H. Pogge-v. Strandmann and I. Geiss, *Die Erforderlichkeit des Unmöglichen: Deutschland am Vorabend des ersten Weltkrieges* (Frankfurt, 1965).

54 Riezler, *Grundzüge*, pp. 191 ff., 201 ff., 214 ff., 219 ff., 229 ff., 246 ff. "The time of coup de mains has passed. Many small, unnoticeable advantages taken together make up a success. . . . Under these circumstances policy is directed toward avoiding the use of force if possible and leaving the decision to the opponent." Since the world political struggle had been transformed into competition for economic advantage and the minds of men, Riezler rejected the personal heroism of the Bismarck legend and concluded provocatively: "In the last analysis the better average decides." For contemporary echoes cf. K. A. von Müller, *Aus den Gärten der Vergangenheit* (Stuttgart, 1952), pp. 541–42 and "Sg" (Franz Sontag) "Grundzüge der Weltpolitik," *AB*, Dec. 29, 1914 and Jan. 16, 1915. See also Paul Rohrbach's laudatory review, agreeing that *"the world political constellation is working in the direction of maintaining peace,"* *Das Grössere Deutschland*, May 10, 1914.

55 Bethmann in conversation with Winterfeld, *Jahreszeiten*, pp. 157 ff. H. Pogge, *Rathenau Tagebuch*, July 25, 1912. Bethmann to Lamprecht, June 21, 1913, printed as appendix to Riezler's *Grundzüge*, pp. 251–52. Jules Cambon to Doumergue, Jan. 28, 29, 1914, *FDs*, 3d ser. 9 : 209 ff. The chancellor's moderate and yet power-political brand of world policy must be analyzed in relationship to the whole phenomenon of liberal imperialism, which deserves a thorough study. See, for instance, the wartime pamphlets, edited by Edwyn Bevin: *The German Empire of Central Africa: As the Basis of a New German World-Policy*, translating a brochure by Emil Zimmermann (New York, 1918); Gerhart von Schulze-Graevernitz, *Deutschland und England* (Berlin, 1922); and Paul Rohrbach's programmatic title essay, "Warum deutsche Weltpolitik?" *Das Grössere Deutschland*, Apr. 5, 1914.

56 Commandant de Civrieux, *Le Germanisme encerclé* (Paris, 1913). Lerchenfeld to

Hertling, June 4, 1914, BHStA, MA I, 957a. Resolution of the presidium of the Pan-German League, Apr. 19, 1914, reprinted in Franz Sontag's article in *AB*, Dec. 19, 1914. Berckheim to Dusch, Mar. 11, 1914, GLAK 233, 34,815. Szögyény reports a similar conversation with William II to Berchtold, Mar. 12, 1914, HHStA, PA III, 171B. Jagow essays, "Gespräch mit Moltke 1914," and "Deutschlands Lage und politische Pläne 1913/14," AA *Nachlass* Jagow. Sverbejev to Sazonov, Apr. 9, 1914, *RDs* 2 : 202–03.

57 Bethmann to Professor Binding, Mar. 30, 1913, DZA Po, Rkz. 1252/1 cited in K. Stenkewitz's, *Gegen Bajonett*, pp. 109–10. Bethmann to crown prince, Nov. 15, 1913, refuting the bellicose Pan-German memorandum by General Gebsattel. H. Pogge-v. Strandmann and I. Geiss, *Die Erforderlichkeit*, pp. 32 ff. Jules Cambon to Poincaré, Feb. 18, 1912, reporting a long conversation with Bethmann, *FDs*, 3d ser. 2 : 53 ff. Vietsch, *Bethmann*, p. 149. Despite the dearth of clues to his private views in the spring of 1914 (conversation with Count Hertling, April 13, 1914, discounting the danger of war, in BHStA MA I 962), there is no indication that Bethmann had changed his ideas about war, especially when compared to its Pan-German glorification by General von Bernhardi, *Deutschland und der nächste Krieg*, rev. ed. (Stuttgart, 1913), which posed the false alternative "*Weltmacht* or Decline?" Cf. also Bernhardi's acid criticism of Bethmann's cultural imperialism: "A chancellor who could write such a letter is not all a man of action. . . . Such a man seems to me little suited to lead the German people on the path of world policy toward a great future, especially under the difficult external circumstances into which his diplomatic art without any positive goal and his powerless peace policy have brought us." Friedrich von Bernhardi, *Eine Weltreise 1911/12 und der Zusammenbruch Deutschlands: Eindrücke und Betrachtungen aus den Jahren 1911 bis 1914 mit einem Nachwort aus dem Jahre 1919* (Leipzig, 1920).

58 Michael Wagebald (pseud.), *Europa in Flammen: Der deutsche Zukunftskrieg von 1909* (Berlin, Oct. 1908), pp. 18 ff., 28 ff., 80 ff., 99 ff., 236 ff. Cf. also Count Ernst von Reuther's earlier call to arms, *Weltfrieden oder Weltkrieg! Wohin geht Deutschlands Weg?* (Berlin, 1907).

Chapter 6

1 A. von Wegerer, *Bibliographie zur Vorgeschichte des Weltkrieges* (Berlin, 1934); M. Gunzenhäuser, "Die Bibliographien zur Geschichte des ersten Weltkrieges," *Schriften der Bibliothek für Zeitgeschichte* (Frankfurt, 1964); and the bibliography of Peter Graf Kielmansegg, *Deutschland und der erste Weltkrieg* (Frankfurt, 1968) introduce the older literature. See also P. Renouvin, *Les Origines immediates de la guerre* (Paris, 1925); Sidney B. Fay, *The Origins of the World War*, 2 vols. (New York, 1928); B. E. Schmitt, *The Coming of the War*, 2 vols. (New York, 1930); and L. Albertini, *Le origini della guerra del 1914*, 3 vols. (Milan, 1942–43). For the *état présent* of the renewed controversy in the wake of Fritz Fischer's provocative works cf. W. J. Mommsen and I. Geiss in the *JCH* 1, nos. 3–4 (1966); James Joll, "The 1914 Debate Continues: Fritz Fischer and His Critics," *Past and Present* 34 (1967) : 100 ff., Hans Herzfeld, *Der Erste Weltkrieg* (Munich, 1968); and Wolfgang Schieder, *Der Erste Weltkrieg: Ursachen, Entstehung und Kriegsziele* (Cologne, 1969). Cf. my own, "The Illusion of Limited War: Chancellor Bethmann Hollweg's Calculated Risk, July 1914," *CEH* 2 (1969) : 48 ff.; and Volker R. Berghahn and Wilhelm Deist, "Kaiserliche Marine und Kriegsausbruch, 1914," *MGM*, no. 1 (1970) : 37 ff.

2 Bethmann to Bülow, June 10, 1915, BA *Nachlass* Bülow. Cf. O. Hammann, *Bilder*

aus der letzten Kaiserzeit (Berlin, 1922), pp. 122 ff. Bethmann protested against "premature criticism" that could only "paralyze those forces of unity which we desperately need for a victorious *Durchhalten*." Cf. also Bethmann to Delbrück, June 16, 1919, DSB *Nachlass* Delbrück. Despite their apologetic tendency, Treutler's memoirs admit the possibility, "that one can have been co-responsible for the war through political and military mistakes." Janssen, ed., *Treutler*, pp. 112 ff.

3 Bethmann to Jagow, June 11, 1919, containing his shock at the disclosure of Grey's assurances to the Russian statesmen at Balmoral, AA *Nachlass* Jagow. Note by Conrad Haussmann, Feb. 24, 1918, about his visit to Hohenfinow, WHStA, J 47, NH 114, cited by W. Steglich, *Die Friedenspolitik der Mittelmächte, 1917–1918* (Wiesbaden, 1964), 1 : 418. Bethmann's rebuttal to Eisner's disclosures, Nov. 27, 1918, in the *DAZ*. Cf. Pius Dirr, *Bayerische Dokumente zum Kriegsausbruch und zum Versailler Schuldspruch* (Munich, 1924) for a comparison between Eisner's versions and the originals. Bethmann interview for Wiegand regarding Gooss's allegations in AA *Nachlass* Jagow, n.d., and Roderich Gooss, *Das Wiener Kabinett und die Entstehung des Weltkriegs* (Vienna, 1919). For the battle of documents cf. also I. Geiss's introduction to Hermann Kantorowicz, *Gutachten zur Kriegsschuldfrage 1914* (Frankfurt, 1967).

4 K. D. Erdmann is presently preparing the long-awaited edition of this document, comparable in importance to the House Diaries for Wilson's biography. Cf. his "Zur Beurteilung Bethmann Hollwegs," *GWU* 15 (1964) : 525–40 and *Die Zeit*, Jan. 16, 1968. Cf. also the selections published by F. Stern, "Bethmann Hollweg and the War: The Limits of Responsibility," in L. Krieger and F. Stern, eds., *The Responsibility of Power* (Garden City, N.Y., 1967), pp. 252–85 and *Die Zeit*, Jan. 2, 1968. For a characterization of Riezler cf. Theodor Heuss, "A Word in Memory of Kurt Riezler," and L. Strauss, "Kurt Riezler, 1882–1955," *Social Research* 23 (1955) : 1–34. Born into a family of prominent South German scholars, Riezler entered the Foreign Service in 1906 after studying the classics and came into Bethmann's inner circle in 1911. According to the chancellor's son Felix, the relationship was that of a bright young man and a skeptical elder statesman whose differences in age, temperament, and responsibility made for scintillating discussions. For his role in German eastern policy after Bethmann's fall, cf. Winfried Baumgart, *Deutsche Ostpolitik 1918: Von Brest Litowsk bis zum Ende des Ersten Weltkrieges* (Munich, 1966), especially p. 209n., with citations from the Bothmer Diary, and my own, "Kurt Riezler and the Failure of German *Ostpolitik*, 1918," *Slavic Review* (1972). After his resignation from the diplomatic service, Riezler was a professor of philosophy at Munich, rector at the University of Frankfurt, and emigrated to the U.S.A. in 1939, where he taught at the New School for Social Research (N.Y.C.) until 1952.

5 Riezler Diary, July 7, 20, Sept. 13, 1914. For a contemporary Anglo-Saxon version of the Bethmann stereotype cf. F. W. Wile, *Men Around the Kaiser* (Indianapolis, 1914), which tags him as "a great schoolmaster" but little else.

6 Riezler Diary, Aug. 21, Oct. 10, 1914. Cf. Hammann's insight in *Bilder*, pp. 66 ff.: "His most difficult struggle was the struggle against himself." Erhard Deutelmoser, "Über Bethmann Hollweg," *Die Weltbühne* 17 (1921) : 61 ff., called him "a man of doubt, a seeker and agonizer," creating the false impression of weakness. "In reality, this was exactly his strength. Bethmann incessantly strove for insight, and when he felt on its firm ground he was not weak but strong."

7 Lerchenfeld to Hertling, June 4, 1914; BHStA MA I 957a, reprinted in Dirr, pp. 110 ff. Bethmann to Lichnowsky, June 16, 1914, GP 39 : 628 ff. For discussions about a new naval increase cf. Müller Diary, May 27 and June 15: "Talk with the chancellor about the chauvinistic reporting of Captain V. Müller, our naval attaché

in London, regarding the Anglo-Russian naval agreement and about the military mission in Constantinople." BA *Nachlass* Müller. The documents on Bethmann's feelings in early summer 1914 are sparse because not until late in May did he reemerge from mourning "after the death of his splendid wife" (ibid.). Cf. also Bethmann to Jagow, AA *Nachlass* Jagow, June 28, 1919: "The British Cabinet has oriented its policy so firmly toward the Entente and the Entente statesmen were so exactly informed of this . . . that the publication of our agreements, especially since the one concerning Portuguese colonies was only a problematic dream and would have been blown up as a defeat in Germany, would never have been able to exert a calming influence on Russia and France."

8 Jagow to Gerhard (Meyer), AA *Nachlass* Jagow, July 6, 1914, arguing for a postponement of a meeting with Grey's secretary, Sir S. G. Tyrrell: "You know that I consider a rapprochement with England, or at least an elimination of all differences, as the solely reasonable policy in the interest of *both* countries. But the English (and especially Grey) are so *closely* involved in the Triple Entente that they fearfully avoid even the appearance of deviating from this course and any too far-reaching advance would only make them shy away." For the reporting of the German ambassador in Belgrade, stressing Serbian complicity, cf. Griesinger to Bethmann, June 30, July 2, 1914, in K. Kautsky, *Die deutschen Dokumente zum Kriegsausbruch 1914* (Berlin, 1927), 1 : 15 ff. Similarly, see Admiral Müller's *Regierte?*, pp. 31–32. Cf. also V. Dedijer, *The Road to Sarajevo* (London, 1967), and Hans Uebersberger, *Oesterreich zwischen Russland und Serbien: Zur Südslawischen Frage und der Entstehung des Ersten Weltkrieges* (Frankfurt, 1958).

9 Bülow, *Denkwürdigkeiten* 3 : 139 ff. Although this episode has an authentic ring, the rest of Bülow's reminiscences on the July crisis, especially pp. 148 ff., Bethmann as "scapegoat," are likely to be spurious. For the conversation with Lichnowsky there is no summary from Bethmann's side, only Bethmann's marginal note requesting a previous discussion with Zimmermann, dated June 27, 1914, *GDs*, pp. 10–11. See also Lichnowsky, *Heading for the Abyss*, pp. 6–7, 16, 71–72, 154 ff. and 157. For the two general staff studies, "The Completion of the Russian Railroad Network" and "The Growing Power of Russia," which were received by Zimmermann on July 5, 1914, cf. AA, Dld 121, no. 31 secr., vol. 2. Cf. also Salza Lichtenau to Vitzthum, July 2, 1914; Geiss, 1 : 71–72. The originals of the German documents are in AA Wk. vols. 1 ff., and Wk. secr., vols. 1 ff., reprinted fairly thoroughly in the Kautsky—Schücking—Montgelas edition. Cf. also BHStA MA III 2691/2 for the originals of Dirr's Bavarian documents, and August Bach, *Deutsche Gesandschaftsberichte zum Kriegsausbruch* (Berlin, 1937) for the Badensian, Saxonian, and Württembergian reports. See also, *FDs*, vols. 39, 10–11; *BDs*, vol. 11; *IBZ*, vols. 4–5; *Oe-U*, vol. 8; Bernhard Schwertfeger, *Amtliche Aktenstücke zur Geschichte der Europäischen Politik 1871–1914* (Berlin, 1925), vol. 2; and M. Boghitschewitsch, *Die Auswärtige Politik Serbiens, 1903–1914* (Berlin, 1928), vols. 1–3. Immanuel Geiss, *Julikrise und Kriegsausbruch*, 2 vols. (Hanover, 1963–64), is a useful compilation of printed sources relating to German policy. Cf. also his revised introduction to the condensed English paperback edition (1968) for his views on the July crisis. For some inaccessible pieces cf. also H. Michaelis and E. Schraepler, *Ursachen und Folgen. Vom deutschen Zusammenbruch 1918 und 1945 bis zur staatlichen Neuordnung Deutschlands in der Gegenwart* (Berlin, 1958), vols. 1 ff. See also the much neglected *Stenographische Berichte über die öffentlichen Verhandlungen des 15. Untersuchungsausschusses der Verfassunggebenden Nationalversammlung* (Berlin, 1920), vol. 2.

10 Bach, pp. 12–13, based upon the Lyncker diary. Bethmann to Tschirschky, July 2, reacting to a telegram of Eiswaldt to Foreign Office, July 1, warning against the

visit (*GDs* 1 : 11 ff.). Cf. Lerchenfeld to Hertling, July 2, 1914, *GDs* 1 : 12 ff. For the effect of the imperial reprimand, see the changed language of the correspondent of the *Frankfurter Zeitung* Gans to the Ballplatz after having been instructed by Tschirschky: "Germany would support the monarchy through thick and thin, whatever it would decide against Serbia. The imperial German ambassador added that the earlier Austria began, the better." Cf. Tschirschky's apologetic telegram to Bethmann, July 4, 1914, and Forgach's memorandum, Geiss 1 : 76–77.

11 Bethmann orally to Thimme (1919), cited in Mommsen, "Die Politik," pp. 284–85. Cf. Saxonian military attaché to minister of war, July 3, 1914, summarizing a conversation with Waldersee: "I have gained the impression that they would consider it favorable if a war would now break out. The situation and chances would not get better. However H.M. is reputed to have spoken in favor of the maintenance of peace." For characterizations of Zimmermann and Stumm cf. Werner von Rheinbaben, *Kaiser, Kanzler, Präsidenten* (Mainz, 1968), pp. 96, 108-09, and Hopman to Tirpitz, July 13, 1914, Berghahn and Deist, "Neue Dokumente," pp. 49–50. Bethmann to Max von Baden, Jan. 17, 1918, regarding the imperialist Reichstag, in E. Zechlin, "Deutschland zwischen Kabinetts und Wirtschaftskrieg," pp. 451 ff. For the bellicosity of one segment of the press cf. Victor Naumann's conversation with Hoyos, July 1, 1914, in Geiss 1 : 60 ff. For the chancellor's position vis-à-vis economic interest groups cf. Fritz Klein, ed., *Deutschland im Ersten Weltkrieg* (Berlin, 1968) 1 : 131 ff. Cf. also Bethmann's memorandum for the first subcommittee of the UA, reprinted in his *Betrachtungen* 2 : 241 ff.

12 For the Austrian background of the Hoyos mission cf. H. Hantsch, *Berchtold* 2 : 569 ff., which indicates that Hoyos first conferred with Zimmermann and orally went far beyond his instructions. Cf. also the disappointing Alexander Hoyos, *Der deutsch-englische Gegensatz und sein Einfluss auf die Balkanpolitik Oesterreich-Ungarns* (Berlin, 1922), pp. 80 ff. Lichnowsky, *Heading for,* p. 16n. Bach, pp. 13 ff. For the Austrian memorandum and covering letter cf. *GDs* 1 : 21 ff. See also Hopman to Tirpitz, July 6, 1914, in Berghahn and Deist, "Neue Dokumente," pp. 45–46. Cf. Szögyény's report of the first conversation with William II and his assurance that "also in this case we can count upon the complete support of Germany. As he had mentioned before, he first had to listen to the chancellor's advice but he did not doubt in the least that Herr von Bethmann Hollweg would completely agree with his opinion." This statement was not as sinister as it may seem since, as Fritz Fischer has shown, Bethmann was in Berlin during all but two days in the week after the murder, and was therefore in constant touch with William II (*Der Krieg der Illusionen,* pp. 688 ff.). Bethmann, *Betrachtungen* 1 : 134 ff. Cf. also UA 1 : 3–23, 79 ff. For the myth of the crown council see G. Craig, *The Politics of the Prussian Army* (New York, 1964), p. 292.

13 Bethmann's reply to Eisner, Dirr, pp. 53 ff. Falkenhayn to Moltke, July 5, "Surely in no case will the next few weeks bring a decision. Much time will go by before the treaty with Bulgaria is signed." Geiss, 1 : 86–87, 92–93, Szögyény to Berchtold, July 6, 1914. Bethmann to Tschirschky, July 6, 1914, the draft in Zimmermann's handwriting. The chancellor struck from the instruction that Germany would support Austria "in all circumstances," a small but significant difference from the more belligerent undersecretary. Bethmann to Waldburg, July 6, AA Wk., vol. 1. In contrast to Szögyény's report, Bethmann's instructions are preoccupied with the diplomatic offensive in the Balkans rather than with the likelihood of war. Cf. also Geiss, 1 and 2, nos. 6, 12, 21, 27, 34, 61, 138, 233, 513, 868, 998, 1063, 1070. Müller Diary, entry for July 7, illustrating the mood of the emperor and the military entourage as well as Hoyos's oral forcefulness, BA *Nachlass* Müller. For the briefings of the military leaders on the morning of July 6, cf. also Geiss

1 : 95 ff. in which, however, tactics and reality are mixed, as in General Bertrab's assurance to Moltke: "To be honest, H.M. considers the matter so far as a purely Balkan question and expresses this opinion, beginning his northern cruise as planned."

14 Bethmann marginalia on a clipping from the *FZ*, July 9, AA Wk., vol. 1. Riezler Diary, July 7, 1914. For the lack of success of Lichnowsky's representations with Grey, cf. also his report to Bethmann, July 6, 1914, which arrived in Berlin July 9 (Geiss 1 : 100 ff.). Cf. also Bethmann's briefing of governmental officials and Reichstag members on Apr. 24, 1913, supporting arms increases, in which he stressed the importance of the Dreibund, the likelihood of British intervention, if not immediately then later, and the need of working for peace. Emphasizing his "good conscience," the chancellor predicted a "world catastrophe," a theme which recurs one year later. Vietsch, *Bethmann*, pp. 154 ff.

15 Riezler Diary, July 7, 8, 1914. This fear of revolution contradicts A. J. Mayer's theory of the "Domestic Causes of the First World War," *The Responsibility of Power*, pp. 268 ff., at least insofar as it concerns Bethmann personally. Cf. also F. Stern, "Bethmann Hollweg und der Krieg; Die Grenzen der Verantwortung," *Recht und Staat in Geschichte und Gegenwart* (Tübingen, 1968), pp. 351–52 for a probing search into the chancellor's mind and psyche.

16 Riezler Diary, July 14, 1914. For the self-conscious relationship of the blank-check decision to earlier policy, cf. Riezler's phrase, "Kiderlen always said we must fight." For the development of the concept of calculated risk, cf. Egmont Zechlin, "Die Illusion vom begrenzten Krieg: Berlin's Fehlkalkulation im Sommer 1914," *Die Zeit*, Sept. 21, 1965, "Probleme des Kriegskalküls und der Kriegsbeendigung im Ersten Weltkrieg," *GWU* 16 (1965): 69 ff., and "Ein Nachwort," in Schieder, *Erster Weltkrieg*, pp. 199 ff. See also Andreas Hillgruber, "Riezler's Theorie des Kalkulierten Risikos," pp. 333 ff.; *Deutschlands Rolle in der Vorgeschichte der beiden Weltkriege* (Göttingen, 1967), pp. 6, 46 ff.; and *Kontinuität und Diskontinuität in der deutschen Aussenpolitik von Bismarck bis Hitler* (Düsseldorf, 1969), pp. 13–14.

17 Clemens von Delbrück, *Die wirtschaftliche Mobilmachung in Deutschland* (Munich, 1924), pp. 96 ff. Cf. also Geiss 1 : 139. Riezler Diary, July 11, 1914: "The chancellor berates the diplomats. The profession spoils people and he trusts neither a domestic nor a foreign one. . . . If he asked one diplomat for information about another, he would tear him apart, even if they were the best of friends." Despite Hammann's "stubborn, strong-headed, and uncomfortable" character, Bethmann refused to sacrifice him to the Foreign Office. "He has a touch of greatness, is capable of grasping the true popular feeling beyond the newspapers and is, should war come, completely indispensable for calling up the people." For German pressure on Vienna to reach a quick decision cf. Szögyény to Berchtold, July 8, 9, 12, 1914. Jagow to Tschirschky, July 11, Jagow to Waldburg, Flotow, July 14, 1914, Geiss 1 : 125 ff. Cf. also Schoen to Hertling, July 9, 1914: "Undersecretary Zimmermann would consider the present moment very opportune for Austria to undertake a revenge campaign [*Rachezug*] against its southern neighbor, and believes certainly war could successfully be localized. But he doubts that Vienna will decide upon this course." Geiss 1 : 40. For the diplomatic offensive in the Balkans cf. Gerard E. Silberstein, *The Troubled Alliance: German-Austrian Relations 1914–1917* (Lexington, Ky., 1970), pp. 16 ff. chiefly concerned with Austro-German Balkan policy.

18 Riezler Diary, July 14, 1914. Riezler was skeptical about Italy, since "it knows the condition of Austria, the success of Russian subversion with all Slavs . . . and underestimates the elasticity of this old state which can bear much more internal

strife than all other crowns. If in case of war England marches immediately, Italy will never join, and it will intervene in the future only if our victory is assured, or it considers it assured." The chancellor's advisor continued his perceptive appraisal: Italy "is horribly afraid of war on our side. It will at most feed on carrion. It cannot participate [unless?] the pacifism of the Socialists unites with the irredentism of the Nationalists." Jagow's instruction to Lichnowsky on "localization" of July 12 was already drafted on July 7, indicating that his rationale was an integral part of the July 5–6 decisions; AA Wk., vol. 1. Cf. also Hopman to Tirpitz, reporting Zimmermann's views, July 13, 1914, in Berghahn and Deist, "Neue Dokumente," pp. 49–50. For the Italian question cf. W. J. Mommsen, "Die Italienische Frage in der Politik des Reichskanzlers Bethmann Hollweg, 1914–1915," *Quellen und Forschungen aus Italienischen Archiven und Bibliotheken* 48 (1968) : 282–308; and Leo Valiani, "Italian-Austro-Hungarian Negotiations, 1914–1915," *JCH* 1 (1966) : 113 ff. and *La dissoluzione dell'Austria Ungeria* (Milan, 1966), pp. 97 ff. For the Austrian decision in favor of war and the German role in it, cf. Norman Stone, "Hungary and the Crisis of July 1914," *JCH* 1 (1966) : 147 ff.; A. J. May, *The Passing of the Hapsburg Monarchy, 1914–1918* (Philadelphia, 1966) 1 : 54 ff., and H. Hantsch, *Berchtold*, pp. 573 ff.

19 Bethmann to Roedern, July 15; AA Wk., vol. 1. Bethmann to William II, July 20, 1914, Geiss 1 : 241 ff. Riezler Diary, July 23, 1914. P. Herre, *Kronprinz Wilhelm*, p. 51. Bethmann's reprimand has not yet been discovered. Riezler continued: "The kaiser does so. The crown prince writes a long letter, demands war, anti-Socialist laws, struggle, and force. Insane slogans. Where are the educated officers who made Prussia great?"

20 Bethmann interview for Wiegand, AA *Nachlass* Jagow: "I believe I remember that especially in the interest of localization we abstained from any influence on the preparation of the Austrian step toward Serbia. We hoped to be able to prevent the Serbian conflict from becoming a European question." Hopman to Tirpitz, July 13, 16, 20, 1914, in Berghahn and Deist, "Neue Dokumente," pp. 49–54. Schoen to Hertling, July 18, 1914, published partially in the original Eisner documents, now Geiss 1 : 212 ff. Circular by Bethmann to Petersburg, Paris, London, July 21, 1914, ibid., pp. 264 ff. Bethmann to Jagow, July 22, 1914, ibid., pp. 282–83. Bethmann rebuttal to Eisner, Dirr, pp. 53 ff. Riezler Diary, July 20, 1914. Cf. also Jagow to Lichnowsky, July 15, 1914: "It is an eminently political question, perhaps the last opportunity to sound the death knell for greater Serbian agitation under relatively favorable circumstances." Cf. also Jagow's even more notorious letter to Lichnowsky of July 18, 1914: "Even now we have not driven Austria to its decision. But we cannot and must not hold back. . . . I want no preventive war, but should the struggle come, we must not run away." Geiss 1 : 175 ff. Cf. also Biedermann to Vitzthum, July 17: "Even if they are not spurred on from here, they are equally not discouraged, and we would rather welcome a forceful step." Ibid., pp. 199–200. Cf. Bethmann to Jagow, March 5, 1920, AA *Nachlass* Jagow.

21 Riezler Diary, July 20, 1914, mentioning the example of Tsingtao, "which as 'cultural center' in east [Asia] is only an end in itself as naval base, militarily and politically untenable," since it provoked Japanese hostility. For the depth of the clash with Tirpitz, embodying the major alternatives for German foreign policy before 1914, cf. another draft rebuttal by Bethmann to Tirpitz's tendentious *Erinnerungen* (Leipzig, 1919) in the BA Kl. Erw., 342–1. "In order to write in Tirpitz's style we have neither banged with the Austrian fist on the table nor driven Austria to march into Serbia." Bethmann also insisted that he did not know if Berchtold had been dead set to march into Serbia: "I was not." Cf. also

John Schrecker, *Imperialism and Chinese Nationalism: Germany in Shantung* (Cambridge, Mass., 1971).

22 Riezler Diary, July 20, 23, 1914. For other German irritations with Austria, cf. Tschirschky to Jagow, May 22, "How often do I pose the question of whether it is still profitable to ally ourselves so firmly with this state structure creaking in all joints and to continue the laborious task of dragging it further." *GP* 39 : 364–65. Cf. also Jagow's laconic rebuttal to Lichnowsky, July 18, 1914, "If you don't like the company, go elsewhere, if you have a choice." Cf. also Jagow's "Austria-Hungary, 1914," in his MS, "Politische Aufsätze," AA *Nachlass* Jagow, GDs 1 : 92. For the whole complex, cf. also Fritz Klein, ed., *Oesterreich-Ungarn in der Weltpolitik 1900–1918* (Berlin, 1965), pp. 155 ff.

23 Riezler Diary, July 23, 1914. Bethmann to Falkenhayn, July 18, in F. Klein, *Deutschland im Ersten Weltkrieg* 1 : 239–40. Cf. also F. Fischer, *Der Krieg der Illusionen*, pp. 698 ff. Hopman to Tirpitz, July 21–4, 1914 in Berghahn and Deist, "Neue Dokumente," pp. 54 ff.

24 Riezler Diary, July 23, 25, 1914. For Germany's clumsy attempts to dissociate itself from the wording of the Austrian note, cf. Jagow to Tschirschky, July 25, and Zimmermann's circular of the same day, Geiss 1 : 342 ff. The next day Jagow refused to associate himself with western efforts to obtain an extension of the ultimatum to Serbia, indicating clearly that Berlin desired at least a local war. Jagow to Lichnowsky, July 25, 1914, Geiss 1 : 404. The night before the chancellor's return to Berlin, Riezler sat "under the great linden trees and pondered everything. What will happen? Will the German nation be saved or perish?"

25 Riezler Diary, July 27, 1914. Bethmann to William II, July 25, AA Wk., vol. 4. For the mood in Berlin cf. Loebell's MS "Erinnerungen," BA *Nachlass* Loebell: "In the next days the city was filled with demonstrations and parades, some for, some against war, causing confusion. I myself appeared at the balcony of the ministry for one parade, assuming that it was a patriotic demonstration, but hurriedly withdrew when I was greeted with the 'International.' Generally the patriotic displays were by far in the majority."

26 Bethmann to William II, July 26, AA Wk., vol. 5. G. A. Müller, *Regierte?*, pp. 32 ff. Bethmann to Pourtalès, Tschirschky, Lichnowsky, and Schoen, July 26, ibid., and Geiss 2 : 31 ff. Cf. also Bethmann's revealing draft circular of July 26 to the German ambassadors, which was sent in somewhat altered form several days later, stressing "justified Austrian self-defense." Should Russia support Serbia "it solely bears the responsibility if a European war arises out of the Austrian-Serbian quarrel, which the other Great Powers are seeking to localize." Geiss 2 : 46–47. Cf. also Graevenitz to Weizsäcker, July 26, 1914, Bach, no. 17, and Schoen to Hertling, July 26, 1914, indicating that Bethmann sought to avoid any Bavarian help in the Austrian mobilization, "since it would appear as a breach of neutrality." Dirr, p. 139.

27 Riezler Diary, July 27, 1914. Cf. I. V. Bestuzhev, "Russian Foreign Policy, February–June, 1914," and H. Rogger, "Russia in 1914," *JCH* 1 (1966): (pb. edition), 88 ff., 229 ff. Cf. also F. Count Pourtalès, *Meine Verhandlungen in St. Petersburg Ende Juli 1914* (Berlin, 1927). For the British change in policy, cf. Lichnowsky to Jagow, July 27, 1914, Geiss 2 : 105 ff., and Grey to Goschen, July 27, 1914, *BDs* 11, no. 176. Cf. also Herbert Butterfield's brilliant exposition of "Sir Edward Grey and the July Crisis, 1914," *Historical Studies* 5 (1965) : 1–25, and the literature cited there. Bethmann to William II, Schoen, Lichnowsky, Tschirschky, AA Wk., vol. 7, Geiss 2 : 102 ff. See especially Bethmann's instruction to Lichnowsky, indicating the limits of cooperation with London: "The more we try to maintain peace in Europe in complete agreement with England, and hopefully

in continuing cooperation with it, . . . the less we can admit the right of Russia or the Triple Entente to take the side of Serbian subversion against Austria." Cf. also the Lynker Diary, July 27, Bach, no. 22 and the Müller Diary for the same day, BA *Nachlass* Müller. For Berlin's initial opposition to British mediation, cf. Szögyény's damning telegram to Berchtold, July 27, 1914, Geiss 2 : 93 ff.

28 William II to Jagow, July 28: "Through it *every reason for war disappears.*" Marginalia by Bethmann on Lichnowsky to Jagow, July 28; Bethmann to Tschirschky, Pourtalès, Lichnowsky, Wangenheim, and William II, July 28, AA Wk., vol. 7 and Geiss 2 : 184 ff. Especially Bethmann to Tschirschky, in the evening of July 28, Geiss 2 : 196 ff. Bethmann to the Prussian ambassadors of the German states, July 28, Geiss 2 : 198 ff. Goschen to Grey, July 28, 1914, *BDs* 11, no. 249. Cf. also Ulrich Trumpener, *Germany and the Ottoman Empire, 1914–1918* (Princeton, 1968), pp. 14 ff.

29 Riezler Diary, July 27, 1914. Südekum to Bethmann, July 29, 1914. Institut für Marxismus-Leninismus beim ZK der SED, *Geschichte der deutschen Arbeiterbewegung* (Berlin, 1966) 2 : 430–31. Bethmann Hollweg to William II, July 29, 1914, cited by E. Zechlin, "Bethmann Hollweg, Kriegsrisiko und SPD, 1914," *Der Monat* 18 (1966) : 17 ff. D. Fricke and H. Radandt, "Neue Dokumente über die Rolle Albert Südekums," *ZfG* 4 (1956) : 757 ff.; Jürgen Kuczynski, *Der Ausbruch der ersten Weltkrieges und die deutsche Sozialdemokratie* (Berlin, 1959); and most recently, D. Groh, "The 'Unpatriotic Socialists' and the State," *JCH* 1 (1966) : 151–78. D. K. Buse, "Ebert and the Coming of World War I: A Month from His Diary," *International Review of Social History* 13 (1968) : 430 ff. Cf. also the revisionist David's note on August 1, "our peace demonstrations of Tuesday evening (the 28th) had been tolerated and even encouraged by Bethmann," E. Matthias and S. Miller, eds., *Das Kriegstagebuch des Reichstagsabgeordneten Eduard David, 1914–1918* (Düsseldorf, 1966), pp. 5 ff.

30 Moltke to Bethmann Hollweg, July 29, 1914, "Zur Beurteilung der politischen Lage," claiming sanctimoniously, "Germany does not want to provoke this horrible war." Geiss 2 : 261 ff. Leuckhart to Carlowitz, July 29, Bach, no. 29, reinforced by Wenninger to Kress, July 29, and Dirr, pp. 220 ff., reporting that the chief of staff favored immediate war: "Against these driving elements the chancellor brakes with all his power and desires to avoid everything which could cause similar measures in France or England and make the stone roll" downhill. Bethmann to Schoen and Pourtalès, July 29, AA Wk., vol. 8, Geiss 2 : 282–83. H. von Zwehl, *Erich von Falkenhayn* (Berlin, 1926), pp. 56 ff.; A. von Tirpitz, *Deutsche Ohnmachtspolitik im Weltkriege* (Hamburg, 1926), pp. 2 ff. and the Müller Diary, entry for July 29, 1914, BA *Nachlass* Müller. Cf. W. J. Mommsen, "Die Politik," pp. 351 ff. For the role of the military, cf. also G. Ritter, *Staatskunst und Kriegshandwerk* (Munich, 1960) 2 : 308, and with an apologetic undertone, "Der Anteil des Militärs an der Kriegskatastrophe von 1914," *HZ* 193 (1961) : 72 ff.

31 Note by Bethmann, July 29, 1914. Cf. *BDs* 11, nos. 293, 305, and 607 for Goschen's surprise. See also L. Cecil, *Albert Ballin: Business and Politics in Imperial Germany, 1888–1918*, pp. 205 ff. On August 1 Ballin reported that Haldane had given him "the impression that England would only be induced to make a martial intervention if Germany were to *swallow* France, in other words, if the balance of power would really be altered by German annexation of French territory." Cf. Riezler, August 15, Lichnowsky, "shaking like a leaf, lacking courage and dignity, and possessing only understanding for the British position," failed to communicate effectively with Berlin. For Prince Henry's report of his impressions in London, cf. his letter to William II, July 28, 1914, Geiss 2 : 200–01.

32 Riezler Diary, August 15, 1914. During the climax of the crisis Riezler took no

474 *Notes to Pages 171–75*

notes, but summarized events two weeks later. Bethmann to Jagow, July 29, 1914: "A policy with a double standard we cannot support as ally" of Austria. Geiss 2 : 264.

33 Riezler Diary, August 15, 1914. Bethmann to Tschirschky at 8, 11, 12:30 P.M., 2:55, 3 A.M. night of July 29/30 to William II, July 30, 6 A.M. and Geiss 2 : 280 ff. Cf. Lerchenfeld to Hertling, July 29, Dirr, no. 47; Varnbüler to Weizsäcker, July 29, and Graevenitz to Weizsäcker, July 29: "The chancellor is still reported to be very optimistic about the maintenance of peace among the great powers." Bach, nos. 40, 41.

34 Bethmann to William II, July 30, 1914, still hopeful: "Should England offer to secure the successes it has proposed to Austria, this could possibly satisfy Vienna." In the second telegram, suggesting the wording of a "Dear Nicky" dispatch to the tsar, Bethmann revealed that German actions in the last stages of the crisis were geared to producing an alibi, stressing that "this telegram will become an especially important document for history. . . ." The four reports of Bethmann's briefing of the ambassadors of the states are sequentially identical, Berckheim to Dusch, Salza Lichtenau to Vitzthum, Varnbüler to Weizsäcker, and Lerchenfeld to Hertling, July 30, Bach, nos. 46 ff. and Dirr, no. 55. The Württembergian military attaché had heard "that during the conference of the highest military and civilian authorities with the kaiser sharply contradictory opinions had emerged; the chancellor still wanted to gain time for the continuation of peaceful negotiations while the minister of war and chief of general staff demanded immediate countermeasures against Russian mobilization and French preparations."

35 Protocol of the session of the Prussian Ministry of State, July 30, 1914, DZA Me, Rep. 90a B III 2b no. 6, vol. 163. Despite military pressure Bethmann accepted only "purely defensive measures." Cf. also Tirpitz, *Ohnmachtspolitik*, p. 5. Zwehl, *Falkenhayn*, pp. 87–88. Bethmann to Tschirschky, July 30, 1914, 11 P.M., July 31, 2:45 A.M., and the earlier draft, not sent. Geiss 2 : 380 ff. Goschen to Grey, July 30, *BDs* 11, no. 329.

36 Riezler Diary, August 18, 1914. Tirpitz, *Ohnmachtspolitik*, pp. 57–58. Bethmann to Tschirschky, Flotow, Lichnowsky, Pourtalès and Schoen, July 31, 1914, Geiss 2 : 461 ff. Goschen to Grey, July 31, *BDs* 11, nos. 336–37. Lyncker Diary, July 31, "the general opinion tended toward making extreme efforts to preserve peace." Bach, p. 35. Cf. H. von Moltke, *Erinnerungen, Briefe und Dokumente, 1877-1916* (Stuttgart, 1922). For Conrad's version of the Moltke telegram, cf. his memoirs, vol. 4, pp. 152 ff., according to which Berchtold incredulously gasped: "That is really something! Who rules: Moltke or Bethmann . . . ?" Cf. also Norman Stone's trenchant analysis of Moltke's extension of the casus foederis in 1909 to include Serbia, and of the unresolved strategic differences in the Dual Alliance: "Moltke-Conrad: Relations between the Austro-Hungarian and German General Staffs, 1909–1914," *HJ* 9 (1966) : 201–208.

37 Protocol of the session of the Federal Council, *GDs*, no. 553, August 1: "It is nothing other than a provocation if (Russia) mobilizes against us while we mediate." For Lerchenfeld's answer and the pessimistic mood, cf. also Loebell's MS "Erinnerungen," 2 : 161. The authorization for war was made easier because in "the military circles here the mood is excellent. Already months ago Chief of General Staff Moltke said that the present moment is militarily so favorable that it will not return in the foreseeable future." Moreover, Bethmann had also communicated the Socialist pledge to support war. Lerchenfeld to Hertling, July 31, Dirr, no. 71. Salza to Vitzthum, Aug. 11, 1914, Bach, no. 74.

38 Zwehl, *Falkenhayn*, pp. 58–59. Lyncker Diary, August 1, Bach, no. 39; Moltke, *Erinnerungen*, pp. 19 ff.; Müller Diary, August 1, BA *Nachlass* Müller; Tirpitz,

Ohnmachtspolitik, pp. 16 ff. Lichnowsky to Jagow, August 1, arrived 4:23 P.M.; Grey "seems to mean . . . if we do not attack France, England will remain neutral and guarantee the passivity of France." For his reversal cf. Lichnowsky to Jagow, August 1, arrival 10 P.M., Bülow, *Denkwürdigkeiten* 3 : 167–68, also echoed in Loebell's MS "Erinnerungen," 2 : 160–61. For the postwar controversy surrounding the Russian declaration of war, cf. Bethmann to Falkenhayn, June 14, 1919; Jagow to Bethmann, June 16, Bethmann to Jagow, June 28, and Bethmann to Jagow, August 15, 1919. Cf. also Jagow to Foerster, June 21, 1926: "We could not wait. The necessity of our strategic position determined our actions." AA *Nachlass* Jagow. For a fresh source on the historic deliberations, cf. the manuscript memoirs of the kaiser's adjutant and Bethmann Hollweg's cousin, Max von Mutius, suggesting that Moltke's personal collapse has been overemphasized. According to Mutius the chief of staff was only chagrined: "I have always feared that. We would have won the campaign against both fronts." BA *Nachlass* Mutius. For a somewhat exaggerated analysis of the importance of the abandonment of the eastern deployment planning, cf. also Adolf Gasser, "Deutschlands Entschluss zum Präventivkrieg 1913–1914," in *Discordia Concors; Festschrift für Edgar Bonjour* (Basel, 1968).

39 Bethmann to Delbrück, February 2, 1919, DSB *Nachlass* Delbrück: "I did not know that the older Moltke had a different (war plan). Personally I doubt whether we could have forced through a decision moving the offensive from West to East." Cf. also Bethmann to Jagow, August 15, 1919, AA *Nachlass* Jagow. Tirpitz, *Ohnmachtspolitik,* pp. 20–21. Cf. also Bethmann's note on December 22, 1912, about Moltke's insistence on the Schlieffen Plan: "Our deployment against France was based on an advance through Belgium, as was well known. This deployment could now be no longer changed." Geiss 2 : 575n. Cf. also E. Zimmermann, "Um Schlieffen's Plan," *Süddeutsche Monatshefte* 27 (1921): 368 ff., showing that Bethmann knew of the plan but failed to realize its full diplomatic implications. See also G. Ritter, *Der Schlieffenplan: Kritik eines Mythos* (Munich, 1956). Lerchenfeld to Hertling, August 2, 1914, Dirr, p. 78. Moltke to Jagow, "Gesichtspunkte militärpolitischer Art," August 2, GDs, no. 662. Bethmann to Lichnowsky, August 2: "Germany, after defending peace to the utmost limit, is being forced by its enemies into the role of a *provocateur* who, to preserve his existence, *must* take up arms." Bethmann to Schoen, Lichnowsky, August 3, 1914, Geiss 2 : 634, 659 ff. Bethmann to the Federal Council, August 1, 1914, Geiss 2 : 545 ff.

40 Pencil note by Bethmann, November 13, 1914; AA Wk., GHQ no. 26. Cf. the report of the chief of the chancellery, A. Wahnschaffe, "Gesamtverantwortung," *BM* 12 (1934) : 660 ff. Goschen's initial dispatch did not contain the "scrap of paper" phrase, only the chancellor's sigh, "But at what a price!" *BDs* 11, no. 667. Later, conservative opponents of the chancellor, such as Minister of the Interior Loebell, claimed that "Bethmann was a broken man" upon receiving the British declaration of war (BA *Nachlass* Loebell, MS "Erinnerungen," 2 : 161), a contention which became the stock-in-trade of the rightist theory that his "policy collapsed like a house of cards." It seems more likely that both the ambassador and the chancellor were moved in the highly charged emotional scene.

41 Müller Diary, August 1, 1914; BA *Nachlass* Müller. Riezler, August 15, 1914. Max von Mutius, MS "Erinnerungen," BA *Nachlass* Mutius. F. Thimme, ed., *Bethmann Hollweg's Kriegsreden* (Stuttgart, 1919), p. 1. For the war enthusiasm, cf. also Ernst Johann, *Innenansicht eines Kriegs: Bilder-Briefe Dokumente, 1914–1918* (Frankfurt, 1968).

42 Wahnschaffe, "Gesamtverantwortung," pp. 661–62. Ph. Scheidemann, *Der Zusammenbruch* (Berlin, 1921), pp. 9–10; E. David, *Kriegstagebuch 1914–1918,* pp. 7–8;

Westarp, *Konservative Politik* 1 : 408–09; Friedrich Payer, *Von Bethmann Hollweg bis Ebert: Erinnerungen und Bilder* (Frankfurt, 1923), pp. 24–25; and E. Pikart, "Der deutsche Reichstag und der Ausbruch des Ersten Weltkrieges," *Der Staat* 5 (1966) : 47–70. Cf. also Szögyény's report to Berchtold, July 1, regarding the fifth anniversary of Bethmann's chancellorship, HHStA, PA III, 171B.

43 Szögyény to Berchtold, August 5, 1914; HHStA, PA III, 171B; Salza to Vitzthum, August 4, 1914, Bach, no. 97; Thimme, *Kriegsreden*, pp. 3 ff.; Riezler, August 15, 1914. According to the Danish deputy H. P. Hanssen (*Diary of a Dying Empire* [Bloomington, Ind., 1955], pp. 25), Bethmann exclaimed, "Whatever may be in store, we believe that August 4, 1914, will for all time remain one of Germany's greatest days!" Cf. also Müller, *Regierte?*, pp. 40–41.

44 Riezler Diary, August 14, 1914. Friedrich Meinecke, *Die deutsche Erhebung von 1914* (Stuttgart, 1914), pp. 9 ff.: "This common heroic effort for the state means a great vote of confidence of the nation and proves that it was healthy in its core and that its policies were basically correct." Bruno Frank, "Stolze Zeit: 1914," first and last stanza cited from Ludwig Reiners, *Der Ewige Brunnen: Ein Volksbuch deutscher Dichtung*, still included in the Munich 1955 edition, p. 458. From the veritable flood of writing only one more sample from Ernst Jäckh: "We trust in the army and navy and in the moral powers of the German people, which in these days of unanimous *Erhebung* manifest themselves." "Der Europäische Krieg," in *Das Grössere Deutschland*, August 8, 1914.

45 Bethmann to Oettingen, August 30, 1914; BA *Nachlass* Oettingen. Bethmann to Eisendecher, August 12, 1919, AA *Nachlass* Eisendecher. Only after the war Bethmann "gained more and more the impression that the antagonisms had become irreconcilable." Especially Grey's assurances to Sazonov in Balmoral seemed "to prove incontrovertibly that the situation was beyond repair; England had laid the Franco-Russian noose around its throat, and Paris and Petersburg were free to decide upon war and peace." Bethmann to Max von Baden, January 17, 1918, E. Zechlin, "Deutschland zwischen," pp. 451 ff.

46 In *Der Erste Weltkrieg*, p. 20, Gerhard Ritter maintained: "It was emphatically a defensive, not an aggressive policy," in a statement representative of the apologist camp. Fischer's pupil Geiss charges, typically of the critics, that "German policy in the July crisis was the missing link between Weltpolitik and the war aims," *Julikrise und Kriegsausbruch* 2 : 731. Cf. my critique of these misleading alternatives in "World Power or Tragic Fate: The *Kriegsschuldfrage* as Historical Neurosis," *CEH* (March, 1972).

47 Bethmann's interview for Wiegand, AA *Nachlass* Jagow. Cf. also L. F. C. Turner, "The Russian Mobilization in 1914," *JCH* 3 (1968) : 65 ff.: "If Russia had refrained from ordering mobilization on July 29, there is a real possibility that the impending catastrophe could have been avoided." For his resentment at Vienna, cf. his telegram to Tschirschky on August 4, 1914, Geiss 2 : 681: "We are forced by Austria's action to conduct war and can expect Austria not to obscure that fact." For his own explanations of the failure of his British policy and "England's guilt," cf. Bethmann to Thimme, June 13, 1918, DSB *Nachlass* Thimme. Bethmann to Delbrück, July 27, 1918, DSB *Nachlass* Delbrück; Bethmann to Jagow, June 11, 1919, AA *Nachlass* Jagow. Cf. also Bethmann's unpublished refutations of Tirpitz's memoirs, BA Kl. Erw. 342, in which the July crisis plays a prominent role. For Moltke's pressure, cf. also Lerchenfeld to Hertling, August 5, 1914, Dirr, no. 83, and Cambon's cutting remark to Bienvenue-Martin, July 27, 1914: "Whatever the chancellor may say [to protest his pacifism], the power of institutions and of the military spirit is here so great that we must be ready for the worst." *FDs* 11, no. 168.

48 Lerchenfeld to Hertling, July 29, 1914, Dirr, no. 47. Grey to Bertie, July 29, 1914, *BDs* 11, no. 283. AA *Nachlass* Jagow, MS "Politische Aufsätze," "Deutschlands Lage und seine politischen Richtlinien 1913–1914," pp. 62 ff., and "Juli 1914 und Kriegsausbruch," pp. 97 ff. For an abortive attempt of the foreign secretary to force revision of the Schlieffen Plan in the spring of 1913, cf. also "Der Durchmarsch durch Belgien," AA *Nachlass* Jagow. Benckendorff to Sazonov, July 26, 1914, Geiss 2 : 57 ff. For a recent perceptive restatement of the entire issue, see Joachim Remak, "1914—The Third Balkan War: Origins Reconsidered," *JMH* 43 (1971) : 353 ff.

49 AA *Nachlass* Jagow, MS "Politische Aufsätze," "Rücktrittsgedanken des Reichskanzlers," p. 67. Bethmann to Weizsäcker, August 30, 1914, *Privatnachlass* Weizsäcker. Riezler Diary, August 15, 1914. Theodor Wolff, *Der Krieg des Pontius Pilatus* (Zurich, 1934), pp. 442–43. "We believed we had to strengthen Austria at a moment when it decided on an active policy. We could not leave it in the lurch," Bethmann pleaded with the journalist on February 5, 1915. He still believed that "Grey could have prevented the war had he declared at the beginning that England would not participate," but admitted strong German complicity. "We have lived lies in our domestic and foreign policy." As "the insane hatred" of the chauvinists had forced his hand, the chancellor concluded: "The war did not arise out of specific diplomatic actions, but rather as a result of popular passion. Here lies part of our guilt, part of the responsibility of the Pan-Germans."

Chapter 7

1 Riezler Diary, Aug. 14, 1914. Hohenlohe to Burian, April 2, 1915. Bethmann speech on the 100th anniversary of Bismarck's birth, HHStA, PA III, 171B.

2 General Keim: "Hammer!" reprinted from the *Tägliche Rundschau*, Aug. 29, 1914 in the *AB*. Paul Rohrbach, "Hie Schuld—Hie Schickung!" *Das grössere Deutschland*, Aug. 8, 1914. During the war the French Socialist S. Grumbach compiled an impressive documentation on the extent of the expansionist wave: *Das Annexionistische Deutschland* (Lausanne, 1917) translated, abbreviated and introduced by J. Ellis Barker as *Germany's Annexationist Aims* (New York, 1917). Cf. also Edwyn Bevan, *German War Aims* (New York, 1918), as well as Ralph Haswell Lutz, *Fall of the German Empire, 1914–1918*, 2 vols. (Stanford, Calif., 1932).

3 Bethmann to Oettingen, Aug. 30, Dec. 12, 1914, BA *Nachlass* Oettingen. Bethmann to Haeckel (?) Feb. 1915, DZA Me, Rep. 77n tit 949, no. 22. For the pressures in favor of annexationism cf. Ebba Dahlin, *French and German Public Opinion on Declared War Aims, 1914–1918* (Stanford, Calif., 1933). Cf. also Hans W. Gatzke's pioneer work, *Germany's Drive to the West* (Baltimore, 1950, pb. 1966) whose initial description of Bethmann as "reluctant annexationist" was more accurate than his assertion in his new foreword that he was "a cool and calculating Machiavellian." Cf. also Erich Volkmann, *Die Annexionsfragen des Weltkrieges*, vol. 12 of *Werk des Untersuchungsausschusses*, 4. Reihe (Berlin, 1929).

4 For the policy of revolutionizing cf. AA Wk., no. 11 with subsignatures for specific countries. Cf. also E. Zechlin, "Friedensbestrebungen und Revolutionierungsversuche," *Aus Politik und Zeitgeschichte*, 1961, 1963, and *Die deutsche Politik und die Juden im Ersten Weltkrieg* (Göttingen, 1969). Cf. also Fischer, *Germany's Aims*, pp. 95 ff., *Der Krieg der Illusionen*, pp. 739 ff.; Ritter, *Die Tragödie der Staatskunst: Bethmann Hollweg als Kriegskanzler, 1914–1917* (Munich, 1964); Gutsche, "Die Beziehungen zwischen der Regierung Bethmann Hollweg und dem Monopolkapital," pp. 6 ff.; F. Klein, ed., *Deutschland im Ersten Weltkrieg*

1 : 351 ff. For the Polish assurances cf. also Count Hutten-Czapski, *Sechzig Jahre* 2 : 150 ff.

5 Tirpitz, *Deutsche Ohnmachtspolitik*, pp. 48, 58 ff. Admiral Hugo von Pohl, *Aus Aufzeichnungen und Briefen während der Kriegszeit* (Berlin, 1920), pp. 7 ff., 18 ff. Bülow, *Erinnerungen* 3 : 148–49. Bethmann to governor in Metz, Sept. 9, 1914, cited by E. Zechlin, "Deutschland zwischen Kabinetts- und Wirtschaftskrieg," pp. 376 ff. On Aug. 28, the new Austrian ambassador, Gottfried Hohenlohe, found Bethmann and Jagow "in a very serious, almost depressed mood, mainly regarding England, since the news" of the sinking of three German battle cruisers no longer left any doubt about the British will to fight. Hohenlohe to Berchtold, Aug. 28, 1914, HHStA, PA III, 171B. Riezler Diary, Aug. 22, 27, 1914, for Bethmann's "fantasy of sparing France and reconciling with it."

6 Riezler Diary, Aug. 18, 21, 1914. The chancellor's assistant was disgusted that there was "nowhere a perspective, nowhere a word beyond the usual routine" of the diplomats. "The system of secrecy is based on fear of recognizing one's incapacity." In the exultation of the August days he pondered about "how difficult it is for the German to get used to the face of world domination which *must* be shown after victory." For the mood of the GHQ, cf. also the Müller Diary, *Regierte?* pp. 48 ff. and the Valentini Diary, Aug. 16 ff. in BA *Nachlass* Thimme. The basic Belgian file is DZA Po, Rkz. no. 2,463. On Sept. 2, the chancellor had already proposed the encouragement of the Flemish movement to the chief of the civil administration. Cf. F. Petri, "Zur Flamenpolitik des Ersten Weltkrieges," *Festschrift für K. Raumer* (Münster, 1966), pp. 513 ff.

7 Riezler Diary, Aug. 22, 1914. Notes by Count Hertling on Aug. 27 and 28, BHStA, MA I, 962. For William II's annexationism cf. his incredible memorandum of May 13, 1917, Grünau to Foreign Office, reprinted in S-G 2 : 194–95. For a thorough investigation of the war aims policy of the federal states cf. K. H. Janssen, *Macht und Verblendung: Die Kriegszielpolitik der deutschen Bundesstaaten, 1914–1918* (Göttingen, 1963).

8 For Erzberger's, Thyssen's, and Röchling's memoranda cf. DZA Po, Rkz. nos. 2,476, 2,477; DZA Me, Rep. 77, tit 885, no. 4, vols. 1 ff., Rep. 89H, 26 no. 11c, as well as the major central war files, AA Wk. secr., vols. 1–38 and DZA Po, Rkz. nos. 2,398 ff., 2,442/10 ff. to 2,446. Bethmann to Erzberger, Sept. 6, 1916 DZA Po, Rkz. no. 2,476 and Bethmann to Dallwitz, AA GHQ no. 214. Cf. also NSDAP Hauptarchiv, Folder 1,341, for copies of Thyssen's memoranda pleading for the annexation of Longwy-Briey in August 1914. For the conceptualization cf. Werner Basler, *Deutschlands Annexionspolitik*, pp. 359 ff.; W. Gutsche, "Die Beziehungen," pp. 35 ff.; "Erst Europa—und dann die Welt," *ZfG* (1964), pp. 746–67; "Zu einigen Fragen der staatsmonopolitischen Verflechtung in den ersten Kriegsjahren am Beispiel der Ausplünderung der belgischen Industrie," *Politik im Krieg* (Berlin, 1964); and "Zu einigen Problemen der Erforschung des ersten Weltkrieges," *ZfMG* 4 (1965) : 67 ff.

9 Zimmermann to Bethmann, Sept. 3, 1914, AA, GHQ 214. W. Gutsche, " 'Mittwochabend' (Delbrück) (MD) Gegründet 1914," in *Die bürgerlichen Parteien in Deutschland* (Leipzig, 1970) 2 : 330 ff. Ernst Jäckh, *Der goldene Pflug*, pp. 184–85. Cf. also the *Nachlässe* of the co-founders Hans Delbrück, DSB and Eugen Schiffer, PrGStA for relevant correspondence. Pogge von Strandmann, *Rathenau Tagebuch*, pp. 185–86. Rathenau's memoranda are in DZA Po, Rkz. no. 2,476 and one is reprinted by M. v. Eynern, *Walther Rathenau: Ein Preussischer Europäer* (Berlin, 1955), pp. 116 ff. Cf. also his truncated *Nachlass* in BA, and E. D. Kollman, "Walther Rathenau and German Foreign Policy, Thought and Actions," *JCEA* (1950) : 127–42 and Peter Berglar, *Walther Rathenau: Seine Zeit—Sein Werk—*

Seine Persönlichkeit (Bremen, 1970). For Delbrück's critique cf. his letter to Bethmann, Sept. 3, 1914, DZA Po, Rkz. no. 2,476.

10 For Wahnschaffe's ideas cf. his commentary on Rechenberg's letter of Aug. 27, 1914, suggesting that the Austro-Polish solution would only be tolerable if Germany secured enough economic advantages, DZA Po, Rkz. 2,476. Bethmann to Delbrück, Aug. 26, 1914, AA, GHQ no. 214. Although Delbrück, in his reply of Sept. 3, thought the annexation of Belgium or Holland unlikely, he was convinced "that we must consider an appropriate widening of their economic relations with us. Similarly we must attempt to arrive at a new settlement with France." For Solf's program cf. his letter of Aug. 28, Sept. 25, 1914, AA, Wk. 15 secr. and Jagow's answer of Oct. 3, 1914, BA *Nachlass* Solf. E. von Vietsch's biography, *Wilhelm Solf: Botschafter zwischen den Zeiten* (Tübingen, 1961) is a straight apology. For the views of the western bureaucracy cf. Mallinckrodt to Bethmann Aug. 31, 1914; Dallwitz to Bethmann, Sept. 3, 1914, as well as Bethmann's reply of Sept. 9, 1914, heavily corrected, asking for further material, AA, GHQ 214. Cf. also Riezler Diary, Aug. 22, 1914, and J. Williamson, *Helfferich*, pp. 117 ff.

11 Riezler to Hammann, Aug. 22, 29, Sept. 5, DZA Po *Nachlass* Hammann, cited by Fischer, *Der Krieg der Illusionen*, pp. 762 ff. Class, *Wider den Strom*, pp. 309 ff.; Kruck, *Alldeutscher Verband*, pp. 71 ff. Cf. also Ritter, "Bethmann Hollweg und die Machtträume deutscher Patrioten im ersten Jahr des Weltkriegs," in *Festschrift für P. E. Schramm* (Munich, 1964) and *Bethmann als Kriegskanzler*, pp. 15 ff. somewhat disappointing. See also K. Schwabe, "Ursprung und Verbreitung des Alldeutschen Annexionismus in der deutschen Professorenschaft im Ersten Weltkrieg," *VJHfZG* (1966): 105 ff. For Wahnschaffe's conversation with Schiffer cf. his letter to Bethmann, Sept. 9, 1914, cited by W. J. Mommsen, "Die Regierung Bethmann Hollweg und die öffentliche Meinung, 1914–1917," ibid. (1969): 117–59.

12 Riezler Diary, Aug. 18, 21, 22, 27, Sept. 1, 1914. Although it is tempting to exaggerate the influence of the chancellor's young assistant when viewing Bethmann through his diary, in the case of the war aims Riezler's impact was considerable, as he was formally charged with the correspondence regarding this topic. Since the chancellor tended toward traditional solutions, the idea of Mitteleuropa as political goal of the war could hardly have originated with him alone.

13 Riezler Diary, Sept. 4, 1914. Bethmann to Loebell, Sept. 8, 1914; BA *Nachlass* Loebell. The chancellor suggested Brandenstein as head "for an eventual government-general of northern France," and added: "I hope he does not have to wait for it too long." Valentini Diary, Sept. 9, 1914, BA *Nachlass* Thimme. See also F. Petri and P. Schöller, "Zur Bereinigung des Franktireur-Problems vom August 1914," *VJHfZG* (1961): 234–48.

14 Bethmann to Delbrück, Sept. 9, 1914, DZA Po, Rkz. no. 2,476. Discovered by Fischer, "Deutsche Kriegsziele," *HZ* (1959): 249 ff. and first published by the East German historian W. Basler, *Deutsche Annexionspolitik*, pp. 381 ff., the September Program is the cornerstone of Fischer's thesis, *Griff nach der Weltmacht*, pp. 110 ff. and was republished by E. Zechlin, "Friedensbestrebungen und Revolutionierungsversuche," *Aus Politik und Zeitgeschichte* (1963): no. 23, 41 ff. Vietsch, *Bethmann*, pp. 201 ff. slights its importance.

15 For the debate on whether the September Program was essentially a means or an end of the war cf. the articles by Fischer and Zechlin collected by Wolfgang Schieder, *Erster Weltkrieg: Ursachen, Entstehung und Kriegsziele*, pp. 29 ff., 149 ff.

16 Riezler Diary, Sept. 9, 13, 23, 1914. For the impressive ancestry of Central European dreams cf. also Henry Cord Meyer, *Mitteleuropa in German Thought and Action, 1815–1945* (The Hague, 1955). For the attitude of the right wing of the Social Democrats toward annexations cf. Eduard David's discussion with Vice-

Chancellor Delbrück, Aug. 24, and with other revisionists, Aug. 29, 1914, *David Tagebuch,* pp. 22 ff., 28 ff.

17 Riezler Diary, Sept. 20, Oct. 7, 1914: "The small and tricky Jagow will slowly attempt to create difficulties on top of difficulties in the customs union question, apparently being half in favor," Riezler predicted. "He is completely old style—as such quite good but *barren.*" For Jagow's attitude cf. also his "Die Frage der Kriegsziele, besonders Belgien betr.," in MS "Politische Aufsätze," AA *Nachlass* Jagow. Delbrück to Bethmann, Sept. 13, 1914; DZA Po, Rkz. no. 2,476. Bethmann to Delbrück, Sept. 19, 1914, ibid. Cf. also Delbrück, *Wirtschaftliche Mobilmachung,* pp. 124 ff. The subsequent negotiations on Mitteleuropa are in DZA Po, Rkz. nos. 403 ff.; DZA Me, Rep. 77, tit. 93 no. 122; and AA, Dld. no. 180 secr., vols. 1 ff. For Bethmann's claim of flexibility cf. Lerchenfeld to Hertling, May 29, 1916; BHStA MA III 2691/9.

18 Riezler Diary, Oct. 6, 9, 11, 12, 27, Nov. 2, 22, 1914. Riezler found no solution to the Belgian problem since "the Netherlands will not take anything. It is impossible to enlarge France. One cannot annex what the military want since seven million cannot be expelled. The events of the war will never be forgotten." On Nov. 8, Riezler discussed Mitteleuropa in Berlin with high officials: "Rechenberg still emotionally advocates a straight customs union with Austria and France, which the smaller states will have to join, a completely new Europe—says if one wants to win much, one has to give up something, even a small part of sovereignty." In contrast, Wahnschaffe and Helfferich proposed "another project . . . preferential tariffs. Double tariffs on the Central European states, minimal tariffs for the most favored nations. . . . Agreement on common maximum duties, perhaps an alliance to fight against American protectionism—creation of a kernel in common customs discussions, etc., around which a unified organization can later crystallize." Riezler preferred the latter alternative with France included, since "this combination leaves open every avenue of political retreat."

19 Bethmann to Loebell, Nov. 14, 1914; BA *Nachlass* Loebell. Bethmann to Weizsäcker, Nov. 10, 1914; *Privatnachlass* Weizsäcker. Bethmann to Hammann, Nov. 14, 1914; DZA Po *Nachlass* Hammann. "Belgium is a hard nut to crack. . . . The right of military occupation in Liège, Namur, Antwerp, in this country which will hate us for a century, as one can only bear, would conjure up St. Bartholomew's eves. The future, if only the far distant one, can bring a partition between us, France, Holland, and Luxembourg." Nevertheless, he added skeptically that France would probably not "want to participate in the rape *now.*" Bethmann to Hertling, Nov. 15, 1914, BHStA MA I 961.

20 Bethmann to Zimmermann, Oct. 18, 1914. Bethmann to Delbrück, Oct. 22, 1914; DZA Po, Rkz. no. 2,476. Bethmann to Delbrück, Nov. 17, 1914. Bethmann to Dallwitz, Nov. 17, 1914; AA, GHQ 214. For the navy's demands cf. Tirpitz to Bethmann, Jan. 20, 1915; DZA Po, Rkz. 2,476 and Tirpitz, *Ohnmachtspolitik,* passim.

21 "Leitsätze zur Sprachregelung für die Presse," Oct. 19, 1914, in Riezler to Foreign Office, cited by W. J. Mommsen, "Die Regierung Bethmann Hollweg und die öffentliche Meinung, 1914–1917," pp. 131 ff. Cf. also Kurt Koszyk, *Deutsche Pressepolitik im Ersten Weltkrieg* (Düsseldorf, 1968). Bethmann to the Prussian Ministry of State, Nov. 28, 1914, DZA Me, Rep. 90a B III 2b no. 6 vol. 163. Bethmann to the Reichstag, Dec. 2, 1914, Thimme, *Kriegsreden,* pp. 23 ff. (with press reaction). Bethmann to Foreign Office, Oct. 11, 1914, DZA Po, Rkz. 2,437/3. Bethmann to Class, Dec. 27, 1914, AA, Dld. no. 169, vol. 5 and Class, *Wider den Strom,* pp. 345 ff. Cf. also the statement by Loebell in his MS "Erinnerungen," 2 : 166: "We agreed not to allow public discussion of the war aims question in parliament and press

until the military situation had created a relatively firm basis for the government's position and seemed to make public debate of the goals of the war fruitful."

22 Hertling's note of his conversation with Bethmann, Dec. 3, 1914; BHStA MA I 962. Bethmann refused the annexation of Belgium, since he did not look forward to having sixty Belgian representatives in the Prussian Landtag. For his conversation with Stresemann and Rötger cf. AA *Nachlass* Stresemann, vol. 139, Dec. 8, 1914; printed by E. Zechlin, "Friedensbestrebungen und Revolutionierungsversuche," *Aus Politik* (1961): no. 24, 335 ff. Cf. also Paul Sweet, "Leaders and policies," *JCEA* (1956), 231 ff., and for National Liberal annexationism in general, Marvin L. Edwards, *Stresemann and the Greater Germany, 1914–1918* (New York, 1963), pp. 54 ff.

23 Riezler Diary, Feb. 6, 11, 17, 1914. Bethmann "complained about the bureaus which do not produce anything politically useful," deploring the lack of vision, energy, and will to power in the Foreign Office. On the other hand, "hardly has Hindenburg won a victory when the National Liberals rush forward to catch a big whale in the war aims debate. What idiots and lying busybodies, Basserman and Paasche. I have to throw up!" Riezler acidly commented on the nationalist hubris. Bethmann to Oettingen, Dec. 14, 1914, BA *Nachlass* Oettingen. Bethmann to Loebell, Jan. 2, 1915, BA *Nachlass* Loebell. Bethmann to Class, Feb. 6, Mar. 31, 1915. *Wider den Strom*, pp. 386, 388 ff. and DZA Po, Rkz. 1,415 ff. Bethmann to Haeckel, Feb. 1915, DZA Me, Rep. 77n, tit. 949 no. 22.

24 Bethmann to Valentini, Mar. 12, 1915; DZA Me, *Nachlass* Valentini, also in Schwertfeger, *Kaiser und Kabinettschef*, pp. 226–27 and Zechlin, "Friedenbestrebungen . . ." (1961), no. 24, 46–47. Bethmann to Loebell, Jan. 2, 1915, BA *Nachlass* Loebell. Bethmann's marginal comment on the petition of the Six Economic Associations of Mar. 11, 1915, DZA Po, Rkz. no. 2441/11; reprinted in facsimile by E. Zechlin in *Sonntagsblatt*, Aug. 2, 1964. Bethmann to Bundesrat, Apr. 8, 1915, Nieser to Kühn, GLAK 233, 34,815. Cf. also Mommsen, "Die Regierung . . . ," pp. 136 ff. See also Riezler Diary, Feb. 27, 1914: "The crown prince has sent an angry telegram because of the *NAZ* article on war aims," in which Bethmann had strongly urged the postponement of debate. "The Pan-Germans should also be allowed to speak freely, since the defeatists were doing so."

25 Riezler Diary, Apr. 1, 8, 1914, based on Wahnschaffe's report: "Excellently done. The chancellor developed the problem [of Alsace-Lorraine] along general lines. Partition. Division. Of course, no increase in power, but grave national task." When Hertling claimed all of Alsace for confessional reasons and Baden and Saxony demurred, "the chancellor let the Bavarians run head on into the other federal states." Cf. also the Nieser report supra. Janssen, *Macht und Verblendung*, pp. 46 ff. and E. Deuerlein, *Der Bundesratsausschus für auswärtige Anlegenheiten 1870–1918* (Regensburg, 1955), pp. 279 ff. See also Bethmann to the Ministry of State, Apr. 10 and Oct. 29, 1915, DZA Me, Rep. 90a B III 2b no. 6, vol. 164.

26 Bethmann to Westarp, Apr. 23, 1915, DZA Po *Nachlass* Westarp. Bethmann to Hirsch, May 4, 1915, ibid. Rkz. no. 2442/12. For Hirsch's industrial connections as well as his rabid annexationism cf. his correspondence with Wahnschaffe in BA Kl. Erw. 427-1 *Nachlassrest* Schifferer. Cf. also Westarp, *Konservative Politik* 2 : 44 ff.

27 Bethmann to Valentini, Mar. 12, 1915, DZA Me, *Nachlass* Valentini. Erzberger to Hertling, Apr. 24, 1915, BHStA MA I 947. To placate Hertling's suspicions, Erzberger stressed "the meeting should under no circumstances have the purpose of creating a chancellor crisis" but only serve to support the aims which Bethmann had repeatedly explained to the party leaders. For the text of the Six Associations' petition, as well as the intellectuals' manifesto, cf. Grumbach, *Das*

Annexionistische Deutschland, pp. 123 ff., 132 ff. See also K. Schwabe, *Wissenschaft und Kriegsmoral: Die deutschen Hochschullehrer und die politischen Grundfragen des ersten Weltkrieges* (Göttingen, 1969). Cf. Fischer, *Griff nach der Weltmacht,* pp. 193 ff.; W. Gutsche, ed., *Deutschland im Ersten Weltkrieg* (Berlin, 1968) 2 : 163 ff. For a slighting of the economic components of the war aims movement cf. also G. Ritter, *Bethmann als Kriegskanzler,* pp. 91 ff.

28 Grumbach, *Das Annexionistische Deutschland,* pp. 409 ff. Cf. also the Delbrück *Nachlass* in BA for the efforts of the bureau Hobohm to combat Pan-German annexationist excesses. Cf. E. Volkmann, *Die Annexionsfragen,* pp. 37 ff. and Gatzke, *Germany's Drive,* pp. 54 ff. Riezler Diary, Mar. 4, Apr. 18, 1915: "Yesterday I was with the chancellor for a long time, explaining to him" the Mitteleuropa scheme based upon the "box system used by holding companies. The German Empire a corporation with Prussia controlling the majority of shares. . . . Hence around Germany a federation in which the *Reich* has the majority as Prussia does in the Empire—so that Prussia also has the leadership in this federation." Because of this grandiose plan Riezler resented "the chauvinists' lack of trust in the chancellor. People have no idea of foreign policy and meddle in it according to their own judgment. This discussion of war aims is ridiculous, since it is all emotionalism." For the chancellor's meeting with the party leaders of the Right cf. Wahnschaffe's protocol of May 13, DZA Po, Rkz. no. 2,398, and Haussmann, *Schlaglichter,* pp. 24 ff.

29 WP, May 17, 1915. Bethmann to Gebsattel, May 13, 1915; Class, *Wider den Strom,* pp. 407–08. Bethmann in the Reichstag, May 28, 1915. Thimme, *Kriegsreden,* pp. 35 ff. Lerchenfeld to Hertling, May 25, 29, 1915, BHStA MA III 2691/5. In conversation with the Bavarian ambassador, Bethmann seemed reluctant to insist on a border rectification toward an Austrian Poland, "which would bring three million Poles and Jews" into the empire. The chancellor imagined a peace in which "Germany attempted to link the smaller neighbor states politically and economically." Cf. also Edwards, *Stresemann,* pp. 59 ff., and Stresemann to Dirr, May 14, and protocol of the audience, May 17, AA *Nachlass* Stresemann 3,056.

30 Riezler Diary, May 22, July 16, 1915: "Of course the naive desire for expansion is false and fatal—but [they demand] everywhere positions which through their military use would increase political power. And now Falkenhayn wants the right of Belgian occupation under any circumstances." Anonymous poem, entitled "Kanzler, jetzt tritt Du hervor!" based on the myth of victory:

> Siegreich drangen unsere Heere
> Vor im Westen, Ost und Süd:
> Seht den Feind! Er weicht, er zittert!
> Er ergibt sich oder flieht!

MS, Hoover Library, Stanford University. According to Hertling's note of July 6, 1915, BHStA MA I 962, Bethmann was convinced "that it is impossible for us to force all enemies to their knees," indicating that German goals had to be reduced accordingly, even if strategic border rectifications in the East and the dependence of Belgium were desirable.

31 Eduard David, *Kriegstagebuch,* pp. 127–28, 137 ff., 141, 144. For the limited annexationism of the Social Democrats cf. Gutsche, *Deutschland im Ersten Weltkrieg* 2 : 262 ff., and Schorske, *German Social Democracy,* pp. 304 ff. For the relevant files cf. DZA Po, Rkz. no. 1394/6 ff. Cf. also E. Matthias, *Die deutsche Sozialdemokratie und der Osten, 1914–1915* (Tübingen, 1954) and A. Ascher, "Imperialists within German Social Democracy prior to 1914," *JCEA* 20 (1960): 397 ff. for the general background.

32 For the clash with the National Liberals, see K. P. Reiss, *Von Bassermann zu*

Stresemann, pp. 195 ff. WP, Aug. 16, 1915. Hohenlohe to Burian, Aug. 23, 31, 1915, HHStA, PA III, 171B. Bethmann to Reichstag, Aug, 19, 1915, Thimme, *Kriegsreden*, pp. 57 ff.: "Germany has never striven for hegemony over Europe." Cf. Wolfgang Benz, "Der 'Fall Mühlon'—Bürgerliche Opposition im Obrigkeitsstaat während des ersten Weltkrieges," *VJHfZG* 18 (1970) : 343 ff.

33 Riezler Diary, Apr. 18, 28, May 22, June 10, Aug. 29, Oct. 4, 11, 16, 1915. At the end of April, "I discussed with Helfferich and the chancellor the question of customs union with Austria. Agreement that everything is a political question; no misgivings in two cases: 1) if Austria emerges victorious, 2) if it is utterly beaten" because in the latter case it could loosely be affiliated with Germany. Riezler considered the problem of German rule especially difficult because "Germany has no modern means of power, has no ideology in its favor, only force." S-G 1 : 124 ff., for the correspondence Bethmann-Falkenhayn beginning in June 1915. Cf. W. Sweet, "Germany, Austria-Hungary and Mitteleuropa: August 1915–April 1916," *Festschrift für Heinrich Benedikt* (Vienna, 1957), pp. 180 ff.; W. Gutsche, "Die Auseinandersetzungen zwischen Falkenhayn und Bethmann Hollweg um das Kriegsziel 'Mitteleuropa' im Spätsommer 1915," *ZfMG* 4 (1965) : 680 ff.; and K. H. Janssen, *Der Kanzler und der General*, pp. 167 ff. Cf. also the Bavarian chargé Schoen's overly sanguine report to Hertling, June 27, 1915, that "regarding war aims both [chancellor and chief of staff] are reputedly in agreement that no 'foul peace' should be concluded and that it continued to be important to remain 'firm.'" BHStA MA III 2691/5. See also the diary of the Prussian Minister of War, Nov. 2, 1915, BA *Nachlass* Wild.

34 AA Dld, no. 180 secr., vols. 1 ff. S-G 1 : 218 ff., protocol by Jagow, Nov. 14, 1915. Riezler Diary, May 16, Oct. 23, Nov. 11, 1915. Bethmann to Prussian Ministry of State, Nov. 18, 1915, DZA Me, Rep. 90a B III 2b no. 6, vol. 164. Cf. also the Bavarian and Mecklenburg protocols of the Bundesrat session, Nov. 30, 1915, in BHStA and DZA Po, Rkz. no. 2399/5. Although he listed indirect dependence of Belgium as well as the creation of a "buffer empire" in the East as desirable, the chancellor cautioned once again: "To formulate such plans now is fruitless, since everything depends upon the military situation at the peace table." Cf. also Fischer, *Griff Nach der Weltmacht*, pp. 244 ff., and Sweet, "Germany, Austria-Hungary and Mitteleuropa," pp. 180 ff., and May, *The Dissolution of the Hapsburg Monarchy* (Philadelphia, 1966).

35 The resolutions of the parties are in Grumbach, *Das Annexionistische Deutschland*, pp. 33 ff., together with much evidence from the contemporary party press. Cf. also Westarp, *Konservative Politik* 2 : 52 ff., especially also the correspondence with Heydebrand in the Westarp *Nachlass* in the possession of Frh. Hiller von Gaertringen, as well as the papers in DZA Po; Hartwig Thieme, *Nationaler Liberalismus in der Krise* (Boppard, 1963), pp. 57 ff. and the material in the Stresemann *Nachlass* in the AA; Epstein, *Erzberger*, pp. 129 ff. and John K. Zeender, "The German Center Party during World War I," *Catholic Historical Review* 42 (1957) : 441 ff. and the material in the Erzberger *Nachlass* in the BA; there is no recent study of the Free Conservatives, but cf. the Kardorff *Nachlass* in the BA; Theodor Heuss, *Naumann*, pp. 362 ff., the Naumann *Nachlass* in the DZA Po and his bestseller, *Mitteleuropa* (Berlin, 1915), released in October, which impressed the chancellor. For Bethmann's attempt to gain the support of the liberal Hansabund when its leaders submitted a manifesto calling for only limited annexations, cf. WP, Sept. 30, 1915. The chancellor "thanked them especially for having found ideas with which I can agree. I cannot reveal the details because we do not know when and from what side peace will come."

36 WP, Nov. 29, 1915, regarding briefings of all the parliamentarians; second WP,

Nov. 29, conference of the chancellor with Spahn, Basserman and Westarp. WP, Dec. 2, 1915 meeting of all party leaders but the Socialists with Bethmann. In the last discussion Bethmann promised he would "attempt to find a more concrete form for our war aims, words which express more exactly that we wish a lasting peace, presupposing that our enemies have no intention of attacking us, and at any rate find us in a strong defensive position." Although the parliamentarians insisted upon using the term *territorial annexations*, Bethmann talked only of "glacis" and countered, "If Russia comes tomorrow and wants to have peace, we shall conclude it."

37　Bethmann to the Reichstag, two speeches of Dec. 9, 1915; Thimme, *Kriegsreden*, pp. 65 ff. For the declaration of the bourgeois parties cf. Grumbach, *Das Annexionistische Deutschland*, pp. 33 ff. Cf. also Gatzke, *Germany's Drive*, pp. 99 ff. Riezler Diary, Dec. 2, 1915: "Dark mood, general insanity. The nations talk past each other—the modern press everywhere prevents a return to sanity. Manipulated mass emotions, children of ignorance and distortion hold the actual power. . . . The present organization of the world contradicts itself in this war: armaments, press demagoguery."

38　Bethmann to Valentini, Dec. 9, 1915, DZA Me, *Nachlass* Valentini. In similar disgust with the rabid annexationism of the heavy industrial press, Bethmann had jotted on the margin of an article of the *Deutsche Tageszeitung*, June 25, 1915: "This senseless whipping up of hatred must cease," cited by Koszyk, *Deutsche Pressepolitik*, p. 162.

39　Bethmann's note of a conversation with Kleist, Buch, and Seydlitz, Jan. 19, 1916, DZA Po, Wk. vol. 6. Riezler Diary, Jan. 19, Feb. 4, 19, Mar. 22, 1916. When Erzberger reported Falkenhayn's desire "to refound Europe through Napoleonic decisions," Riezler commented caustically, "He doesn't know how and where, and would miss the target like the worst dilettante." Similarly, he hoped that "the Pan-German movement will crest in this war, and that it cannot do if it is suppressed. The nation must pass through this seizure to free itself from it."

40　Bethmann to Erich Marcks, Mar. 16, 1916, DZA Po, Rkz. no. 2404/2. The chancellor promised that "the time will be ripe to speak when the end or the direction from which it will come is visible. . . . But until then, we must be satisfied, knowing that it is an immense achievement if we defend ourselves successfully against the dangers threatening us in past and present."

41　Riezler Diary, Feb. 19, Mar. 26, 1916. Bethmann to the press, Mar. 13, 1916, protocol in BA *Nachlass* Thimme; cited by W. J. Mommsen, "Die Regierung Bethmann," pp. 143–44. Bethmann to the Reichstag, Apr. 5; Thimme, *Kriegsreden*, pp. 97 ff. Bethmann note, Apr. 13, 1916, DZA Po, Rkz. nos. 2437/9 ff. Velics to Burian, Mar. 19, 1916, citing a conversation between Bethmann and Hertling, HHStA, PA III, 172B. Bavarian protocol of the session of the Bundesrat, Aug. 9, 1916, BHStA MA I 966. Bethmann to Carl Andres, July 18, 1916, DZA Po, Rkz. no. 2444/4.

42　Bethmann to Prussian Ministry of State, Aug. 19, 1916, DZA Me, Rep. 90a B III 2b no. 6, vol. 165. WP of Bethmann briefing of Prussian Conservatives, Aug. 5, 1916. Riezler Diary, June 17, 1916: "In case of victory this [chauvinism] must be eradicated—if Germany is to go the only possible way to European hegemony, the federative one. This path only Bethmann can find—he alone can mold the public spirit accordingly." Ibid., July 13, 1916: "That these people are still fishing in muddy waters! That those who believed in getting rich quick with annexationist schemes in 1914 are still sticking together and messing around in Belgium, etc. And Bülow!? Impossible to tell if more impudent or dumb." WP, of party leader briefing July 17, 1916. Cf. Haussmann, *Schlaglichter*, pp. 63 ff.

43 Riezler Diary, Aug. 10, 1916. Lerchenfeld to Dandl, July 7, 1916, describing the chances of the *Deutscher Nationalausschuss*, BHStA MA III 2691/10. Stieglitz to Vitzthum, May 31, 1916, SHStA, AM 1,090. Protocol of meeting on the opening of war aims debate, Nov. 7, 1916, DZA Po, RdI, no. 12,270; Bethmann to Prussian Ministry of State, Nov. 23, 1916, DZA Po, RdI, no. 12,271. Also Walter Nicolai, *Nachrichtendienst, Presse und Volksstimmung im Weltkrieg* (Berlin, 1920), p. 115. Cf. also Mommsen, "Die Regierung Bethmann," pp. 154 ff., Gutsche, *Deutschland im Ersten Weltkrieg* 2 : 498 ff., Koszyk, *Deutsche Pressepolitik*, pp. 194 ff., and H. Weber, *Ludendorff und die Monopole: Deutsche Kriegspolitik 1916–1918* (Berlin, 1966).

44 Riezler Diary, Nov. 22, Dec. 2, 1916: "The constitution of Mitteleuropa. The chancellor correctly says one should not emphasize this line too much. Otherwise we weld the others together. The chancellor thinks the development has to lead in this direction, but it cannot be done with the military." Riezler countered, "Hegemony itself can be forced through but never the caudinian yoke of its formal recognition." Note by Bethmann, Oct. 18, 1916, regarding the conversations with Burian; note of Jagow, Oct. 18, 1916; Bethmann to Ferdinand I, Oct. 23, 1916; Bethmann to German Embassy in Vienna, Oct. 28, 1916, as well as the rest of the correspondence in S-G 1 : 517 ff. Cf. also Bethmann's detailed presentation to the Prussian Ministry of State, Oct. 27, 1916, DZA Me, Rep. 90a B III 2b no. 6, vol. 165.

45 Bethmann to Hindenburg, Nov. 4, 1916; Grünau to Foreign Office, Nov. 5, 1916; Bethmann to Grünau, Nov. 6, 1916; Austrian note of peace conditions, Nov. 15, 1916; Bethmann note, Nov. 16; Jagow note, Nov. 21, 1916; all in S-G 1 : 542 ff. Bethmann to Prussian Ministry of State, Dec. 14, 1916, DZA Me, Rep. 90a B III 2b no. 6, vol. 165. Briefing of party leaders, Dec. 11, 1916, WP. Cf. also Hertling to Loessl, Nov. 3, 1916, with a list of peace conditions, BHStA MA I 975. Cf. also Fischer, *Griff nach der Weltmacht*, pp. 396 ff., 416 ff., and Wolfgang Steglich, *Bündnissicherung oder Verständigungsfrieden* (Göttingen, 1958).

46 Riezler Diary, Dec. 29, 1916, Jan. 6, 9, 1917. Riezler was frustrated that "the immense future possibilities like Poland, economic alliance with Austria, etc. fail partly because of the difficulty of implementation, partly because of the resistance and narrowness of the ministries. Not the interests of the toy industry but generosity should shape Mitteleuropa, since an isolated small Germany can only be defended for a short time in the heart of Europe, and remains prey to the gravest danger, and cannot have a really great future." Cf. also Hindenburg to Bethmann, Dec. 13; Holtzendorff to Bethmann, Dec. 24, 1916; S-G 1 : 630 ff.

47 Bethmann to Valentini, Dec. 31, 1916, DZA Me *Nachlass* Valentini and Schwertfeger, *Kaiser und Kabinettschef*, pp. 241 ff. Bethmann to Hindenburg, Jan. 4, 1917; draft instruction to Bernstorff, Jan. 4, 1917; Bethmann to Bernstorff, Jan. 29, 1917, in S-G 1 : 658 ff. For the influence of the submarine question on war aims cf. also Karl E. Birnbaum, *Peace Moves and U-Boat Warfare* (Uppsala, 1958).

48 Riezler Diary, Mar. 11, 1917. Bethmann to the Reichstag, Feb. 27, 1917; Thimme, *Kriegsreden*, pp. 192 ff. Cf also Bethmann to the Reichstag, Mar. 14, 1917; ibid., pp. 215 ff.

49 Note by Colloredo-Mansfeld on Mar. 16, 1917, regarding the Austro-German war aims discussions; unsigned note of Mar. 26, 1917, of the second conference together with a résumé signed by Czernin and Bethmann, Mar. 27, 1917. In this meeting Bethmann indicated: "As utmost minimum we can concede a small boundary rectification to France in exchange for Briey and content ourselves with getting Belgium into our hands economically without annexations." Cf. also Bethmann to William II, May 14, 1917, and joint note by Bethmann and Czernin, May 18,

1917, about Austro-German war aims in the Balkans, in which Germany proposed a "great neo-Serbia and Northern Albania both closely allied to Austria" and if Lithuania, Courland, and Poland were included in the German sphere, Rumania would fall to Austria, S-G 2 : 32 ff., 50 ff. and 199 ff. Cf. also Rudolf Neck, "Das 'Wiener Dokument' vom 27. 3. 1917," *Mitteilungen des österreichischen Staatsarchivs* 7 (1954) : 294 ff., Wolfgang Steglich, *Die Friedenspolitik der Mittelmächte 1917–1918* (Wiesbaden, 1964) 1 : 43 ff., and H. Lehmann, "Czernin's Friedenspolitik, 1916–1918," *WaG* (1963) : 47 ff.

50 Riezler Diary, Apr. 1, 13, 1917: "If the war lasts through the summer the commune will rise in Russia and a peace of international socialism will be negotiated between Haase and Chkeidze." For Czerin's pessimistic memorandum warning "that in late summer or fall peace has to be concluded at any price," cf. S-G 2 : 104 ff. Bethmann to Vienna, Apr. 13; Bethmann to Hindenburg, Apr. 16; Bethmann to Grünau, Apr. 18, counseling against "extensive war aims discussions in the German press"; Bethmann to William II, May 4, 1917; all ibid., pp. 99 ff. Cf. also the WP of the war aims conference of the Prussian ministers, Apr. 21, 1917. For the policy of autonomy cf. also Bernhard Mann, *Die baltischen Länder in der deutschen Kriegszielpublizistik 1914–1918* (Tübingen, 1965) and Gerd Linde, *Die deutsche Politik in Litauen im Ersten Weltkrieg* (Wiesbaden, 1965).

51 Hindenburg to Bethmann, Apr. 5, calling for an internal agreement; Bethmann to Hindenburg, Apr. 16, refusing discussions; Hindenburg to Bethmann, Apr. 20; William II to Bethmann, Apr. 21, enraged upon reading the Socialist resolution in the *Vorwärts*, Apr. 20, accepting the Russian slogan verbatim; Grünau to Bethmann, Apr. 24, the text of the Kreuznach protocol; all in S-G 2 : 80 ff. For the originals cf. AA, Wk. 15 secr., and AA, Wk. no. 2, vol. 1 ff. and DZA Po, Rkz. no. 2,477. Cf. also Müller Diary, *Regierte?*, pp. 278–79. For the significance of the Kreuznach conference cf. Fischer, *Griff nach der Weltmacht*, pp. 447 ff.; Ritter, *Bethmann als Kriegskanzler*, pp. 503 ff.; A. J. Mayer, *Wilson vs. Lenin: Political Origins of the New Diplomacy 1917–1918* (Cleveland, 1963), pp. 106 ff. and K. Epstein, "The Development of German-Austrian War Aims in the Spring of 1917," *JCEA* 17 (1957) : 24 ff. See also the Valentini Diary, Apr. 21, BA *Nachlass* Thimme: "Was late *called to H.M.*, where *Field Marshal Hindenburg demands fall of Bethmann*, because of *Vorwärts*. I was successful in restoring calm."

52 Riezler Diary, May 8, 1917, reflecting on "the chancellor's heroic struggle against the soldiers." S-G 2 : 149 ff. For Bethmann's postscript cf. DZA Po, Rkz. no. 2,445, May 1, 1917, first published by Westarp, *Konservative Politik* 2 : 85. WP of Bundesrat session May 8, 1917. Cf. also Müller, *Regierte?* pp. 278–79: "Valentini was quite right when he called the proceedings 'childish.' " See also Bethmann to Hertling, Jan. 26, 1918, AA, Dld 122, no. 16, vol. 9, claiming that the ultimate protocol was already much reduced by his resistance. Cf. also the emotional debate between Hans Herzfeld and Fritz Fischer in the *HZ* (1960), passim, W. Basler, *Deutsche Annexionspolitik*, pp. 66 ff., and W. Gutsche, ed., *Deutschland im Ersten Weltkrieg* 2 : 735 ff.

53 David, *Tagebuch*, May 7, 1917, p. 227. Riezler Diary, May 8, 9, 13, 19, 1917. WP of party leader briefing, May 3, 1917. While Stresemann called for a clear disassociation from the Left, Payer countered; "Maintain the middle line!" For a detailed account of internal developments in the spring of 1917, cf. also a draft fragment of Bethmann's memoirs, BA *Nachlass* Thimme, no. 61. See also Edwards, *Stresemann*, pp. 135 ff. Westarp, *Konservative Politik* 2 : 87 ff. "The interpellation is only a symptom of the increased agitation against my policy during the last week," Bethmann wrote to Valentini on May 3, making Conservatives, heavy industry, and the military responsible for the agitation: "The situation is very tense."

54 Bethmann to the Reichstag, May 15, 1917, Thimme, *Kriegsreden*, pp. 237 ff., citing the Center Party organ *Germania* for the slogan "bloc of the middle." Hohenlohe to Czernin, May 15, Larisch to Czernin, May 21, 1917, HHStA, PA III, 173.

55 Bethmann to Hindenburg, June 25, 1917, DZA Po, Rkz. no. 2446. WP party leader briefing, July 2, 1917. Lerchenfeld to Loessl, July 9, 1917, reporting a visit of Valentini, who argued that the parliamentary chancellor crisis had been overcome for the time being, BHStA MA I 969. For the collapse of confidence in Bethmann cf. W. J. Mommsen, "L'Opinion allemande et la chute du gouvernement Bethmann-Hollweg en Juillet 1917," *Revue d'histoire moderne et contemporaine* (1968), pp. 39 ff.

56 L. Quessel, "Bethmann Hollweg's Annexionismus," *Sozialistische Monatshefte* (1919), pp. 1037 ff. Silesius (pseud.), "Gedanken über die Politik des Reichskanzlers Bethmann Hollweg," *Deutschlands Erneuerung* (1917), pp. 398 ff. For the paradoxical double majority cf. also the forthcoming study by John L. Snell regarding German parliamentarization previewed in "The World of German Democracy, 1789–1914," *The Historian* 31 (1969): 521 ff. See also Lerchenfeld's sagacious appraisal of Bethmann's policy in his report to Hertling, Oct. 24, 1915, BHStA, MA III 2691/7. Bethmann to Hertling, Jan. 26, 1918; AA, Dld 122, no. 16, vol. 9. Bethmann to Friedrich Meinecke, Aug. 25, 1915, PrGStA *Nachlass* Meinecke; Bethmann to Hans Delbrück, Sept. 8, 1917, DSB *Nachlass* Delbrück: "It is correct that I have never made our peace conditions precisely clear. I did so on purpose," not out of expediency alone. "Even today I consider a detailed announcement of our war aims impossible. This coalition war is too complicated for that. One can only rely upon general formulas that are naturally imprecise." At most, some provisions could be made public, "as I did negatively concerning Belgium. If I demanded guarantees against Belgium's use by our enemies as a constant threat to Germany, this expression could be interpreted in many ways."

57 Riezler Diary, Nov. 22, 1916. Cf. also Jacques Droz, *L'Europe centrale: Evolution historique de l'idée de 'Mitteleuropa'* (Paris, 1960), and for the attempted implementation in Belgium and Poland see my Appendix.

58 For the goals of the Entente cf. A. J. P. Taylor, "The War Aims of the Allies in the First World War," in *Essays Presented to Sir Lewis Namier* (London, 1956), pp. 475 ff. and Pierre Renouvin, "Die Kriegsziele der französischen Regierung, 1914–1918," *GWU* (1966), pp. 129 ff. Because of the recent opening of the archives, research on western war aims is still in its infancy. Cf. also Bethmann to Delbrück, Aug. 5, 12, 1918, DSB *Nachlass* Delbrück: "The promise of a complete restoration [of Belgium] was impossible at that time even in your opinion." Hence Bethmann had to use the expression *real guarantees* to describe his aims: "Moreover, the form of those hypothetical securities depended naturally upon the military situation at peacetime, which was neither then nor now easy to determine and could for that reason never be fixed." Even in 1918 the chancellor remained skeptical that the restitution of Belgium "would have sufficed to bring peace . . . I doubt it." Riezler Diary, May 9, 1917, Aug. 1, 1916. The chancellor's assistant considered the crucial "mistake of German policy that it pursued these three goals simultaneously and insecurely vacillated for two decades among these motives under the influence of a politically uneducated, predominantly emotionally determined public spirit."

Chapter 8

1 Ph. Scheidemann, *Memoirs* 1 : 239, 294 ff. Bethmann, *Betrachtungen* 2 : 56–57. C. Haussmann, *Schlaglichter*, p. 65. Bethmann to Weizsäcker, Aug. 30, 1914,

Privatnachlass Weizsäcker. Cf. W. Stadelmann, "Friedensversuche im ersten Jahre des Weltkrieges," *HZ* (1937), pp. 485 ff.; E. Hölzle, "Das Experiment des Friedens im Ersten Weltkrieg, 1914–1917," *GWU* (1962), pp. 465–522; and E. Zechlin, "Friedensbestrebungen und Revolutionierungsversuche," *Aus Politik und Zeitgeschichte* (1961, 1963); Jacques Bariéty, "L'Allemagne et les problèmes de la paix pendant la première guerre mondiale," *Revue historique* 233 (1965) : 369 ff. and 239 (1968) : 456 ff., and Guy Pedrocini, *Les Négociations secrètes pendant la grande guerre* (Paris, 1968). Despite these special studies, the diplomacy of the Great War has been neglected by historians. Z. A. B. Zeman, *The Gentlemen Negotiators: A Diplomatic History of World War I* (New York, 1971) is only a beginning.

2   Riezler Diary, Aug. 18, Sept. 9, 12, Oct. 1, 4, 7, 1914. Bethmann to Vienna, Aug. 22, 1914 in AA, Dld. 128, no. 1, vol. 34; Bethmann to AA, Sept. 7, 1914, AA, Wk. secr. vol. 1. Cf. Leo Valiani, "Italian-Austro-Hungarian Negotiations 1914/15," *JCH* 1, no. 3 (1966) : 113 ff.; Glen Torrey, "Rumania and the Belligerents, 1914–1918", ibid., pp. 171 ff.; Gerard Silberstein, "The Serbian Campaign of 1915: Its Diplomatic Background," *AHR* 73 (1967) : 51 ff.; Ulrich Trumpener, "German Military Aid to Turkey in 1914," *JMH* 32 (1960) : 145 ff. and "Liman von Sanders and the German-Ottoman Alliance," *JCH* 1, no. 4 (1966) : 179 ff. Cf. also W. M. Carlgren, *Neutralität oder Allianz: Deutschlands Beziehungen zu Schweden in den Anfangsjahren des ersten Weltkrieges* (Uppsala, 1962), and Paul Herre, *Die Kleinen Staaten Europas und die Entstehung des Weltkrieges* (Munich, 1937).

3   Bethmann to AA, Sept. 12; Bethmann to Berchtold, Nov. 23, Zimmermann note, Sept. 9, 1914; in the basic file on peace moves, AA, Wk. no. 2 secr., vols. 1 ff., the backbone of André Scherer's and Jacques Grunwald's *L'Allemagne et les problèmes de la paix pendant la première guerre mondiale,* 2 vols. (Paris, 1962, 1966). For Gerard's unreliable account, see *Face to Face with Kaiserism* (New York, 1918).

4   Riezler Diary, Oct. 1, 4, 6, 27, 28, 1914. Bethmann to Haussmann, Nov. 14, 1914, WHStA *Nachlass* Haussmann. Bethmann considered the French "closest to us, at least complementarily." Cf. also E. Zechlin, "Probleme des Kriegskalküls und der Kriegsbeendigung im ersten Weltkrieg," *GWU* 16 (1965) : 69 ff.; F. Fischer, *Krieg der Illusionen,* pp. 775 ff., and P. Renouvin, "Die öffentliche Meinung in Frankreich während des Krieges, 1914–1918," *VJHfZG* 18 (1970) : 239 ff.

5   Riezler Diary, Oct. 25, 28, 30, Nov. 2, 1914. Bethmann to Wangenheim, July 31, Aug. 10, Bethmann to AA, Nov. 5, 1915, cited by Ulrich Trumpener, *Germany and the Ottoman Empire, 1914–1918* (Princeton, 1968), pp. 16 ff. Cf. also Gerard E. Silberstein's slightly misnamed, *The Troubled Alliance: German-Austrian Relations 1914–1917* (Lexington, Ky., 1970), pp. 73 ff. and "The Central Powers and the Second Turkish Alliance, 1915," *Slavic Review* 24 (1965), pp. 77 ff. See also W. W. Gottlieb, *Studies in Secret Diplomacy during the First World War* (London, 1957), pp. 34 ff., and for the Ottoman Empire as war aim, Lothar Rathmann, *Stossrichtung Nahost, 1914–1918* (Berlin, 1963), pp. 19 ff. Since the policy of revolutionizing was carried on below the chancellor's level, it has been systematically slighted in this account. Cf. Zeman, *Gentlemen Negotiators,* pp. 83 ff. and Zechlin, *Juden,* pp. 116 ff.

6   Bethmann to Weizsäcker, Nov. 10, 1914, *Privatnachlass* Weizsäcker: "I no longer consider a long duration of the war as unfavorable as in the beginning." The chancellor thought "we will have to have much patience, although it seems at times impossible that such a life-and-death struggle of the nations can go on forever." Cf. his letters to Hammann, Nov. 14, 1914, DZA Po *Nachlass* Hammann and to Hertling, Nov. 15, 1914, BHStA, MA I, 961.

7   Riezler Diary, Nov. 22, 26, 1914. In Riezler's mind the alternatives were clear: "We

have peace if we give in, drop Austria or Turkey, but then we will become a vassal of Russia." He predicted a similar result if Germany sacrificed its naval plans and "world political ambitions vis-à-vis England, only this is more bearable, since it is less dangerous for our existence." Because one or the other might be Germany's fate, "the heroic attempt to secure an untouchable position as world power of the first rank through this war is nearly impossible and therefore the people are so touching and tragic in their striving." Nevertheless the minimal goal remained "a break-up of the coalition, the covering of our western flank for a future war against the East, and if impossible, the economic weakening of East and West." But all practical methods, such as Mitteleuropa, "the inheritance of Britain," or "reconciliation with England" would either fail because of chauvinism, the unpolitical soldiers, or the pressure of the navy.

8 Bethmann to Zimmermann, Nov. 19, 1914, the chancellor's fundamental rationale in favor of separate peace, S-G 1 : 15 ff.: "Taking everything into account, despite all confidence, one must call the situation serious." For Zimmermann's detailed critique of separate peace with Russia, cf. his memorandum of Nov. 27, 1914, S-G 1 : 26 ff. See also K. H. Janssen, *Der Kanzler und der General: Die Führungskrise um Bethmann Hollweg und Falkenhayn 1914–1916* (Berlin, 1967), pp. 49 ff.; G. Ritter, *Bethmann Hollweg als Kriegskanzler*, pp. 61 ff.; F. Fischer, *Griff nach der Weltmacht*, pp. 217 ff.; F. Klein, *Deutschland im Ersten Weltkrieg* 1 : 380 ff., and P. Sweet, "Leaders and Policies," *JCEA* (1956), pp. 229 ff. Cf. also Bethmann to the Socialists: "Do you imagine I would not make peace tomorrow were it possible with either France or Russia?" Scheidemann, *Memoirs* 1 : 275.

9 Riezler Diary, Nov. 26, 29, Dec. 12, 1914. Riezler counseled Bethmann "to stall . . . , not to refuse mediation but rather let circumstances render it impossible." According to Andersen, "Grey wanted to concede a sphere of influence to Germany in China." Bethmann to AA, Nov. 25, 27, draft response of the German government approved by Zimmermann and Bethmann, Nov. 30, Bethmann to Ballin, Dec. 25, 1914, all in S-G 1 : 25 ff. Cf. also E. Zechlin, "Friedensbestrebungen," passim, and Carlgren, *Neutralität oder Allianz*, pp. 84 ff.

10 Riezler Diary, Dec. 24, 29, 1914, Jan. 2, 7, 11, Feb. 6, 1915. The chancellor's assistant noted in late December a spurious "offer of a Frenchman to get us an indispensable success in order to liberate France from England," which promptly failed. Cf. Jacques de Launay, *Secrètes diplomatiques 1914–1918* (Brussels, 1963). For the first time he seriously questioned victory, since he feared "separate peace by Austria which, blinded by the gods, is capable of any stupidity," but they would have to cede Galicia. Bethmann to Grand Duke of Mecklenburg, Dec. 15, 1914, DZA Po, Rkz. 2442/10; Bethmann to Loebell, Jan. 2, BA *Nachlass* Loebell; Bethmann to AA, Jan. 6, Bethmann to Copenhagen, Mar. 6, 1915, in S-G 1 : 68–69.

11 Riezler Diary, Mar. 7, 9, 11, 14, 17, 30, 1915: "Stumm tells me the chancellor is thinking of peace. . . . The chancellor said the tsar is reputed to want peace, but fears we would demand all of Poland. Rantzau is instructed to speak to Scavenius about economic concessions and boundary rectifications which we would claim from Russia." While the Andersen mission was failing "Witte died. . . . This man didn't love us." Bethmann to Treutler, Mar. 14, DZA Po, Wk. vol. 3; Bethmann to Treutler, Mar. 17, 18, 1915, S-G 1 : 76–77; and April 4, 1915, reprinted by Janssen, ed., *Treutler*, pp. 227 ff.

12 E. M. House diaries, Mar. 27, 1915, House Collection, Yale University. Bethmann's report of Mar. 28, 1915, S-G 1 : 84, as well as Jagow's note, Mar. 23, 1915, ibid., pp. 80–81 show that the discussion never went beyond generalities. Cf. also Charles Seymour, *The Intimate Papers of Colonel House* (Boston, 1926–28) 1 : 414, for the American envoy's general impression that the Germans were "narrowly selfish in

their purposes and have no broad outlook as to the general good of mankind." Cf. also Gerard's optimistic report to Bryan, Feb. 11, 1915, *FRUS*, 1915, pp. 9–10.

13 Bethmann to Hutten-Czapski, Apr. 21, 1915, DZA Po *Nachlass* Hutten. Riezler Diary, Aug. 22, Oct. 25, 30, Nov. 8, 26, Dec. 13, 1914, Jan. 11, 17, Feb. 17, 1915. Bülow's mission was undercut by Austrian "distrust that he wants to garner cheap successes at Vienna's cost, and by Hapsburg pride and confidence now that we have promised them help in the Carpathians." Cf. Bethmann to Hammann, Nov. 14, 1914, DZA Po *Nachlass* Hammann. Cf. also Bülow, *Denkwürdigkeiten* 3 : 189 ff. and K. Epstein, *Matthias Erzberger*, pp. 140–41, and W. J. Mommsen's authoritative, "Die italienische Frage in der Politik des Reichskanzlers von Bethmann Hollweg, 1914–1915," *Quellen und Forschungen aus italienischen Archiven und Bibliotheken* 48 (1968) : 282 ff.

14 Riezler Diary, Feb. 20, 21, 27, Mar. 5, 7, 20, 1915. The chancellor's assistant speculated whether "Francis Joseph's advisors do not consciously steer toward the collapse of the monarchy or feel that Austria can only save its independence toward us through a breach of faith and future enmity?" Now the "Austrians always claim that things are better than Bülow reports. He wants to give the Italians a present in order to be fêted in Rome." Riezler was appalled by "the kaiser and high nobility through whose inherited political hubris Austria will perish." Bethmann to Prussian Ministry of State, Feb. 17, 27, 1915, sessions of the Prussian Ministry of State on the Silesian offer, full protocols in BA *Nachlass* Heinrichs. H. Hantsch, *Berchtold*, vol. 2. Cf. also Egmont Zechlin, "Das 'schlesische Angebot' und die italienische Kriegsgefahr 1915," *GWU* 14 (1963) : 533 ff.; and E. Rosen, "Giovanni Giolitti und die italienische Politik im ersten Weltkrieg," *HZ* 194 (1962) : 327 ff.

15 Riezler Diary, Mar. 20, Apr. 1, 4, 8, 13, 18, 28, May 10, 16, 22, 1915. Riezler enjoyed "Sonnino's word to Erzberger speaking with St. Francis, *bis dat qui cito dat,*" to which the Center party leader replied, "*bis accipit qui cito accipit.*" Ultimately, he did not know who was more to blame, "Burian-Slurian who always assures one he will grasp the psychological moment and seizes it so well that he misses it for hours," or Italian rapacity, which insisted on the immediate cession of the Trentino. For the larger perspectives cf. A. J. May, *The Passing of the Hapsburg Monarchy, 1914–1918* 1 : 170 ff.; L. Valiani, *La Dissoluzione dell'Austria Ungheria* (Milan, 1966), pp. 97 ff., and Brunello Vigezzi, *L'Italia di fronte alla prima guerra mondiale* (Milan, 1966) 1 : 94 ff.

16 Riezler Diary, May 22, 31, 1915. Bethmann to party leaders, May 13, 15, 27, WP; Bethmann to Bundesratsausschuss May 24, 1915, WP and Lerchenfeld to Loessl, May 23, BHStA, MA I 967b. See also Bethmann's encouraging letter to Bülow, Apr. 1, 1915, BA *Nachlass* Bülow and the apologetic epistle of June 10, 1915, in Hammann, *Bilder*, p. 122. Bethmann to Prussian Ministry of State, Apr. 10, 1915, DZA Me, Rep. 90a B III 2b no. 6, vol. 164. Bethmann to Reichstag, May 18, announcing the Austrian concessions and May 28, 1915, Thimme, *Kriegsreden*, pp. 29 ff. For the repercussions on his domestic position, cf. W. J. Mommsen, "Die Regierung Bethmann Hollweg und die öffentliche Meinung," pp. 138 ff.; and W. Gutsche, *Deutschland im Ersten Weltkrieg* 2 : 207 ff.

17 Bethmann to Valentini, Mar. 3, DZA Me *Nachlass* Valentini. Note by Bethmann about conversation with Andersen, who had "nothing positive to report," Apr. 9; Bethmann to Copenhagen June 1, stressing that we must do everything "to split Russia from the Entente . . . [since] only through breaking the coalition can peace be attained." Bethmann to Treutler, June 3; Bethmann note of conversation with Tisza, June 18; note by Bethmann, June 19; Bethmann to AA, June 25; Bethmann to Copenhagen, July 9, 1915; all in S-G 1 : 93 ff. Riezler

Diary, July 7, 1915. Bethmann to Hertling, July 2, 1915, BHStA MA I 962. Bethmann to Weizsäcker, July 3, 1915, *Privatnachlass* Weizsäcker. "Domestic fermentation is increasing in Russia, but its meaning and effects cannot be determined. In England the Independent Labor Party strongly works for peace, insiders claim with rising success. But the general development can hardly be predicted at this time."

18   Bethmann to Falkenhayn, July 30; Bethmann to Copenhagen, July 31; Bethmann to Treutler, Aug. 4; note by Bethmann, Aug. 9; Bethmann to Copenhagen, Sept. 2, 1915, all in S-G 1 : 146 ff. Cf. also Bethmann to Hindenburg, Aug. 10, 1915, DZA Po, Rkz. 2398/4. For Bethmann's skepticism about separate peace with Russia, cf. Hertling's note of a conversation July 6, 1915, BHStA MA I 962. Riezler Diary, July 11, 12, 21, 24, 1915. Riezler mused about the "slow rise of international peace wishes," predicting a large pacifist movement after the war, and noted "the maneuvering of all socialist parties, each attempting to evoke the call for peace in the other." Regarding the "gesture of liberation" toward Poland, "the chancellor objected that it makes the still existing chance for separate peace with Russia more difficult." Cf. Bethmann to Reichstag, Aug. 9, 1915, Thimme, *Kriegsreden,* pp. 37 ff. Cf. also Bethmann to Delbrück, Sept. 20, 1919, retracing the separate peace efforts in 1915, *Preussische Jahrbücher* (1919), pp. 114–16, and Erwin Hölzle, *Der Osten im ersten Weltkriege* (Leipzig, 1944).

19   Riezler Diary, July 7, 11, 1915: "In the train [I talked] long with the chancellor: Emperor and Falkenhayn must understand that the key is Bulgaria, that peace is not possible, as long as the Balkan hope still shines for France and Russia." Ibid., July 28, Aug. 15, 23, Sept. 10, 27, 1915: The effect of the Bulgarian entry on Russia was "chaos, but nevertheless hardly declining army strength. From there peace is possible overnight—but more probably nobody is capable of such a decision any more. More likely is peace from England after the solution of the Dardanelles question." Bethmann briefing of party leaders, Aug. 16, Sept. 27, 1915, WPs. Bethmann in the Prussian Ministry of State, Sept. 21, 1915, DZA Me, Rep. 90a B III 2b no. 6, vol. 164. Cf. also Gerard Silberstein, *The Troubled Alliance,* pp. 150 ff., "The Serbian Campaign of 1915: Its Military Implications," *International Review of History and Political Science* 3 (1966) : 115 ff., and Janssen, *Kanzler und General,* pp. 148 ff.

20   Riezler Diary, Oct. 4, 23, Nov. 5, 1915: "What a terrible instrument is the press and the practice of appealing to mass instincts in their atmosphere of ignorance. It is the characteristic of modern politics that it unleashes forces which cannot be called back." But "the desire for peace" of the "unpolitical Socialists" equally complicated the statesmen's task. For the Belgian negotiations cf. Bethmann to Hertling, Aug. 17, 1915, AA, Wk. no. 20a secr., 1–3. See also Albert I to Törring, Oct. 30 and Törring to Jagow, Nov. 28, Dec. 1, 1915, S-G 1 : 196 ff. Marginal note by Bethmann on a report by Romberg, Jan. 2, 1916, ibid., pp. 245–46. Bethmann to Haussmann, Oct. 29, 1915, WHStA *Nachlass* Haussmann.

21   Riezler Diary, Dec. 2, 1915. Bethmann to the party leaders, Nov. 29, and Dec. 1, WPs. Bethmann to Bundesrat, Nov. 30, 1915, summary by Lerchenfeld and Mecklenburg ambassador, BHStA MA I 966. Also Bethmann to Reichstag, Dec. 9, 1915, Thimme, *Kriegsreden,* pp. 65 ff. Cf. also Matthias and Miller, *David Tagebuch,* pp. 144 ff.; Scheidemann, *Der Zusammenbruch,* pp. 26 ff.; Viktor Bredt, *Der Deutsche Reichstag im Weltkrieg* (Berlin, 1926); C. Haussmann, *Schlaglichter,* pp. 52 ff.; and E. Matthias and E. Pikart, *Reichstagsfraktion* 2 : 80 ff.

22   Note by Prussian Minister of War Wild von Hohenborn in his diary, Nov. 2, 1915: "I can only emphasize that I could think of nothing more dangerous. The idea is completely impossible!" BA *Nachlass* Wild. Riezler Diary, Dec. 24, 1915, Jan. 11,

13, Feb. 6, 1916. Bethmann to Wach, Sept. 24, 1915, DZA Po, Rkz. 2444/1. At the same time Bethmann was upset about the harsh Austrian demands on Montenegro because "whoever in the present situation does not build golden bridges to an enemy suing for peace but wants to strangle him, is capable of committing any stupidity." Lerchenfeld to Hertling, Jan. 21, 1916, BHStA MA I 957b. Cf. also Bethmann to Treutler, November 17, 1915, expressing skepticism about general or separate peace, in Janssen, ed., *Treutler,* pp. 233 ff.

23 E. M. House Diary, Jan. 27, 28, 1916, Yale University. Cf. also Bethmann's note of Jan. 28, 1916, S-G 1 : 264–65. To House's remark that "in England there was much confidence in him, Jagow, Zimmermann, and Solf but distrust in the war party, I emphasized with much determination that between myself and the emperor there stood nothing and nobody, which impressed him visibly." Riezler Diary, May 7, 1916. Cf. also Ernest R. May, *The World War and American Isolation 1914–1917* (Cambridge, Mass., 1959), pp. 352–53.

24 Bethmann to Prince William, Apr. 22, 1916, S-G 1 : 309 ff. Bethmann to Loebell, May 9, July 1, 1916, BA *Nachlass* Loebell. Bethmann to Bundesrat, Mar. 15, 1916, Lerchenfeld report, BHStA MA I 966. Also Bethmann to party leaders, Mar. 14, 1916, WP. Bethmann to Reichstag, Apr. 5, 1916, Thimme, *Kriegsreden,* pp. 94 ff.: "Gentlemen, when on December last I declared our *willingness to talk about peace,* I said that I could nowhere see the same readiness in the enemy countries. The events of the meantime have proven that I was right."

25 Bethmann note, May 14, Aug. 9, 1915; marginalia by Bethmann, May 7; Lucius to AA, Mar. 14, 1916, S-G 1 : 103 ff., 286 ff. Riezler Diary, Sept. 13, 1914: "The Japanese exact the highest conditions for their help, free immigration into the British colonies in the Pacific, free hand in China, etc. I have counseled to extend the little finger to the Japanese so that they can keep two irons in the fire until the end." Ibid., May 7, June 17, 1916. Cf. also Bethmann to Andres, July 18, 1916, DZA Po, Rkz. 2444/4. Bethmann to William II, Aug. 16, 1916, S-G 1 : 433 ff. See also E. Hölzle, "Deutschland und die Wegscheide des Ersten Weltkrieges." In *Geschichtliche Kräfte und Entscheidungen* (Wiesbaden, 1953), pp. 266 ff.

26 Riezler Diary, Aug. 22, Sept. 9, 22, 1914, May 22, 1915, June 29, 1916: "The Austrians are beaten. The hopes in Paris are revived. Italy relieved. . . . Our mood very serious." Ibid., July 4, Aug. 10, 30, Sept. 21, 1916. Bethmann to Weizsäcker, Sept. 18, 1916, *Privatnachlass* Weizsäcker: "Stürmer's position seems seriously shaken. If he falls, it means a victory for England. If he succeeds in surviving and makes someone like Botkin foreign minister, this could be interpreted as a slow emancipation from Britain." In general he "did not dare speak about future possibilities. The military situation is too unstable." Cf. also Carl Mühlmann, *Oberste Heeresleitung und Balkan im Weltkrieg* (Berlin, 1942), and Silberstein, *The Troubled Alliance,* pp. 198 ff. In early August "the chancellor did not abandon hope that the fall would bring the end of the war," but late the same month he informed Lerchenfeld "that in contrast to his collaborators he had expected the Rumanian declaration of war against Austria after the Italian one against Germany had become known." Lerchenfeld to Hertling, Aug. 2, 13, 28, 1916, BHStA MA III 2691/6–10 and MA I 958.

27 Bethmann to Prussian Ministry of State, Aug. 19, 28, 1916, DZA Me, Rep. 90a B III 2b no. 6, vol. 165. Bethmann to Bundesrat, Aug. 8 and 9, Aug. 28, 1916, WPs and Lerchenfeld reports BHStA MA I 966. Also Bethmann to party leaders, July 17, Aug. 5, Sept. 5, 1916, WPs. Bethmann to Reichstag, Sept. 28, 1916, Thimme, *Kriegsreden,* pp. 130 ff. Bethmann to AA, Aug. 23, Bethmann to William II, Oct. 2, 3, Bethmann to Hindenburg, Oct. 10, 1916, S-G 1 : 456 ff. Cf. Fritz Epstein, "Die deutsche Ostpolitik im ersten Weltkrieg," *JGOE* (1962), pp. 381 ff.

28 Riezler Diary, Nov. 3, 1915. Note by Bethmann of conversation with Burian, Oct. 18, Bethmann to Vienna, Oct. 28, Nov. 1, Bethmann to William II, Nov. 4, Bethmann to Grünau, Nov. 11 ff. Originals in AA, Wk. no. 23 secr., vols. 1 ff., reprinted by S-G 1 : 517 ff. Bethmann to Haussmann, Nov. 4, 1916, WHStA *Nachlass* Haussmann and *Schlaglichter*, pp. 72 ff. Bethmann to Prussian Ministry of State, Oct. 24, 1916, DZA Me, Rep. 90a B III 2b no. 6, vol. 165. Bethmann to Reichstag, Nov. 9, 1916, Thimme, *Kriegsreden*, pp. 163 ff. Matthias and Miller, *Davids Kriegstagebuch*, pp. 208–09. Lerchenfeld to King Ludwig, Nov. 12, 1916, BHStA MA III 2691 /11. Second Investigating Committee of the German Nationalversammlung, *Aktenstücke zur Friedensaktion Wilsons 1916–1917* (Berlin, 1919) and Bethmann Hollweg, *Friedensangebot und U-Bootkrieg* (Berlin, 1919). Cf. also Bethmann's repeated statements to Gerard, beginning with May 2, 1916, *FRUS* (1916), pp. 27, 55, 68–69, and 255.

29 Erzberger to Hertling, reporting a conversation with Bethmann, Aug. 3, 1915, BHStA MA I 947. Lerchenfeld and Wahnschaffe protocols of session of Bundesrat, Oct. 30 and 31; Lerchenfeld report of session of Dec. 11, 1916, ibid. Riezler Diary, Nov. 3, Dec. 9, 1916. The chancellor's assistant was working on a draft speech that attempted to be at the same time firm and conciliatory. Note by Admiral Müller in his diary, Aug. 25 of conversation with Bethmann, *Regierte der Kaiser?*, p. 215. Bethmann to Prussian Ministry of State, Oct. 24, 1916, DZA Me, Rep. 90a B III 2b no. 6, vol. 165. For the question of Bethmann's sincerity cf. G. Ritter, *Kriegskanzler*, pp. 319 ff.; Fischer, *Germany's Aims*, pp. 319 ff.; and Vietsch, *Bethmann*, p. 245, citing a letter to Zorn: "After this horrible war in all nations a strong movement will demand, with elementary power, that everything possible be done to secure world peace. It will be Germany's task not to follow but to lead, and such a policy will not only be in its own interest but in that of mankind."

30 Bethmann to Bundesrat, Oct. 30, 31, and Dec. 11; Bethmann to party leaders, Oct. 7, Dec. 11, WPs; Bethmann to Prussian Ministry of State, Oct. 27, Dec. 11, 1916, DZA Me, Rep. 90a B III 2b no. 6, vol. 165. For background and objectives of the peace move cf. Wolfgang Steglich, *Bündnissicherung oder Verständigungsfrieden: Untersuchungen zu dem Friedensangebot der Mittelmächte vom 12. Dezember 1918* (Göttingen, 1958), especially pp. 80 ff., for Bethmann's marginal note: "The assumption that we could reach better peace conditions through continuing the war would appear as boasting to our enemies" and would only become reality should America accept unrestricted submarine warfare and England be really defeated by it. Cf. also Bethmann to Haussmann, Dec. 14, 1916, WHStA *Nachlass* Haussmann.

31 Bethmann to Bernstorff, Aug. 18, accepting Wilson's mediation; Bethmann to William II, Sept. 23, calling for rapid American action; Bethmann to Hindenburg, Nov. 27, doubting the likelihood of Wilson's move; Bethmann to Vitzthum, Dec. 23, explaining the reasons for not waiting for the US president, S-G 1 : 438 ff. Cf. also Westarp, *Konservative Politik* 2 : 74 ff.; Matthias-Pikart, *Reichstagsfraktion* 2 : 240 ff.; and Erzberger, *Erlebnisse im Weltkriege*, pp. 228 ff. The National Liberals were enraged by the fait accompli; the Conservatives disliked the initiative; the Center Party saw it as advantage that Germany would "forestall all neutrals, especially Wilson"; and the Progressives generally agreed; only the Socialists were genuinely pleased. For the connection between peace and escalation cf. Karl E. Birnbaum, *Peace Moves and U-Boat Warfare: A Study of Imperial Germany's Policy towards the United States, April 18, 1916–January 9, 1917* (Uppsala, 1958), pp. 218 ff.

32 Bethmann to the Reichstag, Dec. 12, 1916, Thimme, *Kriegsreden*, pp. 176 ff. The text of the German note is already in G. Lowes Dickinson, *Documents and State-*

ments Relating to Peace Proposals and War Aims, December 1916–November 1918
(London, 1919), pp. 1 ff. See also the drafts of Nov. 14, Bethmann to Grünau, Dec.
4, 5, Bethmann memo, Dec. 9, and text of note, Dec. 12, S-G 1 : 557 ff. Riezler
Diary, Dec. 13, adding ominously: "Now we must begin the submarine matter rationally and reasonably." Bethmann to Loebell, Dec. 14, 1916, BA *Nachlass* Loebell.
Lerchenfeld to Hertling, Dec. 5, 12, 1916, BHStA MA III 2691/11. Matthias-Miller,
David Tagebuch, p. 234. For a virulent contemporary attack on Bethmann's
pacifism of power" cf. Richard Grelling, "Bethmann, der 'Pazifist,' " pt. 2 in *Wissen
und Leben* 10, nos. 6–7 (1916): "The proffered peace is a peace without pacifism.
. . . Under the green olive branch with which the chancellor graces his head the
peaked helmet is clearly visible."

33 Riezler Diary, Dec. 29, 1916: "Apparently the Entente cannot quickly agree on a
reply. . . . With half an answer it will be exceedingly difficult to hold our allies
together and we will not be able to respond too weakly, i.e. in a manner which
does not endanger the negotiations" because the OHL "judges as always from the
papers, without political experience, and already considers the offer refused."
Ibid., Jan. 6, 1917: "Of course Austria is inclined toward weakness, and initially
answered in the press less firmly than we. They must be propped up once more
even if it will be a last bluff." Bethmann to Vienna, Dec. 15, Bethmann to
Lersner, Dec. 19, 1916; Bethmann to William II, Jan. 2, Bethmann to Hindenburg, Jan. 4, draft instruction by Bethmann, Jan. 4, protocol of a German-Austrian
conference, Jan. 9, 1917; Bethmann to Törring, Jan. 13, 1917: "Moreover the
political situation at present seems so unclear that I do not promise myself any
success from further steps with King Albert." All in S-G 1 : 617 ff. Bethmann to
Haussmann, Dec. 28, 1916, WHStA *Nachlass* Haussmann. For the German and
Entente notes see Dickinson, *Peace Proposals and War Aims*, pp. 7 ff.

34 Phrase used by Bethmann in his interrogation by the second Investigating Committee of the Nationalversammlung, *Stenographische Berichte*, pp. 158 ff. Cf. also
the partly typewritten "Entwurf eines Artikels für *NAZ*" in the preserved fragment of his papers, BA Kl. Erw. 342-1. Grew to Lansing, Nov. 22, Dec. 21, 1916,
FRUS (1916), pp. 68–69, 129 ff. Bethmann note, Nov. 22, 1916, AA Wk. 18 secr.,
vol. 12. Bethmann interview for Hale, Nov. 30, 1916, in Schulthess's *GK* (1916),
1 : 560–61. For Bethmann's intentions see Vitzthum's note of Dec. 11, and for
Zimmermann see Nostitz to Vitzthum, Dec. 14, 1916, SHStA, Berlin 301. For the
precipitous German answer to Wilson, conciliatory in tone but negative in substance (concerning the president as mediator and the publication of conditions),
cf. Zimmermann to Lersner, Dec. 24, 1916, S-G 1 : 639–40: "We have decided on a
response to his note according to our peace move but expressing clearly that we
want to negotiate directly with our enemies." Cf. also J. Williamson, *Helfferich*,
pp. 187 ff.

35 Bethmann to Prussian Ministry of State, Jan. 15, 1917, DZA Me, Rep. 90a B III
2b no. 6, vol. 166. Bethmann to Bundesrat, Jan. 16, Jan. 31, WP and Lerchenfeld
report, BHStA MA I 958: "The chancellor pointed to the German peace offer of
December 12 and said it was the enemy's fault that the war was continuing. There
is no point in discussing the peace conditions contained in their answer to Wilson."
Riezler Diary, Jan. 11, 31, February 18, 1917: "The blindness, ignorance, and
stupidity of the Entente statesmen is beyond measure," since Balfour had feigned
surprised innocence, claiming that the language of the Entente reply was "only the
customary and necessary bluff. Fate in the guise of human dumbness." Bethmann
to Washington, Jan. 28, 1917, S-G 1 : 685 ff., and 2. UA, *Aktenstücke zur Friedensaktion Wilsons*, pp. 45 ff., Bethmann to Bernstorff, Jan. 16, 1917.

36 Arthur S. Link, *Wilson* 5 : 290 ff.; E. R. May, *The World War*, pp. 387 ff., and

Daniel L. Smith, *The Great Departure: the United States and World War I* (New York, 1965).

37 Riezler Diary, Mar. 8, Apr. 6, 1917. Unsigned protocol of Austro-German conference, Mar. 16, 26; Bethmann to William II, May 14; Bethmann marginal note on Wedel to Foreign Office, May 30, 1917; all in S-G 2 : 36 ff. Count Ottokar Czernin, *In the World War* (New York, 1920), pp. 163 ff. R. A. Kann, *Die Sixtusaffaire und die geheimen Friedensverhandlungen Österreich-Ungarns im Ersten Weltkriege* (Vienna, 1966); F. Engel-Janosi, "Über den Friedenswillen Kaiser Karls," in *Virtu Fideque* (Vienna, 1965), pp. 37 ff.; H. Lehmann, "Czernin's Friedenspolitik 1916–1918," *WaG* (1963), pp. 47–59, and A. J. May, *The Passing of the Hapsburg Monarchy* 1 : 486 ff. Bethmann to Hertling, Mar. 5, 1917, S-G 2 : 26 ff. Cf. also W. Steglich, *Die Friedenspolitik der Mittelmächte, 1917/18* (Wiesbaden, 1964), pp. 43 ff.

38 Riezler Diary, Mar. 18, 28; "If hunger comes and peace not with it, then we will get conditions which must lead to revolution if they last. We must reach peace with the present Russian government, since the next will probably be socialist and proclaim an international socialist peace." Ibid., Apr. 3, May 13, 1917. Riezler preferred "making a deal with the present people" to waiting for a socialist constituent assembly, since it "will take too long." Bethmann to Reichstag, Mar. 29, 1917, Thimme, *Kriegsreden*, pp. 225 ff., Bethmann to Eisendecher, Apr. 6, 1917, AA *Nachlass* Eisendecher. Bethmann to Valentini, Apr. 10, 1917, DZA Me, Rep. 89H, I Preussen no. 1, Bethmann to Hertling, Apr. 11, 1917, BHStA, MA I, 961. Cf. Zimmermann's statements of Mar. 19, 1917, HHStA, PA III, 173V. See also Leo Stern, *Die Auswirkungen der grossen sozialistischen Oktoberrevolution auf Deutschland* (Berlin, 1959), vol. 4/II, pp. 411 ff.

39 Riezler Diary, Apr. 4, 11, 1917: "Better news from Russia. Unfortunately its complete disintegration does not help our present need, since it does not yet mean peace. If we only still had some breath left!" Bethmann to William II, Apr. 11, 1917, AA, Wk. no. 2 secr, vol. 32. Cf. also W. Hahlweg, *Lenins Rückkehr nach Russland 1917* (Leyden, 1957) and Z. A. B. Zeman, *Germany and the Revolution in Russia, 1915–1918* (London, 1958).

40 Riezler Diary, Apr. 14, 1917: "Strange situation—we are on the brink of catastrophe or victory. Since yesterday much commotion because of the modest and toned-down declaration of war of Prince Lvov." Bethmann to Grünau, Apr. 12, Bethmann to Vienna, Apr. 13, Bethmann to Hindenburg, Apr. 16, Bethmann to William II, May 4, 1917, S-G 2 : 94 ff. Cf. also *NAZ*, Apr. 15, 1917, and W. Steglich, *Friedenspolitik*, pp. 59 ff.; F. Fischer, *Griff nach der Weltmacht*, pp. 419 ff.; G. Ritter, *Kriegskanzler*, pp. 492 ff., and Gutsche, *Deutschland im Ersten Weltkrieg* 2 : 735 ff. Cf. also M. Erzberger, *Erlebnisse im Weltkrieg*, pp. 231 ff.

41 Lersner to AA, Apr. 29, with Bethmann marginalia of the same day, approving the negotiations on the presupposition "*that a representative of the foreign office take part*." Hohenlohe to Bethmann, Apr. 29, with note by Bethmann, Apr. 30; Bethmann to Grünau, May 7; Ludendorff to Zimmermann, May 30, 1917, all in S-G 2 : 162 ff. Bethmann to party leaders, May 5, 1917, WP; Bethmann to Bundesrat, May 8, 1917, DZA Po, Rkz. 2445. Bethmann to Reichstag, May 15, 1917, Thimme, *Kriegsreden*, pp. 238 ff. Riezler Diary, May 1, 19, June 14, 1917. Winterfeld-Menkin, *Jahreszeiten*, pp. 217 ff., and Matthias-Miller, *David Tagebuch*, pp. 228 ff. See also Lerchenfeld to Hertling, May 15, 1917, BHStA MA I 958.

42 Riezler Diary, June 6, 1917: "If the chancellor undertakes to enlighten William II or the OHL about the situation then the provincial insane asylum answers that the chancellor is caving in. . . . Desperate situation." Lerchenfeld to Hertling, June 9, to Loessl, June 28, 1917, and Bethmann to Hertling, Mar. 27, 1917, BHStA

MA I 958, 977, and 961. Bethmann to Hindenburg, June 25, 1917, DZA Po, Rkz. 2,446. Bethmann, "Friedensmöglichkeiten im Frühsommer 1917," *DAZ*, Feb. 29, 1920; Bethmann, *Betrachtungen* 2 : 296 ff. Steglich, *Friedenspolitik*, pp. 117 ff. Cf. also Felix von Bethmann Hollweg, letter of Feb. 11, 1968: "Pacelli, who was a friend of my brother-in-law Count Zech when he was Nuncio and the latter was ambassador in Munich, has confirmed to him after the war that my father's guess that the papal peace feeler was inspired by England was correct, and the answers given by my father had been considered a suitable basis for peace. . . . It was a great tragedy that my father, when in the last resort the effect of submarine warfare which he had approved led to the English démarche with the Pope and created a tangible possibility for peace, was forced out of office for German domestic reasons." Cf. also M. v. Hagen, "Die päpstliche Friedensvermittlung 1917," *HZ* 177 (1954) : 517 ff.

43   For Bethmann's reaction to the Stockholm conference cf. his marginalia to Grünau's dispatch, May 1, 1917. Despite Riezler's fears that "our bumbling cosmopolitans will be taken for a ride," Bethmann endorsed the Socialists' participation so "that they will learn from the disappointment which they will encounter there and they will listen less to the siren song of the internationalists." Riezler Diary, Apr. 25, 1917. See also M. Fainsod, *International Socialism and the War* (London, 1957) and Matthias-Miller, *David Tagebuch*, pp. 238 ff. Schoen to Hertling, May 3, 1917, BHStA MA III 2691/13; Bethmann to the party leaders, July 2, 1917, WP; Bethmann in the Hauptausschuss, July 7, 9, in L. Stern, *Auswirkungen*, 4/II, pp. 471 ff. Lerchenfeld to Loessl, July 6, 1917, BHStA MA I 969 and Larisch to Czernin, July 7, 1917, HHStA, PA III, 173. Cf. also Haussmann, *Schlaglichter*, pp. 95 ff. and the extensive compilation by Matthias-Morsey, *IFA* 1 : 110 ff. as well as Erzberger, *Erlebnisse*, pp. 251 ff.; Scheidemann, *Zusammenbruch*, pp. 80 ff.; and Westarp, *Konservative Politik* 2 : 335 ff. For the growing peace pressure of the war-weary masses cf. W. Richter, *Gewerkschaften, Monopolkapital und Staat* (Berlin, 1959); H. Wohlgemuth, *Burgkrieg, nicht Burgfriede!* (Berlin, 1963); and Gutsche, *Deutschland im Ersten Weltkrieg* 2 : 625 ff.

44   Bethmann to Hans Delbrück, Sept. 8, 1918, DSB *Nachlass* Delbrück. Bethmann note, Apr. 13, 1916, DZA Po, Rkz. 2437/10. General Graevenitz to Weizsäcker, note of a conversation with Bethmann, March 5/6, 1916, *Privatnachlass* Weizsäcker, courtesy of Professor Leonidas Hill. Bethmann, *Betrachtungen* 2 : 54–55.

45   Riezler Diary, May 8, June 14, 1917. Bethmann to Hans Delbrück, Sept. 8, Aug. 5, 12, 1918, Feb. 1, 1919, DSB *Nachlass* Delbrück. Bethmann to Friedrich Naumann, Nov. 13, 1917, DZA Po *Nachlass* Naumann; Bethmann to Prince Max von Baden, Jan. 17, 1918, cited by Zechlin, "Deutschland zwischen," *HZ* (1964), pp. 452 ff. For the domestic obstacles to a compromise peace cf. the anonymous poem "A rotten peace?" (MS Hoover Library, Stanford University) decrying the "false harbingers of peace":

> Die Besten des Volkes kämpfen,
> Da draussen im Feindesland,
> Zu Hause regieren die Mucker
> Und reden Unverstand.

and asking for "Germany's proud eagle":

> Wann treibt der sie zu Paaren
> Mit mächtigem Flügelschlag?
> Dort draussen—Siegesfanfaren!
> Wann wird im Innern Tag?

46 Marginal note by Bethmann on a telegram by Brockdorff-Rantzau, Jan. 12, 1916, S-G 1 : 252–53. Riezler Diary, Apr. 3, 25, 1917. Bethmann to Delbrück, Feb. 1, 1919, DSB *Nachlass* Delbrück. Bethmann to Jäckh, Dec. 20, 1917, in Jäckh, *Goldener Pflug* 2 : 11 ff. Cf. also Hans Delbrück, *Krieg und Politik* (Berlin, 1919) 2 : 269 ff.; E. Reventlow, *Von Potsdam nach Doorn*, pp. 432 ff.; and Veit Valentin, *Deutschlands Aussenpolitik*, pp. 332 ff.: "Had Bethmann still stood at the helm of the government, undoubtedly he would not have given such a maladroit answer to the British peace gesture" as his successor Michaelis did.

Chapter 9

1 Bethmann to Weizsäcker, Aug. 30, Nov. 10, 1914, *Privatnachlass* Weizsäcker. Bethmann to Hammann, Nov. 14, DZA Po *Nachlass* Hammann. Bethmann to Oettingen, Dec. 14, BA *Nachlass* Oettingen. Bethmann to Loebell, Jan. 2, 1915, BA *Nachlass* Loebell. Bethmann to Haussmann, Jan. 6, 1915, WHStA *Nachlass* Haussmann: "This is not the time for grief. We all must have only one thought and look forward." Bethmann to Eisendecher, Jan. 18; AA *Nachlass* Eisendecher. For moving letters regarding the funeral arrangements cf. Bethmann to Hutten-Czapski, Mar. 15, Apr. 21 ff., 1915, DZA Po *Nachlass* Hutten.

2 Riezler Diary, Aug. 21, Nov. 2, 1914: "Frictions will get wilder and wilder." Bethmann to Oettingen, Dec. 14, 1914, BA *Nachlass* Oettingen. Müller, *Regierte?*, pp. 68 ff. For the general problem cf. also Bethmann, *Betrachtungen* 2 : 37 ff. Gordon A. Craig, *The Politics of the Prussian Army*, pp. 299 ff.; Alfred Vagts, *A History of Militarism* (New York, 1937), pp. 229 ff.; and the magisterial, if unidimensional, volume 3 of Gerhard Ritter's *Staatskunst und Kriegshandwerk*, called *Die Tragödie der Staatskunst: Bethmann Hollweg als Kriegskanzler, 1914–1917* (Munich, 1964), passim.

3 Riezler Diary, Aug. 22, Oct. 1, 6, 22, 1914. The chancellor's assistant called Tirpitz "a Renaissance personality. Actually he and his gang are responsible for the whole constellation because they prevented any agreement with Haldane three years ago; but they lie so much." For a similar critique cf. Janssen, ed., *Treutler*, pp. 177 ff. Alfred von Tirpitz, *Deutsche Ohnmachtspolitik*, pp. 40 ff.; Hugo von Pohl, *Aus Aufzeichnungen und Briefen*, pp. 7 ff.; and Marinearchiv, *Der Krieg zur See, 1914–1918*, 1st ser., vol. 1, *Der Krieg in der Nordsee* (Berlin, 1920).

4 Bethmann to Loebell, Sept. 8, 1914, BA *Nachlass* Loebell. Riezler Diary, Sept. 9, 13: "I cannot shake the impression that French leadership is superior to ours. Nevertheless there is no cause for fear because of our splendid average." One week later he mused: "Apparently tactical mistakes have been made and now everything is being thrown to the right wing," while on September 30 he agonized over "the still undecided battle, the continuing possibility of encirclement on the right." Only on October 12 could it no longer be denied that "our command in the West apparently lacked genius" and the Schlieffen gamble was failing. Cf. also Reichsarchiv, *Der Weltkrieg, 1914 bis 1918* (Berlin, 1925–44), especially vol. 4, *Der Marne Feldzug: Die Schlacht*, pp. 508 ff., and for the extensive literature of the subsequent controversy, G. Jäschke, "Zum Problem der Marneschlacht von 1914," *HZ* 190 (1960) : 311 ff.

5 Valentini Diary, Sept. 9 ff.; BA *Nachlass* Thimme. Bethmann to AA, Sept. 19, 1914; AA, Wk. secr., vol 1. H. von Moltke, *Erinnerungen, Briefe, Dokumente*, pp. 304 ff.; Erich von Falkenhayn, *Die Oberste Heeresleitung, 1914–1916, in ihren wichtigsten Entschliessungen* (Berlin, 1920), pp. 1 ff.; and Erich Ludendorff, *Meine Kriegserinnerungen, 1914–1918* (Berlin, 1919), pp. 32 ff. Bethmann to Hertling, Nov. 15, BHStA MA I 961. Bethmann to Hammann, Nov. 14, DZA Po

Nachlass Hammann. Bethmann to Weizsäcker, Nov. 10, 1914, *Privatnachlass* Weizsäcker. Riezler Diary, Sept. 23: "This morning the chancellor was unbearable, despite the news of the submarine which had sunk three British cruisers. His complaining is turning into a mania. When I present him with foreign press clippings which speak of an inner tiring of France, he becomes quite rude and says 'I don't believe anything anymore.' " Cf. also Janssen, ed., *Treutler,* pp. 16 ff.: "The battle of the Marne and the failure of Moltke formed *the* great turning point in the kaiser's life."

6 Riezler Diary, Nov. 8, 22, 26, Dec. 5, 1914, Oct. 16, 1915. Part of the disagreement hinged on a different assessment of priorities: "Apparently [Falkenhayn] wants war against England, saying that if we eliminate France and Russia cheaply, we would overcome England. But how, if that fails? Then the entire war would be lost." Cf. also K. H. Janssen, *Der Kanzler und der General: Die Führungskrise um Bethmann Hollweg und Falkenhayn, 19714–1916* (Göttingen, 1967), pp. 56 ff. and Hans von Zwehl, *Erich von Falkenhayn* (Berlin, 1926).

7 Riezler Diary, Dec. 12, 31, 1914, Jan. 2, 7, 1915. Bethmann memorandum for Wahnschaffe of conversation with William II, Jan. 7, 1915, BA *Nachlass* Haeften, first published by E. Zechlin, "Friedensbestrebungen," pp. 49 ff. Cf. also Ritter, *Kriegskanzler,* pp. 66 ff.; Fischer, *Griff,* pp. 217 ff.; Gutsche, *Deutschland* 2 : 62 ff. and E. Zechlin, "Ludendorff im Jahre 1915. Unveröffentlichte Briefe," *HZ* 211 (1970): 316 ff.

8 Riezler Diary, Jan. 25, 1915. Valentini Diary, Jan. 3 ff., BA *Nachlass* Thimme. G. Jagow, "Die Frage eines Wechsels der OHL, January 1915," in AA *Nachlass* Jagow, MS "Politische Aufsätze." Bethmann to Wahnschaffe, Jan. 13, 1915, DZA Po, Rkz. 2,398/1. Bethmann to Lyncker, Jan. 14, 1915, BA, Kl. Erw. 342-1. Cf. also the MS "Erinnerungen" of William II's adjutant, Max von Mutius, BA *Nachlass* Mutius and Müller, *Regierte?,* p. 82. Bethmann to Treutler, April 4, 1915, in Janssen, ed., *Treutler,* pp. 227 ff.

9 For the delineation of military and civilian spheres cf. the correspondence between Bethmann and Falkenhayn, culminating in the chancellor's letter of Oct. 18, 1915, AA, Dld. 122, no. 16 secr. Cf. the material in the AA, Wk. secr. vols. 2 ff., especially Bethmann to Foreign Office, Nov. 26, 1914 and Bethmann to Falkenhayn, Mar. 17, 1915. See also Lerchenfeld to Hertling July 8, 1915, BHStA MA III 2691/5. Riezler Diary, Mar. 30, Apr. 4, May 22, June 4, 10, July 7, 11, 12, 28, 1915. Bethmann to Weizsäcker, July 3, 1915, *Privatnachlass* Weizsäcker. Cf. also Bethmann to Treutler, Mar. 14, 1915, DZA Po, Rkz, Wk. vol. 3 and Bethmann to Hutten-Czapski, Apr. 21, 1915, ibid., *Nachlass* Hutten. Gerard Silberstein, "The Serbian Campaign 1915: Its Military Implications," *International Review of History and Political Science* 3 (1966) : 115 ff.

10 Bethmann to Eisendecher, January 18, 1915, AA *Nachlass* Eisendecher. Riezler Diary, Oct. 11, 1914, Mar. 30, Apr. 1, July 11, Oct. 16, 1915. Wild von Hohenborn, MS "Tagebuch," Dec. 16, 1915, as well as frequent similar references in his correspondence to his wife, BA *Nachlass* Wild. Bethmann to Valentini, Aug. 11, 1915, DZA Me *Nachlass* Valentini. Cf. also Wilhelm Groener, *Lebenserinnerungen: Jugend-Generalstab-Weltkrieg* (Göttingen, 1957) ed. Hiller von Gaertringen; Crown Prince Rupprecht von Bayern, *Mein Kriegstagebuch,* vols. 1 and 2 (Berlin, 1929); and Albrecht von Thaer, "Generalstabsdienst an der Front und in der OHL," in *Abhandlungen der Akademie der Wissenschaften in Göttingen, Phil.-Hist. Klasse,* vol. 3 ed. by S. Kähler. See also Janssen, ed., *Treutler,* pp. 173 ff. for the ambassador's effort to mediate.

11 Pohl to Bethmann, Nov. 7, 1914; Bethmann to Foreign Office, Nov. 21, 1914; Bethmann memorandum, Dec. 27, 1914; partially reprinted in Arno Spindler, *Der*

Handelskrieg mit U-Booten (Berlin, 1932) 1 : 53 ff. For the originals cf. AA, Wk. no. 18 secr. and Wk. no. 18 secr. adhib. no. 1. Cf. also Karl E. Birnbaum, *Peace Moves and U-boat Warfare,* pp. 22 ff., unfortunately lacking detail before April 1916. Cf. also H. von Pohl, *Aus Aufzeichnungen und Briefen,* and especially A. von Tirpitz, *Deutsche Ohnmachtspolitik,* pp. 281 ff. Andreas Michelsen, *Der U-Bootskrieg, 1914–1918* (Leipzig, 1925) is little more than a navalist polemic.

12 The issue of the Zeppelin bombing of London paralleled submarine warfare since, like Tirpitz, Count Zeppelin had caught the fancy of a vindictive public demanding the punishment of "perfidious Albion." Bethmann would only allow the bombing of strategic targets, considering retaliation against civilians morally and politically indefensible, since it stiffened the British will to fight. The affair led to a highly controversial exchange of letters, exploited by the anti-Bethmann fronde, collected in DZA Po, Rkz. 2,448/2.

13 Memorandum by the Admiralty, Jan. 7, 1915, cited in Spindler, *Handelskrieg* 1 : 58 ff. Müller, *Regierte?,* pp. 79 ff. Riezler Diary, Dec. 23(?) 1914, Jan. 17, 1915, the first entry referring to the Wiegand interview: "Pohl is enraged about it. Moreover he has himself celebrated as future chancellor." For the text of the interview cf. Tirpitz, *Ohnmachtspolitik,* pp. 621 ff. Cf. also the otherwise so reliable Ernest R. May, *The World War and American Isolation, 1914–1917* (Cambridge, Mass. 1959), p. 116 n. 11 for a slight misreading of Gothic type, i.e. not *verstören* but *zerstören* in the original. The spate of prosubmarine memoranda is in Spindler, *Handelskrieg* 1 : 225 ff. and in B. Kaulisch, "Denkschriften zum U-Boot-Krieg, 1914–1916," *ZfMG* (1970), pp. 693–704.

14 Curiously enough there is no contemporary document on the decisive conference of Feb. 1, 1915. For an attempt at reconstruction cf. Spindler, *Handelskrieg* 1 : 78 ff. On Feb. 6 the young Riezler noted only: "Finally the submarine blockade—perhaps it will have some success anyway." Stresemann to Rippler, Feb. 15, 1915, encouraged by a letter from Captain Capelle of the same day: "For myself I confidently look forward to the use of the submarines in the intended manner." Stresemann *Nachlass,* FO microfilm roll 3,055. Valentini Diary, Feb. 4, 1915, BA *Nachlass* Thimme. For Müller's resentful reaction (he had been circumvented in the decision), cf. *Regierte?,* pp. 87–88. The only direct clue to Bethmann's personal role is the passage cited from an undated refutation of Tirpitz's memoirs (written after 1919 and before the second volume of the *Betrachtungen*), which indicates that he was consulted only in preliminary discussions, but that the decisive *Immediatvortrag* occurred without his presence; BA, Kl. Erw. 342-1. Riezler Diary, Feb. 17. For a vivid narrative of how the navy brass stampeded William II into a decision when he could not consult the civilian leadership, see Janssen, ed., *Treutler,* pp. 192 ff.

15 Bryan to Gerard, Feb. 10, 1915, *FRUS* (1915), pp. 98 ff. Riezler Diary, Feb. 17: "During the last days [the chancellor] has been in such a [gloomy] mood . . . that I almost despair in the possibility of propping up this man bereft of joy and surrounded by sorrows." The "good note to America in the submarine question is the work of Helfferich. Kriege's draft was impossible." Ibid., Feb. 27. For Bethmann's view of the British blockade cf. his interview with Dr. Holtermann of the *Aftenposten,* Feb. 9, 1915, Schulthess's *GK* (1915), 1 : 80–81. The German answer is in Gerard to Bryan, Feb. 17, 1915, *FRUS* (1915), pp. 112 ff. Spindler, *Handelskrieg* 1 : 114 ff. Müller, *Regierte?,* pp. 90 ff. Riezler Diary, Mar. 20, 30, urging "the chancellor to direct a grand note with historical themes to the Americans, starting with the U-boat blockade, going through the entire escalation of breaches of international law, and culminating in starvation and the therefore necessary evacuation of Belgium." Bethmann to Bundesrat, Apr. 7, 1915,

Deuerlein, *Bundesratsausschuss*, pp. 279 ff. For a detailed and compelling exposition of the American point of view cf. Arthur S. Link, *Wilson: The Struggle
for Neutrality, 1914–1915* (Princeton, 1960), pp. 322 ff.

16 Bethmann to Bachmann, May 6, 1915, Spindler, *Handelskrieg* 2 : 86 ff., 98 ff.
Müller, *Regierte?*, pp. 101 ff. J. H. Bernstorff, *Deutschland und Amerika* (Berlin,
1920), pp. 126 ff.; James W. Gerard, *My Four Years in Germany* (New York, 1917);
J. C. Grew, *Turbulent Era: A Diplomatic Record of Forty Years 1904–1945*, vol. 1
(Boston, 1952); L. Cecil, *Albert Ballin*, pp. 248 ff.; Birnbaum, *Peace Moves*, pp.
27 ff.; and E. R. May, *The World War*, pp. 133 ff. For the American note Bryan to
Gerard, May 13, 1915, see *FRUS* (1915), pp. 393 ff., and Link, *Wilson* 3 : 380 ff.
Bethmann to parliamentary leaders, May 13, 27, 1915, WP. For the first German
reply, dated May 29, cf. *FRUS* (1915), pp. 419 ff. See also Jagow's interview with a
UP representative on June 2, 1915, Schulthess's *GK* (1915), 1 : 210–11.

17 Bethmann to Treutler, May 29, 1915, AA, Wk. no. 18 secr., vol. 2. Tirpitz note,
May 30, 1915, *Deutsche Ohnmachtspolitik*, pp. 346 ff. Riezler Diary, May 31,
June 10, 1915. Spindler, *Handelskrieg*, pp. 99 ff. Müller, *Regierte?*, pp. 105 ff. Cf.
Valentini Diary, Aug. 30, 1915, BA *Nachlass* Thimme.

18 Lansing to Gerard, June 9, 1915, *FRUS*, 1915, pp. 436 ff. Riezler Diary, June 10,
June 23, 1915: "Fortunately the chancellor can defend his attitude toward America
with the agreement of the *milites* on land." Bachmann notes of conference in the
chancellery, June 22, 1915, in Tirpitz, *Deutsche Ohnmachtspolitik*, pp. 364 ff. Bethmann to Hertling, July 2, BHStA MA I 961, Müller, *Regierte?*, pp. 110 ff. Lansing
to Gerard, July 8, 1915, *FRUS* (1915), p. 462 and Gerard to Lansing, July 8, 1915,
ibid., pp. 463 ff. Jagow to Bachmann, June 21, 1915, AA, Wk. 18 secr., 2 and Bethmann to Weizsäcker, July 3, 1915, *Privatnachlass* Weizsäcker: "I do not know the
plans of the American government after Bryan's resignation, and I am completely
in the dark." He had to rely on private information "interesting, but meanwhile
outdated." For the background in Washington cf. Link, *Wilson* 3 : 42 ff. and May,
The World War, pp. 137 ff. Cf. also Spindler, *Handelskrieg* 2 : 171 ff.; Bernstorff,
Deutschland, pp. 159 ff. For the submarine petition of the six industrial organizations of June 28, 1915, cf. the Stresemann Papers, roll 3,056.

19 Lansing to Gerard, July 21, *FRUS* (1915), pp. 480 ff. Riezler Diary, July 12, "renewed
fracas with the navy," Aug. 28, 29, 1915. Helfferich to Bethmann, Aug. 5, 1915. Cf.
also Helfferich, *Der Weltkrieg*, pp. 317 ff., in general quite accurate, and J. Williamson, *Helfferich*, pp. 156 ff. Müller, *Regierte?*, pp. 121 ff., 125 ff. Bethmann to Tirpitz, Aug. 6, 1915, and conference of Aug. 26, *Deutsche Ohnmachtspolitik*, pp.
384 ff. Spindler, *Handelskrieg* 2 : 190 ff., 268 ff. Bethmann to Treutler, Aug. 25,
1915, AA, Wk. 18a, 12.

20 Tirpitz to William II, Aug. 27, 1915. *Deutsche Ohnmachtspolitik*, pp. 409 ff. Riezler
Diary, Sept. 2, 10, 1915: "The imperial naval office agitates continually, paints
Holtzendorff as defeatist, and claims that before his appointment he handed in a
memorandum arguing against establishing ourselves at the coast of Flanders, which
is untrue." Valentini Diary, August 28, 1915, BA *Nachlass* Thimme; Müller, *Regierte?*, pp. 126 ff. For domestic reasons the chancellor "was visibly relieved that
Tirpitz will stay on but aghast that another big liner . . . had been torpedoed."
Bethmann to party leaders, Nov. 29, 1915, WP. Bethmann to Hertling, Sept. 10,
1915, BHStA MA I 968. Cf. also Lerchenfeld to Hertling, Sept. 6, 8, 10, 1915, ibid.
and Hohenlohe to Burian, Sept. 6, 1915, HHStA, PA III, 171B.

21 Bethmann to Hutten-Czapski, Aug. 30, 1915, DZA Po *Nachlass* Hutten. Bethmann
to Treutler, Aug. 29, 1915; Bethmann to Holtzendorff, Sept. 2, 1915; and Bethmann
to William II, Sept. 9, 1915, AA, Wk. 18 secr., 3. For Bethmann's personal reaction
to the facts of the Arabic case cf. his pencil note of (Sept.?) 16, 1915, AA, Wk. no.

18a, 12. Cf. also his marginal note on Bernstorff to AA, Oct. 19, 1915, AA, Wk. no. 18a, 13. For Bernstorff's increasing concessions cf. Aug. 24, Sept. 1, 8, and Oct. 6, as well as Gerard's reports of the struggle in Berlin and Jagow's final statement, cf. *FRUS* (1915), pp. 524 ff., 603 ff., Bernstorff, *Deutschland und Amerika*, p. 164. See also Link, *Wilson* 3 : 572 ff.; May, *The World War*, pp. 218 ff.; and Birnbaum, *Peace Moves*, pp. 32 ff. Spindler, *Handelskrieg* 2 : 286 ff.

22 Riezler Diary, Dec. 19, 1915: "None of these actions is decisive. Meanwhile everyone bleeds to death." Ibid., Jan. 11, 1916. Bethmann to Oettingen, Sept. 4, 1915, AA *Nachlass* Oettingen. That cooperation with Holtzendorff might not last forever is clear from Bethmann's marginalia to the Chief of the Admiral Staff's letter of Oct. 27, 1915, denouncing his desire for the resumption of unrestricted submarine warfare against *all* enemy ships as "a surprising and apparently utterly impracticable proposal. We have not made the concession to refrain from torpedoing liners without warning in September to withdraw it in November." AA, Wk. 18 secr., 4. Bethmann to Wild von Hohenborn, Nov. 29, 1915, DZA Po, Rkz. 2398/5, also Lerchenfeld to Hertling, Dec. 14, 1915, BHStA MA III 2691/7.

23 Riezler Diary, Jan. 11, 13, 1916. Müller, *Regierte?*, pp. 145 ff. Tirpitz, *Deutsche Ohnmachtspolitik*, pp. 450 ff.; Spindler, *Handelskrieg* 3 : 71 ff., especially Bethmann's conference with Holtzendorff, Jan. 8, 1915. Janssen, *Kanzler und General*, pp. 184 ff. Bethmann memorandum, Jan. 19, 1916, AA, Wk. 18 secr. adhib. 1, 1, reprinted by Birnbaum in *Peace Moves*, pp. 145 ff.

24 Holtzendorff to Bethmann, Jan. 7, 1916, cited in Spindler, *Handelskrieg* 3 : 72 ff. Riezler Diary, Jan. 18: "Last night with the chancellor. To myself and Zech he read the excellent, restrained, and thoughtful memorandum which he has drawn up in the submarine question. In his own way he brings up all reasons against it slowly and deliberately, and emphasizes primarily that the expected decrease of enemy tonnage will be cancelled by a possible increase of 3½ million tons which Germany has in American ports." January 26, February 1, 4, 6, 1916. His assistant did "not know why he perhaps still wants to run this enormous risk . . . I suspect that his chief argument is unconsciously his shyness in refusing that means which all military advisors of the emperor profess not to be able to do without, and his lack of anything to end the war by the end of 1916." Müller, *Regierte?*, pp. 147 ff. Bethmann to Treutler, Jan. 21, 1916, AA, Wk. 18 secr. adhib. 1, 1. For a completely new piece of evidence on the submarine struggle in early 1916, cf. Bethmann's "Aufzeichnung" (corrected in some other handwriting) in the BA Kl. Erw. 342-1, especially for his audience with William II on Feb. 3, 1916. See also Lerchenfeld to Hertling, Jan. 28, 1916, BHStA MA III 2691/8.

25 Gerard to Lansing, Jan. 29, 1916, in *FRUS* (1916), pp. 154 ff. Riezler Diary, Feb. 6, 1916. Müller, *Regierte?*, pp. 151 ff. Bethmann interview with Wiegand, Feb. 9, 1916, in Schulthess's *GK*, 1916, p. 38. Link, *Wilson* 4 : 95 ff., 158 ff. Lansing to Gerard, Feb. 17, 1916, in *FRUS* (1916), p. 173. Spindler, *Handelskrieg* 3 : 87 ff. for the new orders and growing popular protests. Bethmann to AA, Feb. 19, 1916, AA, Wk. 18 secr., 6. Riezler Diary, Feb. 11, 1916: "Strange, as soon as the Conservatives begin to move against the government, all commissars in Prussia, from ministers down to secret counsellors, shake their heads in fear." Riezler could only barely prevent the publication of the hostile resolution of the commission: "These people would never dare that if they did not think the government weak, because of the incredible timidity of the majority of the officials and the chancellor's manner of remaining considerate until the last possible moment." Cf. also Schulthess's *GK* 1 : (1916), 38–39, and Stresemann's undated note of a submarine session with the chancellor early in 1916, as well as the meeting of Feb. 19, 1916, in Stresemann Papers, reel 3,064. See also the petition of the industrial organizations in favor

of submarine warfare of Jan. 20, 1916, ibid. and Larisch to Burian, Feb. 14, HHStA
PA III 172, as well as Lerchenfeld to King Ludwig, Feb. 19, 1916, BHStA MA III
2631/8. May, *The World War*, pp. 253 ff. The domestic underpinnings of the submarine struggle have been too much neglected by historical scholarship.

26 Bethmann to Zimmermann, Feb. 19, 1916, AA, Wk. 18 secr. adhib. 1, 2, Riezler
Diary, Feb. 22, 1916. The chancellor's assistant called silent torpedoing a "criminal
policy" in contrast to the "desperado policy" of an open announcement, and
counseled Bethmann to resign if he lost in the submarine struggle. Cf. Bethmann,
"Aufzeichnung," BA Kl. Erw. 342–1: "The political leadership could not effectively counter this agitation, since the possibility of a conflict with America existed
even without submarine warfare," and in that case exact "figures on the actual
number of submarines . . . proving the impossibility of forcing England to its
knees, would have worsened morale in the country considerably." Bethmann to
Jagow, Feb. 24, 1916, and Bethmann's long memorandum, written earlier but dated
on Feb. 29, 1916, in AA, Wk. 18 secr. 7. For analysis cf. Birnbaum, *Peace Moves*,
pp. 51 ff.; Ritter, *Kriegskanzler*, pp. 199 ff.; Fischer, *Griff*, pp. 361 ff.; J. Williamson,
Helfferich, pp. 158–59; and Baldur Kaulisch, "Die Auseinandersetzungen über den
uncingeschränkten U-Boot-Krieg innerhalb der herrschenden Klassen im zweiten
Halbjahr 1916 und seine Eröffnung im Februar 1917," *Politik im Krieg*, pp. 90 ff.,
also Bethmann to the Prussian Ministry of State, Feb. 15, 1916, DZA Me, Rep. 90a,
B III 2b no. 6, vol. 165.

27 Riezler Diary, Feb. 22: "I do not believe that the kaiser will decide against the
chancellor if he is firm. . . . The navy rejects all compromise forms of submarine
warfare, exceptions for liners and neutrals, with ever new excuses. Of course there
is something foul there." The chancellor's assistant was appalled by the "lack of
conscience of the agitators, the people believe we have 60–200 U-boats, and in fact
we have 15 big ones, which alone can be used for blockading the Atlantic." Ibid.,
Feb. 29: "The question is clear: With the given number of submarines, nothing
can be done that means war with America. The greatest difficulty is the temper
of the chief of general staff, who declares we have no other means of victory and
we must end the war within six to eight months." Cf. also the increasingly alarmist
reports of Lerchenfeld to Hertling, Feb. 21, 26, 28, BHStA MA III 2691/8, and
Hohenlohe to Burian, Mar. 8, 1916, HHStA PA III 172. Kühlmann to AA, Feb.
23, 1916, and the other correspondence in AA, Wk. 18 secr. adhib. 1, 2 ff.

28 Riezler Diary, Mar. 7, 1916: "Falkenhayn was very wild." Riezler speculated that
he had been put up to it by Minister of War Wild, who "boasted of it. That one
is in general an utterly inferior chap, a repulsive parasite, etc." Bethmann
"Aufzeichnung," BA Kl. Erw. 342–1. Cf. also the fascinating undated note by Bethmann regarding submarine warfare, probably used as the basis for his report to
the emperor, which lists nine major reasons against the decision; and Bethmann
to Jagow, Mar. 5, 1916, reporting the result. AA, Wk. 18 secr. abhib. 1, 4. Janssen,
ed., *Treutler*, pp. 196 ff., 238 ff., and Müller, *Regierte?*, pp. 159 ff. Valentini Diary,
Mar. 4, 1916, BA *Nachlass* Thimme. Tirpitz, *Deutsche Ohnmachtspolitik*, pp. 485 ff.
Spindler, *Handelskrieg* 3 : 101 ff. Birnbaum, *Peace Moves*, pp. 61 ff. Bethmann to
AA, Mar. 4, 1916, AA, Wk. 18, secr., 6. Cf. also Holtzendorff's summary to
Graevenitz: "First diplomacy, then U-boat war." Graevenitz to Weizäcker, Mar. 5/6,
1916, *Privatnachlass* Weizäcker, courtesy of Professor Leonidas Hill.

29 Bethmann "Aufzeichnung," BA Kl. Erw., 342-1. Riezler Diary, Mar. 7: "The agitation is really too incredible—it is being done quite openly. Navy officers appeared
at the *Lokalanzeiger* and attempted to get it to change its line by offering seduc-
tive publishing contracts." Ibid., Mar. 10: "The U-boat agitation in the press has
been stopped by Falkenhayn, who understands the emperor's position." For the

pressure of Bethmann's intimates cf. the numerous Wahnschaffe telegrams, Mar. 2 ff., 1916, in AA, Wk. 18, secr. adhib. 1, 4, as well as Bethmann to Tirpitz, Mar. 5, 1916, ibid., Bethmann circular to the major embassies, Mar. 16, giving the "campaign emanating in the RMA" as reason for the Grand Admiral's dismissal. Cf. Lerchenfeld to King Ludwig, Mar. 4, 1916, BHStA MA III 2691/8, and Hohenlohe to Burian, Mar. 15, 1916, HHStA PA III 172: "The grave responsibility of the chancellor and the F.O. lies rather in their failure to act as 'master in their own house' in time." Tirpitz, *Deutsche Ohnmachtspolitik*, pp. 488 ff., 635 ff. Helfferich, *Der Weltkrieg*, pp. 328 ff. Müller, *Regierte?*, pp. 163 ff. See also the Valentini Diary, Mar. 9, 1916, BA *Nachlass* Thimme, and Wild's notes in his own papers, ibid.

30 Riezler Diary, Mar. 10: "The domestic shock will pass and the agitators will be forced to pipe down." Mar. 15, 19: "What has this unfortunate man with the beard, lying mouth, and spongy face actually done? He created the navy and opinion in favor of it—the latter politically a fatal misleading of public thinking—the former falsely built and unrealistically thought out (risk theory)." Mar. 26: "Strange. Tirpitz is basically a charlatan. The people admire in him the will they miss in Bethmann." Cf. also Stresemann's comments refuting Max Weber's anti-submarine memorandum of Mar. 14, 1916, and the notes of the Berlin representative of the *Hamburger Kurier*, Mar. 19, 1916, on Bethmann's press briefing, Stresemann Papers, reel 3,064. Bethmann to the party leaders, Mar. 14, 1916, the first major submarine debate with the parliamentarians, WP. Bethmann to Prussian Ministry of State, Mar. 15, 1916, DZA Me, Rep. 90a B III 2b no. 6, 165; Bethmann to Bundesrat, Mar. 15, BHStA MA I 966; May, *The World War*, pp. 266 ff.

31 Riezler Diary, Mar. 30, 1916: "Heydebrand, Bassermann, Westarp are nevertheless evil Jesuits. The chancellor was impressive and adroit [in the Budget Commission]. Everything was directed toward calming things down." Minutes of the *Haushaltsausschuss* meeting, Mar. 28/29, 1916, and Stresemann's notes as well as typewritten explanation of the National Liberal submarine resolution and notes of negotiations with Bethmann, Stresemann Papers, reels 3,062, 3,064; Lerchenfeld to Hertling, Mar. 14, 17, 29, 1916, BHStA MA III 2691/8. See also Velics to Burian, Mar. 19, 1916, and Hohenlohe to Burian, Mar. 20, 29, 1916, HHStA, PA III, 172B. See also Bethmann's reports to Treutler, Mar. 17 ff., 1916, AA. Wk. 18 secr. adhib. 1, 5, and Bethmann to Treutler, Mar. 22, 30, 1916, AA, Wk. no. 18 secr., 9. Cf. also Gerard's reports to Lansing, Mar. 18 ff., *FRUS* (1916), pp. 208 ff. Tirpitz, *Ohnmachtspolitik*, pp. 511 ff. has a whole series of testimonials. See also H. P. Hanssen, *Diary of a Dying Empire*, pp. 135 ff., and Bethmann to Valentini, Mar. 26, 1916, DZA Me, Rep. 89H, 1 Gen. 6. Cf. Westarp, *Konservative Politik* 2 : 124 ff.; Erzberger, *Erlebnisse*, 213 ff.; and Haussmann, *Schlaglichter*, pp. 58 ff.

32 Riezler Diary, Apr. 15, 24: "It is better not to run the risk and to make a grand gesture, without regard for the fools at home, to reestablish international law unilaterally and to make the U. S. responsible for reaffirming it in general," Apr. 28, 1916. Bethmann to Reichstag, Apr. 5, 1916, his first major submarine speech, in Thimme, *Kriegsreden*, Apr. 5, 1916. Link, *Wilson* 4 : 233 ff.; Lansing to Gerard, Apr. 18, 1918, and following documents, *FRUS* (1916), pp. 232 ff. Bethmann marginalia on German note to U.S., Apr. 10; Bethmann to Treutler, Apr. 23, demanding postponement of the campaign since the situation had not changed; Bethmann to Jagow, Apr. 21, sketching the outlines of the German answer; and Bethmann marginalia on letter from Hohenlohe, Apr. 24, 1916, all in AA, Wk. 18 secr., 11. Cf. also Bethmann note for report to H.M. Apr. 18, 1916, Wk. 18 secr. adhib. 1, 5. Lerchenfeld to King Ludwig, Apr. 26, 1916, BHStA, MA III 2691/9, and Hohenlohe to Burian, Apr. 10, 1916, HHStA, 172B. Cf. also Müller, *Regierte?*, pp. 168 ff.; Spindler, *Handelskieg* 3 : 159 ff.; and Birnbaum, *Peace Moves*, pp. 75 ff.

33 Bethmann note of conference, Apr. 26, as well as the ensuing correspondence with Jagow and Treutler, AA, Wk. 18 secr. adhib. 1, 5. Riezler Diary, Apr. 28, 29: "If we settle once and for all with America, peace is probable this year even without submarine warfare. Hope: Wilson's pressure on England and Japan's on Russia." Apr. 30: "I believe the American ambassador considers us half insane. He does not see why we choke on [our answers] so much and is quite right in saying: 'You will win the war anyway,' and repeats that Wilson would be forced to move against England after the settlement of this question, and justifies it." Riezler noted, "The kaiser is very impressed by this attitude of the chief of staff, especially by the trump of Verdun, and wavers between both. The chancellor, too, has suffered from this attempt to make him responsible for Verdun." May 7, 1916. Lerchenfeld to Hertling, May 3, 1916, BHStA MA I 957b. Müller, *Regierte?*, pp. 170 ff. Valentini Diary, Apr. 22 ff., BA *Nachlass* Thimme. Wild von Hohenborn Diary, May 2 ff., 1916, especially resentful about Falkenhayn's ill-timed resignation: "Falkenhayn is and remains a weakling when the chips are down." Spindler, *Handelskrieg* 3 : 141 ff. Tirpitz, *Deutsche Ohnmachtspolitik*, pp. 529 ff. Helfferich, *Weltkrieg*, pp. 329 ff.

34 Riezler Diary, May 7, June 29. Zimmermann briefing of the press, May 5, as well as Stresemann's notes of a conversation with the Undersecretary, May 14, 1916, Stresemann Papers, reel 3,062. Bethmann to Bundesrat, May 4, 1916, BHStA MA III 2691/9. Bethmann to parliamentary leaders, July 17, 1916, WP. Bethmann to Reichstag, June 6, 1916, Thimme, *Kriegsreden*, pp. 123 ff. Cf. also Bethmann's draft telegrams of May 5 concerning Wilson's mediation and his long marginalia on a cable from Jagow, May 12, 1916, in AA, Wk. 18 secr., 16; and his telegram to Holtzendorff, June 13, 1916; his marginalia on a Holtzendorff letter on July 13; his reply to the chief of the admiral staff of July 18; and his letter to Müller of Aug. 7, ibid., vols. 18 ff. Cf. also Gerard's long report of May 3, the German note (May 4), Lansing's reply (May 8), and Gerard's translation of the *Kölnische Zeitung* story, May 8, 1916, in *FRUS* (1916), pp. 255 ff. Link, *Wilson* 4 : 259 ff. Müller, *Regierte?*, pp. 175 ff. Spindler, *Handelskrieg* 3 : 200 ff.; Bethmann to Bundesrat, Aug. 8/9, 1916, BHStA MA I 966; Bethmann to parliamentary leaders Aug. 5, 1916, WP. Bethmann to William II, May 23, 1916, AA, Wk. 18 secr. adhib. 1, 5. Lerchenfeld to Hertling, May 2, 6, 1916, BHStA MA III 2691/9. Birnbaum, *Peace Moves*, pp. 89 ff.

35 Müller, *Regierte?*, pp. 185 ff., 200 ff., Bethmann to Valentini, June 14, 1916, DZA Me *Nachlass* Valentini, and Schwertfeger, ed., *Kaiser und Kabinettschef*, pp. 228 ff. Riezler Diary, June 29, 1916. Wild Diary, June 17, 1916, BA *Nachlass* Wild. Janssen, *Kanzler und General*, pp. 210 ff., and "Der Wechsel in der Obersten Heeresleitung 1916," *VJHfZG* (1959), pp. 337 ff. Cf. also Valentini Diary, June 24 ff., BA *Nachlass* Thimme. Lerchenfeld to Dandl, June 19, 1916, BHStA MA III 2691/9. For Treutler's role and dismissal as scapegoat cf. Janssen, ed., *Treutler*, 212 ff.

36 Bethmann to Valentini, July 4, 10; Valentini to Bethmann, July 6, 1916, DZA Me *Nachlass* Valentini. Riezler Diary, Aug. 1, 1916: "Uncertain weeks; horrible battles. Military mistakes everywhere—struggle over Hindenburg's supreme command in the East. . . . The chancellor, with his usual skill with the emperor, finally pushed everything through." Müller, *Regierte?*, pp. 204 ff. Valentini Diary, July 22 ff., 1916, BA *Nachlass* Thimme. Wild Diary, July 24 ff., BA *Nachlass* Wild. Cf. also Bethmann to William II, July 23, 1916, AA, GHQ no. 225; and especially the whole correspondence between Bethmann and Grünau (the new FO representative in GHQ) July 8 ff., 1916, AA, GHQ no. 254. The official history, *Der Weltkrieg 1914 bis 1918*, 10 : 634 ff., underplays Bethmann's pivotal role, while Falkenhayn, *Die OHL*, pp. 240–41, and Ludendorff, *Meine Kriegserinnerungen*, pp. 180 ff., are

studiously cryptic. Cf. Groener, *Lebenserinnerungen*, pp. 310 ff. for more rewarding excerpts. Cf. also Lerchenfeld to Hertling, July 16, 31, Aug. 2, 1916, BHStA MA I 958 and MA III 2691/10.

37 Riezler Diary, Aug. 30, 1916. Valentini Diary, Aug. 21 ff., 1916, BA *Nachlass* Thimme. Müller, *Regierte?*, pp. 214 ff. Wild Diary, Aug. 24 ff., 1916, BA *Nachlass* Wild. Bethmann to Weizsäcker, Sept. 18, 1916, *Privatnachlass* Weizsäcker. Lerchenfeld to Hertling, Aug. 30, 1916, BHStA MA I 958; and Hohenlohe to Burian, Sept. 4, 1916, HHStA, PA III, 172B. For the relief of military circles, cf. Crown Prince Rupprecht, *Kriegstagebuch*, vol. 2. See also G. von Jagow, "Der Wechsel in der OHL, 1916," in MS "Politische Aufsätze," AA *Nachlass* Jagow. Cf. also Ritter, *Kriegskanzler*, pp. 225 ff., and Mommsen, "Die Regierung," pp. 147–48.

38 Riezler Diary, Apr. 30, 1916: "What is dangerous in our militarism—is the lack of education of the ruling caste." Bethmann to Valentini, July 4, 10, 1916, DZA Me *Nachlass* Valentini. Lerchenfeld to Hertling, Aug. 30, 1916, BHStA MA I 958. For the strength of the Hindenburg myth cf. Stresemann to Freigang, Sept. 16, 1916, Stresemann Papers, reel 3,065. Janssen, *Kanzler und General*, pp. 253 ff.; Vietsch, *Bethmann*, p. 235, for a chancellor complaint to Oettingen about the gambler Falkenhayn; and Gutsche, *Deutschland* 2 : 407 ff., which misses the irony of Bethmann's role in the structural crisis, intended to reassert the primacy of moderation and having in effect the opposite result.

39 Riezler Diary, Sept. 21, Nov. 3, 22, 1916: "Jagow cut off. The chancellor has been vacillating for a long time. Helfferich, Stumm, Wahnschaffe [were for it], and in the end gruff telegrams by the kaiser and Valentini's advice. Despite his energy, Zimmermann is a much weaker number. I fear that Ludendorff has agitated with the emperor." Ibid., Dec. 2, 1916. Cf. also Jagow, "Mein Rücktritt" and "Hindenburg" in his *Nachlass* AA, MS "Politische Aufsätze." Stresemann to Freigang, Sept. 11, 1916, Stresemann Papers, reel 3,065. For the increasing number of clashes cf. the Müller and Valentini diaries, the central war files of Foreign Office and Chancellery, Ludendorff, *Meine Kriegserinnerungen*, pp. 187 ff., and Helfferich, *Weltkrieg*, pp. 276 ff. Cf. also Ritter, *Kriegskanzler*, pp. 251 ff.; H. Weber, *Ludendorff und die Monopole*, pp. 41 ff.; and D. J. Goodspeed, *Ludendorff: Soldat, Diktator, Revolutionär* (Gütersloh, 1968).

40 Riezler Diary, Aug. 30: "With failure [I foresee] an extension of the war and a horrible ending—which without it could still hopefully be a draw. Most difficult of all decisions. If the possibilities are not too small, dare it—the nation will be ruined for a century by an unbearably bad peace if this weapon in which the people believe has not been used." Bethmann to Bundesrat, Aug. 28, Lerchenfeld protocol BHStA MA III 2691/10; to parliamentary leaders, Sept. 5, WP; and to Ministry of State, Aug. 19, 28, 1916, DZA Me, Rep 90a B III 2b no. 6, vol. 165. Riezler Diary, Sept. 21, 1916. Spindler, *Handelskrieg* 3 : 209 ff., minutes of a meeting on Aug. 31, 1916. Bethmann to Holtzendorff, Sept. 16, 1916, AA, Wk. 18 secr., 20. Bethmann to Bernstorff, Sept. 2, 1916, 2. UA., *Aktenstücke zur Friedensaktion Wilsons* 1 : 14. Müller, *Regierte?*, pp. 221 ff. Bethmann to Weizsäcker, Sept. 18, 1916, *Privatnachlass* Weizsäcker. Bethmann to Grünau, Oct. 1, and to Hindenburg, Oct. 6, 1916, AA, Wk. 16 secr., 20. Birnbaum, *Peace Moves*, pp. 151 ff. and J. Williamson, *Helfferich*, pp. 162 ff.

41 For the connection between the submarine agitation, the war aims movement, and the fronde, see also Dirk Stegmann, *Die Erben Bismarcks: Parteien und Verbände in der Spätphase des Wilhelminischen Deutschlands. Sammlungspolitik 1897–1918* (Cologne, 1970), pp. 471 ff. Bethmann to Reichstag, Sept. 28, 1916, Thimme, *Kriegsreden*, pp. 140 ff. Kohl, Minutes of Budget Committee, Oct. 2, 1916, BHStA MA III 2691/11. Lerchenfeld to Hertling, Oct. 7, 17, and Erzberger to

Hertling, Oct. 8, 1916, ibid., MA I 947 and MA 95,448. Larisch to Burian, Oct. 9, 13, 1916, HHStA, PA III, 172. Stresemann notes on session of Hauptausschuss, Oct. 20, 1916, Stresemann Papers, reel 3,063. For the exact transcript cf. DZA Po, Rtg. 1,301; and for the mood see H. P. Hanssen, *Diary*, pp. 144 ff. Cf. also the WP of Bethmann's session with the parliamentarians on Oct. 7, 1916. For the meeting of the *Unabhängige Ausschuss für einen deutschen Frieden* cf. the extensive minutes in Nostitz to Vitzthum, Oct. 18, 1916, SHStA as well as the shorter typewritten report in the AA, Wk. 18 secr., 21. For the significance of the Center Party resolution cf. K. Epstein, *Erzberger*, pp. 180 ff. and his criticism of W. Bongard, *Die Zentrumsresolution vom 7. Oktober 1916* (Cologne, 1917). Cf. Westarp, *Konservative Politik* 2 : 131 ff.; Erzberger, *Erlebnisse*, pp. 217 ff.; and Haussmann, *Schlaglichter*, pp. 63 ff.

42 For the power of the slogan "Submarines Go!" cf. the anonymous poem calling for the miracle weapon, for respect for the spirit of the navy, for fulfilling Tirpitz's legacy, for the unleashing of the Zeppelins, and for bold action by the kaiser:

> Mitleid ist Sünde, für Weiber gut
> Handelt es sich um des Volkes Blut.
> Hier, wo es Sein order Nichtsein heisst,
> Ziemt ein rücksichtsloser, kühn-männlicher Geist!
> Deutschland, eh Hunger Dich zwingt auf die Knie,
> Nimm deine Waffe und brauche sie,
> Deine furchtbarste Waffe, der Feinde Graus!
> U-boote raus, heraus!

Cf. Bethmann's testimony, *Friedensangebot und Ubootskrieg, passim*. Ludendorff, *Urkunden der* OHL, pp. 301 ff. Holtzendorff to Müller, Dec. 15, 1916, Müller, *Regierte?*, pp. 242 ff. For the complex interrelationship between peace and escalation cf. Birnbaum, *Peace Moves*, pp. 201 ff. and Link, *Wilson* 5 : 194 ff. See also Riezler Diary, Dec. 9, 1916: "It will be difficult as introduction to the submarines. It will take quite some time until the no comes and then only half—illusions and hope will long remain in suspense and will be used against the U-boats for a long time." Cf. also Janssen, ed., *Treutler*, pp. 208 ff.

43 Bethmann to Bundesrat, Dec. 11, Lerchenfeld protocol, BHStA MA I 958; Bethmann to parliamentary leaders, Dec. 11, WP. Riezler Diary, Dec. 29, 1916: "Strange man, great energy, wonderful strategist, political child, totally uneducated, discovering the most self-evident and also often erroneous things as new truths, but thoroughly loyal." The chancellor's assistant foresaw clearly that "things are getting worse all the time and the period of the greatest questions and most immediate differences between politics and warfare is still to come." Lersner to Bethmann, Dec. 22, 26; Bethmann to Lersner, Dec. 23, 26, 1916, AA, Wk. 18, secr., 25, and 2. UA., *Aktenstücke* 4 : 221 ff. Bethmann to Valentini, Dec. 31, 1916, DZA Me *Nachlass* Valentini. Valentini Diary, Jan. 2, BA *Nachlass* Thimme. Riezler Diary, Jan. 6, 1917. Helfferich, *Weltkrieg*, pp. 361 ff. Müller, *Regierte?*, pp. 245 ff. According to Treutler's successor Grünau, the cracks were papered over once more but "the tension had gone quite far."

44 Riezler Diary, Jan. 9, 1916: "It has suddenly come out that the navy wrote to the OHL on the 22d [of December] that armed enemy freighters do not matter and no increase can be gained by including them. Before it had always pressed for that. To the chancellor the admiralty said nothing about this and calmly attended the conference of the 29th in Pless where the note was agreed upon. Stranger yet, the OHL, which had received the navy letter on the 22d, did not

show it on the 29th—probably because of an accidental foul-up." Riezler was at a loss: "I don't know what will happen now. Strange, but after all previous experience I cannot see this as anything but a slow gliding into unrestricted submarine warfare despite all talk. Great tension about how the decision will go." Holtzendorff to Zimmermann, Jan. 6, 1917, with the admirality *Denkschrift* of Dec. 22. 1916. Helfferich, *Weltkrieg*, pp. 364 ff., and Williamson, *Helfferich*, pp. 190 ff. The dearth of documentation before the decision is typical of Bethmann, who, when not clear about a course of action, liked to withdraw into himself and commit nothing to paper. Cf. also Stresemann to Bassermann, Dec. 28, 1916: "Our cause is prospering. I am convinced that we must use every means for utmost energy in our conduct of the war," Stresemann Papers, reel 3,061.

45 Riezler Diary, Jan. 10, 1917: "We all have the feeling that this question was hanging over us like fate. If history followed the laws of tragedy, Germany should perish because of this fatal error, symbolizing all its previous mistakes. Today submarine warfare may be right and successful; that it was insanity in 1916 will be proven even in the best case by the threefold number of boats in 1917." Müller, *Regierte?*, pp. 247 ff. Valentini Diary, Jan. 9: "Grave discussions, Bethmann very excited." BA *Nachlass* Thimme. *Kaiser und Kabinettschef*, pp. 147 ff. Spindler, *Handelskrieg* 3 : 372 ff. Tirpitz, *Deutsche Ohnmachtspolitik*, pp. 591 ff. Ludendorff, *Urkunden der OHL*, pp. 322 ff. for the protocol of the first meeting with the military. Wahnschaffe to Bethmann, Jan. 9, 1917 (transmitting Helfferich's counter-memorandum), 2. UA, *Aktenstücke*, pp. 226 ff. Protocol of military conference on Jan. 8, and of crown council of Jan. 9, 1917, ibid., 318 ff. Helfferich, *Weltkrieg*, pp. 365 ff. Treutler explained the chancellor's reversal by his fear that a decision against unrestricted submarine warfare "could cost the kaiser his throne." Janssen, ed., *Treutler*, pp. 211 ff.

46 Riezler Diary, Jan. 10, 11, 31, 1917. Lerchenfeld to Hertling, Jan. 25, 1917, BHStA MA I 958. The Bavarian ambassador also advised the chancellor to continue in office. Müller, *Regierte?*, pp. 249 ff. Valentini Diary, Jan. 10 ff., 1917, BA *Nachlass* Thimme: "I am convinced that Bethmann's resignation is at present politically harmful." Bethmann's explanation to General Eisenhardt-Rothe, *Im Banne der Persönlichkeit* (Berlin, 1931), pp. 53 ff. Bethmann to Weizsäcker, Jan. 23, 1917, *Privatnachlass* Weizsäcker. For the significance of the decision cf. Link, *Wilson* 5 : 239 ff.; May, *World War*, pp. 413 ff.; Birnbaum, *Peace Moves*, pp. 304 ff.; Ritter, *Kriegskanzler*, pp. 349 ff.; Fischer, *Griff*, pp. 387 ff.; and Kaulisch, "Die Auseinandersetzungen," *Politik im Krieg*, pp. 111 ff. For Bethmann's resulting breakdown cf. Zech to Treutler, January 14, 1917, in Janssen, ed., *Treutler*, pp. 247–48.

47 Riezler Diary, Jan. 10, 11, 31, 1917. Bethmann to Prussian Ministry of State, Jan. 15, 1917, DZA Me, Rep. 90a B III 2b no. 6, vol. 166. Bethmann to Bundesrat, Jan. 16, and Jan. 31, Lerchenfeld summary, BHStA MA I 966 and WP. Bethmann to *Hauptausschuss*, Jan. 31, 1917, DZA Po, Rtg. 1307, and H. P. Hanssen, *Diary*, pp. 161 ff.: Bethmann's "voice was hoarse and rough. It was evidently very painful for him to plead for a policy which formerly he had passionately opposed. . . . *In the past* it would have been indefensible to begin submarine warfare, but *now* it would be indefensible *not* to conduct it. That was the opinion of our High Command as well as of our allies." Bethmann to Valentini, Jan. 22, 1917, DZA Me *Nachlass* Valentini. Cf. also Westarp, *Konservative Politik* 2 : 148 ff.; Haussmann, *Schlaglichter*, pp. 80 ff.; Scheidemann, *Zusammenbruch*, pp. 45 ff.; and Erzberger, *Erlebnisse*, pp. 220 ff.

48 Czernin, *In the World War*, pp. 131 ff. Link, *Wilson* 5 : 265 ff. Müller, *Regierte?*, pp. 252 ff. Bernstorff to Zimmermann, Jan. 27, and Bethmann to Bernstorff, Jan. 19, 2. UA, *Aktenstücke*, pp. 73 ff. Bernstorff, *Deutschland und Amerika*, pp. 353 ff.

Bethmann's testimony before the Investigating Commission, 2. UA, *Stenographische Berichte*, pp. 164 ff., 656 ff., 724 ff. Bethmann, "Entwurf für einen Artikel," BA Kl. Erw. 342–1. Riezler Diary, Jan. 31, 1917: "Zimmermann talked himself to death in the commission today, as fraternity student and boor. That is a statesman! How could the chancellor let Jagow go—he is just weak!" Thimme, *Kriegsreden*, pp. 187 ff. for an abbreviated version of his speech to the Budget Committee on Jan. 31, 1917. Cf. also his answer to a letter of workers and employees, Jan. 18, 1917, stressing the need for unity and *Durchhalten*, Schulthess's *GK* (1917), 1 : 30–31.

49 Riezler Diary, Jan. 31, 1917. Gerard to Lansing, Jan. 30, and Bernstorff to Lansing, Jan. 31, 1917, *FRUS* (1917), pp. 97 ff. Gerard to Lansing, Feb. 4, reporting a conversation with Bethmann, ibid., p. 114. Link, *Wilson* 5 : 290 ff. May, *The World War*, pp. 416 ff. The reasons for Wilson's failure to halt escalation on the level of armed neutrality and his decision to force the issue with Berlin are still somewhat obscure. Bethmann circular, Feb. 5, 1917, and his earlier draft in mid-January (n.d.), AA, Wk. 18 secr., 24, 27. Bethmann to Weizsäcker, Feb. 19, 1917: "You know how seriously I have always taken the American danger," but he went on to persuade the Württemberg premier nevertheless. *Privatnachlass* Weizsäcker. The slim study by Jürgen Möckelmann, *Deutsch-Amerikanische Beziehungen in der Krise* (Frankfurt, 1967), focuses only on German-Americans.

50 Riezler Diary, Feb. 14, 18, 20, 1917: "China's declaration of war is very sad for our Germans there and for our future. Is a more active policy of Wilson behind it?" Bethmann to Reichstag, Feb. 27, and less hopefully on Mar. 29, 1917. Thimme, *Kriegsreden*, pp. 196 ff., 227 ff. Riezler Diary, Mar. 4, 1917. Wolff Telegraph Bureau release about "an alleged attempt of reconciliation between the U. S. and Germany," Feb. 13, 1917 and *NAZ* article, "Fair Dealing," Mar. 8, 1917; Schulthess's *GK* (1917), 1 : 109–10, 265 ff., Link, *Wilson* 5 : 308 ff. Lerchenfeld to Hertling, Mar. 20, 1917, BHStA MA I 958. Zimmermann to Bernstorff, Jan. 16, 1917, and William II marginalia on letter from Holtzendorff, Mar. 18, 1917, 2. UA, *Aktenstücke*, pp. 335 ff. Lansing circular, Apr. 2, 1917, *FRUS* (1917), pp. 194 ff. Bethmann to Hertling, Mar. 27, 1917, BHStA MA I 976; and to Eisendecher, Apr. 6, 1917, AA *Nachlass* Eisendecher. Cf. B. Tuchmann, *The Zimmermann Telegram* (New York, 1959); F. Katz, "Die deutsche Verschwörung in Mexiko, 1914–1916," *Politik im Krieg*, pp. 118 ff.; and his *Deutschland, Diaz und die mexikanische Revolution: Die deutsche Politik in Mexiko, 1870–1920* (Berlin, 1964). For the American declaration of war in general, cf. the literature cited in Daniel M. Smith, *American Intervention 1917: Sentiment, Self-Interest or Ideals?* (Boston, 1966). For a scurrilous right-wing attack, feeding on the gaps and ambiguities of the Wilsonian case, cf. Heinrich Härtle, *Amerikas Krieg gegen Deutschland: Wilson gegen Wilhelm II—Roosevelt gegen Hitler* (Göttingen, 1968), pp. 86 ff.

51 Bethmann to Valentini, Apr. 10, 1917; DZA Me, Rep. 89H, I Prussia 1. Bethmann to Hertling, Apr. 11, 1917, BHStA MA I 961. Riezler Diary, Apr. 1, 1917: "The entire continent of Europe will doubtlessly starve in 1918—England will survive with American help and will win despite the submarines in 1918—because not only the opponents but also the allies will have collapsed. . . . The losses are higher than one had thought. In the long run this thing cannot be trusted." Apr. 6, 13, June 14, 1917. Müller, *Regierte?*, pp. 275 ff. Bethmann to Bundesrat, May 8, 1917, WP. Lerchenfeld to Hertling, June 9, 1917, BHStA MA I 958. Bethmann to Hindenburg, June 25, 1917, DZA Po, Rkz. 2,446. Bethmann to parliamentarians, July 2, 1917, WP and July 6, 9, 1917, H. P. Hanssen, *Diary*, pp. 201 ff. Lerchenfeld to Loessl, July 6, 1917, BHStA MA I 969. For the role the submarine issue played in the collapse of confidence in Bethmann cf. Stresemann's correspondence with

Ballin, June 27 and July 2, 1917, Stresemann Papers, reel 3,066 and Williamson, *Helfferich*, pp. 219 ff. For the performance of the submarines cf. Michelsen, *U-Bootskrieg*, pp. 196 ff.

52 Riezler Diary, Jan. 31, Feb. 25, 1917: "Strange are the ambition and lack of scruples of the military. In their personal politics all are much more amoral than the politicians. The cause is probably their one-sided education toward the officer's type [directed at] dash, resolution, and honor." On Mar. 11, 1917, Riezler denounced the Right's "alliance with Ludendorff, presently the most indispensable and therefore most powerful man." Valentini Diary, Jan. 25 ff., 1917, BA *Nachlass* Thimme. The conflict between Bethmann and the third OHL permeated all issues by the spring of 1917, but for one especially revealing instance cf. the irate correspondence between Bethmann and Ludendorff in June 1917 regarding the fate of Alsace-Lorraine, DZA Me, Rep. 89H, I Elsass-Lothringen, no. 6, vol. 3. Bethmann to Valentini, Dec. 31, 1916, ibid., *Nachlass* Valentini.

53 Riezler Diary, Apr. 24, 1916 and Apr. 13, 1917. Bethmann to Thimme, Oct. 12, 1918, BA *Nachlass* Thimme. Bethmann to Delbrück, Sept. 10, 1918, DSB *Nachlass* Delbrück. Bethmann to Rassow, July 20, 1920, *Privatnachlass* Rassow. Graevenitz to Weizsäcker, Mar. 5/6, 1916, *Privatnachlass* Weizsäcker. For a sustained defense of the chancellor's policies against the attacks of the historian Eduard Meyer, cf. Riezler's explanatory letters in DZA Po, Rkz. 2,410.

Chapter 10

1 Oscar A. H. Schmitz, *Das wirkliche Deutschland: Die Wiedergeburt durch den Krieg* (Munich, 1915). Friedrich Meinecke, *Die deutsche Erhebung von 1914* (Stuttgart, 1914). Ernst O. Borkowsky, *Unser Heiliger Krieg* (Weimar, 1914). Cf. also Adolf von Harnack's sigh: "We have rewon our dear, beloved, magnificent *fatherland*" in the series of *Deutsche Reden in schwerer Zeit*, printed as pamphlets (Berlin, 1914 ff.). For the phrase *the ideas of 1914* cf. also F. Ringer, *The Decline of the German Mandarins: The German Academic Community 1890–1933* (Cambridge, Mass., 1969), pp. 180 ff. Riezler Diary, Sept. 30, 1914.

2 Bethmann to Weizsäcker, Nov. 10, 1914; *Privatnachlass* Weizsäcker. Bethmann to the Prussian Ministry of State, Aug. 15, 1914, DZA Me, Rep. 90a B III 2b no. 6, vol. 163. Theodor Heuss, *Naumann*, pp. 430 ff. W. J. Mommsen, "Die Regierung Bethmann Hollweg und die öffentliche Meinung, 1914–1917," *VJHfZG* (1969), pp. 117-18. Cf. also Johanna Schellenberg, "Probleme der Burgfriedenspolitik im ersten Weltkrieg—Zur innenpolitischen Strategie und Taktik der herrschenden Klassen Deutschlands von 1914 bis 1916," (Dissertation, East Berlin, 1967) and Wilhelm Deist, *Militär und Innenpolitik im Weltkrieg 1914–1918*, 2 vols. (Düsseldorf, 1970). Tentative because of its insufficient documentation, Rudolf Koschnitzke, "Die Innenpolitik des Reichskanzlers von Bethmann Hollweg," (Dissertation, Kiel, 1951) is the only study of Bethmann's wartime domestic policy.

3 Conrad Haussmann, *Schlaglichter: Reichstagsbriefe und Aufzeichnungen* (Frankfurt, 1924), ed. U. Zeller, pp. 9 ff. Riezler Diary, Sept. 13, Oct. 1, 1914. See also D. Stegmann, *Die Erben Bismarcks*, pp. 449 ff. Matthias and Miller, eds., *David Tagebuch*, pp. 10 ff., Cl. von Delbrück, *Wirtschaftliche Mobilmachung*, pp. 115 ff.; Philip Scheidemann, *Memoiren eines Sozialdemokraten* (Dresden, 1928), 1 : 243 ff.; Cuno von Westarp, *Konservative Politik* 2 : 23 ff.; F. Payer, *Von Bethmann Hollweg bis Ebert*, pp. 24 ff.; and Karl Bachem, *Vorgeschichte, Geschichte und Politik der deutschen Zentrumspartei* 8 : 123 ff. For David's demands cf. Delbrück to Bethmann, Sept. 13, 1914; DZA Po, Rkz. no. 2,476 and Jürgen Kuczynksi, *Der Ausbruch des ersten Weltkrieges und die deutsche Sozialdemokratie* (Berlin, 1957),

pp. 207 ff. For the results of the German national assembly committee's investigation into the causes of the domestic collapse cf. *WUA*, 4th ser., vols. 5, 7, 9, and especially vol. 8, containing Bredt's monographic brief, *Der deutsche Reichstag im Weltkrieg* (Berlin, 1926).

4   Riezler Diary, Sept. 25, 1914. Bethmann to Haussmann, Oct. 4, 1914, cited by G. Ritter, *Kriegskanzler*, pp. 32–33. Bethmann to Delbrück, Sept. 12, 1914: "There is no doubt that the present war will pose completely new and difficult tasks in domestic policy after its conclusion." DZA Me, Rep. 90a, tit I i, no. 2, Abt. D, vol. 1. Bethmann to Delbrück, Sept. 19, 1914, DZA Po, Rkz. 2,476. Delbrück to the party leaders of the lower Prussian house, Oct. 21, 1914, cited in Gutsche, "Bethmann Hollweg und die Politik der 'Neuorientierung': Zur innenpolitischen Strategie und Taktik der deutschen Reichsregierung während des ersten Weltkrieges," *ZfG* (1965), pp. 209 ff. Cf. also Scheidemann, *Memoiren* 1 : 310 ff. and Westarp, *Konservative Politik* 2 : 219 ff.

5   Riezler Diary, Sept. 25: "I am supposed to write a memorandum on this entire question and am brooding. Dissolving the Reichstag with the justification of new tasks and a new time [seems] a questionable [choice]. The war indemnity [should be used] as the final solution of our financial mess [by creating state] monopolies with the help of the reparations." Ibid., Oct. 7, 1914: "This morning Delbrück arrived with Wahnschaffe. At tea he talked about the regulation of our economy by the state and the question of supplies. The government has to do everything now, distribute raw materials to industry and organize exports. . . . Only the confiscation of unearned income to be introduced gradually is still missing." *Ibid.*, Oct. 11, 22, 1914. For the economic questions cf. Albrecht Mendelsson Bartholdy, *The War and German Society* (London, 1937); Gerald D. Feldman, "Fondements sociaux de la mobilisation économique en Allemagne (1914–1916)," *Annales* (Jan., 1970); and Williamson, *Helfferich*, pp. 126 ff.

6   The entries of the Riezler Diary, as on Sept. 25, 30, 1914, about a "memorandum on domestic policy," the index of the volume of documents in which it is found, the identity of the type-face with that of the September Program, and Riezler's initials indicate that the October Memorandum originated with the chancellor's assistant and not with the Secretariat of the Interior. Cf. W. Richter, *Gewerkschaften*, p. 50 for the source of the error, repeated by G. Feldman in his authoritative *Army, Industry and Labour in Germany, 1914–1918* (Princeton, 1966), pp. 119 ff. and by implication also by Fritz Klein, ed., *Deutschland im ersten Weltkrieg* 1 : 425 ff. The document is in DZA Po, Rkz. 2,476, with the markings Rk. 410, pr. October 27, 1914, z.d.A. Ri(ezler) 28/10 (1914).

7   Ibid. Pogge-v. Strandmann, ed., *Walter Rathenau Tagebuch*, pp. 185-86; D. Stegmann, *Die Erben Bismarcks*, 63 ff.; K. Helfferich, *Der Weltkrieg*, pp. 146 ff. See also J. Schellenberg, "Probleme," pp. 82 ff.

8   Ibid. Although, unlike the September Program, Bethmann did not sign the October Memorandum, he can be presumed to have been in close sympathy with its aims.

9   Riezler Diary, Nov. 8, 1914. In the government he found "much enthusiasm for work, initiative, help toward all sides, far better than during peacetime because there is no parliament any longer and more discipline." Ibid., Dec. 5: "Bethmann's Reichstag speech. A really great impression." Bethmann to Ministry of State, Nov. 28, 1914, DZA Me, Rep. 90a B III 2b no. 6, vol. 163. Protocol of the Socialist Reichstag fraction meeting, Nov. 30, 1914, and Heine to Vollmar, Dec. 10, 1914, in E. Matthias and E. Pikart, *Die Reichstagsfraktion der deutschen Sozialdemokratie 1898 bis 1918* (Düsseldorf, 1966) 2 : 6 ff. Haussmann, *Schlaglichter*, pp. 12 ff.; Scheidemann, *Memoirs* 1 : 274 ff., Matthias-Miller, *David Tagebuch*, pp. 64 ff.,

76 ff.; and H. P. Hanssen, *Diary of a Dying Empire*, pp. 83 ff. Bethmann to Reichstag, Dec. 2, 1914, in Thimme, *Kriegsreden*, pp. 13 ff. Bethmann to Oettingen, Dec. 14, 1914, BA *Nachlass* Oettingen.

10 Riezler Diary, Jan. 2, 1915. Bethmann to Wahnschaffe, New Year's, 1915, in Hammann, *Bilder*, pp. 74 ff. Bethmann to Loebell, Feb. 2, 1915. The chief files on Prussian electoral reform are in DZA Po, Rkz. no. 1,072 ff., 2,275; RdI, 15,925; DZA Me, Rep. 77 tit 496a, no. 184, vols. 1–3; no. 186, vols. 1–2 and Beiakten vol. 1; tit 496b, no. 125, vol. 1; Rep. 169 D I b AH Stv. J. no. 53; and in AA, Preussen 2, no. 3, vol. 5. Cf. also the accurate Ludwig Bergsträsser, *Die preussische Wahlrechtsfrage im Kriege und die Entstehung der Osterbotschaft 1917* (Tübingen, 1929), pp. 9 ff.; the testimony of ex-minister Loebell of Nov. 13, 1926, WUA 4th ser., vol. 7, pt. 2, pp. 190 ff.; and its critical review by the former chief of the chancellery, Wahnschaffe, "Reichskanzler von Bethmann Hollweg und die preussische Wahlreform," *Deutsche Revue* (1922), pp. 193 ff. Reinhard Patemann, *Der Kampf um die preussische Wahlreform im Ersten Weltkrieg* (Düsseldorf, 1964), though providing much material on the press, is generally derivative.

11 Riezler Diary, Dec. 25, 1914: "Yesterday long in the garden with the chancellor. He asked me what will happen after the war? Will there be an uprising against the throne because of the *Kommandogewalt?* Will all the old pettiness return? He was nevertheless correct in speaking of liberation and of a new time without the old oppressive atmosphere." His assistant suggested a "new social policy under the motto of careers open to talent," a liberal slogan which Bethmann had used already as Prussian minister of the interior. "He said he could not understand how one could go on living after this war. Weighed down heavily, as always a strange man." Ibid., Feb. 6, 1915: "The chancellor says after the war new men and a new spirit are necessary, free from the opinions in which the older generation grew up; he keeps on repeating this, and considering the immense transformation of relationships, it contains much truth." Ibid., Feb. 17, 1915.

12 Riezler Diary, Mar. 15, June 6, 23, 1915. Haussmann, *Schlaglichter*, pp. 26 ff., 30 ff. and 42 ff. Admitting that "I, too, often suffer from the chasm" between Reichstag and government, Bethmann nevertheless skeptically queried: "As if this [transition to the parliamentary system] would only depend upon orders." Matthias-Miller, *David Tagebuch*, p. 106. For reaffirmations of the Neuorientierung and postponement of any changes in February 1915, cf. Scheidemann, *Memoirs* 1 : 268 ff; Hanssen, *Diary*, pp. 99 ff.; and Hohenlohe to Burian, Mar. 12, 1915, HHStA, PA III, 171B.

13 The hasty but substantially accurate protocols of Wahnschaffe regarding these meetings (beginning in May 1915) are in DZA Po, Rkz. 1,843 and 2,398 ff., 2,442 ff., 2444 ff., the war files of the Chancellery. Because they are not complete, it is impossible to reconstruct with absolute certainty *all* such conferences, but according to parliamentary memoir evidence there seem to have been meetings on Aug. 3, Nov. 30, 1914; Mar. 8, May 13, 26, 27, Aug. 16, Nov. 29, Dec. 2, 1915; Mar. 14, May 21, 27, July 17, Aug. 5, Sept. 5, Oct. 7, Dec. 11, 12, 1916; May 3, July 2, 1917. In general these sessions took place before every Reichstag speech of the chancellor, although sometimes when a larger and still confidential audience was required Bethmann spoke to the *Hauptausschuss* instead, as on Nov. 9, 1916, Jan. 31, July 7 and 9, 1917, DZA Po, Rtg. Prot. Budg. Komm. nos. 1301, 1307 and 1314. Cf. also Mommsen, "Die Regierung Bethmann," pp. 139 ff., and the incomplete list of Matthias-Pikart, *Reichstagsfraktion* 2 : 530.

14 Riezler Diary, Mar. 30, 1915: "The workers are very tired of the war. The Socialists are on the way to splitting themselves." Scheidemann, *Memoirs* 1 : 297 ff., *Zusammenbruch*, pp. 24 ff. Riezler Diary, Mar. 4, 1915. Musing about the chancel-

lor's claim that he was more democratic than his assistant, Riezler noted: "Strange man. Of course he is basically right. . . . The time of the beauty of the masses is coming." Matthias-Miller, *David Tagebuch*, pp. 123, 132, 137 ff. and Matthias-Pikart, *Reichstagsfraktion* 2 : 22, 43 ff. While Bethmann intended to strengthen the progovernment wing in the party, the Socialists wanted "to drive the chancellor forward" to their goals of negotiated peace and reform.

15 For the Berger memorandum, Loebell's proposals, and the first draft law, cf. DZA Po, Rkz. 1,072. Cf. the account in Loebell's unpublished MS "Memoirs," 2 : 184 ff., BA *Nachlass* Loebell. See also Bethmann's marginal note on Loebell's letter of Sept. 3, 1915: "Question: Shall disabled veterans be counted among the taxpayers even if they do not pay taxes?" and Bethmann to William II, Aug. 30, 1915, as well as the emperor's comment "Correct!" on Lobell's assertion that "no reform of Prussian suffrage can take the path of the Reichstag vote." DZA Po, Rkz. 1,072; DZA Me, Rep. 77, tit 496 a, no. 184, vol. 1 and Rep. 90a, A 8, ld 1, adh. I of vol. 13, Westarp, *Konservative Politik* 2 : 256–57, and Bethmann, *Betrachtungen* 2 : 31 ff. Riezler Diary, July 17: "He thinks much about leaving out such tax-based votes; I counseled taking such low rates that theoretically every worker can obtain them (3,000 or 5,000 Mks.), moreover to give all those who took part in the campaign plural votes anyway." Ibid., July 28, 1915. Cf. also Bethmann to Oettingen, Sept. 4, 1915: "The leading men of the future must—with us, too—be reborn from the inner strength of the people. That will not go without convulsions." BA *Nachlass* Oettingen.

16 Loebell memorandum "on the domestic political development during the war," Nov. 22, 1915, published by J. Schellenberg, *Jahrbuch für Geschichte* (Berlin, 1967), pp. 229 ff. Bethmann Hollweg to Valentini, Dec. 9, 1915, DZA Me *Nachlass* Valentini no. 2, now also reprinted by W. Deist, *Militär und Innenpolitik* 1 : 272 ff.

17 Ibid., Westarp, *Konservative Politik* 2 : 283 ff., Gutsche, *Deutschland im Ersten Weltkrieg* 2 : 241–42. Cf. also Valentini's diary entry of Dec. 26, 1915: "The chancellor is concerned about electoral reform and submarine warfare." BA *Nachlass* Thimme.

18 Haussmann, *Schlaglichter*, pp. 49 ff. Scheidemann, *Memoirs* 1 : 324ff.: "In Germany when the Diet opens there is a speech from the Throne. I will see how far one can go. In the Reichstag I cannot speak about Prussia's electoral law." Riezler Diary, Jan. 3: "The Prussian ministers are nervous. At home everything is ossified." Ibid. Jan. 11, 1916. Bethmann to Prussian Ministry of State, Jan. 3, 1916, DZA Me, Rep. 90a B III 2b no. 6, vol. 165. Bethmann to William II, Jan. 13, DZA Po, Rkz. 1,072, Schulthess's *GK* (1916) 1 : 10 ff. Hohenlohe to Burian, Jan. 18, 25, 1916, HHStA, PA III, 172B. Westarp, *Konservative Politik* 2 : 257 ff. and Bergsträsser, *Preussische Wahlrechtsfrage*, pp. 67 ff.

19 Riezler Diary, Mar. 26, 1915: "Food problems. The first of June the potatoes will be finished. It *must* become possible *to supply* meat cheaply instead." Ibid., Jan. 18; "Germany after the war: How will it be? . . . The busybody politicians at home are horrible and have remained with their old nonsense. No new ideas except from the Socialists." Ibid., Jan. 19, and Mar. 26, 1916. Matthias-Miller, *David Tagebuch*, p. 144. Bethmann to Hausmann, Oct. 29, 1915, WHStA *Nachlass* Haussmann. Bethmann to the Prussian Ministry of State, Feb. 2, 6, May 18, June 3, July 16, Oct. 25, Nov. 13, 1915, DZA Me, Rep. 90a B III 2b no. 6, vol. 164. Bethmann response to a Socialist Landtag interpellation about the food scarcity, Oct. 8, 1915, and to a Socialist Reichstag question on Nov. 12, 1915; Bethmann to the *Landwirtschaftsrat*, Nov. 27, 1915, all in Schulthess's *GK* (1915) 1 : 521, 552, 563. Cf. also Westarp, *Konservative Politik* 2 : 365 ff., Elard von Oldenburg-

Januschau, *Erinnerungen* (Leipzig, 1936), pp. 145 ff.; and August Skalweit, *Die deutsche Kriegsernährungswirtschaft* (Stuttgart, 1927).

20 Riezler Diary, Jan. 26, Mar. 15, 19, 22, 26, 30, 1916. For the Socialist split cf. Carl Schorske, *German Social Democracy,* 308 ff.; Matthias-Pikart, *Reichstagsfraktion* 2 : 170 ff., and Hohenlohe to Burian, Mar. 30, 1916, HHStA PA III, 172B. See Bredt, *Der Reichstag im Weltkriege,* pp. 65 ff., and Bethmann to Prussian Ministry of State, Apr. 11, 1916, DZA Me, Rep. 90a B III 2b no. 6, vol. 165. Cf. also Walther Barthel, *Die Linken in der Deutschen Sozialdemokratie,* p. 292, and the material in DZA Po, Rkz. 1,395/6 ff.

21 Bethmann to the Prussian Ministry of State, Dec. 11, 1915, Feb. 27, and Apr. 11, 1916. DZA Me, Rep. 90a B III 2b no. 6, vols. 164–65. With a bit of specious logic the chancellor insisted that neither this nor any other reform was "a payoff for the Socialists" but "a consequence of the facts at hand." Schulthess's *GK* (1916) 1 : 284 ff.; Westarp, *Konservative Politik* 2 : 222 ff.; Matthias-Pikart, *Reichstagsfraktion* 2 : 186 ff.; Feldmann, *Army, Industry and Labor,* pp. 121 ff.; Paul Umbreit, *Der Krieg und die Arbeitsverhältnisse: Die deutschen Gewerkschaften im Kriege* (Stuttgart, 1928), pp. 137 ff.; and H. J. Varain, *Freie Gewerkschaften, Sozialdemokratie und Staat: Die Politik der Generalkommission unter der Führung Carl Legiens, 1890–1920* (Düsseldorf, 1956). Cf. also Hohenlohe to Burian, June 15, 1916, HHStA, PA III, 172.

22 Lerchenfeld to Dandl, June 19, 1916, BHStA MA III 2691/9. Helfferich, *Welt-krieg,* pp. 235 ff. Riezler Diary, May 16, 1916: "Helfferich—good as vice-chancellor —he will appear as the only possible successor [but that] does not hinder the chancellor, who is becoming more and more independent of all personal and domestic political considerations." Cf. also Hohenlohe to Burian, May 22, 1916, HHStA, PA III, 172B and Williamson, *Helfferich,* pp. 151 ff. Thimme, *Kriegs-reden,* pp. 112 ff. Riezler Diary, June 14, 1916. F. Meinecke, *Strassburg—Frei-burg—Berlin,* pp. 213 ff. Bethmann to Harnack, June 14, 1916, DZA Po, 2,446, en-couraging his suggestion of cultural reform. In his conversations Riezler found the union leaders "excellent fellows, objective, moderate, thoughtful, easily ac-cessible." Regarding the Neuorientierung he believed "that we can achieve much good together with them—yes, it would be a sin to rebuff so much force and energy." But since Helfferich "pulled strongly to the Right because he feels socially weak toward that side and is not independent enough . . . and also too ambitious," his desire to introduce state socialism through monopolies remained a pipe dream. Riezler Diary, July 4, 7, Sept. 21, 1916.

23 Undated draft by Colonel Bauer, BA *Nachlass* Bauer, reprinted in W. Deist, *Militär und Innenpolitik* 1 : 482 ff., Ludendorff to Bethmann, Sept. 13, 1916, in *Urkunden der OHL,* pp. 61 ff. Bethmann to Ludendorff, Sept. 17, 30, 1916, in DZA Po, Rkz. no. 2398/8 ff. See also Oberst Bauer, *Der grosse Krieg,* pp. 120 ff.; Wilhelm Groener, *Lebenserinnerungen,* pp. 553 ff.; Ludendorff, *Kriegserinnerungen,* pp. 259 ff.; Helfferich, *Weltkrieg,* pp. 276 ff.; and Williamson, *Helfferich,* pp. 171 ff. Robert B. Armeson, *Total Warfare and Compulsory Labor: A Study of the Mili-tary-Industrial Complex in Germany during World War One* (The Hague, 1964) and H. Weber, *Ludendorff und die Monopole,* pp. 39 ff. are sketchy; Gerald Feld-man, *Army, Industry and Labor,* pp. 149 ff. is more reliable.

24 Groener, *Lebenserinnerungen,* pp. 342 ff. Groener notes of conversation with Beth-mann, Oct. 26, 1916, *Nachlass* Groener, reprinted in Deist, *Militär und Innen-politik* 1 : 500 ff. Wild von Hohenborn, MS "Tagebuch," Oct. 29, 1916, BA *Nachlass* Wild. Ludendorff to Bethmann, Oct. 7, 10, 11; Bethmann to Ludendorff, Oct. 12; Bethmann to state governments, Oct. 12; Bethmann to Hindenburg, Oct.

15, 1916, DZA Po, Rkz. 2398/8. OHL to Bethmann, Oct. 23; Bethmann to Wahnschaffe, Oct. 26, 1916, ibid. See also Lerchenfeld to King Ludwig, Nov. 12, 24, 1916, BHStA MA III 2691/11. Cf. Ritter, *Kriegskanzler*, pp. 417 ff.

25 Wahnschaffe protocol of ministerial conference with Groener, Oct. 29, DZA Po, Rkz. 2398/8 and Groener report to OHL, Oct. 29, 1916, *Nachlass* Groener, published by Deist, *Militär und Innenpolitik* 1 : 502 ff. William II to Bethmann, Nov. 4, 1916, S-G 1 : 561. Bethmann to William II, Nov. 4, 1916, AA, Wk. no. 23 secr., vol. 1; William II to Bethmann, Nov. 6, AA, Wk. secr., vol. 34. Bethmann to Hindenburg, Nov. 7, 1916, DZA Po, Rkz. 2398/9, containing also notes on the Groener-Helfferich negotiations with parliamentary leaders. Bethmann to Prussian Ministry of State, Nov. 1, 10, 1916, DZA Me, Rep. 90a B III 2b no. 6, vol. 165. Bethmann to Grünau, Nov. 17, 1916, DZA Po, Rkz. 2398/9. Cf. also Müller, *Regierte?*, p. 233: "Tension between Bethmann and Hindenburg."

26 Schulthess's *GK* (1916) 1 : 483, 551 ff. This attempt at increasing parliamentary control paralleled the transformation of the Budget Committee into the Chief Committee of the Reichstag charged with advising the government on foreign policy. Since Bethmann did not want to provoke an open rupture with parliament, he acquiesced without ceding any influence, but according to Hohenlohe "it is being considered as the first step on the path of parliamentarization." Hohenlohe to Burian, Oct. 29, Nov. 5, 1916, HHStA, PA III, 172. Cf. Westarp, *Konservative Politik* 2 : 246–47. See also Williamson, *Helfferich*, pp. 179 ff.

27 Socialist agreement to the Auxiliary Service Law was by no means a foregone conclusion, as the protocols of the caucus debates (Nov. 23 ff.) reveal. Matthias-Pikart, *Reichstagsfraktion*, pp. 231 ff. Bethmann to the Prussian Ministry of State, Nov. 26, Dec. 1, 4, DZA Me, Rep. 90a B III 2b no. 6, vol. 165. Bethmann to William II, Dec. 2; Bethmann to Valentini, Dec. 3; Bethmann to Legien, Dec. 11, 1916, DZA Po, Rkz. 2398/9. Bethmann to the Reichstag, Nov. 29, 1916; Thimme, *Kriegsreden*, pp. 172 ff. Cf. the protocols of the Budget Committee, DZA Po, Reichstag nos. 1,307 ff., and H. von Stein, *Erlebnisse und Betrachtungen aus der Zeit des Weltkrieges* (Leipzig, 1919), pp. 93–94. See also Gutsche, *Deutschland im Ersten Weltkrieg* 2 : 461 ff.; and Feldmann, *Army, Industry and Labor*, pp. 217 ff.

28 Riezler Diary, Feb. 14, 18, 1917: "In the transportation crisis Ludendorff seems finally to have understood that even the soldiers have made mistakes and that nothing can be done with the commanding dilettantes. Breitenbach has made very reasonable proposals (against the military central transportation office) and they have been accepted." Riezler Diary, Feb. 25: "Groener covered himself months ago with pessimistic predictions, perhaps because he sensed that the so-called Hindenburg program forced upon the economy demands too much from transportation. . . . Now he can say that the others were at fault." Bethmann to Hindenburg, Mar. 15, 1917, in AA GHQ, no. 227, reprinted by Deist, *Militär und Innenpolitik* 1 : 576–77.

29 Memorandum by Colonel Bauer, "Remarks about the chancellor: Our government has failed during the war. 1) It neglected to mobilize the resources of the country at the right time and thereby now endangers the outcome of the struggle. 2) It has created fatal circumstances at home. 3) It has not been able to defend our standing abroad despite all successes of our arms." BA *Nachlass* Bauer. Colonel Merz to Hertling, Feb. 15, 1917; Grünau to Bethmann, Mar. 14; Bethmann to Hindenburg, Mar. 14, 21; Hindenburg to Bethmann, Mar. 17, 24, 1917, AA GHQ, no. 245, reprinted in Deist, *Militär und Innenpolitik* 2 : 662 ff. In a cutting telegram Bethmann warned the OHL that "responsibility in a political sense exists only for political measures of the government," which were his own domain, and that any military statement to the press describing the degrees of participation in

the formulation of certain policies would be a grave violation of the *Kommando-gewalt*. Despite Hindenburg's irate answer the chancellor insisted that "the dragging of Y. E. into the political arena and playing off your authority against the government is the central tactic of the opponents of the cabinet."

30 Bethmann Hollweg manuscript, BA *Nachlass* Thimme, no. 61. Although it is written in the first person, ostensibly by the ex-chancellor, Wahnschaffe in his correspondence with Thimme (June 11, 1936) referred to a manuscript written by himself to help Bethmann prepare the *Betrachtungen*. It is therefore highly probable that this narrative is the chief of the imperial chancellery's work. Riezler Diary, Jan. 31, Feb. 14, 25, 1917. "The modesty and patriotism of the Socialists are touching—but if the government were to anger them they would quickly evaporate." Ibid., Feb. 28, 1917. Bethmann to the Prussian Ministry of State, Oct. 24, 1916, DZA Me, 90a B III 2b no. 6, vol. 165. Scheidemann, *Zusammenbruch*, pp. 37 ff. and Riezler Diary, Feb. 25, 1917, about the abortive "attempt to induce the Socialists . . . to say something halfhearted in favor of the monarchy." Bethmann to Reichstag, Feb. 27, 1917, Thimme, *Kriegsreden*, pp. 192 ff. Cf. also Westarp, *Konservative Politik* 2 : 228 ff.

31 Riezler Diary, Mar. 4, 8, 1917: "Great domestic debacle. Schorlemer and Michaelis speak in the Landtag without restraint. The *Lokalanzeiger* campaigns for Schorlemer against Batocki. The latter fights the former in the *Vossische Zeitung*. . . . This is all the fault of the chancellor who, if he does not want to lose all respect, must do something. It is high time for him to hang a few ministerial scalps on his belt." Westarp, *Konservative Politik* 2 : 389, and Hohenlohe to Czernin, Mar. 12, 1917, HHStA, PA III, 173.

32 Schulthess's *GK* (1917) 1 : 272 ff., 288 ff. Riezler Diary, Mar. 18, 1917: "The tactical situation was favorable, since the entire Lower House was angry against the House of Lords, and the Conservatives, disoriented, resentful about the tactical mistake of the Upper Chamber, did not know what to do. . . . Now all the sleepy-heads who call themselves liberal should organize and create a youthful popular movement. My last evening with the Progressives was not very confidence-inspiring; they are quite reasonable and benevolent, but somewhat antiquated." Thimme, *Kriegsreden*, pp. 214 ff. Wahnschaffe MS, pp. 7 ff. Haussmann, *Schlaglichter*, pp. 91 ff. Larisch to Czernin, Mar. 16, 1917, HHStA, PA III, 173.

33 Riezler Diary, Mar. 18, 1917: "The first news was a radiogram intercepted on Wednesday in which the Kronstadt garrison asked whom it should obey; H.M. telephoned it to Bethmann in the evening, but the doubts were great and we all considered the immediate victory of reaction assured, since the information indicated that everything was still undecided. It is possible that the chancellor was thereby strengthened in his conviction to speak, but it was certainly not decisive after everything which had been discussed during the last week concerning a necessary gesture to the Left." Ibid., Mar. 25, 28, 1917. Scheidemann, *Memoirs*, 1 : 337 ff. and *Zusammenbruch*, pp. 39 ff., for the rationale that "the chancellor, with his fear of the Right, should not forget to be a little afraid of the people also." Matthias-Miller, *David Tagebuch*, p. 222. Müller, *Regierte?*, pp. 265–66. Bethmann to Stein, Mar. 28, 1917, DZA Po, Wk. vol. 12. Zech to Grünau, Mar. 28, 1917, reprinted by Deist, *Militär und Innenpolitik* 2 : 691–92. Cf. also the documents in Leo Stern, ed., *Die Auswirkungen der grossen sozialistischen Oktoberrevolution auf Deutschland* (Berlin, 1959), vol. 4/II, pp. 381 ff.

34 Bethmann to Grünau, Mar. 28, 1917, AA, GHQ no. 245, reprinted by Deist, *Militär und Innenpolitik* 2 : 694. Wahnschaffe MS, pp. 15 ff., calling the Stresemann speech "a turning point in the history of his party." Schulthess's *GK* (1917) 1 : 349 ff., 356 ff. Stresemann to Bassermann, Mar. 31, Apr. 9, 1917, AA *Nachlass*

Stresemann, 3,061. Hartwig Thieme, *Nationaler Liberalismus in der Krise: Die nationalliberale Fraktion des Preussischen Abgeordnetenhauses 1914–1918* (Boppard, 1963), pp. 99 ff. Bethmann to Reichstag, Mar. 29, 1917; Thimme, *Kriegsreden,* pp. 223 ff. Westarp, *Konservative Politik* 2 : 248 ff. Riezler Diary, Mar. 28, 1917: "Very precarious situation in the Reichstag. . . . Extraordinarily adroit and honest speech of the chancellor in a damnably difficult situation." Hohenlohe to Czernin, Mar. 29, Apr. 4, 1917, HHStA, PA III, 173. Cf. also Bredt, *Reichstag im Weltkriege,* pp. 162 ff.

35 Bethmann to Eisendecher, Apr. 6, 1917, AA *Nachlass* Eisendecher; Wahnschaffe MS, pp. 20 ff. "The atmosphere had to be relieved immediately," and since the military situation offered no prospect of victory, "there remained only a political action." Czernin, *In the World War,* pp. 163 ff. Riezler Diary, Apr. 1, 1917: "The crown must lead, otherwise it will be run over. Good that the old Prussia will be broken; it is only disgusting that such repulsive busybodies as Müller-Meiningen are to represent freedom." Bethmann to Loebell, Apr. 11, 1917, BA *Nachlass* Loebell. Riezler Diary, Apr. 3, 1917. Lerchenfeld to Hertling, Apr. 5, 1917, BHStA, MA I, 947: "The chancellor is fairly sympathetic to the idea" of Reichstag suffrage, but Erzberger predicted severe political struggles. Cf. also Bergsträsser, *Die preussische Wahlrechtsfrage,* pp. 130 ff.

36 Riezler Diary, Apr. 3, 1917: "People who a fortnight ago still thought and said that a free Prussian suffrage should never be given, now fret and complain that it should be granted quickly." Müller, *Regierte?* pp. 270 ff. found the chancellor "very pessimistic regarding the domestic situation, especially because much wheat and barley had spoiled. The Russian Revolution was having quite an effect on the masses." Wahnschaffe MS, pp. 20 ff. Valentini Diary, Apr. 2, 1917, BA *Nachlass* Thimme. Riezler Diary, Apr. 4, 1917. Grünau to Bethmann, Apr. 4, 1917, DZA Po, Rkz. 1,073. Bethmann to William II, Apr. 4, 1917, AA GHQ, no. 247, reprinted in Deist, *Militär und Innenpolitik* 2 : 702–03. The different drafts of the Easter Message are in DZA Po, Rkz. 1,073. Cf. also Bergsträsser, *Preussische Wahlrechtsfrage,* pp. 144 ff.; Patemann, *Der Kampf,* pp. 58 ff., and Bredt, *Reichstag im Weltkriege,* pp. 180 ff.

37 Session of the Prussian Ministry of State, Apr. 5, 1917, DZA Me, Rep. 90a B III 2b no. 6, vol. 165, printed in excerpts in Stern, *Auswirkungen,* 4/II, pp. 409 ff. For the conflict with Loebell cf. also Bethmann to Wahnschaffe, Apr. 2 and Bethmann to Valentini, Apr. 4, 1917, DZA Po, Rkz. 1,073. Cf. also Loebell MS "Memoirs," 2 : 187 ff., BA *Nachlass* Loebell and Westarp, *Konservative Politik* 2 : 263 ff. Hohenlohe to Czernin, Apr. 6, HHStA, PA III, 173. See also Williamson, *Helfferich,* pp. 201 ff.

38 Valentini Diary, Apr. 4 ff., BA *Nachlass* Thimme, Müller, *Regierte?,* pp. 271 ff. Grünau to Bethmann, Apr. 5, 6, 7, 1917, DZA Po, Rkz. 1,073, warning, "I once more urgently advise not making the reform without Loebell, whose cooperation is politically important and who cannot be replaced." Wahnschaffe MS, pp. 22 ff. Prussian Ministry of State, Apr. 6, 1917, DZA Me, Rep. 90a B III 2b no. 6, vol. 165. Riezler Diary, Apr. 6, 1917: "If things go well much will be gained by this reticence because one can then concede equal suffrage instead of parliamentary government and postpone the rest." Wahnschaffe, "Preussische Wahlreform," pp. 195 ff. Wahnschaffe to Bethmann, Apr. 7, 1917: "The draft decided on has the advantage of not immediately provoking the resistance of important circles, but it can only have a calming effect on the lower classes, if it opens *the door to equal suffrage* and can be interpreted in that manner," DZA Po, Rkz. 1,073. Although Wahnschaffe testified that the emperor would have vetoed any more radical

measures, Bergsträsser in retrospect considered this "a decisive mistake in the entire action." *WUA*, 4th ser., vol. 7, pt. 1, pp. 238 ff.

39 Bethmann to Valentini, Apr. 10, 1917, DZA Me, Rep. 89H, I Preussen 1. Bethmann to Breitenbach, Apr. 11 and to Hertling, Apr. 11, 1917; press briefing in the Chancellery, Apr. 7; Bethmann to Treutler, Apr. 8 ff., all in DZA Po, Rkz. 1,073. Grünau to Bethmann, Apr. 11, 1917, reporting William's enthusiasm, AA, Wk. 2 secr., vol. 32. Helfferich, *Weltkrieg*, pp. 434 ff. and Matthias-Miller, *David Tagebuch*, p. 123: "Not completely satisfactory; the 'Prussian spirit' remains very slow; but it is a great step forward." Cf. also Hohenlohe to Czernin, Apr. 11, 1917, reluctantly admitting success, HHStA, PA III, 173, and Schoen to Hertling, Apr. 11, 1917, BHStA MA III 2691/13, calling it a masterstroke and proof "how correct Bethmann was . . . in conducting a policy which had the working classes behind it." Cf. also Bergsträsser, *Preussische Wahlrechtsfrage*, pp. 154 ff. (who unaccountably stops with the Easter Message) and Patemann, *Kampf*, pp. 63 ff. See also Gutsche, *Deutschland im ersten Weltkrieg*, 2 : 728 ff. and Mommsen, "Die Regierung Bethmann," pp. 156 ff., who pays too little attention to the constitutional conflict.

40 Riezler Diary, Apr. 10, 11, 16, 19, 1917: "Rapid worsening of the situation: we will hardly escape without an explosion. The strikes show that starving masses, confused by the Russian Revolution, cannot be contained any longer." Ibid., Apr. 20, 1917. Wahnschaffe MS, pp. 28 ff. Heinrich Scheel, "Der Aprilstreik 1917 in Berlin," in A. Schreiner, ed., *Revolutionäre Ereignisse und Probleme in Deutschland während der Periode der Grossen Sozialistischen Oktoberrevolution 1917/18* (Berlin, 1957), pp. 24 ff. Schulthess's *GK* (1917) 1 : 410 ff.; Scheidemann, *Zusammenbruch*, pp. 63 ff.; Müller, *Regierte?*, pp. 277 ff. Valentini Diary, Apr. 21 ff., BA *Nachlass* Thimme. Bethmann circular, Apr. 24, 1917, cited in Wahnschaffe MS, pp. 29–30. Riezler Diary, May 1, 1917. Cf. Hohenlohe's detailed reports to Czernin of Apr. 23, 26, and May 4, 1917, mentioning the figure of 150,000 workers, HHStA, PA III, 173, and Schoen to Hertling, Apr. 17, 1917, BHStA MA III 2691/13. See also A. J. Mayer, *Wilson vs. Lenin*, pp. 122 ff.

41 Bethmann to Hertling, Apr. 11, 1917, BHStA MA III 2691/13. Schulthess's *GK* (1917) 1 : 470. Hanssen, *Diary*, pp. 192 ff. Riezler Diary, May 1, 8, 9, 1917: "Horrible situation. The parliaments at each others' throats. The Upper House wants to go against the Constitutional Committee, which can only be restrained with utmost effort." Wahnschaffe MS, pp. 41 ff. For Bethmann's views on parliamentary government cf. his statement in the Prussian Ministry of State, May 1, 1917, DZA Me, Rep. 90a B III 2b no. 6, vol. 165, and his conversation with his conservative cousin Vitzthum, Mar. 29, 1917: "What does parliamentarianism mean? One cannot resolve by law to introduce parliamentary government, but it exists when conditions themselves produce it." The exclusion of the crown from government was inevitable because "the general development points toward the gradual introduction of parliamentarianism even in Germany." SHStA Berlin 273. Cf. also Hertling's note of May 5 of Bethmann's assurances to the minister presidents of the states, BHStA MA I 962. William to Bethmann, May 12, 1917, AA GHQ, 247, reprinted in Deist, *Militär und Innenpolitik* 2 : 748 ff. Cf. also the exchange of telegrams between Bethmann and the cabinet chiefs, May 5 ff. DZA Po, Rkz. 1,073 printed by Westarp, *Konservative Politik* 2 : 243 ff. Matthias-Miller, *David Tagebuch*, pp. 226–27. Helfferich, *Weltkrieg*, pp. 435 ff. Cf. also the alarmed reports of Hohenlohe to Czernin, May 12, 14, 1917, HHStA, PA III, 173, and Schoen to Hertling, May 3, 1917 and Hertling to Dandl, May 5, 1917, BHStA, MA III 2691/14 and MA I 975.

42 Riezler Diary, May 8, 9, 13, 1917: "The chancellor is back from GHQ. The crisis

expected by the fronde has not happened . . . a change of ministers is of course impossible right now—hence we must attempt to muddle on." Bethmann to Reichstag, May 15, 1917. Thimme, *Kriegsreden*, pp. 237 ff. Wahnschaffe MS, pp. 45 ff. Riezler Diary, May 19, 1917: "Pressure for a coalition ministry of parliamentarians. That is not necessary. It is better to draw the best qualified people from private life. Meinecke as minister of culture, resuming the great Prussian tradition of Humboldt, Gneisenau, and Stein." Müller, *Regierte?*, pp. 282 ff. Lerchenfeld to Hertling, May 15, 1917, BHStA MA I 958 and Larisch to Czernin, May 21, 1917, HHStA, PA III, 173.

43 Loebell MS, "Erinnerungen," 2 : 188 ff. Bethmann to Loebell, Apr. 11, 1917, BA *Nachlass* Loebell. Riezler Diary, May 19, 1917. Wahnschaffe MS, pp. 48 ff. Bethmann to Valentini, May 20; Loebell votum, May 10; Lentze votum, May 11, DZA Po, Rkz. 1,073. Bethmann to Prussian Ministry of State, May 23, DZA Me, Rep. 90a B III 2b no. 6, vol. 165. Wahnschaffe, "Wahlrechtsreform," pp. 195 ff. Westarp, *Konservative Politik* 2 : 267 ff. For the text of Loebell's plural suffrage proposal *WUA*, 4th ser., vol. 7, pt. 2, pp. 190 ff. Picking up Bethmann's slogan "Free path to the capable" as basis of a voting system halfway between class and universal suffrage, Loebell envisaged one basic and one age vote (over fifty, three children) accessible to all, but introduced additional votes for property, income, independence, and education weighted in favor of rural landed property over urban enterprise. Theoretically open to "the best electors within each social stratum," the proposal was constructed to reduce the Socialist vote from 33 percent to 25 percent and to take away 50 of the 200 Conservative seats but to assure the parties of the Right a solid majority in the Landtag. See also Patemann, *Kampf*, pp. 79 ff.

44 Riezler Diary, June 9, 1917: "If the people identify the OHL with the Pan-Germans or if it becomes known that the chancellor is deprived of any freedom of action at home or abroad by the generals, there will be an uprising against the system of militarism and the beginning of the collapse." Since "the chancellor will lose should he threaten to resign, Gallwitz [?] become his successor, [and] Austria declare that it cannot subscribe to such a policy, a storm of protest will be unleashed at home and the war will be lost." Bauer note on conversation with Roedern, June 20, 1917, BA *Nachlass* Bauer; Bethmann to Hindenburg, June 25, 1917, DZA Po, Rkz. 2,446, also in Ludendorff, *Urkunden*, pp. 397 ff. and reprinted with Hindenburg's acid marginalia by Deist, *Militär und Innenpolitik* 2 : 769 ff. Excerpted notes by Merz von Quirnheim, July 9, 1917, ibid., pp. 782 ff. Wahnschaffe MS, pp. 54 ff. Müller, *Regierte?*, pp. 295–96.

45 Riezler Diary, June 9, 1917: "It is an unspeakably horrid situation that the generals can bring liars like the grain dealer Weil to the emperor to report on submarine warfare, that Hindenburg and Ludendorff are so uneducated, that the people are dividing into supporters of a victorious and a bad peace, that the uniformed dilettantes, caught up in their sport, judge everything emotionally, reveling in power and so-called toughness, and no one is able to offer a cool assessment of the situation and at any moment a blind bunch of fools can turn the domestic situation topsy-turvy: *Pauvre Allemagne!*" Larisch to Czernin, June 20, 30, July 2, 5, 1917, HHStA, PA III, 173. Wahnschaffe MS, pp. 31 ff. Schulthess's *GK* (1917) 1 : 591 ff. for Heydebrand's bitter Herford speech; ibid., pp. 601 ff., 641–42 for the National Liberal position; ibid., pp. 631 ff. for the *Preussentag* of the Progressives; and ibid., pp. 658–59 for the Socialist view. Scheidemann, *Zusammenbruch*, pp. 158 ff.; Matthias-Miller, *David Tagebuch*, pp. 236 ff.; and Matthias-Pikart, *Reichstagsfraktion* 2 : 263 ff.

46 Bethmann memorandum on conversation with William II, June 29, 1917, cited

in full in Wahnschaffe MS, pp. 59 ff., 68–69. Müller, *Regierte?*, p. 298: "The chancellor for one and one-half hours paces back and forth in the garden with the kaiser, describes the difficult domestic situation, and proposes a parliamentary minister (Spahn) as concession to the liberal tendencies. That is refused." Valentini Diary, June 29–30, BA *Nachlass* Thimme. Bethmann, *Betrachtungen* 2 : 219 ff. The conditional promise of parliamentarization insufficiently communicated to the leaders of the Left was so quickly devoured by the crisis of confidence in the government that only the *David Tagebuch*, p. 238 (June 30, 1917) records the plan, and the secondary literature has consistently slighted the issue. Cf. E. Matthias and R. Morsey, *Der interfraktionelle Ausschuss, 1917–1918* (Düsseldorf, 1959), vol. 1, pt. 1, pp. xxv ff., and G. Ritter, *Kriegskanzler*, 557 ff.

47 Wahnschaffe MS, pp. 69 ff. Scheidemann, *Zusammenbruch*, pp. 82 ff. Payer, *Von Bethmann*, pp. 28–29. Heuss, *Naumann*, pp. 472 ff. Bethmann to parliamentary leaders, WP, July 2, 1917. Matthias-Miller, *David Tagebuch*, p. 239; Helfferich, *Weltkriege*, pp. 438 ff.; Erzberger, *Erlebnisse im Weltkrieg*, pp. 251 ff.; Westarp, *Konservative Politik* 2 : 336 ff. Bethmann to Prussian Ministry of State, July 2, 1917, DZA Me, Rep. 90a B III 2b no. 6, vol. 165. Bethmann to Valentini, July 3, 1917, DZA Po, Rkz. no. 2398/10. See also W. J. Mommsen, "La chute du gouvernement Bethmann Hollweg en juillet 1917," *Revue d'histoire moderne et contemporaine* (1968), pp. 50 ff.

48 Wahnschaffe MS, pp. 75 ff. Schulthess's *GK* (1917) 1 : 668–69. Hanssen, *Diary*, pp. 194 ff. DZA Po, Rtg. no. 1,314 for the minutes of the Budget Committee. Bethmann to Valentini, July 5, 1917, DZA Me, Rep. 89H, I Preussen 1. As he telegraphed to William II on July 6, he still hoped to calm the excitement with a Reichstag speech, "inspired with a firm tone." DZA Po, Rkz. 1,074. Cf. also Patemann, *Kampf*, pp. 85 ff., and Williamson, *Helfferich*, pp. 214 ff. Bethmann's resolve was also strengthened by a petition of Hans Delbrück's liberal conservative circle in favor of equal suffrage, Schulthess's *GK* (1917) 1 : 666–67.

49 Erzberger, *Erlebnisse im Weltkriege*, pp. 225 ff.; Epstein, *Erzberger*, pp. 204 ff.; Haussmann, *Schlaglichter*, pp. 95 ff.; Scheidemann, *Zusammenbruch*, pp. 85–86; Hanssen, *Diary*, pp. 201 ff.; Matthias-Miller, *David Tagebuch*, pp. 240–41; Payer, *Von Bethmann*, pp. 29–30, and for the motives cf. also the discussions in the Erzberger trial and the investigating committee *WUA*, 4th ser., vol. 7/1, pp. 217 ff., 7/2, pp. 227 ff. Wahnschaffe MS, pp. 91 ff. When Bethmann complained that the Center Party leader had "ambushed him like Ziethen," Erzberger replied that he had only intended to create a majority for the chancellor's policy. Cf. also Matthias-Morsey, *IFA*, 1 : xxix ff.; for the demands of the interparty committee see ibid., pp. 3 ff., Wahnschaffe MS, p. 84, Payer, *Von Bethmann*, pp. 30–31 and Matthias-Pikart, *Reichstagsfraktion* 2 : 280 ff. Cf. also Lerchenfeld to Loessl, July 6, 1917: "I have the impression that Erzberger, who earlier was a strong supporter of Bethmann, intends to get out, not from personal motives . . . but because he sincerely believes that policy should be conducted differently." BHStA MA I 969. Larisch to Czernin, July 6, 7, 1917, HHSTA, PA III, 173. See also Udo Bermbach, *Vorformen parlamentarischer Kabinettsbildung in Deutschland: Der Interfraktionelle Ausschuss 1917–1918 und die Parlamentarisierung der Reichsregierung* (Cologne, 1967), pp. 54 ff.

50 Wahnschaffe MS, pp. 84 ff. Hanssen, *Diary*, pp. 207 ff. Protocols of the Budget Committee, DZA Po, Rtg. nos. 1,314 ff. Müller, *Regierte?*, pp. 300 ff. Valentini Diary, July 7 ff., 1917, BA *Nachlass* Thimme. Schwertfeger, *Kaiser und Kabinettschef*, pp. 157 ff. Memorandum by Mertz von Quirnheim, July 9, 1917, in Deist, *Militär und Innenpolitik*, 2 : 782 ff. Bethmann to the Prussian Ministry of State, July 8, 1917, DZA Me, Rep. 90a B III 2b no. 6, vol. 165. Helfferich, *Weltkrieg*, pp.

442 ff. Loebell, MS "Erinnerungen," 2 : 189–90. Wahnschaffe, "Wahlrechtsreform," pp. 201 ff. Cf. also William II's statement to the Bavarian ambassador: "He, the kaiser, is for the time being for plural suffrage, the chancellor for equal votes," Lerchenfeld to King Ludwig, July 8, 1917, BHStA MA I 969. See also Larisch to Czernin, July 7, 8, 1917, HHStA, PA III, 173, and Nostitz to Vitzthum, July 7, 1917, in Stern, *Auswirkungen*, 4/II, pp. 581 ff.

51 Wahnschaffe MS, pp. 85 ff., 118 ff. Hanssen, *Diary*, pp. 216 ff. DZA Po, protocols of the Budget Committee, Rtg. no. 1,314 ff. Matthias-Miller, *David Tagebuch*, p. 242. For the crown council cf. DZA Me, Rep. 90a B III 2b no. 3, vol. 6. Loebell resented being outmaneuvered through the crown council "to which all state secretaries of the empire had been invited, although it was a purely Prussian matter and only the Prussian Ministers possessed a seat and a vote." MS, "Erinnerungen," 2 : 190, recording an alignment of ten to six in favor, while the Prussian ministers lined up five to three against! Ultimately, Breitenbach's judgment "that we would suffer a severe defeat with the plural suffrage suggested by the minister of the interior" prevailed. Cf. Helfferich, *Weltkrieg*, pp. 445–46; Schwertfeger, *Kaiser und Kabinettschef*, pp. 160–61; Westarp, *Konservative Politik* 2 : 271 ff.; Stern, *Auswirkungen*, 4/II, pp. 588 ff.; and Patemann, *Kampf*, pp. 90 ff. Cf. also Lerchenfeld to Loessl, July 9, 10, 1917, BHStA MA I 969: "The outcome of the crisis depends upon the kaiser's decision," adding that if electoral reform and parliamentarization were granted, Bethmann, "can probably remain." Hohenlohe to Czernin, July 9, 10, 1917, HHStA, PA III, 173 ff.

52 Bethmann memorandum, DZA Po, Rkz. 2403/5, July 11, 1917, cited in full in the Wahnschaffe MS, pp. 86 ff. Müller, *Regierte?*, pp. 302–03. Valentini Diary, July 10, 1917, BA *Nachlass* Thimme. Loebell MS, "Erinnerungen," pp. 190–91. Payer, *Von Bethmann*, pp. 30–31. Haussmann, *Schlaglichter*, pp. 104 ff. Scheidemann, *Zusammenbruch*, pp. 88 ff. Matthias-Morsey, *IFA*, 1 : 28 ff. Matthias-Pikart, *Reichstagsfraktion* 2 : 290 ff. In his *Erlebnisse im Weltkriege*, p. 259. Erzberger commented perceptively, "The chancellor made the mistake of isolating himself too much from parliament and devoting himself almost exclusively to the kaiser." Since Bethmann only darkly hinted about his struggle with the emperor and the conservative advisors, the deputies received the misleading impression that he was not actively working for reform, and their frustration vented itself in statements like that of Socialist Hoffmann: "With Bethmann one can no longer make any policy. In the three great areas of nutrition, domestic reform, and peace he has brought nothing but disappointments." Matthias-Pikart, *Reichstagsfraktion* 2 : 274 ff.

53 Wahnschaffe MS, pp. 88 ff.: "I have attempted to show that I was already convinced of the necessity of proclaiming the decision in favor of equal suffrage before the chancellor crisis erupted, and that after my proposal was accepted I offered my resignation." Bethmann to Prussian Ministry of State, July 11, 1917, DZA Me, Rep. 90a B III 2b no. 6, vol. 165. Helfferich, *Weltkrieg*, pp. 447 ff. Wahnschaffe, "Wahlrechtsreform," pp. 203–04. Scheidemann, *Zusammenbruch*, pp. 90 ff. Haussmann, *Schlaglichter*, pp. 118 ff. Payer, *Von Bethmann*, p. 31. Schwertfeger, *Kaiser und Kabinettschef*, pp. 162–63. Schulthess's *GK* (1917) 1 : 687–88. Cf. also Lerchenfeld to Ludwig, July 12, 1917, BHStA MA I 969, and Hohenlohe to Czernin, July 11, 1917, both agreeing that "the chancellor crisis has been overcome." For the *Reichsrat* scheme cf. also Matthias-Morsey, *IFA*, 1 : 45 ff., and Williamson, *Helfferich*, pp. 226 ff.

54 Hanssen, *Diary*, pp. 228 ff. Haussmann, *Schlaglichter*, pp. 119 ff. Payer, *Von Bethmann*, pp. 31 ff. Scheidemann, *Zusammenbruch*, pp. 90–91. Matthias-Miller, *David Tagebuch*, pp. 243–44. *Kreuzzeitung*, July 12, publishing a resolution of the

Conservative Party condemning equal suffrage. *Alldeutsche Blätter,* July 14, 1917. More serious was the defection of the *Berliner Tageblatt* and the *Frankfurter Zeitung* cited in Mommsen, "Die deutsche öffentliche Meinung und der Zusammenbruch des Regierungssystems Bethmann Hollweg im Juli 1917," *GWU* 19 (1968) : 656 ff. Cf. also Patemann, *Kampf,* pp. 93 ff. For the crown prince intrigue cf. notes by Mertz von Quirnheim, n.d., reprinted by Deist, *Militär und Innenpolitik,* 2 : 790; Bauer, *Der Grosse Krieg,* pp. 141 ff.; Ludendorff, *Urkunden der OHL,* pp. 408 ff.; and Westarp, *Konservative Politik* 2 : 354 ff. For the generals' ultimatum cf. Wahnschaffe MS, pp. 150 ff.; Valentini Diary, July 12, 1917, BA *Nachlass* Thimme.

55 Scheidemann to Socialist caucus, reporting on his last conversation with Bethmann, July 19, 1917, in Matthias-Pikart, *Reichstagsfraktion* 2 : 307. Cf. also David's sudden insight: "In general a good outcome; much gained in the first effort; but it would have been more, if Bethmann had remained." Matthias-Miller, *David Tagebuch,* p. 249. Riezler Diary, Dec. 4, 1916. Bethmann to Max von Baden, Jan. 17, 1918, reprinted by E. Zechlin, "Deutschland zwischen," pp. 456 ff. Cf. also Bethmann's revealing confession to Oettingen, Mar. 30, 1917, cited by E. Vietsch, *Bethmann,* p. 265, and his letter to Undersecretary Drews of Dec. 15, 1917: "In the last analysis it is revolution which the government attempts to bring about in the form of an evolution, and it will make sparks fly." BA *Nachlass* Drews.

56 Bethmann replying to Stresemann's criticism in the Budget Committee on July 9, 1917, Wahnschaffe MS, pp. 144–45. Riezler Diary, Jan. 19, Nov. 3, 1916: "Yesterday [I spoke] long with the chancellor, who considers a really decisive policy with a sensible foreign line only possible with the Left, but this is hardly practicable for us because of the kaiser, the Prussian bureaucracy, and the navy." Ibid., Apr. 10, 25, May 19, 1917. Bethmann to Naumann, Nov. 13, 1917, DZA Po *Nachlass* Naumann. Wahnschaffe MS, p. 160. Cf. also Koschnitzke, "Innenpolitik," pp. 282 ff.; Gutsche, *Deutschland im Ersten Weltkrieg* 2 : 746 ff.; Fischer, *Weltmacht,* pp. 516 ff.; Ritter, *Kriegskanzler,* pp. 576 ff.; and Mommsen, "Regierung Bethmann," pp. 158–59.

Chapter 11

1 Bethmann to Delbrück, Sept. 8, 1917, DSB *Nachlass* Delbrück. Bethmann to Eickhoff, Sept. 27, 1911; Bethmann to Delbrück, June 10, 1911: "Our system has special problems but it can be successful if government and parties attempt to work together practically without aping foreign formulas." Bethmann to Schwerin-Löwitz, July 1, 1911, all in DZA Po, Rkz. 1,391. Bethmann to Loebell, Aug. 16, and Nov. 20, 1911, in DZA Po, Rkz. 1,391/5. Cf. Bethmann to Hutten-Czapski, Sept. 15, 1910; Bethmann to Bassermann, Jan. 21, 1913; and Bethmann to Schlepp, Apr. 9, 1914: "I consider it a service to the future of German liberalism if liberal men oppose blurring the distinction with socialism." DZA Po, Rkz. 1,394.

2 Bethmann marginalia on an article of the *Vossische Zeitung,* "Der Reichskanzler als Handlanger," July 18, 1914, DZA Po, Rkz. 1,392. Bethmann to William II, Apr. 15, 1910, DZA, Rkz. 1,395; Bethmann to minister of the interior, May 5, 1913, authorizing inconclusive discussions regarding the prevention of the "influx of Socialist ideas into the army reserve" DZA Po, Rkz. 1,395/8; Bethmann to William II, July 29, 1914; Bethmann to Südekum, July 30, 1914, sending his "deep thanks" for the "communications . . . which were of great value for me;" Wahnschaffe note of his conversation with deputy Cohen, Oct. 2, 1914, all in DZA Po, 1,395/9. Bethmann marginalia on a *Kreuzzeitung* reprint of a speech by Octavio von Zedlitz-Neukirch, June 26, 1916, DZA Po, Rkz. 1,392. Wahnschaffe to Batocki, June 28,

1915, DZA Po, Rkz. 1,395/10. Cf. also W. J. Mommsen, "Die Regierung Bethmann Hollweg und die öffentliche Meinung 1914–1917," *VJHfZG* (1969), pp. 117 ff.

3 Bethmann to Falkenhayn, July 18, 1914, DZA Po, RdI, no. 12,215/1, cited by Johanna Schellenberg, "Die Herausbildung der Militärdiktatur in den ersten Jahren des Krieges," in *Politik im Krieg*, pp. 22 ff. Memorandum of a Dr. Schulze on the chancellor's legal responsibility under the state of siege law, initialed by Bethmann Nov. 28, 1914, DZA Po, Rkz. 2,398/1. Bethmann to Prussian Ministry of State, Nov. 12, 1915, reprinted among other documents on the state of siege by W. Deist, *Militär und Innenpolitik im Weltkrieg, 1914–1918* (Düsseldorf, 1970), 1 : 33 ff. See also Johanna Schellenberg, "Probleme der Burgfriedenspolitik im ersten Weltkrieg—zur innenpolitischen Strategie und Taktik der herrschenden Klassen Deutschlands von 1914 bis 1916" (Dissertation, Berlin, 1967), chap. one.

4 Bethmann to AA, Aug. 31 (two telegrams), AA GHQ, no. 240 and AA Wk no. 8, vol. 8, cited in Deist, *Militär*, 1 : 70, n. 4. Riezler to AA, draft guidelines, Oct. 19, 1914, AA GHQ, no. 284, ibid., pp. 78 ff. Wandel circular to the commanding generals, Nov. 9, 1914, ibid., pp. 81 ff. Riezler Diary, Nov. 11, 1914. Bethmann to Hammann, Nov. 14, 1914: "The *Deutsche Tageszeitung* is horrible; almost as repulsive as the *Lokalanzeiger*. If Germany is to look like this after the war may God have mercy upon us." DZA Po *Nachlass* Hammann. Cf. also Bethmann to Kessel, Sept. 21, 1914, AA Wk. no. 8, vol. 21, and to Zimmermann, Oct. 26, 1914, ibid., vol. 45. See also the disappointing Kurt Koszyk, *Deutsche Pressepolitik im Ersten Weltkrieg* (Düsseldorf, 1968), pp. 22–23, 68 ff.

5 Phrase from one of the *Stimmungsberichte* of the Prussian Ministry of the Interior, drafted by the conservative journalist Berger, covering Oct. 1914, DZA Po, Rkz. 2,437/3. Cf. Kurt Mühsam, *Wie wir belogen wurden: Die amtliche Irreführung des deutschen Volkes* (Munich, 1918); and Walter Vogel, "Die Organisation der amtlichen Presse- und Propagandapolitik des Deutschen Reiches," *Zeitungswissenschaft* 16 (1941): 26 ff. The memoirs of the participants: Otto Hammann, *Bilder*, pp. 124 ff.; Matthias Erzberger, *Erlebnisse*, pp. 1 ff.; W. Nicolai, *Nachrichtendienst, Presse und Volksstimmung im Weltkrieg* (Berlin, 1920), pp. 51 ff.; and E. Deutelmoser, "Die amtliche Einwirkung auf die deutsche Öffentlichkeit im Kriege," *Deutsche Nation* I (1919): 18 ff. are generally uninformative.

6 "Bestimmungen über die Verwertung der in den Pressekonferenzen angegebenen Informationen," Oct. 27, 1914, AA, Wk. no. 8, vol. 41, reprinted in Deist, *Militär* 1 : 76 ff. For a partial file of protocols of the press briefings cf. DZA Po, Rkz. 2,241. On May 21, 1915, Ambassador Mumm, the Foreign Office spokesman, advised "against engaging in the unleashing of a popular war against the entire Italian nation" in order not to destroy the chance for separate peace at a later time. When editor Neumann of the *Lokalanzeiger* criticized the "usual weakness of the Wilhelmstrasse" in rude terms and only partially apologized, Mumm noted: "I would consider it high time to have the *Lokalanzeiger* instructed that it generally has to orient its line according to the policy of the chancellor." DZA Po, Rkz. 2,437/5.

7 Bethmann to Loebell, Oct. 11, 1914, DZA Po, Rkz. 2,466/4. Cf. also Wahnschaffe's marginalia on Loebell's "morale report" of Sept. 30 and his critical note regarding the *Stimmungsbericht* of Nov. 3, 1914, DZA Po, Rkz. 2,437/3 and 2,437/4. Bethmann to Loebell, Jan. 2, 1915, BA *Nachlass* Loebell. Bethmann marginalia on the annexationist petition of the *Kriegsausschuss der deutschen Industrie*, Mar. 11, 1915, DZA, Rkz. 2,441/11, cited by Mommsen, "Die Regierung," pp. 135–36. For impressive evidence of popular sympathy for the chancellor cf. the twelve-volume file of declarations of support in the DZA Po, Rkz. 1,749/3 to 1,749/14. See also

Riezler Diary, Feb. 17, 1915: "Hammann is supposed to be freed from his other duties in order to prepare the ground for domestic action."

8 Riezler Diary, Oct. 22, 1914. Westarp, *Konservative Politik*, 2 : 307–08. Riezler Diary, Oct. 30, Nov. 8, 26, Dec. 12: "The people are sad because not all their fondest dreams are ripening. They fear that if the war does not end well because of bad leadership, revolution will break out." Bethmann to Treutler, April 4, 1915, in Janssen, ed., *Treutler*, pp. 227 ff. Cf. Stresemann to Wedel, Jan. 16, 1915: "With Bethmann and Wahnschaffe, we will never become a world empire." AA *Nachlass* Stresemann, 3,055. For the gradual formation of the anti-chancellor movement cf. H. Class, *Wider den Strom*, pp. 301 ff.; Hermann Dewitz, *Von Bismarck bis Bethmann: Innenpolitische Rückblicke eines Konservativen* (Berlin, 1919), pp. 60 ff.; Elard von Oldenburg-Januschau, *Erinnerungen* (Leipzig, 1936), pp. 126 ff. See also A. Kruck, *Geschichte des Alldeutschen Verbandes*, 73 ff.; W. Gutsche, "Die Beziehungen," pp. 355 ff.; D. Stegmann, *Sammlungspolitik*, pp. 414 ff.; and for a fresh conceptual framework, A. J. Mayer, *Dynamics of Counterrevolution in Europe, 1870–1956* (New York, 1971).

9 Liebknecht statement in the session of the Socialist Reichstag caucus, Feb. 21, 1915, protocol Giebel, reprinted by Matthias-Pikart, *Reichstagsfraktion*, 2 : 29 ff. Riezler Diary, Jan. 20, Feb. 6, 17, 1917. "What a spectacle—the unconscious Germanization of social democracy, in which the most German idealism had caught itself in the barbed wire of dogmas imported from France and England in the 1860s." Bethmann marginal note on a memorandum by Riezler regarding the treatment of Liebknecht, Jan. 14, 1915: "If the revisionists leave the intransigents too long uncurbed, the danger arises that the radicals will gain ascendancy, especially since the general public mood is deteriorating." Bethmann note of conversation with Kessel, Feb. 7, and a Wahnschaffe memorandum, Feb. 4, 1915, DZA Po, Rkz. 1,395/9. Bethmann to Loebell, July 21; Bethmann to Fendrich, Sept. 11, 1915; both in DZA Po. Rkz. 1,395/10. Cf. also W. Barthel, *Die Linken in der deutschen Sozialdemokratie*, pp. 219 ff. and W. Wohlgemuth, *Burgkrieg, nicht Burgfriede! Der Kampf Karl Liebknechts, Rosa Luxemburgs und ihrer Anhänger um die Rettung der deutschen Nation in den Jahren 1914–1916* (Berlin, 1963), pp. 117 ff.

10 Riezler Diary, Mar. 4, Apr. 28, May 22, 1915: "The world presents a horrible spectacle: The collapse of idealism; paroxysms of hatred; base power of modernity; the ignorance of the mob in the hands of the press combines." Bethmann to Hutten-Czapski, Apr. 21, 1915, DZA Po *Nachlass* Hutten. Bethmann to Hirsch, May 5, 1915, DZA Po, Rkz. 2,442/12. Bethmann to parliamentary leaders, May 13 and to industrialists, May 17, 1915, WPs. Cf. also Stresemann's justification of the petition of the industrial organizations to Peter, Mar 1, 1915, and the revealing correspondence between Hirsch and Erzberger, Mar. 28 ff. about the extent of the chancellor's annexationism, Stresemann Papers, reels 3,055 and 3,062. Cf. Westarp, *Konservative Politik*, 2 : 161 ff.; Haussmann, *Schlaglichter*, pp. 24 ff., 31 ff., 35 ff. See also F. Fischer, *Griff*, pp. 180 ff. and John A. Moses, "Pan-Germanism and the German Professors 1914–1918," *Australian Journal of Politics and History* 15 (1969) : 45 ff.

11 Riezler memorandum on the Pan-German fronde, Sept. 15, 1916, DZA Po, Rkz. 1,418. Bethmann to Class, Feb. 6, 1915, Class, *Wider den Strom*, pp. 386 ff. Cf. also Riezler's unsent draft letter to the Pan-German leader, Dec. 27, 1914: "In our times the political leadership needs the understanding cooperation of public opinion and its makers, but can only win the battle if every single man on the political front does not act according to his personal impulse but determines

timing and manner of public demonstrations according to the wishes of the government, even if its reasons are not known to him." AA, Dld 169, vol. 5. Cf. also Bethmann to Class, Mar. 31, 1915: "Every patriot who is not at the front must subordinate his personal opinions about the future to the need of the moment and must eschew agitation as long as the responsible authorities consider it inopportune." To do otherwise would be a "grave violation of his duty to the crown." Ibid., pp. 388 ff. Bethmann to Prussian minister of war, Feb. 26, 1915, AA, Dld 169, vol. 7, reprinted in Deist, *Militär*, 1 : 228 ff.

12 Bethmann to Gebsattel, May 13, 1915 (draft by Riezler). Bethmann note rejecting the claims of Conservative publicist Strantz, Aug. 14, 1915, DZA Po, Rkz. 1,415 and 1,416. Bethmann to Hertling, July 2, 1915, BHStA MA I 961. For attempts to exploit particularist sentiment cf. Hertling to Lerchenfeld, Mar. 29, 1915; Hertling to Bethmann, Dec. 9, 1915, ibid. MA I 957b; the material in the Saxonian file AM 1,090 on Bethmann in the SHStA; the chancellor's correspondence with Weizsäcker and Eisendecher; and the Badensian documents in GLAK 233, 34,815-16. Cf. also Janssen, *Macht und Verblendung*, pp. 58 ff. Riezler Diary, June 23, 1916; Wahnschaffe to Valentini, June 29, 1915, DZA Me, Rep. 92.

13 Bethmann to Kessel, June 22, 1915; Eugen Zimmermann to Bethmann, June 19, 1915. Wahnschaffe to Oertel, June 29, 1915; Bethmann to Ebert and Scheidemann, July 11, 1915; Bethmann marginal comments on article of *Vorwärts*, Sept. 1, 1915, "Nutzniesser des Krieges," revealing his bias: "The attacks against the agrarians will probably have to be refuted." All in DZA Po, Rkz. 2,437/6 and 2,437/7. Cf. also Bethmann to Prince Max von Baden, Mar. 13, 1915, refusing to allow the distribution of an article by H. S. Chamberlain in order not to create a precedent, DZA Po, Rkz. 2,398/2. Cf. also Bethmann's reaction to Ballin's complaint of July 9 about the suppression of an article by the pacifist von Truppel: "Only for military articles do we have preventive censorship." DZA Po, Rkz. 2,398/3. Cabinet order of William II, Aug. 4, 1915, and the draft organizational charts for *Kriegspresseamt* and *Oberzensurstelle* of Sept. 1915, reprinted in Deist, *Militär*, 1 : 101 ff., 289 ff. Cf. also Koszyk, *Pressepolitik*, passim.

14 Riezler Diary, July 24, Aug. 18, 23, 1915, and DZA Po, Rkz. 2,447/3, "Die Intrigen des Abgeordneten Bassermann und nationalliberale Kundgebungen gegen den Reichskanzler," for Bassermann to Buhl, n.d.; WP Aug. 2 of the chancellor's conference with the Liberal party leaders; Bassermann to Bethmann, Aug. 2; *Nationalliberale Korrespondenz*, Aug. 16; and Bethmann to Hertling, Aug. 14, 1916. Cf. also the material in the Schiffer Papers in PrGStA and Stresemann Papers, reel 3,055, reprinted in K. P. Reiss, *Von Bassermann zu Stresemann*, pp. 195 ff.; E. Schiffer, *Ein Leben*, pp. 186 ff.; Haussmann, *Schlaglichter*, pp. 40 ff.; WP of parliamentary leader briefing, Aug. 16, 1915; Thimme, *Kriegsreden*, pp. 37 ff.; H. Thieme, *Nationaler Liberalismus in der Krise*, pp. 64 ff.; and Mommsen, "Regierung," pp. 139 ff. Bethmann to Oettingen, Sept. 4, 1915, BA *Nachlass* Oettingen.

15 For his concern with the development of the Socialists and the ineffectiveness of the revisionists, cf. Bethmann to Weizsäcker, July 3, 1915, *Privatnachlass* Weizsäcker. Riezler *Diary*, Aug. 29, 1915: "Unable to forget the Russo-German community of interest, the Conservatives invoke Bismarck and maintain that we have no political differences with Russia (true: as little as the lamb with the wolf) —they are pale with fright over Poland. The National Liberals have nothing more to offer because their best ideas have become common currency . . . ; totally empty, concealing their sterility with hollow boasts, they are activated by personal gain, vanity, careerism, thirst for power, and by the patronage of heavy industry, attracting men like Stresemann and Fuhrmann" ibid., Sept. 27, 1915. For the

chancellor's view at the end of 1915, cf. Bethmann to Valentini, Dec. 2, 1915, DZA Me, Rep. 92, Valentini no. 2. Hohenlohe to Burian, Aug. 16, 1915, HHStA, PA III, 171B. "None of these parties, no matter how much they disagree with Bethmann, would presently risk a chancellor crisis, if only because they would be unable to present a successor."

16 Riezler memorandum on Pan-German fronde, Sept. 15, 1916, DZA Po, Rkz. 1,418. Riezler Diary, Jan. 18, Feb. 22, 1915. Bethmann to Falkenhayn, Feb. 5, 23, 1916, AA, Wk. 18 secr., adhib. 1, vols. 1 and 2. Bethmann marginalia on Wild letter of Mar. 5, 1916, DZA Po, Rkz. 2,437/9. Bethmann to the press, Mar. 13, 1916, DZA Po *Nachlass* Hammann, cited by Mommsen, "Regierung," pp. 143–44 and the note of the editor of the *Hamburger Kurier*, Mar. 19, 1916 in the Stresemann Papers, reel 3,064. For the party leader briefings cf. WP, Mar. 14, 1916 and Stresemann notes, n.d., Feb. 19 and Mar. 28, 1915, in his Papers, reel 3,064. Cf. also Hanssen, *Diary*, pp. 135 ff.; Haussmann, *Schlaglichter*, pp. 58 ff.; and Westarp, *Konservative Politik*, 2 : 118 ff. Bethmann to Valentini, Mar. 26, 1916, DZA Me, Rep 89H, I Gen 6. Valentini Diary, Mar. 28, 29, 1916, BA *Nachlass* Thimme. Riezler Diary, Mar. 25, 26, 1915; and Müller, *Regierte?*, pp. 155 ff., 163 ff., quoting Valentini's fear that Bethmann might resign: "The kaiser will not drop him, but the chancellor himself will come and say he has not the necessary confidence of the German people and it would be better if he went."

17 Riezler Diary, Apr. 15, 28, 1916. Bethmann to Treutler, March 24, 1916, reprinted in Janssen, ed., *Treutler*, pp. 240 ff. Bethmann to Strachwitz, July 23, 1916, DZA Po, Rkz. 2,444/4: "It is very harmful for our morale if the people are told time and again that the government does not fully use our weapons because it desires an understanding with England or it does not permit the debate of our war aims because it lacks well defined goals." Loebell to Bethmann, Feb. 4, with his marginalia Feb. 5, 1916; Bethmann note, Mar. 13, 1916; DZA Po, Rkz. 2,437/9. Olberg to Wahnschaffe, Apr. 4, 1916, regarding the permission of "very general discussions" about the chancellor's war aims speech. Cf. also Wahnschaffe's marginalia on letter of Wandel, Apr. 8, 1916: "Loebell's proposal runs directly counter to the interests of the *political* leadership." Bethmann to the ministers of state, Apr. 22, 1916, suggesting that "new guidelines will prove sufficient." Bethmann to Falkenhayn, July 4, and to Luckwaldt, June 7, 1916; Bethmann to William II, June 9, 1916; Bethmann to the Imperial Press Association, June 10, 1916; all in DZA Po, Rkz. 2,437/10.

18 Wolfgang Kapp, *Die Nationalen Kreise und der Reichskanzler* (Königsberg, May 1916). For the official correspondence regarding the "Kapp affair" cf. also DZA Po, Rkz. no. 799. Wahnschaffe dotted the margins of the pamphlet with exclamations like: "Unheard of . . . trite . . . the navy doesn't even believe that itself . . . outrageous," etc. Kapp to Bethmann, June 6, 18, complaining about the "grave personal affront"; protocol of the session of the Ministry of State, June 20; Trott Zu Solz, compromise declaration of June 23; and Bethmann to Buch, June 22, 1916. Cf. Oldenburg-Januschau, *Erinnerungen*, p. 175; Westarp, *Konservative Politik* 2 : 169 ff. Cf. also the counterpamphlet by Georg Wagner, editor of the *Posner Neueste Nachrichten*, ingeniously entitled "Ver'kapp'te Feinde im Reich": "He and his supporters are afraid of the '*Neuorientierung* of domestic policy'. These gentlemen correctly fear for their power position which they occupied before the war in Prussia-Germany." DZA Po, Rkz. 1,417/2. Cf. also Bethmann's characteristic marginalia on the complaint of the *Freie Vaterländische Vereinigung* (a moderate bourgeois organization fighting the Pan-Germans) of July 31, 1916, that the military had forbidden the foundation of a local chapter: "It is unbearable that the deputy commanding general in Stettin, together with the

Pommersche Tagespost, conducts an independent policy for the benefit of Pomeranian Junkers," DZA Po, Rkz. 2,437/10. Cf. also Hohenlohe to Burian, Aug. 3, 1916 and Müller, *Regierte?,* p. 197.

19 Junius Alter, alias Franz Sontag, *Das deutsche Reich auf dem Wege zur geschichtlichen Episode* (Munich, 1916), reprinted in slightly changed form as an anonymous broadside by "three Germans" at Pentecost 1916, under the title *Deutsche Reichspolitik seit 14. Juli 1909.* Although, despite repeated house searchings, the police failed to discover the person behind the pseudonym, they intercepted the correspondence of the volkish publisher Lehmann with Hans Liebig, March 28, 1916: "For our chancellor, too, the hour of judgment will come." Hans von Liebig, "Zu neuen Ufern," summer 1915; *Die Politik von Bethmann Hollweg* two vols. bound in one (Munich, 1916); a copy of the third volume, *Das B-System als Sieger,* printed in April 1917, is in the DZA Po, Rkz. 1419. In his brochure, *Reichsverderber* (Berlin, 1921), he claimed: "The bitterness with which Bethmann fought against the Pan-Germans was striking. This was the only struggle during the war which he led firmly and energetically." Bethmann to Wild, Apr. 1916 (cessat), DZA Po, Rkz. 1,417; Heinrich Class, *Vertrocknete Herzen?* (Easter 1916, n.p.); Heinrich Pudor, under the letterhead of the swastika, representing a largely imaginary German volkish council, sued the chancellor for treason, June 30, 1917, DZA Po, Rkz. 1,420. For Hirsch's increasingly acrimonious correspondence with Wahnschaffe, circulated in mimeographed form, cf. BA, Kl. Erw. 381–2 and DZA Po *Nachlass* Westarp. For another anti-Bethmann pamphlet see ibid. Kl. Erw. 427–1. The Zeppelin-Bethmann correspondence was also eventually published as a broadside, DZA Po, Rkz. 2,448/2. Bacmeister's attacks in the Rhineland papers were also widely read, prompting the chancellor to comment on an article in *Der Tag,* Aug. 31, 1916, "Bassermann should keep his party in line!" For a running collection of material on the fronde cf. also DZA Po, Rkz. 1,416 ff. Cf. also Koszyk, *Pressepolitik,* pp. 152 ff.

20 The extraordinarily perceptive analysis of Bavarian Minister of War Kress, Aug. 5, 1916, is in the BHStA MA 95,448, recently also reprinted by Deist, *Militär,* 1 : 406 ff. Cf. also Wahnschaffe to Valentini, Aug. 3, 1916: "This miserable talk would not have to be taken so seriously if the unscrupled propaganda did not cause a nearly fatal confusion in the minds of true patriots." DZA Po, Rkz. 2,437/ 10. Cf. also Riezler's brilliant memorandum on the Pan-German fronde, Sept. 15, 1916, ibid., Rkz. 1,418, which almost verbally agrees with his diary, June 17, 1916: "Deep chasm between Prussia and the rest because of the insatiable and not yet discredited faith in blind force. The Conservatives speculate *à la baisse,*" predicting a dire end to the war and blaming the chancellor. For the partiality of the legal system, foreshadowing Weimar, cf. the *Berliner Tageblatt* article on a fine of 30 Mks for the chairman of the *Vaterländische Schriftenverband,* Aug. 18, 1916, to which Bethmann remarked, "The court could have reduced the penalty to 1.50 Mks in order not to hit too hard the poor 'factory owner' who distributed a pamphlet directed against the crown."

21 K. H. Schädlich, "Der Unabhängige Ausschuss für einen deutschen Frieden," *Politik im Krieg,* pp. 50 ff.; Dietrich Schäfer, *Mein Leben* (1926, n.p.); and D. Stegmann, *Sammlungspolitik,* pp. 463 ff. For the thrust of the anti-Bethmann propaganda see the anonymous poem MS in the Hoover Library, Stanford University, charging that Germany's fate would not change for the better:

> Bis *der* kommt, den im Gezänke
> Der Parteien das Volk erfleht,

Dessen Geistes Sturmesbrausen
Eitler Zwerge Spur verweht.

Dann erst finden Ruh die Toten,
Für die Heimat hingemäht.
Dann, erst dann, Du Volk der Helden,
Ernte, was mit Blut gesät.

22 Bethmann to Thimme, June 18, 1916, thanking the librarian of the Prussian Herrenhaus for the collected work, *Der innere Frieden des deutschen Volkes,* DZA Po, Rkz. 2,437/10. Riezler Diary, June 17, 1916. Bethmann to Wahnschaffe, June 1, 1916, DZA Po, Rkz. 1,417/1. Thimme, *Kriegsreden,* pp. 122 ff. For the intense debate provoked by Bethmann's denunciation cf. the press clippings in SHStA, AM, 1,093. Westarp to Lisske, June 13, 1916, DZA Po, Rkz. 1,391/1. Bassermann to Haussmann, Sept. 23, 1916, ibid., Rkz. 1,418. Bethmann's marginal comment on letter of Lisske, June 20, 1916, ibid., Rkz. 1391/1. Westarp, *Konservative Politik,* 2 : 168 ff.; and Matthias-Miller, *David Tagebuch,* p. 181: "A bold, strong stroke against the Right. Bethmann has grown."

23 Bethmann meeting with party leaders, July 17, 1916, WP; Bethmann conference with Conservative party members of the Upper House, Aug. 5, 1916, WP. Lerchenfeld protocol of the session of the Bundesrat, Aug. 8/9, BHStA MA I 966, and protocol of the Prussian Ministry of State, Aug. 19, DZA Me, Rep. 90a B III 2b no. 6, vol. 165. Cf. also Riezler Diary, Aug. 30: "The result of the district attorney's investigation against the Pan-Germans [reveals] the insanity of these people, their lack of moral scruples—it would be disastrous if they looked like they were right." Hohenlohe to Burian, Sept. 25, 1916, HHStA, PA III, 172.

24 Bethmann to Kessel, Aug. 4, 1916: "The proof for the contagious effect of this agitation *is the silly but often repeated slander that I regret our naval victory at Jutland*" (italicized phrase struck from the final draft). Bethmann to Kessel, Aug. 5, 1916, calling for the lifting of the prohibition of the *Berliner Tageblatt* in order not to make the liberal paper a martyr. Bethmann to Kessel, Sept. 10, 1916, DZA Po, Rkz. 2,437/10. Cf. also Bethmann to Moltke, Jan. 6, 1916, protesting that "an officer has raised . . . false and grave accusations against a high official and used them in a manner which I consider utterly despicable." DZA Po, Rkz. 1,416. Bethmann note Aug. 18, 1916, Bethmann to Capelle, Sept. 6, 1916, and Wahnschaffe note for Bethmann's conversation with editor Giesen, Oct. 20, 1916, DZA Po, Rkz. 1,417/2 ff. Cf. Müller, *Regierte?,* pp. 213–14.

25 Bethmann to Hertling, July 26, Sept. 27, 1916, DZA Po, Rkz. 2,444/5. Eichmann (?) notes on the deputy ministerial conferences in the chancellery concerned with the improvement of morale on Aug. 31, Sept. 2, and Oct. 5, 1916, and Riezler's draft of an introductory speech revealing the government program: "Gravity of the situation. The people must keep their heads up. No new central office. Every ministry in its area and in its manner." DZA Po, Rkz. 2,437/11 f. Cf. Deist, *Militär,* 1 : 313 ff. for a meeting between the *Kulturbund* and officials on June 24, 1916, admiralty protocols of the following sessions, and a draft of the content of the *Deutsche Kriegsnachrichten.* Cf. also Mommsen, "Regierung," pp. 151–52.

26 Wahnschaffe to Bodenhausen, July 16, 1916. Bethmann to Wedel, July 18, 1916, Nationalausschuss resolution of Nov. 12, 1916, calling for a peace "guaranteeing full security for us and our allies in the future as well as the free unfolding of our forces, corresponding to the immense sacrifices in blood and property and the successes of our weapons and promising guarantees for its permanence." DZA Po, Rkz. 2,448 and 2,448/1. Bethmann to Wach, Oct. 21, 1916, DZA Po, Rkz.

1418/1. Cf. also Lerchenfeld to Dandl, July 7, 1916, BHStA MA III 2691/10, and the entry in *Die bürgerlichen Parteien in Deutschland* (Berlin, 1968–70), vols. 1 and 2 for "Mittwochabend," "Deutsche Gesellschaft 1914," "Freie Vaterländische Vereinigung," its ideological predecessors. Cf. also Stegmann, *Sammlungspolitik*, pp. 477–78.

27 Bethmann to Valentini, July 4, 10, 1916. Bethmann to Kessel, July 7, 1916: "The consciously and tenaciously pursued desire to work toward a chancellor crisis is not the decisive point, despite its determining influence on the attitude of the party." (This section, like the quote from the first Valentini letter in the text, was stricken in the final draft.) DZA Po, Rkz. 1,392. Valentini to Bethmann, July 7, Nov. 17, 1916, DZA Me, Rep. 92, vol. 2. Bethmann to Treutler, July 2, 1916, in Janssen, ed., *Treutler*, pp. 244 ff. Cf. also the entry in the Valentini Diary, Nov. 13, 1916, BA *Nachlass* Thimme and Müller, *Regierte?*, p. 235. Cf. also Westarp, *Konservative Politik* 2 : 312 ff., and for his meeting with the chancellor of Dec. 23, 1916, pp. 316 ff. Cf. also Vitzthum's note of concern "about the growing alienation between the chancellor and the parties of order," July 20, 1916. Nostitz to Vitzthum, Aug. 3, 1916, concluding that "the cause of the antagonism between Conservatives and the chancellor undoubtedly lies in the area of domestic policy." Cf. also Nostitz to Vitzthum, Sept. 25, 27, 1916, all in SHStA, AM, 1,090. Because of the discontent of the Right, Bülow attempted to reactivate his candidacy for chancellorship in the summer of 1916 with the cleverly written apology, *Deutsche Politik* (Berlin, 1916). Hohenlohe to Burian, Dec. 22, 1916, HHStA, PA III, 172.

28 For the appointment of the third OHL cf. Mommsen, "Regierung," pp. 147 ff. Riezler to Bodenhausen, Sept. 9, 1916, DZA Po, Rkz. 2,448/1. Bethmann to Wach, Oct. 10, 1916, DZA Po, Rkz. 1,418. Bassermann to Stresemann, Sept. 23, 1916, Stresemann Papers, reel 3,061. Cf. also Stresemann to Körting, Nov. 20, 1916, rejecting renewed assaults since "hasty attacks against the chancellor have only the opposite result." Ibid., 3,065. For detailed reports of the UA mass meeting in the Reichstag, cf. Nostitz to Vitzthum, Oct. 18, SHStA, AM 1,090, Larisch to Burian, Oct. 4, 1916, HHStA, PA III, 172, and Lerchenfeld to Hertling, Oct. 17, 1916, BHStA MA 95,448. Riezler Diary, Nov. 22 and Dec. 9, 1916. Bethmann to Hindenburg, Jan. 16, Feb. 10, 24, 27, 1917, DZA Po, Rkz. 2,438, complaining about Groener's attacks against Breitenbach as "violation of the appearance of governmental unity . . . without which the prestige of the administration cannot be maintained." Cf. also Ludendorff to Zimmermann, Dec. 28, 1916 (the *Vortrupp* case), and the correspondence between Bethmann and Hindenburg, Mar. 14 ff., 1917, concerning public responsibility for government actions, in Deist, *Militär*, 2 : 553 ff., 672 ff. Cf. also Koszyk, *Pressepolitik*, pp. 31 ff.

29 Ludendorff to Bethmann, Nov. 8, 1916. Bethmann to Loebell and Stein (cessat), Nov. 10, 1916, DZA Po, Rkz. 2,438. Cf. Bethmann to Loebell, Sept. 10, 1916 (still opposed to a lifting of the ban). Ibid. 2,437/12. For the previous situation cf. Olberg guidelines, Aug. 1, 1916. See also the decisive memorandum of the head of the *Kriegspresseamt* of Oct. 5, and notes of an official in the Secretariat of the Interior, Nov. 8 regarding a deputy ministerial conference on the subject, and Helfferich draft telegram, Nov. 11, stating the decision of a second meeting, DZA Po, RdI 12,270. Cf. also Deist, *Militär*, 1 : 431 ff. Bethmann to Hindenburg, Nov. 11, 1916. The new guidelines only prohibited "1) any propaganda against the opinions and motives of others, 2) any argumentation which amounts to the influencing of the conduct of war, and 3) any disturbance of the relations to our allies" to which the word *neutrals* was added. DZA Po, Rkz. 2,438.

30 Bethmann to the Ministry of State, Nov. 23, 1916. Bethmann to William II, Nov. 21, 1916. Bethmann to Valentini, Nov. 21, 1916, Bethmann to Hindenburg, Jan.

16, 1917. Deutelmoser to Bethmann, Feb. 5, 1917, containing the protocols of the press briefings on Nov. 25 ff., 1916, DZA Po, Rkz. 2,438 and 2,439. Cf. also Mommsen, "Regierung," pp. 151 ff. Gutsche, *Deutschland im ersten Weltkrieg*, 2 : 498 ff. Although there is little direct evidence on the motives of Bethmann's ultimate change of mind, it is clear that from the beginning his entourage attempted "to get the war aims debate liberalized. In the end everything can regulate itself only through free discussion," as Riezler noted on Dec. 2, 1915, in his diary.

31 Riezler Diary, Feb. 18, 1917. Ebert in the Socialist caucus session, Feb. 22, 1917; Matthias-Pikart, *Reichstagsfraktion*, pp. 242 ff.; Scheidemann, *Memoirs*, 1 : 332 ff.; Riezler Diary, Feb. 25, Mar. 8, 1917. See also Hohenlohe's incisive dispatch to Czernin, Feb. 26, 1917. Cf. Wahnschaffe MS, pp. 5 ff., stressing the psychological effects of the turnip winter and the transportation and fuel crisis. Cf. also Bethmann to Valentini, Feb. 11, 1917, complaining about William II's authorization of military distribution of H. S. Chamberlain's article, "The Will to Victory," as "such an obviously tendentious incident that it must . . . hasten the disorganization of our domestic conditions, to a degree which should not be underestimated." Schwertfeger, *Kaiser und Kabinettschef*, pp. 247 ff.

32 Riezler Diary, Feb. 20, 24, Mar. 4, 1917. The chancellor's aide feared that "Haussmann would say too much, especially about the touchy subject of Duisberg who . . . said much that he can only know from the OHL," but hoped that his "words would impress Ludendorff and serve him as warning." The entire material relating to the Adlon meeting is in the DZA Me, Rep. 92, vol. 26, together with William II to Valentini, Feb. 25, a stinging rebuke of the fronde. On Feb. 28 Valentini noted in his diary: "Because of the Duisberg speech and the Adlon meeting the cabinet chiefs are supposed to write to Hindenburg and Knorr." BA *Nachlass* Thimme. Haussmann, *Schlaglichter*, pp. 85 ff.; Scheidemann, *Memoirs*, 1 : 339 ff.; Westarp, *Konservative Politik*, 2 : 170–71; Müller, *Regierte?*, pp. 262–63. Cf. also Tirpitz, *Deutsche Ohnmachtspolitik*, p. 598 and Schulthess's *GK* (1917), 1 : 183, 229 ff.

33 Riezler Diary, Mar. 11, 1917. Colonel Bauer, "Bemerkungen über den Reichskanzler," Mar. 6; "Die Stellung des Reichskanzlers," middle of March; and "Über die Zukunft Deutschlands," late April 1917, in BA *Nachlass* Bauer, reprinted in Deist, *Militär*, 1 : 579 ff. and 2 : 673 ff. and 716 ff. Cf. also Grünau to AA, Mar. 14, 1917, ibid., 2 : 670 ff. Oberst Bauer, *Der grosse Krieg in Feld und Heimat*, pp. 133 ff.; E. Ludendorff, *Meine Kriegserinnerungen, 1914–1918* (Berlin, 1919), pp. 355 ff.; G. Ritter, *Kriegskanzler*, pp. 503 ff.; and H. Weber, *Ludendorff und die Monopole*, pp. 67 ff. Cf. also Hohenlohe to Czernin, Mar. 21, 1917, HHStA, PA III, 173. Stresemann to Bassermann, Apr. 9, 1917: "Bethmann's position is presently very dubious. . . . The entire GHQ stands almost unanimously against him. . . . The emperor vacillates because he wants to avoid a break with the Socialists and believes that Bethmann still controls them, for which he is very grateful." Stresemann Papers, reel 3,061. For the running battle between chancellor and OHL see the entries of the Valentini Diary for spring 1917, BA *Nachlass* Thimme and Müller, *Regierte?*, pp. 265 ff.

34 Riezler Diary, Mar. 18, 25, 28, Apr. 13, 1917; Vitzthum to Nostitz, Mar. 29, 1917, SHStA, AM, Ber 273; Schulthess's *GK* (1917), 1 : 396 ff. C. Schorske, *German Social Democracy*, pp. 312 ff.; L. Stern, *Der Einfluss der grossen sozialistischen Oktoberrevolution*, 4/II, pp. 406 ff.; Gutsche, *Deutschland im Ersten Weltkrieg*, 2 : 625 ff.; Hohenlohe to Czernin, Mar. 30, Apr. 23 ff., 1917, HHStA, PA III, 172B. Schoen to Hertling, Apr. 17; note by Hartz, Apr. 23, 1917, BHStA MA III 2691/13 and MA I 975; Riezler Diary, Apr. 13, 16, 19, 25, 1917. Bethmann to Stein, Mar. 26, 1917,

and Wahnschaffe Protocol of meeting Mar. 21, 1917, to discuss countermeasures against the deterioration of morale following the Russian Revolution, DZA Po, Rkz. 2,349. Cf. also Mommsen, "L'opinion allemande et la chute du gouvernement Bethmann Hollweg en juillet 1917," *Revue d'histoire moderne et contemporaine* (1968), pp. 46 ff. For the larger perspectives cf. also A. J. Mayer, *Political Origins of the New Diplomacy, 1917–1918* (New Haven, 1959) and the essays in Hellmuth Rössler, ed., *Weltwende 1917: Monarchie—Weltrevolution—Demokratie* (Göttingen, 1965).

35   Wahnschaffe MS, pp. 44 ff. Hohenlohe to Czernin, May 12, Larisch to Czernin, June 20, 1917, HHStA, PA III, 173; Schoen to Hertling, May 3, 5; Lerchenfeld to Hertling, May 15, June 9, 1917, BHStA MA I 958; Nostitz to Vitzthum, May 12, 1917, SHStA AM, 1,090. Riezler Diary, Apr. 20, May 8, 9, 13, 1917. Cf. also Williamson, *Helfferich*, pp. 211 ff.

36   French governmental circular, *L'Allemagne véritable* (Feb. 1917), DZA Po, Rkz. 1,418/2. Cf. also Michaelis to Lersner, Sept. 1, 1917, and the surrounding correspondence for the question of the authenticity of the document. Cf. also Bethmann to Gebsattel, May 10, 1917 (cessat) pointing to the "advantage which the attentive enemy has been able to draw and hopes to draw in the future from this agitation of secret and open broadsides," DZA Po, Rkz. 1,418/2, Riezler Diary, June 9, 1916. Cf. also Egan to Lansing, May 16, reporting the latest information of Wiegand, NA. "There is widespread general dissatisfaction with the chancellor. All agreed only on one point, namely that he must go." The American journalist concluded that the emperor's immediate entourage was "extremely reactionary" and "accuses the chancellor of being too weak and coquetting with Socialists," while more liberal forces in GHQ and Berlin deplored his "Mexican blunder and failure to make any separate peace with Russia." See Pogge-v. Strandmann, ed., *Rathenau Tagebuch*, May 5, 1917, pp. 213 ff., conversation with Bethmann.

37   Erzberger note on Bethmann's fall, July 15, 1917, BA *Nachlass* Bülow, no. 73. Erzberger, *Erlebnisse*, pp. 251 ff.; Epstein, *Erzberger*, pp. 204 ff.; Matthias-Morsey, *IFA*, 1 : xxviii ff.; *Erzberger Prozess* (Berlin, 1920), passim; Scheidemann, *Zusammenbruch*, pp. 85 ff.; Haussmann, *Schlaglichter*, pp. 96 ff.; Westarp, *Konservative Politik*, 2 : 343 ff.; Helfferich, *Weltkrieg*, pp. 443 ff.; Hanssen, *Diary*, pp. 201 ff.; *WUA*, vol. 7, passim, and Magnus von Braun, *Von Ostpreussen bis Texas* (Stallhamm, 1955), pp. 109 ff. Wahnschaffe MS, pp. 69 ff., 91 ff. According to an entry of July 24, 1917, Riezler filled a separate notebook with comments on the July crisis, which did not survive; hence his remarks are rather sketchy. Cf. also Larisch to Czernin, July 7 ff., 1917, HHStA, PA III, 173 and Lerchenfeld to Loessl, Ludwig, and Hertling, July 6 ff., 1917, BHStA MA I 969 and MA III 2691/14 for accurate and detailed reports. For a file of press clippings that demonstrate the crisis of morale cf. SHStA AM, 1,092. Cf. Egan to Lansing, July 9, 1917, NA: "The internal political storm which is now sweeping through Germany seems every hour more severe," quoting the *Hamburger Fremdenblatt* on "the bankruptcy of the system." See also Mommsen, "La chute," pp. 50 ff. who slights the intrigue.

38   Wahnschaffe MS, pp. 94 ff. Matthias-Morsey, *IFA*, 1 : 12 ff.; Haussmann, *Schlaglichter*, pp. 100 ff.; Payer, *Von Bethmann*, pp. 29 ff.; Scheidemann, *Zusammenbruch*, pp. 86 ff.; Matthias-Pikart, *Reichstagsfraktion*, pp. 283 ff.; Matthias-Miller, *David Tagebuch*, pp. 240 ff.; Helfferich, *Weltkrieg*, pp. 444 ff.; and Hanssen, *Diary*, pp. 207 ff. Cf. also DZA Po, Rtg. no. 1,314 for the full stenographic report of the Budget Committee session.

39   Hindenburg to William II, June 27, 1917: "The gravest concern is the decline of public morale; it must be raised, otherwise we will lose the war." The OHL frankly doubted "whether the chancellor is capable of correctly solving these

tasks." Note by Colonel Mertz von Quirnheim, "Der Kampf gegen den Reichs-kanzler," July 9, and excerpt of letter of July 7, 1917, reprinted by Deist, *Militär*, 2 : 782 ff. Wahnschaffe MS, pp. 109 ff.: "I had no objections to briefing the parliamentarians on military matters." Copies of Hindenburg to William II, July 7; and Wahnschaffe to Ludendorff, July 8, 1917. Erzberger note July 15, 1917, BA *Nachlass* Bülow, no. 73. Cf. also Valentini Diary, July 6 ff., 1917, BA *Nachlass* Thimme and Müller, *Regierte?*, pp. 300 ff. G. Ritter, *Kriegskanzler*, pp. 560 ff. Cf. also Wahnschaffe to Valentini, already on May 24, 1917, DZA Me, Rep. 92 "I have only small hope that [the chancellor] will succeed in maintaining his au-thority as firmly as this horribly serious time demands. The struggle with the OHL is here known to every journalist and parliamentarian." Cf. also Hinden-burg to Bethmann, July 7, 1917 (cessat), AA *Nachlass* Hintze, material of the 2. UA.

40 Colonel Bauer, résumé, "Bethmann Hollweg's Sturz," BA *Nachlass* Bauer. Stresemann, "Material für die Darstellung der Krisis," July 1917, Stresemann Papers, reel 3,075, both reprinted by Matthias-Mosey, *IFA* 1 : 73 ff. Erzberger note on Bethmann's fall, July 15, 1917, BA *Nachlass* Bülow, no. 73. Wahnschaffe MS, pp. 114 ff. Matthias-Mosey, *IFA*, 1 : 14 ff.; Haussmann, *Schlaglichter*, pp. 103 ff.; Scheidemann, *Zusammenbruch*, pp. 87–88; Westarp, *Konservative Politik*, 2 : 350 ff.; Matthias-Miller, *David Tagebuch*, pp. 241 ff.; Hanssen, *Diary*, pp. 216 ff. Cf. also Larisch to Czernin, July 8, 1917, HHStA, PA III, 173. Lerchenfeld to King Ludwig, July 8, 1917, reporting an audience with William II in which the am-bassador stressed the confidence of the states in Bethmann. Although "his power of decision is not very great, this is compensated by many valuable traits. . . . To call a conservative chancellor now appears to me downright dangerous." BHStA MA I 969.

41 Wahnschaffe MS, pp. 118 ff. DZA Po, Rtg no. 1,314. Hanssen, *Diary*, pp. 216 ff. Lerchenfeld to Loessl, July 9, 1917, reporting assurances from Valentini, with the caveat, "There is yet another pending issue which could lead to a chancellor crisis—the difference between chancellor and OHL regarding war aims." BHStA MA I 969. Hohenlohe to Czernin, July 10, 1917, HHStA, PA III, 173. Helfferich *Weltkrieg*, pp. 448–49; Valentini Diary, July 9 ff., 1917, BA *Nachlass* Thimme, and Müller, *Regierte?*, pp. 301 ff.: "The responsibility for this entire dangerous crisis rests in Valentini's opinion—and also in mine—with the OHL who has taken the lead in the Pan-German antichancellor agitation." Cf. also Stovall's contradictory dispatch to Lansing, July 12, 1917, NA, indicating Zimmermann's and Helfferich's falls as likely: "Majority of papers believe that chancellor will remain in view of his strong position with Emperor but all-German and con-servative papers consider his position shaky and mention Counts Hertling and Bernstorff as most probable successors."

42 Matthias-Miller, *David Tagebuch*, pp. 243–44; Scheidemann, *Zusammenbruch*, pp. 88 ff.; Haussmann, *Schlaglichter*, pp. 115 ff.; Westarp, *Konservative Politik*, 2 : 353 ff. Matthias-Morsey, *IFA* 1 : 110 ff. for a textual comparison of the four successive drafts of the peace resolution. Wahnschaffe MS, pp. 154 ff. Stresemann, "Material für die Darstellung der Krisis," July 1917, Stresemann Papers, reel 3,075. Erzberger note on Bethmann's fall, July 15, 1917, *Nachlass* Bülow, no. 73. Valentini Diary, July 10 ff., 1917, BA *Nachlass* Thimme and Müller, *Regierte?*, pp. 302 ff. Pogge-v. Strandmann, *Rathenau Tagebuch*, July 12, 1917, "Zweites Gespräch mit Ludendorff," pp. 216 ff., where Rathenau proposed that Ludendorff himself take over the political leadership; the quartermaster general, with surprising insight into his own limitations, rejected the suggestion. For the reversal of the progres-sive press cf. Egan to Lansing, July 14, 1917, NA: "All seem to agree that the

Prussian suffrage proclamation leaves the crisis still unsolved and that nothing short of the fate [*sic*] of the chancellor . . . will quiet the agitation." Erzberger, *Erlebnisse*, pp. 261 ff. Hohenlohe to Czernin, July 10, 11, 1917, HHStA, PA III, 173 and Lerchenfeld to Loessl, July 10, 11, 1917, BHStA MA I 969. See also Theodor Wolff, *Der Marsch durch zwei Jahrzehnte* (Amsterdam, 1936), pp. 144 ff.

43   Memorandum of the crown prince regarding "Die Ereignisse in Berlin, Juli 11–13" written on July 18, 1917, DZA Po, Rkz. 2,403/5 (providing the basis for Herre, *Kronprinz Wilhelm*, pp. 87 ff.). Cf. also ibid. for a short note of Helfferich regarding the July crisis, and for the pencil drafts of Bethmann's notes on his resignation, July 11, and July 14, 1917, reprinted in *WUA*, 2 : 153. Cf. also Bauer, *Der grosse Krieg*, pp. 141–42; Ludendorff, *Urkunden der OHL*, 408 ff.; Payer, *Von Bethmann*, pp. 31–32; Haussmann, *Schlaglichter*, pp. 121 ff.; Erzberger, *Erlebnisse*, pp. 262 ff.; Westarp, *Konservative Politik*, 2 : 357 ff.; Helfferich, *Weltkrieg*, p. 450; Williamson, *Helfferich*, pp. 225 ff.; Schwertfeger, *Kaiser und Kabinettschef*, pp. 164–65; and Matthias-Morsey, *IFA*, 1 : 56 ff. Wahnschaffe MS, pp. 152 ff. and Valentini Diary, July 12, 1917, BA *Nachlass* Thimme. Cf. also Lerchenfeld to King Ludwig, reporting an audience with William II, July 12, 1917, BHStA MA I 969. See also R. F. Hopwood, "Czernin and the Fall of Bethmann Hollweg," *Canadian History* (1967), pp. 49 ff. Riezler Diary, Oct. 3, 1917: "Maltzahn boasted of having handpicked the parliamentarians whom the crown prince received. Moreover, Bauer had immediately welcomed him and instructed him—hence the question to the party leaders: 'Do you believe Bethmann to be a hindrance to peace?' which David, the ass, affirmed."

44   Stresemann, "Material für die Darstellung der Krisis," July 1917, Stresemann Papers, reel 3,075. Bauer résumé, July 1917, BA *Nachlass* Bauer. Erzberger notes on the chancellor crisis, July 15, 1917, BA *Nachlass* Bülow, no. 73. Bethmann notes on his resignation, July 14, 1917, DZA Po, Rkz. 2,403/5. Wahnschaffe MS, pp. 153 ff. Ludendorff to Lyncker, Hindenburg to Lyncker, July 12, 1917, AA *Nachlass* Hintze, papers of the 2d Investigating Committee of the National Assembly. Crown Prince memorandum, July 18, 1917, DZA Po, Rkz. 1,403/5. Valentini Diary, July 12, 1917, BA *Nachlass* Thimme and Müller, *Regierte?*, pp. 302–03. Cf. also Riezler Diary, Aug. 4, 1917, for Bethmann's first statement that "he [would] not cling to his office" if the OHL threatened to resign. Cf. also Mertz to Hertling, July 12, 1917 BHStA MA I 969, and the excerpt from Mertz's memoirs regarding the crisis, in Deist, *Militär*, 2 : 790 ff.

45   Bethmann note, July 14, DZA Po, Rkz. 2,403/5. Wahnschaffe MS, pp. 154 ff. Bethmann to William II, July 12 (late in the evening), 1917, initialed by the emperor on the morning of July 13, 1917, DZA Me, Rep. 89H, I Gen 6, vol. 2. For Hertling's trip to Berlin cf. his telegram to Loessel, July 13, and Lerchenfeld to King Ludwig, July 14, 1917, BHStA MA I 969 as well as Hertling's letters to his wife and son, July 1917, in his *Nachlass* BA. Valentini Diary, July 13, 1917, BA *Nachlass* Thimme and his narrative, "Zwei Kanzlerwechsel im Jahre 1917," ibid., Kl. Erw. 341-1. Bethmann to William II, July 13, 1917, DZA Me, Rep. 89H, II Dt. Reich, no. 1. Crown Prince memorandum, July 18, 1917, accompanied by a letter to William II, July 13, 1917, DZA Po, Rkz. 2,403/5: "At least I assume that you cannot permit a government with only the Left in the interest of the crown." Helfferich, *Weltkrieg*, pp. 451 ff.; Bethmann, *Betrachtungen*, 2 : 227 ff.; Georg Michaelis, *Für Volk und Staat* (Berlin, 1922), pp. 321 ff.; Payer, *Von Bethmann*, pp. 34 ff. and Braun, *Von Ostpreussen*, pp. 114 ff. Riezler Diary, Aug. 4, 1917: "Few will understand the heroic honesty of his action." Cf. also Stresemann to Fuss, July 14, 1917: "The last days have brought the deepest psychological ex-

citement of my political career. . . . I hope, however, that Bethmann's removal will benefit the fatherland." Stresemann Papers, reel 3,075.

46 Bethmann to Rassow, Aug. 26, 1917, *Privatnachlass* Rassow. Müller, *Regierte?*, pp. 303 ff. recording Bethmann's ruminations on the day of his fall. Valentini to Bethmann, July 14, 1917, transmitting the official notice of his dismissal, DZA Me, Rep. 89H, II Dt. Reich, no. 1. Lerchenfeld speech to the Bundesrat, July 18, 1917, and Bethmann's reply, BHStA, MA, 95,150 and Nostitz to Vitzthum, July 18, 1917, SHStA AM, 273. Cf. also *Norddeutsche Allgemeine Zeitung*, July 14, 1917, "Zum Kanzlerwechsel." Cf. also Nieser to Dusch, July 9 ff., 1917, GLAK 233, no. 34,823. Bethmann to Delbrück, Sept. 8, 1917, DSB, *Nachlass* Delbrück. Bethmann to Naumann, July 17, Nov. 13, 1917, DZA Po *Nachlass* Naumann. Cf. also O. Hammann, *Bilder*, pp. 77–78 for Bethmann's comments about the "hatred of the generals" at his last meal with Wahnschaffe, Heilbron, Riezler, Helfferich, and August Stein. For the limited degree of continuity in personnel, cf. Williamson, *Helfferich*, pp. 229 ff.

47 Diary of the sailor Stumpf, *WUA*, vol. 10/II, 250. Westarp, *Konservative Politik*, 2 : 361–62. Testimony by the son of Spahn to the Reichstag investigating committee, *WUA*, vol. 7, pt. 2, pp. 234 ff. For Stresemann's apologia cf. ibid., pp. 302 ff.; for Bredt's conclusion, vol. 6, 7/I, pp. 86 ff.; for Scheidemann's version, ibid., p. 277; and for Schwertfeger's verdict, ibid., p. 370. Wahnschaffe MS, pp. 159 ff. and Nostitz's penetrating analysis in his dispatches to Vitzthum, July 21 and 22, 1917, SHStA AM 273. For the larger context cf. also Mommsen, "La chute," pp. 51 ff.; Vietsch, *Bethmann Hollweg*, pp. 270 ff.; Gutsche, *Deutschland im Ersten Weltkrieg*, 2 : 753 ff.; Ritter, *Kriegskanzler*, pp. 584 ff.; and Fischer, *Griff nach der Weltmacht*, pp. 516 ff. According to Bethmann's oral communication to Rassow in 1920, *Privatnachlass* Rassow, the kaiser responded to the military ultimatum with the outcry, "Now there is nothing left for me to do but abdicate!"

Chapter 12

1 Bethmann to Eisendecher, July 20, Dec. 19, AA *Nachlass* Eisendecher; Bethmann to Naumann, July 17, DZA Po *Nachlass* Naumann; Bethmann to Weizsäcker, Aug. 6, *Privatnachlass* Weizsäcker; Bethmann to Valentini, July 17, 1917, DZA Me *Nachlass* Valentini. Cf. also Bethmann to Haussmann, July 16: "Thanking you for your friendly letter I wish to express my gratitude for your help during these difficult times and ask you to continue working toward bringing the struggle at home and abroad to an end beneficial to the whole nation." WHStA *Nachlass* Haussmann.

2 Bethmann to Valentini, Dec. 3, DZA Me *Nachlass* Valentini. Bethmann to Eisendecher, Dec. 19, AA *Nachlass* Eisendecher. Bethmann to Oettingen, August 31, BA *Nachlass* Oettingen. Bethmann to Treutler, July 16, 1917, in Janssen, ed., *Treutler*, p. 249. Bethmann to Weizsäcker, Aug. 6, *Privatnachlass* Weizsäcker. The ex-chancellor thanked the Württemberg premier "for all the loyal support which you have given me over so many difficult years. . . . In contrast to the political parties, I have always been spoiled undeservedly by the worthy state governments." Bethmann to Hammann, Oct. 29, 1917, DZA Po *Nachlass* Hammann.

3 Bethmann to Valentini, Dec. 3, 1917, DZA Me *Nachlass* Valentini. Bethmann to Oettingen, Sept. 10, Nov. 30, 1917, BA *Nachlass* Oettingen. Riezler Diary, Aug. 4, 1917. Bethmann was "very well, unpretentious, without pose, and just impressive." Friedrich Meinecke, *Strassburg*, pp. 232 ff., 246 ff.

4 Bethmann to Oettingen, Aug. 31, 1917, BA *Nachlass* Oettingen. Bethmann to

Eisendecher, Jan. 18, 1918, AA *Nachlass* Eisendecher. Bethmann to Hammann, Oct. 29, 1917, DZA Po *Nachlass* Hammann. Although agreeing with the moderate aims of the *Volksbund für Freiheit und Vaterland*, Bethmann refused to join in order not to compromise it with his name. Riezler Diary, Oct. 3, 1917, and Jan. 14, 1918. Bethmann to Thimme, Nov. 28, BA *Nachlass* Thimme, Bethmann to Haussmann, Nov. 28, 1917, WHStA *Nachlass* Haussmann: "We must live through the great revolution which this war means for us, too, honestly and rationally. Quod Deus bene vertat!" Cf. also Georg Michaelis, *Für Volk und Staat* (Berlin, 1922) and K. Graf von Hertling, *Ein Jahr in der Reichskanzlei* (Freiburg, 1919), passim.

5 Bethmann to Valentini, Dec. 3, 1917, Jan. 17, 1918, DZA Me *Nachlass* Valentini. Cf. also Valentini Diary and his *Aufzeichnungen*, BA *Nachlass* Thimme for the successive chancellor crises. Bethmann to Oettingen, Jan. 3, 1918, BA *Nachlass* Oettingen. See Gerhard Ritter's last volume of *Staatskunst und Kriegshandwerk: Die Herrschaft des deutschen Militarismus und die Katastrophe von 1918* (Munich, 1969).

6 Bethmann to Eisendecher, Dec. 19, 1917, Jan. 18, 1918, AA *Nachlass* Eisendecher: "It is good that such words have been spoken from such an important position— and *can* be spoken." Bethmann to Max von Baden, published in *Erinnerungen und Dokumente* (Stuttgart, 1927), p. 179. Bethmann to Max von Baden, Jan. 17, 1918, original in AA, Dld 122, no. 16, vol. 8, reprinted by Egmont Zechlin in "Deutschland zwischen," *HZ* 199 (1964) : 347 ff. The second letter is also commonly called Bethmann's "political testament."

7 Bethmann to Hertling, Jan. 26, 1918, AA, Dld 122, no. 16, vol. 9. (See also the anonymous draft article "Geschichtsfälschungen" in BA, Kl. Erw. 342-1 on Bethmann's autonomy policy.) Bethmann to Oettingen, Jan. 3, 1918, BA *Nachlass* Oettingen. Cf. also R. von Kühlmann, *Erinnerungen*, pp. 511 ff. and K. F. Nowak, *Die Aufzeichnungen des Generalmajors Max von Hoffmann* (Berlin, 1929) 1 : 184–85. See F. Fischer, *Griff nach der Weltmacht*, pp. 621 ff., and J. Petzold, ed., *Deutschland in Ersten Weltkrieg*, vol. 3.

8 Bethmann to Weizsäcker, Dec. 27, 1917, *Privatnachlass* Weizsäcker. Bethmann to Valentini, Jan. 17, 1918, DZA Me *Nachlass* Valentini. Bethmann to Oettingen, Feb. 29, 1918, BA *Nachlass* Oettingen. Bethmann to Solf, Aug. 29, 1918, ibid., *Nachlass* Solf. Riezler Diary, Feb. 11, Apr. 15, 1918. See also Müller, *Regierte?*, pp. 345–46. Cf. John Wheeler-Bennet, *The Forgotten Peace* (London, 1938); Steglich, *Die Friedenspolitik*, pp. 232 ff.; W. Halweg, *Der Diktatfrieden von Brest-Litowsk 1918 und die bolschewistische Weltrevolution* (Münster, 1960); W. Baumgart, *Deutsche Ostpolitik 1918* (Munich, 1966); and my own, "Kurt Riezler and the Failure of German *Ostpolitik*, 1918," *Slavic Review* (1972).

9 Bethmann to Haussmann, June 29, 1918, WHStA *Nachlass* Haussmann. Bethmann to Naumann, July 24, 1918, DZA Po *Nachlass* Naumann. Bethmann to Oettingen, Feb. 28, 1918, BA *Nachlass* Oettingen. Bethmann to Delbrück, Sept. 10, 1918, DSB *Nachlass* Delbrück.

10 Riezler Diary, Sept. 24, 1918. Bethmann to Delbrück, July 27, 1918, DSB *Nachlass* Delbrück. Cf. also Bethmann to Oettingen, May 28, 1918: "Today's army report announces the victory of Chemin des Dames. Splendid, if only it will bring peace closer!" Cf. also his letters of June 3 and July 20, 1918, BA *Nachlass* Oettingen. For the failure of the last offensive cf. also Ludendorff, *Kriegserinnerungen*, pp. 473 ff. and H. Meier-Welcker, "Die deutsche Führung an der Westfront im Frühsommer 1918," *WaG* 21 (1961) : 164 ff. Bethmann to Treutler, September 29, 1918, in Janssen, ed., *Treutler*, pp. 253–54.

11 Bethmann to Oettingen, Oct. 7, 1918, BA *Nachlass* Oettingen. For the causes of

the collapse cf. also the work of the Reichstag's commission of inquiry, subcommittee four, Hoover Institute, Stanford, as well as E. Matthias and R. Morsey, *Die Regierung des Prinzen Max von Baden*, 2 vols. (Düsseldorf, 1962); H. Michaelis and E. Schräpler, eds., *Der Militärische Zusammenbruch und das Ende des Kaiserreichs* (Berlin, 1958); *UF*, vol. 1 and the official *Amtliche Urkunden zur Vorgeschichte des Waffenstillstandes* (Berlin, 1924).

12 Riezler Diary, Oct. 2, Nov. 12, 1918: "Chaos reigns . . . the garrison is dissolved, and the only question is which workers' and soldiers' soviet will win out. Will Liebknecht with a handful of fanatics succeed in taking the scarcely defended centers of power?" Bethmann to Valentini, Dec. 2, 1918, DZA Me *Nachlass* Valentini. Bethmann to Oettingen, Nov. 18, 1918, BA *Nachlass* Oettingen: "The Entente will know how to foil the Anschluss of Austria to Germany and, while not immediately annexing the left bank of the Rhine, will sever it de facto. What remains will be impoverished and enslaved. They will form a League of Nations and accept us, not as equal but as serf. I do not believe in rapid peace."

13 Bethmann to Valentini, Dec. 2, 1918, DZA Me *Nachlass* Valentini. Bethmann to Oettingen, Nov. 18, 30, Dec. 7, 1918, BA *Nachlass* Oettingen: "I do not abandon my belief in the power of our people and count on the fact that we will be spared extensive bolshevism. For the moment I am not discontent with the domestic situation." Bethmann to Kardorff, Dec. 4, 1918, BA *Nachlass* Kardorff. Bethmann to Delbrück, Dec. 7, 1918, DSB *Nachlass* Delbrück. Cf. also A. J. Ryder, *The German Revolution of 1918: A Study of German Socialism in War and Revolt* (London, 1967); Daniel Horn, *The German Naval Mutinies of World War I* (New Brunswick, N.J., 1969); and E. Matthias and S. Miller, *Die Regierung der Volksbeauftragten*, 2 vols. (Düsseldorf, 1969).

14 Bethmann to Haussmann, Dec. 5, 1918, WHStA *Nachlass* Haussmann. Bethmann to Oettingen, Nov. 30, Dec. 7, 1918, BA *Nachlass* Oettingen: "Nobody can say what the enemy will leave us. Wilson continues to be mysterious. Even if he should be full of goodwill his position with his own Republicans and the chauvinist Entente is difficult." Bethmann to Kardorff, Jan. 2, 1919, BA *Nachlass* Kardoff. Bethmann to Jagow, March 24, 1919, AA *Nachlass* Jagow. Cf. also A. Rosenberg, *The Birth of the German Republic* (London, 1931).

15 Bethmann to Thimme, Sept. 15, Nov. 28, 1917, June 13, 1918, BA *Nachlass* Thimme. Cf. also Thimme's rebuttal, "Bethmann als militärischer Kanzler," *Berliner Tageblatt*, Sept. 16, 1917. Bethmann to Delbrück, July 27, Aug. 5, 12, Sept. 8, 1918, Jan. 2, 1919, DSB *Nachlass* Delbrück. Bethmann to Eisendecher, Aug. 12, 1919, AA *Nachlass* Eisendecher. Bethmann to Naumann, Nov. 13, 1917, DZA Po *Nachlass* Naumann.

16 For the editorial correspondence between Bethmann and Thimme on the wartime speeches cf. BA *Nachlass* Thimme, especially Jan. 29, Feb. 14, 16, June 13, Oct. 12, 1918, Mar. 19, 1919 ff. Friedrich Thimme, *Bethmann Hollwegs Kriegsreden* (Stuttgart, 1919), with a sizeable introduction, pp. xiii–lxii. Several editions had already been published as propaganda in German and other languages by the semiofficial house of Reimar Hobbing, but Thimme's set was remarkably complete, except for Bethmann's last speech in the *Hauptausschuss* of July 9, 1917, which the chancellor considered too unfinished. Cf. also Bethmann to Thimme, Aug. 15, Sept. 9, 1919; and Bethmann to Heilbron, Feb. 16, 1918, BA, Kl. Erw. 342-1.

17 Wahnschaffe to Delbrück, Aug. 22, 1918, DSB *Nachlass* Delbrück. The bulk of the correspondence regarding the memoirs is in the AA *Nachlass* Jagow, such as Bethmann to Jagow, Dec. 20, 1918, Mar. 30, Apr. 5, June 28, 1919. There are also occasional pieces in BA *Nachlass* Thimme, such as the letter of Mar. 19, 1919. Theobold von Bethmann Hollweg, *Betrachtungen zum Weltkriege* pt. 1, *Vor dem*

Kriege (Berlin, 1919), especially pp. 187 ff., his conclusion appended after the publication of the peace conditions. The English edition, translated by George Young, appeared as *Reflections on the World War* in 1920, and the French version in 1924 with a new preface, dated May 1919: "The world has never yet seen so appalling an apparatus for the oppression of a vanquished nation."

18 Bethmann to Jagow, June 28, 1919, AA *Nachlass* Jagow: "Today Theodor Wolff [reviewed it] in a scarcely decent and truthful manner; Thimme in the *Deutsche Politik* I find weak, as well as Naumann in the *Hilfe*. . . . From Oncken I received a sympathetic letter even factually often in agreement." Hans von Liebig, "Bethmann's Betrachtungen," *Deutschlands Erneuerung* 6 (1922): 697 ff. Heydebrand, "Bethmann und seine Betrachtungen zum Weltkriege," *Konservative Monatsschrift* 79 (1921): 285 ff.; H. Dreyhaus, "Kriegsdenkwürdigkeiten," *Forschungen zur Brandenburgischen und Preussischen Geschichte* 33 (1921): 423 ff.; G. Stresemann, "Betrachtungen zum Weltkriege," *Deutsche Stimmen* (1919), pp. 569 ff.; K. von Landmann, "Bethmann's Kriegsbetrachtungen," *Allgemeine Rundschau* 19 (1922): 65–66. W. Schotte, "Politische Korrespondenz," *Preussische Jahrbücher* 179 (1920): 155 ff.; H. O. Meisner, ibid., pp. 148 ff.; O. Trautmann, "Bethmann's Betrachtungen," *Die Grenzboten* (1919), pp. 285 ff.; B. Cirmeni, "Die Schuld am Kriege," *Deutsche Revue* 46 (1921): 1 ff.; and L. Quessel, "Bethmann's Annexionismus," *Sozialistische Monatshefte* 53 (1919): 1037 ff.

19 For the Eisner publication cf. Dirr, *Bayr. Dok.*, passim. Bethmann's interview was with Colonel Schwertfeger on Nov. 25, 1918, published two days later in the *DAZ:* "Herr von Bethmann Hollweg über die bayerischen Dokumente," BA *Nachlass* Schwertfeger. Cf. also A. Mitchell, *Die Revolution in Bayern, 1918–1919* (Munich, 1967).

20 Bethmann to Jagow, May 20, June 11, 28, Aug. 15, 1919, AA *Nachlass* Jagow. "With Heilbron I have established a central clearing office." For the coordinated efforts against the "war guilt lie" cf. I. Geiss's introduction to H. Kantorowicz's *Gutachten zur Kriegsschuldfrage 1914* (Stuttgart, 1967). Bethmann to Delbrück, June 16, 1919, DSB *Nachlass* Delbrück. For the entire complex cf. Richard M. Watt, *The Kings Depart: The Tragedy of Germany—Versailles and the German Revolution* (New York, 1968).

21 Bethmann to Jagow, June 14, 28, July 13, Aug. 15, Sept. 25, 1919; Bethmann to Falkenhayn, June 14, 1919; Jagow to Bethmann, June 16, 1919, AA *Nachlass* Jagow. Bethmann to Schwertfeger, July 5, 1919, BA *Nachlass* Schwertfeger. Cf. E. von Falkenhayn, *Die Oberste Heeresleitung 1914–1916 in ihren wichtigsten Entschliessungen* (Berlin, 1919), almost completely nonpolitical. See in contrast E. Ludendorff, *Meine Kriegserinnerungen* (Berlin, 1919), *Die Urkunden der OHL* (Berlin, 1920), and *Kriegsführung und Politik* (Berlin, 1922). For Bethmann's refutation of one of the key military charges, the mistaken declaration of war against Russia, cf. his correspondence with General Kuhl, Apr. 7, 27, 1920, published by August Bach, "August 1914: Ein aufschlussreicher Briefwechsel," *BM* 17 (1939): 663–73.

22 Bethmann and Jagow, Aug. 15, Oct. 4, 11, 15, 1919, AA *Nachlass* Jagow. Bethmann to Hammann, Sept. 29, 1919, DZA Po *Nachlass* Hammann. Bethmann to Valentini, Jan. 17, 1920, DZA Me *Nachlass* Valentini. Cf. also A. Tirpitz, *Erinnerungen* (Leipzig, 1919), and *Politische Dokumente*, 2 vols. (Hamburg, 1926); H. Pohl, *Aus Aufzeichnungen und Briefen während der Kriegszeit* (Berlin, 1920); various articles by Müller; G. Jagow, *Ursachen und Ausbruch des Weltkrieges* (Berlin, 1919); K. Helfferich, *Der Weltkrieg*, 3 vols. (Berlin, 1919), which disappointed the chancellor; and O. Hammann, *Bilder aus der letzten Kaiserzeit* (Berlin, 1919).

23 Bethmann to Rassow, Dec. 3, 1920, *Privatnachlass* Rassow. A comparison of the

two drafts of Bethmann's rebuttal to Tirpitz, n.d., reveal that he wrestled incon-
clusively with the problem of combatting the admiral's claims. The first, BA,
Kl. Erw. 243-2 is in the form of a letter to the editor, from internal evidence pre-
dating the second volume of the *Betrachtungen* and centered upon the July crisis,
the lack of action of the German navy, unrestricted submarine warfare, and his
personal animosity. The second version in ibid. 342 is in the form of a chapter of
his memoirs, entitled "Naval Policy" and subheaded "Herr Tirpitz's Memoirs,"
and a more extensive and detailed refutation of the same points.

24 Bethmann to Jagow, Sept. 25, Oct. 4, 1919, "Bethmann's interview for Wiegand
concerning Gooss's book," copy in AA *Nachlass* Jagow, n.d. Cf. also Roderich
Gooss, *Das Wiener Kabinett und die Entstehung des Weltkrieges* (Vienna, 1919).
For Bethmann's criticism of the charges of German ambassador to England,
Lichnowsky, *Meine Londoner Mission* (Berlin, 1919), cf. Bethmann to Jagow, June
28, 1919. AA *Nachlass* Jagow.

25 Bethmann to Jagow, Oct. 11, 26, AA *Nachlass* Jagow. Bethmann to Hutten, Dec.
9, 1919, DZA Po *Nachlass* Hutten-Czapski. For the stenographic reports of the
hearings cf. the Hoover Institution copy of the *Untersuchungsausschuss über die
Weltkriegsverantwortlichkeit* 2d subcommittee. For the text of Bethmann's statement cf. his pamphlet, *Friedensangebot und U-Bootkrieg: Wortlaut der Aussage
des früheren Reichskanzlers im Untersuchungsausschuss* (Berlin, 1919). To the ex-
chancellor's taste the "questioning was depressing . . . and my general impressions of Berlin utterly negative." See also E. Fischer-Baling, "Der Untersuchungsausschuss für die Schuldfrage des ersten Weltkrieges," in *Aus Geschichte und Politik*
(Düsseldorf, 1954), pp. 117–37, and Williamson, *Helfferich*, pp. 303 ff.

26 Bethmann to Valentini, Dec. 6, 1919, DZA Me *Nachlass* Valentini. Bethmann
to Oettingen, Dec. 7, 1919, BA *Nachlass* Oettingen for his repeated complaint:
"It remains impossible for me to accept the brutality of the Entente and our
lack of dignity." Cf. also the graphic description of M. J. Bonn, *Wandering
Scholar* (London, 1949), pp. 242 ff. and P. Rassow, "Bethmann's Vernehmung,"
Deutsche Politik (1920), pp. 616 ff.

27 Karl Kautsky, *Die deutschen Dokumente zum Kriegsausbruch,* 5 vols. (Berlin,
1919) and *Wie der Weltkrieg entstand* (Berlin, 1919). Bethmann to Jagow, Nov.
26, 1919, Jan. 9, 18, 20, Feb. 3, 20, 1920. Bethmann to Quarck (chairman), n.d., AA
Nachlass Jagow. "Bethmann Hollweg zu den Randbemerkungen des Kaisers,"
Tägliche Rundschau, Dec. 14, 1919. Bethmann's testimony is reprinted in the
Betrachtungen, 2 : 241 ff., "Denkschrift des Reichskanzlers: Der österreichisch-
serbische Streit."

28 Bethmann to Jagow, Sept. 19, 1919, a five-point rebuttal of conservative charges,
Sept. 25, 1919, Feb. 20, 1920, AA *Nachlass* Jagow; Bethmann to Delbrück, Sept.
20, 1919, reprinted in the *Preussische Jahrbücher* as "Das 'Friedensangebot' von
1915," 178 (1919) : 114 ff. Bethmann to Pourtalès, July 26, Aug. 7, 1920, AA
Nachlass Pourtalès. Bethmann, "Friedensmöglichkeiten im Frühsommer 1917,"
DAZ, Feb. 29, 1920. Cf. also Rassow's notes of a conversation with Bethmann, Sept.
9, 1920, *Privatnachlass* Rassow.

29 Anonymous, *Der Erzberger Prozess: Stenographische Berichte* (Berlin, 1920), pp.
691 ff., 712 ff., 731 ff., 838 ff., 1135 ff. Bethmann to Jagow, Mar. 5, 1920. Cf. also K.
Epstein, *Erzberger*, pp. 392 ff., and Williamson, *Helfferich*, pp. 313–14. Bethmann
quoted by Oettingen in his diary, late in 1919, as cited by Vietsch, *Bethmann*,
p. 286. Cf. also Johannes Erger, *Der Kapp-Lüttwitz Putsch* (Düsseldorf, 1967).

30 Bethmann to Thimme, Aug. 15, Sept. 6, 1919, BA *Nachlass* Thimme. Bethmann to
Valentini, Dec. 6, 1919, Jan. 17, Nov. 12, 1920, DZA Me *Nachlass* Valentini.
Bethmann to Oettingen, Sept. 22, Dec. 7, 1919, June 25, 1920, BA *Nachlass*

Oettingen, complaining that "my second volume is naturally retarded through the commission of inquiry, which does not hurt it in many respects."

31 Bethmann to Rassow, July 20, 30, Aug. 18, 26, Sept. 14, 30, Oct. 25, Dec. 3, and conversation of Sept. 9, 1920. *Privatnachlass* Rassow. Bethmann to Valentini, Nov. 12, Dec. 11, 1920, DZA Me *Nachlass* Valentini. Bethmann to Oettingen, Sept. 16, 1920, BA *Nachlass* Oettingen. Cf. the introduction of Felix von Bethmann Hollweg to vol. 2, *Betrachtungen zum Weltkriege: Während des Krieges* (Berlin, 1922), delayed by concurrent foreign editions. The reception of the memoir in the former Entente was highly critical, and reviewers berated him as "one of the chief personalities of a second-rate age." Th. Barclay, "Bethmann Hollweg's Personal Recollections," *Fortnightly Review* 108 : 217 ff. and D. J. Hill, "Considerations . . ." in *American Journal of International Law* 19 : 650–51. See also Felix von Bethmann Hollweg to Oettingen, Jan. 29, 1921, BA *Nachlass* Oettingen.

32 Bethmann to Oettingen, Sept. 22, Dec. 7, 1919 ("Life goes on somehow"), and Dec. 16, 1920. "On Nov. 28 we dedicated a memorial for the fallen warriors at the end of the long linden avenue. . . . Modest and powerful, completely fitting into the landscape, I find it artistically beautiful." Bethmann to Hutten-Czapski, Mar. 29, Dec, 22, 1920, DZA Po *Nachlass* Hutten. Bethmann to Pourtalès, July 26, 1920, AA *Nachlass* Pourtalès.

33 Bethmann to Valentini, Dec. 11, 1920, DZA Me *Nachlass* Valentini: "I can delight in the mood of the human beings with whom I live. Hence: Merry Christmas. We are one year further and it could have been worse." Bethmann to Hutten-Czapski, Dec. 22, 1920, DZA Po *Nachlass* Hutten.

34 Felix von Bethmann Hollweg to Oettingen, Jan. 29, 1921, AA *Nachlass* Oettingen. For an affidavit of Bethmann's personal physician on the cause of death, cf. the Thimme *Nachlass* BA. F. Thimme, "Zu Bethmann Hollweg's Gedächtnis," *Deutsche Politik* (1921), pp. 81 ff. Pastor Passow, "Zum Gedächtnis des Reichskanzlers Bethmann-Hollweg," BA, Kl. Erw. 342-1. Oettingen to Bethmann, Dec. 30, 1920, BA *Nachlass* Oettingen: "The enclosed weak poem will, in case you do not already know it, bring you a smile."

35 For a survey of the obituaries in the leading papers cf. *Das Echo,* Jan. 20, 1921, which summarized: "The tragedy of Bethmann's life, the eternal split between wanting and achieving, is expressed in almost the entire press of Right and Left. Recognition of his outstanding *personal* traits is combined with more or less sharp condemnation of his domestic and foreign policy: A brave man, but no chancellor! The *passiveness* of his nature is almost everywhere correctly seen, and judged according to the ideology of the sheet." Cf. also F. Kern, "Bethmann's Schatten," *Grenzboten* 4 (1921) : 361 ff.; A. von Wahl, condemning Bethmann as "foreign element in Prussia," *Deutsche Literaturzeitung* 33 (1922) : 825 ff. H. Eisele, "Bethmann Hollweg," *Allgemeine Rundschau,* Jan. 15, 1921; B. Guttmann and R. Kirchner, *Bethmann—Tirpitz—Ludendorff* (Frankfurt, 1919); H. Kranold, "Bethmann Hollweg," *Sozialistische Monatshefte* 56 (1921) : 3 ff. Cf. also G. Erenyi, "Bethmann Hollweg und Ludendorff," *Die Gegenwart* (1921), pp. 358 ff. and W. Herzog, "Bethmann Hollweg," *Das Forum* (1921), pp. 89 ff.

36 Kurt Riezler, "Bethmann Hollweg: Ein Nachruf," *Deutsche Politik* (1921), pp. 125 ff. Legationsrat Heilbron, "Gedenkworte," delivered at the annual meeting of the Bethmann circle, Nov. 29, 1928. For further eulogies cf. the correspondence and papers in the Thimme and Solf *Nachlässe,* BA. Note by Oettingen in his diary, Dec. 17, 1917, cited by Vietsch, *Bethmann,* p. 281.

Chapter 13

1 Ernst Troeltsch, "Nachruf auf Bethmann Hollweg," *Der Kunstwart* (1921), pp.
289 ff. Martin Spahn, "Die deutsche Kriegsliteratur," *Hochland*, vol. 18, pt. 2
(1921) : 108 ff. Obituary on Bethmann Hollweg in the *Frankfurter Zeitung*, Jan. 4,
1921.

2 Kurt Riezler, "Bethmann Hollweg," *Deutsche Politik* (1921), pp. 125 ff. Troeltsch,
"Nachruf," pp. 289 ff.; Erhard Deutelmoser, "Über Bethmann Hollweg," *Die Weltbühne* 17 (1921) : 61 ff.; Adalbert Wahl, "Zwei Kriegsreichskanzler," *Deutsche Literaturzeitung* 43 (1922) : 825 ff.; *Neue Züricher Zeitung*, "Zum Tode Bethmann Hollwegs," Jan. 5, 1921.

3 Troeltsch, "Nachruf," pp. 289 ff.; Friedrich Thimme, "Zu Bethmann Hollwegs
Gedächtnis," *Deutsche Politik* (1921), pp. 81 ff.; obituary of the Independent
Socialist paper, *Die Freiheit*, Jan. 3, 1921. For a fresh and sympathetic view of
his aims cf. Hans Herzfeld, *Der Erste Weltkrieg* (Munich, 1968), pp. 29 ff.

4 Troeltsch, "Nachruf," pp. 289 ff.; Kurt Riezler, "Bethmann Hollweg," pp. 125 ff.;
Neue Züricher Zeitung, Jan. 5, 1921; *Die Freiheit*, Jan. 3, 1921. For Bethmann's
frustration in implementing his reforming plans cf. his letter to Oettingen on
Oct. 7, 1918: "I have been nurturing these ideas for years and suffered from them
because I was unable to put them into practice and only reaped hatred and scorn."
BA *Nachlass* Oettingen.

5 For some recent reexaminations of the general problem of imperialism, cf. George
Lichtheim, *Imperialism* (New York, 1971) and W. J. Mommsen, *Das Zeitalter des
Imperialismus* (Frankfurt, 1969). For further leads regarding Imperial Germany,
see Gustav Schmidt, "Deutschland am Vorabend des Ersten Weltkrieges," in Michael
Stürmer, ed., *Das kaiserliche Deutschland* (Düsseldorf, 1970), pp. 397 ff.; Volker R.
Berghahn, "Das Kaiserreich in der Sackgasse, "*Neue Politische Literatur* 16 (1971):
494–506; and F. Klein, "Neue Veröffentlichungen in der BRD zu Geschichte und
Vorgeschichte des ersten Weltkrieges," *Zfg* 20 (1972) : 203–16.

6 Johannes Ziekursch, *Politische Geschichte des neuen deutschen Kaiserreiches*, vol.
3: *Das Zeitalter Wilhelms II* (Frankfurt, 1930), pp. 221 ff. and Erich Eyck, *Das
persönliche Regiment Wilhelms II: Politische Geschichte des deutschen Kaiserreiches von 1890 bis 1914* (Erlenbach-Zurich, 1948), pp. 779 ff.: "He is a truly tragic
figure because he found no compromise between the two imperatives which lived
in him. As statesman and patriot he considered himself bound to a policy which
he could not defend as a moral human being. . . . It was Bethmann's misfortune
that he was put at the helm of a people whose leading men considered themselves
political realists."

7 Riezler, "Bethmann Hollweg," pp. 129–30. J. G. Fichte, *Addresses to the German
Nation*, ed. G. A. Kelley (New York, 1968), pp. 118–19. A. Wach, *Staatsmoral und
Politik* (Leipzig, 1916), pp. 13 ff. For the whole complex cf. also L. Krieger's and
F. Stern's epilogue to *The Responsibility of Power*, pp. 445 ff. and H. H. Gerth and
C. Wright Mills, eds., *From Max Weber: Essays in Sociology* (New York, 1958),
p. 120.

8 For Treutler's sketch: "Never resolved, always full of misgivings, [Bethmann was] a
perfectionist, a decent, noble man who despised all intrigue" cf. Janssen, ed.,
Treutler, pp. 172–73. Riezler, "Bethmann Hollweg," pp. 129–30. Typical of the
lack of alternatives to Imperial Germany's collapse was Bethmann's first letter after
his fall to Oettingen, Aug. 31, 1917, BA *Nachlass* Oettingen: "Even today it is my
conviction that I was on the right track. The triumphant raging of my enemies will
not make me doubt that. To be sure, I have stumbled in its execution and I shall

not be jealous if my successor has better luck. But I doubt that he will be able to change our fundamental course."

Appendix

1 Riezler Diary, Apr. 18, 1915. Jagow to Solf, two letters of Aug. 25, 1914, BA *Nachlass* Solf.

2 Riezler Diary, Aug. 21, 22, 27, Sept. 1, 1914. Bethmann to Delbrück, Aug. 23, 26, "instruction for the chief of the civil administration," DZA Po, Rkz. no. 2,463. "Die Frage der 'Kriegsziele,' namentlich Belgiens," MS "Politische Aufsätze," *Nachlass* Jagow. Cf. also L. von Köhler, *Die Staatsverwaltung der besetzten Gebiete: Belgien* (Berlin, 1927) and J. Pirenne and M. Vauthier, *La Législation et l'administration allemandes en Belgique* (Paris, 1925). For the background of this question see Horst Lademacher, *Die belgische Neutralität als Problem der europäischen Politik* (Bonn, 1970).

3 Riezler Diary, Sept. 1, Oct. 6, 7, 9, 11, 19, 1914. Bethmann to Weizäcker, Nov. 10, 1914, *Privatnachlass* Weizsäcker. F. Petri and P. Schöller, "Zur Bereinigung des Franktireur-Problems vom August 1914," *VJHfZG* (1961), pp. 234 ff. See also H. Pirenne, *La Belgique et la guerre mondiale* (Brussels, 1929) and A. Henry, *Etudes sur l'occupation allemande en Belgique* (Brussels, 1920). Cf. also DZA Po, RdI. 19,388, 19,495, and 19,523 ff. for further files on German policy.

4 Bethmann to Weizsäcker, Nov. 10, *Privatnachlass* Weizsäcker. Bethmann to Hammann, Nov. 14, DZA Po *Nachlass* Hammann; Bethmann to Hertling, Nov. 15, 1915, BHStA MA I 961. Jagow to Solf, Oct. 3, 1914, BA *Nachlass* Solf. Riezler Diary, Dec. 13, 1914: "Protector of freedom for the small states, economic hegemony, etc." Feb. 6, 17, Apr. 18, May 16, June 10, 1915. F. Meinecke, *Erinnerungen*, pp. 216 ff. Cf. also G. Ritter, *Kriegskanzler*, pp. 434 ff. and F. Fischer, *Griff*, pp. 321 ff.

5 Bethmann to Falkenhayn, Feb. 23, DZA Po, Rkz. no. 2,442/10. Wild von Hohenborn Diary, Nov. 1, 1915, BA *Nachlass* Wild. Heinrichs Protocol, June 19, 1915, BA *Nachlass* Heinrichs. Riezler Diary, Oct. 16, 1915. For the basic economic files on Belgium cf. DZA Po, RdI. 19,523 ff. A. Tirpitz, *Deutsche Ohnmachtspolitik*, pp. 191 ff. O v. Lancken-Wakenitz, *Meine Dreissig Dienstjahre* (Berlin, 1931), pp. 213 ff. See also W. Gutsche, "Zu einigen Fragen der staatsmonopolistischen Verflechtung in den ersten Kriegsjahren am Beispiel der Ausplünderung der belgischen Industrie und der Zwangsdeportation von Belgiern," in *Politik im Krieg*, pp. 66 ff.

6 Bethmann note, Jan. 1, 1916, S-G 1 : 243. Bethmann to Sandt, Sept. 2, 1914, DZA Po, Rkz. no. 2,463. Bethmann to Bissing, Dec. 16, 1914, S-G 1 : 35–36. Bethmann to Bissing, Jan. 6, 1916, AA Wk no. 20a secr., vol. 1. Cf. also Bissing to William II, May 3, 1915, DZA Me, Rep. 89H, VI Europa no. 2, vol. 2. R. P. Oszwald, "Freiherr von Bissing," *Deutsches Biographisches Jahrbuch* (Berlin, 1921), pp. 34 ff. See also F. Petri, "Zur Flamenpolitik des 1. Weltkrieges: Ungelöste Fragen und Aufgaben," *Festschrift für K. Raumer* (Münster, 1966), pp. 513 ff. For the possibility of Karl Lamprecht's influence on Bethmann in a pro-Flemisch direction, cf. also the study in preparation by Dr. U. Lewald.

7 Riezler Diary, Mar. 19, 1916, Feb. 18, 24, 1917. Wahnschaffe Protocol of a conference, Feb. 7, 1917; Bethmann to Grünau, Feb. 8, 1919, S-G 2 : 2 ff., also in AA Belgien 63 vols. 9 ff. Bethmann in the Reichstag, Apr. 5, 1916: "Germany cannot again leave the long oppressed Flemish nation to French influence." Thimme, *Kriegsreden*, pp. 91 ff., 211 ff.

8 Bethmann statements to the Reichstag committee of inquiry, *Stenographische Berichte über die öffentlichen Verhandlungen des 2. Untersuchungsausschusses* (Ber-

lin, 1919), pp. 217 ff. Ludendorff, *Urkunden der OHL*, pp. 124 ff. Bethmann to Delbrück, Jan. 24, 1917, DZA Po, RdI. 19,388. Bethmann to Hertling, Mar. 5, 1917, BHStA MA I 961. Gutsche, "Zu einigen Fragen," pp. 82 ff. A. Henry, *Etudes sur l'occupation*, pp. 81 ff.

9 Commission d'enquête sur les violations des règles du droit des gens, des lois et des coutumes de la guerre. *Rapports et documents d'enquête* (Brussels, 1923), 1–4, especially vol. 4. *Rapports d'ensemble et conclusions*. A full-scale study of German Belgian policy with all its diplomatic and economic ramifications and weighing intent against execution must still be undertaken.

10 Bethmann to Delbrück, Nov. 3, 1914. Riezler Diary, Aug. 18, 21, 1914. Hutten-Czapski, *Sechzig Jahre* 2 : 152–53. The key files are AA Wk no. 20c secr., vols. 1–16; DZA Po, RdI. 19,685 (for the State Council); and DZA Me, Rep. 77, Tit no. 1884, no. 1, vols. 1 ff.; Pep. 77 Tit 875, no. 10 adhib. 5, vols. 1 ff. and Rep. 89H, VI Europa no. 21. Cf. also Eldon Ray Burke, *Polish Policy of the Central Powers During the World War* (Chicago, 1936); Titus Komarnicki, *Rebirth of the Polish Republic* (London, 1957); Werner Conze, *Polnische Nation und deutsche Politik im Ersten Weltkrieg* (Cologne, 1958), and E. Zechlin, *Die deutsche Politik und die Juden im ersten Weltkrieg* (Göttingen, 1969).

11 Bethmann to Stockholm, July 3; Bethmann to Treutler, Aug. 4, 1915, S-G 1 : 148 ff. Bethmann to Hindenburg, Aug. 17, 1915, cited from a manuscript in the AA *Nachlass* Jagow written by *Geheimrat* Heilbron to serve as basis of Bethmann's Polish remarks in his memoirs (hereafter cited as Heilbron), pp. 8 ff. An equally important source is the collection, "Verhandlungen über die Entstehung eines selbständigen Königreich Polens, Aug. 4, 1915 bis Nov. 4, 1916," also in AA *Nachlass* Jagow, containing the most important documents of Bethmann's Polish policy (hereafter cited as *Verhandlungen*). For the frontier strip cf. also I. Geiss, *Der polnische Grenzstreifen, 1914–1918* (Lübeck, 1960) and "Der polnische Grenzstreifen: Wilhelminische Expansionspläne im Lichte heutiger Geschichtsforschung," *Der Monat* 171 (1962) : 58 ff., as well as W. Basler, *Deutsche Annexionspolitik*, passim.

12 Heilbron, pp. 7–8. Riezler Diary, Jan. 25, Mar. 3, July 7, 16, 21, 28, Aug. 18, 19, 23, 1915. Wolfgang von Kries, "Deutsche Staatsverwaltung in Russisch-Polen," *Preussische Jahrbücher* 235 (1934) : 221 ff. "Die wirtschaftliche Ausnutzung des Generalgouvernements Warschau," ibid. 235 (1934) : 130 ff. Cf. also Leon Grosfeld, "La Pologne dans les plans impérialistes allemands pendant la grande guerre 1914–1918 et l'acte du 5 novembre 1916," *La Pologne au Xe Congrès International des sciences historiques à Rome* (Warsaw, 1955), pp. 327 ff. and M. Handelsman, *La Pologne: Sa vie économique et sociale pendant la guerre* (Paris, 1933).

13 Bethmann note of conversation with Burian, Aug. 13, Bethmann to Falkenhayn, Sept. 5, 11, 16; Bethmann to Jagow, Oct. 13, memorandum by Jagow, Oct. 25; Note by Jagow of German-Austrian negotiations, Nov. 14, 1915, all in S-G 1 : 161 ff., Heilbron, pp. 10 ff., and *Verhandlungen*, pp. 5 ff. Riezler Diary, Aug. 29, Sept. 10, 23, Oct. 11, 1915. Baron Stephan von Burian, *Austria in Dissolution* (New York, 1925), pp. 80–81 and Arthur J. May, *The Passing of the Hapsburg Monarchy, 1914–1918*, 1 : 157 ff.

14 Riezler Diary, Oct. 26, 27, 29, Nov. 2, 5, 26, Dec. 19, 21, 1915, Jan. 3, 1916. Cf. also Richard Perdelwitz, *Die Polen im Weltkriege und die internationale Politik* (Leipzig, 1939) and Stanizlav Filasiewicz, *La question polonaise pendant la guerre mondiale* (Paris, 1920).

15 Bethmann to Beseler, Jan. 6, 1916, in Conze, *Polnische Nation*, pp. 145 ff. Treutler to Bethmann (transmitting Falkenhayn's desires), Jan. 23, 1916, S-G 1 : 259. Ludendorff to Zimmermann, Oct. 20, 1915. *Verhandlungen*, p. 27. Heilbron, pp.

12 ff. Hutten-Czapski, *Sechzig Jahre* 2 : 360 ff. Mutius to Jagow, Feb. 16, 21, 24, 26, Mar. 8, 14 ff., 1916, AA Wk 20a secr., vol. 1a. Riezler Diary, Jan. 26, Feb. 4, 17, 1916. Beseler to Bethmann, Feb. 6, Bethmann to Beseler, Feb. 21, Bethmann to Hindenburg, Apr. 6, 1916, Heilbron, pp. 14 ff.

16   Riezler Diary, Mar. 10, Apr. 15, June 14, 17, July 4, Aug. 1, 8, 1916. Bethmann to Treutler, Apr. 10, Jagow to Treutler (reporting negotiations with Burian), Apr. 16, Jagow to Tschirschky, May 29, June 19, note by Burian, July, Bethmann to Tschirschky, July 30, unsigned note, Aug. 12 (detailing the Austro-German talks), Bethmann to Beseler, Aug. 13, 1916, S-G 1 : 298 ff., *Verhandlungen*, pp. 50 ff. Beseler to Bethmann Mar. 2, July 11, Kries memorandum, Mar. 7, Bethmann to Beseler July 19, Aug. 8, notes of a conference on Polish frontier strip, Aug. 9, Bethmann to Hindenburg, Aug. 17, 1916, Heilbron, pp. 18 ff. Bethmann to the Prussian Ministry of State, Aug. 19, 1916, DZA Me, Rep. 90a B III 2b no. 6, vol. 165.

17   Falkenhayn to Bethmann, July 19; Bethmann to Falkenhayn, July 20; Ludendorff to Zimmermann, July 17, S-G 1 : 411 ff. *Verhandlungen*, pp. 84 ff. Bethmann to Bundesrat, Aug. 8/9, WP and Deuerlein, *Bundesratsausschuss*, pp. 287 ff. Beseler to Bethmann, Aug. 2, Bethmann to Foreign Office, Sept. 10, Bethmann to Beseler Sept. 9; notes of a conference on Sept. 17, 1916. Heilbron, pp. 28 ff., *Verhandlungen*, pp. 160 ff. AA Wk no. 20c secr., vol. 4. Protocol of negotiations in Pless, Oct. 19, Jagow circular Oct. 22, S-G 1 : 492 ff. Riezler Diary, Sept. 21, 1916. Burian, *Austria in Dissolution*, pp. 105 ff.

18   Bethmann to William II, Oct. 2, Bethmann to Hindenburg, Oct. 4, 10, 1916, S-G 1 : 488–89. Bethmann meeting with parliamentary leaders, Sept. 29, Oct. 10, 21, 1916, Heilbron, pp. 39–40. *Verhandlungen*, pp. 22 ff., Bethmann to Prussian Ministry of State, Oct. 8 and 24, 1916, DZA Me, Rep. 90a B III 2b no. 6, vol. 164. Bethmann's conversation with Bavarian ambassador, Lerchenfeld to Hertling, Oct. 21, 1916, BHStA MA III 2691/11. Cf. Westarp, *Conservative Politik*, 2 : 67 ff.

19   Riezler Diary, Oct. 29, Nov. 3, 1916. Bethmann comment on OHL demand, Oct. 30, 1916. Bethmann reception of Studnicki, Nov. 1, 1916. Beseler proclamation text in Grünau to Jagow, Nov. 4, 1916. Description of Warsaw scene on Nov. 5, 1916, in Heilbron, pp. 49–50, *Verhandlungen*, pp. 370–71. For the Polish response cf. Conze, *Polnische Nation*, pp. 226 ff.

20   Bethmann briefing of 43 press representatives, Oct. 29, 1916, Heilbron, pp. 49–50. Bethmann to Bundesrat, Oct. 30/31, WP, Lerchenfeld summary BHStA MA I 966 and Deuerlein, *Bundesratsausschuss*, pp. 292 ff. Bethmann to party leaders, in the Hauptausschuss of the Reichstag, Nov. 9, 1916, Thimme, *Kriegsreden*, p. 165 for a fragment, DZA Po, Rkz. 2398/9 for the original.

21   Riezler Diary, Nov. 3, 22, 1916, Feb. 14, 18, 28, Mar. 11, 1917. Heilbron, pp. 50 ff. Schoen to Hertling, Feb. 21, 1917, BHStA MA III 2691/17. For further correspondence cf. AA, Wk no. 20c secr., vols. 9 ff.

22   Riezler Diary, Nov. 22, 1916, Jan. 9, Mar. 8, 1917. Conze, *Polnische Nation*, pp. 265 ff. Prussian Ministry of State, Mar. 15, 1917, DZA Me, Rep. 90a B 2b III no. 6, vol. 166, pp. 87 ff.

23   Riezler Diary, Nov. 22, 1916, Mar. 10, May 13, Aug. 4, 1917. Protocol of Austro-German conference, Jan. 6, 1917, S-G 1 : 663–64. Noske to Zimmermann, transmitting Bethmann–Beseler–William II accord, June 23, 1917, S-G 2 : 236–37. Cf. also AA, Wk no. 20c secr., vols. 11 ff. Count Ottokar Czernin, *In the World War* (New York, 1920), pp. 222 ff. Cf. also Arthur Hausner, *Die Polenpolitik der Mittelmächte und die österreichisch-ungarische Militärverwaltung in Polen während des ersten Weltkrieges* (Vienna, 1935).

24   Gottlieb Jagow, "Polen," MS "Politische Aufsätze," AA *Nachlass* Jagow. Bethmann

Hollweg, *Betrachtungen,* 2 : 87 ff. Cf. also F. Gregory Campbell, "The Kaiser and *Mitteleuropa* in October 1918," *CEH* 2 (1969) : 376 ff.

25 Gerd Linde, *Die deutsche Politik in Litauen im ersten Weltkrieg* (Wiesbaden, 1965). Bernhard Mann, *Die baltischen Länder in der deutschen Kriegszielpublizistik 1914–1918* (Tübingen, 1965). For the larger perspectives cf. L. Dehio, *Gleichgewicht oder Hegemonie?* (Krefeld, 1948); R. Wittram, *Das Nationale als europäisches Problem* (Göttingen, 1954); G. Ritter, *Das deutsche Problem* (Munich, 1962); and A. Hillgruber, *Kontinuität und Diskontinuität in der deutschen Aussenpolitik von Bismarck bis Hitler* (Düsseldorf, 1969).

Note on Sources

A synthetical study dealing with a major figure whose tenure of office equals two American presidential terms can only cut a bold swath through the forest of public and private documentation, without any pretense of completeness. Nevertheless, strategic cuts, if they proceed from a general conceptual design that consciously tries to cover all important points, can hope to render visible the large outlines and chief features of the underlying landscape. Although the abundance of published material, such as *Die Grosse Politik,* is enough to discourage any but the foolhardy, the student of Imperial Germany must penetrate beyond the printed word into the Alice in Wonderland world of archives. Only the handwritten line can convey the freshness of a decision. Moreover, without seeing individual paraphs, corrections, varying drafts, and marginal comments—often deleted in publication—it is impossible to reconstruct the nuances of a policy, the substantial as well as tactical differences between the people involved. Even in such a well-mined area as the Second Reich, there is still the occasional joy of individual discovery, or at least the sudden insight that can spring from recognizing the position of a document in relation to a whole series of papers. Lastly, the elusive motivation for official policies only emerges from going beyond bureaucratic files into the personal papers of the participants.

Despite the chaotic course of German history responsible for the destruction of the Bethmann *Nachlass,* the public record is remarkably complete. The Deutsche Zentralarchiv Postdam, which holds the documents of the imperial chancellery on all of Bethmann's major policies, is of crucial importance for German domestic politics and war aims. The files of the imperial Secretariat of the Interior provide the material for his tenure from 1907 to 1909, while the protocols of the Budget Committee shed light on the attitude of the Reichstag, and the *Nachlässe* of Hammann, Naumann, and Hutten-Czapski contain valuable letters. The second section of the Deutsche Zentralarchiv, located in Merseburg, is of similar importance for Prussian politics during Bethmann's tenure. The archives of the Ministry of the Interior possess much evidence of his early governmental career, as well as of his initiatives as the head of the bureau-

cracy from 1905 to 1907. The holdings of the Civil Cabinet are crucial for the chancellor's relationship to the emperor and also offer
much evidence on specific questions. The corrected reports of the
sessions of the Prussian Ministry of State, though somewhat condensed, are invaluable to understanding the decision-making of the
cabinet; and the personal papers of Rudolf von Valentini include
a considerable correspondence with Bethmann and his collaborators.
The Prussian files sheltered from the bombing in the West are collected in the Hauptstaatsarchiv in Dahlem and complement the
Merseburg set with a sizeable segment on the *Staatsministerium* and
the Meinecke, Schiemann, and Schiffer papers.

For foreign policy, the Politische Archiv des Auswärtigen Amtes
in Bonn is still the chief source. Although the documents collected
under Bethmann's name are generally disappointing, the rich files
include much unpublished material on prewar policy, and while
they offer few surprises regarding the outbreak of the war, do possess
important collections on German war aims and peace moves, as well
as the chancellor's correspondence with the GHQ, which cuts across
many questions. The stenographic reports of the Reichstag Commission of Inquiry and the revealing *Nachlässe* of Eisendecher, Jagow,
Pourtalès, Hintze, and Stresemann round out the picture. Although
they contain only fragments of the imperial documents for this
period, the Federal Archives in Coblenz have the best collection of
personal papers of the bureaucrats, parliamentarians, and generals of
German history (the latter now transferred to the military archives
in Freiburg, which also house the remainder of the imperial naval
archives). Aside from relatively extensive holdings on Bauer, Bülow,
Erzberger, Hertling, Loebell, Schwertfeger, Solf, and Thimme, there
are the Müller, Mutius, Delbrück, and Wild von Hohenborn diaries
or manuscript memoirs, as well as the recovered fragments of the
Bethmann *Nachlass* and the Oettingen correspondence.

Beyond these central collections, the archives of the individual
states are a rich source. Among them, the Bavarian ambassadorial
reports from Berlin and the specific subject files (containing several
Bethmann letters) are the best known. But the Badensian dispatches
offer perhaps a more detailed day-to-day record of the moods of the
Foreign Office and a substantially complete set of minutes for the
meetings of the Foreign Affairs Committee of the Bundesrat. Aside
from the diplomatic holdings, the Württembergian archives also
contain the important Conrad Haussmann papers, including corre-

spondence with the chancellor. Often overlooked, the records of the Saxonian government in Dresden have a well-informed set of ambassadorial letters, a clipping file on the chancellor, and notes of his conversations with his cousin, Count Vitzthum. Last but not least, the Prussian state archives for Brandenburg house a few papers on the *Landratsamt* in Freienwalde as well as the central provincial administration. The manuscript section of the Deutsche Staatsbibliothek in Berlin also possesses the majority of the Delbrück papers as well as the *Nachlass* of Adolf von Harnack.

Among the non-German archives, the Austrian Haus- Hof- und Staatsarchiv in Vienna, though sometimes reluctant to part with its riches, has the most extensive materials on German affairs. The diplomatic dispatches from Berlin comment in detail on domestic politics, but the holdings on foreign policy are dispersed in individual subject drawers. The Kiderlen-Waechter papers in the E. M. House Collection at Yale University go considerably beyond the published version. The American ambassadorial reports from Berlin, available in the National Archives, vary drastically with the perceptiveness of their authors but add an interesting noncontinental perspective on German developments.

More difficult to track down, but ultimately most rewarding, are the papers of prominent Wilhelmian figures still in private possession. The Bethmann family has fragments that shed light on the chancellor's youth and estate, as well as an impressive folder of photographs. Frau Professor Rassow has preserved the correspondence between her husband and the ex-chancellor and interesting notes of several conversations. Freifrau von Weizsäcker graciously aids scholars in consulting the *Nachlass* of her father, which contains Bethmann letters and some official Württemberg papers. Kurt Riezler's daughter keeps a copy of her father's controversial diary. Since some sources, such as the Oettingen diaries, remained inaccessible, the present note is by no means an exhaustive list and only hopes to whet scholarly appetites and to serve as a rough guide for further research.

Index

References to end notes give chapter number, colon, and then note number.

Achenbach, President von, 41–42

Adlon meeting, 367–68, 11:32

Aerenthal, Count Alois Lexa von, 110, 111, 116, 132

Agadir, 122

Agrarian pressure groups (e.g. *Bund der Landwirte*), 42, 44, 320

Albania, 133, 136, 137, 138, 141, 168, 244

Albert (king of Belgium), 244, 409

Algeciras, conference of, 109, 120, 126

Alldeutsche Blätter, 346

Alldeutscher Verband, 112. *See also* Pan-Germans

Alsace-Lorraine, 114, 120, 159, 164, 306, 311; Bethmann and reform of, 80–81, 89, 106, 311. *See also* Peace Moves; War aims, German; Zabern affair

Ambassadors' conference in London, 135–36, 138, 141

Andersen, Hans Niels, 236–38, 243, 263

Andrassy, Count Julius von, 292

Anglo-German naval rivalry. *See* Anglo-German relations; England; Germany; Haldane mission

Anglo-German relations, 58–59, 109, 141–43, 391; Bethmann's initiative for rapprochement, 112–16, 118; during Morocco crisis, 122–24, 126; Haldane mission, 126–30, 169–70; during Balkan wars, 133–39. *See also* England

Angola, 128, 142, 145, 152

Annexationism. *See* Belgium; Poland; War aims

Anti-Semitism, 104, 373, 415, 420

Antwerp, 189, 193, 199, 201, 221

Arabic (ship): sinking of, 278–79

Arbeitskammern (chambers of work), 57, 68

Arnim, Bernhard von, 72

Asquith, Herbert Henry, 404

Associations law (*Vereinsgesetz*), 54–56, 68, 322

Austria-Hungary, 109, 291–92, 303, 339, 393; and Balkans, 116–18, 131–39; ultimatum to Serbia, 162–66, 391, 393. *See also* July crisis; Peace moves; War aims; War responsibility

Austro-German relations, 82–83, 109, 113, 116–17, 130–39, 272, 291–92, 412–21; and the blank check, 149, 153–55, 160

Austro-Italian relations, 131–32

Austro-Russian relations, 116–18, 131–38, 140–41

Auxiliary service law. *See also* Hindenburg program

Bachmann, Gustav, 276, 279

Bacmeister, Walter, 360

Baden, Prince Max von, 383, 384, 386

Bagdad railroad, 109, 115, 117, 128, 130, 142, 152, 157, 186

Balkans, 116, 118, 138–42, 270, 295–96. *See also* July crisis; Peace moves; War aims

Balkan wars, 95–96, 109, 132–39

Ballin, Albert, 68, 113, 170, 191, 237, 375

Bassermann, Ernst, 84, 87, 91, 94, 95, 102, 106, 124, 179, 206, 209, 249, 271, 286–87, 290, 302, 314, 315, 317, 349, 356, 357, 362, 364. *See also* National Liberal Party

Batocki, Adolf von, 321, 328, 332

Bauer, Max, 323, 10:29, 338, 368–69, 373, 375, 376

Bebel, August, 84, 91, 97, 106, 124, 152. *See also* Social Democratic Party

Belgium, 170, 175–76, 179, 272, 367, 374, 404–12, 423. *See also* Peace moves; War aims

Benckendorff, Count Alexander, 184

Benedict XV (pope), 259. *See also* Catholicism

Benguella railroad, 145

Berchtold, Count Leopold von, 132–34, 136, 138, 154, 160, 168, 170, 172, 182, 237, 240, 413